CONTENTS

Fundamentals of Real Estate Appraisal

William L. Ventolo, Jr. & Martha R. Williams, JD

Sam Martin, PhD, DREI, Consulting Editor

Thirteenth Edition

President: Dr. Andrew Temte
Executive Director, Real Estate Education: Melissa Kleeman-Moy
Development Editor: Adam Bissen

FUNDAMENTALS OF REAL ESTATE APPRAISAL THIRTEENTH EDITION

Published by DF Institute, Inc., d/b/a Dearborn Real Estate Education
332 Front St. S., Suite 501
La Crosse, WI 54601

Printed in the United States of America

First revision, April 2019

ISBN: 978-1-4754-6380-4

PREFACE

This thirteenth edition of *Fundamentals of Real Estate Appraisal* continues to cover all of the topics included in the Basic Appraisal Principles and Basic Appraisal Procedures course requirements established by the Appraiser Qualifications Board of the Appraisal Foundation.

As with other areas of real estate practice, the professional appraiser must keep pace with the demands of the marketplace. Technological advances have affected all facets of the real estate sales transaction, from the real estate broker's first client contact to closing. Despite the availability of vast databases of market information, however, there is no substitute for the well-reasoned opinion of a competent appraiser. Of course, the skill and judgment required to make a reliable appraisal must begin with a thorough knowledge of appraisal principles and procedures.

Fundamentals of Real Estate Appraisal is designed to help the student relate appraisal theory and technique to practice.

- Each unit begins with a list of the key terms used in the unit. Because students may not study the units in chronological order, important terms are emphasized whenever appropriate—not just the first time they appear in the text.
- Learning objectives help alert the student to the goals of the course material.
- Information on real estate and the real estate industry is designed to give the student the necessary background in how real estate is defined, marketed, and valued.
- Explanations of the basic approaches to appraising are thorough, yet concise.
- Frequent practical examples, including use of forms and data grids, help bring the real world of appraising to the reader.
- The many exercises and review questions used in the text increase its usefulness as a practical, hands-on tool by requiring reader participation.

The emphasis throughout this book is on the ways in which appraisal theory and practice come together and, above all, on the importance of the appraiser's objectivity in forming an opinion of value. Fannie Mae's Appraiser Independence Requirements are included in the first unit, setting the tone for the rest of the book.

ABOUT THE AUTHORS

William L. Ventolo, Jr., a former vice president of Development Systems Corporation and its subsidiary, Real Estate Education Company, received his master of science in psychology from the University of Pittsburgh. He has developed and authored numerous industrial training programs and manuals, including a comprehensive dealership accounting correspondence course used by the Ford Motor Company. In addition to *Fundamentals of Real Estate Appraisal*, he has authored or coauthored many trade books and textbooks, including *The Art of Real Estate Appraisal*, *How to Use the Uniform Residential Appraisal Report*, *Mastering Real Estate Mathematics*, *Residential Construction*, *Your Home Inspection Guide*, and *Principles of Accounting*. He resides in Nokomis, Florida.

Martha R. Williams, who received her juris doctorate from the University of Texas, is an author and educator and has practiced law in Texas and California. In addition to *Fundamentals of Real Estate Appraisal*, she is author or coauthor of *The Art of Real Estate Appraisal*, *How to Use the Uniform Residential Appraisal Report*, *California Mortgage Loan Brokerage*, *California Real Estate Principles*, other textbooks, and numerous electronic courses. A former officer of the Real Estate Educators Association and the Association of Illinois Real Estate Educators, she resides in Elburn, Illinois.

ABOUT THE CONSULTING EDITOR

Sam Martin received his PhD in Education from Walden University and has earned the Distinguished Real Estate Instructor (DREI) designation from the Real Estate Educators Association. An appraisal and real estate educator since 1988, he holds Illinois Certified Residential Real Estate Appraiser, Real Estate Managing Broker, Prelicense educator, and real estate CE educator licenses. He is also a Certified Uniform Standards of Professional Practice instructor and the owner of SamTheTutor.com, Inc. He has taught for the Chicago Association of REALTORS®, REALTOR® University, Triton College, and the University of Phoenix. He has written an advanced appraisal textbook used in certification courses and developed advanced valuation online courses. He is a member of the Illinois Coalition of Appraisal Professionals and the Real Estate Educators Association, is Past President of the Association of Illinois Real Estate Educators, and is on the Board of Directors of the Illinois Association for Educational Communication and Technology.

ACKNOWLEDGMENTS

The authors wish to thank those who participated in the preparation of the thirteenth edition of *Fundamentals of Real Estate Appraisal.*

The consulting editor for this edition was Sam Martin, PhD, DREI, who also reviewed the ninth edition.

Maureen Sweeney, SRA, AI-RRS, IFA, provided the sample appraisal used in Unit 15.

The twelfth edition was reviewed by Douglas G. Winner, Certified General Real Estate Appraiser, MMA, CDA, GRI, REALTOR®, real estate and appraisal author and instructor, AQB-certified *USPAP* instructor, and president of All Property Appraisal Corporation.

The tenth edition was reviewed by Thurza Andrew and Jody Hooper. Building codes official John E. Spurgeon, MCP, helped update the cost figures.

Dennis S. Tosh, PhD, who holds the J. Ed Turner Chair of Real Estate and is associate professor of finance at the University of Mississippi, and William B. Rayburn, PhD, associate professor of finance at the University of Mississippi, served as consulting editors for earlier editions.

Terry V. Grissom, MBA, PhD, MAI, CRE, served as consulting editor for the fifth and sixth editions, offering the insight of his years of appraisal practice and skill as an educator.

James H. Boykin, PhD, MAI, SREA, served as consulting editor on earlier editions of this book, and his assistance was always appreciated. Earlier editions were reviewed by Richard Ransom Andrews, Carol Bohling, Robert W. Chaapel, Linda W. Chandler, Jane Chiavacci, Diana M. De Fonzo, Clay Estes, Larry E. Foote, Donald A. Gabriel, Robert C. Gorman, Ron Guiberson, George R. Harrison, Gary Hoagland, Robert Houseman, Kennard P. Howell, Alan Hummel, James E. Jacobs, David J. January, Donald B. Johnson, Paul Johnson, Lowell Knapp, Frank W. Kovats, Timothy W. Lalli, Craig Larabee, Joseph H. Martin, Robert S. Martin, John F. Mikusas, Michael Milgrim, Robert L. Montney, Mark A. Munizzo, Lisa Musial, Henry E. Ormonde, Leroy Richards, Kenneth E. Ritter, Michael L. Robinson, Lawrence Sager, Richard Sorenson, Margaret E. Sprencz, Paul C. Sprencz, Bryan K. Swartwood, Jr., Ralph Tamper, Milton J. Tharp, Douglas G. Winner, and Terrence M. Zajac.

In addition to those mentioned, numerous instructors, students, and real estate professionals have offered many useful comments and suggestions over the years. We thank all who have contacted us and welcome additional comments on this edition.

Finally, the authors thank the staff of Dearborn Real Estate Education for their diligence in once again bringing the manuscript through the production process.

William L. Ventolo, Jr.

Martha R. Williams, JD

1

UNIT ONE

THE APPRAISAL PROFESSION

LEARNING OBJECTIVES

When you have completed this unit, you will be able to

- describe the types of assignments that an appraiser can receive,
- explain how the savings and loan crisis of the 1980s led to appraiser licensing,
- name the organization that assists Congress by developing appraiser and appraisal criteria,
- identify and explain the qualification criteria for the four categories of appraiser licensing,
- recognize other federal regulations that have an impact on appraisal practice, and
- list the major appraisal trade groups.

KEY TERMS

- Appraisal Foundation
- appraisal management companies (AMCs)
- Appraisal Practices Board (APB)
- appraisal report
- Appraisal Standards Board (ASB)
- appraiser
- Appraiser Independence Requirements
- Appraiser Qualifications Board (AQB)
- computer-assisted mass appraisal (CAMA)
- Department of Veterans Affairs (VA)
- Dodd-Frank Wall Street Reform and Consumer Protection Act (Dodd-Frank)
- Economic Stimulus Act of 2008
- Fannie Mae
- Federal Deposit Insurance Corporation (FDIC)
- Federal Housing Administration (FHA)
- Federal Housing Finance Agency (FHFA)
- Financial Institutions Reform, Recovery, and Enforcement Act of 1989 (FIRREA)
- Freddie Mac
- government-sponsored enterprises (GSEs)
- House Price Index (HPI)
- Housing and Economic Recovery Act of 2008 (HERA)
- House Finance Board
- Office of Thrift Supervision (OTS)
- opinion of property value
- scope of work
- subprime lending crisis
- Truth in Lending Act (TILA)
- *Uniform Standards of Professional Appraisal Practice (USPAP)*

OVERVIEW

More than a half-century of prosperity following the end of World War II and the subsequent demand for housing caused the overall value of real estate to rise dramatically in the United States. Even though prices dipped somewhat in recessionary periods in various market areas, the trend continued on an upward curve, finally peaking in most parts of the country in early 2007. Then, the lowered credit requirements and a too-broad range of loan products brought a cascade of loan and market failures. As the country entered 2012, foreclosures continued to dominate sales statistics, despite record-low interest rates.

WEB LINK
www.fhfa.gov

According to what was then the Office of Federal Housing Enterprise Oversight (OFHEO), and is now the **Federal Housing Finance Agency (FHFA)**, the price of the average U.S. residence increased almost 47% from 2002 to 2007. By October 2011, however, FHFA reported that the **House Prince Index (HPI)**, an indicator of house price trends in various regions of the United States, had declined to 19.2% below its April 2007 peak and was about the same as the February 2004 index level. Most parts of the country have seen housing values rebound since then, but some areas are still experiencing sluggish growth. Perhaps more significant is the decline in the percentage of homeowners. According to the U.S. Census Bureau, 69.2% of households were headed by homeowners as of June 2004. In contrast, the homeownership rate in 2016 was 63.4%.

WEB LINK
www.census.gov

The appraiser's analysis always takes into account the fact that market demand fluctuates, whatever the underlying reason. Not every property will increase in value, particularly over the short term, and some may lose value.

After many years of debate, the federal government mandated state-regulated appraiser licensing or certification for specified federally related real estate transactions. The major impetus for this action came with the enactment by Congress of the Financial Institutions Reform, Recovery, and Enforcement Act of 1989 (FIRREA). Some states require licensing or certification for *all* transactions.

This unit takes a look at the appraiser's role and discusses some of the qualifications that can help ensure a reliable, credible appraisal. The unit also covers licensing and certification requirements and includes discussion of *the Uniform Standards of Professional Appraisal Practice (USPAP)*.

■ THE APPRAISER'S WORK

The professional real estate **appraiser** provides an opinion of the value of an interest in real property (land and/or buildings). Value may be sought for any number of reasons, such as setting a sales price or determining insurance coverage. The appraiser's client can be a buyer, a seller, a lender or other company, an attorney or estate administrator, a public agency, or a real estate broker. Although real estate brokers make many informal estimates of value, it is common practice to rely on the practiced judgment of a professional whose sole interest is in providing a well-founded, unbiased opinion of value.

The **scope of work** that is required for the appraisal assignment, as established by the client and the appraiser, will determine the extent of the research and analysis that the appraiser will perform to complete the appraisal. An appraiser's **opinion of property value** usually is in writing and may be a letter simply stating the appraiser's opinion of value. Most often, however, it is a longer document called an **appraisal report**. The proper steps must be taken to arrive at the value conclusion, regardless of the method used to report it. The appraiser must conduct a thorough study of the appraised property, its geographical area, historical values, and economic trends. The appraiser must be able to read a legal description and recognize the exact boundaries of the subject property. The appraiser also must have some knowledge of building construction to recognize the quality and condition of the structures on the subject property.

The appraiser must know market conditions—why some properties are more desirable than others—as well as how to analyze income and expense statements in order to determine a property's potential earnings.

In short, the appraiser needs some of the expertise of the surveyor, the builder, the broker, the accountant, the economist, and the mortgage lender. Because an appraisal takes into account the many market factors that influence a property's value, an experienced appraiser can make an important contribution to any real estate transaction.

Assignments Available

The service of a qualified appraiser is a recognized essential in many situations. In a real estate transaction involving either the sale or the lease of real property, an appraisal may be desired to

- help set the seller's asking price;

- help a buyer determine the fairness of the asking price;
- set a value for real property when it is part of an estate;
- estimate the relative values of properties being traded;
- set value on property involved in corporate mergers, acquisitions, liquidations, or bankruptcies;
- determine the amount of a mortgage loan; or
- set rental rates.

In addition, other uses of real estate requiring appraisals include

- determining building insurance value;
- determining the effect on value of construction defects as part of a legal proceeding;
- determining property losses due to fire, storm damage, earthquake, or other disaster;
- assessing property for taxes;
- setting gift or inheritance taxes;
- estimating remodeling costs;
- valuing property as part of a marital dissolution;
- valuing property in an arbitration of a dispute;
- determining development costs;
- discovering a vacant property's most profitable use;
- ascertaining whether the present use of a property is its most profitable use; and
- establishing a value for property in a condemnation proceeding.

As time goes on, more and more of these appraisal activities have come to rely on computerized research and databases. An example is the technique called **computer-assisted mass appraisal (CAMA)**, useful when thousands of properties are reassessed for tax purposes. The more complex the property, however, the more the training and skill of the appraiser become a vital part of the valuation process.

Employment Opportunities

The types of appraisals noted previously give some indication of employment opportunities available to professional real estate appraisers.

The appraiser may be self-employed, working as a sole practitioner, or perhaps using the services of a staff of other appraisers. Large **appraisal management companies (AMCs)** have offices in major cities coast to coast, making use of the services of hundreds of appraisers, who usually act as independent contractors.

Aside from appraisal management companies, other sources of employment are open to appraisers and, in many cases, to appraiser trainees. Appraisers' reports are used as a basis for establishing a variety of tax and condemnation values. Federal agencies, such as the **Federal Housing Administration (FHA)**, which is part of the

WEB LINK

www.hud.gov
www.va.gov

Department of Housing and Urban Development (HUD), and the **Department of Veterans Affairs (VA)**, appraise properties before insuring or guaranteeing mortgage loans. All agencies involved in such matters as road construction, urban renewal, conservation, and parkland employ appraisers.

Large industrial organizations, retail and wholesale chains, and restaurant franchises hire appraisers to serve their real estate departments by inspecting and judging the condition of land and buildings before entering into purchase or lease agreements. Individuals considering the purchase or lease of real estate may hire an appraiser directly. If the appraisal will be used as part of a federally related transaction, the services of a licensed or certified appraiser probably will be required. Some states require that all appraisers be licensed or certified—even for transactions that are not federally related. Some clients also impose this requirement.

The importance of objective, accurate appraisals cannot be overstated. The wide range of activities for which the appraiser's services are required eventually touches the life of every citizen.

Appraiser Compensation

The majority of real estate appraisals are market valuations of single-family homes and are performed by self-employed appraisers. A self-employed appraiser works for a specified fee paid by the party by whom the appraiser is hired. In an increasingly common relationship, the appraiser is hired (as an independent contractor or employee) by an appraisal management company that contracts with a lender or other client to provide appraisal services as needed. Federal regulations enacted after the recent housing market downturn, which are discussed later in this unit, now require a layer of oversight between lenders and appraisers to avoid the risk of collusion to produce inflated appraisal values.

Appraisal fees are based on the time required to complete the appraisal process and report (the more complex the property or appraisal report required, the higher the fee will be), but they are also subject to negotiation between the appraiser and the party for whom the appraisal is prepared. Fees are thus subject to a balance between the appraiser's overhead and expenses on one hand and market competition on the other hand. Under no circumstances should the appraiser's fee depend on the final opinion of value, to avoid even the appearance of a conflict of interest. The appraiser's fee also cannot be based on a stipulated or subsequent event.

Exercise 1-1

Should an appraiser's compensation be based on the value of the property being appraised? Why or why not?

Check your answer against the one in the answer key at the back of the book.

LICENSING AND CERTIFICATION

Some of the greatest influences on the status of the real estate appraiser came during the two decades of the 20th century in which the United States experienced its greatest economic challenges. The Great Depression of the 1930s gave birth to both the Society of Residential Appraisers, as part of the United States Savings and Loan League, and the American Institute of Real Estate Appraisers, under the auspices of the National Association of Real Estate Boards (now the National Association of REALTORS®).

The decade of the 1980s brought many examples of economic upheaval, from the cyclic escalation and subsequent decline of real estate prices in California to the devastated marketplaces of the oil-belt states and the Northeast. These and other economic factors contributed to, and in turn were affected by, the collapse of many savings and loan institutions, which ultimately led to the licensing of real estate appraisers.

The decade began with great promise. The Depository Institutions Deregulation and Monetary Control Act of 1980 greatly expanded the activities of depository institutions and raised the level of federally insured accounts to $100,000. With deregulation, however, came many abuses by institutions that were ineptly and sometimes fraudulently managed. It was an era of increased competition, yet many savings and loan associations were strapped with long-term mortgage loans that yielded considerably less income than was necessary to offer the high short-term interest rates that would attract and keep depositors. To compensate, many institutions began to finance projects based on limited market analysis—projects that would have been risky ventures in the best of markets. Unfortunately, political and economic forces did not work in favor of the risk-takers. The Tax Reform Act of 1986 (TRA '86) eliminated the tax incentives for many investments, and the economies of the oil-belt states took a downturn. The resulting crash of real estate prices in many parts of the country proved to be the mortal blow for many overextended institutions.

Other factors contributing to the savings and loan crisis were carelessness and sometimes outright fraud in the preparation of real estate appraisals. Before the savings and loan crisis, no state required appraiser licensing or certification, and only a few states provided for voluntary certification of real estate appraisers or appraisals. At most, some states required that real estate appraisers have a real estate agent's license. This easygoing state of affairs was to be dramatically altered, however, by the federal government.

FIRREA

Congress took action to rescue the failed and failing savings and loans and to initiate procedures that would help prevent another such disaster by passing the **Financial Institutions Reform, Recovery, and Enforcement Act of 1989 (FIRREA)**. FIRREA established the **Office of Thrift Supervision (OTS)** and the **Housing Finance Board** to supervise the savings and loans, a responsibility that had previously belonged to the Federal Home Loan Bank Board. The Federal Savings and Loan Insurance Corporation (FSLIC) was disbanded, and the **Federal Deposit Insurance Corporation (FDIC)** was made responsible for insuring all deposits in participating savings and loan associations as well as deposits in the participating banks it already insured.

Appraiser Licensing

One of the most important actions taken by Congress through FIRREA was the requirement that as of July 1, 1991 (later extended to January 1, 1993), all "federally related real estate appraisals" be performed only by appraisers licensed or certified (as required) by the state in which the real estate is located.

An appraisal by a certified appraiser is required for properties with a transaction value of more than $1 million or complex one- to four-unit residential properties with a transaction value greater than $250,000. A property is considered complex if the property itself, its form of ownership, or the market conditions are atypical.

Licensed status generally is required for appraisals of one- to four-unit residential property, unless the size or complexity of the property indicates that a certified appraiser is necessary. Federal agency directives have indicated that appraisals of nonresidential property and complex residential property with a transaction value less than $250,000 also may be handled by licensed rather than certified appraisers.

In October 1992, Congress passed legislation that requires that any agency seeking to establish a *de minimis* value—a minimum valuation threshold below which appraiser licensing or certification is not required—determine in writing that the threshold set would not threaten the safety and soundness of lending institutions. This threshold was raised from $100,000 to $250,000, effective June 7, 1994. In 2018, FDIC raised the threshold for appraisal of nonresidential properties to $500,000, and other agencies are expected to follow suit. Currently, Fannie Mae, Freddie Mac, the Department of Housing and Urban Development (HUD), and the VA still require the use of state-licensed or state-certified appraisers for every appraisal, as do many lenders and other appraisal clients.

The Appraisal Foundation

WEB LINK

www.appraisalfoundation.org

FIRREA stipulates that state appraiser licensing and certification qualifications and appraisal standards meet or exceed those of the **Appraisal Standards Board (ASB)** and the **Appraiser Qualifications Board (AQB)** of the **Appraisal Foundation**, a nonprofit corporation established in 1987 and headquartered in Washington, D.C. Some appraiser education and experience criteria discussed in the next part of this unit are recommendations, but others are required in order to qualify the appraiser to handle a federally related transaction.

WEB LINK

www.uspap.org

The ASB is responsible for establishing the rules for developing an appraisal and reporting its results. It has issued the ***Uniform Standards of Professional Appraisal Practice (USPAP)***, which has been adopted by all major appraisal groups.

The AQB is responsible for establishing the qualifications for states to follow in the licensing, certification, and recertification of appraisers.

In response to the mortgage lending crisis of recent years, the board of trustees of the Appraisal Foundation formed the **Appraisal Practices Board (APB)** on July 1, 2010. According to an APB press release, the APB was created "to issue voluntary timely guidance to appraisers on emerging valuation issues that are occurring in the marketplace." The guidance is intended to assist appraisers, appraiser regulators, and educators. The initial projects of the APB indicate its concerns. As of October 2014, the APB has issued valuation advisories on adjusting comparable sales for seller concessions, residential appraising in a declining market, identifying comparable properties, and identifying comparable properties in automated valuation models for mass appraisal. All APB valuation advisories can be found at the APB website, accessed through www.appraisalfoundation.org.

Announcement of future activities, public meetings, and publications of the Appraisal Foundation and its boards can be found at its website.

As of August 2017, the appraisal organizations that sponsor the Appraisal Foundation include the American Society of Appraisers, American Society of Farm Managers and Rural Appraisers, Appraisers Association of America, Columbia Society of Real Estate Appraisers, Instituto de Evaluadores de Puerto Rico, International Association of Assessing Officers, International Society of Appraisers, International Right of Way Association, Massachusetts Board of Real Estate Appraisers, National Association of Independent Fee Appraisers, and the North Carolina Professional Appraisers Coalition. Affiliate sponsors include the American Bankers Association, Farm Credit Council, and National Association of REALTORS®. The Royal Institution of Chartered Surveyors is an international sponsor.

Qualifications of an Appraiser

The real estate appraiser's primary qualifications are education and experience. Figure 1.1 lists the AQB licensing and certification criteria for all licensing categories. The criteria set minimum standards, which may be exceeded by state standards. Check with your state's appraiser regulatory agency for applicable rules. The Appraisal Subcommittee of the Federal Financial Institutions Examination Council maintains a directory of state appraiser regulatory programs at www.asc.gov/State-Appraiser-Regulatory-Programs/Statecontactinformation.aspx.

WEB LINK

www.asc.gov/State-Appraiser-Regulatory-Programs/Statecontactinformation.aspx

Appraiser qualification requirements undergo continuous review and revision. Applicants must fulfill both education and experience requirements before taking a qualifying examination, which is required of all licensing categories except appraiser trainee. For the appraiser trainee, all courses must be taken within the five-year period before the trainee application is submitted. The appraiser trainee is allowed to have more than one supervising appraiser, and both appraiser trainee and supervising appraiser(s) must complete a special course explaining their responsibilities in fulfilling that relationship before it begins. All coursework at all levels must include an examination. A written, proctored examination is required for all qualifying education distance course offerings; the exam can be written on paper or administered electronically on a computer workstation or other device. As of January 1, 2017, background checks are required as part of the application process for all licensing categories and are also encouraged for all existing licensees.

Education

The coursework and experience levels established by the Appraiser Qualifications Board of the Appraisal Foundation for licensing and certification set the standard for appraiser education and training. Each state adopts its own requirements, which may be even more demanding. Programs offered by professional associations such as the Appraisal Institute and National Association of Independent Fee

Appraisers must meet individual state requirements in order to offer courses that can be used for credit toward licensing or continuing education in those states.

Colleges and private schools also offer courses in real estate appraising topics, but there are many other courses at both high school and college levels that can be useful for the prospective or practicing appraiser. Some subjects included in basic appraisal courses could benefit from more study. Appraisers must be able to work easily with mathematical computations, because they will be computing land and building dimensions and construction costs and performing all the steps necessary to determine investment income. For this last subject, a knowledge of accounting techniques is invaluable. A course in statistics (required for a certified appraiser) can help any appraiser in researching trend indicators, such as those found in census and economic reports, as well as in the overall analysis of data collected.

Because the appraiser must be able to recognize and draw conclusions from the driving forces behind population movements and economic trends, economics and city planning courses are useful. A knowledge of building construction or engineering will help the appraiser recognize and value building components.

General real estate courses of interest to appraisers, and available through colleges and private schools, are geared primarily to prospective real estate salespeople and brokers, who must be licensed by their state real estate offices. Many real estate appraisers enter the field in this way—gaining the experience of handling real estate transactions and learning firsthand how the market operates.

Overlaying all the courses and practical experience is the necessity to become technologically proficient. The modern appraisal office relies heavily on electronic data gathering, recording, analysis, and reporting. This topic will be discussed in greater detail later in this unit.

Experience

The novice appraiser is likely to begin as a state-licensed trainee who is permitted to work only under the direct supervision of a licensed or certified appraiser. Prospective appraisers, who may perform only the range of duties authorized by the supervising appraiser's credential, can then develop the competence to warrant being hired for their appraisal skill. Government agencies and some financial institutions may have their own appraiser training programs.

Objectivity

Above all, the appraiser must remain objective in considering all of the factors relevant to the appraisal assignment. Any personal interest in the outcome of the appraisal must be revealed to the client, as indicated in the certification mandated by Standards Rule 2-3 of *USPAP*. As a practical matter, it is in the appraiser's best interest to avoid any assignment that might create an appearance of impropriety.

An appraiser's main credential will ultimately be the expertise that comes with performing numerous appraisals. The competent appraiser will also maintain a high level of professional practice by keeping up to date on developments in the field, reading appraisal and related publications, and attending seminars and conferences, in addition to fulfilling continuing education requirements.

FIGURE 1.1

AQB Real Property Appraiser Qualification Criteria (Effective May 1, 2018)

Category	Scope of Practice	Education Hours and Courses	College-Level Courses	Experience
Appraiser trainee	Appraisal of those properties that the supervising certified appraiser is permitted by current credential and that the supervising appraiser is qualified to appraise	75 hours consisting of the basic core curriculum: ■ Basic Appraisal Principles—30 hours ■ Basic Appraisal Procedures—30 hours ■ National *USPAP* course or its equivalent—15 hours (also satisfied by the holding of a valid real estate appraiser license or certification)	None	None
Licensed real property appraiser	Appraisal of noncomplex properties of one to four residential units having a transaction value less than $1 million and complex properties of one to four residential units having a transaction value less than $250,000; does not include appraisal of subdivisions for which a development analysis/ appraisal is necessary	150 hours consisting of the basic core curriculum, plus the following: ■ Residential Market Analysis and Highest and Best Use—15 hours ■ Residential Appraiser Site Valuation and Cost Approach—15 hours ■ Residential Sales Comparison and Income Approaches—30 hours ■ Residential Report Writing and Case Studies—15 hours (also satisfied by the holding of a valid real estate appraiser certification)	None	1,000 hours of experience in no fewer than six months
Certified residential real property appraiser	Appraisal of properties of one to four residential units without regard to value or complexity, and vacant or unimproved land best used for one- to four-family properties; does not include the appraisal of subdivisions for which a development analysis/ appraisal is necessary	200 hours consisting of the basic core curriculum, plus the 75 hours of courses for the Licensed Residential Real Property Appraiser, plus: ■ Statistics, Modeling, and Finance—15 hours ■ Advanced Residential Applications and Case Studies—15 hours ■ Appraisal Specialty Real Estate and Appraisal Subject Matter Electives—20 hours	Bachelor's degree or higher (in any field) from an accredited college or university or one of five other options, including an associate's degree in a field of study related to business administration, accounting, finance, economics, or real estate	1,500 hours of experience in no fewer than 12 months
Certified general real property appraiser	Appraisal of all types of real property	300 hours consisting of the basic core curriculum, plus: ■ General Appraiser Market Analysis and Highest and Best Use—30 hours ■ Statistics, Modeling and Finance—15 hours ■ General Appraiser Sales Comparison Approach—30 hours ■ General Appraiser Site Valuation and Cost Approach—30 hours ■ General Appraiser Income Approach—60 hours ■ General Appraiser Report Writing and Case Studies—30 hours ■ Appraisal Subject Matter Electives—30 hours	Bachelor's degree or higher (in any field) from an accredited college or university	3,000 hours of experience in no fewer than 18 months, of which 1,500 hours must be in nonresidential appraisal work

Exercise 1-2

Which of the following courses would benefit a professional appraiser? Why or why not?

Real estate finance

Land-use planning

Real estate law

Real estate economics

Statistics

Real estate principles

Demographics

Information systems

Check your answer against the one in the answer key at the back of the book.

■ OTHER FEDERAL REGULATION

Ownership and use of real estate are the subjects of an increasing number of federal laws and administrative regulations.

Fair Housing

The important role of all real estate professionals in providing access to housing for every resident of the United States has been recognized by Congress. The Fair Housing Amendments Act of 1988, effective March 12, 1989, prohibits discrimination in the selling, brokering, or appraising of residential real property because of race, color, religion, sex, handicap, familial status, or national origin. The subject of fair housing will be covered in greater detail in Unit 8, "Data Collection."

Environmental Concerns

Regulations affecting buildings that may contain lead-based paint or other contaminants are evidence of a heightened awareness of building construction and land development issues that affect the health and safety of occupants and others. Some of these topics will be covered in Unit 7, "Building Construction and the Environment."

Subprime Lending Crisis

The **subprime lending crisis** that has been in evidence since 2007 has caused increased scrutiny of the entire lending process, including the appraisal of mortgaged property. The crisis was precipitated by what turned out to be a disastrous combination of strong market demand heightened by investors seeking an alternative to the stock market, low interest rates, overly generous loan-qualifying practices that made loans available to borrowers with relatively low credit scores (the no-doc loan didn't even require verification of the borrower's income), and a range of loan products that offered absurdly low initial interest rates or required payment of interest only. One of the most tempting loan products was the 2/28 adjustable-rate mortgage (ARM), which offered an initial low interest rate for the first two years of the loan; the option ARM even gave the borrower the choice of not paying the interest owed, which was added to the loan balance. The assumption by borrowers (incorrectly, as it turned out) was that property appreciation would justify a refinance of the loan before the higher rate kicked in.

By the second half of 2006, many borrowers found that they could not make the new, higher loan payments that kicked in after the initial two-year period and started defaulting on their mortgages. Other borrowers found that they were left with loan balances greater than the market values of their homes—the condition known as being upside down or under water—and simply walked away from their properties. Some mortgage foreclosures were attributed to fraudulent transactions, many of which included fraudulent appraisals that misstated property values in order to defraud a lender. In some cases, an appraisal purported to appraise a property that didn't exist, providing the basis for what prosecutors call the air loan. Information on the activities of the Federal Bureau of Investigation in investigating and prosecuting cases of mortgage fraud, including descriptions of the most common fraud schemes, can be found at www.fbi.gov/about-us/investigate/white_collar/mortgage-fraud.

WEB LINK

www.fbi.gov/about-us/investigate/white_collar/mortgage-fraud

Legislation

Congress took action by passing several pieces of legislation designed to boost the economy, including the **Housing and Economic Recovery Act of 2008 (HERA)**. The law increased the levels at which the FHA or the VA could insure or guarantee loans, and also increased the levels at which loans could be sold on the secondary mortgage market (one of the ways in which lenders acquire more funds for lending).

All mortgage loans now face heightened scrutiny by lenders who seek to verify that both borrower and property qualify for the requested loan. Borrower qualification can be shown by the credit report and verification of income. Property qualification can be demonstrated by an objective appraisal based on market conditions and not wishful thinking. Appraisal standards have never been so important.

HERA also created the **Federal Housing Finance Agency (FHFA)** by merging the Office of Federal Housing Enterprise Oversight (OFHEO) and the Federal Housing Finance Board (FHFB). FHFA is now the regulator and conservator of **Fannie Mae** and **Freddie Mac**, and the regulator of the 12 Federal Home Loan Banks. Fannie Mae and Freddie Mac are **government-sponsored enterprises (GSEs)** that form the secondary mortgage market by purchasing mortgages from banks and packaging them for sale as securities on public exchanges. The role played by the GSEs in the housing crisis will be discussed in more detail in Unit 5, "The Real Estate Marketplace."

WEB LINK

www.fhfa.gov
www.fanniemae.com
www.freddiemac.com

Appraiser Independence Requirements

The subprime lending crisis, and resulting investigations into mortgage lending fraud by both federal and state officials, has resulted in new requirements designed to insure the objectivity of appraisals of secured property. The latest directive from Fannie Mae includes the **Appraiser Independence Requirements,** which are shown in Figure 1.2; they took effect October 15, 2010, and apply to loans sold to Fannie Mae. The 2010 enactment of the **Dodd-Frank Wall Street Reform and Consumer Protection Act (Dodd-Frank)** requires changes to the **Truth in Lending Act (TILA)** and other legislation that prohibit coercion and other actions designed to influence appraisals. As of September 2016, 40 states have enacted comprehensive laws to regulate appraisal management companies.

Professional Standards of Practice

The major appraisal associations have been leaders in establishing standards of appraisal practice, as well as in defining ethical conduct by members of the profession. In 1985, representatives from nine appraisal groups formed the Ad Hoc Committee on Uniform Standards of Professional Appraisal Practice:

- American Institute of Real Estate Appraisers (since merged with the Society of Real Estate Appraisers and now known as the Appraisal Institute)
- American Society of Appraisers
- American Society of Farm Managers and Rural Appraisers
- Appraisal Institute of Canada
- International Association of Assessing Officers
- International Right of Way Association
- National Association of Independent Fee Appraisers
- National Society of Real Estate Appraisers
- Society of Real Estate Appraisers

The standards, published in 1987 and amended regularly since then, cover real estate, personal property, and business appraisals, as well as other topics. They are now the *Uniform Standards of Professional Appraisal Practice*, as interpreted and amended by the Appraisal Standards Board of the Appraisal Foundation. *USPAP* Standards 1, 2, and 3 cover real property appraisal, real property appraisal reporting, and review appraisal. While this book is not intended to instruct students in *USPAP*, sections of *USPAP* will be referred to throughout this book to help students understand how topics covered relate to current appraisal requirements.

WEB LINK
www.uspap.org

Keep in mind that the contents of *USPAP* are subject to ongoing review and modification by the Appraisal Standards Board of the Appraisal Foundation, currently on a two-year cycle. The complete text of the current *Uniform Standards of Professional Appraisal Practice* can be found at www.uspap.org.

FIGURE 1.2
Appraiser Independence Requirements

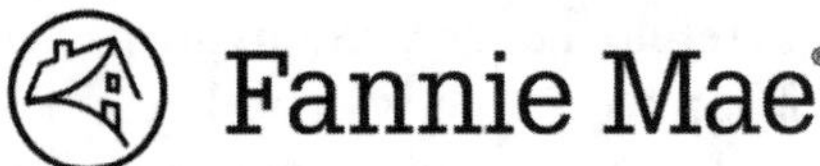

Appraiser Independence Requirements

October 15, 2010
(Reposted April 2017 for reformatting)

I. Appraiser Independence Safeguards

A. An "appraiser" must be, at a minimum, licensed or certified by the State in which the property to be appraised is located.

B. No employee, director, officer, or agent of the Seller, or any other third party acting as joint venture partner, independent contractor, appraisal company, appraisal management company, or partner on behalf of the Seller, shall influence or attempt to influence the development, reporting, result, or review of an appraisal through coercion, extortion, collusion, compensation, inducement, intimidation, bribery, or in any other manner including but not limited to:

(1) Withholding or threatening to withhold timely payment or partial payment for an appraisal report;

(2) Withholding or threatening to withhold future business for an appraiser, or demoting or terminating or threatening to demote or terminate an appraiser;

(3) Expressly or impliedly promising future business, promotions, or increased compensation for an appraiser;

(4) Conditioning the ordering of an appraisal report or the payment of an appraisal fee or salary or bonus on the opinion, conclusion, or valuation to be reached, or on a preliminary value estimate requested from an appraiser;

(5) Requesting that an appraiser provide an estimated, predetermined, or desired valuation in an appraisal report prior to the completion of the appraisal report, or requesting that an appraiser provide estimated values or comparable sales at any time prior to the appraiser's completion of an appraisal report;

(6) Providing to an appraiser an anticipated, estimated, encouraged, or desired value for a subject property or a proposed or target amount to be loaned to the Borrower, except that a copy of the sales contract for purchase transactions may be provided;

(7) Providing to an appraiser, appraisal company, appraisal management company, or any entity or person related to the appraiser, appraisal company, or appraisal management company, stock or other financial or non-financial benefits;

(8) Removing an appraiser from a list of qualified appraisers, or adding an appraiser to an exclusionary list of disapproved appraisers, in connection with the influencing or attempting to influence an appraisal as described in Paragraph B above (this prohibition does not preclude the management of appraiser lists for bona fide administrative or quality-control reasons based on written policy); and

(9) Any other act or practice that impairs or attempts to impair an appraiser's independence, objectivity, or impartiality or violates law or regulation, including, but not limited to, the Truth in Lending Act (TILA) and Regulation

FIGURE 1.2
Appraiser Independence Requirements (continued)

II. Acceptability of Subsequent Appraisals

A Seller must not order, obtain, use, or pay for a second or subsequent appraisal in connection with a Mortgage financing transaction unless: (i) there is a reasonable basis to believe that the initial appraisal was flawed or tainted and such basis is clearly and appropriately noted in the Mortgage file, or (ii) such appraisal is done pursuant to written, pre- established bona fide pre- or post-funding appraisal review or quality control processes or underwriting guidelines, and so long as the Seller adheres to a policy of selecting the most reliable appraisal, rather than the appraisal that states the highest value, or (iii) a second appraisal is required by law.

III. Borrower Receipt of Appraisal

The Seller shall ensure that the Borrower is provided a copy of any appraisal report concerning the Borrower's subject property promptly upon completion at no additional cost to the Borrower, and in any event no less than three days prior to the closing of the Mortgage. The Borrower may waive this three-day requirement if such waiver is obtained at least three days prior to the closing of the Mortgage. The Seller may provide the Borrower at closing, a revised copy of an appraisal and information as to the nature of any revisions, so long as the revisions had no impact on value.

The Seller may require the Borrower to reimburse the Seller for the cost of the appraisal.

IV. Appraiser Engagement

A. The Seller or any third party specifically authorized by the Seller (including, but not limited to, appraisal companies, appraisal management companies, and Correspondent lenders) shall be responsible for selecting, retaining, and providing for payment of all compensation to the appraiser. The Seller will not accept any appraisal report completed by an appraiser selected, retained, or compensated in any manner by any other third party (including Mortgage Brokers and real estate agents).

B. There must be separation of a Seller's sales or Mortgage production functions and appraisal functions. An employee of the Seller in the sales or Mortgage production function shall have no involvement in the operations of the appraisal function.

(1) Certain parties are prohibited from:

(a) Selecting, retaining, recommending, or influencing the selection of any appraiser for a particular appraisal assignment or for inclusion on a list or panel of appraisers approved or forbidden to perform appraisals for the Seller; and

(b) Having any substantive communications with an appraiser or appraisal management company relating to or having an impact on valuation, including ordering or managing an appraisal assignment.

These parties are:

(i) All members of the Seller's Mortgage production staff;

(ii) Any person who is compensated on a commission basis upon the successful completion of a Mortgage; and

(iii) Any person whose immediate supervisor is not independent of the Mortgage production staff and process.

Seller personnel not described in Section IV.B(1)(i) through (iii) above are not subject to the restrictions described above, and may engage in communications with an appraiser. In addition, any party, including the parties described in Section IV.B 1 (i) through (iii) above, may request that an appraiser provide additional information or explanation about the basis for a valuation, or correct objective factual errors in an appraisal report.

FIGURE 1.2
Appraiser Independence Requirements (continued)

(2) If absolute lines of independence cannot be achieved as a result of the Seller's small size and limited staff, the Seller must be able to clearly demonstrate that it has prudent safeguards to isolate its collateral evaluation process from influence or interference from its Mortgage production process.

C. Any employee of the Seller (or if the Seller retains an appraisal company or appraisal management company, any employee of that company) tasked with selecting appraisers for an approved panel or substantive appraisal review must be:

(1) Appropriately trained and qualified in the area of real estate appraisals; and

(2) In the case of an employee of the Seller, wholly independent of the Mortgage production staff and process.

V. Use of Appraisal Reports by In-House Appraisers or Affiliated Appraisers

A. In underwriting a Mortgage, the Seller may use an appraisal report:

(1) Prepared by an appraiser employed by:

(a) The Seller;

(b) An affiliate of the Seller;

(c) An entity that is owned, in whole or in part, by the Seller; or

(d) An entity that owns, in whole or in part, the Seller.

(2) Prepared by an appraiser employed, engaged as an independent contractor, or otherwise retained by an appraisal company or any appraisal management company affiliated with, or that owns or is owned, in whole or in part, by the Seller or an affiliate of the Seller, provided that the Seller complies with the provisions of these Appraiser Independence Requirements.

B. The Seller also may use in-house staff appraisers to:

(1) Order appraisals;

(2) Conduct appraisal reviews or other quality control, whether pre-funding or post- funding;

(3) Develop, deploy, or use internal Automated Valuation Models; or

(4) Prepare appraisals in connection with transactions other than Mortgage origination transactions (e.g., Mortgage workouts), if the Seller complies with the provisions of these Appraiser Independence Requirements.

VI. Transfer of Appraisals

A Seller may deliver to Fannie Mae a conventional Mortgage with an appraisal prepared by an appraiser selected by another lender, including where a Mortgage Broker has facilitated the Mortgage application (but not ordered the appraisal). The Seller delivering the loan to Fannie Mae makes all representations and warranties to Fannie Mae regarding the appraisal set forth in the Mortgage Selling and Servicing Contract, the Selling Guide and related documents, including the representation that the appraisal is obtained in a manner consistent with these Appraiser Independence Requirements.

VII. Referrals of Appraisal Misconduct Reports

Any Seller that has a reasonable basis to believe an appraiser or appraisal management company is violating applicable laws, or is otherwise engaging in unethical conduct, shall promptly refer the matter to the applicable State appraiser certifying and licensing agency or other relevant regulatory bodies.

Figure 1.2
Appraiser Independence Requirements (continued)

VIII. Compliance

Sellers must adopt written policies and procedures implementing these Appraiser Independence Requirements, including, but not limited to, adequate training and disciplinary rules on appraiser independence, including the principles detailed in Section I. Additionally, Sellers must ensure that any third parties, such as appraisal management companies or Correspondent lenders, used in conjunction with the sale and delivery of a Mortgage to Fannie Mae are also in compliance with these Appraiser Independence Requirements.

WEB LINK

www.appraisalfoundation.org

Any proposed changes to the standards, as well as information of value to both appraisers and consumers, can be found at www.appraisalfoundation.org.

Exercise 1-3

1. The federal legislation that resulted in state licensing and certification of appraisers in federally related transactions was
   a. the Internal Revenue Code.
   b. FIRREA.
   c. FDIC.
   d. FSLIC.
2. In federally related appraisals, state appraiser certification qualifications must meet or exceed those of
   a. the Appraisal Standards Board.
   b. the Appraiser Qualifications Board.
   c. the Appraisal Practices Board.
3. Guidance on emerging valuation issues in the marketplace is issued by
   a. the Appraisal Standards Board.
   b. the Appraiser Qualifications Board.
   c. the Appraisal Practices Board.
4. Fannie Mae requires the use of a state-licensed or state-certified appraiser only
   a. for appraisals of property with a transaction value of more than $250,000.
   b. for all Fannie Mae–related transactions.

Check your answers against those in the answer key at the back of the book.

■ PROFESSIONAL GROUPS

Trade Associations

As a way of establishing professional credentials and keeping up to date in the appraisal field, the appraiser may seek membership in one of the appraisal professional groups. Such organizations usually have regular meetings, publish professional journals, hold seminars, and conduct appraisal courses. Usually, they have education, experience, and examination requirements for membership. Often, news updates and legislative announcements are published on an organization's website and are available to the public.

The major appraisal and related associations follow, along with their member designations. Requirements for membership vary widely, with some being substantially more rigorous than others. Readers are urged to carefully evaluate the benefits of membership in any appraisal organization.

WEB LINK
www.appraisers.org

American Society of Appraisers, Herndon, Virginia

www.appraisers.org

Member designations: AM (Accredited Member) and ASA (Accredited Senior Appraiser)

WEB LINK
www.asfmra.org

American Society of Farm Managers and Rural Appraisers, Inc., Denver, Colorado

www.asfmra.org

Member designations: AFM (Accredited Farm Manager), ARA (Accredited Rural Appraiser), RPRA (Real Property Review Appraiser), AAC (Accredited Agricultural Consultant)

WEB LINK
www.appraisalinstitute.org

Appraisal Institute, Chicago, Illinois

www.appraisalinstitute.org

Publisher of *The Appraisal Journal and Valuation* magazine, as well as a number of special reports and books

Member designations: MAI (member experienced in the valuation and evaluation of commercial, industrial, residential, and other types of property, and who advises clients on real estate investment decisions) and SRA (member experienced in the analysis and valuation of residential real property)

WEB LINK
www.aicanada.org

Appraisal Institute of Canada, Winnipeg, Manitoba, Canada

www.aicanada.org

Publisher of *Canadian Property Valuation*

Member designations: CRA (Canadian Residential Appraiser) and AACI (Accredited Appraiser Canadian Institute)

WEB LINK
www.iaao.org

International Association of Assessing Officers, Chicago, Illinois

www.iaao.org

Publisher of the *Journal of Property Tax Assessment & Administration* and *Fair & Equitable* magazine, as well as many specialized booklets and manuals

Member designations: AAS (Assessment Administration Specialist), CAE (Certified Assessment Evaluator), CMS (Cadastral Mapping Specialist), PPS (Personal Property Specialist), RES (Residential Evaluation Specialist)

WEB LINK
www.irwaonline.org

International Right of Way Association, Inglewood, California

www.irwaonline.org

Publisher of *Right of Way* magazine

Member designations: ARWP (Associate Right of Way Professional), RWA (Right of Way Agent), RWP (Right of Way Professional), SR/WA (Senior Right of Way Professional)

WEB LINK
www.naifa.com

National Association of Independent Fee Appraisers, Inc., Chicago, Illinois

www.naifa.com

Publisher of *Appraiser's Voice*

Member designations: IFA (member), IFAA (agriculture member), IFAS (senior member), and IFAC (appraiser counselor)

WEB LINK
www.nraiappraisers.com

National Residential Appraisers Institute, Amherst, Ohio

www.nraiappraisers.com

Member designations: CMDA (Certified Market Data Analyst), GSA (Graduate Senior Appraiser), SCA (Senior Certified Appraiser), and SLA (Senior Licensed Appraiser)

WEB LINK
www.nsrea.org

National Society of Real Estate Appraisers, Inc., Cleveland, Ohio

www.nsrea.org

Publisher of *National Report*

Member designations: RA (Residential Appraiser), CRA (Certified Real Estate Appraiser), and MREA (Master Real Estate Appraiser)

WEB LINK
www.ncpac.us

North Carolina Professional Appraisers Coalition, Garner, North Carolina

www.ncpac.us

Member designation: CDA (Coalition Designated Appraiser)

Political Action Groups

WEB LINK
www.nationalappraisalcoalition.org/findacoalition.html

With the great number of recent legislative and administrative changes that impact appraisers, organizations of appraisers that focus on political advocacy have been formed in approximately 20 states. A current list of these groups can be found at the National Appraisal Coalition website: www.nationalappraisalcoalition.org/findacoalition.html.

■ THE MODERN APPRAISAL OFFICE

With the increasing availability and range of use of small, easily programmed computers and other devices, the appraiser must be acquainted with a variety of appraisal-based applications. Keeping up to date with advances in technology is crucial. The professional appraiser must keep up with competitors to support the best interests of clients. To do that, the appraiser should be prepared to read articles about technological advances in appraisal journals, be alert to reviews of new products, watch training videos, and take both classroom and online courses. A few technology considerations are mentioned next.

The Backup System

Digitized information that is created and may exist only in electronic form is a boon to the appraiser, but it can also be the appraiser's worst nightmare in the event of a power failure, mechanical malfunction, or incursion by a computer virus. Ensuring against a power failure can be as simple as having a battery (not just a power surge protector) to which a computer is connected to provide a secondary power supply. A program that provides an automatic backup of files nightly can prevent a catastrophic loss of data. The backup can be downloaded to a separate hard drive or server located onsite, but an offsite source for data storage offers even greater protection. Off-site (cloud) services are plentiful, convenient, and inexpensive. Such offsite services help the appraiser comply with *USPAP* obligations such as the Record Keeping Rule, which requires appraisers to keep appraisal records for a minimum of five years. If the appraiser loses a workfile, the fault rests with the appraiser. As software has become more sophisticated, most programs automatically back up the user's work at regular intervals during the workday, minimizing any data loss. The installation and ongoing use of an antivirus program is essential for all computers and other communication devices.

The Internet

Use of the internet for research and data collection is growing exponentially every year, as more and more sources, including multiple listing services, provide online access to their databases. The number of government offices allowing access to public records is also growing. Information on national, regional, and local economic, employment, and other trends is readily available. Services specialize in data on various types of commercial and residential properties; some of these sources are listed in Unit 8, "Data Collection." Despite numerous data sources, however, not all information available is up to date or accurately reported. *USPAP* requires that appraisers verify all information used in the appraisal report.

Geographic Information Systems (GIS)

Modern geographic information systems (GIS) can be used to locate the subject of the appraisal, comparable properties, and additional landmarks useful in the appraisal. GIS data can also be used to locate properties relative to floodplains and wetlands. Satellite-based mapping systems have been used for as long as satellites have orbited the earth. From their initial military and weather technology-based applications, mapping systems based on latitude and longitude have entered the commercial marketplace. Commercial services now provide digital reference maps that provide overlays of national, regional, and local data and are capable of incorporating the appraiser's own data. The cost of such maps depends on the source and method of transmission.

The Camera

Appraisers used to rely on instant cameras for their appraisals. Over time, appraisal requirements increased, and appraisers turned to 35-millimeter photography. With advances in technology, appraisers then turned to digital imaging. The first digital cameras were large, unwieldy, and produced low-resolution images. Modern smartphones have camera functions that are vastly superior. With a digital camera equipped with a memory card of sufficient capacity or wireless access to a computer, the appraiser can import images directly to an appraisal report. If the report is transmitted electronically, the photos are incorporated into the report to be viewed on the recipient's screen. *Note*: Because some courts and government agencies still require printed appraisal reports with separate, professionally reproduced photos, some appraisers choose to use a 35-millimeter film camera as well as a digital camera. The purpose of the appraisal will dictate the appropriate format.

Measuring Devices

Gone are the days when appraisers used measuring wheels and tape measures. Now, appraisers use modern laser tape devices that can measure buildings with greater accuracy and can be used even in inclement weather, such as fog. Using Bluetooth technology, such laser tapes can upload dimensions directly into appraisal software that can produce a floor plan. This increases the appraiser's speed and accuracy, which reduces liability.

Use of Technology

The use of appropriate resources, including internet access, can help an appraiser function more efficiently and more accurately, but these tools serve only as aids to the appraiser. There never will be a substitute for the skilled and informed judgment of a professional appraiser.

Exercise 1-4

What are some things an appraiser can do to ensure an efficient, reliable source of information and data storage?

Check your answer against the one in the answer key at the back of the book.

■ SUMMARY

The skills required of the professional appraiser touch on most areas of real estate practice. The best-qualified appraiser will have some of the abilities of an economist, city planner, surveyor, real estate developer, builder, and broker. Familiarity with appraisal-based computer applications is a necessity.

Impartiality, knowledge of appraising fundamentals, and the quality of judgment that comes only with experience are the professional appraiser's chief credentials. Real estate appraisers' impartiality is essential to insure that their prerogatives are not abused. The appraiser's knowledge and experience provide the basis for an accurate appraisal. Employment opportunities include both private and public sectors, and an appraiser may be called on for a variety of purposes.

Only state-licensed or state-certified appraisers are allowed to perform real property appraisals in certain federally related transactions. By helping to better define the role and responsibilities of the real estate appraiser, federal and state regulations enhance the qualifications of those who seek licensing or certification to improve the level of appraisal services available.

Federal laws and regulations on such topics as fair housing and environmental issues are of increasing concern to appraisers. The subprime lending crisis of the first decade of this century resulted in legislation that increased loan limitations for federally insured and guaranteed loans and also increased the limits on loans that can be purchased on the secondary mortgage market. Fannie Mae issued Appraiser Independence Requirements, and the Dodd-Frank Act resulted in new regulations designed to avoid coercion of appraisers.

The professional appraisal societies provide excellent sources of appraisal information. Today's appraiser makes use of such resources to stay abreast of both legal requirements and technological innovations.

■ Review Questions

1. List at *LEAST* five general course areas that would benefit a real estate appraiser, in addition to real estate courses.

2. The federal agency that now insures deposits in financial institutions is
   a. FDIC.
   b. FSLIC.
   c. RTC.
   d. FIRREA.

3. All the following areas of federal regulation affect appraisers *EXCEPT*
   a. appraiser licensing.
   b. fair housing.
   c. Congressional Budget Office (CBO).
   d. lead-based paint.

4. Appraiser qualifications that meet federal guidelines come from
   a. the Appraiser Qualifications Board.
   b. the Appraisal Standards Board.
   c. the Resolution Trust Corporation.
   d. the Appraisal Institute.

5. Every state must enact legislation to provide for appraiser licensing and certification that is consistent with criteria established by
   a. the Federal National Mortgage Association.
   b. the Appraiser Qualifications Board of the Appraisal Foundation.
   c. the Resolution Trust Corporation.
   d. the Appraisal Institute.

6. The purpose of *USPAP* is to
   a. delay government regulation.
   b. present information that will be meaningful to the client and will not be misleading in the marketplace.
   c. guarantee professionalism in appraisers.
   d. present information that will be useful to appraisers.

7. A certified appraiser is required for federally related transactions involving property valued at more than
   a. $250,000.
   b. $500,000.
   c. $750,000.
   d. $1,000,000.

8. The Federal Housing Finance Agency was created by
   a. the Financial Institutions Reform, Recovery, and Enforcement Act of 1989.
   b. the Housing and Economic Recovery Act of 2008.
   c. the Tax Reform Act of 1986.
   d. the Fair Housing Amendments Act of 1988.

9. The appraisal coursework required by the AQB for a certified general real estate appraiser totals
   a. 75 hours.
   b. 150 hours.
   c. 300 hours.
   d. 500 hours.

10. An appraisal is
    a. an opinion of value.
    b. an estimate of value.
    c. the highest price.
    d. whatever the buyer and seller agree on.

11. An appraiser
    a. estimates price.
    b. estimates value.
    c. renders an opinion of value.
    d. renders an opinion of cost.

12. The scope of work
    a. protects the public.
    b. establishes what the appraiser should do in the assignment.
    c. is an optional component of the appraisal assignment.
    d. is established by the client.

13. To ensure the credibility of the appraisal, the appraiser must be
    a. objective.
    b. a novice.
    c. under the supervision of another appraiser.
    d. working in a team of appraisers.

14. All of the following are valid methods to keep up with changes in technology *EXCEPT*
    a. taking college courses.
    b. taking appraisal courses.
    c. word of mouth from friends.
    d. watching internet videos about technology.

15. The purpose of the *Uniform Standards of Professional Appraisal Practice (USPAP)* is to
    a. increase appraisal fees.
    b. enhance public trust in appraisal.
    c. increase the appraiser's business.
    d. make appraiser licensing national.

16. The appraisal coursework required for a certified residential appraiser is
    a. 75 hours.
    b. 150 hours.
    c. 200 hours.
    d. 300 hours.

17. Appraisers are licensed by
    a. the federal government.
    b. the government of the state in which the appraiser resides.
    c. the government of the state in which the subject property is located.
    d. the National Association of REALTORS®.

18. Licensing of appraisers protects
    a. the public.
    b. the appraiser.
    c. the Appraisal Foundation.
    d. the state.

19. The appraiser can accurately locate the property being appraised using
    a. a compass.
    b. a digital camera.
    c. a backup system.
    d. a geographic information system (GIS).

20. Joining a professional trade association
    a. can help an appraiser keep up to date with the appraisal field.
    b. is required by federal law.
    c. is required by the law of the state in which the appraiser is practicing.
    d. guarantees the appraiser will find work.

Check your answers against those in the answer key at the back of the book.

UNIT TWO

APPRAISAL MATH AND STATISTICS

■ LEARNING OBJECTIVES

When you have completed this unit, you will be able to

- convert percentages to decimals, decimals to percentages, and fractions to decimals;
- solve percentage problems;
- calculate the area of squares, rectangles, triangles, and irregular closed figures;
- convert various units of measure;
- compute the amount of living area in a house;
- compute the volume of triangular prisms;
- define terms used in the study of statistics;
- interpret and analyze statistical data when presented in an array and frequency distribution;
- calculate the mean, median, and mode;
- distinguish between the formula for finding the standard deviation of an entire population and the formula for finding the standard deviation of a sample;
- calculate the range, average deviation, and standard deviation;
- prepare statistical data in the form of tables, bar charts, histograms, and line graphs; and
- describe regression analysis.

■ KEY TERMS

aggregate
area
array
average deviation
bell curve
compound interest
decimal
fraction
frequency distribution
mean
measure of central tendency
measure of dispersion
median
mode
normal distribution
outlier
percent
parameter
population
random sample
range
regression analysis
sample
simple interest
skewness
square foot
standard deviation
variate

■ OVERVIEW

Math is used every day in the real estate business. Sometimes it involves a simple measurement of land area. At other times, it involves a complex investment analysis that requires sophisticated computers programmed with compound interest schedules and multiple regression tables.

This unit covers some of the basics of real estate math. You will learn to work with percentages, decimals, and fractions, as is routine with the appraiser. In addition, this unit provides a review of the mathematics involved in computing area and volume. A home appraisal generally requires the use of area in some way. When comparing properties, for example, the appraiser must be able to determine the size of a lot in square feet, the amount of floor space in a room or house, and the construction cost per square foot of various components of the house.

Many boundaries, lots, and houses are irregularly shaped; that is, they are not rectangular. Appraisers should know how to compute the area (and volume, where applicable) of just about any shape they may encounter.

Other mathematical computations with which the appraiser should be familiar, such as compound interest, are also discussed. The unit ends with a brief introduction to statistics. Statistical analysis has particular application to the work of the appraiser because appraisers are continually drawing inferences about populations or markets from samples.

Because readers will have varying degrees of knowledge and experience in math computations, the questions at the end of this unit may be used to review such computations. They will indicate whether all the material in this unit should be studied.

■ CALCULATORS

Calculators are a great aid in the real estate business, and you should know how to use one. State licensing exams generally allow you to use a silent, handheld calculator, as long as it does not have a printout tape. A common four-function calculator (+, –, ×, ÷, plus % and √ keys) is sufficient for most problems you will encounter on the job or on exams. Most models have the ability to store and recall numbers in a built-in memory, which reduces the need to write down answers to be used in subsequent calculations.

If you plan to buy a new calculator, however, a good-quality financial calculator might be a better choice. This type of calculator has a memory and is also capable of performing all the mathematical and financial operations you will probably need. A financial calculator will include these additional function keys:

Key	Function
n	Number of interest compounding periods
i	Amount of interest per compounding period
PMT	Payment
PV	Present value
FV	Future value

These five keys on the financial calculator can handle almost every conceivable problem dealing with finance. Although proficiency with the calculator does not guarantee success on exams or on the job, there is little doubt that it does provide a critical edge.

PERCENTAGES

Percent (%) means per hundred or per hundred parts. For example, 50% means 50 parts out of a total of 100 parts (100 parts equals 1 whole), and 100% means all 100 of the 100 total parts, or 1 whole unit.

Converting Percentages to Decimals

To change a percentage to a **decimal**, move the decimal point two places to the left and drop the percent sign (%). All numbers have a decimal point, although it is usually not shown when only zeros follow it.

IN PRACTICE

99 is really 99.0
6 is really 6.0
$1 is the same as $1.00

So, percentages can be readily converted to decimals.

99% = 99.0% = 0.990 = 0.99
6% = 6.0% = 0.060 = 0.06
70% = 70.0% = 0.700 = 0.70

Note: Adding zeros to the right of a decimal point after the last digit does not change the value of the number.

Converting Decimals to Percentages

This process is the reverse of the one you just completed. Move the decimal point two places to the right and add the % sign.

IN PRACTICE

0.10 = 10%
1.00 = 100%
0.98 = 98%
0.987 = 98.7%

Converting Fractions to Decimals

A proper **fraction** is one whose top number is less than its bottom number. Its value is always less than 1.

Examples: $\frac{1}{4}$ $\frac{1}{2}$ $\frac{3}{17}$ $\frac{9}{100}$

The top number in a fraction is called the numerator. The bottom number in a fraction is called the denominator.

To convert a proper fraction to a decimal, divide the fraction's numerator by its denominator.

$\frac{5}{8}$

$5 \div 8 = 0.625$

Exercise 2-1

Convert the following fractions to decimals.

$\frac{2}{5}$

$\frac{37}{100}$

$\frac{1}{6}$

Check your answers against those in the answer key at the back of the book.

Percentage Problems

Percentage problems usually involve three elements: percent (rate), total, and part.

IN PRACTICE

Percent		Total		Part
10%	of	100	is	10

IN PRACTICE

Look at the example that follows. A problem involving percentages is really a multiplication problem. To solve this problem, you first convert the percentage to a decimal, and then multiply.

What is 20% of 150?

150 × 20% = ?
20% = 0.20
150 × 0.20 = 30

Answer: 20% of 150 is 30.

A generalized formula for solving percentage problems is

$$\text{Total} \times \text{Percent} = \text{Part}$$

To solve a percentage problem, you must know the value of two of the elements of this formula. The value that you must find is called the unknown (most often shown in the formula as *x*).

IN PRACTICE

If 25% of the houses in your area are less than 10 years old and there are 600 houses, how many houses are less than 10 years old?

Total × Percent = Part
600 × 25% = x
600 × 0.25 = 150

Two additional formulas can be derived from the basic formula total × percent = part. The following diagram will help you remember them:

$$\frac{\text{Part}}{\text{Total} \times \text{Percent}}$$

Because part is over percent in the diagram, you make a fraction of these two elements when looking for a total:

$$\text{Total} = \frac{\text{Part}}{\text{Percent}}$$

Because part is over total, you make a fraction of these two elements when looking for a percentage:

$$\text{Percent} = \frac{\text{Part}}{\text{Total}}$$

Because percent and total are both in the lower part of the diagram, multiply these two to get the part:

$$\text{Part} = \text{Total} \times \text{Percent}$$

IN PRACTICE

If 25% of the houses in your area are less than 10 years old and this amounts to 150 houses, how many houses are there in your area?

Solution: State the formula.

$$\text{Total} = \frac{\text{Part}}{\text{Percent}}$$

Substitute values.

$$\text{Total} = \frac{150}{0.25}$$

Solve the problem.
Total = 600

IN PRACTICE

There are 600 houses in your area, and 150 of them are less than 10 years old. What percentage of the houses are less than 10 years old?

Solution:

$$\text{Percent} = \frac{\text{Part}}{\text{Total}}$$

$$\text{Total} = \frac{150}{600}$$

Percent = 0.25 or 25%

Problem-Solving Strategy

Let's take a look at how to solve word problems. Here's the five-step strategy you should use:

1. Read the problem carefully.
2. Analyze the problem, pick out the important factors, and put those factors into a simplified question, disregarding unimportant factors.
3. Choose the proper formula for the problem.
4. Substitute the figures for the elements of the formula.
5. Solve the problem.

If you use this strategy throughout this unit and wherever it applies in this text, you'll have an easier time with word problems.

IN PRACTICE

Consider an example that applies the five-step strategy to a typical real estate problem.

1. Read the following problem carefully.

   A house sold for $140,600, which was 95% of the original list price. At what price was the house originally listed?

2. Analyze the problem, pick out the important factors, and put those factors into a question.

   $140,600 is 95% of what?

3. Choose the proper formula for the problem.

$$\text{Total} = \frac{\text{Part}}{\text{Percent}}$$

4. Substitute the figures for the elements of the formula.

$$\text{Total} = \frac{\$140{,}600}{0.95}$$

5. Solve the problem.

Total = $148,000

Let's try another problem, one that you'll deal with in units on income capitalization. Assume a property earns a net operating income of $26,250 per year. What percentage of net operating income (rate) is this, if the property is valued at $210,000?

You can solve this problem using these capitalization formulas:

$$\frac{\text{Income}}{\text{Value} \times \text{Rate}}$$

$$\frac{\text{Part}}{\text{Total} \times \text{Percent}}$$

Both formulas are really the same. Think of total as value, part as income, and percent as rate.

Solution: Restate the problem:

What percentage of $210,000 is $26,250?

What formula will you use?

$$\text{Rate} = \frac{\text{Income}}{\text{Value}} \quad \text{or} \quad R = \frac{I}{V}$$

Solve the problem:

$$\$26{,}250 \div \$210{,}000 = 0.125 \text{ or } 12.5\%$$

As you have seen, in working with problems involving percentages, there are several ways of stating the same relationship.

For example, you can say that

$$P = B \times R$$

where
P is the percentage of the whole
B is the base, or whole
R is the rate

Or

$$I = RV$$

where
I is the amount of income
R is the rate
V is the value or whole

Or

$$\text{Part} = \text{Whole} \times \text{Rate}$$

Or

$$\text{Part} = \text{Total} \times \text{Percent}$$

IN PRACTICE

To find out how many square feet are in 20% of an acre, you must first know how many square feet are in an acre. This number is 43,560. The problem can be solved by using any of the preceding formulas.

Part = Whole × Rate
Part = 43,560 sq. ft. × 20%
Part = 43,560 sq. ft. × 0.20
Part = 8,712 sq. ft.

Exercise 2-2

If houses in your area have increased in value 8% during the past year and the average price of houses sold last year was $190,000, what is the average price of houses sold today?

A house purchased for $250,000 sold a few years later. The seller received $340,000 after deducting sale expenses. What percentage profit did the seller make on the investment?

Check your answers against those in the answer key at the back of the book.

■ INTEREST

Interest is the cost of using someone else's money. A person who borrows money is required to repay the loan plus a charge for interest. This charge will depend on the amount borrowed (principal), the length of time the money is used (time), and the percentage of interest agreed on (rate). Repayment, then, involves the return of the principal plus a return on the principal, called interest.

There are two types of interest: simple interest and compound interest.

Simple Interest

Simple interest is interest earned on only the original principal, not on the accrued interest. Interest is always payable for a particular period, whether daily, monthly, annually, or based on some other schedule. With simple interest, the amount earned at the end of each period is withdrawn or placed in a separate account.

The formula for computing simple interest is

$$\text{Principal} \times \text{Rate} \times \text{Time} = \text{Interest}$$

For example, the interest owed on a loan of $1,000 for 180 days at a rate of 10% per year is $1,000 × 0.10 × (180⁄360), which can be simplified to $1,000 × 0.10 × ½, which equals $50.

The formula for computing simple interest is used to determine the amount of up-front points (also called discount points) that a lender may require as part of the fee for a mortgage loan.

For example, a loan in the amount of $160,000 may require payment of two points at the time of closing. In that case, the borrower must be prepared to pay $160,000 × 2%, which is $160,000 × 0.02, or $3,200, to the lender as a condition of receiving the loan.

In computing a loan's annual percentage rate (APR) for federal mortgage loan disclosure purposes, one point (1%) paid at the time of origination is considered roughly equal to a one-eighth increase in the rate charged over the life of the loan. This means that if a loan of $160,000 at an interest rate of 5% requires a payment of two points up front, the annual percentage rate—the actual interest rate paid—is closer to 5¼%. This figure is computed by adding 5% + (2 × ⅛%), which is 5% + 2⁄8%, which can be simplified to 5¼%.

Compound Interest

The term **compound interest** means that the interest is periodically added to the principal, and in effect the new balance (principal plus interest) draws interest. The annual interest rate may be calculated at different intervals, such as annually, semiannually, quarterly, monthly, or daily. When the interest comes due during the compounding period (for instance, at the end of the month), the interest is calculated and accrues, or is added to the principal.

IN PRACTICE

A savings account with a starting balance of $20,000 earns compound interest at 2% per year compounded annually. To determine how much money will be in the account at the end of two years, follow these steps:

1. Calculate the interest for the first earning period
   $20,000 × 1.02 = $20,400

2. Calculate the interest for the next earning period on the new principal balance
   $20,400 × 1.02 = $20,808

The balance at the end of two years is $20,808.

Calculating the Functions of One Dollar

The annuity and other capitalization techniques covered in Unit 14 will require the use of a financial calculator, such as the HP 12C. Before calculators greatly simplified calculations, an appraiser could make use of tables of factors derived from formulas that represent the change in return on an investment over time at various interest rates.

There are six functions of an investment of one dollar that are traditionally used in finance, and they are an integral part of appraisal analysis. The six functions of one dollar are:

1. **The Future Value of $1**

   Put a dollar in the bank and watch it grow.

2. **The Future Value of $1 per Period**

   Put a dollar in the bank every period and watch it grow.

3. **The Sinking Fund Factor**

   How much must be set aside in the bank now so that a dollar is saved over time?

4. **The Present Value of $1**

   If you expect to earn a dollar at some future date, what is that dollar worth now?

5. **The Present Value of $1 per Period**

   If you expect to earn a dollar every period, what are those dollars worth now?

6. **The Payment to Amortize $1**

   If you borrow a dollar, how much must be paid (in principal and interest) every period to pay off the loan?

Hewlett Packard first marketed the HP 12C financial calculator in 1981; the version sold today is essentially unchanged. The calculator uses a system called reverse Polish notation (RPN) to perform basic functions, such as those listed here.

Addition. To add 1 to 1, the keystrokes are: 1 [enter] 1 [+]. The display reads 2.

Subtraction. To subtract 4 from 10, the keystrokes are 10 [enter] 4 [–]. The display reads 6.

Multiplication. To multiply 5 times 4, the keystrokes are 5 [enter] 4 [×]. The display reads 20.

Division. To divide 20 by 5, the keystrokes are 20 [enter] 5 [÷]. The display reads 4.

If you are using the HP 12C, you will note that there is no key with the equal sign (=). The HP 12C does not require one, which eliminates an extra key stroke and also provides the advantage that one calculation can be made after another without interruption or reentering the last display.

In Unit 14, "Direct and Yield Capitalization," we will look at elementary financial function problems using the HP 12C.

Exercise 2-3

An account is opened with a deposit of $30,000. If interest is compounded at an annual rate of 2%, and no withdrawals are made, what will be the account balance at the end of three years?

Check your answer against the one in the answer key at the back of the book.

■ AREA AND VOLUME

Many mathematical computations occur throughout the appraisal of any structure, from the simplest one-room warehouse to the most complex apartment or office building. The appraiser must find the square footage of the appraised site, the number of square feet of usable structure space, and the total square feet of the ground area the structure covers. In addition, one of the methods used in the cost approach to appraisal requires the measurement of cubic feet of space occupied by the structure.

The appraiser should know how to compute the area (and volume, where applicable) of any shape. Property boundaries, particularly those measured by the method known as metes and bounds (also called courses and distances), often are not regularly shaped, and structures usually are not.

Area of Squares and Rectangles

To review some basics about shapes and measurements:

The space inside a two-dimensional shape is called its **area**.

A right angle is the angle formed by one-fourth of a circle. Because a full circle is 360 degrees and one-fourth of 360 degrees is 90 degrees, a right angle is a 90-degree angle.

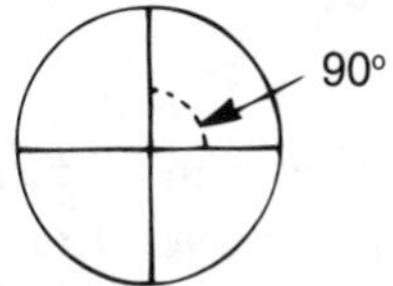

A rectangle is a closed figure with four sides that are at right angles to each other.

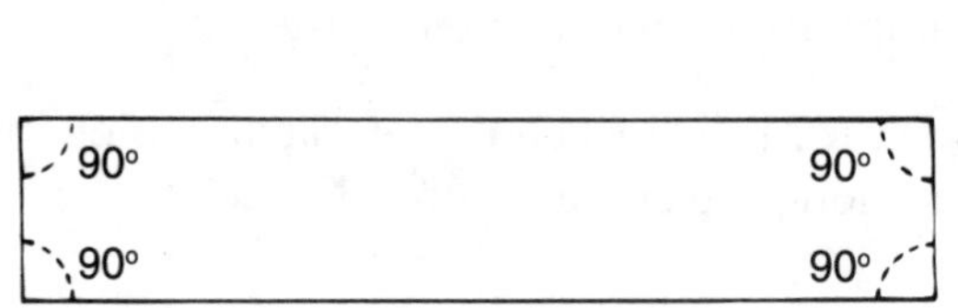

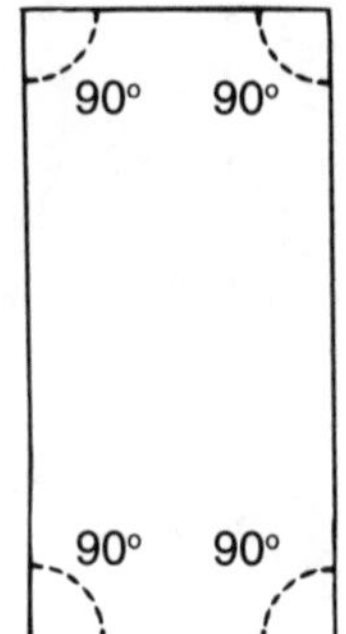

A square is a rectangle with four sides of equal length. A square with sides each one inch long is a square inch. A square with sides each one foot long is a **square foot**.

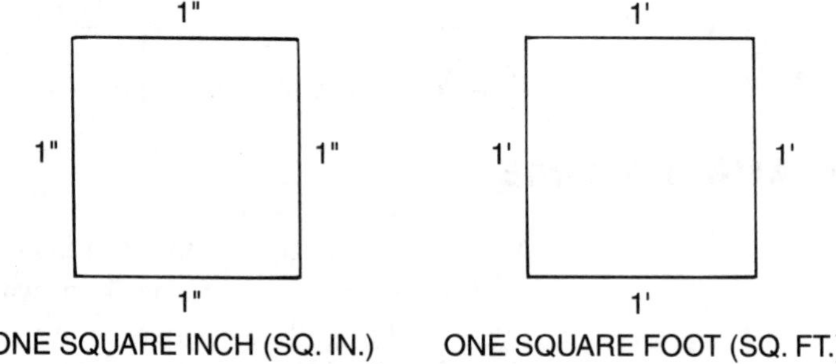

Note: The symbol for inch is ". The symbol for foot is '. The abbreviations are in. and ft.

The following formula may be used to compute the area of any rectangle:

$$\text{Area} = \text{Length} \times \text{Width}$$

$$A = L \times W$$

The area of the following rectangle, using the formula, is 5" × 6", or 30 square inches.

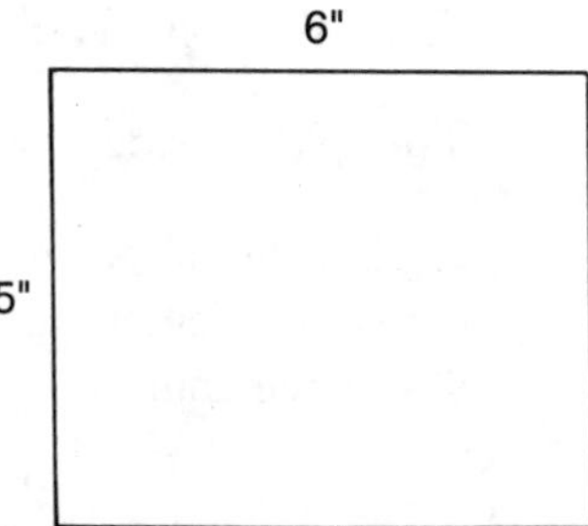

The term *30 inches* refers to a straight line 30 inches long. The term *30 square inches* refers to the area of a specific figure. When inches are multiplied by inches, the answer is in square inches. Likewise, when feet are multiplied by feet, the answer is in square feet.

Square feet are sometimes expressed by using the exponent ^{2}; for example, 10 $ft.^2$ is read 10 feet squared and means 10' × 10', or 100 square feet.

An exponent indicates how many times the number, or unit of measurement, is multiplied by itself. This is called the power of the number or unit of measure. The exponent is indicated at the upper right of the original number or unit of measurement (for example, 10^3 would equal 10 × 10 × 10; 10^4 is 10 × 10 × 10 × 10).

In the following image, the area of the rectangle at the left is 4' × 6', or 24 square feet. The area of the square at the right is 5 yards × 5 yards, or 25 square yards.

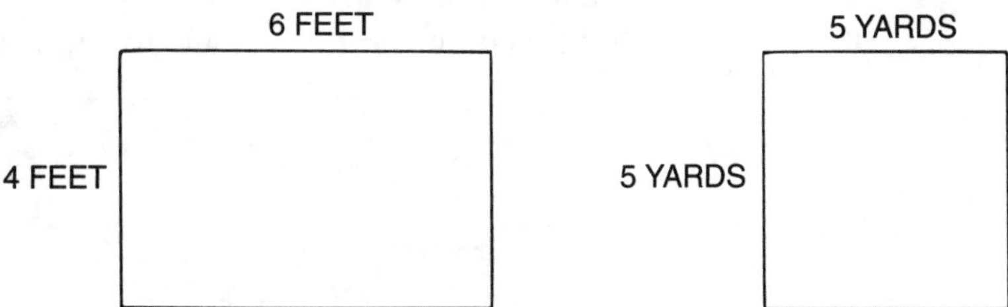

IN PRACTICE

To provide storage space for its vehicles, a business has leased a vacant lot that measures 60 feet by 160 feet. How much rent will the business pay per year if the lot rents for $0.35 per square foot per year?

To solve this problem, the area of the lot must be computed first.

$$A = L \times W = 160' \times 60' = 9{,}600 \text{ sq. ft.}$$

The number of square feet is then multiplied by the price per square foot to get the total rent.

$$9{,}600 \times \$0.35 = \$3{,}360$$

Front foot vs. area

In certain situations, a tract of land may be priced at $X per front foot. Typically, this occurs when the land faces something desirable, such as a main street, a river, or a lake, thus making the frontage the major element of value.

For example, consider the following tract of land facing (fronting on) a lake.

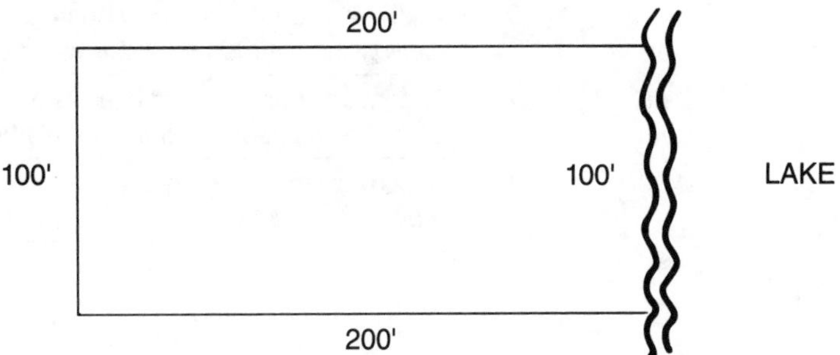

The area of the lot is 20,000 square feet (100' × 200'). If this lot sells for $100,000, its price could be shown as $5 per square foot ($100,000 ÷ 20,000 square feet) or $1,000 per front foot ($100,000 ÷ 100 front feet).

Conversions—using like measures for area

When area is computed, all dimensions used must be given in the same kind of unit. When a formula is used to find an area, units of the same kind must be used for each element of the formula, with the answer as square units of that kind. So inches must be multiplied by inches to arrive at square inches, feet must be multiplied by feet to arrive at square feet, and yards must be multiplied by yards to arrive at square yards.

If the two dimensions to be multiplied are in different units of measure, one of the units of measure must be converted to the other. The following chart shows how to convert one unit of measure to another.

12 inches = 1 foot 36 inches = 1 yard 3 feet = 1 yard	
To convert feet to inches, *multiply the number of feet by 12.*	(*ft.* × 12 = in.)
To convert inches to feet, *divide the number of inches by 12.*	(*in.* ÷ 12 = ft.)
To convert yards to feet, *multiply the number of yards by 3.*	(*yd.* × 3 = ft.)
To convert feet to yards, *divide the number of feet by 3.*	(*ft.* ÷ 3 = yd.)
To convert yards to inches, *multiply the number of yards by 36.*	(*yd.* × 36 = in.)
To convert inches to yards, *divide the number of inches by 36.*	(*in.* ÷ 36 = yd.)

To convert square inches, square feet, and square yards, use the following chart:

To convert square feet to square inches, *multiply the number of square feet by 144.*	(*sq. ft.* × 144 = sq. in.)
To convert square inches to square feet, *divide the number of square inches by 144.*	(*sq. in.* ÷ 144 = sq. ft.)
To convert square yards to square feet, *multiply the number of square yards by 9.*	(*sq. yd.* × 9 = sq. ft.)
To convert square feet to square yards, *divide the number of square feet by 9.*	(*sq. ft.* ÷ 9 = sq. yd.)
To convert square yards to square inches, *multiply the number of square yards by 1,296.*	(*sq. yd.* × 1,296 = sq. in.)
To convert square inches to square yards, *divide the number of square inches by 1,296.*	(*sq. in.* ÷ 1,296 = sq. yd.)
To convert acres into square feet, *multiply the number of acres by 43,560.*	(*acres* × 43,560 = sq. ft.)

Exercise 2-4

Solve the following problems:

12" × 3'= ____________ square feet or ____________ square inches

15" × 1.5' = ____________ square feet or ____________ square inches

72" × 7' = ____________ square feet or ____________ square inches

What is the area of the square below in square inches?

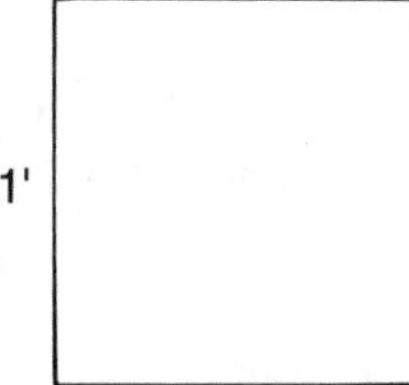

1,512 square inches = ____________ square feet.

A house is on a lot that is 75 feet by 125 feet. What is the area of the lot?

Check your answers against those in the answer key at the back of the book.

Area of Triangles

A triangle is a closed figure with three straight sides and three angles. The word *tri* means three.

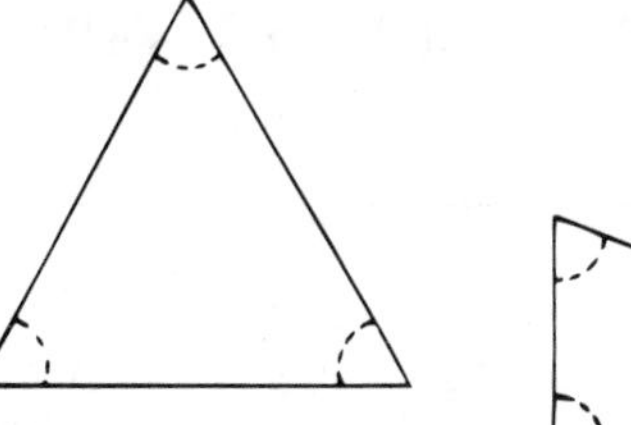

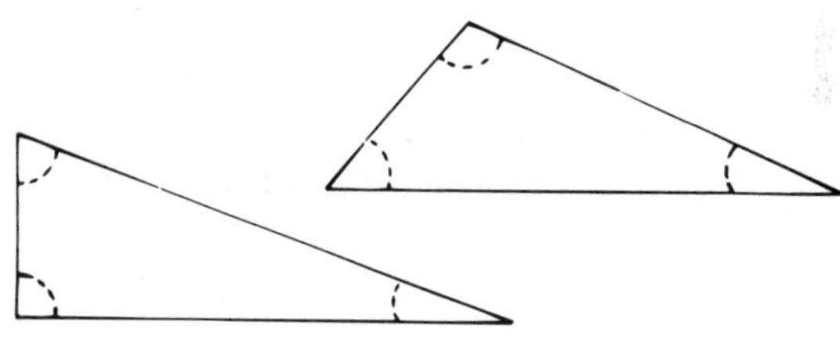

In the following figure, the 4-square-inch at the left has been cut in half by a straight line drawn between its opposite corners to make two equal triangles. When one of the triangles is placed on a square-inch grid, it is seen to contain ½ sq. in. + ½ sq. in. + 1 sq. in., or 2 sq. in.

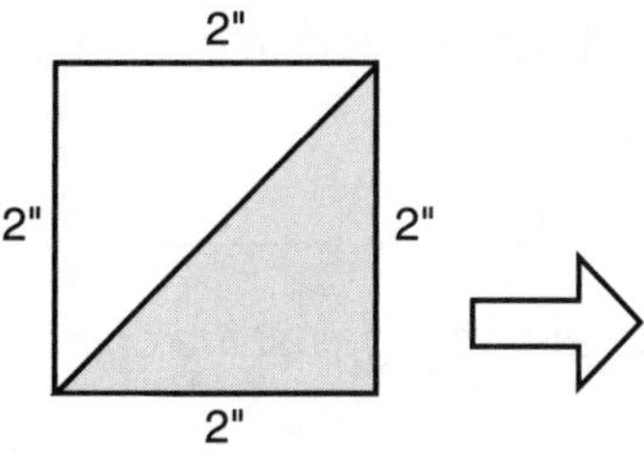

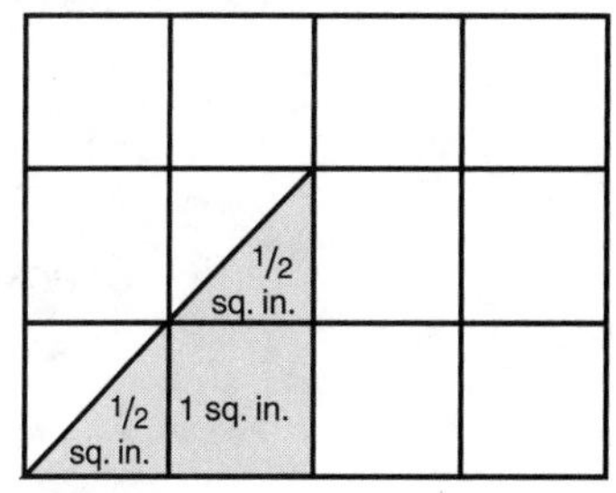

The area of the following triangle is 4½ sq. ft.

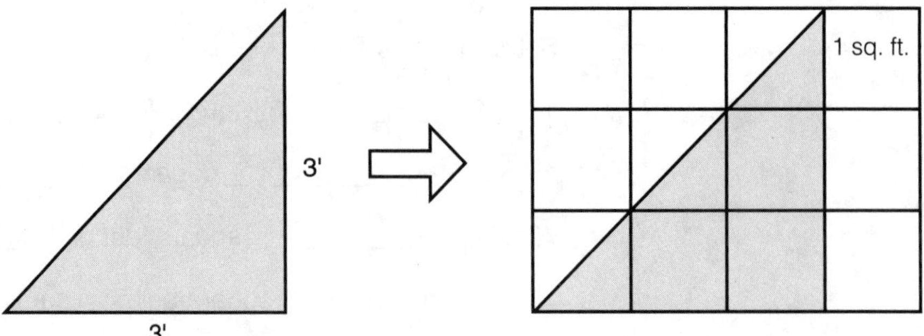

The square-unit grid is too cumbersome for computing large areas. It is more convenient to use the following formula for finding the area of a triangle:

$$\text{Area of triangle A} = \tfrac{1}{2}(\text{Base} \times \text{Height})$$

$$A = \tfrac{1}{2}(BH)$$

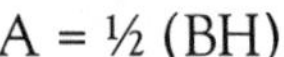

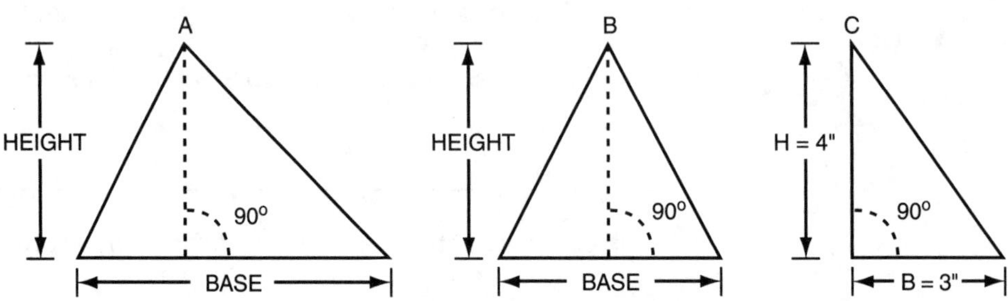

The base is the side on which the triangle sits. The height is the straight-line distance from the tip of the uppermost angle to the base. The height line must form a 90-degree angle to the base. The area of triangle C is:

$$A = \tfrac{1}{2}(BH) = \tfrac{1}{2}(3" \times 4") = \tfrac{1}{2}(12 \text{ sq. in.}) = 6 \text{ sq. in.}$$

Exercise 2-5

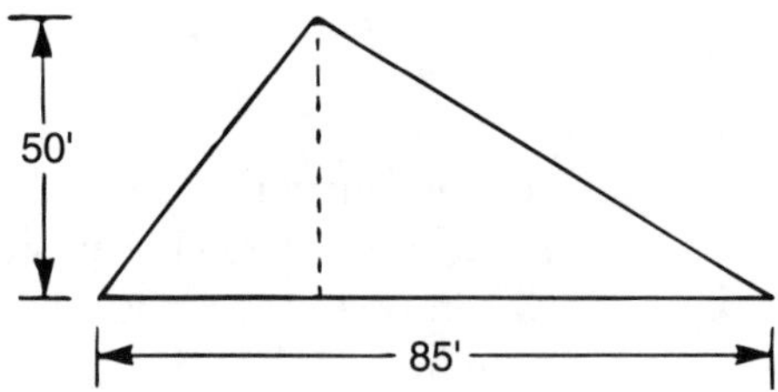

The diagram shows a lakefront lot. Compute its area.

Check your answer against the one in the answer key at the back of the book.

Area of Irregular Closed Figures

Here is a drawing of two neighboring lots.

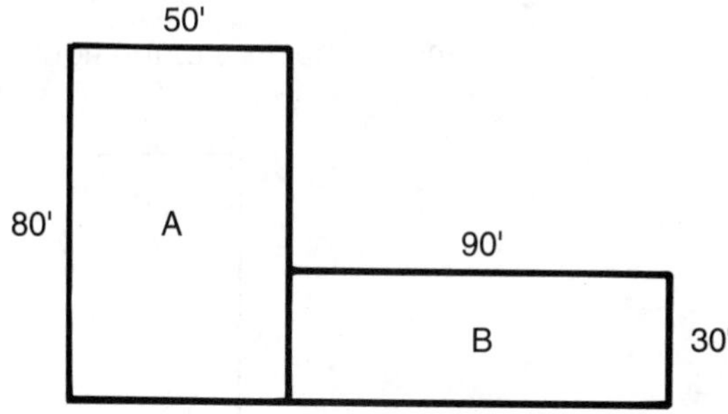

To find the total area of both lots:

Lot A = 50' × 80' = 4,000 sq. ft.

Lot B = 90' × 30' = 2,700 sq. ft.

Both lots = 4,000 sq. ft. + 2,700 sq. ft. = 6,700 sq. ft.

Two rectangles can be made by drawing one straight line inside Figure 1 in the following image. There are two possible positions for the added line, as shown in Figures 2 and 3.

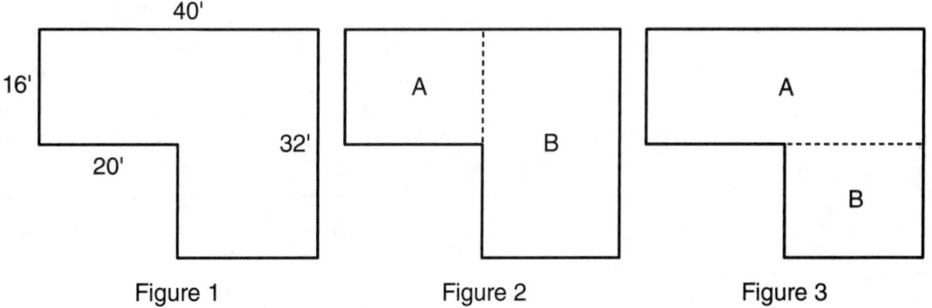

Figure 1 Figure 2 Figure 3

Using the measurements given in Figure 1, the total area of the figure may be computed in one of two ways:

Area of A = 20' × 16' = 320 sq. ft.

Area of B = 32' × (40' – 20') = 32' × 20' = 640 sq. ft.

Total area = 320 sq. ft. + 640 sq. ft. = 960 sq. ft.

Or

Area of A = 40' × 16' = 640 sq. ft.

Area of B = (40' – 20') × (32' – 16') = 20' × 16' = 320 sq. ft.

Total area = 640 sq. ft. + 320 sq. ft. = 960 sq. ft.

The area of an irregular figure can be found by dividing it into regular figures, computing the area of each, and adding all of the areas together to obtain the total area.

Exercise 2-6

This figure has been divided into rectangles, as shown by the broken lines.

Compute the area of the figure.

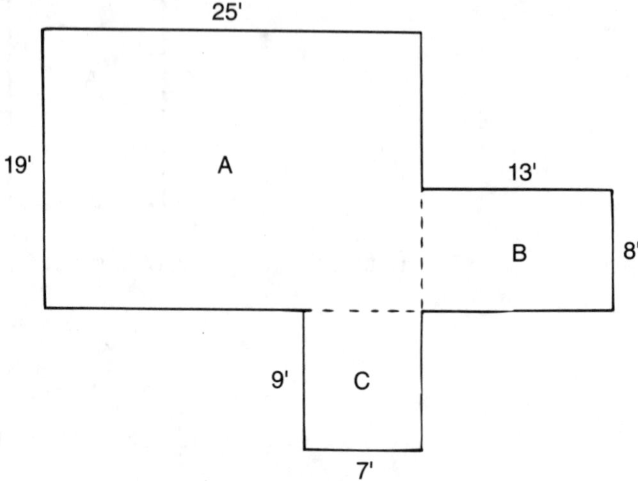

Make a rectangle and a triangle by drawing a single line through the following figure, and then compute the area of the figure.

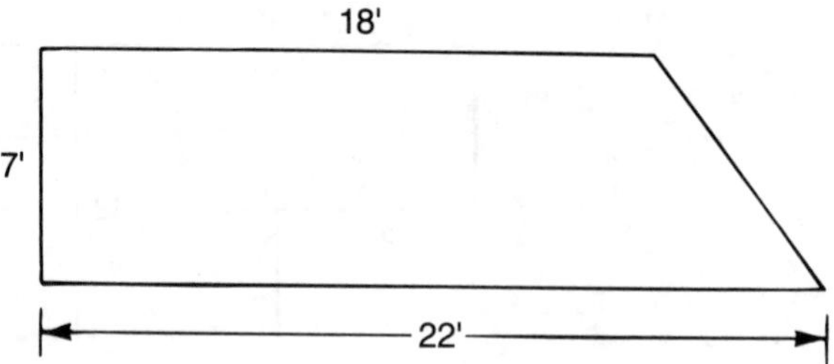

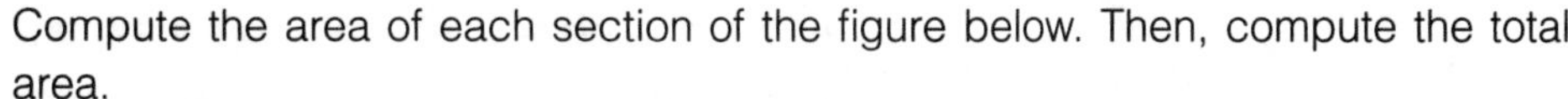

Compute the area of each section of the figure below. Then, compute the total area.

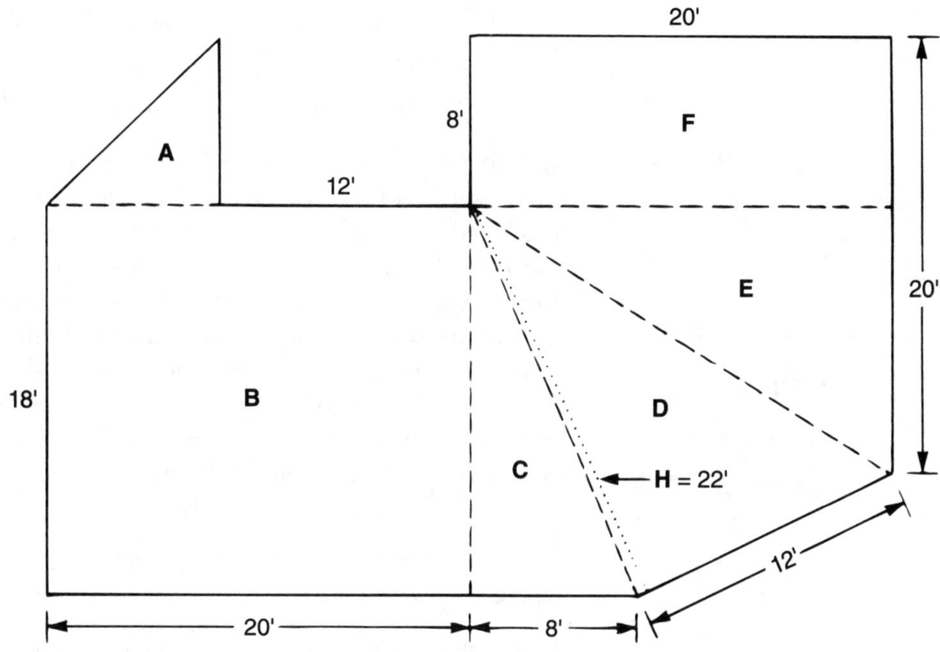

Check your answers against those in the answer key at the back of the book.

Living Area Calculations

Real estate appraisers frequently must compute the amount of living area in a house. The living area of a house is the area enclosed by the outside dimensions of the heated and air-conditioned portions of the house. This excludes open porches, garages, and such.

When measuring a house in preparation for calculating the living area, these steps should be followed:

1. Draw a sketch of the foundation.
2. Measure all outside walls.
3. If the house has an attached garage, treat the inside garage walls that are common to the house as outside walls of the house.
4. Measure the garage.
5. Convert inches to tenths of a foot (so that the same units of measurement are used in the calculations).

   Many appraisers use a tape measure marked with feet and tenths of a foot rather than feet and inches, which saves time and reduces the risk of errors.
6. Before leaving the house, check to see that net dimensions of opposite sides are equal. If not, remeasure.

7. Section off your sketch into rectangles.
8. Calculate the area of each rectangle.
9. Add up the areas, being careful to subtract the area of the garage, if necessary.
10. Before leaving the house, always recheck the dimensions.

In 1996, the American National Standards Institute (ANSI) adopted the standard for measurement of floor area of single-family houses and condominiums that was developed by the NAHB Research Center (now called the National Innovation Labs), a subsidiary of the National Association of Home Builders. Before then, there was no uniform standard for home measurement, though there was a standard for measurement of floor area in office buildings. The text of the most recent version of the standard applicable to single-family houses and condominiums, known as ANSI Z765-2003, can be found at http://krec.ky.gov/legal/legal%20 docs/calc_sqfootage.pdf. The appraiser should be familiar with this document, as well as the method commonly used by local real estate agents and appraisers.

WEB LINK

http://krec.ky.gov/legal/legal%20docs/calc_sqfootage.pdf

Exercise 2-7

What is the living area of the house shown in the sketch below? Follow the steps listed previously and remember to compute each area separately.

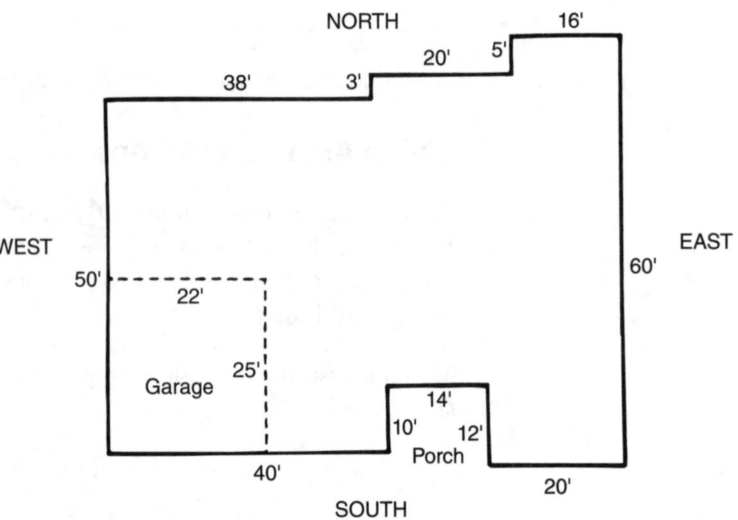

Check your answer against the one in the answer key at the back of the book.

Volume

When a shape has more than one side and encloses a space, the shape has volume, defined as the space that a three-dimensional object occupies.

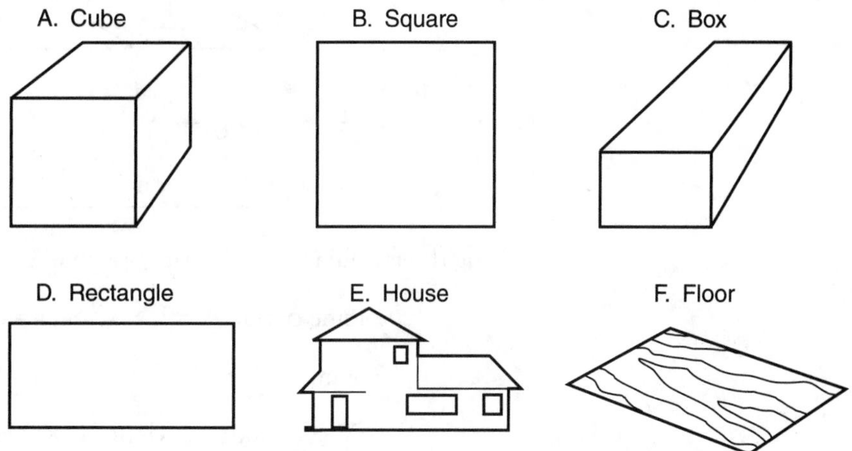

Of these shapes, A, C, and E have volume; B, D, and F have area only.

Flat shapes—squares, rectangles, triangles, et cetera—do not have volume. Flat shapes have two dimensions (length and width or height), and shapes with volume have three dimensions (length, width, and height).

Technically speaking, each shape with three dimensions can also be measured in terms of its surface area. For example, a bedroom has volume because it has three dimensions—length, width, and height; however, one wall can be measured as surface area, or Area = Length × Width.

Cubic units

A cube is made up of six squares. Look at the six sides of the following cube.

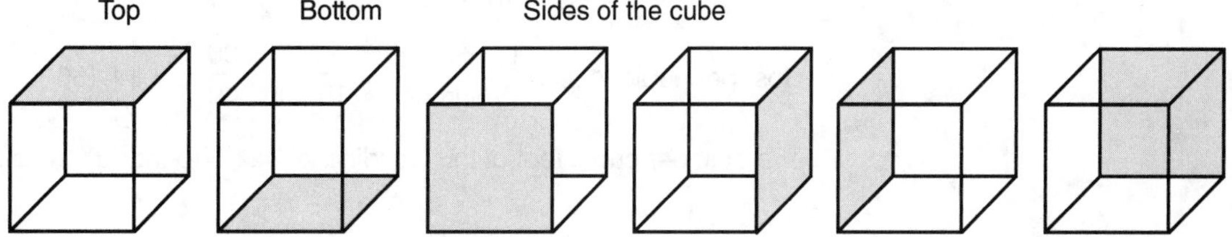

Volume is measured in cubic units. Each side of the cube below measures one inch, so the figure is one cubic inch, or 1 cu. in.

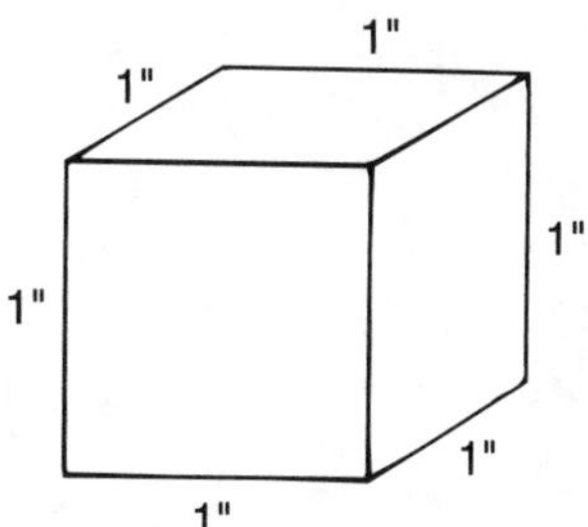

There are four cubic feet in the figure below. The exponent 3 may also be used to express cubic feet; that is, 1 $ft.^3$ is one cubic foot.

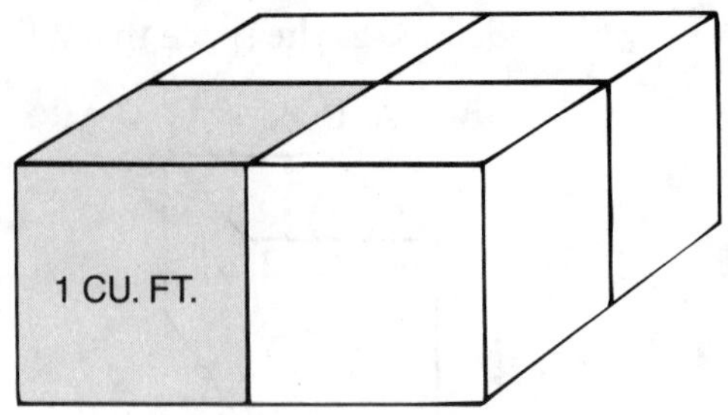

Using the formula for computing volume:

Volume of box A = L × W × H = 6" × 3" × 9" = 162 cu. in.

Volume of box B = L × W × H = 9' × 6' × 3' = 162 cu. ft.

V (volume) = L (length) × W (width) × H (height)

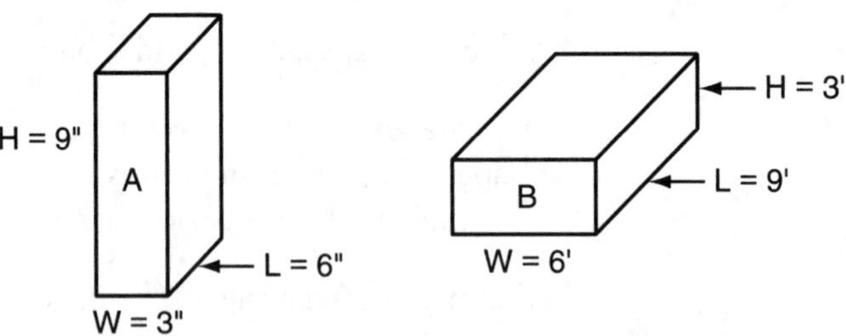

IN PRACTICE

A building's construction cost was $450,000. The building is 60 feet long, 45 feet wide, and 40 feet high, including the basement. What was the cost of this building per cubic foot?

V = L × W × H = 60' × 45' × 40' = 108,000 cu. ft.

$$\text{Cost per cubic foot} = \frac{\text{Total cost}}{\text{Volume}} = \frac{\$450{,}000}{108{,}000 \text{ cu ft}} = \$4.166$$

The cost per cubic foot of this building is $4.17 (rounded).

Conversions—using like measures for volume

To convert cubic inches, cubic feet, and cubic yards, use the following chart.

To convert cubic feet to cubic inches, *multiply the number of cubic feet by 1,728.*	(*cu. ft.* × 1,728 = cu. in.)
To convert cubic inches to cubic feet, *divide the number of cubic inches by 1,7728.*	(*cu. in.* ÷ 1,728 = cu. ft.)
To convert cubic yards to cubic feet, *multiply the number of cubic yards by 27.*	(*cu. yd.* × 27 = cu. ft.)
To convert cubic feet to cubic yards, divide the *number of cubic feet by 27.*	(*cu. ft.* ÷ 27 = cu. yd.)
To convert cubic yards to cubic inches, *multiply the number of cubic yards by 46,656.*	(*cu. yd.* × 46,656 = cu. in.)
To convert cubic inches to cubic yards, *divide the number of cubic inches by 46,656.*	(*cu. in.* ÷ 46,656 = cu. yd.)

IN PRACTICE

How many cubic yards of space are there in a flat-roofed house that is 30 feet long, 18 feet wide, and 10 feet high?

$$V = L \times W \times H = 30' \times 18' \times 10' = 5{,}400 \text{ cu. ft.}$$
$$\text{cu. yd.} = \text{cu. ft.} \div 27 = 5{,}400 \text{ cu. ft.} \div 27 = 200 \text{ cu. yd.}$$

Volume of triangular prisms

To compute the volume of a three-dimensional triangular figure, called a prism (e.g., an A-frame house), use the following formula:

$$\text{Volume} = ½(B \times H \times W)$$

To compute the volume of the following house, first divide the house into two shapes, S and T.

Find the volume of S.

$$V = ½(B \times H \times W) = ½(22' \times 8' \times 35') = ½(6{,}160 \text{ cu. ft.}) = 3{,}080 \text{ cu. ft.}$$

Find the volume of T.

$$V = 22' \times 35' \times 10' = 7{,}700 \text{ cu. ft.}$$

Total volumes S and T.

$$3{,}080 \text{ cu. ft.} + 7{,}700 \text{ cu. ft.} = 10{,}780 \text{ cu. ft.}$$

Exercise 2-8

Complete the following problems:

1. 8' × 7' = __________ sq. ft. = __________ sq. in. = __________ sq. yd.

2. 9' × 3' × 2' = __________ cu. ft. = __________ cu. in. = __________ cu. yd.

3. Find the total ground area covered by a building with the perimeter measurements shown in the following figure.

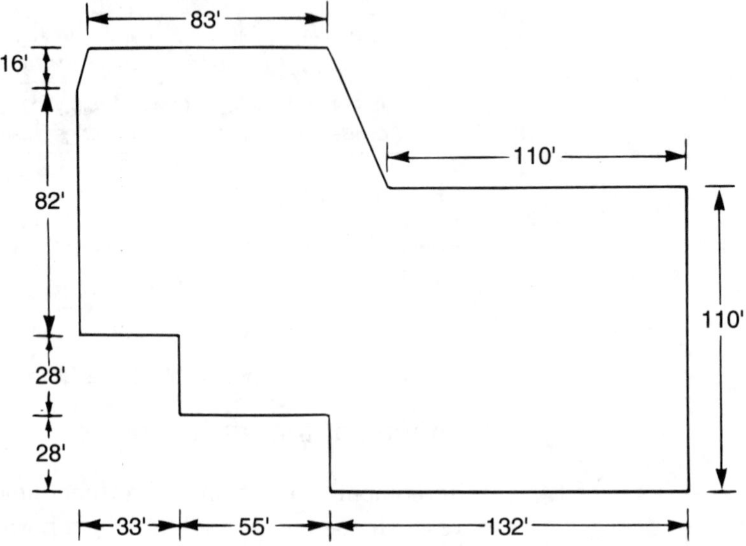

4. The building shown here has a construction cost of $45 per cubic yard. What is the total cost of this building?

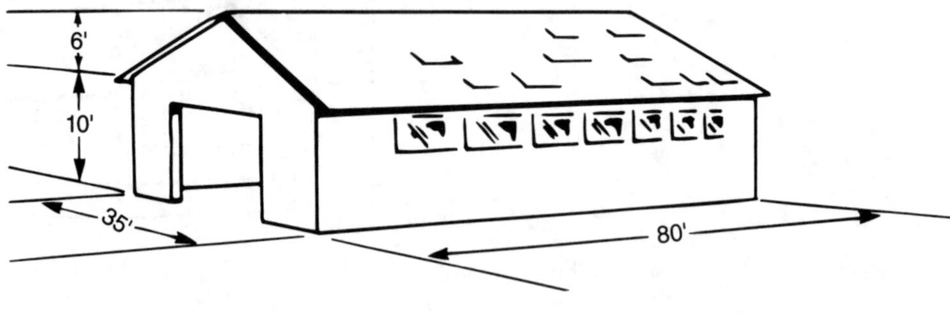

Check your answers against those in the answer key at the back of the book.

STATISTICS

Statistics is the science of collecting, classifying, and interpreting information based on the number of things. Economists often use statistics to support theories and conclusions. Appraisers, too, can use statistics to support the assumptions that allow an estimate of value. Some of the commonly used statistical terms are defined in the following paragraphs.

Population and Sample

In the language of statistics, a **variate** is a single item in a group. One single-family home is a variate. All variates in a group make up a **population**. For example, in Pittsburgh, Pennsylvania, the population of single-family homes consists of all the single-family homes in that city.

Appraisers are rarely, if ever, able to deal with the total population. It may be too expensive or too time-consuming to gather the details on all the population. The appraiser must, therefore, rely on a **sample** of the population. A sample is defined as some of the population or some of the variates in that population. A sample must be large enough to accurately represent the population but small enough to be manageable.

Random sampling

A **random sample** is one in which every variate in the population is chosen by chance and therefore has an equal probability of being picked. By using random sampling, the likelihood of bias is reduced. A biased sample is one in which some variates in the population are more likely to be included than others.

Sample size

The size of the sample is simply the number of variates in the sample. For example, if 20 single-family houses were used by an appraiser to represent the market, then the sample size is equal to 20. The larger the sample, the more certain you can be that it accurately reflects the population.

Parameter and aggregate

A single number or attribute, called a **parameter**, can be used to describe an entire group or population of variates. For example, all the house sales in a community in a given year can be described by the total dollar amount of all the sales. The total, or sum, of all variates is called an **aggregate**.

Organization of Numerical Data

To facilitate interpretation and analysis, statistical data must be arranged or grouped in an orderly way. There are two principal methods of arranging numerical data. In one method, each of the various values or variates is presented in order of size. This arrangement is called an **array**. In the second method of arranging numerical data, called a **frequency distribution**, the values are grouped to show the frequency with which each size or class occurs.

The dollar amounts $100,000, $102,000, $150,000, $175,000, $150,000, $165,000, $150,000, $100,000, and $150,000, which represent home sales in a neighborhood, have less meaning when presented in this unorganized manner than when presented in an array (Figure 2.1) or in a frequency distribution (Figure 2.2).

Measures of Central Tendency

In analyzing data, the first task is to describe the information in precise terms of measurement. Basic concepts of measurement used in statistics include measures of central tendency. A **measure of central tendency** describes the typical variate in a population. For example, the typical sales price for a single-family home and the typical rent for a square foot of office space are measures of central tendency.

FIGURE 2.1
An Array

House Sales
$175,000
165,000
150,000
150,000
150,000
150,000
102,000
100,000
100,000
Number of sales: 9

FIGURE 2.2
Frequency Distribution

Sales	Frequency
$175,000	1
165,000	1
150,000	4
102,000	1
100,000	2
Number of sales:	9

Three common statistical measures are the mean, the median, and the mode. All three measure central tendency and are used to identify the typical item or variate in a population or sample.

Mean

The **mean** is the average—that is, the sum of the variates divided by the number of variates. For example, in Figure 2.1, the mean price of the houses sold is $1,242,000 divided by 9, or $138,000.

Median

The **median** is found by dividing the number of variates into two equal groups. If the number of variates is odd, the median is the single variate at the middle. If the number of variates is even, the median is the arithmetic mean of the two variates closest to the middle from each end. In Figure 2.1, the median home price is $150,000.

Mode

The **mode** is the most frequently occurring variate. In Figure 2.2, the mode is $150,000.

Selecting a measure of central tendency

Before appraisers select one measure of central tendency, they should consider the following:

- The arithmetic mean is the most familiar measure of central tendency and can be conveyed to a client quickly and easily.
- The arithmetic mean is affected by extreme values called **outliers**, and might not represent any of the variates in a population. For example, the arithmetic mean of 5, 10, 15, 20, and 500 (outlier) is 110.
- When the outlier value of 500 is taken out of the calculation, the mean of the sample is only 12.5.
- The median is not affected by extreme variates as is the arithmetic mean. For example, the median in the previous item is 15. So, in samples of population where the variances are great, the median is a much better indicator than the average, or mean.
- The mode might represent an actual situation. For example, the population of apartments per building might have an arithmetic mean of 11.25, a median of 12.5, and a mode of 12. It is more realistic to discuss 12 units per building than 11.25 or 12.5. The mode, therefore, is most useful when a number of units have the same value.

Measures of Dispersion

Obtaining representative values other than measures of central tendency is often desirable. A **measure of dispersion** may be computed to measure the spread of the data; that is, to determine whether variates are grouped closely about the mean or median or are widely scattered or dispersed. In other words, a measure of dispersion describes the variance in a data set. Three common measures of dispersion are the range, the average deviation, and the standard deviation.

Range

The **range** is a measure of the difference between the highest and lowest variates. The range of prices in Figure 2.1 is $175,000 minus $100,000, or $75,000.

Average deviation

The deviation is the measure of how widely the individual variates in a population vary. The **average deviation** measures how far the average variate differs from the mean. The formula for the average deviation finds the mean of the sum of the absolute differences (plus and minus signs are ignored) of each of the variates from the mean of the variates. The average deviation is also called the average absolute deviation because absolute differences are used, making all the values positive.

In Figure 2.3, the average deviation is 5.78 (52 ÷ 9). This means that, on the average, the test scores deviated from the mean by 5.78 points.

Standard deviation

The **standard deviation** measures the differences between individual variates and the entire population by taking the square root of the sum of the squared differences between each variate and the mean of all the variates in the population, divided by the number of variates in the population. The formula for standard deviation is

$$\sigma = \sqrt{\frac{\sum (x-\mu)^2}{N}}$$

and is read,

> the standard deviation (σ) equals the square root ($\sqrt{}$) of the sum (Σ) of X minus the mean (μ) squared, divided by the number of items or variates (N).

Substituting figures in the formula (Figure 2.3):

> The sum of X minus the mean squared is 428 divided by 9 equals 47.56; the square root of 47.56 is 6.896, rounded to 6.90 (σ).

Note: The formula for computing the standard deviation in this example holds true only when the entire population is considered. If a sample of a population is used, as is typically the case in real estate appraising, the sum of the squared differences from the mean is divided by the number of variates in the sample minus one. One is subtracted from the number of variates in a sample to adjust for the one degree of freedom that is lost when the mean is computed. The formula for finding the standard deviation of a sample is

Sample	Population
$s = \sqrt{\frac{\sum (x-\bar{x})^2}{n-1}}$	$\sigma = \sqrt{\frac{\sum (x-\mu)^2}{N}}$

Notice the use of the different symbols in the formula when a sample rather than the total population is used:

> s = the sample standard deviation
> x = an individual variate in a sample
> $\bar{x}$ = the sample mean
> n = the number of variates in a sample

FIGURE 2.3
Average Deviation and Standard Deviation

	Scores on Real Estate Test	Deviations from Mean	Squares of Deviation
	94	12	144
	91	9	81
	85	3	9
	84	2	4
	82	0	0
	78	–4	16
	77	–5	25
	75	–7	49
	72	–10	100
Total	738	52	428

Mean = 82 (738 ÷ 9)
Median = 82
Mode: In the illustrated population of test scores there is no mode.
Range = 22
Average Deviation = 5.78 (52 ÷ 9)
Standard Deviation = 6.90 (√ of 428 ÷ 9)

Graphic Presentation of Data

Statistical presentation of data is generally in the form of tables, bar charts, histograms, and line graphs. Figure 2.4 lists the square foot construction costs for single-family homes. The first column shows dollars per square foot, and the second column the number of homes built in the square foot cost range indicated. The figures are totaled.

The same statistical data is presented in Figure 2.5 in a bar chart. Charts are often more informative than tables. A table is simply a list of the data; the chart gives a picture, and the data is more easily interpreted. The bar chart in Figure 2.5 and the histogram in Figure 2.6 both present a picture. All three are graphic presentations of statistics.

The histogram in Figure 2.6 is like a bar chart in a vertical position, but the bars or blocks on the histogram are contiguous and all are equal in width.

In the line graph shown in Figure 2.7, each point in the series of information on square foot construction costs is plotted, and the points are connected by a line. The line may be solid or dotted, and several items may be shown on the same graph. For example, in Figure 2.7 a dotted line could also be plotted to present construction costs per square foot in the year 2017 and 2018.

These are all simple illustrations. Tables, bar charts, histograms, and line graphs can be used to illustrate a variety of complex data pertaining to real estate. These may include population, operating statements, building permits issued, real estate taxes, traffic count, expense ratios, rents, land costs, comparable sales data, and other items of information.

Normal Distribution

Suppose an appraiser wants to indicate the range of sales prices or other data lying between any given numbers. In ordinary computation, range merely describes the difference between the highest and lowest price; it does not lend itself to further analysis. This limitation can be overcome by the use of a statistical approach; the appraiser calculates the standard deviation of dispersion within the population.

FIGURE 2.4
Table Showing Square Foot Construction Costs for Single-Family Homes—2016

Dollars per Square Foot	Number of Houses
60	20
70	25
80	30
90	35
100	40
110	45
120	40
130	35
140	30
150	25
160	20
Total	345

FIGURE 2.5
Bar Chart

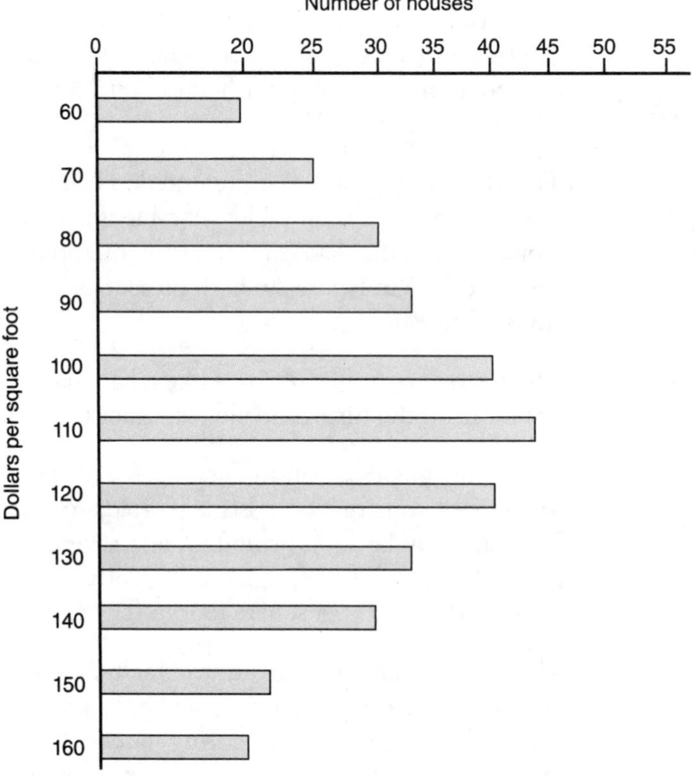

To illustrate, in a **normal distribution** of values, the shape assumed would be a normal curve, or **bell curve**, as shown in Figure 2.8.

In the normal curve, we know how much of any given area lies within given standard deviations from the mean. The mean deviation tells how much on the average each individual score varies from its own mean. The usefulness of standard deviation lies in the fact that approximately 34% of the population will fall between the mean and one standard deviation. Therefore, 68% of the population will fall between plus or minus one standard deviation, approximately 95% between plus or minus two standard deviations, and almost 100% between plus or minus three standard deviations. With this information, the appraiser can apply the normal distribution to many situations.

FIGURE 2.6
Histogram

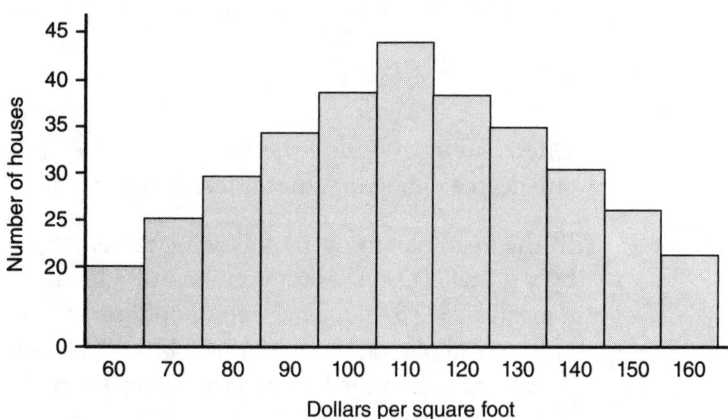

FIGURE 2.7
Line Graph

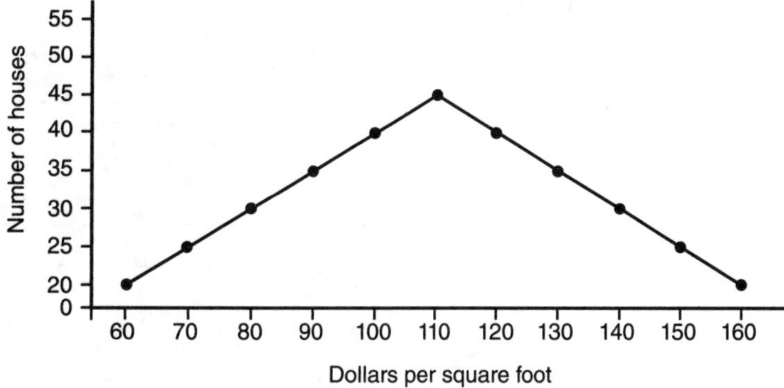

IN PRACTICE

A sample of five houses has sales prices of $175,000, $170,000, $185,000, $180,000, and $180,000. The standard deviation is $5,701, and the mean is $178,000. Therefore, on the average, each house differs from the mean by $5,701.

The formula for finding the standard deviation based on these facts is

$$s = \sqrt{\frac{\sum (x - \bar{x})^2}{n - 1}}$$

Where,

s = the sample standard deviation
Σ = sum of
x = an individual variate in sample
$\bar{x}$ = mean of sample
n = number of variates in sample

FIGURE 2.8
Normal Curve

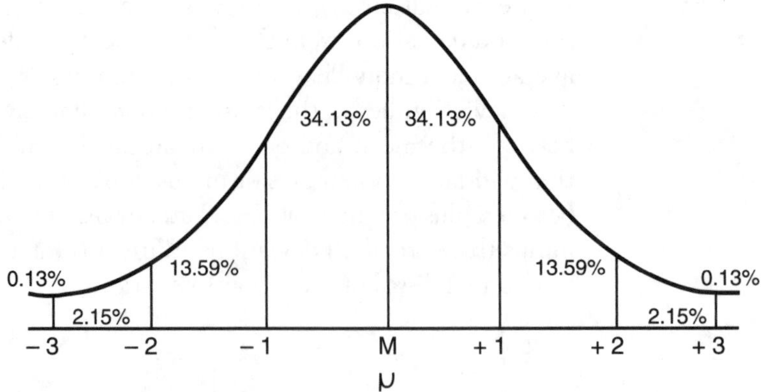

One is subtracted from the number of observations in a sample to adjust for the one degree of freedom that is lost when the mean is calculated.

In the first column of the following table, the sum of the house sales represented by *x* is $890,000. This total is then divided by 5 (the number of *x*s), resulting in a mean of $178,000. The second column is found by subtracting the mean from *x*. For example, on the first line $170,000 minus $178,000 equals minus $8,000. The third column is *x* minus the mean squared. On the first line, for example, *x* minus the mean squared (minus $8,000) when squared equals $64,000,000. The third column is then totaled to obtain the sum of *x* minus the mean squared, or $130,000,000.

x	$(x - \bar{x})$	$(x - \bar{x})^2$
$170,000	–$8,000	$64,000,000
175,000	–3,000	9,000,000
180,000	2,000	4,000,000
180,000	2,000	4,000,000
185,000	7,000	49,000,000
890,000		Total = $130,000,000

Mean = $890,000 ÷ 5 = $178,000

Substituting figures in the formula:

$$s = \sqrt{130{,}000{,}000 \div 4}$$

$$s = \sqrt{32{,}500{,}000}$$

$$s = \$5{,}701$$

Exercise 2-9

Compute the sample standard deviation of the following data set:

25, 15, 18, 12, 28

Check your answers against those in the answer key at the back of the book.

Skewness

Skewness is a measure of symmetry in a distribution, or more accurately, the lack of symmetry. A distribution is symmetric if it looks the same to the left or right of the center point of a bell-shaped curve, as shown in Figure 2.9. If the data is perfectly symmetrical, the mean, median, and mode are of equal value.

A positively skewed distribution has a longer tail to the right, and the mean is greater than the median, which is greater than the mode (Figure 2.10). If the distribution has a longer tail to the left, it is negatively skewed, and the mode is greater than the median, which is greater than the mean.

Regression Analysis—An Old Technique with a New Use

The availability of ever cheaper and more powerful personal computers has elevated an old theoretical valuation technique to the cutting edge of appraisal technology—one that is within the means of even the smallest appraisal office. This technique is called multiple linear regression analysis.

Regression analysis makes use of basic principles of statistics, some of which are discussed in this unit, to analyze comparable sales and determine line-item adjustments. A single regression analysis can consist of millions of individual calculations. Software with built-in regression analysis can enter recommended adjustment values automatically as the appraiser completes the URAR form. The result is not only to make the appraisal process more efficient but also to give the appraiser's value conclusion a high degree of accuracy, even in a difficult rural market lacking ready access to good comparable sales data.

With the aid of regression analysis, appraisers can make subtle predictions about the market that would be impossible otherwise. Perhaps more important is the level of accuracy possible because the technique provides detailed statistical justification for the values derived.

FIGURE 2.9
Bell-Shaped Curve

Normal Distribution
If the data is perfectly symmetrical the mean, median, and mode are all equal.

Mean
Median
Mode

FIGURE 2.10
Positively and Negatively Skewed Distributions

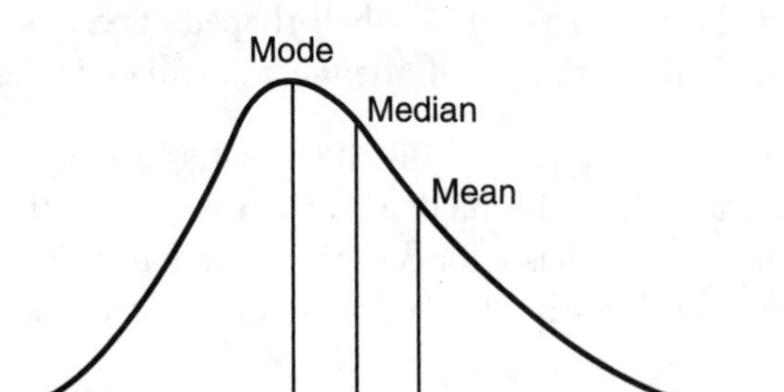

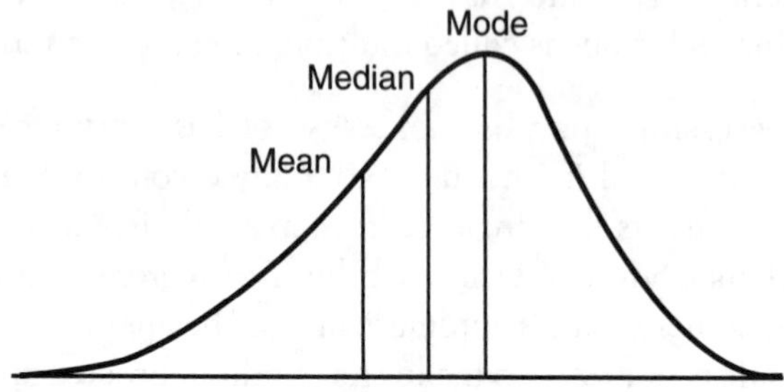

A thorough treatment of the use of regression analysis in appraising is beyond the scope of this text, but books, courses, and other materials explaining how to use this technique are available.

■ SUMMARY

Many mathematical concepts are involved in the study of appraisal, ranging from simple arithmetic to sophisticated statistical techniques.

In statistical analysis, three common measures of central tendency are used—the mean, the median, and the mode. The arithmetic mean is calculated by summing the data and dividing it by the number of items or variates. The mean is influenced by extremes or outliers; that is, exceptionally high or low values will inordinately affect the mean. If the data is skewed or strung out further to the left or right, the mean will be shifted in the same direction. The median is the middle value in an array of numbers. It is not affected by extremes, but it is affected by the data being skewed to the low or the high sides. The mode is the number which occurs most frequently in a series. The data tends to cluster about the mode.

A measure of dispersion describes differences in a population. This measure may be the range, average deviation, or standard deviation. The standard deviation is the most accurate measure of dispersion, assuming a normal distribution. In statistical analysis, normal distribution is represented by a bell-shaped curve.

Random sampling implies that any one item or variate selected from a population has the same chance of being selected as any other. Regression analysis makes use of limited data to interpret market forces.

■ Review Questions

1. A property has an assessed value of $45,000. If the assessment is 36% of market value, what is the market value?

2. A property valued at $200,000 produces a net operating income of $24,000 per year. What percentage of value (rate) does this property earn?

3. Find the total area of the figure below.

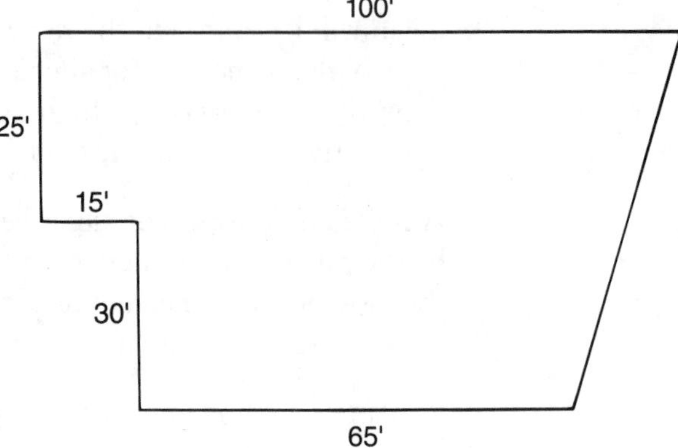

4. The house below would cost $2.75 per cubic foot to build. What would be the total cost, at that price?

5. What is the total area of the figure below in square feet?

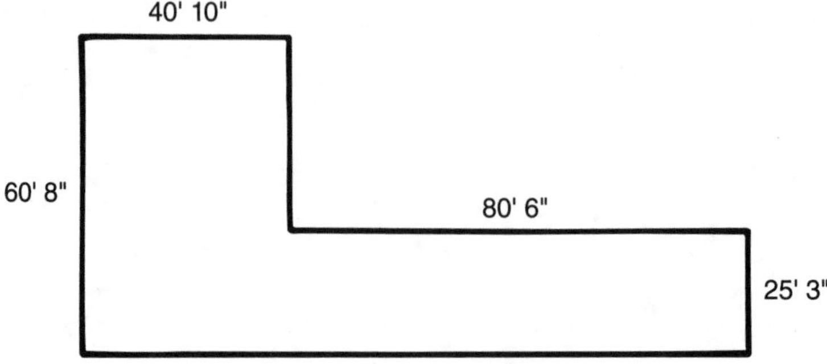

6. What is the living area of the house shown in the sketch below?

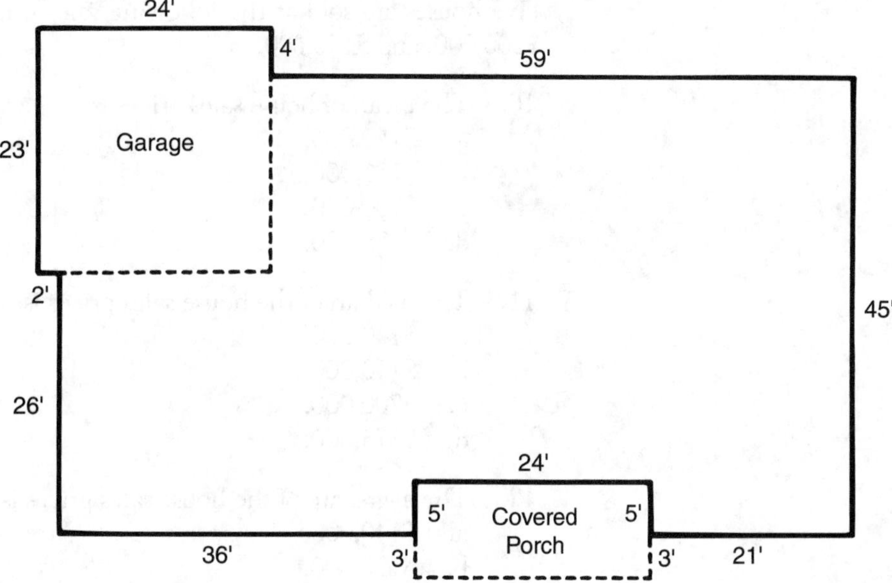

7. The average of all variates is
   a. the mean.
   b. the mode.
   c. the median.
   d. the range.

8. The center of all variates is
   a. the mean.
   b. the mode.
   c. the median.
   d. the range.

9. The difference between the highest and lowest variates is
   a. the mean.
   b. the mode.
   c. the median
   d. the range.

Use the following information for questions 10 through 12.

Five houses are sold at the following sales prices: $100,000, $75,000, $175,000, $200,000, and $150,000.

10. The mean of house sales prices is
    a. $140,000.
    b. $150,000.
    c. $700,000.
    d. $175,000.

11. The median of the house sales prices is
    a. $140,000.
    b. $150,000.
    c. $700,000.
    d. $175,000.

12. The aggregate of the house sales prices is
    a. $140,000.
    b. $150,000.
    c. $175,000.
    d. $700,000.

13. The factor used to convert square feet to square yards is
    a. 3.
    b. 9.
    c. 18.
    d. 27.

14. The factor used to convert cubic feet to cubic yards is
    a. 3.
    b. 9.
    c. 18.
    d. 27.

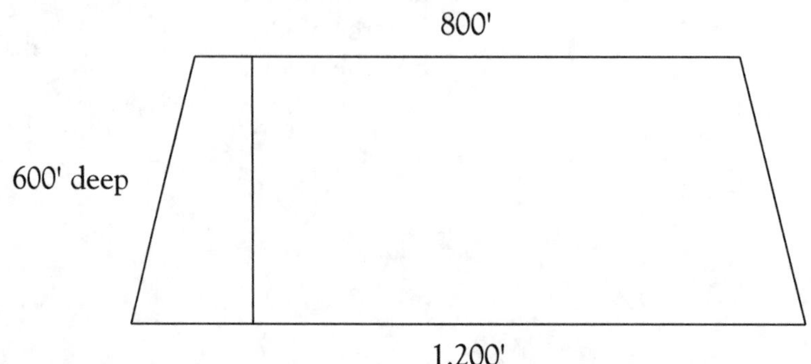

15. What is the area of the lot drawn above?
    a. 500,000 sq. ft.
    b. 600,000 sq. ft.
    c. 700,000 sq. ft.
    d. 800,000 sq. ft.

16. What is the area of a lot with the dimensions shown above in acres?
    a. 13.8
    b. 14.8
    c. 15.8
    d. 16.8

17. In a positively skewed distribution, the mean will be
    a. less than the mode.
    b. less than the median.
    c. greater than the median.
    d. the same as the mode.

18. In a negatively skewed distribution, the mode will be
    a. greater than the mean.
    b. less than the median.
    c. less than the mean.
    d. the same as the median.

19. Extreme values in a data set are referred to as
    a. measures of variability.
    b. outliers.
    c. weighted averages.
    d. deviations.

20. The mean, median, and mode are all equal
    a. if the data is negatively skewed.
    b. in a bimodal distribution.
    c. if the data is positively skewed.
    d. if the data follows a normal distribution.

Check your answers against those in the answer key at the back of the book.

UNIT THREE

REAL ESTATE AND ITS APPRAISAL

■ LEARNING OBJECTIVES

When you have completed this unit, you will be able to

- state what an appraisal is;
- identify the components of real estate;
- list the considerations in determining whether an item is a fixture;
- distinguish between public and private restrictions on land use;
- explain the methods that are used to create a legal description of land;
- define the types of freehold estate;
- define the types of nonfreehold estate;
- explain other interests in real estate, such as the easement and license; and
- distinguish the various forms of real estate co-ownership.

KEY TERMS

appraisal
bundle of rights
community property
condominium
cooperative
corporation
covenants, conditions, and restrictions (CC&Rs)
easement
eminent domain
encroachment
escheat
fee simple estate
fixture
freehold estate
joint tenancy
land
leasehold estate
leased fee estate
license
life estate
lot and block system
metes and bounds system
personal property
planned unit development (PUD)
police power
private restrictions
public restrictions
real estate
real property
rectangular survey system
reversion
site
taxation
tenancy by the entirety
tenancy in common (TIC)
tenancy in partnership
trust

OVERVIEW

Appraising has always been a unique part of the real estate industry. The appraiser's estimate of property value has a significant effect on many aspects of a real estate transaction, whether the transaction involves a sale, transfer, mortgage loan, lease, property tax assessment, or some other purpose. The appraiser must act as a disinterested third party; for this reason, the appraiser's compensation is not based on the estimated value of the property being appraised. With no vested interest in the estimation of value, the appraiser should be able to objectively evaluate the property's relative merits, appeal, and value.

This unit defines some of the terms that will be used throughout this book, including *appraisal*, *land*, *site*, *real estate*, *real property*, and *personal property*. The term *fixture* is defined, and the legal tests for determining when an item is a fixture to real estate are provided.

You will learn how a parcel of real estate is described, how it may be owned, how its use may be restricted, and how title may be transferred.

BASIC CONCEPTS

What Is a Real Estate Appraisal?

As defined in *USPAP*, an **appraisal** is the act or process of developing an opinion of value.

An appraisal can be described more fully as

- an opinion or estimate of value,
- for a specific purpose,
- for a specific person,
- of a specific property,

- as of a specific date,
- based on established facts.

An appraisal includes a description of the property under consideration, the appraiser's opinion of the property's condition, its utility for a given purpose, and/or its probable monetary value on the open market. The term *appraisal* is used to refer to both the process by which the appraiser reaches certain conclusions (*USPAP* Standard 1) and the written report in which those conclusions are communicated (*USPAP* Standard 2). With an objective, well-researched, and carefully documented appraisal, all parties involved, whether in a sale, lease, or other transaction, are aided in the decision-making process.

A reliable opinion of value is sought for many different reasons. A seller wants to know the value of real estate owned to determine an appropriate selling price, a prospective buyer wants to pay no more than necessary, and a broker wants to realize the maximum commission. Financial institutions, which need appraisals to assist in their underwriting decisions regardless of the loan amount, insist on an appraisal to determine the amount of money to lend to a credit applicant. The loan-to-value ratio will be based on the sales price or appraised value, whichever is less. An appraisal can help determine appropriate lease payments, particularly when a large commercial property is leased for a long term. Appraisals are also used to estimate value for taxation and insurance purposes and in condemnation proceedings.

To understand how real estate is appraised, you should know how the term *real estate* is defined.

Real Estate and Real Property

Real estate is defined as the land itself and all things permanently attached to it. The definition of real estate typically includes the following:

- Land
- Fixtures (attachments) to land
- Anything incidental or appurtenant to land that benefits the landowner, such as an easement right to use your neighbor's driveway for access to your property
- Anything else that is considered immovable (part of the real estate) by law, except for cultivated crops (called emblements) and other severable (removable) things that are sold by a contract of sale that complies with the laws regulating the sale of goods

Land

The earth's surface, including everything under or on it, is considered **land**. The substances under the earth's surface may be more valuable than the surface itself. Mineral rights to solid substances (such as coal and iron ore), as well as those that must be removed from beneath the surface to be reduced to possession (such as oil and gas), may be transferred independently of the rest of the land. Water rights provide access to our increasingly important surface and underground water supplies.

When land is improved by the addition of streets, utilities (water, gas, electricity), sewers, and other services, it becomes a **site** and may be considered suitable for building purposes.

Within limitations, the air rights above the earth's surface are also considered the landowner's property. Transferable development rights of airspace have facilitated construction of highrise buildings.

Fixtures

A **fixture** is anything permanently attached to land. Fixtures include natural things that are attached by roots, such as trees and bushes, and manmade things, such as fences and buildings.

Ordinarily, improvements to real estate, including both landscaping and structures, are considered fixtures. In determining whether a specific item is a fixture, and thus part of the real estate, courts will consider the following, which can be remembered by the acronym *MARIA*:

- Method by which the item is attached—how permanent the attachment is and the resulting economic burden of removal;
- Adaptability of the item for the land's ordinary use;
- Relationship of the parties;
- Intention of the person in placing the item on the land; and
- Agreement of the parties.

If a seller of real estate has attached something to the land, that item will be considered a fixture unless the sales contract provides otherwise or the courts determine it is not a fixture according to the criteria listed previously. The appraiser must indicate whether fixtures are included in the property appraisal.

Trade fixtures

A determination of whether an item is a fixture may also be important when property is leased. An item owned and attached to a rental space or building by a tenant and used for business purposes is called a trade or chattel fixture. Some examples of trade fixtures are gas station pumps, restaurant equipment, store shelves, and the exercise equipment in a health club.

If the tenant places an item on the land, to whom will the item belong when the lease terminates? Landlord and tenant are free to make whatever agreement they desire with regard to ownership of trade fixtures. If they have made no lease agreement or if the lease is silent on the subject of a particular fixture, state law will determine ownership of the fixture and thus whether it may be removed by the tenant.

Tenants usually may remove a trade fixture before the end of the lease term if the fixture was installed for purposes of trade, manufacture, ornament, or domestic use, and if it can be removed without damage to the premises. Otherwise, tenants are generally allowed to remove the fixture only if the tenant believed in good faith that the fixture could be installed and subsequently removed. Of course, tenants who are allowed to remove a trade fixture must pay for any resulting property damage. A trade fixture that is not removed becomes the property of the landlord.

Bundle of rights

The owner of real estate has the power to do certain things with it. These rights of ownership, often called the **bundle of rights**, include the rights to use, rent, sell, or give away the real estate, as well as to choose not to exercise any of these rights.

In some states, the rights of ownership of real estate are referred to as **real property**. In other states, the rights of ownership are included within the definition of real estate, and the terms *real estate* and *real property* are synonymous.

Traditionally, appraisers have distinguished between real estate (the land and buildings) and real property (the legal rights of ownership). In current practice, however, the terms *real estate* and *real property* are frequently used interchangeably, as is the case in this text.

The rights inherent in the ownership of real estate are what may be bought and sold in a real property transaction. In an appraisal, the rights being appraised must be stated because any limitation on the rights of ownership may affect property value. There are property rights that are reserved by law for public (government) exercise and thus limit an owner's full enjoyment of ownership rights. There also may be private restrictions on the use of real property.

Public restrictions

There are four public or governmental restrictions that limit the ownership of real estate. They are (1) taxation, (2) eminent domain, (3) escheat, and (4) police power.

The right of **taxation** enables the government to collect taxes and to sell the property if the taxes are not paid. In many states, growing pressure to increase state or local government funds, or reduce a burgeoning deficit, has placed additional strain on property owners. *Ad valorem* (according to value) taxation historically has taken the form of property taxes based on assessed value. In addition to charges required to maintain state and local services, special assessments for particular neighborhood or regional improvements, separately itemized on property tax bills, are becoming increasingly popular. One reason for the high cost of land for new buildings in many areas is the rising level of development fees used to build roads, sewer systems, and other infrastructure improvements, as well as schools, parks, and other public spaces. Such costs are, of course, passed on to the homebuyer or investor. Even in areas where property tax rates are well defined, added exactions by local governing authorities, even when they don't appear on an itemized tax bill, may have a significant effect on building cost and cost of ownership.

Private property may be taken for public use, on payment of just compensation, by the right of **eminent domain**. If the owner of real property dies leaving no qualified heirs, ownership of the property may revert to the state by the right of **escheat**. The **police power** of government enables it to establish zoning ordinances, building codes, and other measures that restrict the use of real estate to protect the health, safety, morals, and general welfare of the public.

Private restrictions

There may be private (nongovernmental) qualifications or limitations on the use of real property, most often because of **covenants, conditions, and restrictions (CC&Rs)** placed in the deed received by the property owner. CC&Rs typically benefit subdivision property owners and owners of condominium units.

The most frequently encountered private limitation on use is the lien created by the security instrument used to finance the purchase of the property. The instruments used to hypothecate (pledge) real estate as security for a debt are the mortgage and the deed of trust. The most significant difference between the two is the method by which each is enforced. A mortgage may require a court-ordered sale to be foreclosed. A deed of trust usually allows the trustee who holds title on behalf of the beneficiary (lender) to sell the property and pay off the underlying debt in the event of default by the trustor (buyer/borrower). Because of statutory protections provided to homeowners and others, the differences between the two forms of security instrument may be more theoretical than practical, and it is common practice to refer to any security interest in real estate as a mortgage.

Personal Property

Any tangible items that are not permanently attached to real estate, and thus are not considered fixtures, are classified as **personal property**. Trade fixtures are included in this category because they are usually owned and installed by the tenant for the tenant's use and are to be removed by the tenant when the lease expires.

Why is it important to know the distinction between fixtures and personal property? If an item is classified as a fixture, it is part of the real estate, and its contribution to value is included in the value estimate. Items of personal property are usually not included in an appraisal.

The attachment necessary for an item to be considered a fixture would ordinarily be such that the item could be removed only by causing serious damage to either the real estate or the item itself. A window air conditioner would ordinarily be considered personal property, but if a hole were cut in a wall expressly for the installation of the air conditioner, the unit would probably be considered part of the real estate. Because the distinction between fixtures and personal property is not always obvious, appraisers should find out how these items are treated in their areas.

The parties involved in a transaction can and should agree on what items are to be considered part of the real estate. In the absence of such an agreement, however, if legal action is necessary, a court will apply the tests of a fixture listed earlier.

Exercise 3-1

Indicate whether each of the following is ordinarily real estate or personal property:

1. Window screens
2. Hot tub installed in wood deck
3. Furnace
4. Plantation shutters
5. Central air-conditioning
6. Kitchen cabinets
7. Child's movable playhouse
8. Portable room heater
9. Rose bushes
10. The right to sell land and any building(s) attached to the land

Why is the distinction between real estate and personal property important to the appraiser?

Check your answers against those in the answer key at the back of the book.

■ LEGAL DESCRIPTIONS OF LAND

A legal description of land is one that describes the land in such a way that a competent surveyor could locate its boundaries using the description.

The three basic methods used to describe land in the United States are the lot and block system, the metes and bounds system, and the rectangular (or government) survey system.

Lot and Block System

The **lot and block system**, also called the lot, block, and tract system and the subdivision system, is the method used to describe most residential and commercial building lots.

Individual parcels are referred to by the tract, block, and lot numbers by which they are identified in the subdivision map filed in the county recorder's office. The description will also name the city and county in which the tract is located and should provide the book and page number in the county recorder's office where the subdivision map appears, as well as the date the map was recorded.

Figure 3.1 shows part of a subdivision in Riverglen, California. The legal description of lot 7 is as follows: "Lot 7, Fertile Acres, Amended 35/38 (as recorded July 14, 1976, Book 186, Page 19 of maps), City of Riverglen, County of Riverside, State of California."

FIGURE 3.1
Subdivision Plat Map

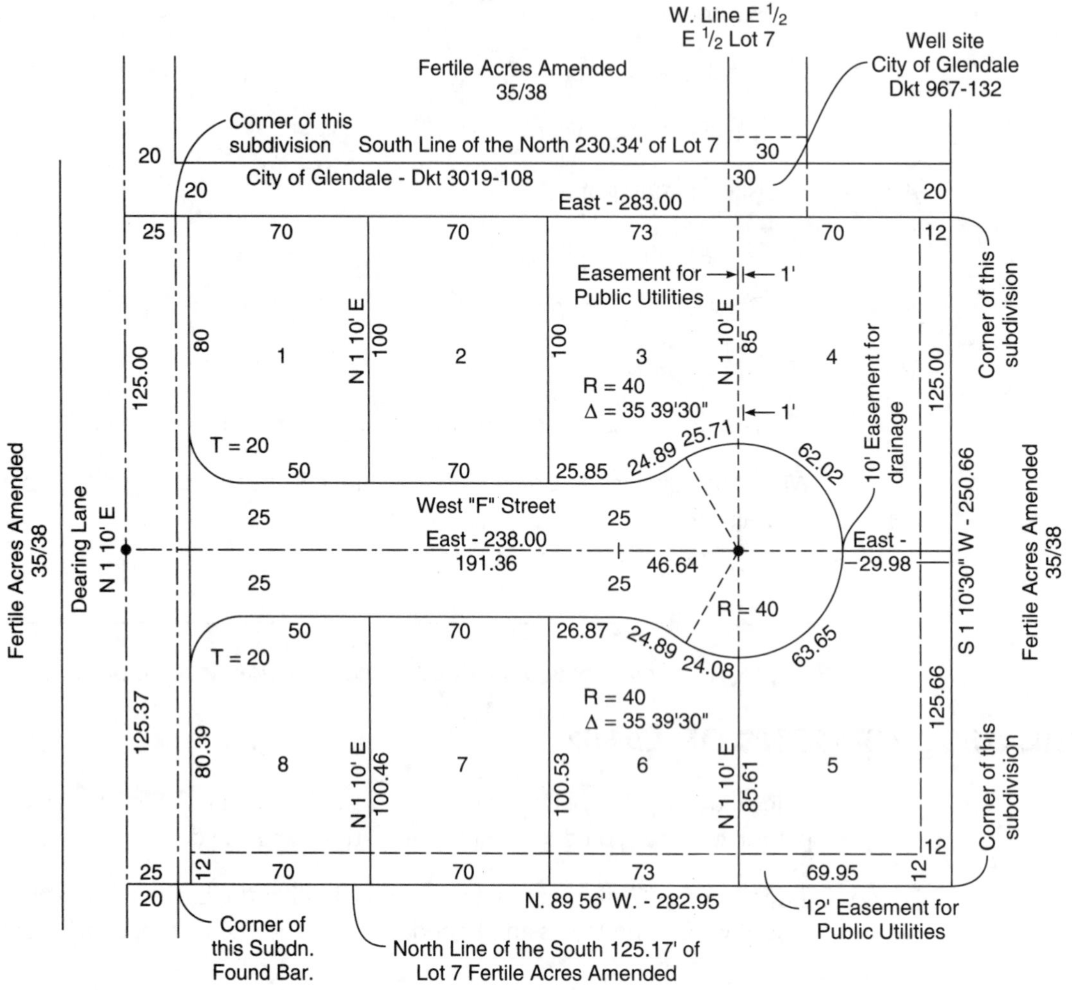

Metes and Bounds System

The **metes and bounds system** is one of the oldest known methods of surveying land in the United States and is used predominantly through the eastern states. A metes and bounds description defines the perimeter of a parcel of land by using measured distances from specified boundary markers.

A metes and bounds description starts at a point of beginning and follows natural or artificial boundaries, called bounds, for measured distances, called metes. Individual monuments or markers may also be referred to in the description. In many areas, points of beginning have been replaced by permanent markers, and the laser transits used by modern surveyors give extremely accurate results.

Because both natural and artificial boundaries or markers may change drastically in only a few years, a metes and bounds description may be quite unreliable. Consider the following early example of such a description (illustrated in Figure 3.2), and you can imagine the difficulties of the landowner who bought the described parcel after the creek had changed its course and one of the roadways mentioned had been plowed under for farming. A tract of land located in the Village of Red Skull was described as follows:

> Beginning at the intersection of the East line of Jones Road and the South line of Skull Drive; thence East along the South line of Skull Drive 200 feet; thence South 15 degrees East 216.5 feet, more or less, to the center thread of Red Skull Creek; thence Northwesterly along the center line of said Creek to its intersection with the East line of Jones Road; thence North 105 feet, more or less, along the East line of Jones Road to the place of beginning.

FIGURE 3.2
Metes and Bounds Tract

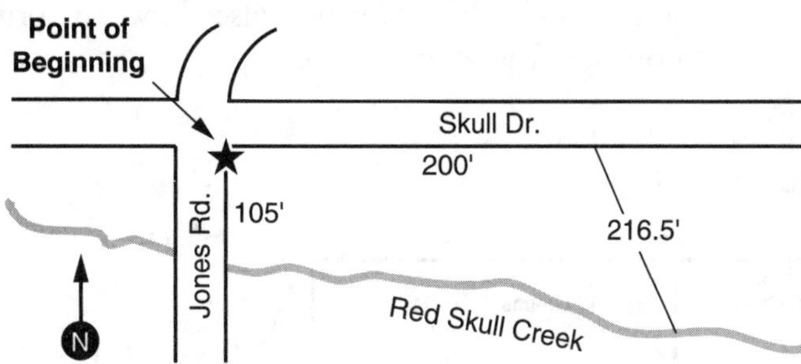

Rectangular Survey System

The **rectangular survey system**, also called the U.S. government survey system and section and township system, is most useful in identifying large tracts of rural property. Land area is divided into townships measured and numbered starting at the intersection of a base line running east to west and a principal meridian running north to south (see Figure 3.3). Lines running east and west, parallel to the base line and spaced six miles apart, are called township lines. An east-west group of townships is called a tier. Lines that run north and south, parallel to the principal meridian, are also six miles apart and are called range lines. When the horizontal township lines and the vertical range lines intersect, they form squares, called townships. A township is divided into 36 sections. A section of land contains 640 acres and is 1 mile square, or 5,280 feet by 5,280 feet.

FIGURE 3.3
Township Lines and Range Lines

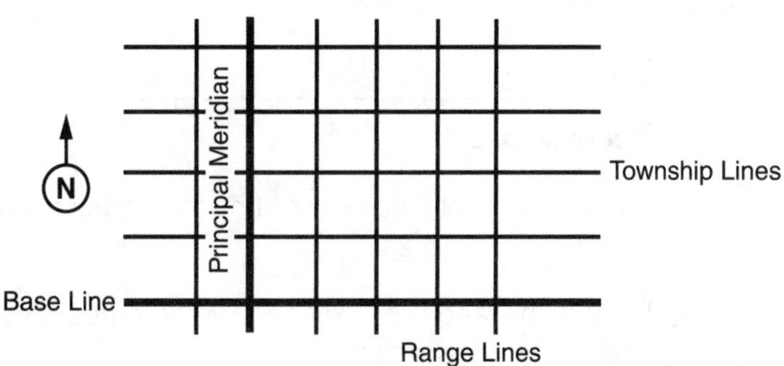

Sections are numbered 1 through 36, as shown to the right in Figure 3.4. Section 1 is always at the northeast, or upper righthand corner of the township. The numbering proceeds right to left, left to right for the next row, right to left for the row after that, et cetera. Each section in a township, in turn, can be divided into halves, quarters, and even smaller parcels based on compass point directions, as shown to the left in Figure 3.4.

The area of a fractional part of a section is found by multiplying the fraction (or fractions) by the number of acres in a section—640. The rectangular survey system description of the 40-acre parcel labeled A in Figure 3.4 is "the NE¼ of the SW¼ of Section 31." If only the legal description is known, the area of the parcel can be found by multiplying as follows: ¼ × ¼ × 640 = 40 acres.

The appraiser should be familiar with all three forms of legal descriptions and know which form or forms are accepted in the area where the appraisal is being conducted (Figure 3.5, which also shows the principal meridians and base lines throughout the United States).

FIGURE 3.4
Sections of a Township

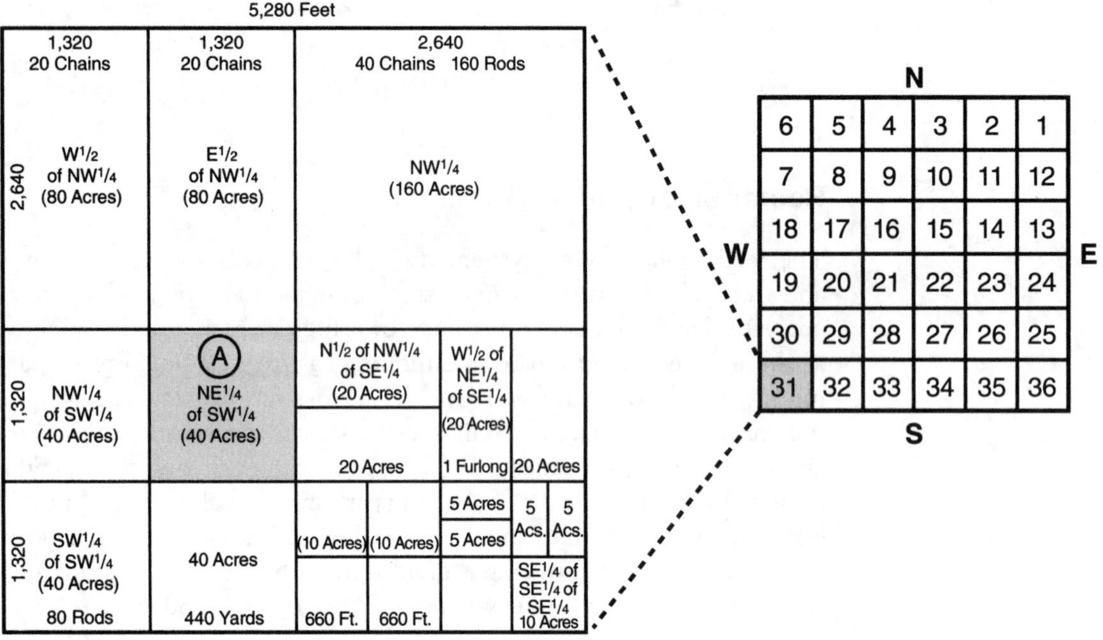

Exercise 3-2

What is the land area covered by the parcel described as the W½ of the SW¼ of the E½ of Section 24?

What is the land area covered by the parcel described as the S½ of Section 10 and N½ of Section 15?

A deed conveyed the NE¼ of Section 18 and the NW¼ of Section 20. Are these parcels contiguous? How many acres were conveyed?

The E½ of the N½ of Section 22 is priced at $7,500 per acre. What is the total price of the parcel?

The S½ of Section 35 of the township is at Tier 1 North and Range 3 East of the grant meridian and base line. What is the half-section adjacent to that parcel to its south?

What is the section to the north of the section described as Section 5, Tier 3 South and Range 5 West?

Check your answers against those in the answer key at the back of the book.

Figure 3.5
Map of United States Showing Meridians and Base Lines

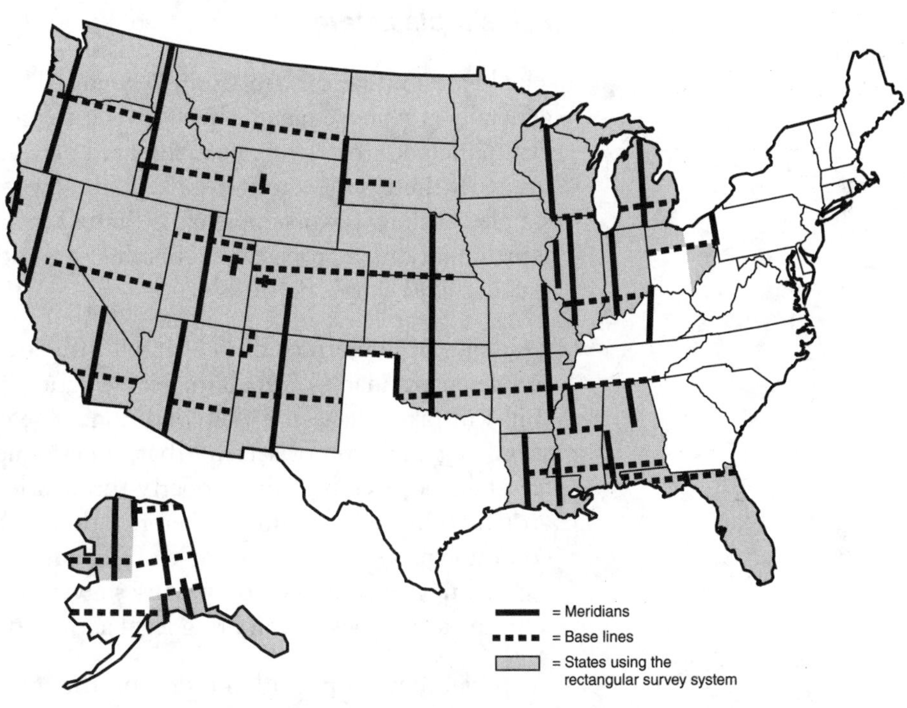

These states generally use the metes and bounds method of legal description:

Maine	Tennessee
Massachusetts	New Hampshire
Connecticut	Georgia
Rhode Island	North Carolina
Vermont	South Carolina
New York	Maryland
Pennsylvania	Virginia
Delaware	West Virginia
New Jersey	Texas
Kentucky	Hawaii

LEGAL RIGHTS AND INTERESTS

The value of real property depends on the kind of property right owned. Although the rights of ownership are spoken of as the "bundle of rights," all the rights are not always owned by the same person or transferred together. Ownership interests in real estate are called estates in land.

Freehold Estates

The highest or most complete form of ownership in medieval times was the **freehold estate**. Holders of freehold estates were not subject to the overlord but could do with the property whatever they chose. Freehold estates are still considered estates of ownership. The person who owns a freehold estate can transfer the right of possession to someone else, as in a lease of the property, but the underlying right of ownership remains with the holder of the freehold estate. There are several types of freehold estate, defined by the length of time they remain in effect.

Fee simple estate

The highest interest in real estate recognized by law is the **fee simple estate**. This generally is what we mean when we refer to property ownership. Fee simple ownership includes the right to use the land now and for an indefinite period in the future. If there are no restrictions on the ownership right, it is considered a fee simple absolute. Ownership that is limited in some way is a fee simple qualified. Any limitation on property use that might result in the loss of the ownership right is called a fee simple defeasible.

Examples of limitations on fee simple title are the condition precedent (or fee simple determinable), stipulating some action that must be taken before ownership will take effect, and the condition subsequent (or fee simple conditional), specifying an action or activity that, if performed, will allow the previous owner to retake possession of the property through legal action. The requirement that an heir achieve a certain age before title can be transferred is an example of a condition precedent. An example of a condition subsequent is a requirement that alcohol not be consumed on premises given to a church; if the condition is broken, the former owner can bring legal action to retake the property.

A special limitation is a limitation on the use of property, written so that if the stated condition is broken, title to the property automatically returns to the former owner without the need for legal action. A gift of property "so long as" it is used for a particular purpose will set up a special limitation.

Most real property appraisals are made on the basis of fee simple ownership—nothing is held back. The holder of a fee simple estate, however, may or may not own all mineral, water, and other rights associated with the land. A condition or other restriction on use of the property also may exist. The appraiser should note any such exclusions or other factors limiting the owner's use of the property as well as their effect on value.

Life estate

A **life estate** is a present, possessory interest that lasts only as long as the life of a stated person or persons. A life estate usually is based on the life of the person who receives it, although it could be based on the life of any named person ("my mother") or persons ("my parents"). When the measuring life is that of anyone other than the holder of the life estate, it is termed a life estate *pur autre vie* (for another's life).

On the death of the person against whose life the term of possession is measured, the land becomes the property of the person named at the time the life estate was created. The ultimate recipient, called the remainderman, holds what is called an estate in remainder during the life of the holder of the life estate. Alternatively, the land could be designated to return to the person who originally gave or transferred the life estate, in which case the original owner's interest during the term of the life estate is called a **reversion**.

A life estate can be transferred by gift, sale, or lease, but its value will depend on the risk associated with its probable termination date. The interest of a remainderman or reversioner can be given away, sold, or leased, but the recipient will have no right of possession until the life estate terminates.

Nonfreehold Estates

Nonfreehold estates are those that convey only a right of use and not the underlying fee simple right of ownership.

Leasehold estate

A nonfreehold estate is also called a **leasehold estate**. A leasehold estate is the interest of the lessee (tenant), who acquires a right to use property by an agreement, called a lease, with the fee simple owner, who is then called the lessor (landlord). The leasehold is an estate of tenancy. It confers a right of use for the term specified in the lease, but it does not convey ownership. A tenant has no underlying fee interest, but the tenant's leasehold estate can have value, such as when the rent paid by the tenant is less than the property's market rent—what it would command if available on the market today.

Leased fee estate

The **leased fee estate** is the interest retained by the landlord who conveys a leasehold estate to a tenant.

Exercise 3-3

1. What estates are created when property is leased?

2. What is the owner's interest in rented real estate?

3. What is the term used to describe an estate that goes back to the original owner on the death of a life tenant?

Check your answers against those in the answer key at the back of the book.

Other Interests

Easement

An **easement** is a real property interest that conveys a limited right of use or enjoyment, such as the right to travel over a parcel of land.

Sometimes an easement benefits the owner of an adjoining parcel of land. In that case, the land benefited by the easement is called the dominant tenement. The land over which the easement runs is called the servient tenement. An easement appurtenant is one that is said to "run with the land," because it is automatically conveyed to a new owner if title to the dominant tenement is transferred. In addition, it does not terminate if title to the servient tenement transfers (Figure 3.6 and Figure 3.7).

An easement in gross belongs to an individual person or business and does not run with any parcel of land. Railroads, oil pipeline companies, and utility companies may make use of easements in gross. They do not own the underlying land but have the right to use it. Because it is considered a "personal" interest, an easement in gross usually cannot be assigned to anyone else and will terminate on the death of its owner.

FIGURE 3.6
Easement Appurtenant

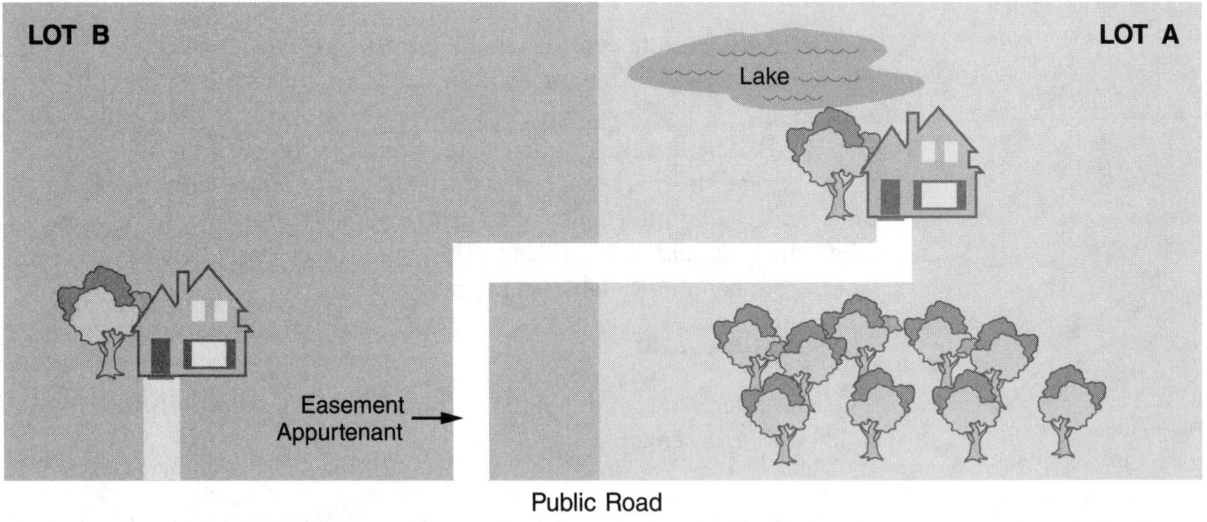

The owner of Lot A has an appurtenant easement across Lot B to gain access to his property from the paved road. In this example, Lot A is dominant and Lot B is servient.

FIGURE 3.7
Easement Appurtenant Gross

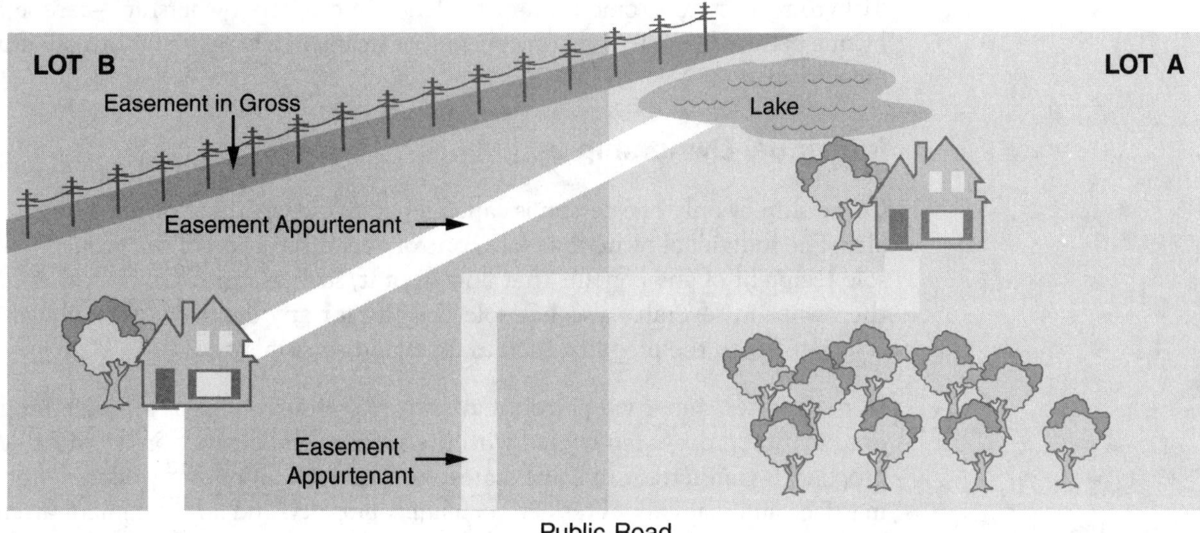

The owner of Lot B has an appurtenant easement across Lot A to gain access to the lake. For that use, Lot B is dominant and Lot A is servient. The utility company has an easement in gross across both parcels of land for its power lines. Note that Lot A also has an appurtenant easement across Lot B for its driveway. In this instance, Lot A is dominant and Lot B is servient.

License

A **license** is a temporary permission to come onto the land of another for a specific purpose. The use of land conveyed by a license is nonexclusive because the holder of a license has no right to keep anyone else from the property. A license can be terminated at any time without notice and is considered personal property rather than real property. An example of a license is the purchase of hunting rights on private property.

Encroachment

An **encroachment** exists when part of an improvement to land extends over the boundary line onto an adjoining parcel. Some encroachments, such as that of a fence that is a few millimeters over the border in a few places, are so slight that they are meaningless to the adjoining property owner. Occasionally, however, even a few inches of encroachment can be a grave matter, particularly when a highrise building in a congested urban area is involved. Then a few inches of encroachment may seriously impede the ability of the adjoining owner to make maximum use of that parcel. What will happen if, for instance, a 30-story building is found to encroach 10 inches onto the neighboring lot? Most likely, the owner of the neighboring lot will be entitled to compensation for the loss in value due to the inability to make full use of the property. That amount may be quite substantial if the encroachment forces the property owner to redesign a proposed structure, particularly if a conflict with the zoning or development approval process arises. An encroachment can also lead to title problems, creating an impediment to a property transfer.

FORMS OF PROPERTY OWNERSHIP

Title to real estate—some form of evidence of property ownership—can be held by one person, by more than one person, or in any of a variety of forms of business ownership.

Individual Ownership

Ownership by only one person is called separate ownership or ownership in severalty. The individual owner has sole control over disposition of the property and is sole recipient of any benefits that flow from it, such as rents. On the other hand, the owner in severalty also has sole liability for any debts or other obligations associated with the property, such as taxes and assessments.

In most states, a married person may own real estate either as separate property or as marital property co-owned with the spouse. The distinction is critical when property is transferred. In some states, for instance, all property acquired during marriage automatically is termed *community property*, and any document attempting to convey such property must be executed (signed) by both spouses.

To avoid problems, the marital status of individuals conveying or receiving real estate always should be indicated on the deed conveying title. Common descriptive terms are *single* (never married), *unmarried* (divorced), *widow* (for surviving wife), and *widower* (for surviving husband).

Separate ownership frequently is used when a business is operated as a sole proprietorship. The sole proprietor's business is conducted in the sole proprietor's name or under a trade name, business income is reported on the sole proprietor's individual income tax return, and the sole proprietor is the only person liable for debts of the business.

Co-Ownership

When two or more people own the same real estate, they are called co-owners or concurrent owners.

Tenancy in common

A **tenancy in common (TIC)** is created when two or more persons take title in which tenancy in common is specified or when no other method of taking title is mentioned.

Tenants in common have unity of possession. This means that each tenant has the right to possession of the entire property and cannot be excluded by the other tenants, even if the tenants own unequal fractional interests in the property. If each of three cotenants owns one-third of a property, each still has the right to use the entire property. If there are four cotenants and one has a 40% interest in the property while each of the other three owns a 20% interest in the property, each still has the right to use the entire property. As a practical matter, cotenants who share a property will often agree on a separate portion for each to use (such as a single flat in a multiunit building), or they may agree on a separate time period during which each will have full use of the property (such as a vacation home). If the cotenants lease the property, each receives a proportionate share of the proceeds less a proportionate share of the expenses.

Tenants in common can transfer their interest by gift or sale or by will at death. The person to whom the property is transferred receives the same fractional interest and right of possession (Figure 3.8). A forced sale or division of the property to dissolve the tenancy can be brought about by a lawsuit known as a partition action. The property will be divided into separate parcels, if possible. If the property must be sold, each cotenant receives a proportionate share of the proceeds less a proportionate share of expenses.

FIGURE 3.8
Tenancy in Common

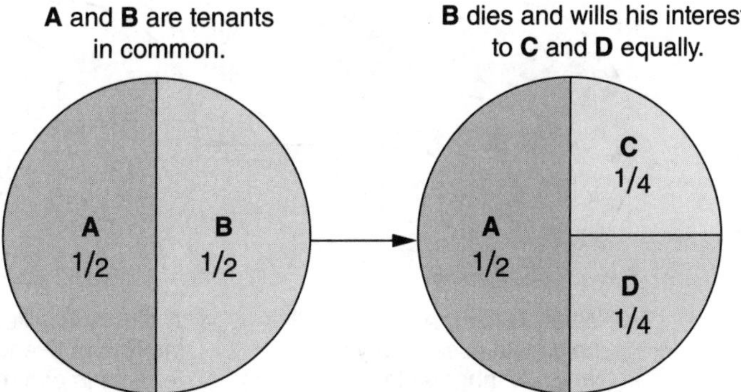

Joint tenancy

A **joint tenancy** is a form of co-ownership that must meet certain legal requirements to be effective. There are four unities of ownership that are traditionally needed to create a joint tenancy—unity of title, time, interest, and possession. A single instrument of conveyance (deed) that transfers title to a specified property must identify all joint tenants at the same time, with each receiving an equal interest (no unequal shares) and present right of possession of the property. If all four unities are present, the joint tenancy will create a right of survivorship (full and undivided ownership) in the last surviving joint tenant.

The most important feature of the joint tenancy is the right of survivorship, which means that joint tenants cannot transfer title to their individual share by will. Even if the interest is specified in the will to go to someone else, the attempted transfer will be ineffectual because the right of the surviving joint tenants is paramount. As each successive joint tenant dies, the surviving joint tenants acquire the deceased tenant's interest. The last survivor takes title in severalty and has all the rights of individual ownership, including the right to pass the property to heirs (Figure 3.9). In most states, the right of survivorship automatically accompanies title taken in a joint tenancy. In other states (such as North Carolina), the right of survivorship must be specifically mentioned in the instrument of conveyance.

FIGURE 3.9
Joint Tenancy with Right of Survivorship

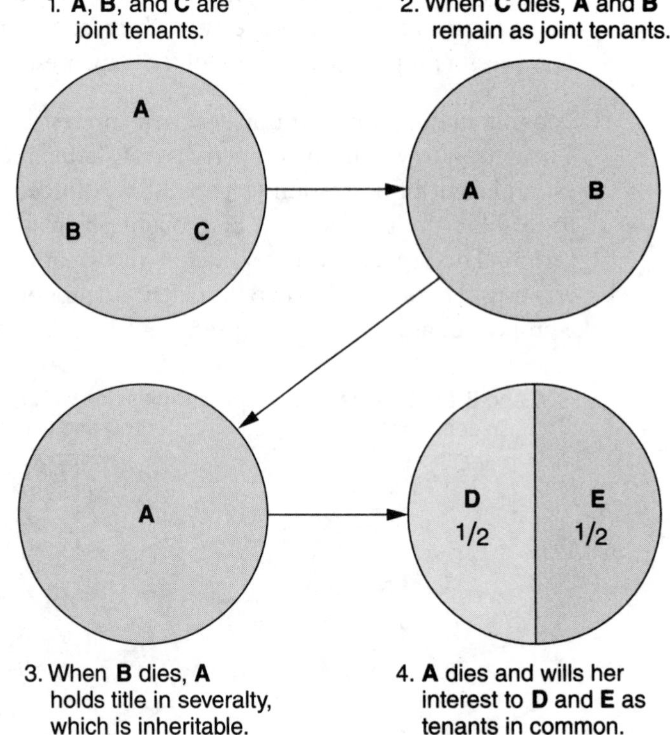

A joint tenant can transfer the interest in the joint tenancy while alive, but not without terminating the joint tenancy with respect to that interest. If there were only two joint tenants originally, the joint tenancy would be completely terminated by a transfer of one joint tenant's interest, and the two owners then would be tenants in common. If there were more than two joint tenants originally, the joint tenancy would remain in effect only for the joint tenants whose interests were not transferred. The remaining joint tenants would have a cotenancy with the new co-owner.

For example, A, B, and C are joint tenants with the right of survivorship in a parcel of real estate. Owner A conveys that interest to D. D now owns a one-third interest in the parcel as a tenant in common with B and C. B and C are still joint tenants as to their respective shares of the property (Figure 3.10).

FIGURE 3.10
Combination of Tenancies

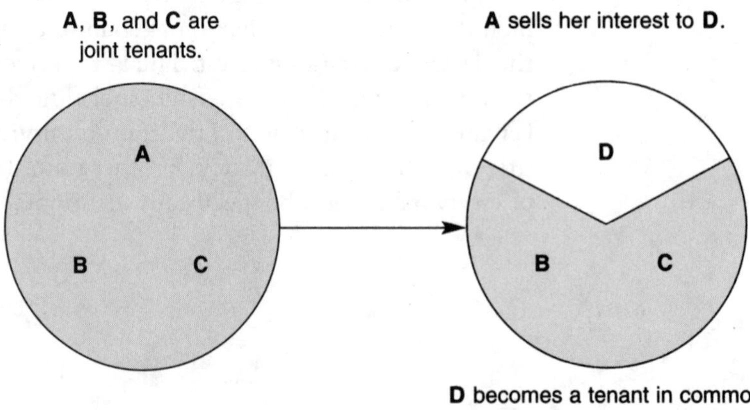

Marital property

As already mentioned, married persons may have a special status as property owners. The forms of marital property ownership vary from state to state, with the two categories described next being the most common.

Community property is all property acquired by either spouse during marriage, except property acquired

- by gift or inheritance,
- with the proceeds of separate property, or
- as income from separate property.

Property that was separate property before the marriage remains separate property afterward. The newest trend in community property states is to allow the spouses to agree in writing to change the "character" of property from separate to community or from community to separate. Community property is a holdover from Spanish law and is found in various forms in Arizona, California, Idaho, Louisiana, Nevada, New Mexico, Texas, Washington, and Wisconsin, and is available as an option to married residents of Alaska. Because it is a form of ownership available only to married couples, community property usually is residential, although some commercial property is owned by spouses as community property.

Tenancy by the entirety is available in some states as a form of marital property ownership in which each spouse has an equal, undivided interest, with title passing to the survivor when one spouse dies. The right of survivorship exists only as long as the marriage, however. In the event of divorce, a tenancy by the entirety automatically becomes a tenancy in common. A tenancy by the entirety also may be terminated by agreement of the spouses or as a result of a legal proceeding brought by a joint creditor of both spouses.

Tenancy in partnership

Two or more persons who carry on a business for profit as partners may own property for partnership purposes in a **tenancy in partnership**. All partners have the right to use the property for partnership purposes. The property can be transferred by the partnership only if the rights of all partners are transferred. Partnership property can be attached only by partnership creditors. When a partner dies, that partner's interest in partnership property goes to the surviving partners, although the heirs of the deceased are entitled to the deceased's share of business profits.

The partnership as a form of business ownership has several special features. No separate income tax is paid by the partnership. Partnership income is distributed to the partners, who are individually responsible for reporting and paying taxes on the income received. Each partner is liable for partnership debts, however.

A commonly used form of real estate partnership is the joint venture, in which the lender contributes the financing while other partners (such as the developer, landowner, construction company, or construction manager) contribute property or expertise.

Exercise 3-4

1. Name two forms of real property ownership characterized by a right of survivorship.
2. What estate indicates that real property is held in sole ownership?
3. What form of real property ownership can defeat a will?

Check your answers against those in the answer key at the back of the book.

Business and Trust Ownership of Real Estate

A **corporation** must follow the laws of the state in which it is incorporated. A domestic corporation is one that does business within the state where it is incorporated; a foreign corporation is one that does business in a state other than the state of incorporation.

Although owned by shareholders, the corporation is recognized as a separate legal entity. As such, it may own, lease, and convey real estate. The day-to-day activities of the corporation are in the hands of its officers, who are under the overall guidance of the board of directors.

A benefit of incorporation is that officers, directors, and shareholders generally are not liable for corporate decisions and corporate debts. A disadvantage of incorporation is that corporate income is taxed twice—first to the corporation, then again to the shareholders when it is distributed as dividends. Income is taxed only once (when it is distributed to shareholders), if the corporation qualifies for treatment under Subchapter S of the Internal Revenue Code.

A nonprofit corporation also can own, lease, and convey real estate, but the corporation is owned by members rather than shareholders.

The limited liability company (LLC) is now recognized by most states. The exact structure and requirements of the LLC vary from state to state, but the LLC generally offers its members the control and income distribution benefits of the general partnership coupled with the reduced liability of the corporation.

A **trust** permits title to real estate to be held by a trustee for the benefit of a beneficiary. The property owner is the trustor, who establishes the trust and conveys title to the trustee, whose powers are defined in the trust document. A trust often is used as a way to convey title on behalf of minor children in the event of a parent's death.

In some states, such as Illinois, use of a land trust is a common way for one or more persons to hold title to avoid encumbering real estate. The trustor usually is named as the beneficiary. Because the interest of a beneficiary is considered personal property and not real estate, a judgment against the beneficiary will not create a lien against the real estate. The land trust usually lasts no longer than 20 years, although the term can be extended by agreement. If the trust term ends or the trustee is unable to locate the beneficiary, the trustee can resign and deed the property to the beneficiary or sell the property and distribute the proceeds to the beneficiary. On the beneficiary's death, title held in the land trust will pass as specified in the beneficiary's will or, if there is no will, to the beneficiary's heirs.

The living trust is gaining popularity as a way to hold title and avoid probate. The trustor places title to both real and personal property in the name of the trustee, but the trustor is also the beneficiary, who has the right to use the property. When the trustor/beneficiary dies, the contingent beneficiaries named in the trust are then entitled to use of the property. A living trust can be set up by a married couple as cotrustors/beneficiaries, with title going to the contingent beneficiaries on the death of the second spouse.

The real estate investment trust (REIT) frequently has been used to secure capital for real estate purchases and pass along the benefits of depreciation and other tax deductions. Those benefits were reduced by the Tax Reform Act of 1986, however.

Special Forms of Ownership

Fee simple ownership of a parcel of real estate generally includes the land as well as all fixtures, such as buildings, attached to it. Sometimes ownership of real estate includes fewer features, and sometimes it includes more.

Condominium

A **condominium** is the absolute ownership of a unit in a multiunit building based on a legal description of the airspace the unit occupies, along with a specified share of the undivided interest in the common areas within the development. Common areas typically include the land itself, walkways, parking spaces, recreation and exercise facilities, hallways, stairs, elevators, and lobbies, as well as the foundation, exterior structure, and roof.

A condominium unit is real property that can be bought, sold, and financed just like a single-family house. The owners usually form an association to manage the commonly held real estate in accordance with detailed rules that specify the relationships among the unit owners and how the condominium operates. The expenses of management and maintenance are divided pro rata among the owners, who pay a monthly fee to the association. On occasion, unit owners may be charged a special assessment to pay for unusual costs that have not been adequately provided for in a reserve fund. Most states require the disclosure of condominium documents to buyers so that they can become aware of all the rules the association has adopted.

The condominium form of ownership has been used for residential apartments as well as for office, retail store, manufacturing, and garage spaces.

Cooperative

Each owner in a **cooperative** project is a shareholder in the corporation that holds title to real estate. Each owner receives the right to exclusive occupancy of part of the property, such as an apartment. Because the individual shares are not considered real estate, cooperative units are not financed individually, although the entire property may be financed.

Planned unit development

The **planned unit development (PUD)** is a type of development, as well as a zoning classification, that features individually owned parcels together with shared common areas. The planned unit development typically provides well-landscaped open areas by allowing greater density in built-up portions of the tract. PUDs have been established for residential, commercial, and industrial uses.

Exercise 3-5

1. What is the highest form of real property ownership?
2. What estates in real property are owned by tenant and landlord?
3. A house on a rural parcel includes an easement over the adjoining property. What is the legal term that describes the adjoining property? What is the legal term that describes the property on which the house is located?
4. Co-owners who have an equal right of possession coupled with a right of survivorship have what form of co-ownership?
5. In what form of property ownership is an exclusive right to an identified segment of airspace conveyed along with an interest in common in the rest of the parcel?

Check your answers against those in the answer key at the back of the book.

■ SUMMARY

An appraisal is the act or process of developing an opinion of value. It provides a description of property as well as the appraiser's opinion of the property's condition, its utility for a given purpose, and/or its probable monetary value on the open market.

Real estate (or real property) includes land, fixtures to land, anything incidental or appurtenant to land (such as an easement right), and anything immovable by law, with certain exceptions. Land includes the earth's surface, what is under the surface (such as minerals and water), and what is above the surface. Land becomes a site suitable for building when utilities are available.

In determining whether something is a fixture to land (and thus part of the real estate), a court will look to the intention of the person who placed the item on the land, the method of attachment, the adaptability of the item for the land's ordinary use, and the agreement and relationship of the parties concerned. An appurtenance is anything used with land for its benefit.

The bundle of rights of ownership of real property are subject to public restrictions, such as taxation, and private restrictions, typically covenants, conditions, and restrictions placed in a property owner's deed. Anything that is not real property is personal property.

The methods by which land can be described include the lot and block system (with reference to a subdivision map), the metes and bounds system (using natural or artificial boundaries), and the rectangular survey system (using townships measured from meridians and base lines by reference to tiers and ranges).

Estates in land include the freehold estates of the fee simple estate and life estate. Nonfreehold estates include the leasehold estate owned by the lessee (tenant) and the leased fee estate owned by the lessor (landlord). Other property interests include the easement that allows a use of another's property and the license that is a temporary permission to enter someone else's property. An encroachment exists when part of an improvement extends onto an adjoining parcel.

Separate ownership is ownership by one person. Business ownership by one person is a sole proprietorship. Forms of co-ownership (ownership by more than one person) include tenancy in common, which has unity of possession, and joint tenancy, which has the four unities of time, title, interest, and possession. In most states, joint tenancy also carries with it the right of survivorship. A partition action can be brought by a co-owner to force a division or sale of the property. Ownership of marital property depends on the laws of the state; some states allow community property and others allow tenancy by the entirety.

A tenancy in partnership can be used by a business partnership to hold title to real estate. A corporation can hold title in its own name as a recognized legal entity. A trust permits title to be held by a trustee for the benefit of a beneficiary. Forms of trust include the land trust, living trust, and real estate investment trust.

A condominium is an ownership interest in airspace, while a cooperative is a shareholder interest in a corporation that holds title to real estate. A planned unit development includes both an individually owned parcel and a shared common area.

■ Review Questions

1. The property of a person who dies leaving no heirs passes to the state by the right of
   a. acquisition.
   b. escheat.
   c. condemnation.
   d. eminent domain.

2. Condemnation of private property for public use is called the right of
   a. seizure.
   b. escheat.
   c. eminent domain.
   d. acquisition.

3. Anything that is *NOT* real property is
   a. real estate.
   b. a fixture.
   c. an appurtenance.
   d. personal property.

4. An appraisal may include
   a. a property description.
   b. an opinion of property condition.
   c. an opinion of market value.
   d. all of these.

5. Real property includes
   a. land.
   b. fixtures and appurtenances to land.
   c. anything immovable by law, with certain exceptions.
   d. all of these.

6. Tenancy by the entirety is a form of
   a. marital property ownership.
   b. tenancy in common.
   c. business property ownership.
   d. ownership in severalty.

7. A landlord has
   a. a fee simple qualified.
   b. a fee simple defeasible.
   c. an estate of tenancy.
   d. a leased fee estate.

8. The four unities required for a joint tenancy are
   a. tenancy, location, title, and possession.
   b. time, title, interest, and possession.
   c. possession, ownership, use, and enjoyment.
   d. title, time, location, and possession.

9. An individually owned parcel includes a share of common areas in
   a. a PUD.
   b. a condominium.
   c. a stock cooperative.
   d. a life estate.

10. A type of real estate featuring ownership of airspace, as well as an interest in common in the entire parcel, is
    a. a PUD.
    b. a condominium.
    c. a stock cooperative.
    d. a life estate.

11. Your children will be MOST likely to inherit Greenacre from you if you have
    a. a life estate.
    b. a defeasible fee.
    c. a remainder.
    d. a special limitation.

12. A life estate is
    a. a present, possessory interest.
    b. a future interest.
    c. an estate of tenancy.
    d. a fee simple defeasible.

13. Property acquired by a spouse during marriage by gift or inheritance is
    a. marital property.
    b. community property.
    c. separate property.
    d. jointly owned property.

14. What are the considerations in determining whether something attached to real property is a fixture?

15. A township is divided into
    a. 160 sections.
    b. 36 sections.
    c. 4 ranges.
    d. 36 meridians.

16. The S½ of NW¼ of Section 16 is a parcel of
    a. 20 acres.
    b. 40 acres.
    c. 80 acres.
    d. 160 acres.

17. A subdivision map is referred to in
    a. the lot and block system.
    b. the lot, block, and tract system.
    c. both of these.
    d. neither of these.

18. A parcel described as the N½ of the SW¼ and the S½ of the NW¼ contains
    a. 80 acres.
    b. 160 acres.
    c. 320 acres.
    d. 640 acres.

19. The type of legal description used primarily in urban areas is
    a. the lot and block system.
    b. the rectangular survey system.
    c. the metes and bounds system.
    d. the meridian datum system.

20. What is the area of the parcel below?

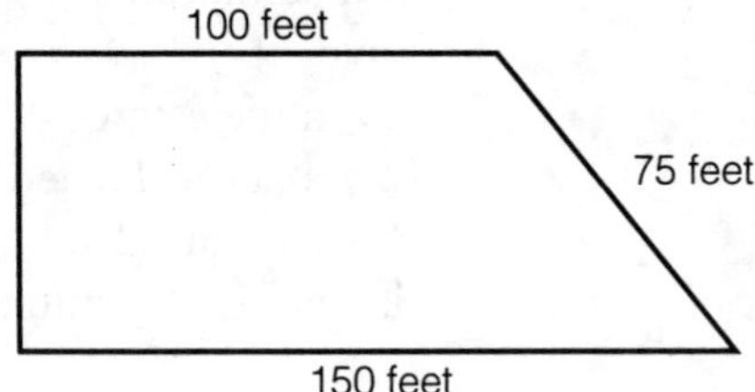

    a. 5,125 sq. ft.
    b. 9,375 sq. ft.
    c. 12,000 sq. ft.
    d. 24,000 sq. ft.

Check your answers against those in the answer key at the back of the book.

UNIT FOUR

REAL ESTATE TRANSACTIONS

■ LEARNING OBJECTIVES

When you have completed this unit, you will be able to

- list commonly used contracts involving real estate,
- explain the elements of a valid contract,
- state the requirements of the statute of frauds,
- describe the ways in which a contract is discharged,
- identify and explain the purpose of the most common types of deed,
- describe important terms of residential and commercial leases, and
- explain the benefits of a ground lease.

■ KEY TERMS

acknowledgement
assignment
bargain and sale deed
breach
chain of title
counteroffer
deed
escalator clause
eviction
fair housing laws
grant deed
gross lease
ground lease
lease
lessee
lessor
net lease
novation
offer to purchase
percentage lease
performance
quitclaim deed
reconveyance deed
recording
reformation
release
rescission
revocation
sheriff's deed
specific performance
statute of frauds
statute of limitations
tax deed
trust deed
warranty deed

OVERVIEW

There can be many roadblocks to a successful real estate transaction. In a real estate sale, one roadblock may be the prospective buyer's failure to qualify for financing, and another may be a problem with the condition of the property that is revealed only after an inspection. Still another roadblock may be a prior property transfer that affects the ownership interest of the present owner, preventing the owner from conveying good title to the buyer. Because the appraiser is interested in any factor that can impede a transaction and possibly affect property value, the appraiser should understand how a sale of real estate is accomplished and how title to real estate is transferred.

In this unit, you will learn the necessary provisions of some of the most frequently encountered documents that are included in a real estate sales transaction, from the provisions of a typical purchase contract to the transfer of title by deed. You also will learn the common provisions of a lease of real property.

THE OFFER TO PURCHASE

The most important step in a successful real estate sale is the real estate sales contract, which typically takes the form of an **offer to purchase** made by the buyer that is accepted by the seller. There are other contracts that also may be part of a real estate purchase, including the following:

- Listing agreement between the seller and the seller's real estate agent, who must be licensed by the state
- Buyer's representation agreement between the buyer and the buyer's real estate agent
- Financing instruments that will enable the buyer to obtain a loan for the purchase
- Escrow agreement that will authorize an escrow agent to arrange for the transfer of funds from buyer to seller and transfer of title from seller to buyer

In addition, the buyer may enter into a contract with one or more inspectors to examine the property, the seller will arrange to pay off any existing financing secured by the property according to the terms of that agreement, and the seller's (listing) agent may provide compensation to the buyer's agent. If property repairs are required, the party responsible for the work will employ someone to perform the work. The lender will hire an appraiser to perform an appraisal to provide assurance that the property's market value is sufficient to support the amount of the loan the lender has been asked to make. The lender will require that title insurance be obtained and will also insist on being named as an "additional insured" or "loss payee" on the borrower's hazard insurance policy.

Of course, there are many incidental contracts that will flow from the purchase transaction, such as the hiring of a moving company to remove the seller's possessions from the property, and another company to bring in the buyer's furnishings. The buyer will want to have the property cleaned before that occurs, and perhaps have some painting done, new carpets installed, et cetera. It is easy to understand why the housing industry is one of the linchpins of the American economy.

Elements of a Valid Contract

No matter how many agreements form some part of the transaction, each will have to contain the following elements required to create a valid contract:

- The parties must have the legal capacity to enter into a binding agreement. If they do not, the contract could be void (never legally valid) or it could be voidable (cancelable) by the person who lacked the capacity to enter into the contract.

IN PRACTICE

A minor cannot make a valid contract for the purchase or sale of real estate, although the minor's legal guardian can do so. Some states allow an emancipated minor to act as an adult. A minor typically becomes emancipated by entering military service, marrying, or successfully petitioning the court for that determination.

- An offer must be made by one party and accepted by the other party to the contract. The offer must be made and accepted freely and voluntarily, without any threat of harm, undue influence, mistake or fraudulent misrepresentation on the part of either party.

IN PRACTICE

Fraud in the inducement is the legal term for the use of improper influence to persuade someone to sign a contract. Foreclosure fraud occurs in this way when a homeowner in distress is persuaded to transfer title to property to someone who promises to help the homeowner avoid foreclosure. The new owner of record then mortgages the property for the maximum amount, absconds with the money, and leaves the person defrauded in worse financial shape than before.

- There must be a lawful object to the contract. A court of law will not enforce a contract to commit a crime.
- Some form of consideration, whether an obligation or payment, must support the contract. This mutuality of contract can be a promise to do something in the future (or refrain from doing something) by one party, with monetary payment to be made by the other party when the promise is performed.
- In some cases, such as a contract for the sale of real estate, the contract may have to be in writing. The state law known as the statute of frauds (discussed in the following box) will specify which contracts have to be in writing.

In addition to contracts that are void or voidable, a contract can be unenforceable if it would violate some law, such as an agreement to commit an unlawful act.

If the person to whom the offer is made returns it to the offeror with a **counteroffer** that changes any of the terms of the original offer, the entire original offer is considered rejected.

Statute of Frauds

The **statute of frauds** is a holdover of the English common law in all states except Louisiana, which adopted the French system of legal codes. The statute of frauds requires a written agreement in any transaction that involves the following:

- The sale of real estate or an interest in real estate
- The lease of real estate for more than one year
- An agreement to employ an agent, broker, or other person to purchase, sell, or lease real estate for more than one year, or find a purchaser, seller, lessee, or lessor of real estate for a term of more than one year
- An agreement by a purchaser of real estate to pay a debt secured by a mortgage or deed of trust on the property purchased, unless the purchaser is assuming an existing debt

An offer can be revoked before it is accepted if the offeree (the person to whom the offer is made) or the offeree's agent receives notice of the **revocation** before acceptance. An exception is made if the offer is supported by some form of consideration (such as payment for an option to purchase real estate), in which case the offer remains open for the term of the option.

Exercise 4-1

Identify the questionable contract elements in each of the following situations:

1. A homeowner has just celebrated her 85th birthday and is suffering from the onset of Alzheimer's disease. Her nephew offers to move into her house to help care for her and she agrees. Within one year, the woman is in a nursing home, and her nephew is the new owner of the house.
2. A father offered his son $10 for every "A" the son received on his report card. The son proudly brought his father a report card with eight A grades, but his father paid him only $50.
3. A painting contractor admired his client's house and told him that he would pay "a million bucks" to live in such a nice house. The client said, "Sold!"
4. A loan officer from a large bank phoned an appraiser and asked for a "ballpark" value on a property in her area, with the promise to give her as much appraisal work as she could handle if she could produce dependable results.

Check your answers against those in the answer key at the back of the book.

Contract Terms

At the very least, the terms of a contract for the sale of real estate should identify the parties unambiguously; state the nature of the transaction; include an adequate description of the property that is the subject of the contract; state the price or the manner in which the price is to be determined, such as by an appraiser's opinion of market value; state any conditions to the performance of either party, such as the buyer securing financing; and specify the time of performance. Even though those items will form the basis for a contract to purchase real estate, many other considerations will be included in the agreement to avoid future misunderstandings and to complete the transaction as efficiently as possible.

Typical provisions of an offer to purchase

The prospective buyer will try to make the offer to purchase as complete and specific as possible. With that goal in mind, the offer to purchase a residential property could be four to eight pages or more and also include other clauses or documents, such as a statement of agency representation, that are required by state or federal law. The offer to purchase will typically include the following:

- Date on which the offer is made
- Name and marital status of the offeror (buyer)
- Identification of the property on which the offer is being made
- Purchase price offered
- Date on which the closing of the sale is to take place
- Date on which the buyer is to receive possession of the property
- Financing terms that are a condition of the offer
- Necessity for an appraisal of the property that meets or exceeds the offered purchase price
- Inspections that the buyer will make and an indication of which party will pay for any required work
- Lead-based paint disclosure by the seller (required by federal and usually state law for buildings constructed before 1978)
- Fixtures or other items to be included in the sale
- Seller to provide clear title to the buyer
- Deadlines for removal of any contingencies
- Final walk-through by the buyer before the closing
- Liquidated damages in the event that the buyer fails to complete the purchase, if allowed by state law
- Dispute resolution, including mediation and possibly subsequent arbitration of disputes
- How escrow is to be established and instructions given to the escrow holder
- The date on which the offer will expire if it is not accepted by the seller
- The signature of the buyer(s)

There will usually also be other disclosures required by state or local law; a statement that the property is being sold in compliance with federal and state fair housing laws; a section indicating how property taxes and other expenses will be prorated at closing (and whether buyer or seller pays for expenses for that day); definitions of the terms used in the contract; provision for payment of attorney fees by the successful party if there is any legal action or proceeding based on the contract; and a statement that "time is of the essence" and that the agreement incorporates any prior negotiations of the parties. If the buyer must sell a present home before completing the transaction, there will also be a sale contingency.

IN PRACTICE

In most residential real estate transactions (particularly those that involve a broker), the parties use a preprinted offer-to-purchase form. If a preprinted contract form is used, by the time the contract negotiations are completed and there is an agreement acceptable to both parties, there may be cross-outs to the form and both typed and handwritten insertions. Any change to the original form should be initialed by the parties. If there is any confusion as to the final version of the contract, the usual order of priority is that

- typed insertions take precedence over preprinted content,
- handwritten insertions take precedence over both typed and preprinted content, and
- specific information takes precedence over general information.

Contract Language

Often, state law will dictate all or part of the contents of a contract or other document related to a residential real estate transaction. Agency and property condition disclosures, notices, and other information will probably be required to follow the wording specified by the law. Sometimes, the required wording must appear in a specific style and size of type.

IN PRACTICE

State law may require that a listing agreement include a statement that "all commission rates are negotiable."

The growing diversity of the population of the United States has created new concerns that the documents involved in a home purchase be understood by consumers. Many states now require that, if the primary language of a client (or customer) of a real estate licensee is a language other than English, documents must be prepared and presented in the client's primary language.

Discharging a Contract

A contract is discharged (terminated) by

- **performance** of the contract terms,
- a **rescission** of the contract agreed to by both parties,
- **release** by one party of the other party's obligation under the contract,
- a **novation** in which a new contract replaces the terms of the original agreement,

- a **reformation** of the contract terms to correct a mistake or change of terms in the original agreement,
- **assignment** of the contract to a new party, unless prohibited by the contract terms, or
- **breach** of the contract terms by one of the parties, in which case the other party may be able to sue for **specific performance** (completion of the contract terms, such as a transfer of title in a sale transaction) or damages (funds to compensate the nonbreaching party for financial loss resulting from the breach).

It may become impossible to perform the terms of the contract, such as when property is destroyed by a natural disaster. In that case, the buyer's purchase of the property will probably be excused.

If there is reason for a party to sue to enforce a contract, the lawsuit must be brought within a specific period of time. A state's **statute of limitations** (another holdover from the English common law) will dictate the deadlines for bringing a legal action. The deadline will depend on the subject of the action; for instance, in California the deadline to bring a lawsuit to enforce a written instrument (such as a contract) is four years from the date of the contract, while the deadline to bring an action based on fraud is three years from the discovery of the fraud. Check with your state for the applicable deadlines in these cases as well as when a legal action may be brought to recover title to real property. On the state's website, enter "statute of limitations."

■ RECORD RETENTION

Primarily because of the possibility of a legal action, most states will require that an appraiser retain all employment contracts or letters of engagement or agreement for appraisal services, as well as copies of all appraisal reports and supporting research, for a specified period.

IN PRACTICE

USPAP's Record Keeping Rule requires that the appraiser prepare a work file for each appraisal, appraisal review, or appraisal consulting assignment. The work file must be in existence prior to the issuance of a written or oral report; a written summary must be added to the work file within a reasonable time after the issuance of an oral report. The work file must contain all of the information specified in *USPAP* and must be retained for at least five years after preparation of the report or at least two years after final disposition of any judicial proceeding in which the appraiser provided testimony related to the assignment, whichever period expires last.

Exercise 4-2

List the terms that should be part of a contract to perform an appraisal of real estate.

Check your answer against the one in the answer key at the back of the book.

■ TRANSFER OF TITLE

Title to real estate generally is conveyed by deed. The requirements for a valid deed and the most frequently used types of deeds are explained next.

Requirements for a Valid Deed

A **deed** is a written instrument by which the owner of real estate intentionally conveys to a purchaser the owner's right, title, or interest in a parcel of real estate. The owner of the real estate is called the grantor, and the person who acquires title is called the grantee.

In order for a deed to be legally valid,

- it must be in writing;
- it must include a description of the parties (full name and marital status);
- the grantor must be legally capable of executing the deed;
- the property must be adequately described;
- it must contain a granting clause using the necessary words of conveyance (such as the word grant);
- it must be signed by the grantor(s); and
- it must be delivered to and accepted by the grantee.

A deed is of no effect if it is not delivered; that is, its delivery cannot be conditional. For instance, the grantor cannot sign the deed and give it to a third person, such as an attorney, with directions to give the deed to the named grantee when the grantee has performed some condition. On the other hand, the deed could be delivered and accepted with a condition placed in the deed itself so that title would be lost if the grantee failed to fulfill the condition.

A deed also has to be accepted by the grantee knowingly. If a homeowner faces foreclosure, just mailing the keys and a deed to the property to the lender does not guarantee that the property will be transferred. The lender must be willing to accept what is termed a *deed in lieu of foreclosure* before the deed will be considered valid. *Note:* Even if the lender accepts the deed, if a sale of the property doesn't cover the remaining loan balance (and costs of sale), the borrower may still be subject to a deficiency judgment.

Types of Deeds

A variety of deeds are used in most states, depending on the purpose of the transaction.

Grant deed

A **grant deed** conveys the grantor's title by use of a granting clause. The grantor makes no express warranties of title, but a grant deed carries implied warranties that the grant's interest has not already been conveyed and that neither the grantor nor anyone who might claim title from the grantor has placed any encumbrance, such as a tax lien, on the property.

Quitclaim deed

A **quitclaim deed** provides the grantee with the least protection of any deed. With a quitclaim deed, the grantor makes no claim to any ownership interest in the described real estate but conveys whatever interest the grantor may own, if any.

Warranty deed

A **warranty deed** warrants expressly that the grantor has good title. With the prevalence of title insurance to protect the buyer in the event that the title turns out not to be good, this form of deed is becoming less common in most states. In some areas of the country, the grant deed has replaced the warranty deed as the most popular form of conveyance.

Bargain and sale deed

A **bargain and sale deed** contains no warranties against encumbrances; it only implies that the grantor holds title and possession of the property. Thus, the grantee has little legal recourse if defects later appear in the title. In some areas, the bargain and sale deed is used in foreclosures and tax sales, in which case the buyer would presumably purchase title insurance for protection.

Trust deed

The **trust deed**, or deed of trust, has already been described as a form of instrument used to hypothecate real estate as security for a debt. The trustor (owner) transfers title to the trustee (impartial third party) to hold for the benefit of the beneficiary (lender) in the event that the trustor defaults before the underlying debt is repaid.

Reconveyance deed

When the trustor under a deed of trust has repaid the underlying debt in full, it is the duty of the beneficiary to notify the trustee so that the property can be deeded back to the trustor by means of a **reconveyance deed**.

Sheriff's deed

A **sheriff's deed**, which contains no warranties, is given to the purchaser of property at a court-ordered sale.

Tax deed

When property is sold by the county tax collector for nonpayment of taxes, the successful purchaser receives a **tax deed**. The quality of the title conveyed by a tax deed varies from state to state according to statutory provisions.

Recordation

A deed can be legally valid even though it is not witnessed, the signature of the grantor is not verified by anyone else, and the deed is not recorded in the county recorder's office. As a practical matter, however, acknowledgment and recording of a deed is a necessity, if only because the lender will require it.

Acknowledgment

To be recorded in the county recorder's office or other repository of title information, most states require that a deed contain an **acknowledgment** of the grantor's signature. Usually, this is accomplished by the stamp (or seal) and signature of a notary public, judge, justice of the peace, court clerk, or other person provided by law.

Recording

Recording is important because it serves as notice to the world of the transfer of title. The deed must be recorded in the appropriate office in the county where the property is located.

When properly recorded, the deed serves to place the grantee in the **chain of title** to the described property. Anyone investigating the title to the property should be able to move backward through the grantee index, tracing the name of the grantor on the present deed as the grantee on the previous deed, et cetera, and then forward through the grantor index to the present grantor. If the name of each grantor and grantee does not appear in exactly the same way on every recorded document conveyed to or from that individual, there may be a missing "link" in the chain.

A fictitious name can be used to receive title, provided the same name is used to convey the property. Title cannot be conveyed to a fictitious person, although title can be conveyed to a corporation because a corporation is a recognized legal entity.

IN PRACTICE

The links in the chain of title show how title was conveyed to the present owner of a property, going back to the earliest recorded document. The chain of title does not reveal the encumbrances that may have been placed on the property and does not serve as evidence that no encumbrances have been recorded.

Exercise 4-3

1. What is the difference between a quitclaim deed and a warranty deed?
2. Why is deed recordation recommended?

Check your answers against those in the answer key at the back of the book.

■ LEASE AGREEMENTS

As you learned in Unit 3, some contracts transfer the right to use real estate rather than the right of ownership. In a **lease** of real estate, the property owner is the **lessor** (landlord) and the party acquiring the right of use is the **lessee** (tenant). The consideration for the right of use usually is the rent paid by the tenant, although sometimes a tenant will provide services, such as maintenance or property management, in exchange for the right to occupy the property. A lease must be in writing if it will not be completed within one year. This includes the period after the lease agreement is signed but before the lease term begins. So, a lease for a nine-month period of occupancy that won't start until four months after the lease is signed must be in writing.

Fair Housing

Because of the number of protections for consumers, most leases and landlord/tenant relationships have stringent legal requirements. Even before there is a signed agreement, federal and state **fair housing laws** will protect the rights of not only the tenant who signs the lease but also any other intended resident of the property. State and local laws may protect more individuals than federal law, which currently prohibits discrimination on the basis of race, color, religion, sex, national origin, handicap, or familial status.

All available units within the prospective tenant's specifications must be shown to the prospect. For example, it's not up to the landlord to decide whether an apartment on an upper floor is suitable for a family with small children. A prospective tenant who has a disability may create an obligation on the part of the landlord to make a required modification, or to allow the tenant to modify the property (but the tenant can be required to return the property to its original condition when the lease terminates).

In addition to all residents of the unit, fair housing protections will extend to guests of the residents. The landlord can't arbitrarily decide to limit the number of visitors a resident may have, particularly if limitations are placed only on some tenants or on some types of visitors.

Residential Leases

State law will provide many other protections as well. The state will require that an agent acting on behalf of the landlord or tenant be licensed. There will be specific disclosures that the landlord must make to a prospective tenant, such as the possible presence of lead-based paint on the premises (federal and possibly also state law) and other possibly hazardous conditions. Other property conditions that may require disclosure are mentioned in Unit 7, "Building Construction and the Environment."

State law is likely to limit the amount of security deposit that the landlord can require of a residential tenant and will specify the conditions under which the security deposit can be returned and how quickly it must be returned after the lease terminates. The condition of the property will be subject to state regulations to ensure that it is habitable and that the tenant's rights are respected if the property requires maintenance or is damaged in a natural disaster. If the tenant or the tenant's guest is injured because of the property's condition, the landlord may be liable for any costs associated with the injury.

Not all of the obligations involved in a residential lease are the landlord's. In addition to paying rent on time, the tenant must keep the premises sanitary and notify the landlord of any property destruction from any cause that is part of the landlord's maintenance responsibility. If the tenant or the tenant's guest damages the property, the tenant may be charged for repairs.

If the tenant breaches the lease by failing to pay rent, or violates the terms of the lease in some other way, such as by conducting an illegal activity on the premises, the landlord can begin the process of **eviction**. The state will specify that the landlord provide notice to the tenant and comply with other requirements, but recognition of the importance of maintaining our housing supply and making it available to consumers usually gives an eviction proceeding priority on a court's docket. If a judgment is rendered in favor of the landlord, the sheriff will be ordered by the court to remove the tenant. If the tenant has abandoned the premises, any of the tenant's possessions left behind that are salvageable usually are placed in storage for a specific period of time, then sold by the sheriff if unclaimed.

IN PRACTICE

In addition to the duties just mentioned, the landlord is responsible for working to insure tenant safety. That responsibility includes installation of proper lighting, repair of broken stairs or uneven walkways, maintenance of security doors and intercom systems, and prompt reporting to police of any criminal activity that poses a threat to residents.

Commercial Leases

A number of lease arrangements can be used for the wide variety of commercial (nonresidential) properties. There are fewer legal protections for the lessee because a commercial property tenant usually is a business person who is considered to be more sophisticated than the typical consumer. The primary concerns covered in a commercial lease include an accurate identification of the property and parties involved in the lease transaction, term of the lease, compensation to the lessor, tenant improvements, and liabilities of the parties.

Commercial buildings may be leased with minimal interior finishing, allowing the layout of work spaces and choice of flooring, wall coverings, and other finishing materials to be accomplished by the tenant—typically at the tenant's expense. The lease will also specify the condition in which the tenant is to leave the property at the termination of the lease, which may depend on the nature of the property improvements. Office cubicles usually are constructed with movable (and removable) panels, and a retail store will use freestanding displays that can be rearranged as needed and removed when necessary. Permanent walls constructed by a tenant will remain part of the structure when the lease terminates, as will light fixtures and most types of flooring, although all will be subject to negotiation.

Lease negotiations will cover building security issues. These include building control and access, security systems, access to passenger and service elevators, parking, and other concerns, as well as who will pay for installation and ongoing expenses of those items.

An important provision of the commercial lease will be the amount of compensation to be received by the lessor, and how that compensation is to be determined. In a **gross lease**, the tenant pays a specified amount of rent over the term of the lease, maintains the premises, and carries insurance on the contents of the leased space, while the landlord is responsible for all expenses associated with property ownership, such as taxes, assessments, and insurance of the structure. Both landlord and tenant will be concerned that there is sufficient liability insurance coverage for any personal injury or property damage that occurs on the premises and will negotiate the kinds of coverage required.

An **escalator clause** in a lease may provide for an increase in rent payments based on increases in a specified index, such as the consumer price index (CPI) or the wholesale price index (WPI).

A **percentage lease** will base rent payments on the income earned by the tenant, with a base amount set as the minimum to be paid.

A **net lease** will include some or all of the expenses of ownership (such as property taxes, assessments, and insurance on the building structure) in the required lease payments; a net lease may also be called a triple-net lease, absolute net lease, or 3N lease.

Ground Leases

Although they are used more frequently with commercial properties, **ground leases** are beginning to attract the attention of residential property developers. With a ground lease, the owner of the land leases the right to erect a structure on the property for a specified term, typically 99 years (which may be the maximum allowed by state law). When the ground lease terminates, the tenant must vacate the premises, and the structure becomes the property of the landlord. Although it may seem that the landlord stands to reap a windfall when the ground lease terminates, the structure may have outlived its useful life and be a burden rather than a benefit to the landlord. If the structure is still viable, it is also likely that the most suitable tenant for the structure in the future will be the tenant who erected the improvements, who may be induced to perform any necessary renovations and begin a new lease term.

The reason the ground lease has become attractive to residential developers is that it can be a way to provide housing at a more affordable cost. Most Americans change their residences a number of times and rent or own at various times. One way to minimize the expense of ownership is to rent, rather than purchase, the land that the living space occupies, and, as a practical matter, an ownership interest that will last for 50 years or longer may be more than enough to satisfy the needs of most homeowners. The ground lease already is common in areas that have limited space and high demand for housing.

IN PRACTICE

Ownership rights in many condominium complexes in Hawaii convey the right to occupy a specified unit subject to the remaining term of a ground lease. Property subject to a ground lease will always be less valuable than property that is owned entirely in fee simple and, as the remaining lease term decreases, the value of the property will decrease correspondingly.

Leasehold and leased fee interests and their appraisal are discussed in Unit 16, "Appraising Partial Interests."

Exercise 4-4

Two friends plan to open a retail store in a small shopping center. They are investing almost all their capital in their inventory. What kind of lease would probably be most attractive to them?

Check your answer against the one in the answer key at the back of the book.

■ SUMMARY

A successful real estate sales transaction will involve many contracts and other documents, such as the offer to purchase, listing agreement, buyer's representation agreement, financing instruments, and escrow agreement, as well as contracts for the engagement of inspectors, contractors, and property appraiser.

To create a valid contract, the parties must have the legal capacity to enter into a binding agreement; an offer made by one party must be accepted by the other party; the contract must have a lawful object; there must be mutuality of contract, which means that there must be some form of consideration or obligation on both sides; and the contract may have to be in writing. If a contract does not meet all of these requirements, it may be voidable, void, or unenforceable. A contract can be revoked before acceptance.

The statute of frauds requires that certain contracts, such as those involving real estate, be in writing. The statute of limitations indicates the time period in which a legal action can be brought.

The terms of an offer to purchase real estate will identify the property, person(s) making the offer, purchase price, date on which the sale is to close, contingencies of the sale (such as financing and satisfactory inspections), fixtures or other items to be included in the sale, mediation or other dispute resolution, liquidated damages if the buyer fails to complete the purchase, and how escrow will be established, among other things. Federal and state law will require compliance with fair housing laws and will also require numerous disclosures to be made during the transaction process. In addition, there may be a requirement that documents be provided in a language other than English.

A contract is discharged by performance, rescission, release, novation, reformation, assignment, or breach, which could result in a suit for specific performance or damages.

State law will probably require that the appraiser retain all contracts for appraisal services, as well as copies of all appraisal reports and supporting research for a specified period of time.

Title is conveyed by deed. A valid deed must be in writing, made by a legally capable grantor, contain a description of the property and parties, have a granting clause, be signed by the grantor, and delivered to and accepted by the grantee knowingly. A deed in lieu of foreclosure may help a borrower avoid foreclosure.

Types of deed include the grant deed, quitclaim deed, warranty deed, bargain and sale deed, trust deed, reconveyance deed, sheriff's deed, and tax deed.

With an acknowledgment of the grantor's signature, recording a deed in the county in which the identified property is located will serve as notice of the ownership of the grantee named in the deed and become a part of the property's chain of title.

A lease between lessor (landlord) and lessee (tenant) can convey the right to use residential or commercial property. Residential lease transactions must meet federal and state requirements, including compliance with fair housing laws. A tenant who breaches the lease terms will be subject to eviction.

A commercial lease will indicate responsibility for tenant improvements and specify the lease payment terms, which could indicate a gross lease, escalator clause, percentage lease, or net lease.

The ground lease is popular with commercial buildings as well as residential buildings in areas of high property demand.

■ Review Questions

1. One of the elements of a valid real estate purchase contract is
   a. legal capacity of the seller.
   b. approval of the lender.
   c. a statement of the listing agent's commission.
   d. the term of the listing.

2. A valid contract requires
   a. parties who are older than 21.
   b. an offer by one party that is delivered to the other party.
   c. an offer by one party that is accepted by the other party.
   d. consideration in the form of a cash payment.

3. A valid contract requires
   a. that the contract be in writing.
   b. a stated objective.
   c. an obligation by both parties.
   d. receipt of monetary payment by one party.

4. A contract for the purchase of real estate must be in writing, according to
   a. the terms of the contract.
   b. the lender's requirements.
   c. the statute of limitations.
   d. the statute of frauds.

5. The statute of frauds applies to a lease of real estate that
   a. will be completed within one year.
   b. will be completed in more than one year.
   c. involves the services of a real estate agent.
   d. includes a security deposit.

6. The form of deed used to return title to real estate to its owner when the debt secured by a deed of trust is paid in full is
   a. the warranty deed.
   b. the reconveyance deed.
   c. the quitclaim deed.
   d. the tax deed.

7. The form of deed that makes no warranties, express or implied, is
   a. the grant deed.
   b. the reconveyance deed.
   c. the quitclaim deed.
   d. the tax deed.

8. A condition to an offer to purchase real estate that is unlikely would involve
   a. the sale of the buyer's current home.
   b. financing for the purchase loan.
   c. inspection of the property.
   d. the lender's approval of the contract.

9. A contract may be discharged by all the following *EXCEPT*
   a. performance of the contract terms.
   b. decision of a third party.
   c. reformation.
   d. novation.

10. A change to the contract terms to correct a mistake is
    a. a reformation.
    b. a rescission.
    c. a novation.
    d. a breach.

11. A default by one of the parties to a contract is
    a. a reformation.
    b. a rescission.
    c. a release.
    d. a breach.

12. The legal action to force a defaulting party to complete a sale transaction is called
    a. assignment of the defaulting party's interest.
    b. partition.
    c. specific performance.
    d. suit to quiet title.

13. Title to real estate generally is conveyed by
    a. life estate.
    b. defeasible fee.
    c. contract.
    d. deed.

14. The form of conveyance that is used to make real estate security for a debt is
    a. the trust deed.
    b. the reconveyance deed.
    c. the bargain and sale deed.
    d. the warranty deed.

15. The deed that contains no warranties against encumbrances but implies that the grantor holds title and possession of the property is
    a. the trust deed.
    b. the sheriff's deed.
    c. the bargain and sale deed.
    d. the quitclaim deed.

16. The deed that returns title to the borrower when a debt has been paid is
    a. the trust deed.
    b. the reconveyance deed.
    c. the bargain and sale deed.
    d. the sheriff's deed.

17. Before a deed can be recorded, *MOST* states require that it be
    a. acknowledged.
    b. signed by the grantee.
    c. accompanied by consideration.
    d. prepared in triplicate.

18. The record of property ownership that can be discovered by examining the history of transfers to the property starting with the present grantee is called
    a. the property petition.
    b. the chain of title.
    c. the summary of grants.
    d. the document decree.

19. *MOST* states have the greatest number of legal protections for
    a. the commercial property lessor.
    b. the commercial property lessee.
    c. the residential property lessor.
    d. the residential property lessee.

20. Rent will increase based on the increase in a specified index under
    a. a gross lease.
    b. an escalator clause.
    c. a percentage lease.
    d. a net lease.

Check your answers against those in the answer key at the back of the book.

UNIT FIVE

THE REAL ESTATE MARKETPLACE

■ LEARNING OBJECTIVES

When you have completed this unit, you will be able to

- discuss the characteristics of real estate markets,
- explain why the market for real estate is not like other markets,
- identify the types of market analysis that help define the market for real estate,
- discuss the ways in which real estate is financed,
- name the elements that create value,
- define market value and explain other types of value,
- identify influences on real estate value, and
- list and explain the basic value principles that must be considered in determining market value.

KEY TERMS

- absorption analysis
- anticipation
- assessed value
- balance
- beneficiary
- capital market
- change
- competition
- conformity
- contribution
- cost
- cost of credit
- decline
- deed of trust
- demand, utility, scarcity, transferability (DUST)
- demography
- effective purchasing power
- equilibrium
- externalities
- feasibility study
- forecasts
- four factors of production
- growth
- highest and best value
- insurable value
- investment value
- law of decreasing returns
- law of increasing returns
- life cycle of property
- market
- market value
- money market
- mortgage
- opportunity cost
- physical, economic, governmental, social (PEGS)
- price
- progression
- regression
- revitilization
- sales price
- segmentation
- substitution
- supply and demand
- surplus productivity
- trustee
- trustor
- value is use

OVERVIEW

The most significant investment for most Americans is the purchase of a home. Whether a detached single-family house, a highrise condominium, a town house, a farm, a ranch, or even a houseboat, such a purchase often is well rewarded at the time of a subsequent sale, when the property's value may have increased substantially over its initial purchase price. At a time of economic downturn, however, and particularly if a resale occurs within only a year or two, the property may not command a high enough sales price to cover both the seller's original purchase price and the expenses of sale (such as a broker's commission).

Of course, commercial property transactions are also important to the parties involved, and commercial property values can be even more volatile than those of other forms of real estate. The favorable economic indicators that encourage office and retail development may lead to overbuilt markets and empty buildings. Commercial property is typically leased, and unfavorable economic conditions can quickly lead to vacant storefronts and lowered lease rates.

In either case, a property appraisal can be valuable in making a final decision on whether to enter a transaction. An appraisal can assure either purchaser or seller that the sales price is reasonable in light of prevailing market conditions.

The forces that create and affect the real estate marketplace are the subjects of this unit. We first examine some of those forces, then define the term *market value*. We conclude with a discussion of some basic economic principles that contribute to real property value.

THE MARKET FOR REAL ESTATE

A **market** is simply a place for selling and buying. While we refer in this text to the local real estate market, in many respects there never can be a truly local real estate market. There may be locally occurring transactions (such as within a neighborhood, city, or county), but all transactions are affected to some extent by the wider market forces within the state, region, and nation. The major forces—population level, strength of the economy, and availability of financing—can be identified separately, yet they are interconnected.

Characteristics of Real Estate Markets

Unlike the market for real estate, other goods and services are said to have efficient markets. The factors that contribute to an efficient market include the following:

- Products that are readily exchangeable for other products of the same kind
- Ample supply of knowledgeable buyers and sellers
- Little or no government regulation influencing value
- Relatively stable prices
- Easy product supply and transfer of title

A market that is at its most efficient is said to be a perfect market. Unfortunately, the market for real estate is far from perfect.

We can begin to define a real estate market by understanding the special factors that influence real estate as a commodity. Every parcel of real estate is considered unique and thus not interchangeable with any other parcel. Buyers and sellers of real estate frequently are unsophisticated and lack knowledge of the factors that make one parcel of real estate more valuable than another. The number of buyers and sellers frequently moves away from a state of equilibrium to create either a seller's market (many more buyers than sellers) or a buyer's market (many more sellers than buyers). Real estate is intensely regulated, with regard both to the uses to which it can be put and to the manner in which its ownership can be transferred. As a result of all these factors, as well as the fact that real estate is immovable, prices can be highly volatile.

Characteristics of land

Because every parcel of real estate is unique and immobile, some of the factors that ordinarily affect supply and demand must receive somewhat different consideration.

A market is simply a forum for buying and selling, that is, a means for bringing together buyer and seller. For products other than real estate, the location of the product to be sold affects shipping costs and is only one of a number of determinants that affect value. The most important single factor in determining real estate value is location. Land cannot be delivered to a location where it is in short supply or warehoused until it is needed. The seller of real estate can improve the property by preparing it for building or by constructing or renovating improvements. The seller also can use advertising and other promotional tools to make the property's availability known to the greatest number of potential buyers. The one thing the seller of real estate cannot do is change the property's location. What the seller can do is make the property more desirable by analyzing the needs and desires of potential buyers and improving the property with those requirements in mind.

Market Analysis

An analysis of the real estate marketplace must include demographic data on the area's residents. **Demography** is the scientific study of population statistics, such as births, deaths, and marriages. The overall market area can be further defined by the process called **segmentation** into specific categories of consumer preferences, including those relating to income, work, leisure activities, and other lifestyle patterns.

By knowing as much as possible about the people who make up the market area, it is possible to predict the probable demand for various types and price levels of housing as well as the commercial and industrial establishments necessary to supply the required products and services. Such **forecasts** are published regularly by various government agencies as well as research centers, industry-related companies, and trade associations.

An **absorption analysis** is a study of the number of units of residential or nonresidential property that can be sold or leased over a given period of time in a defined location. Existing space inventory must be considered in light of present demand and current or projected space surplus. In short, is there a need for new space? That question is not easy to answer. Recent decades have shown that there will always be boom-and-bust cycles in which demand for properties results in overbuilding or inflated price levels that cannot be sustained. The overbuilding of the commercial real estate market in the 1980s left many urban areas with a supply of office space that did not approach acceptable occupancy levels until the mid-1990s. The booming residential real estate market of the first part of this century, helped by low interest rates and adjustable-rate mortgages, was followed by the subprime lending crisis and resulted in a record number of foreclosures and many vacant homes.

An absorption analysis usually is performed as part of a **feasibility study**, used to predict the likely success of a proposed real estate development. The feasibility study also includes a cost analysis of the proposed construction and projected return to investors.

Of course, the most complete statistics and best analyses are useless without a thoroughly up-to-date knowledge of the political climate and government forces, both local and otherwise, that may result in regulations affecting property ownership and use. A feasibility study of area growth projections for a new subdivision is incomplete if it does not take into account a proposed highway expansion adjacent to the site. Without that knowledge, the use proposed by the owner or prospective purchaser might be meaningless. With that knowledge, a recommendation that the proposed use change from residential to commercial could result in a project several times as valuable.

The Cost of Credit

Few buyers of real estate could afford, or would prefer, to pay all cash for property. Interest paid on a loan used to purchase real estate is the **cost of credit** to the borrower. When the cost of credit is high, borrowers cannot qualify to buy property that would be affordable when financing is not as expensive. The cost of credit to borrowers thus has a direct impact on the price that can be paid for property.

The cost of credit depends on the availability of funds in relation to the number of potential borrowers. Credit is said to be "tight" when there is not enough financing to accommodate all prospective borrowers.

Sources of capital

A **money market** fund consists of short-term financing instruments. These include U.S. Treasury bills, notes, and other government securities; municipal notes; certificates of deposit; commercial paper (corporate borrowing to finance current operations); Eurodollars (funds deposited outside the United States); and others. Because short-term loans are much in demand in the real estate industry for construction financing and other interim or "bridge" loans, rates available on the money market usually have a major impact on real estate development.

The **capital market** is the term used to describe the trading of longer-term financing instruments such as mortgages, deeds of trust, bonds, stocks, and other obligations generally maturing in more than one year. There is no one location or institution that comprises either the money market or the capital market and no sharp line of demarcation in the kinds of instruments handled by each.

Competing investments

Investors generally fall into one of two groups, debt investors and equity investors. Debt investors are the more conservative of the two groups because they take a passive rather than an active role in management of their investments and demand a security interest in property being financed. Equity investors, who make use of what is termed venture capital, take a more active, though unsecured, role in the investment.

How Real Estate Is Financed

The lien on real estate demanded by the debt investor may take the form of either a mortgage or a deed of trust, both of which are explained in the following paragraphs. It is important to note that even though the mortgage and deed of trust are different types of security instruments, the term mortgage is also used to refer to any instrument by which real estate is made security for a debt.

Mortgage terms and concepts

The security instrument is the document that hypothecates the real property that serves as the lender's assurance that the debt incurred will be repaid. Personal property (anything that doesn't qualify as real estate) can be pledged by a security instrument, rather than hypothecated. One difference between the two forms of security is that possession of personal property pledged to secure payment of a debt may be turned over to the creditor. When real estate is used as security, the debtor usually retains possession.

A **mortgage** creates a lien in favor of the mortgagee (lender) on the property of the mortgagor (property owner). The lien is enforced by the mortgagee if the mortgagor fails to meet the obligations imposed by the promissory note that states the terms of the loan agreement. Enforcement of a mortgage may be through a judicial foreclosure, which requires a court hearing, or by a sale on behalf of the mortgagee, if provided for in the mortgage instrument.

A **deed of trust**, or trust deed, is an actual transfer of title from the **trustor** (property owner, who is the borrower and who retains equitable title to the property) to a **trustee** (neutral third party, who acquires legal title with a power of sale that benefits the lender) to be held on behalf of the lender, known as the **beneficiary**. When the debt is repaid, the beneficiary notifies the trustee, who issues a reconveyance deed that returns legal title to the trustor. If the trustor defaults, the trustee may sell the property to repay the underlying debt.

Mortgage payment plans

A mortgage debt (any debt secured by real estate, whether the security instrument used is a mortgage or deed of trust) can be repaid through various payment plans.

Repayment of a mortgage debt usually requires payment of both principal (the amount borrowed) and interest (the charge for the borrowing). The interest rate can be fixed (the same for the life of the loan) or adjustable (varying according to an established index, such as the rate on six-month Treasury bills or the average cost of funds of FDIC-insured institutions). With either fixed-rate or adjustable-rate loans, the lender's effective yield (and the borrower's effective cost) often is increased by some form of buydown, an advance payment of interest called points or discount points. Each point equals 1% of the loan amount and effectively adds ⅛% to the interest rate paid by the borrower.

Types of mortgages

The fully amortized *fixed-rate mortgage* requires regular payments of both principal and interest so that the loan is fully paid off at the end of the loan term. With the *adjustable-rate mortgage*, individual payments can rise or fall as the interest rate rises or falls in step with the index used.

The *graduated payment mortgage* provides lower monthly payments in the early years of the loan term, with gradual increases over five to 10 years, after which payments level off for the remainder of the loan term. The *growing equity mortgage* provides a fixed interest rate but an increasing payment amount, allowing for a more rapid payoff.

The *reverse annuity mortgage*, available to those aged 62 or older, provides a lump sum or a monthly payment to a homeowner using a previously mortgage-free (or mostly mortgage-free) home as collateral, with the entire loan amount plus interest due at the end of the loan term. The *shared appreciation mortgage* offers a below-market interest rate and lower payments in exchange for the transfer of some equity from borrower to lender.

Elements That Create Value

For real estate or any commodity to have value, the four elements that create value must be present. These elements are **demand**, **utility**, **scarcity**, and **transferability (DUST)**. The element of demand is present when someone wants the property and has the financial ability to purchase it. Utility means that the property can serve a useful purpose. Scarcity is present when the property is in short supply relative to demand. Transferability means that title to the property can be moved readily from one person or entity to another. When all four elements of value are present, property has a value that may be estimated by an appraiser.

The elements that create value can be broken down even further. Demand is a function of *desire*, or a buyer wanting to acquire something, and **effective purchasing power**, which is the buyer's ability to pay for the item desired. Just because a buyer wants something does not mean that the buyer can afford it. Does the buyer have the financial resources to pull out a checkbook and pay for the item that way, or is the buyer able to finance the purchase? Desire and purchasing power must be in equilibrium. Even if there is desire for a particular type of property in a marketplace, if prospective buyers have little cash, or financing is hard to procure, sales will be curtailed and values will drop.

IN PRACTICE

A penthouse condominium in a very desirable area is listed for sale for $5 million. The listing gets plenty of hits on its internet listing and regular requests for showings, but attracts no offers. In fact, many people in the housing market might wish to buy the unit (desire), but it is likely that none of those interested can afford it at the asking price (effective purchasing power). Once the price of the unit is lowered to an acceptable level for this market, desire and effective purchasing power will be matched, equilibrium will be met, and the unit will probably sell.

Types of Value

When a good or service can be used to acquire another good or service, the commodities have what is termed *value in exchange*. A marketplace exists when there is no impediment to the ready exchange of goods or services. Most often, goods or services are exchanged for their equivalent in legal tender—money. The cost to the owner of an item includes the labor and materials required to produce it. The amount of money required to bring about the exchange is the **price** paid for the good or service. As you will learn later in this unit, the price paid or cost to a subsequent owner of a good or service will be affected by both the number of potential purchasers (demand) and quantity of the goods or services (supply). Because it reflects conditions in the marketplace, value in exchange is what is described as **market value**.

Many regulatory agencies and other government units, as well as individuals, incorporate into their real estate decision criteria a variety of objectives and policies that are perceived as influencing value. These criteria often define a type of value, such as one of those listed in the following. Nevertheless, they are typically anchored to a value-in-exchange concept, usually represented by a market value definition. The types of value defined may include the following:

- Appraised value
- Assessed value
- Book value
- Capitalized value
- Cash value
- Depreciated value
- Exchange value
- Going concern value
- Improved value
- Inheritance tax value
- Insurable value
- Investment value
- Leased fee value
- Leasehold value
- Liquidation value
- Market value
- Mortgage loan value
- Rental value
- Replacement value
- Retrospective value
- Salvage value
- Value in use

To appraise property means to provide an opinion of the dollar amount that represents one of the property's values. Appraisers for banks, savings associations, or other lenders will probably be seeking the market value of the properties they inspect for mortgage loan purposes. Depreciated cost (value) is used in one appraising approach to form an opinion of market value; rental value may be used in another. In a divorce or other court proceeding, the parties may be interested in a property's value at some point in the past—its retrospective value. City and county real estate taxes are based on assessed value.

Definition of market value

The *Uniform Standards of Professional Appraisal Practice* defines **market value** as

> a type of value, stated as an opinion, that presumes the transfer of a property (i.e., a right of ownership or a bundle of such rights), as of a certain date, under specific conditions set forth in the definition of the term identified by the appraiser as applicable in an appraisal.

USPAP thus requires the appraiser to state the specific conditions under which market value is determined. Those conditions generally will concern the

- relationship, knowledge, and motivation of the parties;
- terms of sale, such as cash or cash equivalent; and
- conditions of sale, such as exposure on a competitive market for a reasonable time prior to sale.

The definition used by Fannie Mae states that market value is

> the most probable price that a property should bring in a competitive and open market under all conditions requisite to a fair sale, the buyer and seller, each acting prudently [and] knowledgeably, and assuming the price is not affected by undue stimulus.

Market value thus typically assumes an arm's-length transaction in which

- buyer and seller are typically motivated;
- both parties are well informed or well advised, and acting in what they consider their best interests;
- a reasonable time is allowed for exposure in the open market;
- payment is made in terms of cash in U.S. dollars or in terms of financial arrangements comparable thereto; and
- the price represents the normal consideration for the property sold unaffected by special or creative financing or sales concessions granted by anyone associated with the sale.

To summarize, market value reflects a transaction in which there are no exceptional factors influencing the buyer, the seller, or the availability of financing. What happens when an unusually high number of properties on the market are in foreclosure or already owned by a lender? In this case, the appraiser must determine what is "normal" for the current market. Unfortunately, foreclosure sales are likely to affect the value of all properties in the area—not just those that were foreclosed or are being sold under imminent threat of foreclosure. In such a market, property condition becomes even more important than usual. If a foreclosed property has suffered from lack of care, or even vandalism, what will be the cost to bring that property up to the condition of other properties?

Sales price

Sales price is what a property actually sells for—its transaction price. This price may differ from market value because many factors can prevent a sale from being an arm's-length transaction. The need of either of the principals (buyer or seller) to close the transaction within a short period of time will limit that party's bargaining power. On the other hand, if a seller receives an offer for less than the asking price, which is the market value of the property, but the offer is made only one week after the property is put on the market, the seller may decide that a quick sale is worth losing the higher price that might be received if the property were left on the market longer. The buyer and the seller may be relatives, friends, or related companies, and one or both could voluntarily limit their bargaining power. Also, the buyer may have a pressing need to acquire the property, such as the need to add to an adjoining site.

Cost

The amount paid for a good or service is its **cost**. The cost to purchase a parcel of real estate may or may not be the same as the *price* it can command when it is sold to someone else. A developer may pay $5 million for a prime downtown lot and another $20 million to construct an office building on the site. If the market is flooded with similar properties and market demand thus is very low, the developer may not recoup the cost of the lot and building when the property is eventually sold.

Investment value

Investment value is the value of a property to a particular investor, considering the investor's cash flow requirements. Cash flow is the amount of income left over after all expenses of ownership have been paid. Different investors will have different income expectations, as well as different expenses of ownership.

Before the Tax Reform Act of 1986 eliminated many of the tax advantages of real estate ownership, a property could be desirable even if it offered a negative cash flow (that is, it cost more to own than the income it produced) in the early period of ownership. The loss generated by the real estate could be used as a deduction to shelter other income from taxation. The amount of loss that can be carried over from real estate investments now has been greatly restricted. Determination of an individual real estate investor's after-tax position requires the services of a tax accountant or attorney.

Other values

Use value is the value of the acquired right to use a property for a specific purpose or in a specific manner. An example is tribal property owned by the Cherokee Nation. A qualified heir would inherit the right to use the property (the possessory interest), but not the real estate itself.

Value in use is property value based on a particular use, often considered as part of a broader operation or process. An example is a driving range adjacent to a golf course. The value-in-use concept offers an analytical framework to support real estate value in the context of a business's overall going-concern value, which also takes into account the intangible but valuable assets of an established, profitable business, such as customer goodwill.

The value determined by a local taxing authority as the basis for *ad valorem* property taxation is called **assessed value**. The amount for which property may be insured is its **insurable value**.

Influences on Real Estate Value

The forces of nature, as well as the human-generated effects of government, economic, and social systems, all affect the value of real estate. The **physical, economic, governmental,** and **social (PEGS)** forces are discussed next.

Physical and environmental

Climatic and other environmental conditions, exacerbated by ill-planned development, can wreak havoc on both land and buildings.

IN PRACTICE

In California, many residential and commercial buildings have been built directly over or in close proximity to known earthquake fault lines. Earthquakes also can occur in many other states, which may not be as well prepared as California to deal with them. In some tornado-prone areas of the Midwest, new subdivisions stand directly in the path of potential catastrophe. In recent decades, multiple hurricanes inflicted heavy damage on communities in Florida, Louisiana, New Jersey, Texas, and other coastal states. Fires have ravaged parts of California, Texas, and Florida.

The range of possible liabilities imposed on property owners for environmental reasons, including the presence or proximity of hazardous substances as well as noise and dangerous conditions, can be overwhelming. A special area of appraisal focused on discovery and analysis of environmental problems has emerged.

Economic

Real estate values tend to move in cycles, mirroring the economy as a whole. With a high level of employment and regular salary increases, demand for housing and other forms of real estate will increase and prices will follow suit. When the unemployment rate rises and wage levels stagnate or decrease, or interest rates (particularly on adjustable-rate loans) increase at a greater rate than anticipated, the number of mortgage loan foreclosures will increase. As more properties become available, yet fewer persons are able to afford them, market values decline. When economic conditions become more favorable, market values are stabilized and, as conditions continue to improve, may begin to rise once again.

Government and legal

The increasing number and complexity of regulations affecting ownership and use of real estate have proven to be major influences on the cost of acquiring and owning real estate. Although an appraiser cannot make a legal judgment, determination of the highest and best use of the property being appraised must always take into account both existing and proposed zoning, which will specify the range of uses available to the property owner.

IN PRACTICE

In some states, property tax exactions require voter approval, which can be difficult to obtain. As a result, increases in development fees have been used to pass new infrastructure costs on to developers and, ultimately, property buyers.

Social

Social influences are gaining increasing recognition as harbingers of future market demand. Although the single-family detached home still is the most desired form of housing, the condominium form of ownership, typically in a multiunit building, has become popular in urban areas. Mixed-use developments providing both residential and retail units have stimulated interest in downtown areas of both large and small cities. As more people show evidence of environmental as well as personal concerns, builders will respond to those desires, as well. The "green" house that makes a minimal impact on the environment is already being built.

Of course, one of the most interesting phenomena of the past several decades has been the influence of the great wave of post–World War II baby boomers born between 1946 and 1964 as they have grown to maturity. The economic effects of this sector of the population have been impossible to ignore. While the baby boomers were children, record levels of building were required to provide them with schools. Universities blossomed with record enrollments. When the baby boomers demanded housing, builders complied. When the baby boomers decided to have their own babies, they created a baby boomlet. As they reach retirement age, baby boomers are creating new opportunities for developers of housing designed to accommodate the needs of seniors. The concept of universal design" includes features to enhance the accessibility of homes and fixtures, which can appeal to homeowners in all age groups.

Exercise 5-1

Which factors are likely to prevent an arm's-length transaction?

1. Seller's immediate job transfer to another city
2. New highway construction
3. Delinquent tax sale
4. Location across the street from a grade school
5. Flooding in crawlspace not revealed by seller
6. Purchase of adjacent property for business expansion

Check your answer against the one in the answer key at the back of the book.

■ BASIC VALUE PRINCIPLES

While some property owners could probably make a fairly accurate guess as to the current value of their properties, they would still be unable to identify all or most of the factors that contribute to that value. The knowledge of precisely what those factors are, and how they influence and can be expected to influence property value, is part of what lends credence to the appraiser's opinion of market value.

The 16 basic value principles discussed next are interrelated, and their relative importance will vary depending on particular local conditions. Supply and demand may be the strongest factor in a popular resort area; in an urban area, a period of economic recession may deter development of new stores. Even climatic or geological conditions are important, as when unexpected heavy rainfall creates the threat of destructive mudslides.

It is the appraiser's task, then, to consider the subject property in light of all the factors applicable to the property's type and location, as well as the purpose of the appraisal. Principles affecting marketability (such as supply and demand) will have greater influence in the sales comparison and cost approaches, while principles affecting productivity (such as opportunity cost) will have the greatest influence in the income approach.

1. Anticipation

According to the principle of **anticipation**, property value may be affected by expectation of a future event. The expectations of a real estate buyer will depend to some extent on the type of property purchased. The buyer of a single-family residence usually expects to take advantage of the property's amenities as a shelter, as well as the prestige value of ownership. In the same way, some owners of commercial property enjoy the use of the facilities in conducting a business on the premises. The ability of the property to generate income is the primary expectation of most buyers of commercial and multifamily residential property. Determining the present value of the future income stream is the basis of the income approach to appraising, discussed in Units 13 and 14.

In addition to the benefits that flow from possession, real estate may offer a benefit that is realized only when property is sold. Real estate has historically proved to be a generally appreciating asset. As such it is usually bought with the expectation of future higher value. This anticipation of higher value is usually fulfilled because land offers a fixed supply to satisfy what has proved to be a continually growing demand. However, anticipation may also lower value if property rights are expected to be restricted or if the property somehow becomes less appealing to prospective buyers.

For example, a residential area scheduled to undergo condemnation for highway construction might represent anticipation in either of its forms. Owners of residential property immediately adjacent to the highway may expect property values to decline as traffic noise and pollution increase. Owners of residential property far enough away from the highway to avoid those problems may expect property values to rise as their property is made more accessible to surrounding business and shopping areas.

Land-use requirements are often anticipated by developers, who wish to be ready with the necessary residential, commercial, or industrial facilities to meet the demand they expect. The predicted need might or might not materialize, however, which is why real estate as an investment still contains an element of risk. In short, real property is very often purchased for its anticipated future benefits, whether for production of income, a tax shelter (to the extent allowed by law), or future appreciation.

2. Balance

Real estate is a unique, immovable product, yet it is affected by the same market forces that influence the production of other, movable items. Land will tend to be at its highest value when the four factors of production (item 8) are in **balance**.

Balance also is the term used to describe a mix of land uses that maximizes land values. With the appropriate proportion of residential, commercial, and other land uses, all properties benefit by the ability of the area to attract and keep both residents and businesses.

3. Change

All property is influenced by the principle of **change**. No physical or economic condition remains constant. Just as real estate is subject to natural phenomena—earthquakes, tornadoes, fires, violent storms, and routine wear and tear by the elements—the real estate business (as any business) is subject to the demands of its market. It is the appraiser's job to keep aware of past and perhaps predictable effects of natural phenomena as well as the changes in the marketplace.

4. Competition

According to the principle of **competition**, when the supply of property in the marketplace is low relative to the demand for such property, creating excess profits for present property owners, the result is to attract more properties to the marketplace.

All types of real estate are subject to the effects of competition in some form. The value of a house will be affected by the number of other, similar houses available in the same area. If only a few properties are competing for the attention of a much larger number of buyers, those properties will command much higher prices than they would if there were many such properties for sale.

Income-producing properties are always susceptible to competition. For example, if demand produces excess profits for a retail store, similar stores will be attracted to the area. This competition tends to mean less profit for the first business. Unless total market demand increases, there probably will not be enough sales to support very many stores, and one or more will be forced out of business. Occasionally, the opposite is true, and additional competitors serve as a stimulus to the area, making a center of trade for the products being sold.

5. Conformity, Progression, and Regression

In general, particularly in residential areas of single-family houses, buildings should follow the principle of **conformity**; that is, they should be similar in design, construction, age, condition, and market appeal to other buildings in the neighborhood.

Nonconformity may work to the advantage or disadvantage of the owner of the nonconforming property. A house that has not been well maintained but is in a neighborhood of well-kept homes will benefit from the overall good impression created by the neighborhood and its probable desirability. This is an example of the principle of **progression**. In an example of the principle of **regression**, a house that has been meticulously maintained but is in a neighborhood of homes that have not received regular repair will suffer from the generally unfavorable impression created. In the same way, an elaborate mansion on a large lot with a spacious lawn will be worth more in a neighborhood of similar homes than it would be in a neighborhood of more modest homes on smaller lots. From the appraiser's viewpoint, the major concern is whether the improvements, or components, are typical.

6. Contribution

In an appraisal for market value, any improvement to a property, whether to vacant land or a building, is worth only what it adds to the property's market value, regardless of the improvement's construction cost. In other words, an improvement's contribution to the value of the entire property is counted, not its intrinsic cost. The principle of **contribution** is easily applied to certain housing improvements. An extensively remodeled kitchen usually will not contribute its entire cost to the value of a house. A second bathroom, however, may well increase a house's value by more than its installation cost.

The principle of conformity may overlap with the principle of contribution and can be quite obvious in older neighborhoods.

IN PRACTICE

If a house's out-of-date asbestos shingle exterior is its major flaw and other houses nearby have wood siding or masonry exterior finishes, the addition of new siding may be worth several times its cost because a hazardous material will be eliminated and the house that was out of date will blend in with those nearby. The appraiser's opinion, therefore, should be governed by a feature's contribution to market value—not by its reported cost.

7. Externalities

The principle of **externalities** states that influences outside a property may have a positive or negative effect on its value. For example, the federal government's direct participation in interest rate controls, in mortgage loan guarantees, in providing tax incentives for rehabilitation of older homes, and so forth, has had a powerful impact on stimulating or retarding the housing supply and increasing or decreasing the level of home ownership. Values of homes and all other types of real property are directly affected by governmental action or inaction. External influences affecting value exist at regional, city, and neighborhood levels. Information on some of these factors is readily available. Crime rates, population density, income level, and even the results of student performance on standardized tests can all be found on the internet.

8. Four Factors of Production

The concept of value cannot exist without consideration of the **four factors of production** (capital, labor, land, and management) and the return required by each in a specific enterprise. Return on capital is characterized as interest or yield. The use of labor requires compensation in the form of wages or salaries. Return on land is rent. Finally, the return to the entrepreneurial risk taker and/or coordinator of an enterprise—the management function—is profit.

9. Life Cycle of Property— GEDR

Ordinary physical deterioration and market demand create a life cycle of four stages through which an improved property will pass: (1) **growth**, when improvements are made and property demand expands; (2) **equilibrium** or stability, when the property undergoes little change; (3) **decline**, when the property requires an increasing amount of upkeep to retain its original utility while demand slackens; and (4) **revitalization** or rehabilitation, which may occur if demand increases, serving to stimulate property renovation. They can be remembered by the acronym *GEDR*.

The principle of growth, equilibrium, decline, and revitalization also applies to an entire neighborhood. Whether it is an area of long-established housing within the city limits, an older close-in suburb, or a new development at the edge of the metropolitan area, a neighborhood will show the effects of the life cycle.

10. Highest and Best Use

Of all the factors that influence market value, the primary consideration is the highest and best use of the real estate. The **highest and best use** of a property is its most profitable legally and physically permitted use—that is, the use that will at present provide the highest property value. The highest and best use evolves from an analysis of the community, neighborhood, site, and improvements.

A highest and best use study may be made to find the most profitable use of a vacant site or to determine the validity of a proposed site utilization. If there already is a structure on the property, the highest and best use study may make one of several assumptions: the site could be considered vacant, with the cost of demolishing the existing structure taken into account when estimating profits from any other use of the site; the cost of refurbishing the existing structure could be considered in light of any increased income that might result; the structure could be considered as is, that is, with no further improvements; and the structure might be considered adaptable to new uses. Every case must be studied on its own merits, considering zoning or other restrictive ordinances as well as current trends.

IN PRACTICE

Many gas stations have closed since the early 1970s. Before that time, if those facilities reopened, most of them would probably have been used again only as gas stations. With the modern trend toward drive-in facilities, from restaurants and dry-cleaning shops to almost every other type of retail outlet, many former gas stations were converted to other types of drive-in businesses. With the present emphasis on the environment and federal and state regulations that require the cleanup of contaminated sites, including the storage tanks and ground contamination found on property that has been used for a gasoline station, such properties are considerably less desirable than those that do not require such extensive remediation.

The depth of analysis required to support the appraiser's conclusion of a property's highest and best use will depend on the nature of the report. A property's highest and best use may also be redefined at a later date, just as its appraised value may fluctuate downward or upward. The process of determining a property's highest and best use is discussed in more detail in Unit 9, "Site Valuation."

11. Law of Increasing Returns

Improvements to land and structures eventually will reach a point at which they will have no positive effect on property values. As long as money spent on such improvements produces a proportionate or greater increase in income or value, the **law of increasing returns** is in effect.

12. Law of Decreasing Returns

At the point when additional property improvements bring no corresponding increase in the property's income or value, the **law of decreasing returns** is operating.

13. Opportunity Cost

In the appraisal of income-producing property, **opportunity cost** is the value differential between alternative investments with differing rates of return. The appraiser considers the alternatives in selecting a rate of return for the property being appraised, which in turn will affect the final value estimate for the property.

14. Substitution

The value of real property is basically determined by using what is called the principle of **substitution**. The price someone is willing to pay for a property is influenced by the cost of acquiring a substitute or comparable property. If the asking price for a house is $495,000, yet a nearby, very similar property is available for only $450,000, no one is likely to offer $495,000 for the first property.

Every appraisal makes use of the principle of substitution to some extent. Its most conspicuous use is in the appraisal of single-family residences using the sales comparison approach. In that approach, the appraiser collects selling price information and other data on homes similar to the property being appraised (called the subject property) that are located in the same or a similar neighborhood and that have sold recently. The appraiser then adjusts the selling prices of those properties to account for significant differences between them and the subject property in size, style, quality of construction, and other factors likely to affect the market value of the property being appraised.

IN PRACTICE

If the subject property has only two bathrooms and an otherwise comparable property in the same neighborhood that has sold recently has three bathrooms, the appraiser will adjust the selling price of the comparable property downward by the market value in that area of a third bathroom. Thus, if the comparable property has sold for $325,000 and the market value of a third bathroom is $16,000, the selling price of the comparable is reduced by $16,000 (to $309,000) to approximate the effect on the subject's estimated market value of the absence of a third bathroom.

If the subject property has a valuable feature that the comparable property lacks, the selling price of the comparable property will be increased to accurately reflect the market value of the subject property. The sales comparison approach is discussed further in Units 8 and 12.

15. Supply and Demand

As with any marketable commodity, the law of **supply and demand** affects real estate. Property values will rise as demand increases and/or supply decreases. The last building lot in a desirable residential development will probably be worth much more than the first lot that was sold in the development, assuming a consistent demand.

The effect of supply and demand is most obvious on the value of older buildings in very desirable areas, usually in cities, where demographic trends (population size and distribution) may bring heavy demand for housing to neighborhoods that have already seriously deteriorated. A building in such an area, even if it required extensive remodeling to meet current building codes, might have increased in value several times because of the increased demand. The property might be valued primarily as a "teardown"—that is, for the potential its site offers for new construction, as permitted by local zoning and building codes. Thus it should be remembered that demand relates to the supply of a particular type of property in a given location—not to property in general.

16. Surplus Productivity

The income capitalization approach to appraising, discussed in Units 13 and 14, makes use of the concept of the residual value of property purchased for investment purposes. If the expenses of ownership (capital, labor, and management) are deducted from net income, the remaining amount is termed **surplus productivity** and is considered the investor's return on the use of the land, or land rent. The expectation of profit is also expressed as the entrepreneurial incentive that motivates a developer to assume the risks involved with taking on a project.

Conclusion

The principles discussed in this unit are the keys to understanding why, when, and how certain factors act to influence the value of real property. The appraiser who understands these principles can form opinions based on knowledge and understanding, not guesswork.

Exercise 5-2

Which basic value principle(s) does each of the following case problems illustrate?

1. A homeowner also owns a vacation home near a small town almost 300 miles from the city in which he lives and works. He doesn't use his vacation house more than three weeks every year. The last time he stayed there, he noticed that a gas station had been built a few hundred yards down the road. After talking to the owner, he discovered that a zoning change had been put into effect to allow construction of a new shopping center on land adjacent to the gas station. While the owner's property was not rezoned, he realizes that it won't be suitable as a vacation retreat once the shopping center is built.

2. A homeowner customized the family room of her new home by adding a cedar-lined steam room, six-person whirlpool spa, and special ventilating system. The homeowner decided that the improvements were justified because even though she knew she would only be living in the home for a few more years, she could realize the worth of the improvements when she sold her home.

3. A structurally sound office building rents for $20 per square foot but lacks air-conditioning. A similar, air-conditioned building in the same neighborhood rents for $25 per square foot.

4. Two drugstores are located on the same city block, and both have had good business for 20 years. One store is modernized with new displays, better lighting, and computerized inventory control. Because the store is part of a chain, remodeling costs are absorbed without a general increase in prices. The other drugstore begins losing customers.

5. A 100-unit apartment building designed for middle-income persons at least 55 years of age is in very good condition. The owners plan extensive remodeling and redecorating to be financed by raising rents as needed. The plans will probably take four years to complete. None of the apartments will be altered, but the building's exterior will be completely redone, and the lobby will be furnished with expensive carpeting, chairs, and a chandelier. The lobby remodeling is done first; the tenants seem pleased, and no major objection is made to the resultant rent increases. After the second year, however, many tenants object to the continued increases and choose not to renew their leases. The owners have difficulty finding new tenants.

6. A single-family neighborhood is located adjacent to property that was recently used for an airport expansion. Excessive noise caused by airplanes flying overhead and the potential danger they create have adversely affected the value of homes in the immediate area.

Check your answers against those in the answer key at the back of the book.

■ SUMMARY

The market for real estate is a product of statewide, regional, and national, as well as local, forces. Population level, the strength of the economy, and the availability of financing all affect the real estate market.

Markets for goods and services are called efficient when the products are readily exchangeable and easily transported, there is an ample supply of buyers and sellers, government regulation has little or no effect on value, and prices are stable. The market for real estate functions differently. Real estate is immobile, unique, and heavily regulated. In addition, buyers and sellers of real estate frequently lack knowledge of the factors that contribute to market value.

Market analysis begins with a study of area demographics. The market is then segmented into areas of preference, and the activities of the people that make up the segments are forecast. A feasibility study of the financial success of a proposed development includes an absorption analysis of the number of units likely to be sold within a specified period of time.

Sources of capital for real estate development include short-term money market funds as well as longer-term capital markets. Debt investors require a security interest in the property financed, while equity investors are willing to take a riskier unsecured role.

Although we commonly refer to any financing instrument as a mortgage, there are differences in the creation and effect of the mortgage and deed of trust. With a mortgage, the property owner is the mortgagor, and the lender is the mortgagee. With a trust deed, the property owner is the trustor, the lender is the beneficiary, and a neutral third party is the trustee, who holds legal title to the secured property until the debt is paid.

The elements of value are demand, utility, scarcity, and transferability. Demand is the result of desire coupled with effective purchasing power.

Value in exchange is the ability of a good or service to command another good or service. Market value is the most probable price real estate should bring in an arm's-length transaction in which neither party is acting under duress; the property has been on the market a reasonable length of time; the property's assets and defects are known to both parties; and there are no unusual circumstances, such as favorable seller financing. Its sales price is what a property actually sells for.

The amount initially paid for a good or service is its cost to the person who owns it. Cost may or may not be the same as the item's estimated market value and its subsequent resale price. Investment value is the value to an individual investor. Value in use is based on a particular use. Assessed value is used for taxation purposes. Insurable value is the amount for which property may be insured. Going-concern value is the value of a business exclusive of the value of the real estate it occupies.

Forces affecting value include the physical and environmental, economic, governmental and legal, and social.

The basic value principles that are among the factors contributing to price increases and decreases include anticipation; change; competition; conformity, progression, and regression; contribution; externalities; the stages of growth, equilibrium, decline, and revitalization; highest and best use; the laws of increasing and decreasing returns; the principle of substitution; and the effects of supply and demand.

The four factors of production are land, labor, capital, and management. When these factors are in balance, land value should be at its highest. Opportunity cost is the difference in value created by differing rates of return. When the expenses of ownership are deducted from net income, the remainder, or surplus productivity, is attributable to land value.

■ Review Questions

1. The scientific study of population statistics is
   a. scientography.
   b. segmentation.
   c. demography.
   d. forecasting.

2. The amount initially paid for a good or service is its
   a. price.
   b. market value.
   c. investment value.
   d. cost.

3. Market value is based on
   a. insurable value.
   b. most probable price.
   c. cost.
   d. value in use.

4. Short-term financing instruments are part of
   a. the money market.
   b. the capital market.
   c. the absorption analysis.
   d. the feasibility study.

5. Longer-term financing instruments are part of
   a. the money market.
   b. the capital market.
   c. the absorption analysis.
   d. the feasibility study.

6. Under a deed of trust, the property owner is
   a. the trustor.
   b. the trustee.
   c. the beneficiary.
   d. the reconveyancer.

7. Under a mortgage, the lender is
   a. the mortgagor.
   b. the mortgagee.
   c. the equity investor.
   d. the reconveyancer.

8. Demand can be broken down into desire and
   a. effective purchasing power.
   b. availability.
   c. gross income.
   d. marketing time.

9. The construction cost to add a new bedroom to a home is $45,000. If the bedroom is added, the value of the property will increase by $30,000. This is an example of
   a. increasing return.
   b. decreasing return.
   c. plottage.
   d. anticipation.

10. The return on a similar investment is considered to determine
    a. opportunity cost.
    b. effective purchasing power.
    c. assemblage.
    d. substitution.

11. The most profitable, legally permitted use of land is referred to as its
    a. market value.
    b. value in use.
    c. highest and best use.
    d. market price.

12. The life cycle of a neighborhood or property includes
    a. no recognizable pattern, as all neighborhoods and properties are unique.
    b. growth, decline, equilibrium, revitalization.
    c. growth, decline, revitalization, equilibrium.
    d. growth, equilibrium, decline, revitalization.

13. Explain the difference between market value and sales price.

Identify the major value principle described in each of the following cases.

14. A less expensive house tends to gain in value because of more expensive neighborhood houses.

15. The value of a property tends to be limited by what it costs to buy another property similar in physical characteristics, function, or income.

16. Plans have been announced for a multi-million-dollar retail and business center to be built next door to a vacant lot you own. Property values in the area of the proposed site will tend to increase as a result of this announcement.

17. The rental value of vacant land can sometimes be greater than it would be if the land were improved with a building.

18. In many downtown areas, parking lots make more profit than older office buildings.

19. An investor will probably pay more for the last 20 lots in an area where the demand for houses is great than for the first 20 lots in the same area.

20. The cost of installing an air-conditioning system in an apartment building is justified only if the rental increase that can be expected as a result of the installation exceeds the amount spent.

Check your answers against those in the answer key at the back of the book.

UNIT SIX

THE APPRAISAL PROCESS

■ LEARNING OBJECTIVES

When you have completed this unit, you will be able to

- identify the steps in the appraisal process,
- explain the importance of determining the appraiser's scope of work,
- define retrospective value,
- describe situations in which a retrospective value appraisal is used, and
- discuss each of the three major approaches to appraising.

■ KEY TERMS

cost approach
Department of Housing and Urban Development (HUD)
depreciation
Fannie Mae
Federal Housing Administration (FHA)
fee simple estate
Freddie Mac
highest and best use
income capitalization approach
leased fee estate
leasehold estate
letter of engagement
life estate
retrospective value
sales comparison approach
scope of work
secondary mortgage market
Uniform Residential Appraisal Report (URAR)
Uniform Standards of Professional Appraisal Practice (USPAP)

■ OVERVIEW

At its simplest, an appraisal presents the appraiser's opinion of a property's probable monetary value on the open market. There is much more involved in even the simplest appraisal than a mere estimate of value, however.

In deriving a final opinion of value the appraiser will use one or more of the approaches to appraising—the sales comparison approach, the cost approach, and the income capitalization approach. The manner in which the appraiser applies a particular approach may be determined by the type of property being appraised and the factors of greatest importance to buyers. A single-family rental house, for instance, would not be appraised using the same method of income valuation as would an office building, even though both properties may produce income.

This unit focuses on the basic definition of each of the value approaches. Also covered are the steps involved in the appraisal process, from the appraisal assignment through the final opinion of value.

■ STEPS IN THE APPRAISAL PROCESS

An appraisal begins with a specific assignment initiated by a **letter of engagement** to the appraiser, such as a request to estimate the market value of a single-family residence being considered for a mortgage loan. From that point, every appraisal requires the organized collection and analysis of data. Specific data about the property, general data about the surrounding area, and data applicable to the appraisal approach being used all must be researched.

The flowchart in Figure 6.1 outlines the eight steps in the appraisal process. The steps, as follows, are described in the following list.

1. *Define the problem.*
2. *Determine the scope of work.* The first two parts of the appraisal process will determine the type and extent of the analysis the appraiser is to perform. The **scope of work** that is required will depend on the property, client, purpose of the appraisal, type and definition of value, effective date of the appraisal, and any conditions to the appraisal assignment. Identifying the appraisal problem includes the following:

   - *Identification and location of the real estate.* The property to be appraised must be identified by a complete legal description as well as a street address.
   - *Property rights to be appraised.* The typical appraisal assignment values the highest interest in real estate recognized by law—referred to as fee simple ownership—but the property interest may be less than full ownership, such as a tenant's interest in a lease or the right to use an easement or right-of-way, or title may be held in partnership, by a corporation, or jointly with other individuals.
   - *Definition of value to be estimated.* Because the word *value* can have many interpretations, the type of value sought should always be defined so the client fully understands the basis for the reported value.

- *Purpose and intended use of the appraisal.* The appraiser and client must agree on what the appraisal is to accomplish. The purpose of an appraisal relates to the type of value that is sought. The purpose of the greatest number of appraisals is to give an opinion of market value. However, appraisals can be made for many other purposes—for example, to find a property's replacement cost or its insurable value.

  The intended use or function of an appraisal is concerned with the reason the appraisal is being made, and the reasons may be varied. An appraisal may be made in a prospective purchase or sale, as the basis of a mortgage loan, to determine "just compensation" where property is taken under the right of eminent domain, to determine the terms of a lease, et cetera.

- *Effective date of the opinion of value.* What will be the effective date of the appraisal? It could be a date in the past, the date the property was inspected by the appraiser, the date the appraisal report was created, or some future date. Because real estate values are constantly changing, an opinion of value is considered valid only for the date specified.

- *Any special limiting conditions.* Normally, appraisals include a statement of qualifying and limiting conditions to protect the appraiser and to inform and protect the client and other users of the appraisal.

FIGURE 6.1
The Appraisal Process

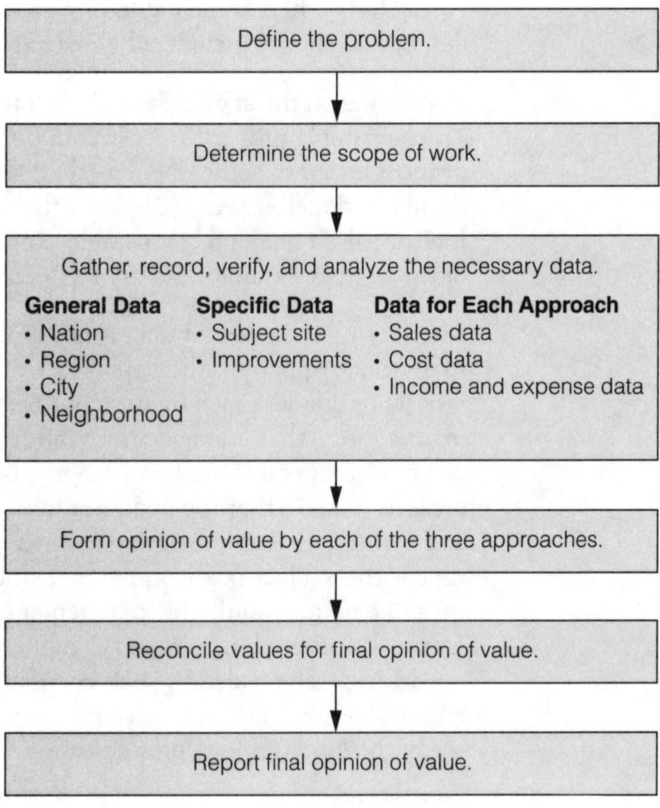

These points will be covered in more detail later in this unit. Once the appraiser knows the property interest to be appraised and why the appraisal is necessary—whether for insurance purposes, to find market value, or simply to determine rental value—the approach(es) best suited to the property can be chosen. Occasionally, only one approach will be appropriate, because it will be the most reliable for some properties.

3. *Gather, record, verify, and analyze the necessary data.* Once the appraiser knows which approach(es) will be used, the information needed can be itemized. The appraiser must be familiar enough with the sources of information to state exactly what the sources for the particular case will be. The types of data needed must be collected and recorded for future use, and the data's accuracy must be verified. This step is the most critical in the appraisal assignment, as it will form the basis for the appraiser's opinion of the property's value.

   The appraiser compiles general data on the geographic and economic features of the nation, region, city, and neighborhood. Property location, as influenced by both natural and economic factors, is often of critical importance.

   Regardless of the interest being appraised, specific data on the subject property (including a detailed physical description) must be obtained. Particularly when comparable properties are to be found, the physical description should include all items likely to affect market value.

   Depending on the approach used, the appraiser also will gather sales data on comparable properties, cost data on construction of a like property, or income and expense data based on the property's history. All sources should be double-checked against other sources, especially when obtaining the sales price of a comparable property. In such a case, at least one of the sources should be a party to the transaction.

   Interpreting the relevant data is just as important as collecting it. In virtually every appraisal, the appraiser will begin this part of the appraisal process by conducting a **highest and best use** analysis that considers the market forces that influence the subject property to determine the property's most profitable use on which to base the final opinion of value. The analysis requires that the appraiser take into account the physical, legal, and locational attributes present in the real estate asset—the property that is the subject of the appraisal—and consider the extent to which those attributes fulfill the requirements of the marketplace. In other words, does the subject property's highest and best use satisfy the human needs that are revealed by such economic indicators as supply, demand, and absorption? The appraiser may conclude that the highest and best use of the land is not its present use.

4. *Form opinion of value by each of the three approaches.* Using the sales comparison approach, the appraiser analyzes available comparable sales data to form an opinion of value for the property under appraisal. In the cost approach, the cost new of property improvements, less depreciation of those improvements, is added to site value. Site value is found by using the sales comparison approach. In the income capitalization approach,

value is based on the rental income the property is capable of earning, after consideration of operating expenses and the property's expected rate of return.

5. *Reconcile values for final opinion of value*. The appraiser must correlate the information and decide what conclusions can be drawn from the volume of collected facts. The appraiser never simply averages differing value determinations. The most relevant approach, based on analysis and judgment, receives the greatest weight in determining the figure that most accurately reflects the value sought.
6. *Report final opinion of value*. Finally, the appraiser presents the conclusion of value in the reporting form requested by the client. As you will see in Unit 15, "Reconciliation and the Appraisal Report," the content of all appraisal reports should follow *USPAP*.

In Unit 8, "Data Collection," you will learn some of the many sources of information used in a real estate appraisal.

BEGINNING THE APPRAISAL PROCESS

Purpose and Use of the Appraisal

The appraiser begins the appraisal process by determining the scope of work required, based on the property being appraised, the type of value sought, and the purpose of the appraisal. Market value is the most frequently sought appraised value. Other types of value are highlighted in Unit 5.

Interests to Be Appraised

The form of legal interest being appraised must always be specified. Unit 3 described the various interests in real property, including fee simple, life estate, leasehold estate, and leased fee estate. Each of these interests can be appraised. The estimated value of the interest depends on the term of the interest, any limitations on property use during that term, whether the interest is transferable, and other factors.

A **fee simple estate**, or fee simple absolute, is the only form of ownership completely free of any other interest or estate. Even the owner of a fee simple absolute estate is subject to zoning and other governmental regulations, however. The appraisal also might be based on a partial interest, such as mineral rights.

A **leasehold estate** always has a definite termination date and can be valued for its remaining term. The **leased fee estate** that is retained by the owner of the fee simple interest also can be valued. Valuation of leasehold and leased fee estate is discussed in Unit 16, "Appraising Partial Interests."

The value of a **life estate** depends on the estimated remaining life span of the person against whose life the estate is measured. If that person is elderly, the life estate obviously has less value than it would if the measuring life were that of a healthy 20-year-old who did not engage in any unusually hazardous activities.

Date of the Opinion of Value

An appraisal may be made as of any date—past, present, or future. Most often, current value is sought, and the appraiser selects the latest date possible. Most appraisers select the date of inspection of the subject property as the effective date of the appraisal. Frequently, the value opinion sought is **retrospective value**, meaning the value as of a specific date in the past. A retrospective valuation is based on knowledge of the market prior to the current date and may be sought for such purposes as a property tax appeal, calculation of estate tax, condemnation proceeding, lease renegotiation, or divorce settlement. To estimate *future value*, the appraiser must extrapolate future market behavior based on current information and projected trends, an extremely difficult task. In any event, to avoid misleading the client, the appraiser should always state the assumptions under which the appraisal is made and any limitations on the use of the appraisal.

Limiting Conditions

www.fanniemae.com
www.fanniemae.com/singlefamily
www.freddiemac.com

Fannie Mae and **Freddie Mac** are the major government-sponsored enterprises (GSEs) that purchase mortgages from primary lenders (such as banks), package the mortgages, and sell the resulting securities on publicly traded exchanges as part of the **secondary mortgage market**. The GSEs and other agencies do not expect an appraisal to be an all-encompassing process or the appraiser to spend an unlimited amount of time in preparing an appraisal report. The latest revision of the **Uniform Residential Appraisal Report (URAR)** form released by Fannie Mae and Freddie Mac incorporates a "Statement of Assumptions and Limiting Conditions" to help define the appraiser's role and specify the conditions under which the appraisal is made. Fannie Mae does not allow additions or deletions to the form when it is used as part of a Fannie Mae–related appraisal. For other transactions, the appraiser may draft a customized set of limiting conditions or add to this list, as appropriate for a particular property. Figure 6.2 shows the last three pages of the six-page URAR form, which replaced all previous versions of the URAR form for Fannie Mae appraisals as of November 1, 2005. The first three pages of the form, which include property information, data analysis, and opinion of value, appear throughout the remainder of this book.

You should note that the "Statement of Assumptions and Limiting Conditions" expressly limits the appraiser's responsibility for discovering and disclosing adverse conditions such as the presence of hazardous wastes and toxic substances on the property. In fact, the statement specifically provides that "the appraisal report must not be considered as an environmental assessment of the property." Nevertheless, in its guidelines for performing appraisals, Fannie Mae requires any lender who is informed by the real estate broker, property seller, purchaser, or any other party to a mortgage transaction that an environmental hazard exists on or near the property to record the information in the mortgage file, disclose it to the appraiser and the borrower, and comply with any other state or local disclosure laws. If the appraiser knows of any hazardous condition, it must be noted and its likely effect on the subject property's value must be commented on. The effect on value is measured by analysis of comparable market data as of the effective date of the appraisal; that is, the appraiser must use market data from properties located in the same affected area.

It is in the appraiser's best interest to learn as much as possible about the types of environmental risks that are likely to be encountered, so that their presence can be considered in the valuation process. Some of these conditions are mentioned in Unit 7, "Building Construction and the Environment." Of course, specific coursework in environmental hazards is necessary for anyone who intends to act as an environmental assessor or auditor.

Above all, the appraiser must disclose the limitations and assumptions under which the appraisal is made. The ***Uniform Standards of Professional Appraisal Practice (USPAP)*** stress in Standards Rule 2-1(c) that each written or oral real property appraisal report must "clearly and accurately disclose any extraordinary assumption, hypothetical condition, or limiting condition that directly affects the appraisal and indicate its impact on value."

The certification statement required by *USPAP* for all written property appraisals is discussed in Unit 15, "Reconciliation and the Appraisal Report."

FHA Appraisals

www.hud.gov
www.hud.gov/offices/hsg/fhahistory.cfm

The **Department of Housing and Urban Development (HUD)** creates standards for **Federal Housing Administration (FHA)** appraisals. Appraisers who do FHA work must complete a three-page form describing, in detail, the physical condition of the home. The standards require that appraisers pinpoint "problems with plumbing, walls, ceilings, roofs, foundations, basements, electrical systems, and heating and air-conditioning systems; soil contamination; the presence of wood-destroying insects; hazards and nuisances near homes (such as oil and gas wells); lead-based paint hazards; and other health and safety problems."

To ensure that appraisers who do FHA work will meet these government standards, the HUD program includes HUD-mandated testing. An appraiser will be certified to do FHA appraisals only after passing the exam.

FIGURE 6.2
Uniform Residential Appraisal Report

Uniform Residential Appraisal Report

File #

This report form is designed to report an appraisal of a one-unit property or a one-unit property with an accessory unit; including a unit in a planned unit development (PUD). This report form is not designed to report an appraisal of a manufactured home or a unit in a condominium or cooperative project.

This appraisal report is subject to the following scope of work, intended use, intended user, definition of market value, statement of assumptions and limiting conditions, and certifications. Modifications, additions, or deletions to the intended use, intended user, definition of market value, or assumptions and limiting conditions are not permitted. The appraiser may expand the scope of work to include any additional research or analysis necessary based on the complexity of this appraisal assignment. Modifications or deletions to the certifications are also not permitted. However, additional certifications that do not constitute material alterations to this appraisal report, such as those required by law or those related to the appraiser's continuing education or membership in an appraisal organization, are permitted.

SCOPE OF WORK: The scope of work for this appraisal is defined by the complexity of this appraisal assignment and the reporting requirements of this appraisal report form, including the following definition of market value, statement of assumptions and limiting conditions, and certifications. The appraiser must, at a minimum: (1) perform a complete visual inspection of the interior and exterior areas of the subject property, (2) inspect the neighborhood, (3) inspect each of the comparable sales from at least the street, (4) research, verify, and analyze data from reliable public and/or private sources, and (5) report his or her analysis, opinions, and conclusions in this appraisal report.

INTENDED USE: The intended use of this appraisal report is for the lender/client to evaluate the property that is the subject of this appraisal for a mortgage finance transaction.

INTENDED USER: The intended user of this appraisal report is the lender/client.

DEFINITION OF MARKET VALUE: The most probable price which a property should bring in a competitive and open market under all conditions requisite to a fair sale, the buyer and seller, each acting prudently, knowledgeably and assuming the price is not affected by undue stimulus. Implicit in this definition is the consummation of a sale as of a specified date and the passing of title from seller to buyer under conditions whereby: (1) buyer and seller are typically motivated; (2) both parties are well informed or well advised, and each acting in what he or she considers his or her own best interest; (3) a reasonable time is allowed for exposure in the open market; (4) payment is made in terms of cash in U. S. dollars or in terms of financial arrangements comparable thereto; and (5) the price represents the normal consideration for the property sold unaffected by special or creative financing or sales concessions* granted by anyone associated with the sale.

*Adjustments to the comparables must be made for special or creative financing or sales concessions. No adjustments are necessary for those costs which are normally paid by sellers as a result of tradition or law in a market area; these costs are readily identifiable since the seller pays these costs in virtually all sales transactions. Special or creative financing adjustments can be made to the comparable property by comparisons to financing terms offered by a third party institutional lender that is not already involved in the property or transaction. Any adjustment should not be calculated on a mechanical dollar for dollar cost of the financing or concession but the dollar amount of any adjustment should approximate the market's reaction to the financing or concessions based on the appraiser's judgment.

STATEMENT OF ASSUMPTIONS AND LIMITING CONDITIONS: The appraiser's certification in this report is subject to the following assumptions and limiting conditions:

1. The appraiser will not be responsible for matters of a legal nature that affect either the property being appraised or the title to it, except for information that he or she became aware of during the research involved in performing this appraisal. The appraiser assumes that the title is good and marketable and will not render any opinions about the title.

2. The appraiser has provided a sketch in this appraisal report to show the approximate dimensions of the improvements. The sketch is included only to assist the reader in visualizing the property and understanding the appraiser's determination of its size.

3. The appraiser has examined the available flood maps that are provided by the Federal Emergency Management Agency (or other data sources) and has noted in this appraisal report whether any portion of the subject site is located in an identified Special Flood Hazard Area. Because the appraiser is not a surveyor, he or she makes no guarantees, express or implied, regarding this determination.

4. The appraiser will not give testimony or appear in court because he or she made an appraisal of the property in question, unless specific arrangements to do so have been made beforehand, or as otherwise required by law.

5. The appraiser has noted in this appraisal report any adverse conditions (such as needed repairs, deterioration, the presence of hazardous wastes, toxic substances, etc.) observed during the inspection of the subject property or that he or she became aware of during the research involved in performing this appraisal. Unless otherwise stated in this appraisal report, the appraiser has no knowledge of any hidden or unapparent physical deficiencies or adverse conditions of the property (such as, but not limited to, needed repairs, deterioration, the presence of hazardous wastes, toxic substances, adverse environmental conditions, etc.) that would make the property less valuable, and has assumed that there are no such conditions and makes no guarantees or warranties, express or implied. The appraiser will not be responsible for any such conditions that do exist or for any engineering or testing that might be required to discover whether such conditions exist. Because the appraiser is not an expert in the field of environmental hazards, this appraisal report must not be considered as an environmental assessment of the property.

6. The appraiser has based his or her appraisal report and valuation conclusion for an appraisal that is subject to satisfactory completion, repairs, or alterations on the assumption that the completion, repairs, or alterations of the subject property will be performed in a professional manner.

Freddie Mac Form 70 March 2005 — Page 4 of 6 — Fannie Mae Form 1004 March 2005

FIGURE 6.2

Uniform Residential Appraisal Report (continued)

Uniform Residential Appraisal Report

File #

APPRAISER'S CERTIFICATION: The Appraiser certifies and agrees that:

1. I have, at a minimum, developed and reported this appraisal in accordance with the scope of work requirements stated in this appraisal report.

2. I performed a complete visual inspection of the interior and exterior areas of the subject property. I reported the condition of the improvements in factual, specific terms. I identified and reported the physical deficiencies that could affect the livability, soundness, or structural integrity of the property.

3. I performed this appraisal in accordance with the requirements of the Uniform Standards of Professional Appraisal Practice that were adopted and promulgated by the Appraisal Standards Board of The Appraisal Foundation and that were in place at the time this appraisal report was prepared.

4. I developed my opinion of the market value of the real property that is the subject of this report based on the sales comparison approach to value. I have adequate comparable market data to develop a reliable sales comparison approach for this appraisal assignment. I further certify that I considered the cost and income approaches to value but did not develop them, unless otherwise indicated in this report.

5. I researched, verified, analyzed, and reported on any current agreement for sale for the subject property, any offering for sale of the subject property in the twelve months prior to the effective date of this appraisal, and the prior sales of the subject property for a minimum of three years prior to the effective date of this appraisal, unless otherwise indicated in this report.

6. I researched, verified, analyzed, and reported on the prior sales of the comparable sales for a minimum of one year prior to the date of sale of the comparable sale, unless otherwise indicated in this report.

7. I selected and used comparable sales that are locationally, physically, and functionally the most similar to the subject property.

8. I have not used comparable sales that were the result of combining a land sale with the contract purchase price of a home that has been built or will be built on the land.

9. I have reported adjustments to the comparable sales that reflect the market's reaction to the differences between the subject property and the comparable sales.

10. I verified, from a disinterested source, all information in this report that was provided by parties who have a financial interest in the sale or financing of the subject property.

11. I have knowledge and experience in appraising this type of property in this market area.

12. I am aware of, and have access to, the necessary and appropriate public and private data sources, such as multiple listing services, tax assessment records, public land records and other such data sources for the area in which the property is located.

13. I obtained the information, estimates, and opinions furnished by other parties and expressed in this appraisal report from reliable sources that I believe to be true and correct.

14. I have taken into consideration the factors that have an impact on value with respect to the subject neighborhood, subject property, and the proximity of the subject property to adverse influences in the development of my opinion of market value. I have noted in this appraisal report any adverse conditions (such as, but not limited to, needed repairs, deterioration, the presence of hazardous wastes, toxic substances, adverse environmental conditions, etc.) observed during the inspection of the subject property or that I became aware of during the research involved in performing this appraisal. I have considered these adverse conditions in my analysis of the property value, and have reported on the effect of the conditions on the value and marketability of the subject property.

15. I have not knowingly withheld any significant information from this appraisal report and, to the best of my knowledge, all statements and information in this appraisal report are true and correct.

16. I stated in this appraisal report my own personal, unbiased, and professional analysis, opinions, and conclusions, which are subject only to the assumptions and limiting conditions in this appraisal report.

17. I have no present or prospective interest in the property that is the subject of this report, and I have no present or prospective personal interest or bias with respect to the participants in the transaction. I did not base, either partially or completely, my analysis and/or opinion of market value in this appraisal report on the race, color, religion, sex, age, marital status, handicap, familial status, or national origin of either the prospective owners or occupants of the subject property or of the present owners or occupants of the properties in the vicinity of the subject property or on any other basis prohibited by law.

18. My employment and/or compensation for performing this appraisal or any future or anticipated appraisals was not conditioned on any agreement or understanding, written or otherwise, that I would report (or present analysis supporting) a predetermined specific value, a predetermined minimum value, a range or direction in value, a value that favors the cause of any party, or the attainment of a specific result or occurrence of a specific subsequent event (such as approval of a pending mortgage loan application).

19. I personally prepared all conclusions and opinions about the real estate that were set forth in this appraisal report. If I relied on significant real property appraisal assistance from any individual or individuals in the performance of this appraisal or the preparation of this appraisal report, I have named such individual(s) and disclosed the specific tasks performed in this appraisal report. I certify that any individual so named is qualified to perform the tasks. I have not authorized anyone to make a change to any item in this appraisal report; therefore, any change made to this appraisal is unauthorized and I will take no responsibility for it.

20. I identified the lender/client in this appraisal report who is the individual, organization, or agent for the organization that ordered and will receive this appraisal report.

Freddie Mac Form 70 March 2005 | Page 5 of 6 | Fannie Mae Form 1004 March 2005

FIGURE 6.2
Uniform Residential Appraisal Report (continued)

Uniform Residential Appraisal Report File

21. The lender/client may disclose or distribute this appraisal report to: the borrower; another lender at the request of the borrower; the mortgagee or its successors and assigns; mortgage insurers; government sponsored enterprises; other secondary market participants; data collection or reporting services; professional appraisal organizations; any department, agency, or instrumentality of the United States; and any state, the District of Columbia, or other jurisdictions; without having to obtain the appraiser's or supervisory appraiser's (if applicable) consent. Such consent must be obtained before this appraisal report may be disclosed or distributed to any other party (including, but not limited to, the public through advertising, public relations, news, sales, or other media).

22. I am aware that any disclosure or distribution of this appraisal report by me or the lender/client may be subject to certain laws and regulations. Further, I am also subject to the provisions of the Uniform Standards of Professional Appraisal Practice that pertain to disclosure or distribution by me.

23. The borrower, another lender at the request of the borrower, the mortgagee or its successors and assigns, mortgage insurers, government sponsored enterprises, and other secondary market participants may rely on this appraisal report as part of any mortgage finance transaction that involves any one or more of these parties.

24. If this appraisal report was transmitted as an "electronic record" containing my "electronic signature," as those terms are defined in applicable federal and/or state laws (excluding audio and video recordings), or a facsimile transmission of this appraisal report containing a copy or representation of my signature, the appraisal report shall be as effective, enforceable and valid as if a paper version of this appraisal report were delivered containing my original hand written signature.

25. Any intentional or negligent misrepresentation(s) contained in this appraisal report may result in civil liability and/or criminal penalties including, but not limited to, fine or imprisonment or both under the provisions of Title 18, United States Code, Section 1001, et seq., or similar state laws.

SUPERVISORY APPRAISER'S CERTIFICATION: The Supervisory Appraiser certifies and agrees that:

1. I directly supervised the appraiser for this appraisal assignment, have read the appraisal report, and agree with the appraiser's analysis, opinions, statements, conclusions, and the appraiser's certification.

2. I accept full responsibility for the contents of this appraisal report including, but not limited to, the appraiser's analysis, opinions, statements, conclusions, and the appraiser's certification.

3. The appraiser identified in this appraisal report is either a sub-contractor or an employee of the supervisory appraiser (or the appraisal firm), is qualified to perform this appraisal, and is acceptable to perform this appraisal under the applicable state law.

4. This appraisal report complies with the Uniform Standards of Professional Appraisal Practice that were adopted and promulgated by the Appraisal Standards Board of The Appraisal Foundation and that were in place at the time this appraisal report was prepared.

5. If this appraisal report was transmitted as an "electronic record" containing my "electronic signature," as those terms are defined in applicable federal and/or state laws (excluding audio and video recordings), or a facsimile transmission of this appraisal report containing a copy or representation of my signature, the appraisal report shall be as effective, enforceable and valid as if a paper version of this appraisal report were delivered containing my original hand written signature.

APPRAISER

Signature ______________________
Name ______________________
Company Name ______________________
Company Address ______________________
____
Telephone Number ______________________
Email Address ______________________
Date of Signature and Report ______________________
Effective Date of Appraisal ______________________
State Certification # ______________________
or State License # ______________________
or Other (describe) ____________ State # ____________
State ______________________
Expiration Date of Certification or License ______________________

ADDRESS OF PROPERTY APPRAISED

____
____

APPRAISED VALUE OF SUBJECT PROPERTY $ ____________

LENDER/CLIENT

Name ______________________
Company Name ______________________
Company Address ______________________
____
Email Address ______________________

SUPERVISORY APPRAISER (ONLY IF REQUIRED)

Signature ______________________
Name ______________________
Company Name ______________________
Company Address ______________________
____
Telephone Number ______________________
Email Address ______________________
Date of Signature ______________________
State Certification # ______________________
or State License # ______________________
State ______________________
Expiration Date of Certification or License ______________________

SUBJECT PROPERTY

☐ Did not inspect subject property
☐ Did inspect exterior of subject property from street
Date of Inspection ______________________
☐ Did inspect interior and exterior of subject property
Date of Inspection ______________________

COMPARABLE SALES

☐ Did not inspect exterior of comparable sales from street
☐ Did inspect exterior of comparable sales from street
Date of Inspection ______________________

■ VALUATION APPROACHES

The basic problem when buying or selling real estate is deciding what it is worth. To derive an opinion of value, the appraiser uses three traditional valuation methods: the sales comparison approach, the cost approach, and the income capitalization approach. Each approach uses many of the principles defined in Unit 5. In addition, each approach has its own terms and principles, some of which will be mentioned briefly in the following summaries of the three approaches. All of them will be explained fully in later units.

Sales Comparison Approach

The **sales comparison approach**, or market data approach, to appraising makes the most direct use of the principle of substitution. The value of a property is considered to be related to the selling prices of properties like it. In the sales comparison approach, then, an opinion of value is obtained by comparing the property being appraised—the subject property—to recent sales of similar, nearby properties, called *comparables* or *comps*. The appraiser finds three to five (or more) comps.[1] The appraiser notes any dissimilar features between the subject property and each of the comps and makes an adjustment for each difference by using the following formula:

Sales price of comparable property	±	Adjustments	=	Indicated value of subject property

The appraiser adds to the sales price of a comparable property the value of a feature present in the subject property but not in the comparable. The appraiser subtracts from the sales price of the comparable property the value of a feature present in the comparable but not in the subject property. Major types of adjustments include those made for physical (on-site) features, locational (off-site) influences, conditions of sale (buyer-seller motivation and financing terms), and time from date of sale. After going through this process for each of the comparable properties, the appraiser assigns a value to the subject property that is the adjusted sales price of the comparable(s) most like the subject.

---

1. The number of sales needed for an accurate estimate of value cannot be easily specified. Most appraisers believe that three to five comparable sales constitute a representative sample—particularly if the sales are very similar, are located close by, and have sold recently. The fewer the sales, the more carefully they should be investigated. If the quality of the data collected is questionable, a larger number of sales should be considered.

   The reason for an appraisal can also influence the number of comparable sales needed. For example, an appraisal used to establish value in a condemnation proceeding would probably require a greater number of comparable sales than one used to establish value for a mortgage loan.

IN PRACTICE

House A, which sold for $355,000, is comparable to house B, the subject property, but has a garage valued at $25,000. House B has no garage. In this case, using the formula for the sales comparison approach, the market value of the subject property would be reached as shown below.

$355,000 – $25,000 = $330,000

House B is valued at $330,000.

IN PRACTICE

House X, the subject property, is 15 years old. A comparable property, house Y, is 15 years old and sold for $270,000 one year prior to this appraisal. Because of changes in market conditions since the sale of house Y, the appraiser has determined that 10% added to the sales price is an accurate reflection of the increase in property values over the year. In this case, using the formula for the sales comparison approach:

$270,000 + (10% × $270,000) = Value of subject property
$270,000 + $27,000 = $297,000

House X is valued at $297,000.

Vacant land is valued in the same way, by finding other comparable properties and adding or subtracting, as necessary, the worth of any amenities present in either the subject or the comparable property and not in the other. Features of vacant land requiring a sales price adjustment might include installation of utilities, composition of soil, terrain, size, shape, zoning, and location. Factors requiring a major sales price adjustment for land zoned for residential use could include location in a flood plain; proximity to undesirable land uses, such as a landfill or industrial area; or high building permit and construction costs in a congested urban or suburban area.

Cost Approach

In the **cost approach**, the appraiser estimates the value of any improvements to the land (such as structures) in terms of their reproduction or replacement cost as though new. The distinction between reproduction and replacement cost is discussed in Unit 10. The appraiser then subtracts any loss in value owing to the depreciation of the improvements. Finally, the appraiser adds an estimate of the value of the site itself, usually found by the sales comparison approach. The rationale of the cost approach is that a knowledgeable buyer will pay no more for a house than the cost of constructing a substitute house on a similar lot and with similar design and amenities. The formula for the cost approach is

Reproduction or replacement cost of improvements – Depreciation on improvement(s) + Site value = Property value

Depreciation may occur through either deterioration (effects of wear and tear or the elements) or obsolescence. Obsolescence can be functional, such as outmoded room layout or design, or external, caused by changes in factors outside the property, such as zoning, the property's highest and best use, or supply and demand.

IN PRACTICE

A house being appraised is similar in size, design, and quality of construction to a new house that has a construction cost of $225,000. The house being appraised has depreciated by 20% due to lack of maintenance and is on a lot valued separately at $40,000. Using the cost approach formula:

$$\$225{,}000 - (20\% \times \$225{,}000) + \$40{,}000 = \text{Property value}$$
$$\$225{,}000 - \$45{,}000 + \$40{,}000 = \$220{,}000$$

The value of the property based on the cost approach is $220,000.

IN PRACTICE

A warehouse that would cost $850,000 to construct today has depreciated 25% in its lifetime and is on land valued at $440,000. What is the property's total estimated value by the cost approach?

$$\$850{,}000 - (25\% \times \$850{,}000) + \$440{,}000 = \text{Property value}$$
$$\$850{,}000 - \$212{,}500 + \$440{,}000 = \$1{,}077{,}500$$

The value of the property based on the cost approach is $1,077,500.

Income Capitalization Approach

The **income capitalization approach** is based on the net income, or investment return, that a buyer expects from the property. The price that the buyer will pay will be determined by the probable return the property will yield from the investment. The income capitalization approach is used primarily for valuing income-producing properties such as apartment buildings, shopping centers, and office buildings.

Remember that the income capitalization approach is based on net operating income—which is usually expressed as an annual amount. Rents are not net operating income. All the expenses of maintaining the building, such as upkeep and management, must be subtracted from effective gross income (scheduled rents plus any other income minus vacancy and collection losses) to realize net operating income.

If a property's net operating income for the year is known, as well as the buyer's anticipated overall rate of return for the investment (stated as a capitalization or "cap" rate), value can be computed by using the following formula:

$$\text{Net operating income} \div \text{Return (capitalization rate)} = \text{Property value}$$

Or:

$$\frac{I}{R} = V$$

The cap rate increases as the risk to the investor increases. The higher the cap rate, the lower the property value, and the lower the cap rate, the higher the property value.

IN PRACTICE

A buyer wants a 6% investment return. He is interested in a medical office building that produces a net operating income of $425,000 per year. What would the buyer be willing to pay for the building?

$$\frac{\$425{,}000}{0.06} = \$7{,}083{,}333$$

The property value that will produce the expected net operating income is $7,083,333.

The return that can be expected based on an estimated level of income and property value can be computed by using a variation of the basic income capitalization formula:

$$\frac{\text{Income}}{\text{Property value}} = \text{Return}$$

Or:

$$\frac{I}{V} = R$$

IN PRACTICE

An investor estimates that a net operating income of $39,300 can be received from a building that will require an investment of $560,000. What is the investor's capitalization rate (return)?

$$\frac{\$39{,}300}{\$560{,}000} = 0.07017$$

The expected return, based on the income alone, is 7%.

A buyer who has only a certain amount to invest and wants a specific rate of return from his investment would use another variation of the formula:

$$\text{Property value} \times \text{Return} = \text{Net operating income}$$

Or:

$$V \times R = I$$

IN PRACTICE

To receive an 8% return from an investment of $700,000, what would be the required net operating income of the purchased property?

$$\$700,000 \times 0.08 = \$56,000$$

The net operating income would have to be $56,000.

Exercise 6-1

Using the formula for the approach specified, solve each of the following appraisal problems.

Sales comparison approach:

House X, in an Arizona community in which swimming pools are highly desired, is being appraised. It is very similar to house Y, but house Y has an in-ground swimming pool and spa valued at $27,000. House Y sold two months ago for $778,000. What is the market value of house X using the formula for the sales comparison approach?

Cost approach:

A retail store, built 15 years ago, has depreciated about 30% overall. It would cost $230,000 to build today, and similar sites are now worth $52,000. What is the market value of this store using the formula for the cost approach?

Income capitalization approach:

An apartment building provides a net annual operating income of $64,500. Investors are expecting a 9% return on this type of investment. What will the asking price be if it is the same as the market value found by the formula for the income capitalization approach?

Check your answers against those in the answer key at the back of the book.

■ RELATIONSHIP OF APPROACHES

The three approaches to real estate appraisal require different kinds of information, which may include data on comparable nearby property sales (sales comparison approach), building cost (cost approach), and investment return (income capitalization approach). The information available will help determine which appraisal method will be given the most validity in the appraiser's opinion of the market value of the subject property.

As a general rule, the sales comparison approach is the most reliable approach with single-family residences; the cost approach is most reliable with non-income-producing properties having a limited market or with special purpose properties; and the income capitalization approach is most reliable with income-producing properties.

Most appraisals will require the use of more than one approach, especially when land value must be distinguished from building value. This is true when the cost approach is used to find building value. There are other instances when land value must be separated from building value, such as for tax valuation purposes. These will be discussed later in this book.

IN PRACTICE

If a 45-year-old school building is to be sold, what approach would be given the most weight in determining its market value?

School buildings are not usually on the market, so there probably would be no recent comparable sales in the vicinity. If the building could be used as office or other rental space as it stood, or with a little remodeling, the income capitalization approach might be feasible. The approach given the most weight, however, would probably be the cost approach, because the high cost of constructing a similar new building would probably be the most significant selling factor.

The next step in the appraisal process is to analyze the value indications from the three approaches to arrive at the best and most supportable opinion of value. This can be either a single dollar figure or a range into which the value most likely will fall. The process the appraiser follows to do this is called reconciliation.

Proper analysis and reconciliation are essential to a good appraisal report. The use of accepted appraisal methods does not in itself produce a sound opinion of value. It must be combined with good judgment on the part of the appraiser, as well as experience in gathering needed information and making thorough analyses and valid interpretations of relevant data.

The reconciliation process is covered in detail in Unit 15, "Reconciliation and the Appraisal Report."

Exercise 6-2

Decide which appraisal approach(es) would normally carry the most weight in valuing each of the following properties:

1. A factory
2. An automobile showroom and garage
3. A public building formerly used as a town hall
4. Farmland surrounded by commercial and industrial developments
5. A one-story retail store in a busy downtown business district
6. An older, single-family residence in a neighborhood rezoned to permit high-rise apartments
7. A medical office building in a business center adjacent to a hospital complex
8. A single-family, owner-occupied residence

9. A place of worship

10. A small abandoned roadside restaurant adjacent to a new apartment complex

---

Check your answers against those in the answer key at the back of the book.

■ SUMMARY

The appraisal process begins with a statement of the problem—the purpose of the appraisal—which will help determine the scope of work required to complete the appraisal assignment. The interest to be appraised, whether a fee simple estate, life estate, leasehold estate, leased fee estate, or some other property interest, must be noted, as well as the client and the reason for the appraisal. By gathering, recording, verifying, and analyzing all the necessary data, the appraiser can form an opinion of value based on knowledge and understanding and not guesswork.

There are three basic approaches to determining the market value of real property. The sales comparison approach makes use of data regarding recently sold properties that are similar to the subject property. The cost approach utilizes the present construction cost of existing improvements less depreciation. The income capitalization approach makes use of the net operating income that may be expected from the property. The appraiser must use the appraisal approaches that are most reasonable in light of the type of property being appraised.

■ REVIEW QUESTIONS

1. The appraisal approach that would be *MOST* useful in valuing single-family residential property is
   a. the sales comparison approach.
   b. the cost approach.
   c. the income capitalization approach.

2. The appraisal approach that normally would be *MOST* useful in valuing investment property is
   a. the sales comparison approach.
   b. the cost approach.
   c. the income capitalization approach.

3. The appraisal approach that normally would be *MOST* useful in valuing public and religious-use properties is
   a. the sales comparison approach.
   b. the cost approach.
   c. the income capitalization approach.

4. The reliability of an appraisal depends on
   a. the knowledge and judgment of the appraiser.
   b. the accuracy of the data used.
   c. both of these.
   d. neither of these.

5. Property A is a single-family residence that sold for $480,000. It is very similar to property B, which you are appraising, except that property A has a two-car garage worth $36,000. Using the formula for the sales comparison approach, calculate the market value of property B.

6. An office building has depreciated 40% since it was built 25 years ago. If it would cost $725,000 to build today, and if similar sites are selling for $175,000, what is the market value of the property using the formula for the cost approach?

7. You are appraising a single-story building producing net operating income of $124,000 per year. If you determine that a 9% return is justified on this investment, what would be your value estimate of the property using the income capitalization approach formula?

8. The appraisal process provides all of the following advantages, *EXCEPT*
   a. increases efficiency.
   b. reduces liability.
   c. increases fees.
   d. assists enforcement agencies.

9. The first step in the appraisal process is to
   a. define the problem.
   b. collect the fee.
   c. collect data about the subject property.
   d. reconcile the values reached by each of the appraisal approaches.

10. The last step in the appraisal process is to
    a. state the problem.
    b. report opinion of value.
    c. reconcile the values reached by each of the appraisal approaches.
    d. collect the fee.

11. The step in the appraisal process that determines what the appraiser should do in an assignment is
    a. define the problem.
    b. gather data.
    c. determine the scope of work.
    d. talk to the client.

12. The date of an appraisal is determined by
    a. the lender.
    b. the client only.
    c. the party who pays the appraiser.
    d. the conversation between the client and the appraiser.

13. The date of the appraisal is also known as
    a. the effective date.
    b. the inspection date.
    c. the calendar date.
    d. the date of the report.

14. Limiting conditions in an appraisal report serve to
    a. limit the client's responsibilities.
    b. limit the appraiser's responsibilities.
    c. protect the public.
    d. limit the appraiser's license.

15. The date of the appraisal can be
    a. any date chosen by the appraiser.
    b. any date chosen by the client.
    c. any date chosen by an agreement between client and appraiser, but can only be a present date.
    d. any date chosen by an agreement between client and appraiser, and can be a past, present, or future date.

16. FNMA and FHLMC are part of
    a. the primary mortgage market.
    b. the secondary mortgage market.
    c. the Federal Housing Administration.
    d. the Federal Reserve System.

17. The three approaches to value are used
    a. on every assignment.
    b. as appropriate, according to the scope of work.
    c. according to the client's instruction.
    d. to increase the appraisal fee.

18. If the NOI stays the same and the cap rate increases, property value
    a. decreases.
    b. increases.
    c. stays the same.
    d. cannot be determined.

19. If the NOI stays the same and the property value increases, the cap rate
    a. decreases.
    b. increases.
    c. stays the same.
    d. cannot be determined.

20. The form used most often for FNMA appraisals is
    a. the VA.
    b. the FHA.
    c. the URAR.
    d. the narrative.

Check your answers against those in the answer key at the back of the book.

7

UNIT SEVEN

BUILDING CONSTRUCTION AND THE ENVIRONMENT

LEARNING OBJECTIVES

When you have completed this unit, you will be able to

- measure the gross living area of a structure;
- compare and contrast: ranch, Cape Cod, two-story, split-level, and split-entry;
- critique a house and lot in terms of its orientation, topography, and view;
- define curb appeal;
- identify the various components of a house from a diagram;
- identify common radon entry routes; and
- explain the term "low-E glass".

■ KEY TERMS

building codes
Cape Cod
curb appeal
Department of Veterans Affairs (VA)
electrical system
Energy Star
Federal Housing Administration (FHA)
fenestration
foundation
framing
green building
gross building area (GBA)
gross leasable area (GLA)
gross living area (GLA)
heating and air-conditioning
insulation
International Code Council (ICC)
Leadership in Energy and Environmental Design (LEED)
low-E glass
manufactured house
orientation
plumbing system
R-value
radon gas
ranch house
solar heating
split-entry
split-level
topography

■ OVERVIEW

Real estate appraisers must know their product to help in deriving a supportable opinion of market value. In terms of residential real estate, this means knowing the construction features that determine quality, show good craftsmanship, and indicate good upkeep or show neglect, especially through visible flaws that could indicate significant structural damage. By being aware of current architectural trends and construction standards, the appraiser can gauge a property's desirability, marketability, and value. The purpose of this unit is to explain the basic construction features of wood-frame residential houses so you can better judge and evaluate them.

Wood-frame construction, whether covered by weatherboarding or veneered with brick or stone, is the type most frequently used in single-family houses. Wood-frame houses are preferred for a number of reasons:

- They are less expensive than other types.
- They can be built rapidly.
- They are easy to insulate against heat or cold.
- Greater flexibility of design is possible, thereby enabling architects and builders to produce a variety of architectural styles.

The following building fundamentals will be considered in this unit:

- State and municipal regulations, such as building codes
- Plans and specifications
- Architectural styles and designs
- Terms and trade vernacular used in residential construction
- The practical approach to recognizing, judging, and comparing the quality of the various house components

This unit also covers some of the environmental issues (such as the presence of asbestos or radon gas) that must be considered by real estate appraisers as well as brokers, developers, lenders, and others involved in real estate transactions.

PART I: BUILDING PLANNING AND DESIGN

■ REGULATION OF RESIDENTIAL CONSTRUCTION

The purpose of **building codes** is to ensure that builders follow minimum requirements for building size and construction. Most building codes require a permit before beginning any new construction or making changes to an existing property, such as remodeling, building an addition, or adding a new improvement, such as a swimming pool. Through the permit requirement, city officials can verify compliance with building codes by examining building plans before construction begins, as well as inspecting the work at various stages. Codes will vary in different regions of the country.

Building codes for the construction industry were established when the Building Officials Conference of America (BOCA) combined with the National Board of Fire Insurance Underwriters to establish rules to ensure both comfort and safety for homeowners. These standards became the forerunners of present municipal building codes. The merger of BOCA and the regional U.S. codes organizations has resulted in formation of the **International Code Council (ICC)**, www.iccsafe.org.

WEB LINK

www.iccsafe.org

The **Federal Housing Administration (FHA)** and **Department of Veterans Affairs (VA)** standards also have served as models for municipal building codes, which place primary importance on materials, structural strength, and safe, sanitary conditions. Such building codes set the minimum construction standards that must be met by builders. HUD established minimum property standards (MPS) for manufactured homes, as well as new single-family homes, multi-family housing, and residential health care facilities. Manufactured homes and other structures must meet local standards for site preparation, foundation, and utility connections.

WEB LINK

www.hud.gov

State and local building codes frequently supplement all of these standards with construction specifications designed to help buildings withstand regional conditions, from climate extremes in northern states to earthquakes in California and hurricanes in Florida.

■ PLANS AND SPECIFICATIONS

Careful plans and specifications are required to comply with building codes. These must be in sufficient detail to direct the builder in assembling the construction materials. Working drawings, called plans or blueprints, show the construction details of the building. Specifications are written statements that establish the items included (such as fixtures), quality of the materials, and workmanship required.

An owner may engage an architect to design a house and prepare plans and specifications for its construction.

Professional architects typically must be licensed by the state(s) in which they practice and may also join a trade association having its own membership requirements, such as the American Institute of Architects (AIA), www.aia.org. The architect's services may include negotiating with the builder and inspecting the progress of the construction, as well as preparing plans and specifications.

WEB LINK

www.aia.org

Architects' fees, usually based on the hours spent on a given project, may vary from 6% to 15% of the total cost of the finished house, depending on the services rendered. The builder typically acts as general contractor, providing day-to-day supervision of the job site in addition to procuring building materials and hiring carpenters, plumbers, electricians, and other subcontractors.

Other specialists may be involved in residential construction, including the mechanical engineer, who provides the heating, air-conditioning, and plumbing plans and specifications; the structural engineer, who ensures that the foundation will support the structure and specifies the amount of steel required for reinforcing the foundation and the type and mix of concrete to be used; and the soil engineer, who may assist in determining the stability of the land on which the foundation is to be built. The soil engineer's investigation, coupled with the structural engineer's knowledge, will determine the details of the foundation.

Building Measurement

The size of a structure being appraised will be stated in the appraisal report and may be a critical factor in the final determination of value. The appraiser should always

- state the basis for the measurement provided in the appraisal report;
- verify all measurements personally; and
- if a multiunit building is involved, base all measurements on the same standard for consistency.

Several commonly used standards of measurements are discussed in the following paragraphs. The residential property standards originated with the federal agency requirements (FHA, VA, Fannie Mae, etc.).

Gross living area

For a single-family detached residence, size is described in terms of **gross living area (GLA)**, defined as the total amount of finished, year-round habitable above-grade (above ground level) space, measured along the building's outside perimeter. Depending on property location, this usually means that all living areas must be heated and/or cooled. Generally, attics, basements, and crawlspaces are not included in the measurement. Local custom may allow inclusion of other space in the calculation, if typical of the area and accepted by property buyers as equivalent to living space. For example, many areas have buildings constructed on hillsides, either upslope (the house is built into the hill at an elevation higher than the roadway) or downslope (the house is built on piers at an elevation lower than the roadway). Gross living area of such homes typically includes lower levels that are not completely above grade on all sides. The best appraisal practice is always to compare properties with others of similar construction.

For condominium apartments, size is described in square footage of interior floor space rather than as outside wall measurement.

Measuring Gross Living Area

Fannie Mae's July 2017 Selling Guide describes how square footage of living area is to be measured:

The most common comparison for one-unit properties, including units in PUD, condo, or co-op projects, is above-grade gross living area. The appraiser must be consistent when he or she calculates and reports the finished above-grade room count and the square feet of gross living area that is above-grade. The need for consistency also applies from report to report. For example, when using the same transaction as a comparable sale in multiple reports, the room count and gross living area should not change.

When calculating gross living area, the following should occur:

- The appraiser should use the exterior building dimensions per floor to calculate the above-grade gross living area of a property.
- For units in condo or co-op projects, the appraiser should use interior perimeter unit dimensions to calculate the gross living area.
- Garages and basements, including those that are partially above-grade, must not be included in the above-grade room count.

Only finished above-grade areas can be used in calculating and reporting of above-grade room count and square footage for the gross living area. Fannie Mae considers a level to be below-grade if any portion of it is below-grade, regardless of the quality of its finish or the window area of any room. Therefore, a walk-out basement with finished rooms would not be included in the above-grade room count. Rooms that are not included in the above-grade room count may add substantially to the value of a property, particularly when the quality of the finish is high. For that reason, the appraiser should report the basement or other partially below-grade areas separately and make appropriate adjustments for them on the Basement & Finished Rooms Below-Grade line in the Sales Comparison Approach adjustment grid.

For consistency in the sales comparison analysis, the appraiser should compare above-grade areas to above-grade areas and below-grade areas to below-grade areas. The appraiser may need to deviate from this approach if the style of the subject property or any of the comparables does not lend itself to such comparisons. For example, a property built into the side of a hill where the lower level is significantly out of ground, the interior finish is equal throughout the house, and the flow and function of the layout is accepted by the local market, may require the gross living area to include both levels. However, in such instances, the appraiser must be consistent throughout the appraisal in his or her analysis and explain the reason for the deviation, clearly describing the comparisons that were made.

Gross building area

For multifamily residences and industrial buildings, size is described in terms of **gross building area (GBA)**, defined as all enclosed floor areas (including both attics and basements), measured along the building's outside perimeter. Interior common areas are included in gross building area, but not exterior common areas, such as open stairways.

Gross leasable area

For shopping centers, size generally is described in terms of square feet of **gross leasable area (GLA)**, defined as total space designed for occupancy and exclusive use of tenants (including basements), measured from outside wall surfaces to the center of shared interior walls.

The size of other multitenant commercial properties, such as office buildings, will be described as local custom dictates or perhaps, according to the negotiating strengths of landlord and tenant. For instance, common areas (and the expense of their maintenance), including lobbies, corridors, and elevator shafts, may be apportioned among tenants on a pro rata basis—that is, in relation to the size of each tenant's exclusive-use space.

■ HOUSE STYLES

Although the details of construction are rigidly specified by building codes, house styles may vary greatly. There are no absolute standards, and real estate values rest on what potential buyers, users, and investors think is desirable as well as on what they consider to be attractive.

House styles can be grouped under two broad categories: traditional and contemporary.

Traditional Styles

Past architectural styles appeal to many prospective homeowners. Within this nostalgic design category, traditionalists have a wide range of individual styles to choose from: Cape Cod, Victorian, and Georgian—to name a few (Figure 7.1). The handling of architectural details gives the traditional house its unique flavor. Fortunately, the detailing for many traditional houses no longer must be handcrafted because good reproductions are now mass produced. Ready-made entrance doors, mantels, moldings, and parquet floors bear a close resemblance to their handcrafted prototypes.

The outward appearance of a house may adhere to a single style or combine several different styles. Materials, scale, and proportion should be consistent within the architectural style. The gingerbread trim that adds to the appeal of a Victorian house will look out of place on a more contemporary design. A brick facade on a Mediterranean style house would be a waste of two good ideas. Over time, a house that is true to its design will mature gracefully and maintain its value.

FIGURE 7.1
Traditional House Styles

Mediterranean

Cape Cod

Victorian

Farm House

Georgian

Contemporary Styles

Although many contemporary houses appear uncomplicated, they are often clever examples of how to make the best use of materials and space (Figure 7.2). A distinctive contemporary look relies on the straightforward expression of the structural system itself for major design impact. One great benefit of contemporary residential architecture is its responsiveness to indoor-outdoor living. Walls of sliding glass doors, large windows, skylights, decks, terraces, and atriums all contribute to this relationship. The contemporary ranch homes by builders such as Joseph Eichler, which were most popular in the several decades after WWII, have seen a resurgence of interest. These midcentury modern homes, as they are called, are now recognized for their attractive designs, open-plan living areas, and use of outdoor spaces to expand living areas.

WEB LINK
www.eichlermidcentury.com

FIGURE 7.2
Contemporary House Style

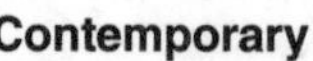
Contemporary

■ HOUSE TYPES

House type refers to the number of and arrangement of a home's living levels. Although variations exist, most home types fall somewhere within the basic categories described next and illustrated in Figure 7.3.

The One-Story House

The one-story house, often called a **ranch house**, has all the habitable rooms on one level (Figure 7.3). Its great advantage is the absence of steps to climb or descend, particularly if the house is built on a concrete slab foundation or over a crawlspace, rather than a basement. Because no headroom is required above the ceiling, the roof of a one-story house is usually pitched low. The low height simplifies construction, too, but this does not necessarily mean a lower cost because foundation and roof areas are larger in proportion to total finished area than in other types of housing. The ranch is one of the easiest houses to maintain.

The One-and-a-Half-Story House

The one-and-a-half-story house, or **Cape Cod**, is actually a two-story house in which the second-floor attic space has sufficient headroom to permit up to half the area to be used as livable floor area. It has two distinct advantages: economy in cost per cubic foot of habitable space and built-in expandability (Figure 7.3).

FIGURE 7.3
Types of Houses: One Story and One and a Half Story

The Two-Story House

The two-story house offers the most living space within an established perimeter; the living area is doubled on the same foundation and under the same roof (Figure 7.4). Certain economies are inherent in the two-story plan: plumbing can be aligned, and winter heating is utilized to the best advantage—heat rises to the second floor after warming the ground floor. More house can be built on a smaller lot with a two- story plan. The roof is smaller, relative to the overall floor area, as is the foundation required.

The Split-Level House

The **split-level house**, which has fallen out of favor, has three separate levels of space (Figure 7.4). The lowest level, situated entirely or partially below the outside finished grade, usually contains the garage, heating and air-conditioning system, and family room. The next area—the one raised a half-flight from the lowest level—is extra space common only to a split-level house. The floor here is even with, or close to, the outside grade; it usually includes the kitchen and main living area. The sleeping level is another half-flight up, above the garage and family room.

The Split-Entry House

The **split-entry** design, sometimes called a raised ranch, is also somewhat outmoded. It is basically a one-story house on an elevated foundation. The resulting greater height makes the lower level a more usable space for recreation rooms, baths, bedrooms, or other uses. In effect, the square footage of the house is doubled at a modest cost increase—merely that of finishing the rooms on the lower level (Figure 7.4). The downside is that there is no extra basement space to use for storage and/or casual activities.

FIGURE 7.4
Types of Houses: Two-Story, Split-Level Styles

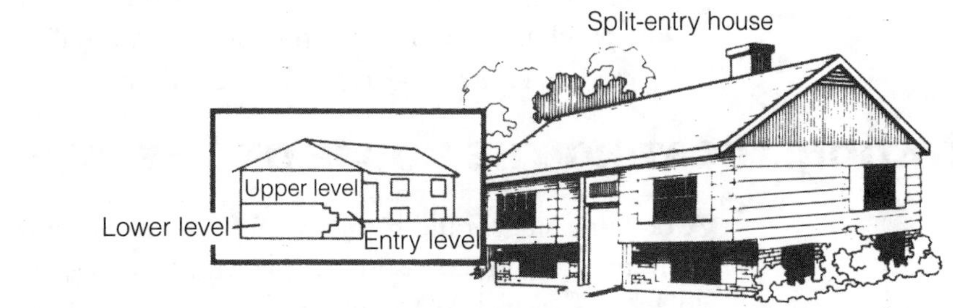

Factory-Built Houses

There are four basic types of factory-built houses, each characterized by the extent of assemblage completed in the factory and whether the house must comply with state and local building codes:

- *Manufactured house*. The **manufactured house** is the most complete of the factory-built houses, available usually in one or two pieces needing only to be anchored to a foundation and connected to utilities. Manufactured homes, as defined by the federal government, must meet the requirements of the Department of Housing and Urban Development. These "HUD Code" homes thus avoid state and local building code requirements, except for site preparation, installation of utilities, and foundation requirements.

- *Modular house*. This type of housing, which must meet state and local building code requirements, comes from the factory in single-room or multiple-room sections, which are then fitted together at the construction site.
- *Panelized house*. Entire wall units, complete with electrical and plumbing installations, are constructed at the factory and transported to the site where final assembly begins. With the foundation laid, the house can be enclosed within a week. State and local building code re-quirements must be met.
- *Precut house*. As the name implies, materials are delivered to the construction site already cut and ready to assemble. Each piece should fit perfectly in its place, eliminating costly time for measuring and cutting materials on site. State and local building code requirements must be met. Precut homes, available until 1940 from the Sears Roebuck catalog, can still be purchased from companies such as Lindal Cedar Homes, though professional contractors typically erect them.

ORIENTATION: LOCATING THE HOUSE ON THE SITE

A building site should be analyzed for its topography; the variations in the sun's path from season to season; the placement, types, and sizes of trees; and the available views, as well as the proximity to neighbors and any sources of noise. Once these factors are studied, the builder can decide on the **orientation** that will allow the house to take full advantage of the site's special characteristics. Both aesthetic and practical considerations come into play. Correct siting on the property can make a house more pleasant to live in and more attractive to buyers. If the property has a slope, the house should probably be located on the highest elevation so that rainwater drains away from the structure; a different placement would require special foundation considerations. A house with correct orientation that is intelligently landscaped, with windows and glass doors in the right places and adequate roof overhang, can save thousands of dollars in heating and air-conditioning bills over the years. The location of a house on its lot also contributes to full-time enjoyment and use of house and grounds. Improper positioning is probably the most common and costly mistake made in house planning today.

Topography

Topography, the "lay of the land," often dictates what style of building may be placed on the site and how the foundation of the building must be designed. A sloping site will require an engineering report to ensure a stable foundation suitable for the overall structure. A steep slope that would be considered impractical for building in some parts of the country may still be considered desirable in those parts of the country where buildable land of any kind is at a premium.

Facing to the South

Ideally, a house should be positioned on the lot so that the main living areas have the best view and also face south. The south side of a house receives five times as much solar heat in the winter as in summer, and the north side receives no solar heat at all during winter months.

Unless some measures of control are used, the same sunshine that helps to heat a house during the winter will make it uncomfortable during the summer. Figure 7.5 shows how this potential problem can be avoided. Because the summer sun is higher in the sky, a wide roof overhang will shade the windows by deflecting the direct heat rays. A roof overhang will not interfere with the sunshine in winter months because the winter sun travels a much lower arc and shines in at a much lower angle than the summer sun.

FIGURE 7.5
Sunlight Exposure

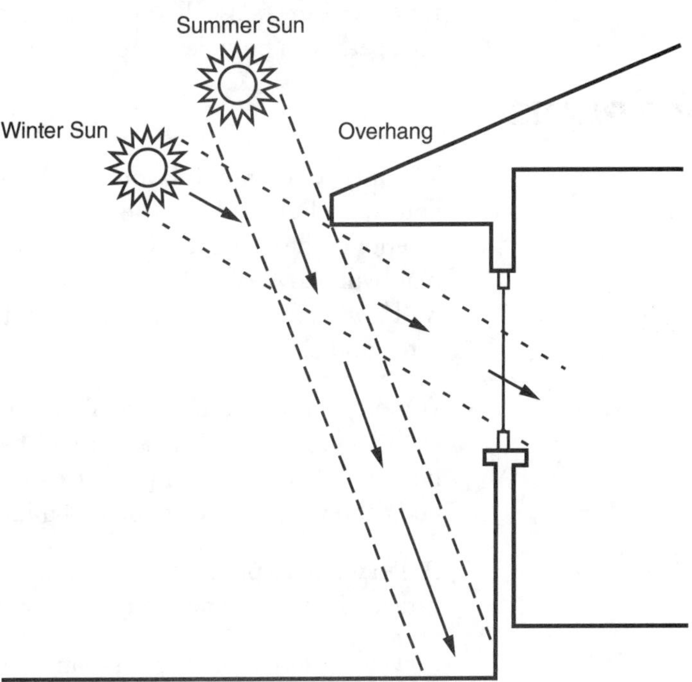

View

A decision on the location of a house can also depend on the view. If the site has an interesting long view to the east or west, it might be wise to take advantage of it, in spite of the sun factor. Even if a site does not have a good long view, a short view of a garden or patio can be just as interesting if carefully planned.

Division of Outdoor Space

Another important step in good site planning is the division of the lot into three different zones: public, service, and private.

The public zone is the area visible from the street—usually the land in front of the house—and consideration should be given to the impression it will make on people driving by or coming to the main entrance. This is called **curb appeal**. Curb appeal refers to a property's overall attractiveness as viewed from the street. A prospective buyer's first impression of a house, and decision on whether or not to view its interior, is likely to be based on its curb appeal. If the lawn is overgrown, weeds are more prominent than shrubbery, the house's paint is peeling, and there are cracks in the driveway, a buyer is likely to be turned off and move on to the next property. A well-maintained exterior space, on the other hand, with an attractive walkway to the main entrance and an inviting front porch, sends a positive message to a prospective buyer.

The service zone consists of the driveway, walkways, storage area for outdoor equipment, and place for trash and recycling containers. The service zone should be designed so deliveries can be made to the preferred entrance without intrusion into the private area.

The private zone is the outdoor living space for the residents. While preferences vary in different geographic areas, an expanse of lawn, patio, garden, deck, barbecue pit or other food-preparation area, and play area often are included in this zone. Architects usually prefer to situate a house as close to the street as zoning laws permit to provide a larger private zone.

HOUSE PLANS

The interior design or layout of a house is central to day-to-day comfort and livability, and also affects the house's market value. A *floor plan* shows what the interior of the house will look like when construction is completed. A basic design plan will show each floor level in the structure, including exterior and interior walls, windows, doors, fireplaces, stairways, appliances, cabinets, plumbing fixtures, and closets.

A more complete architectural or building plan will show exact specifications of each building component and will be the blueprint for the construction of the building. A scale of ¼-inch to 1 foot is used for construction plans, with symbols and abbreviations used to detail building components.

A landscaping plan will show placement of any separate structures, such as a garage, shed, or swimming pool, as well as trees, shrubbery, and planting beds.

A wide variety of floor plans can be viewed on the internet by entering "house plans" in any search engine.

Exercise 7-1

1. List some economic advantages basic to the following house types:
   a. One-and-a-half-story house
   b. Two-story house
   c. Split-entry house
2. How can the orientation of a house on its lot contribute to monetary savings and the enjoyment of the house and its grounds?
3. What is the scale most often used for building features in a construction plan?
4. What is the definition of curb appeal?
5. Why do architects prefer to place a house as close to the front of a lot as zoning laws permit?

Check your answers against those in the answer key at the back of the book.

PART II: CONSTRUCTION DETAILS

Basic knowledge of building construction will help the appraiser identify the factors that contribute to building quality and, ultimately, value.

Throughout this section of the unit, certain terms will be followed by a bracketed number. The number refers to the corresponding term in the house diagram at the end of this unit (Figure 7.15), which provides an overall picture of how housing components fit together into the end product. For example, footing [1] means the component labeled 1 in the house diagram.

■ FOUNDATIONS

The **foundation** of the house is the substructure on which the superstructure rests. The term *foundation* includes the footings, foundation walls, columns, pilasters, slab, and all other parts that provide support for the house and transmit the load of the superstructure to the underlying earth. Foundations are constructed of cut stone, stone and brick, concrete block, or poured concrete. Poured concrete is the most common foundation material because of its strength and resistance to moisture. The two major types of foundations are concrete slab and pier and beam, shown, respectively, in Figure 7.6 and Figure 7.7.

Concrete Slab

A concrete slab foundation is composed of a concrete slab supported around the perimeter and in the center by concrete beams sunk into the earth. It is made of poured concrete reinforced with steel rods. The foundation slab rests directly on the earth, with only a waterproofing membrane between the concrete and the ground. Foundations formed by a single pouring of concrete are monolithic, while those in which the footings and the slab are poured separately are called floating.

FIGURE 7.6
Concrete Slab Foundations

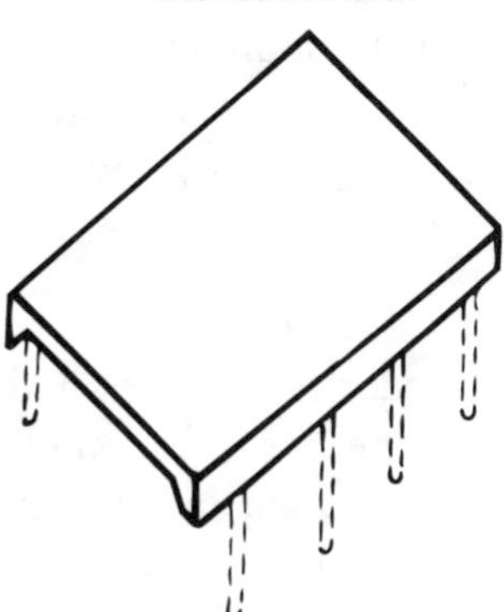

FIGURE 7.7
Pier and Beam Foundation

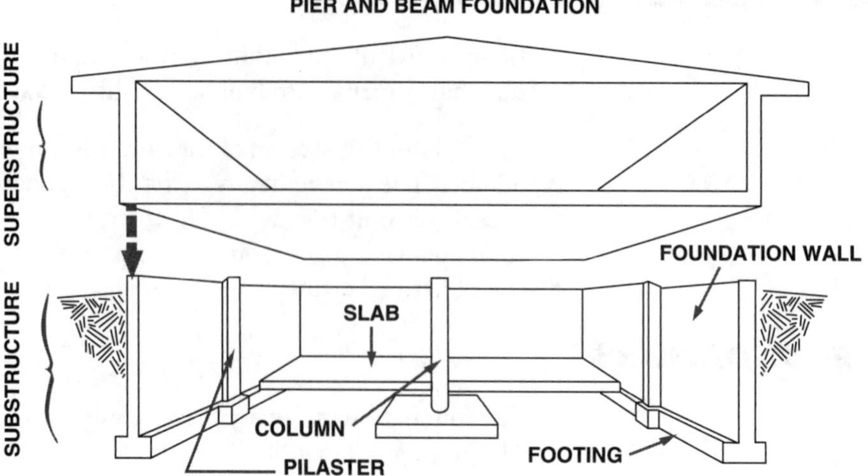

Pier and Beam

In a pier and beam foundation, the foundation slab rests on a series of isolated columns, called piers, that extend above ground level. The space between the ground and the foundation is called the crawlspace. Each support of a pier and beam foundation consists of a pier [55], or column, resting on a footing [57], or base. The pier, in turn, supports the sill [8], which is attached to the pier by an anchor bolt [7]. The floor joists [10] that provide the major support for the flooring are placed perpendicular to and on top of the sills.

Termite Protection

The earth is infested with termites, extremely active antlike insects that are very destructive to wood. Before the slab for the foundation is poured, the ground should be chemically treated to poison termites and thus prevent them from coming up through or around the foundation and into the wooden structure. The chemical treatment of the lumber used for sills and beams and the installation of metal termite shields [9] also provides protection.

Radon Gas

Radon gas is a colorless, odorless, tasteless radioactive gas that comes from the natural breakdown of uranium. It can be found in most rocks and soils. Outdoors, it mixes with the air and is found in low concentrations that are harmless to people. Indoors, however, it can accumulate and build up to dangerous levels that can increase the risk of lung cancer.

How does radon get into a house? The amount of radon in a home depends on the home's construction and the concentration of radon in the soil underneath it. Figure 7.8 shows how radon can enter a home through dirt floors, cracks in concrete foundations, floors and walls, floor drains, tiny cracks or pores in hollow block walls, loose-fitting pipes, exhaust fans, sump pumps, and many other unsuspected places, even the water supply.

FIGURE 7.8
Common Radon Entry Routes

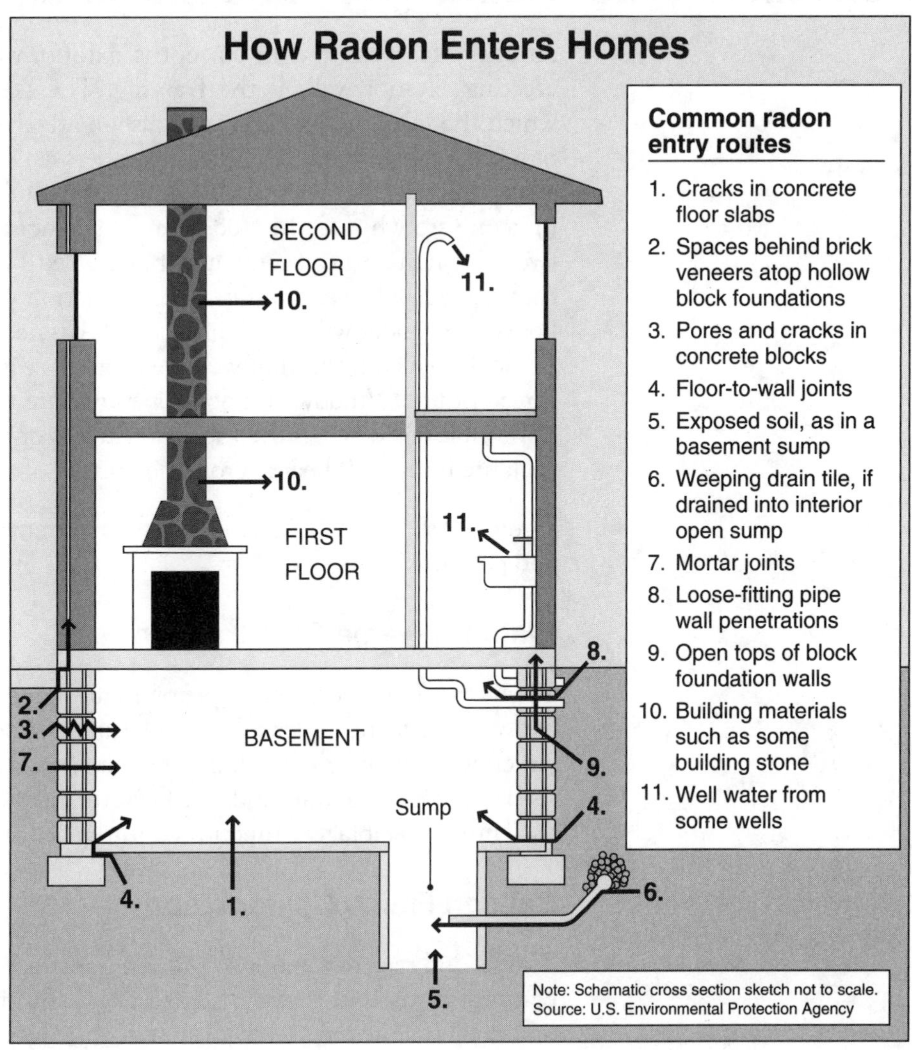

A lot of the variation in radon levels has to do with the "airtightness" of a house: the more energy-efficient a home is, the more likely it will have higher radon levels. The average house has one complete air exchange every six to seven hours; that is, about four times a day all the air from inside the house is exchanged with outside air. The tighter the house, the more likely it is that the air exchange will come from beneath the house from the air over the soil, which may contain high levels of radon gas.

In areas in which radon levels may be above a designated safe level (currently, 4.0 pCi/L, which is 4 picocuries of radon per liter of air), it is common practice to request a radon test before a home sale. If necessary, a radon mitigation system (essentially, a ventilation system to insure adequate air exchange in the basement of a building) can be installed, with the cost negotiated between buyer and seller. More homes are being tested before construction is completed so that a mitigation system can be installed as soon as possible. In response to the awareness of radon problems, the National Action Radon Plan was created by the EPA and released in November 2015, with the goal of reducing radon risk in 5 million homes and prospectively saving 3,200 lives annually by 2020.

WEB LINK
www.epa.gov/radon

■ EXTERIOR STRUCTURAL WALLS AND FRAMING

After the foundation is in place, the exterior walls are erected. The first step in erecting exterior walls is the **framing**. The skeleton members of a building to which the interior and exterior walls are attached are called its frame. The walls of a frame are formed by vertical members called studs [15], which are spaced at even intervals and are attached to the sill. Building codes typically require that for a one-story house, the stud spacing may not exceed 24 inches on center. For a two-story house, the spacing may not exceed 16 inches. Studs rest on plates [12] that are secured to and rest on the foundation wall [4]. In constructing walls and floors, the builder will install firestops [43] as needed or required. These are boards or blocks nailed horizontally between studs or joists to stop drafts and retard the spread of fire. Window and door openings are framed in with wood boards. The horizontal board across the top of a window or door opening is called the header [26]; the horizontal board across the bottom of the opening is called the sill.

Figure 7.9 shows three basic types of wood frame construction: platform, balloon, and post and beam.

Platform Frame Construction

Today the most common type of frame construction for both one-story and two-story residential structures is platform frame construction. In platform construction, only one floor is built at a time, and each floor serves as a platform for the next story. The wall studs are first attached to the upper and lower plates, and the entire assemblage is then raised into place and anchored to the sill.

Balloon Frame Construction

The second type of framing is balloon frame construction, which differs from the platform method in that the studs extend continuously to the ceiling of the second floor. The second floor joists rest on ledger boards or ribbon boards set into the interior edge of the studs. The balloon method gives a smooth, unbroken wall surface on each floor level, thus alleviating the unevenness that sometimes results from settling when the platform method is used. The balloon method is usually employed when the exterior finish will be brick, stone veneer, or stucco.

Post and Beam Frame Construction

Many contemporary-style buildings utilize post and beam frame construction. With this method, the ceiling planks are supported on beams that rest on posts placed at intervals inside the house. Because the posts provide some of the ceiling support, rooms can be built with larger spans of space between the supporting side walls. In some houses, the beams are left exposed, and the posts and beams are stained to serve as part of the decor.

FIGURE 7.9
Frame Construction Types

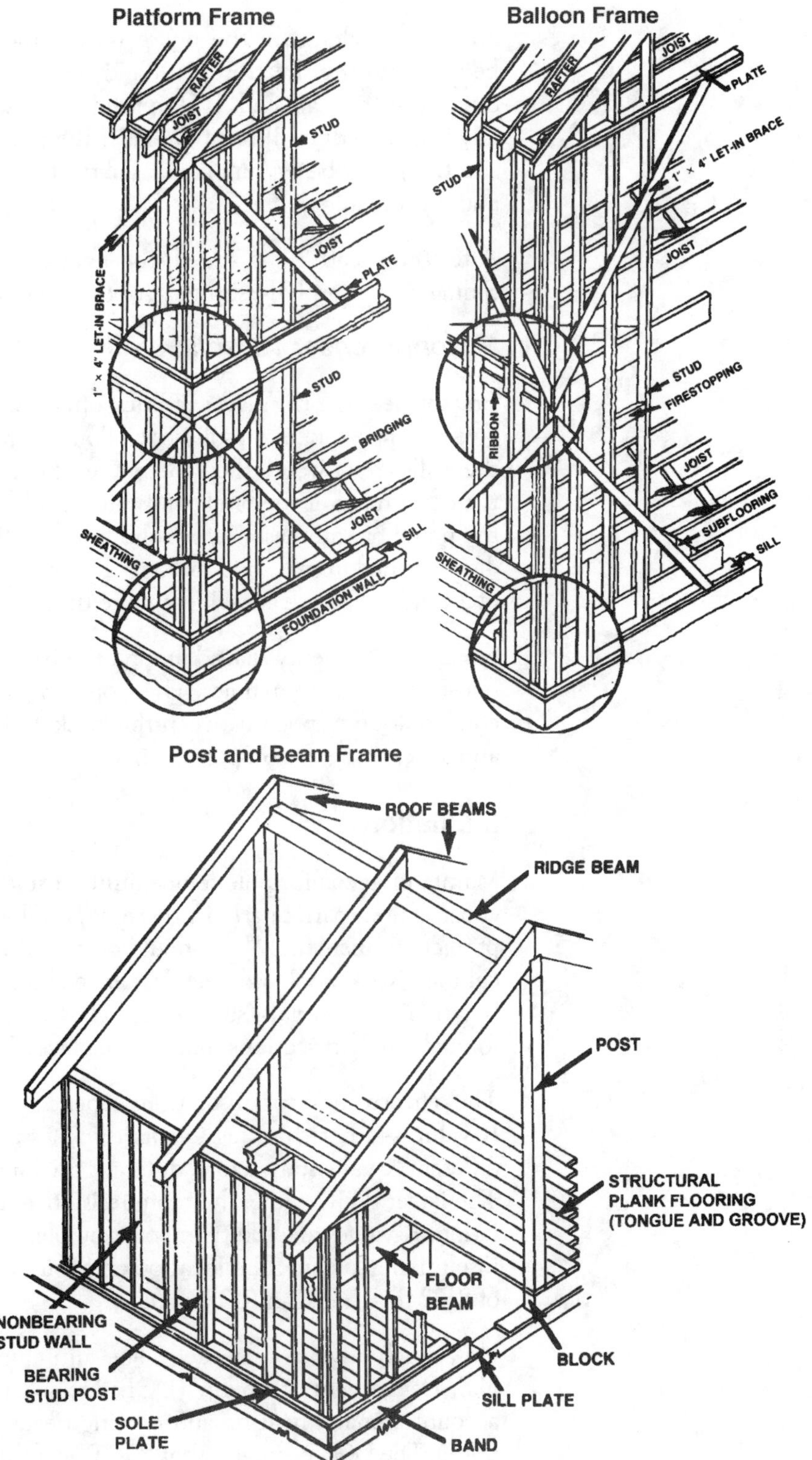

Exterior Walls

After the skeleton of the house is constructed, the exterior wall surface must be built and the sheathing [19] and siding [20] applied. The sheathing is nailed directly to the wall studs [15] to form the base for the siding. Sheathing is generally insulated drywall or plywood. If the house is to have a masonry veneer, the sheathing may be gypsum board. Fabricated sheathings are available in both strip and sheet material.

After the sheathing is added, the final exterior layer, called siding, is applied. Siding may be asphalt, shingles, wood, aluminum, stone, brick, or other material.

Masonry veneer vs. solid brick

Brick veneer is a thin layer of brick often used as a covering on a frame house to give the appearance of a solid brick house. If the masonry is merely decorative and the walls are of wood, then the house has masonry veneer exterior finishing. On the other hand, if the brick walls provide the support for the roof structure, then the house has all masonry, or solid brick, walls. A masonry veneer house may be distinguished from a solid masonry house by the thickness of the walls; the walls of a veneered house are seldom more than eight inches thick.

Small outlets evenly spaced around the base of the masonry perimeter of a brick house are called weep holes. These openings provide an outlet for any moisture or condensation trapped between the brick and the sheathing of the exterior walls and are essential for proper ventilation.

Insulation

Maintaining comfortable temperatures inside the home is an important factor in construction, particularly in these days of high-cost energy. To ensure adequate protection, **insulation** [17] should be placed in the exterior walls and upper floor ceilings. Rock wool and fiberglass are commonly used insulation materials. Combinations of materials, such as fiberglass wrapped in aluminum foil or rock wool formed into batt sections that can be placed between the studs, are also available.

The effectiveness of insulation depends on its resistance to heat flow—its **R-value**—rather than just on its thickness. Different insulating materials have different R-values; therefore, different thicknesses are required to do the same job. The larger the R-value, the more resistance to heat flow and the better the insulation. R-values are additive. For example, if you already have an R-13 value of insulation in a particular location and you want it to be R-35, you can use a layer of R-22 to achieve an R-35 value.

How much R-value is needed? The minimum R-value recommendations of the U.S. Department of Energy (DOE) are specific to ZIP code areas and take into account climate, heating and cooling needs, types of heating used, and energy prices. The DOE estimates that 50–70% of the energy used in the average American home is for heating and cooling. Yet most of the houses in the United States are not insulated to recommended levels. In an attic insulation study, for example, it was found that the average insulation level in attics is about R-20, but the DOE recommends an average of R-40. The DOE guidelines cover other areas of the home as well, including ceilings, floors, exterior walls, and crawlspaces. Because

WEB LINK

www.energy.gov

insulation is relatively inexpensive, the cost/benefit ratio makes increased insulation levels worthwhile.

Information about DOE programs can be found at www.energy.gov.

Asbestos and urea-formaldehyde foam insulation

WEB LINK

www.epa.gov

Two kinds of home insulation to avoid using are asbestos and urea-formaldehyde foam insulation, or UFFI. Asbestos insulation, embedded in ceilings and walls by builders of another era, is no longer used because it is believed to cause the cancer called mesothelioma if its fibers get into the lungs; symptoms can take as long as 30 years to appear. UFFI also may be a potential health hazard, and its use is banned in the United States. It often emits noxious odors and toxic fumes, causing nausea and other irritations if inhaled. If you suspect a house has either asbestos or urea-formaldehyde foam insulation, consult a qualified inspector to examine all questionable areas. More information about both of these substances can be found at www.epa.gov.

■ ROOF FRAMING

Residential roofs are made in several styles, including gable, saltbox, hip, and flat, as shown in Figure 7.10 includes the rafters [30], sheathing [40], and exterior trim or frieze board [42].

■ ROOF COVERINGS

The roof is a key design element, as well as a barrier against rain and snow. There is a wide variety of roofing materials to choose from, including asphalt shingles, wood shingles, and shakes, tile, metal, slate, and concrete.

Exterior Trim

The overhang of a pitched roof that extends beyond the exterior walls of the house is called an eave [24], or cornice, shown in Figure 7.11. The cornice is composed of the soffit, the frieze board, the fascia board, and the extended rafters. The frieze board [42] is the exterior wood-trim board used to finish the exterior wall between the top of the siding or masonry and eave, or overhang, of the roof framing. The fascia board is an exterior wood trim used along the line of the butt end of the rafters where the roof overhangs the structural walls. The overhang of the cornice provides a decorative touch to the exterior of a house as well as some protection from sun and rain.

FIGURE 7.10
Roof Designs

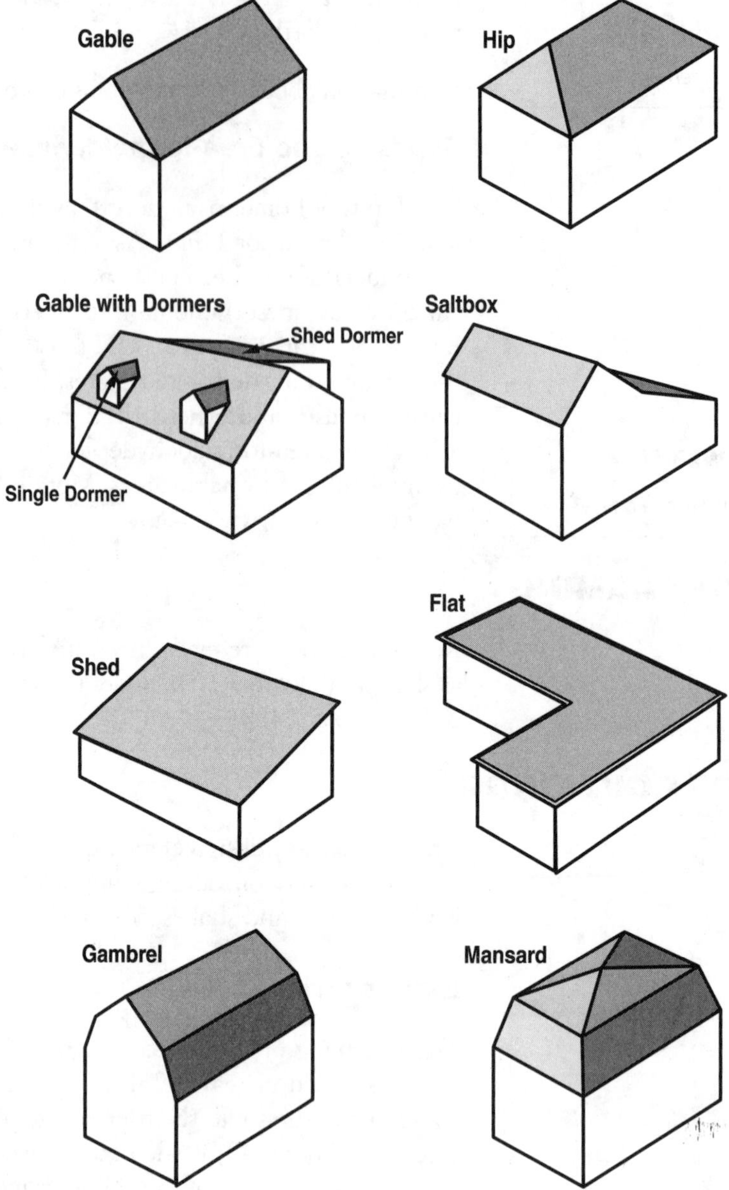

FIGURE 7.11
Eave or Cornice

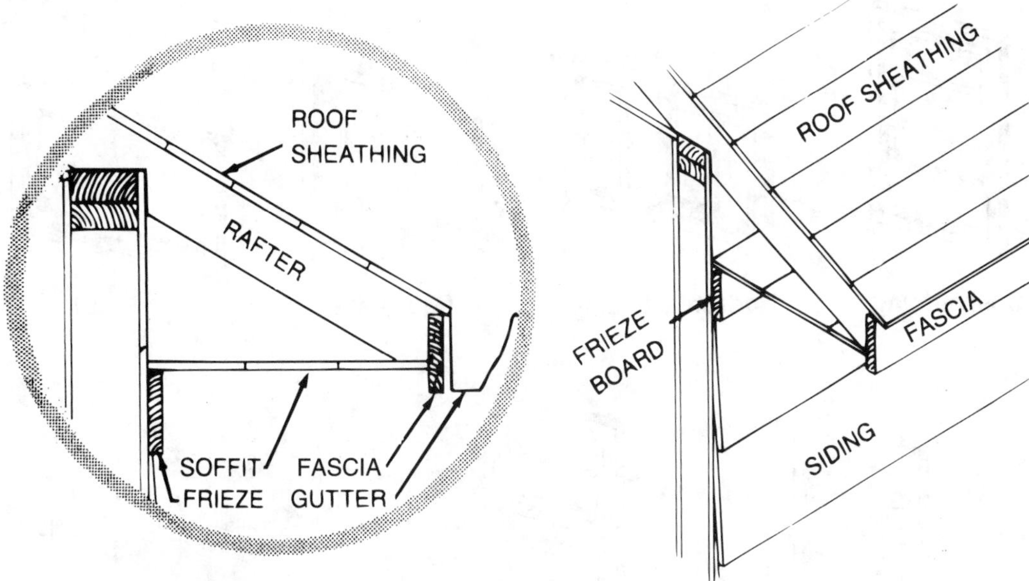

■ EXTERIOR WINDOWS AND DOORS

Windows and doors contribute to the overall tone of a house, as well as provide a specific function. The term **fenestration** refers to the design and placement of windows, doors, and other exterior openings of a building. Skillfully placed doors regulate traffic patterns through the house and provide protection from intruders. Windows, in turn, admit light and a view of the exterior.

Types of Windows

Windows, shown in Figure 7.12, come in a wide variety of types and sizes, in both wood and metal (usually aluminum). Wood is preferred where temperatures fall below freezing. Although metal windows require less maintenance than wood, the frames get colder in winter and panes frost and drip from moisture condensation.

Windows may be sliding, swinging, or fixed. A window might span more than one category if part of it is fixed and another part slides.

Sliding windows

The double-hung window and the single-hung window are still the most common for new construction and for remodeling, particularly in traditional houses. The double-hung window has an upper and lower sash, both of which slide vertically along separate tracks. This arrangement allows cool air to come in at the bottom and warm air to go out through the top. Unfortunately, only half the window can be opened at any one time for ventilation, and it cannot be left open during a hard rain. Single-hung models also feature an upper and lower sash, but only the lower sash is operative. The horizontal sliding window moves back and forth on tracks. As with the double- and single-hung types, only 50% of this window may be opened for fresh air, although sliding windows usually provide more light and a better view.

FIGURE 7.12
Types of Windows

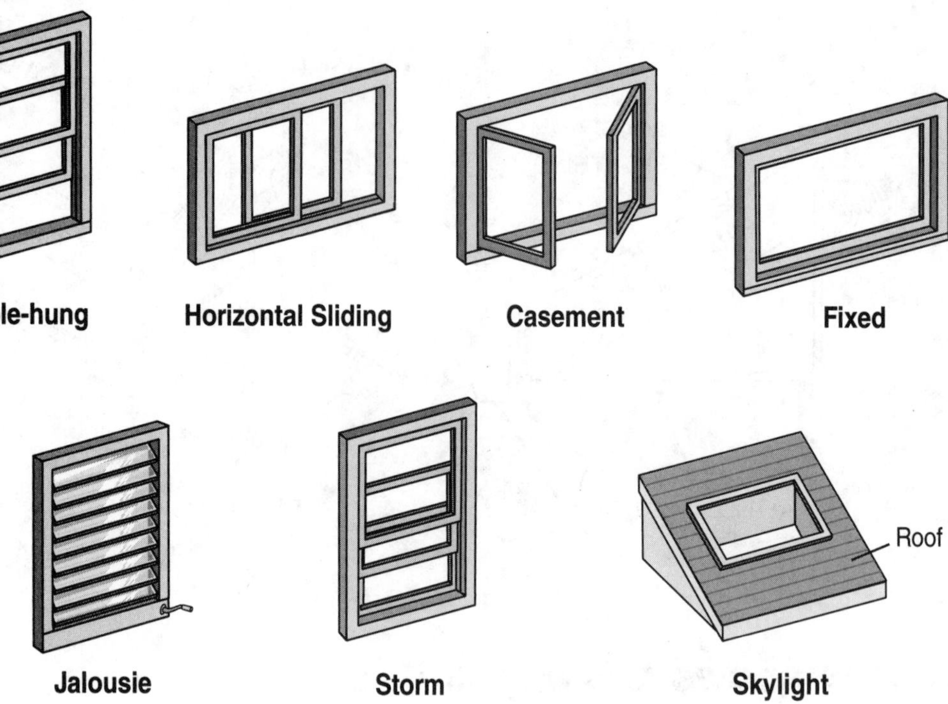

Swinging windows

Casements and jalousies are two common types of swinging windows. Casement windows are hinged at the side and open outward. One advantage of the casement window is that the entire window can be opened for ventilation. Jalousie or louver windows consist of a series of overlapping horizontal glass louvers that pivot together in a common frame and are opened and closed with a lever or crank. In a sun room or sun porch, the jalousie combines protection from the weather with maximum ventilation.

Fixed windows

A fixed window usually consists of a wood sash with a large single pane of insulated glass that cannot be opened for ventilation. It provides natural light and at the same time gives a clear view of the outside. Fixed windows are often used in combination with other windows.

Storm windows

A winter necessity in most parts of the country, storm windows fit on either the inside or the outside of the prime windows. Storm windows are usually made of aluminum, although older houses sometimes have wooden ones and newer houses may have the vinyl type.

Storm windows can reduce summer air-conditioning bills, as well as winter heating costs. Many homeowners who have air-conditioning now leave their storm windows on year-round.

The extraordinary damage created by recent hurricanes has resulted in new window glass and covering requirements in Florida and other states. The appraiser should be aware of the impact of these and other requirements on market value.

Skylights

Skylights can bring both natural illumination and the heat of the sun into rooms. A skylight lets about five times as much daylight into an area as a window of the same size. As a result, a skylight can make a small space appear brighter and larger than it actually is. A skylight is also an excellent way to bring light into a room with an obstructed or unsightly view.

Energy-Efficient Windows

Because of dramatic improvements in the thermal performance of glass, along with improved window construction techniques, homeowners can save energy without sacrificing natural light and expansive views.

A standard energy rating, called an R-value, measures window efficiency. The higher the R-value, the better the thermal efficiency. High efficiency ratings are achieved largely through the use of low-emissivity glass, or **low-E glass**. Low-E refers to a number of glazing techniques that significantly improve the energy performance of glass. These include using double or triple panes, filling the air pockets between panes with argon gas, and using window films.

In addition, proper installation, weatherstripping, and adequate caulking are crucial. For example, a 1⁄16-inch crack around a three-by five-foot window is equivalent to having a brick-size hole in the wall.

Noise Pollution

Windows can leak sound, just as pipes can leak water. Factors ranging from window design and materials to installation techniques affect the noise levels in homes. In general, though, energy-efficient windows cut down on the amount of sound entering a home.

Air absorbs sound and glass carries it. As a result, double- or triple-pane windows absorb more sound waves than do single-pane windows. Wood and vinyl frames absorb more sound than aluminum frames. In addition, applying soft materials such as foam or caulking around the frame will increase sound absorption even more.

Types of Doors

Exterior doors are made from wood or metal and are usually 1¾ inches thick. Interior doors usually have a thickness of 1⅜ inches.

Doors are most often classified by construction and appearance—the four most common types are flush, panel, sliding glass, and storm and screen (Figure 7.13).

FIGURE 7.13
Types of Doors

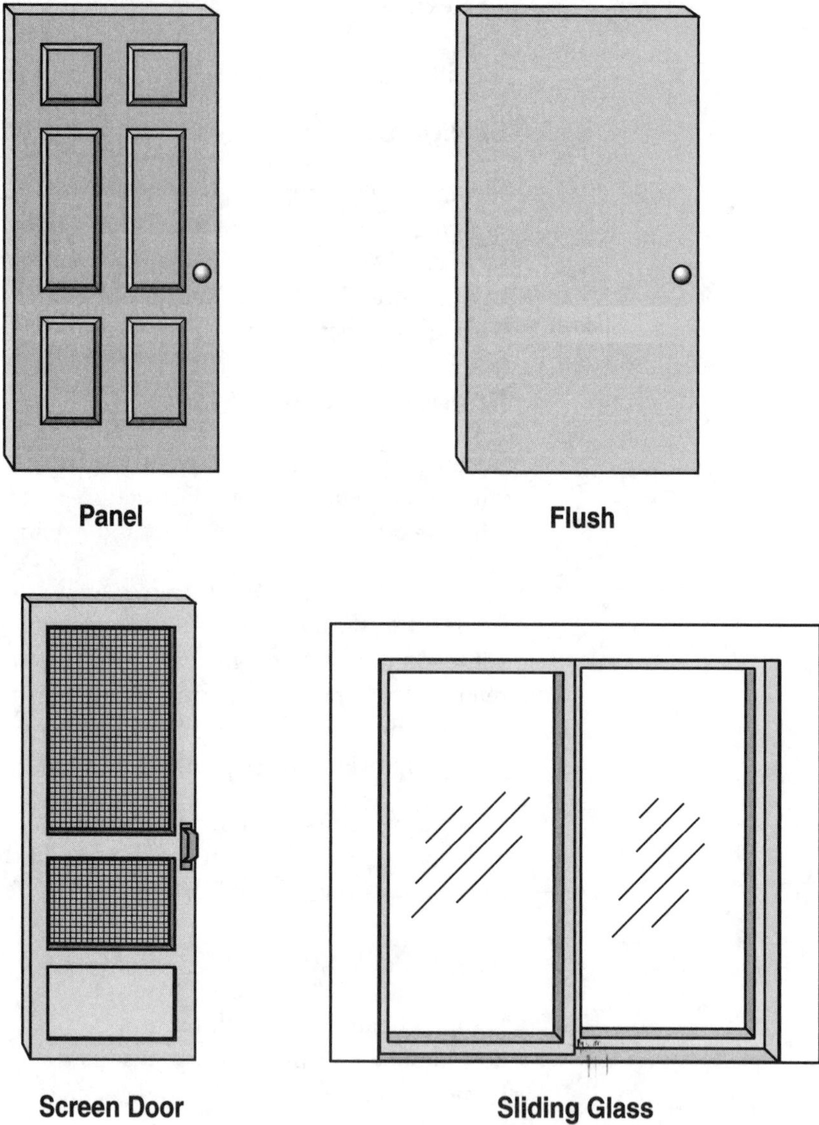

Flush doors

Flush doors are most often constructed of hardwood-face panels bonded to solid cores or hollow cores of light framework. Solid cores are generally preferred for exterior doors because they provide better heat and sound insulation and are more resistant to warping. Hollow-core doors are about one-third as heavy as the solid-core type and are commonly used for interior locations, where heat and sound insulation are not critical.

Panel doors

Available in a variety of designs, panel doors may be used for either interior or exterior application. They consist of stiles (solid vertical members of wood or metal) and rails (solid horizontal members of wood or metal) enclosing flat plywood or raised wood panel fillers or, in some types, a combination of wood and glass panels.

Sliding glass doors

Sliding glass doors have at least one fixed panel and one or more panels that slide in a frame of wood or metal. Like a window sash, the door panels are composed of stiles and rails and may hold either single or insulating glass.

Storm and screen doors

Storm doors are made either with fixed glass panels, to improve weather resistance, or with both screen and glass inserts, to permit ventilation and insect control. In areas with moderate year-round temperatures, screen doors (without glass inserts) are frequently used. Combination doors combine the functions of both storm and screen doors with interchangeable glass and screen panels. Self-storing storm doors contain the equivalent of a two-track window, accommodating two inserts in one track and another in the adjacent track. The glass and screen inserts slide up and down, just as they do in a vertical storm window.

Location of Exterior Doors

Exterior doors control passage in and out of the house. The main entrance door, usually the most attractive and most prominent door, should be located on the street side of the house. The goal is to create a good first impression and make the entry easy to find. The service door leads outside from rooms such as the kitchen, utility room, basement, or garage and is important for good traffic flow in the house. The patio door ties together indoors and outdoors and usually opens from a family room or dining area onto a patio, deck, or terrace.

An exterior door must be tight fitting, weather-stripped to prevent air leaks, and able to offer security against intruders.

■ INTERIOR WALLS AND FINISHING

Interior walls are the partitioning dividers for individual rooms and are usually covered with plasterboard [46], although the older, more expensive process of covering strips of wood lath with plaster also may be used. The terms *drywall* and *wallboard* are synonymous with plasterboard. Plasterboard is finished by a process known as taping and floating. Tape covers the joints between the sheets of plasterboard. Floating is the smoothing out of the walls by the application of a plaster texture over the taped joints and rough edges where nails attach the plasterboard to the wall studs. Texturing created by a heavy layer of a plaster-like finish coat may be applied with a roller onto the plasterboard prior to painting.

The final features added to a home include floor covering, trim, cabinet work, and wall finishings of paint, wallpaper, or paneling.

Floor coverings of vinyl, asphalt tile, wood (either in strips or blocks), carpet, brick, stone, or terrazzo tile are applied over the wood or concrete subflooring.

Trim masks the joints between the walls and ceiling and gives a finished decorator touch to the room. Trim, which is usually wood, should be selected in a style that is complementary to the overall decor of the house.

Lead-Based Paint

The presence of lead in paint used in housing is of major concern because of the danger of lead exposure to adults and especially children. The danger to adults includes high blood pressure, memory and concentration problems, and difficulty during pregnancy. The danger to children includes damage to the brain and nervous system, behavior and learning problems, slowed growth, and hearing loss. Deteriorating paint releases lead; renovations can release large amounts of lead into the home as well as the surrounding soil. Encapsulation using special paints that prevent lead from leaching through to the surface may be the best preventative.

As of 1978, the use of lead-based paint in housing has been prohibited by the federal government. It has been estimated that 83% of homes built prior to 1978 (64 million homes in all) contain lead-based paint. The Residential Lead-Based Paint Hazard Reduction Act of 1992 requires disclosure of the possible presence of lead-based paint in homes built before 1978. As of September 6, 1996, sellers and landlords owning five or more residential dwelling units must comply with disclosure requirements; the law went into effect on December 6, 1996, for sellers and landlords owning four or fewer residential dwelling units. Compliance is the responsibility of the Environmental Protection Agency (EPA). Information on legal requirements is available from the National Lead Information Center, (800) 424-5323, or *www2.epa.gov/lead/forms/lead-hotline-national-lead-information-center*, as well as EPA branches and state health departments.

WEB LINK

www2.epa.gov/lead/forms/lead-hotline-national-lead-information-center

While the law does not require that the seller or landlord conduct any testing or hazard reduction, the seller or landlord must disclose any known presence of lead and provide copies of available lead hazard evaluations and reports. The prospective buyer or renter must

- receive an EPA disclosure pamphlet (or state-approved alternative),
- have 10 days in which to arrange a property inspection, and
- sign a lead warning statement and acknowledgment.

Real estate agents must inform the seller or the landlord of the requirements, make sure that the buyer or the renter has received the necessary documentation, and retain the signed disclosure/acknowledgment statement for three years.

What is the impact of the disclosure law on the market value of affected homes? Because all homes in a given neighborhood, being of roughly the same age and quality of construction, may contain lead-based paint, prospective homebuyers and renters may have little practical alternative.

Cabinet work may be built on the job but is usually prefabricated in the mill. Cabinets should be well constructed to open and close properly and should correspond with the style of the house.

Wall finishing is one of the most important decorator items in the home. Paint and wallpaper should be selected for both beauty and utility. Ceramic, granite, marble, glass, concrete, manufactured stone, and other materials are used as wall, counter, or floor coverings in kitchens, bathrooms, and other rooms.

PLUMBING

The **plumbing system** in a house is actually a number of separate systems, each designed to serve a special function. The water supply system brings water to the house from the city main or from a well and distributes hot and cold water through two sets of pipes. The drainage system collects waste and used water from fixtures and carries it away to a central point for disposal outside the house. The vent piping system carries out of the house all sewer gases that develop in drainage lines. It also equalizes air pressure within the waste system so that waste will flow away and not back up into fixtures. The waste collecting system is needed only when the main waste drain in the house is lower than sewer level under the street or when the house has more than one drainage system. The house connection pipe system, a single pipe, is the waste connection from the house to the city sewer line, to a septic tank, or to some other waste disposal facility.

Plumbing must be installed subject to strict inspections and in accordance with local building codes, which dictate the materials to be used and the method of installation. Sewer pipes are of cast iron, concrete, or plastic, while water pipes are of copper, plastic, or galvanized iron. Recently, wrought-drawn copper and plastic have been used more frequently because they eliminate piping joints in the foundation slab.

Plumbing Fixtures

Bathtubs, toilets, and sinks are made of cast iron or pressed steel coated with enamel, as well as ceramic, glass, and other materials. Plumbing fixtures have relatively long lives and often are replaced because of their obsolete style long before they have worn out.

Water Heaters

A water heater is basically an insulated metal tank that does just what its name implies. Water is almost always heated by gas or electricity. The size needed will depend on several factors including the number of people in the household, the hot water consumption during peak use periods for activities such as bathing or laundering, the recovery time required by the tank, and fuel costs in the area. Manufacturers recommend that the tank be placed closest to the point of use.

Water heaters are available in several capacities for residential use, ranging from 17 gallons up to 80 gallons. After water is heated to a predetermined temperature, the heater automatically shuts off. When hot water is drained off, cold water replaces it, and the heating unit turns on automatically. An on-demand system, which means that the water isn't heated until it is required, is gaining popularity because of its potential energy savings.

HEATING AND AIR-CONDITIONING

Warm-air heating systems are most prevalent in today's houses. A forced warm-air system consists of a furnace, warm-air distributing ducts, and ducts for the return of cool air. All supply ducts should be well insulated and joints and other openings taped to prevent air leaks.

Bacteria, Fungi, and Molds

These biological agents live in air ducts, air-conditioning and heating units, and humidifiers and between wallboards and drywall. They can cause disease, allergic reactions, and respiratory illness.

The appraiser may not have the knowledge or experience needed to determine the cost of correcting environmental problems such as those discussed in this unit. What the appraiser can do, however, is conduct a conscien-tious inspection of the subject property and recommend that the client bring in a qualified environmental consultant if contamination is suspected.

Even after an environmental problem has been corrected, however, the property may still suffer from what appraisers call *stigmatization*. This term refers to a continuing decline in the value of a property because of a falsely perceived environmental problem—that is, a stigmatized property may continue to lose value even though the environmental problem has been fixed or perhaps never even existed.

Stigmatization can also refer to property that has acquired an undesirable reputation because of some event that occurred on or near it, such as a violent crime or personal tragedy. A rumor suggesting that a house is haunted is another example of stigmatization.

Stigmatization issues are not about a property's physical defects but rather about opinions or perceptions, however misguided, that brand the property as undesirable. Certain issues may be the subject of state laws intended to protect property owners, in which case the appraiser could be held liable for improper disclosure. The appraiser should seek legal counsel when dealing with such properties.

Each furnace has a capacity rated in British Thermal Units (BTUs). The number of BTUs given represents the furnace's heat output from gas, oil, or electric firing. A heating and cooling engineer can determine the cubic area of the house, as well as its construction, insulation, and window and door sizes. From this data, the engineer can compute the furnace capacity required to provide heat for the house in the coldest possible weather.

All gas pipes for heating and cooking are made of black iron. Gas pipes are installed in the walls or overhead in the attic, where adequate ventilation is possible. They are never placed in the slab.

Almost all new homes today are centrally air-conditioned. Air-conditioning units are rated either in BTUs or in tons. Twelve thousand BTUs are the equivalent of a one-ton capacity. An engineer can determine the measurements and problems inherent in the construction and layout of the space and from this information can specify the cooling capacity required to adequately service the space or house.

Combination heating and cooling systems are common in new homes. The most prevalent is the conventional warm-air heating system with a cooling unit attached. The same ducts and blower that distribute warm air are used to distribute cool air. The cooling unit is similar to a large air conditioner.

Many heating experts believe the heat pump will eventually replace today's conventional combination heating and cooling systems. The small heat pump is a single piece of equipment that uses the same components for heating or cooling. The most commonly used system for small heat pumps takes heat out of the ground or air in winter to warm the air in the house and takes warm air out of the house in summer, replacing it with cooler air. The main drawback to the heat pump has been its initial cost. Once installed, however, it operates very economically and requires little maintenance. It works most efficiently in climates where winter weather is not severe, but new improvements make it adequate even in northern states.

Solar Heating

The increased demand for fossil fuels has forced builders to look for new sources of energy. One of the most promising sources of heat for residential buildings is solar energy. There are two methods for gathering solar energy: passive and active. Figure 7.5 shows the simplest form of **solar heating**—a passive system in which windows on the south side of a house take advantage of winter sunlight. A passive system can be improved inside the house by using water-filled containers that are warmed by the sun during the day and radiate warmth into the room during the night. Such a system takes up space inside the home, however, and is not compatible with most decorating schemes. If those considerations are unimportant and if there is adequate available sunlight, a passive solar heating system can be installed easily and at low cost.

Most solar heating units suitable for residential use are active systems that operate by gathering the heat from the sun's rays with one or more solar collectors, as shown in Figure 7.14. Water or air is forced through a series of pipes in the solar collector to be heated by the sun's rays. The hot air or water is then stored in a heavily insulated storage tank until it is needed to heat the house. The heat production of a solar system is limited by both storage capacity and the need for good (sunny) weather, which means that most such systems must have an independent heating unit for backup. There is as yet no economical system that uses solar power to air-condition a home. Solar heaters for swimming pools continue to provide a low-cost way of heating pool water.

FIGURE 7.14
Active Solar Water Heating System

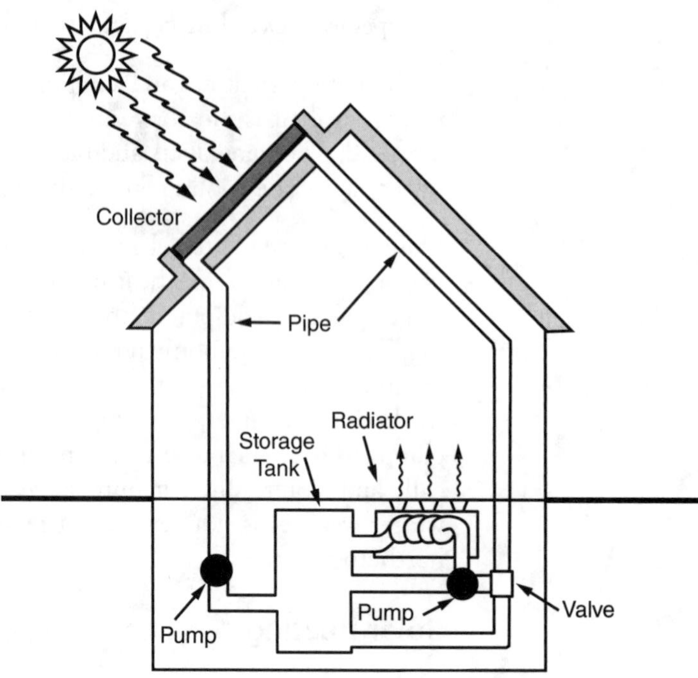

■ ELECTRICAL SYSTEM

A good residential **electrical system** has three important characteristics. First, it must meet all National Electrical Code (NEC) safety requirements: each major appliance should have its own circuit, and lighting circuits should be isolated from electrical equipment that causes fluctuations in voltage. Second, the system must meet the home's existing needs and have the capacity to accommodate room additions and new appliances. Finally, it should be convenient; there should be enough switches, lights, and outlets located so that occupants will not have to walk in the dark or use extension cords.

Electrical service from the power company is brought into the home through the transformer and the meter into a circuit breaker box (or a fuse panel in older homes). The circuit breaker box is the distribution panel for the many electrical circuits in the house. In case of a power overload, the heat generated by the additional flow of electrical power will cause the circuit breaker to open at the breaker box, thus reducing the possibility of electrical fires. The architect or the builder is responsible for adhering to local building codes, which regulate electrical wiring. All electrical installations are inspected by the local building authorities, which assures the homeowner of the system's compliance with the building codes.

Power Requirements

Residential wiring circuits are rated by the voltage they are designed to carry. In the past, most residences were wired for only 110-volt capacity. Today, because of the many built-in appliances in use, 220-volt to 240-volt service is generally necessary. Amperage, the strength of a current expressed in amperes, is shown on the circuit breaker panel. The circuit breaker panel (or fuse panel) should have a capacity of at least 100 amperes. A larger service (150 to 200 or more amperes) may be needed if there is electric heat, an electric range, or if the house has more than 3,000 square feet. New wiring will be required if the existing board is only 30 to 60 amperes in capacity. If there are fewer than eight or 10 circuits, it will probably be necessary to add more. Each circuit is represented by a separate circuit breaker or fuse. A house with a lot of electrical equipment may require 15 to 20 or more circuits.

Electromagnetic Fields

While the power of lightning is unmistakable, most people fail to realize that electricity is always around us and that the earth's magnetic field creates measurable electrical currents no matter where we are. While there is as yet no conclusive evidence of any harmful effects of electromagnetic fields (EMFs), some studies have suggested a correlation between high levels of EMFs and certain types of cancers, such as leukemia. It should be noted that the EMFs linked to a slight increase in incidence of leukemia in one study were produced by continued exposure to high-voltage transmission lines, and not to the kind of fields created by ordinary home wiring and appliances. The most recent study to date indicates that there are, in fact, no measurable effects of even prolonged exposure to high-voltage transmission lines. Nevertheless, public perception of a problem (even if in error) may have an effect on the value of property located close to high-voltage transmission lines.

In the United States, high-voltage transmission lines operate at voltages between 50 and 765 kilovolts (kV), with each kV equal to 1,000 volts. Distribution lines that feed off transmission lines operate at less than 50 kV. Both types of lines carry considerably more power than the ordinary household system of 240 volts. To err on the side of safety, even with regard to ordinary household current and appliances, local utility companies are beginning to offer EMF assessments in which measurements of EMFs are made throughout the home. As a simple precaution, for instance, residents may be warned against having appliances, such as a clock radio or telephone, too close to the head of a bed or other location where prolonged exposure is possible.

Green Building

A **green building** is a structure that is designed, sited, built, maintained, operated, and removed—basically, the complete building life cycle—to meet certain objectives, such as protecting the occupants' health and using energy, water, and other resources more efficiently to help reduce the negative impact on the environment.

WEB LINK
www.usgbc.org

The United States Green Building Council (USGBC) has developed the **Leadership in Energy and Environmental Design (LEED)** green building rating system, which is the nationally accepted benchmark for the design, construction, and operation of high performance green buildings. Information about the rating system and resources can be found at www.usgbc.org.

WEB LINK
www.energystar.gov

The United States Environmental Protection Agency's **Energy Star** program rates commercial buildings for energy efficiency and provides Energy Star qualifications for new homes that meet its standards for energy efficient building design. Information is available at www.energystar.gov.

Exercise 7-2

1. Where are solid-core and hollow-core doors generally used? Why?
2. Two of the separate plumbing systems in a house are the vent piping system and the water supply system. What is the purpose of each?
3. What is the major disadvantage of the heat pump?
4. List three important characteristics of a residential electrical system.
5. What is the basic difference between balloon and platform construction? Which is preferred?
6. Define the following features of residential construction and give the purpose of each:
   a. Firestopping
   b. Circuit breaker box
   c. Insulation
   d. Monolithic slab
   e. Sill

Check your answers against those in the answer key at the back of the book.

Basic Building Terms

The following building terms and concepts were introduced or discussed in this unit. If you are not sure of the meaning or application of any of these terms, restudy that section of the unit.

110-volt wiring
220-volt wiring
amperage
anchor bolt
architectural style
asbestos
balloon frame
BTUs
building code
building plan (blueprint)
building specifications
casement window
circuit breaker box
collar beam
concrete slab foundation
cornice
crawlspace
double-hung window
drainage system
eave
electromagnetic fields (EMFs)
exposed rafter roof framing
fascia board
fenestration
firestops
floating
floating slab
floor joist
flush doors
footing
foundation wall
frame
framing
green building
frieze board
insulation
jalousie window
joist and rafter roof
lead-based paint
monolithic slab
panel doors
pedestal
pier
pier and beam foundation
piling
plate
platform frame
plasterboard
post and beam frame
rafter
rails
ribbon board
ridge
R-value
sheathing
siding
sill (beam)
sliding window
solar collector
solar heating
stiles
stud
taping
truss roof framing
urea-formaldehyde
veneer
vent piping system
weep hole

■ SUMMARY

To appraise real estate successfully, an appraiser must know the fundamentals of building construction, from the design and approval process to basic construction techniques and materials. Carefully prepared plans and specifications must adhere to at least the minimum construction standards established by local building codes. Appropriate engineering is necessary to determine site and foundation requirements.

A variety of house styles fall within the two broad categories of traditional and contemporary, with budget, space, and living requirements dictating size. A house should be oriented to take maximum advantage of its site, including the potential for solar heat.

The typical wood-frame house will make use of construction techniques based on a concrete slab or pier and beam foundation. A wide variety of exterior and interior wall finishes is available to suit homeowner requirements. Doors and windows also offer opportunities for individualization.

Plumbing fixtures must take into account the type of water available while suiting the needs of the residents. The choice of heating and/or cooling system is also important. The electrical system should be adequate for present as well as anticipated usage.

Environmental hazards, such as asbestos, radon gas, urea-formaldehyde foam insulation, lead-based paint, and mold and other biological contaminants can negatively affect the value of real estate. Appraisers are not expected to be experts in the detection of hazardous substances. If any of these conditions are suspected, a formal environmental assessment may be recommended and the appraisal made subject to the results of that determination.

A new field called green building is gaining momentum to help reduce and to ultimately eliminate the impact of buildings on the environment and human health.

FIGURE 7.15
Anatomy of a House

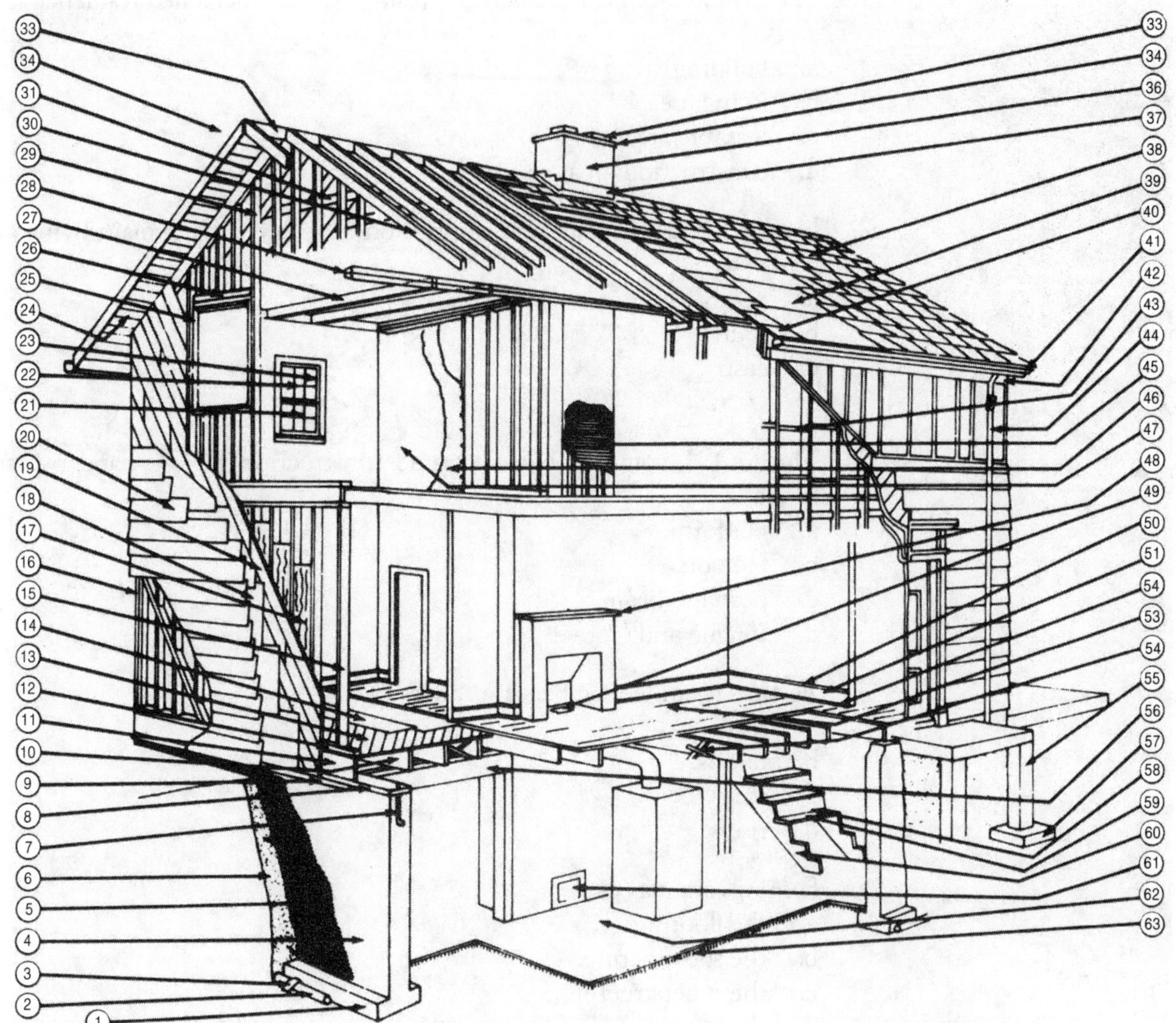

1. FOOTING
2. FOUNDATION DRAIN TILE
3. CRUSHED WASHED STONE
4. FOUNDATION WALL
5. DAMPPROOFING OR WEATHERPROOFING
6. BACKFILL
7. ANCHOR BOLT
8. SILL PLATE
9. TERMITE SHIELD
10. FLOOR JOIST
11. BAND OR BOX BEAM
12. SOLE PLATE
13. SUBFLOORING
14. BUILDING PAPER
15. WALL STUD
16. CORNER STUDS
17. INSULATION
18. HOUSE WRAP
19. WALL SHEATHING
20. SIDING
21. MULLION
22. MUNTIN
23. WINDOW SASH
24. EAVE (ROOF PROJECTION)
25. WINDOW JAMB TRIM
26. WINDOW HEADER
27. CEILING JOIST
28. TOP AND TIE PLATES
29. GABLE STUD
30. RAFTERS
31. COLLAR TIES
32. GABLE END OF ROOF
33. RIDGE BEAM
34. CHIMNEY FLUES
35. CHIMNEY CAP
36. CHIMNEY
37. CHIMNEY FLASHING
38. ROOFING SHINGLES
39. ROOFING FELT/ICE AND WATER MEMBRANE
40. ROOF SHEATHING
41. EAVE TROUGH OR GUTTER
42. FRIEZE BOARD
43. FIRESTOP
44. DOWNSPOUT
45. LATHS
46. PLASTERBOARD
47. PLASTER FINISH
48. MANTEL
49. ASH DUMP
50. BASE TOP MOULDING
51. BASEBOARD
52. SHOE MOULDING
53. FINISH MOULDING
54. CROSS BRIDGING
55. PIER
56. GIRDER
57. FOOTING
58. RISER
59. TREAD
60. STRINGER
61. CLEANOUT DOOR
62. CONCRETE BASEMENT FLOOR
63. CRUSHED WASHED STONE

■ REVIEW QUESTIONS

1. The standard of measurement for a single-family detached residence is the gross
   a. building area.
   b. living area.
   c. leasable area.
   d. construction area.

2. Ideally, a house should be positioned on its lot so that the main living areas face
   a. north.
   b. south.
   c. east.
   d. west.

3. The *MOST* common type of frame construction for one- and two-story houses is
   a. platform.
   b. balloon.
   c. post and beam.
   d. tongue and groove.

4. Vertical framing members are called
   a. joists.
   b. rafters.
   c. studs.
   d. risers.

5. Footings are part of
   a. the flooring.
   b. the substructure.
   c. the superstructure.
   d. the frieze board.

6. The skeleton members of a building to which the interior and exterior walls are attached are called its
   a. foundation walls.
   b. siding.
   c. framing.
   d. sheathing.

7. The interface between the roof and chimney is called
   a. a footing.
   b. the foundation.
   c. flashing.
   d. lattice.

8. Electrical towers create
   a. electromagnetic fields.
   b. magnetic charges.
   c. thermal inductions.
   d. flooding.

9. The efficiency of insulation is measured by its
   a. SEER value.
   b. R value.
   c. amperage.
   d. BTUs.

10. The power of an electrical line is measured in
    a. amperage.
    b. R value.
    c. SEER value.
    d. BTUs.

11. Circuit breakers
    a. protect the electrical lines from overload.
    b. protect the plumbing from leaks.
    c. alert the homeowner when there is a break-in.
    d. notify the fire department when there is a short in an electrical line.

12. Plumbing fixtures are
    a. removed by a property seller.
    b. real property.
    c. chattel.
    d. treated as personal property in a real estate transaction.

13. As of what year did the federal government ban the use of lead-based paint in housing?
    a. 1988
    b. 1998
    c. There is no ban on lead-based paint
    d. 1978

14. When earth touches wood, a major problem could be
    a. spiders.
    b. beetles.
    c. termites.
    d. radon.

15. Gross living area (GLA) is measured
    a. using interior dimensions.
    b. using exterior dimensions.
    c. only in cubic feet.
    d. only in square feet.

For each of the following, describe the construction technique illustrated in Figure 7.15.

16. Foundation wall framing

17. Exterior walls

18. Interior walls

19. Window

20. Floor coverings

Check your answers against those in the answer key at the back of the book.

UNIT EIGHT

DATA COLLECTION

LEARNING OBJECTIVES

When you have completed this unit, you will be able to

- identify the steps in the appraisal process,
- use the Data Bank to determine and find information,
- evaluate the characteristics of a neighborhood,
- describe the four stages in the life cycle of a neighborhood,
- complete the Neighborhood, Site, and Improvements sections of the URAR form,
- explain what is meant by an arm's-length transaction,
- calculate the cash equivalency of a property sale, and
- explain how the Uniform Appraisal Dataset affects the appraisal report.

KEY TERMS

air rights
arm's-length transaction
assemblage
cash equivalency
contract rent
conventional lender
Data Bank
data source list
depreciation
easement
economic base
external obselescence
functional obsolescence
GEDR (growth, equilibruim, decline, and revitalization)
leased fee
leasehold interest
market rent
mineral rights
neighborhood boundaries
physical deterioration
plottage
sales comparison approach
scheduled rent
seller financing
stages of life cycle
tax base
Uniform Appraisal Dataset (UAD)

■ OVERVIEW

At every step in the appraisal process, an appraiser makes use of data that has been collected and carefully analyzed for its applicability to the property being appraised. In this unit, you will review the steps in the appraisal process that require the collection of a variety of data from a variety of sources. You will examine a suggested data bank of sources, which you may supplement.

You will also learn how to use forms to help ensure the collection of adequate data regarding the subject property's neighborhood, as well as the subject site and building.

In this unit, you will begin to trace the progress of a typical appraisal using the sales comparison approach by following the applicable steps outlined in the appraisal flowchart introduced in Unit 6. A single-family residence and lot will be discussed as the sales comparison method and the general techniques used in valuing vacant sites are covered in this unit and Units 9 and 12. At the end of Unit 12, you will be given the information needed to complete your own appraisal analysis of a single-family residence using the sales comparison approach.

■ IDENTIFY THE PROBLEM

Prior to accepting an assignment, the appraiser must determine whether he or she has the skills to perform the job competently. According to *USPAP*'s Competency Rule, an appraiser who lacks the necessary knowledge or experience to perform a specific appraisal service must disclose this fact to the client before accepting the job. The appraiser may still accept the assignment, however, by indicating how the competence necessary to complete the assignment will be acquired, such as by associating with a qualified appraiser or retaining someone who, in fact, does possess the required knowledge or experience.

Of course, an appraiser may accept an assignment and not realize until later that the job is beyond the appraiser's skill level or that the assignment will require more time than the appraiser has available in order to produce competent results. At the point of such discovery, the appraiser is obligated to notify the client and should also indicate the steps that will be taken to become competent, if the assignment is to be completed.

Once the competency issue has been settled, the first step in the appraisal process is to define the problem. The appraiser begins by

- identifying the subject property by its mailing address and by its more precise legal description,
- identifying the property rights to be appraised,
- identifying the client and other intended users of the report,
- identifying the intended use of the report,
- defining the value sought—most often the market value for a prospective sale or loan,
- specifying the effective date of the appraisal—usually a date near or on the day the property is inspected, and
- determining any conditions limiting the scope of use of the appraisal.

Throughout this book, we will assume that the appraiser's task is to determine the market value of the subject property.

Property Rights Conveyed

The majority of residential appraisals are of property held in fee simple ownership; that is, all of the rights of ownership are held by the current property owner. Sometimes, however, the different rights of ownership are separated and held by more than one person.

A frequent example of separation of rights of ownership of residential property involves **mineral rights**. In areas that are suspected of containing oil or gas deposits, a transfer of title to real estate frequently will withhold mineral rights, title to which is retained by the transferor (the person making the transfer). The right to test for and remove the minerals may never be exercised; however, the fact that mineral rights have been separated from the other rights of ownership should be noted by the appraiser. The appraiser should also note any effect that less than fee simple ownership may be expected to have on value. If all properties in the area carry a similar reservation of mineral or other rights, there is likely to be little or no effect on market value.

A common example of a transfer of only a partial interest in commercial property is the transfer of developmental **air rights**. The fact that air rights can be transferred separately may allow a developer to accumulate the development rights of several different parcels to erect a single building that would otherwise violate zoning building height restrictions. The property from which development rights have been transferred will have its value reduced accordingly.

An **easement** creates a benefit to the dominant tenement (the land to which the easement provides ingress and egress) and a detriment to the servient tenement (the land over which the easement runs).

The full rights of ownership also include the right to dispose of the property, such as by sale, lease, or will. If the property has already been leased, however, the **leased fee** estate retained by the lessor (landlord) must be valued in light of the existing lease. The lessee—the holder of the lease—has the **leasehold interest** at the contract or **scheduled rent** agreed to between lessor and lessee. The leasehold interest will have value depending on the relationship of the **contract rent** to the prevailing **market rent** (an estimate of a property's rent potential). If market rents are higher than the rent the current lease provides, the difference between them determines the value of the leasehold interest.

In all of these examples, an appraisal must take into account the exact property interest that is being valued.

Exercise 8-1

The exercises in this unit and in Unit 12 give you information on the sample appraisal you will be carrying out as you study the sales comparison approach. You are to complete each exercise, referring to the explanation just covered, if needed. Then, check your results against those given in the Answer Key at the back of this book. If necessary, correct your responses before proceeding to the next text discussion.

The single-family residence located at 2130 West Franklin Street, Midstate, Illinois, is to be appraised as part of a loan refinancing. State the problem, indicating the value that is being sought and the appraisal method that will be used to achieve it.

Check your answer against the one in the answer key at the back of the book.

■ DETERMINE THE SCOPE OF WORK

Scope of work encompasses the amount and type of information researched and the analysis applied in the appraisal development process. The appraisal report must present enough information to allow the client and other intended users to understand it.

The appraiser's scope of work normally is considered acceptable when it matches or exceeds what the client and other users expect, and when the appraiser has performed the assignment in line with what peers would do under the same or similar assignments.

In the second step of the appraisal process, the appraiser determines the kinds of data that must be collected and the sources of that data. Regardless of the specific appraisal approach used, certain data must always be obtained—information about the region, city, and neighborhood, as well as facts about the property being appraised. When the sales comparison approach is used, sales data on comparable properties also must be obtained.

■ GATHER, RECORD, VERIFY, AND ANALYZE THE NECESSARY DATA

The appraisal process, as discussed in Unit 6, requires the collection or verification of data at almost every stage. Knowledge of the sources of available data and their reliability is essential if an appraisal is to be performed properly.

In step 3 of the appraisal process, as shown in the flowchart in Figure 6.1, five categories of data are needed to form a reliable opinion of value:

- General data on the geographic and economic features of the nation, region, city, and neighborhood
- Specific data on the subject site and improvements—including a detailed physical description
- Sales data on comparable properties—to apply the sales comparison approach

- Cost data on construction of a like property and accrued depreciation data on the subject property—to apply the cost approach
- Income and expense data from properties similar to the subject—to apply the income capitalization approach; sales and income data from properties similar to the subject that have been sold in the same market area and were rented at the time of the sale—to apply the gross rent multiplier method, a form of income approach for residential properties

Without knowledge of the sources and reliability of available data, the appraiser would be unable to perform the job properly. The appraisal report must contain a detailed description of the work performed, in accordance with *USPAP* requirements. The type of property being appraised will dictate the kinds of data that must be collected. A factory in an industrial area, for instance, will require more services than a home in a residential area. Thus, the appraiser makes an integrated analysis, moving from general data to data required for the specific appraisal approach, always keeping the subject property in mind.

Uniform Appraisal Dataset

The subprime mortgage crisis pointed out the need to enhance the quality of the data that is at the heart of the appraisal process, as well as to make it more consistent. At the direction of FHFA, Fannie Mae and Freddie Mac have, among other projects, worked together to develop the Uniform Appraisal Dataset (UAD). As of September 1, 2011, the UAD applies to all data elements required to complete the

- Uniform Residential Appraisal Report (Fannie Mae Form 1004);
- Individual Condominium Unit Appraisal Report (Fannie Mae Form 1073);
- Exterior-Only Inspection Individual Condominium Unit Appraisal Report (Fannie Mae Form 1075); and
- Exterior-Only Inspection Residential Appraisal Report (Fannie Mae Form 2055).

WEB LINK

www.fanniemae.com/singlefamily/uniform-appraisal-dataset

The UAD thus applies to conventional mortgage loans sold to Fannie Mae and Freddie Mac and will be referred to in this unit as well as in later units of this book.

THE DATA BANK

This section introduces you to some of the many sources of information available to appraisers as well as to property owners. By learning as much as possible about the economic, political, social, and environmental conditions of the area where a property is located, the appraiser can begin to assimilate the information needed to make an informed judgment, that is, one based on the appropriate indicators of market value.

Figure 8.1 is the **Data Bank**. You will be referring to it throughout the rest of this book to help you determine the types of information required for an appraisal and where the information can be found.

FIGURE 8.1
Data Bank

DATA SOURCE LIST

1. Personal inspection
2. Seller
3. Buyer
4. Broker
5. Salesperson
6. Register of deeds
7. Title reports
8. Transfer maps or books
9. Leases
10. Mortgages
11. Banks and other lending institutions
12. City hall or county courthouse
13. Assessor's office
14. Published information on transfers, leases, or assessed valuation
15. Property managers or owners
16. Building and architectural plans
17. Accountants
18. Financial statements
19. Building architects, contractors, and engineers
20. County or city engineering commission
21. Regional or county government officials
22. Area planning commissions
23. Highway commissioner's office, road commission
24. Newspaper and magazine articles
25. Multiple-listing systems
26. Cost manuals (state, local, private)
27. Local material suppliers
28. Public utility companies
29. United States Bureau of the Census
30. Department of Commerce
31. Federal Housing Administration
32. Local chamber of commerce
33. Government councils
34. Local board of REALTORS®
35. National, state, or local association of home builders
36. Public transportation officials
37. Other appraisers
38. Professional journals
39. Railroad and transit authorities or companies
40. Labor organizations
41. Employment agencies
42. Plats
43. Neighbors
44. Area maps (topographic,soil)
45. Airlines and bus lines, moving companies
46.
47.
48.
49.
50.

A. REGIONAL, CITY, NEIGHBORHOOD DATA

Types of Information	Sources
Topograph	44
Natural resources	32, 44
Climate	32
Public transportation:	
Air	32, 45
Rail	39, 45
Bus	36, 45
Subway	36, 45
Route maps	1, 36
Expressways	23, 44
Traffic paterns	12, 20, 22, 23, 36
Population trends	22, 24, 29, 32, 33
Family size	22
Zoning	12, 20, 22
Building codes	12, 19, 20
Political organization, policies, and personnel	12, 21
Employment level	11, 32, 33, 40
Professions, trades, or skills required	32
Level of business activity and growth	11, 24, 32
Average family income	22, 29, 30, 32
Rents and lease features	9, 15, 34
Percentage of vacancies	4, 31, 34
New building (amount and kind)	15, 24, 30, 34, 35
Building permits issues	12, 20
Bank deposits and loans	11, 32
Perentage of home ownership	4, 29, 34
Tax structure and rates	12, 13
Building permits issued	12, 20

Types of Information	Sources
Electrical power consumption and new hookups	28
Assessments	12, 13
Utilites or improvements available (streets, curbs, sidewalks; water; electricity; telephone; gas; sewers)	12, 28
Percent built up	12, 34
Neighborhood boundaries	1, 4, 12, 42
Predominant type of building	1, 13, 19, 22
Typical age of buildings	1,13, 15, 19
Condition of buildings	1, 22, 33, 37
Price range of typical properties	4, 7, 15, 31, 34
Marketability	4, 15
Life cycles	4, 37
Land value trend	4, 13, 37
Location of facilities: schools; shopping; recreational; cultural; religious	1, 22, 44
Avenues of approach	1, 20
Types of services offered	28
Availability of personnel	22, 32
Employee amenities (shopping, eating, and banking facilities)	1
Marketing area	22, 32
Competition	1, 32
Types of industry (light, heavy)	32
Sources of raw materials	32
Hazards and nuisances	1, 43
Deed restrictions	6, 7
Changing use of area	4, 24

FIGURE 8.1
Data Bank (continued)

B. SITE DATA	
Types of Information	**Sources**
Legal description	6
Dimensions and area	1, 6, 42
Street frontage	1, 6, 42
Location in block	6, 42
Topography	6, 44
Topsoil and drainage	19, 44
Landscaping	1
Improvements:	
Streets, curbs, sidewalks	1, 12, 20
Water; electricity; telphone; gas	28
Sewers	1, 12, 20
Tax rates and assessed valuation	12, 13
Liens and special assessments	7, 13
Zoning, codes, or regulations	12, 20, 22
Easements and encroachments	6
Status of title	7

C. BUILDING DATA	
Types of Information	**Sources**
Architectural style	1
Date of construction and additions	6, 13, 20
Placement of building on land	1, 20, 44
Dimensions and floor area	16, 42
Floor plans(s)	16, 20
Construction materials used (exterior and interior)	16, 19, 27
Utilities available	1, 28, 32
Interior utility and other installations:	1, 13, 16
Heating and air-conditioning	
Plumbing	
Wiring	
Special equipment, such as elevators	
Exceptions to zoning, codes, or regulations	6, 20, 22
Status of title	7
Mortgages and liens	6, 11
Condition of building	1, 13, 22

D. SALES AND COST DATA	
Types of Information	**Sources**
Date of sale	1 to 6, 25
Sales price	1 to 6, 25
Name of buyer and seller	1 to 6, 25
Deed book and page	6, 8, 37
Reasons for sale and purchase	2 to 5
Building reproduction cost	19, 26, 27, 40
Building replacement cost	19, 26, 27, 40
Depreciation factors:	1, 16, 19, 22, 26
Physical deterioration	
Functional obsolescence	
External obsolescence	

E. INCOME AND EXPENSE DATA	
Types of Information	**Sources**
Income data (both subject and comparable properties):	
Annual income	18
Current lease terms	1, 15
Occupancy history	15, 18
Collection loss history	15, 18
Fixed expense data (both subject and comparable properties):	13, 15, 18, 38
Real estate taxes	
Insurance	
Operating expense data (both subject and comparable properties):	13, 15, 18, 35
Management	
Payroll	
Legal and accounting	
Maintenance	
Repairs	
Supplies	
Painting and decorating	
Fuel	
Electricity	
Miscellaneous	
Reserves for replacement	1, 18, 26

Surfing the Net

Of course, no source list would be current without reference to the many sources now accessible via the internet. From its beginnings 50 years ago as a way for military information to be transmitted, then a method of communication for university researchers, the internet has been segmented into the electronic access routes that we now call the web and is accessible to virtually anyone with a computer or smart phone.

Federal agencies, states, and many municipalities now have their own websites and provide a continually replenished supply of census, employment, building, and other data.

Throughout the text and in the first appendix, we have provided the names and web addresses of those organizations we feel would be most useful to an appraiser. No doubt you will add many more websites to the list as you progress through your study of appraising.

The Data Source List

The first part of the Data Bank lists 45 typical sources that supply the information required for a real estate appraisal. You can add to the list in the spaces numbered 46 through 50. Many of the sources have websites that provide a convenient way to access updated information.

The Data Bank also contains eight lists that indicate the most appropriate sources for the various types of data necessary at every step in the appraisal process. Each type of listed information is keyed to one or more of the 45 sources of information itemized in the source list. You can add references to any other sources that you have found useful. Here's how the Data Bank works.

IN PRACTICE

In inspecting a site in a new subdivision, you notice that construction work has begun along both sides of the roadway. There are no workers present to question, however. How can you find out what kind of work is under way?

In Data Bank List B, "Site Data," you look up "Improvements" and find four possible sources of information—source list numbers 1, 12, 20, and 28. The sources are (1) personal inspection, (12) city hall or county courthouse, (20) county or city engineering commission, and (28) public utility companies. Because you have already inspected the property personally, you would contact the other sources, the most pertinent one first. In this case, the county or city engineering commission probably could tell you the reason for the construction activity. There may be a website on which announcements of construction activity are posted. If the activity involves a private project, the department that issues building permits should have the information that you want.

National and regional trends

The real estate marketplace may be defined primarily by local custom and needs, but it is strongly influenced by national and regional matters. An important area of national influence is real estate financing. The secondary market in residential mortgages and the necessity to market some commercial properties on a national basis also have given real estate financing a truly national perspective.

Demographic studies have revealed both short-term and long-term patterns in population movements across the country. Workers generally will follow employment opportunities, and in the 1970s and 1980s the oil states (Texas, Louisiana, Oklahoma, and Colorado) attracted a great many former auto and steel industry personnel from states like Michigan, Ohio, and Pennsylvania. When the oil industry also proved vulnerable, some workers stayed on, but others returned to their former places of residence. The latest energy boom has been in states, such as Texas, Montana, and the Dakotas, permitting extraction of oil and natural gas from shale rock. Information on the energy industry is available from the U.S. Energy Information Administration, www.eia.gov.

www.eia.gov

The same phenomenon occurred at the beginning of this century, when some of the high-flying high-tech companies in the San Francisco Bay Area succumbed to the effects of too much competition and vastly overoptimistic market projections. We have seen the cycle begin again, as successful companies like Google and Facebook have revitalized the job market in Silicon Valley, but have made the San Francisco Peninsula one of the most expensive places to live in the United States.

Factors other than employment also dictate population shifts. The demographics of an aging populace indicate that a certain percentage of retirees from the Midwest and Northeast continue to choose to relocate to an affordable warmer climate, such as Arizona, Florida, Nevada, and North Carolina, contributing to the rapid population growth in those areas.

The national economy affects the real estate marketplace most visibly during periods of recession and inflation. When demand for goods and services declines on a national basis, it may be impossible for a region or state to avoid at least some of the consequences.

Economic base

The level of business activity in a community—particularly activity that brings income into the community from surrounding areas—defines its **economic base**. A range of businesses, from retail stores and professional offices to small-scale and large-scale manufacturing plants, can provide employment opportunities as well as the resources that allow local residents and businesses to spend their funds on local goods and services. A community's economic base also helps determine the **tax base** from which the community can draw financial support for establishment and maintenance of infrastructure (roads, bridges) and services essential to both businesses and residents.

Communities that do not have a substantial economic base in relation to their overall size are less able to provide the facilities and services that attract new residents and businesses. The "bedroom suburb" that relies on neighboring towns for products and services also must rely on the willingness and ability of residents to carry a tax load sufficient to meet local needs. The community with a reasonable amount of retail business development benefits from sales tax and other tax revenue. Furthermore, with a strong economic base, a community becomes more desirable for both businesses and residents, and that desirability is reflected in higher property values.

Examination of a community's economic base tells an appraiser something about the community's long-term economic viability and, thus, its likely ability to sustain real estate values.

Local area and neighborhood

Even communities with only a few thousand residents may have well-differentiated geographic and neighborhood divisions. In this age of the tract house, neighborhoods within large communities generally are referred to by the name under which the tract was subdivided or sold. Sometimes a business district defines a local area or neighborhood. Housing growth tends to radiate outward from the business hub.

Access to shopping, schools, and places of employment are all factors that make one area or neighborhood more desirable than another. The defined boundaries of a neighborhood also are important in determining whether other properties can be considered "comparable" to the property being appraised. Later in this unit, you will learn the property characteristics (building size, quality of construction, etc.) the appraiser tries to match when considering sales of recently sold properties. Location is the most important factor in comparing other properties with the subject.

Site and improvements

Individual building lots often are more valuable when combined with other lots in a single parcel. **Assemblage** is the process of combining adjacent lots, and the increase in value that may result from ownership of the larger parcel is called **plottage**. Individual lot owners are compensated for their properties at least partly on the basis of the ultimate value of the assembled parcel. The last properties to be sold tend to command a higher price than those first sold. Nevertheless, there has been more than one example of the last holdout who wanted such an outrageous price that the offer to purchase was rescinded. More than one office or apartment project has been redesigned around a small home or business building whose owner overestimated the developer's budget and patience.

A highest and best use study should take into account the site's present zoning, physical characteristics, and existing structures. Even a relatively new building in good condition may warrant destruction if a larger building with greater profit potential can be erected on the same site.

Agricultural land entails special considerations. Soil and water testing will reveal the suitability of the land for specific crops as well as the presence of any contaminants. The necessity and availability of water for irrigation and the drainage capacity of the soil also must be taken into account. If the site contains wetlands, they may be subject to federal supervision. Other federal and state regulations may limit agricultural land use to defined purposes.

Exercise 8-2

Refer to the Data Bank in Figure 8.1 and list the source(s) for the following:

1. Lot size
2. New construction in the area
3. Proposed zoning changes
4. Population size
5. Nearest schools and places of worship
6. Municipal services
7. Recent zoning changes
8. Utility easements
9. Property tax assessment

Check your answers against those in the answer key at the back of the book.

■ DATA FORMS

Use of well-drafted forms can help an appraisal proceed much more smoothly, efficiently, and accurately and ensure that no details of the property, its location, or the information required for each of the appraisal techniques are overlooked. Many appraisers have developed their own forms, or make use of forms created by their clients, to provide a level of standardization and quality control for the finished appraisal report.

The rest of this unit includes sections of the Uniform Residential Appraisal Report (URAR) form that are used to collect and record data on the neighborhood, site, and subject property's improvements. An appraiser also would have considerable data on the region and city and would have to update that information when needed. Part of an appraiser's job is to keep up to date on economic indicators such as employment level and business starts (or failures), as well as political trends that could signal governmental policy changes affecting property values. The more aware an appraiser is of economic influences and trends, the easier it will be to identify and understand the factors that affect the value of a property.

Neighborhood Data

As both consumers and appraisers know, location has a direct effect on the market value of property and will greatly influence a person's enjoyment of the property and provide the relief of knowing that a sound investment has been made. It is the appraiser's job to build an accurate profile of the neighborhood. The appraiser knows which areas are experiencing declining interest and which neighborhoods are "hot," not based on a hunch but on solid, quantifiable data. Each appraisal won't require entirely new data; once compiled and analyzed, information will be updated only as often as warranted, depending on market conditions.

Use of a form, such as the Neighborhood section of the URAR form shown in Figure 8.2, can help the appraiser gather some of the basic information needed for every appraisal report. Data Bank List A of Figure 8.1 supplies sources for much of the neighborhood information needed, but a considerable amount of fieldwork still is necessary.

FIGURE 8.2
Neighborhood Data

NEIGHBORHOOD

Note: Race and the racial composition of the neighborhood are not appraisal factors.											
Neighborhood Characteristics				**One-Unit Housing Trends**				**One-Unit Housing**		**Present Land Use %**	
Location	☐ Urban	☐ Suburban	☐ Rural	Property Values	☐ Increasing	☐ Stable	☐ Declining	PRICE	AGE	One-Unit	%
Built-Up	☐ Over 75%	☐ 25–75%	☐ Under 25%	Demand/Supply	☐ Shortage	☐ In Balance	☐ Over Supply	$ (000)	(yrs)	2-4 Unit	%
Growth	☐ Rapid	☐ Stable	☐ Slow	Marketing Time	☐ Under 3 mths	☐ 3–6 mths	☐ Over 6 mths	Low		Multi-Family	%
Neighborhood Boundaries								High		Commercial	%
								Pred.		Other	%
Neighborhood Description											
Market Conditions (including support for the above conclusions)											

IN PRACTICE

When checking a neighborhood, the appraiser should note the general condition of all houses in the area. Are the homes large or small? How well are the properties landscaped? Are the lawns well kept? Do the surrounding houses complement each other architecturally? Answers to these questions tell much about the quality of life in the neighborhood. In most cases, visual inspection should disclose whether the neighborhood is likely to retain its character and value or to decline gradually. Not only is a thorough, firsthand knowledge of the area of tremendous value to an appraiser, it is essential for an accurate determination of the property's value.

Although most of the categories of neighborhood data are self-explanatory, some require background knowledge if the appraiser is to record them accurately. **Neighborhood boundaries,** for instance, are determined by considering the following:

- Natural boundaries (actual physical barriers—ravines, lakes, rivers, and highways or other major traffic arteries)
- Differences in land use (changes in zoning from residential to commercial or parkland)
- Subdivision borders; in some newer subdivisions, neighborhood boundaries are established by a gated entry and walled perimeter
- Average value or age of homes; larger subdivisions may set aside blocks or larger areas for properties of different price ranges
- availability of amenities, such as lake access
- Senior housing, although there may be distinct neighborhoods even within a senior housing development based on home style, price range, or proximity to amenities, such as a golf course

When recording neighborhood data, the appraiser records the street name or other identifiable dividing line and notes the type of area adjacent to the subject neighborhood at that boundary. A residential property adjacent to a park usually has a higher value than a similar property adjacent to a shopping center, for instance.

When an appraiser compares properties to form an opinion of value, it is critical that the properties come from the same neighborhood or very similar neighborhoods. The attributes of the surrounding area are just as important as the size, quality of construction, and features of the house being appraised.

Stages of life cycle—GEDR

Just as with individual properties, a typical neighborhood goes through four distinct periods in its life: growth, equilibrium (also called stability), decline, and revitalization (also called rehabilitation), which can be remembered as **GEDR**.

When an area is first developed, property values usually increase until few vacant building sites remain. At that point, the houses in the neighborhood tend to stabilize at their highest monetary value, and prices rarely fluctuate downward. As the years go by, however, and the effects of property deterioration become visible, the area usually declines in both value and desirability. The process of decline can be accelerated by the availability of new housing nearby, successive ownership of homes by lower-income residents who may not be able to afford the increasing maintenance costs of older homes, and the conversion of some properties to rental units, which may not be properly maintained. As properties decrease in value, some may even be put to a different use, such as light industry, which in turn further decreases the attractiveness of the surrounding neighborhood for residential use. The neighborhood's life cycle may start over again due to revitalization—a period when demand increases, providing the stimulus needed for property renovation.

IN PRACTICE

The pattern described previously is the result of general economic growth coupled with increasing consumer demand and the availability of land for housing and commercial development. In recent years, this pattern has been subjected to volatile market conditions, most recently the increase in property foreclosures stemming from the subprime lending crisis. The areas that had seen the greatest property appreciation—California, Florida, and Nevada—also experienced the greatest number of foreclosures in 2007 and 2008. From January 2007 to January 2008, California had more than a 400% increase in the number of foreclosures.

Demand is not the only influence on property values. In some areas, housing growth may be deliberately limited for environmental or other reasons. When development to meet housing needs is limited, the period of equilibrium of existing houses may be much longer than would otherwise be the case. In other words, homeowners are more likely to repair or remodel their present housing when they can't afford to buy new housing elsewhere, or it simply is unavailable.

Knowledge of the existence of all these factors, how they are interrelated, and how they impact property values is part of the appraiser's job. In short, the appraiser must be sensitive to all determinants of value, including economic, social, and governmental influences, to accurately gauge their effect on neighborhood and property desirability.

Proximity to hazards and nuisances

The proximity of the neighborhood, or any part of it, to hazards or nuisances has become very important. The more we learn about environmental conditions, the more likely we are to discover factors that are injurious to health or safety. The mere potential for danger (such as that created by chemical storage facilities) may have the effect of lowering property values in nearby areas. The appraiser should be aware of any existing or potential hazard, as well as ones that have been alleviated (such as factory smoke pollution that may have been drastically reduced).

As a general rule, every prospective property developer in every part of the country should arrange for an independent, thorough analysis of the soil and any existing structures to determine the presence of contaminants. Some of these, such as radon gas, are described in Unit 7, "Building Construction and the Environment." Unless the contaminant can be easily remedied at a reasonable cost, the best way for a property buyer to avoid a problem may be to avoid contaminated property, if possible.

IN PRACTICE

Unless a contaminant is readily apparent, an appraiser who is not specially trained to conduct an environmental assessment should not offer an opinion on the presence or absence of materials that may be deemed hazardous. Nevertheless, there may be other property detriments or nuisances, such as location in an airport flight path, that should be noted, and their impact on value considered.

Not all nuisances are readily apparent, and some are annoyances rather than hazards to health and safety. Then, too, what is acceptable to one person may be a nuisance to another. The house near the train track that most people avoid because of the noise and potential danger might be attractive to a train buff. The appraiser must analyze each condition to determine whether it has an effect on value by researching the market.

Exercise 8-3

Fill out the URAR Neighborhood section that appears in Figure 8.2 with the information supplied here. All the information pertains to the sample appraisal you will complete in this unit and in Unit 12. When you have finished, check your completed form against the one given in the answer key at the back of the book. Correct all errors and fill in all missing pieces of information on your form.

The neighborhood map, Figure 8.3, shows the location of 2130 West Franklin Street, Midstate, Illinois, the subject of the sample appraisal. For this appraisal, you can assume that the subdivision is the neighborhood under analysis.

Figure 8.3
Neighborhood Map

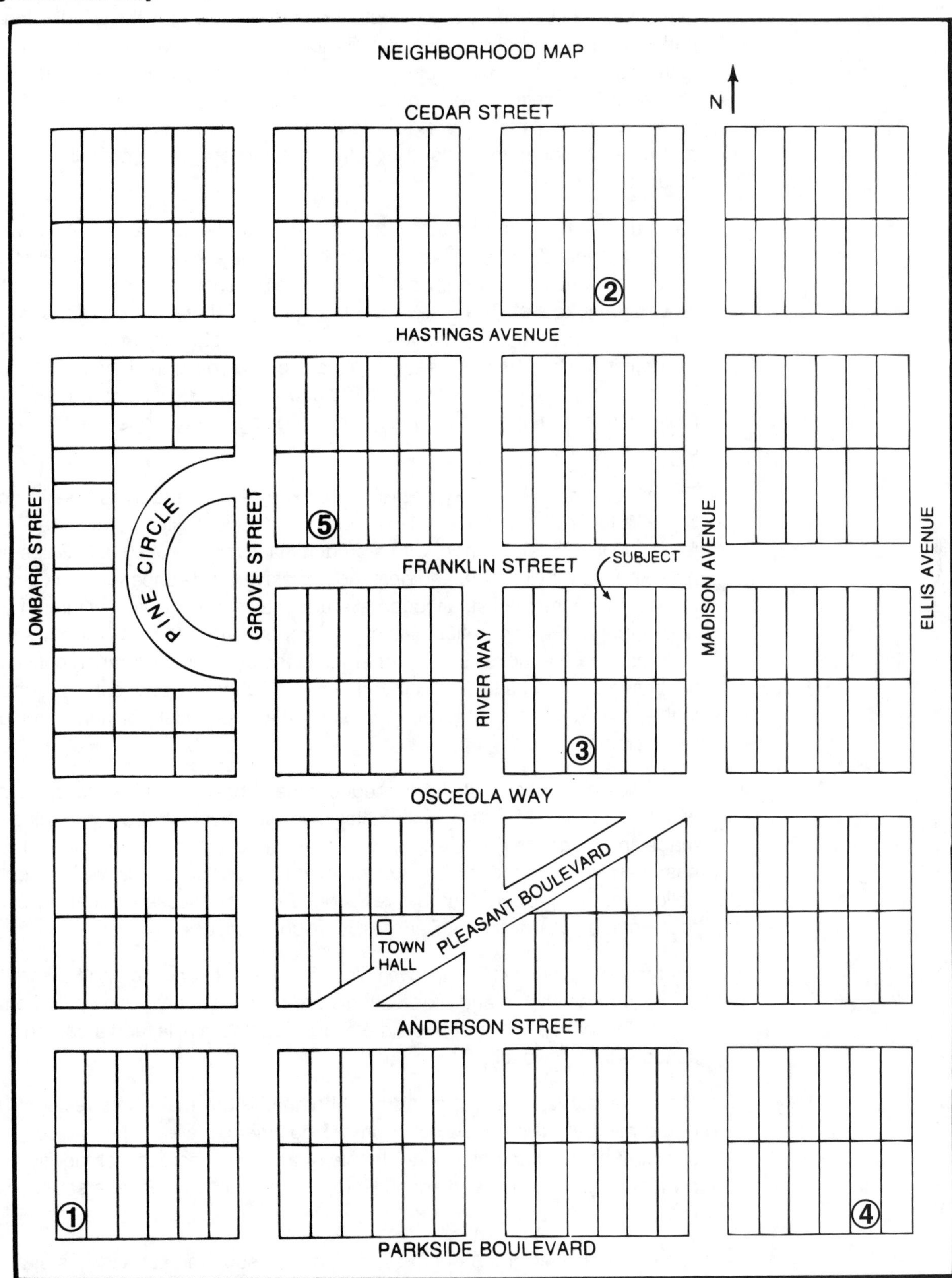

Midstate is a city of just over 100,000 people. The boundaries of the subdivision are Lombard Street, Cedar Street, Ellis Avenue, and Parkside Boulevard. Parkside forms a natural boundary to the south, because it separates the subdivision from parkland. Lombard divides the subdivision from expensive highrise apartments to the west, forming another boundary. Ellis to the east separates the subdivision from an area of retail stores, and Cedar Street to the north provides a boundary between the single-family residences of the subdivision and a business district and area of moderately priced apartments. Parkland is gently rolling; built-up areas are level.

This subdivision is still known locally as the "Gunderson" area, which was its name at its founding, but it has since been incorporated as a part of Midstate. In the subdivision map, fewer than 1% of the lots are shown as vacant, and sales of those are infrequent. The area has a few two- and three-unit buildings on Lombard Street that are about 20 years old, but the single-family homes have been built within the last 15 to 22 years, and the average age of the houses is 18 years. The apartment buildings average $700,000 to $900,000 in value, make up no more than 1% of the entire neighborhood, and usually have one apartment that is owner-occupied.

The area is considered very desirable for middle-income families (yearly income $50,000 to $75,000). About 2% of homes are rented. Home values are in the $260,000 to $380,000 range, with a predominant value of $290,000. Sales prices have kept up with inflation, and demand has stayed in balance with the number of homes put on the market, although average marketing time is now three months, due primarily to seasonal fluctuation. The property at 2130 West Franklin is typical of at least several dozen other properties in the area, all brick ranch houses with full basements and attached garages, on lots 50 feet by 200 feet. Other houses in the area are either split-level or two-story, the latter usually having aluminum or wood siding.

All utilities have been installed throughout the subdivision, and assessments for water and sewer lines, sidewalk installation, and asphalt street surfacing were made and paid for eight years ago when the improvements were made. The area has been incorporated, so it has city fire and police services as well as garbage collection. The property tax rate is $5 per $100 of assessed valuation, comparable to rates charged in similar nearby neighborhoods.

There is a community hospital two miles southeast at Parkside and Saginaw, and public grade schools and high schools are no more than ¾ of a mile from any home. Two private grade schools are available within a mile, and a parochial high school is within two miles.

The average size of families in this neighborhood is 3.7. Many area residents work in the nearby business district or in the commercial area, where a concentration of 40 retail stores as well as theaters and other recreational facilities offers a wide range of goods and services. Business and commercial areas are within two miles.

There is a smaller group of stores, including a supermarket and gas station, at Madison and Cedar streets and a public library branch at Cedar and Grove. Only about 1% of properties are devoted to commercial use.

A superhighway two miles away that bisects the central business district of Midstate connects the area to major interstate routes. There is no public transportation. The highest concentration of office and retail buildings in the business district is no more than 15 minutes by car from any house in the area, and the commercial area takes about the same time to reach. Emergency medical facilities are within a ten-minute drive of any home.

There are no health hazards within the neighborhood, either from industry or natural impediments. The busiest street through the neighborhood, Madison, is still mainly residential and generally quiet. No change from current land use is predicted, and there are no nuisances, such as noise-producing factories or construction yards.

The information should be filled in on the URAR Neighborhood Data section in Figure 8.2. When you have finished, check your form against the completed one in the Answer Key at the back of the book. Correct all errors and fill in all missing pieces of information on your form.

Check your answers against those in the answer key at the back of the book.

Site Data

The Site section of the URAR form shown in Figure 8.4 can be used to record the information needed to describe the subject site.

The Site Visit

Any visit to the subject property requires the permission of the property owner.

Even if the appraiser inspects only the exterior of structures or walks the property boundaries, to do so without permission can be considered trespassing.

Always contact the owner first. If the property is occupied by a tenant or anyone else other than the owner, you should make sure that your visit is anticipated, for your own protection as well as out of respect for the property occupants.

FIGURE 8.4
Site Data

SITE

Dimensions | Area | Shape | View

Specific Zoning Classification | Zoning Description

Zoning Compliance ☐ Legal ☐ Legal Nonconforming (Grandfathered Use) ☐ No Zoning ☐ Illegal (describe)

Is the highest and best use of the subject property as improved (or as proposed per plans and specifications) the present use? ☐ Yes ☐ No If No, describe

Utilities	Public	Other (describe)		Public	Other (describe)	Off-site Improvements—Type	Public	Private
Electricity	☐	☐	Water	☐	☐	Street	☐	☐
Gas	☐	☐	Sanitary Sewer	☐	☐	Alley	☐	☐

FEMA Special Flood Hazard Area ☐ Yes ☐ No FEMA Flood Zone | FEMA Map # | FEMA Map Date

Are the utilities and off-site improvements typical for the market area? ☐ Yes ☐ No If No, describe

Are there any adverse site conditions or external factors (easements, encroachments, environmental conditions, land uses, etc.)? ☐ Yes ☐ No If Yes, describe

The appraiser begins by obtaining a complete and legally accurate description of the property's location and making a sketch to show the property's approximate shape and street location. A public building or other landmark also could be shown on the sketch to help locate the site. The topography (surface features) of the site should be noted as well as the existence of any natural hazards, such as location in or near a floodplain, earthquake fault zone, or other potentially dangerous condition.

The UAD specifies how the size of the subject property is to be noted. If the site is less than one acre, its size must be reported in square feet, shown as a whole number followed by "sf"; for example, 27840 sq. ft. If the site is one acre or greater, its size must be reported in acreage to two decimal places followed by "ac"; for example, 3.40 ac. The total size of the entire site must be entered and no other data is permitted.

The UAD also specifies how the view from the subject property can be indicated. There will be an overall view rating of neutral (N), beneficial (B), or adverse (A), followed by an abbreviation indicating one or more view factors that contribute to the overall rating. The choices are:

- Water view (Wtr)
- Pastoral view (Pstrl)
- Woods view (Woods)
- Park view (Prk)
- Golf course view (Glfvw)
- City view skyline view (CtySky)
- Mountain view (Mtn)
- Residential view (Res)
- City street view (CtyStr)
- Industrial view (Ind)
- Power lines (PwrLn)
- Limited Sight (LtdSght)
- Other

For example, the description entered for a home on a golf course could be "B;Glfvw" and the description of a home with a less desirable view of a manufacturing facility could be "A;Ind". If the view is indicated as "Other", the description entered must allow the reader of the report to understand what the view is, using language that is more specific than just "typical" or "average." For example, the view from a property located next to a railroad track could be shown as "A;RRtracks". The text must fit within the space provided and also must be entered in exactly the same way in the comparable sales grid for the subject property.

As much as possible, comparable properties should reflect the same site attributes as the subject property. A house with an expansive view of a golf course is best compared to other houses with similar views.

Special considerations in appraisal of agricultural properties include investigation of soil and water quality as well as water supply and drainage.

Knowledge of the subject site's zoning, which will affect its future use, is necessary, as is knowledge of the current zoning of surrounding areas. A site zoned for a single-family residence may be poorly used for that purpose if the neighborhood is declining and multiunit buildings are being built nearby. In such a case, the feasibility of changing the zoning to multiunit residential construction might be analyzed by making a highest and best use study.

Any easements or deed restrictions should be noted. Any part of the site that cannot be used for building purposes should be clearly designated, along with any other limitation on site use. Such limitations could raise or lower site value.

IN PRACTICE

An easement may allow airspace or below-ground space for present or future utility installations or a right-of-way for others to travel over the property. A deed restriction, usually established by the property's subdivider, may specify the size of lots used for building, the type or style of building constructed, setbacks from property lines, or other factors designed to increase the subdivision's homogeneity and thus stabilize property values.

Finally, the appraiser should describe any land area held in common with other property owners. A subdivision may be divided into relatively small building parcels to allow space for a greenbelt (a landscaped area available for the use of all property owners), sports facilities (such as a swimming pool, tennis court, or golf course), and even a clubhouse. The proximity of such features to the subject property should also be noted.

Exercise 8-4

The following information is applicable to the sample site at 2130 West Franklin Street. Use it to fill in the Site section of the URAR form in.

The legal description of the lot is

> Lot 114 in Block 2 of Gunderson Subdivision, being part of the Northwest ¼ of the Southeast ¼ of Section 4, Township 37 North, Range 18, East of the Third Principal Meridian as recorded in the Office of the Registrar of Titles of Grove County, Illinois, on April 27, 1990.

The lot is 50 feet by 200 feet, rectangular, with 50 feet of street frontage. (The first lot dimension given is usually street frontage.) There are mercury vapor streetlights but no alley. The driveway, which is 24 feet wide and 30 feet long, is paved with asphalt. The public sidewalk and curb are concrete. The land is level, with good soil and a view of the tree-lined street, typical of lots in the area.

Neither storm nor sanitary sewers have ever overflowed, and the property is not located in a Federal Emergency Management Agency (FEMA) Special Flood Hazard Area. An easement line runs across the rear 10 feet of the property. The property is zoned R-1 for single-family residential use, its present use. Deed restrictions stipulate that the house must be no closer than 10 feet to side property lines, 30 feet to the street, and 50 feet from the rear property line. The current structure does not violate these restrictions. Water, gas, electric, and telephone lines have been installed. The lot is attractively landscaped, with low evergreen shrubbery across the front of the house and a view of the tree-lined parkway (the space between the sidewalk and curb). The backyard has several fruit trees. There is no evidence of any encroachment or nearby adverse land use.

When you have completed your Site Data form, check it against the one in the answer key at the back of the book. Correct any errors and fill in any omissions on your form.

Check your answers against those in the answer key at the back of the book.

Building Data

The Improvements section of the URAR form in Figure 8.5 can be used to appraise a single-family residence, conforming to the UAD requirements.

FIGURE 8.5
Building Data

IMPROVEMENTS

General Description		Foundation		Exterior Description	materials/condition	Interior	materials/condition
Units ☐ One ☐ One with Accessory Unit		☐ Concrete Slab ☐ Crawl Space		Foundation Walls		Floors	
# of Stories		☐ Full Basement ☐ Partial Basement		Exterior Walls		Walls	
Type ☐ Det. ☐ Att. ☐ S-Det./End Unit		Basement Area	sq. ft.	Roof Surface		Trim/Finish	
☐ Existing ☐ Proposed ☐ Under Const.		Basement Finish	%	Gutters & Downspouts		Bath Floor	
Design (Style)		☐ Outside Entry/Exit ☐ Sump Pump		Window Type		Bath Wainscot	
Year Built		Evidence of ☐ Infestation		Storm Sash/Insulated		Car Storage ☐ None	
Effective Age (Yrs)		☐ Dampness ☐ Settlement		Screens		☐ Driveway # of Cars	
Attic	☐ None	Heating ☐ FWA ☐ HWBB ☐ Radiant		Amenities	☐ Woodstove(s) #	Driveway Surface	
☐ Drop Stair	☐ Stairs	☐ Other	Fuel	☐ Fireplace(s) #	☐ Fence	☐ Garage # of Cars	
☐ Floor	☐ Scuttle	Cooling ☐ Central Air Conditioning		☐ Patio/Deck	☐ Porch	☐ Carport # of Cars	
☐ Finished	☐ Heated	☐ Individual	☐ Other	☐ Pool	☐ Other	☐ Att. ☐ Det. ☐ Built-in	

Appliances ☐ Refrigerator ☐ Range/Oven ☐ Dishwasher ☐ Disposal ☐ Microwave ☐ Washer/Dryer ☐ Other (describe)

Finished area **above** grade contains: Rooms Bedrooms Bath(s) Square Feet of Gross Living Area Above Grade

Additional features (special energy efficient items, etc.)

Describe the condition of the property (including needed repairs, deterioration, renovations, remodeling, etc.).

Are there any physical deficiencies or adverse conditions that affect the livability, soundness, or structural integrity of the property? ☐ Yes ☐ No If Yes, describe

Does the property generally conform to the neighborhood (functional utility, style, condition, use, construction, etc.)? ☐ Yes ☐ No If No, describe

Exterior features

Even before entering a single-family house, the appraiser is called on to make certain value judgments. Approaching the house from the street, the appraiser mentally records a first impression of the house, its orientation, and how it fits in with the surrounding area. At the same time, the appraiser notes and records information about the landscaping. Next, the external construction materials (for the foundation, outside walls, roof, driveway, etc.) are listed and the condition of each, as well as the general external condition of the building, is rated. Finally, the appraiser measures each structure on the site, sketches its dimensions, and computes its area in square feet.

The appraiser enters the architectural style or design that best describes the house, such as "Colonial" or "Farmhouse," but without using terms that are vague or merely descriptive of the building materials, such as "Typical" or "Brick." Design names can vary from community to community. The year the subject was built is indicated by a four-digit number for the year. If the appraiser is unable to ascertain the exact year of construction, an estimation of the year of construction must be entered, preceded by a tilde (~); for example, "~1950".

Interior features

Once in the house, the appraiser notes and evaluates major construction details and fixtures, particularly the interior finish, the kind of floors, walls and doors, the condition and adequacy of kitchen cabinets, the type and condition of heating and air-conditioning systems, rooms with special features (such as a wet bar or fireplace), and any other features that indicate the quality of the construction. The appraiser also observes the general condition of the house—for evidence of recent remodeling, the presence of cracked plaster, sagging floors, or any other signs of deterioration—and records room dimensions and total square footage. The appraiser should inquire about the presence of any substance requiring disclosure, such as lead-based paint.

A basement is indicated by its size in square feet, expressed as up to five digits in whole numbers only, and the percentage of the basement that is finished, indicated by a whole number of up to three digits. If there is no basement, the numeral zero (0) is entered in both fields. The appraiser should indicate the heating and cooling types, or enter "None" if none is present. The appropriate boxes are checked to indicate amenities available; if there are no fireplaces or woodstoves, the numeral zero (0) is entered. The appraiser enters "None" in the appropriate space if there is no patio/deck, pool, fence, porch, or other amenity. The appraiser indicates the number of vehicles that can be accommodated by the type of parking space available; if none is available, the appraiser enters the numeral zero (0).

The number of rooms of each type is entered. The number of full and partial baths above grade is entered, separated by a period, with full baths indicated first. For example, three full baths and two half baths are shown as "3.2". A three-quarter bath (shower but no tub) is counted as a full bath in all cases. Quarter baths (toilet only) are not included in bathroom count.

The appraiser describes the condition of the property by using one of the UAD-required grades, which is entered in exactly the same way in the Sales Comparison Approach section of the URAR form. The grades are listed in Figure 8.6.

FIGURE 8.6
Condition Entries

C1—Improvements all have been very recently constructed, show no physical depreciation, and have not previously been occupied.

C2—Virtually all building components are new or have been recently repaired, refinished, or rehabilitated. The improvements feature no deferred maintenance, little or no physical depreciation, and require no repairs.

C3—Improvements are well-maintained and feature limited physical depreciation due to normal wear and tear. Some components, but not every major building component, may be updated or recently rehabilitated.

C4—Improvements feature some minor deferred maintenance and physical deterioration due to normal wear and tear. All major building components have been adequately maintained and are functionally adequate, requiring only minimal repairs to building components and mechanical systems, and cosmetic repairs.

C5—Improvements feature obvious deferred maintenance and are in need of some significant repairs. Functional utility and overall livability is somewhat diminished due to condition, but the dwelling remains useable and functional as a residence.

C6—Improvements have substantial damage or deferred maintenance with deficiencies or defects that are severe enough to affect safety, soundness, or structural integrity.

In addition to a general condition rating, the appraiser must indicate whether any material work has been done to the kitchen(s) or bathroom(s) in the prior 15 years. If there have been none, the entry "No updates in the prior 15 years" must be made. If there has been any update, additional information for kitchens and bathrooms must be provided. If there has been work performed, the appraiser indicates whether the level of work completed is updated, not updated, or remodeled. The time frame indicated for completion of work is less than 1 year ago, 1 to 5 years ago, 6 to 10 years ago, 11 to 15 years ago, or time frame unknown. For example, condition could be indicated as "C4; No updates in the prior 15 years;" and be followed by a general description of property condition.

Depreciation

The appraiser then notes the general condition of the building, giving consideration to three kinds of **depreciation**:

Physical deterioration. The effects of ordinary wear and tear and the action of the elements.

Functional obsolescence. The absence or inadequacy of features in the design, layout, or construction of the building that are currently desired by purchasers, or the presence of features that have become unfashionable or unnecessary. Fixtures such as bathtubs or vanities fall into this category. A kitchen without updated cabinets, countertops, and appliances would be less desirable in most areas.

External obsolescence (formerly called environmental, economic, or locational obsolescence). A feature made undesirable or unnecessary because of conditions outside the property. A change of zoning from residential to commercial might make a single-family house obsolete if such usage does not fully utilize (take full monetary advantage of) the site.

The kinds of depreciation and how each affects the value of the property are explained in greater detail in the units on the specific appraisal approaches. When the appraiser first records building data, it is enough to make a general estimate of the degree of physical deterioration, functional obsolescence, or external obsolescence present in the property.

Multiunit buildings

In appraising a multiunit residential building, the appraiser records the building data in the same way as for a single-family house, except a multiunit building will have more information to evaluate, possibly in many categories. If apartment and room sizes are standard, this work will be greatly simplified. If there are units of many different sizes, however, each apartment must be recorded. In such a case, a floor-by-floor room breakdown would not be as useful as an apartment-by-apartment breakdown. Because most multiunit apartments are standardized, a typical floor plan that indicates the size, placement, and layout of the apartments would be the easiest and best way to show them.

There are some physical features that an appraiser may not be able to learn about a house or apartment building without breaking into walls, but if a checklist of items to be inspected, such as those in Figure 8.5, is prepared in advance, most of the building's deficiencies as well as its special features can be identified. If the appraiser can supply all of the required information and knows enough about construction to recognize and record any features not itemized on the list, he or she will have as thorough an analysis of the building as required for any appraisal method.

As you go through the rest of this book, you will be entering data in all of the forms presented in this unit. You may review this unit whenever necessary. If you have difficulty computing building or lot areas, refer to Unit 2, which covers the mathematics involved in area and volume problems.

Exercise 8-5

The following information is applicable to the sample single-family residence at 2130 West Franklin Street. Use it to complete the Improvements section of the URAR form that appears in Figure 8.5.

The subject was built in 1995 and is a seven-room brick ranch house with a concrete foundation. It has double-hung wood windows, wood doors, and aluminum combination storm and screen windows and doors. The general outside appearance and appeal of the house are good. The wood trim was recently painted. The black mineral-fiber roof shingles are in good condition, as are the aluminum gutters and downspouts. The attached two-car garage is also brick. The driveway is asphalt. The house has a full basement with a 100,000 BTU gas forced-air furnace, which is in good condition, and a central air-conditioning unit, also in good condition. There are no special energy-efficient items. The basement has a concrete floor and walls, is finished with a suspended ceiling, drywall, and tile flooring over 50% of its 1,825 square feet of area, and has no outside entry. There is a sump pump in the basement and no evidence of flooding. The wiring is 220-volt.

The house has a living room, dining room, kitchen, three bedrooms, two full bathrooms, and one half-bath. The kitchen has 12 feet of oak cabinets with a built-in double-basin stainless steel sink with garbage disposal, dishwasher, stainless steel range with oven and hood with exhaust fan, and stainless steel refrigerator. All appliances will be sold with the house.

The general condition of the interior living area is very good. The walls and ceilings are ½-inch drywall. All the walls are painted, as is the trim. Doors are wood, six panel. Floors are hardwood, with wall-to-wall carpeting in living and dining rooms, and ceramic tile in kitchen, family room, and both bathrooms. Each full bathroom has a built-in tub and shower, lavatory with vanity, mirrored cabinet, and toilet with wall-hung tank. The half-bath has a vanity lavatory and toilet. All bathroom fixtures are white.

The house has a total of 1,825 square feet of gross living space, calculated from its exterior dimensions, and is functionally adequate. Based on its general condition, the house has an effective age of 20 years. There is no evidence of any adverse environmental condition on or near the property.

Check your completed Improvements section against the one in the Answer Key at the back of the book. Correct any errors and fill in any omissions.

Check your answers against those in the answer key at the back of the book.

■ DATA FOR SALES COMPARISON APPROACH

The **sales comparison approach** is the most widely used appraisal method for valuing residential property and vacant land. Using this approach, the appraiser collects sales data on comparable nearby properties that have sold recently, then makes market-derived adjustments reflecting individual differences between the subject and comparables. After necessary adjustments have been made, the appraiser selects the resultant value indication that best reflects the market value of the subject property. As a formula, the sales comparison approach is as follows:

$$\text{Sales price of comparable property} \pm \text{Adjustments} = \text{Indicated value of subject property}$$

The sales comparison approach relies on the principle of substitution, which was defined in Unit 5. If a property identical to the one being appraised was sold recently, its sales price should be a good indicator of the price that could be commanded by the property that is the subject of the appraisal. In practice, however, the appraiser's job is not nearly as simple as that statement might suggest.

IN PRACTICE

Every parcel of real estate is considered unique. Even with properties of the same design and construction built on adjacent building lots, there always will be some features that make one property different from the other. Over time, as successive owners maintain the properties in their own fashion and decorate or remodel in keeping with their tastes, the properties will become less and less similar in appearance and function. The newly built homes on unlandscaped lots that start out looking like identical twins will be quite readily distinguishable after a very short time.

The best an appraiser can do is learn as much as possible about the property being appraised so that other recently sold properties can be found that are as close as possible to the appraised property in as many features as can be identified. It is important to remember that the appraiser making an opinion of market value is making an opinion only. There is no guarantee that the indicated market value will be realized in a future sale of the appraised property. Because the sales comparison approach makes use of market data, it is also called the market data or direct market comparison approach.

IN PRACTICE

The sales comparison approach can be used for many types of property, but it is particularly useful in the appraisal of a single-family residence because a home purchase generally is made by an owner/occupant who is unconcerned about the property's potential cash flow as a rental unit. Typically, what is most important to the home purchaser is the market value of the property relative to the value of other similar properties in the neighborhood, most of which typically also are owner-occupied. Of course, even owner/occupants are concerned with their financial ability to carry the costs of owning a home, from mortgage and tax payments to utility bills and ordinary costs of maintenance. Owner/occupants, however, do not expect the property's potential rental value to cover all those costs. As a result, the sales price of a single-family home may be somewhat higher than its projected investment value, which is based on the cash flow the property can produce.

After all details about the subject property are known, data can be collected on sales of comparable properties. Only recent sales should be considered; they must have been arm's-length transactions, and the properties sold must be substantially similar to the subject property.

Recent Sales

To be considered in an application of the sales comparison approach, a property sale should have occurred fairly close in time to the date of appraisal. The acceptability of the sale from a time standpoint will depend on the number of sales that have taken place and the volatility of the marketplace. Within a normal market, sales no more than six months before the date of appraisal generally are acceptable. In a slow-moving market, the appraiser may have to refer to comparable sales from as long as a year earlier. In that event, the appraiser probably will need to make an adjustment to allow for the time factor. If other types of properties have increased in value over the same period, a general rise in prices may be indicated. The appraiser must determine whether the property in question is part of the general trend and, if it is, adjust the sales price of the comparable accordingly. This adjustment answers the question, "How much would this comparable property probably sell for in today's market?"

For some purposes, such as an appraisal for a federal agency, there may be a definite time limit on the sale date of comparable properties. Even if there is no time imposed by the client or agency for whom the report is being prepared, the appraiser must be alert to market trends, including both the number of overall sales and the changes in market value.

In a period of depressed prices, the task of finding recent sales of comparable properties can be even more difficult for the appraiser of commercial property. In the best of times, in most areas commercial property sales simply are not as numerous as residential property sales, and it may be impossible for the appraiser to locate property sales that have occurred within even a year or more. The difficulty of the task is compounded if the commercial property is so unusual or has been so customized that no true comparable is available. This is one reason why the sales comparison approach may not be the best appraisal method to use for a commercial property.

The preceding discussion should make it obvious why the study of economics is a necessity for the appraiser, who must be able to recognize economic forces in order to identify possible trends and then apply that knowledge to the facts of the appraisal. The appraiser isn't expected to second-guess the marketplace, but must be able to define its present condition and draw the appropriate conclusions.

Similar Features

In selecting comparable properties, the appraiser will be limited to sales that have occurred in the neighborhood or immediate vicinity. Because most new residential construction occurs within subdivisions developed entirely or predominantly by a single builder, finding recent sales that conform to the subject property's specifications generally presents no difficulty. The appraiser's task becomes more arduous when dealing with properties that are atypical because of either the site or the structure.

Today, when 100-lot home developments are common and some are many times that size, it may be hard to believe that such mass-produced housing is a fairly recent historical phenomenon. Through the 1930s, homes generally were designed and constructed individually for a particular client. The availability of long-term financing following the New Deal reforms of the 1930s, coupled with the severe housing shortage that followed World War II, created the perfect conditions for a new type of development.

Levittown, New York, built in the late 1940s, marked the first extensive application to home-building of the economies of material purchasing and labor specialization that had been so successful in the birth of the automobile industry. By standardizing home specifications and making the most efficient use of work crews that moved from house to house on a well-coordinated schedule, William Levitt was able to offer modestly priced housing at a time when the need was great. Similar subdivisions across the country soon offered a practical, affordable version of the American dream.

Many people find the uniformity of some subdivisions aesthetically unpleasing, but such uniformity is a delight for the real estate appraiser. Over the years, tract builders have tried to make homes more distinctive (or "semicustomized," as they are described in advertising) by offering a range of layout and finishing material options, but most subdivision homes retain their basic similarity of form and function. Finding comparable property sales in such a neighborhood rarely is an arduous task.

The appraiser's task is more complicated when the subject property is truly distinctive, either because it has been individually designed and constructed or because the site offers special features. Then, the appraiser must accurately examine and describe the subject property to find comparables that come as close as possible to as many of the property specifications as possible. The most important features to compare will be those that have the greatest effect on value, whether positively or negatively. If the house is the design of a leading architect, and that fact is a desirable and valuable feature, the best possible comparable will be another house designed by the same architect. If the property is on a beachfront, the location may be the single most influential component of the property's value.

Site characteristics that have the greatest effect on value include location, size, view, topography, availability of utilities, and presence of mature trees and other plantings.

IN PRACTICE

If the most outstanding feature of a property is the view, the best comparable will be a property with a similar view. If the site has a steep downhill slope, with no space flat enough for a garden or outdoor play area, the ideal comparable will be a house on a similarly restrictive lot.

If comparables that match the property's most important (valuable) feature(s) cannot be found, the value of the feature(s) must be estimated and used as an adjustment to the sales price of each of the selected comparables.

Though adjustments may be made for some differences between the subject property and the comparables, most of the following factors should be similar:

- Style of house
- Age
- Number of rooms, bedrooms, and baths
- Size of lot
- Size of building
- Terms of sale
- Type of construction
- General condition

If at all possible, the comparable properties should be from the same neighborhood as the subject property. Specific data, similar to that collected for the subject property, should be collected for completed sales of at least three comparable properties. Often, sales data on more than those three will have to be studied, because the first three properties the appraiser analyzes may not fit the general requirements listed above well enough to be used in the appraisal. What is important is that the sales chosen provide adequate support for a value conclusion. An analysis of the sales properties not used directly in the report may be helpful in establishing neighborhood values, price trends, and time adjustments.

Financing Terms

The terms of sale are of great importance, particularly if the buyer has assumed an existing loan or if the seller has helped finance the purchase. The seller may take back a note on part of the purchase price (secured by a mortgage or trust deed on the property) at an interest rate lower than the prevailing market rate. The seller may also "buy down" the buyer's high interest rate on a new loan by paying the lender part of the interest on the amount borrowed in a lump sum at the time of the sale. The argument has been made that in a buydown, the sales price has been effectively reduced by the amount the seller has paid to the lender. In any event, the sales price should be considered in light of the cost to the buyer reflected in the method used to finance the purchase. If the buyer obtained a new conventional (non-government-backed) loan and paid the remainder of the purchase price in cash, it would be sufficient to note that fact.

Ideally, because comparable properties should have comparable terms of sale, no adjustment for that factor will be necessary. If the appraiser has no choice but to use properties with varying financing terms, the selling prices could be adjusted to reflect those variances by using a **cash equivalency** technique. With one version of this technique, the appraiser compares the monthly payment to be made by the buyer with the required monthly payment on a new loan in the same principal amount, at the prevailing interest rate as of the sale date. The resulting percentage is applied to the amount of the purchase price represented by the principal of the low-interest loan. When this reduced amount is added to the amount paid in cash by the buyer to the seller, the result is an adjusted sales price that compensates for the effects of below-market-rate financing.

IN PRACTICE

The total purchase price of a property was $200,000. The buyer made total cash payments of $50,000 and also assumed the seller's mortgage, which had a remaining principal balance of $150,000, bearing an interest rate of 5%, with monthly payments of $858.91. As of the date of sale, the mortgage had a remaining term of 20 years. Prevailing mortgages on a loan of equal amount and for a like term, as of the sale date, required a 6% interest rate with monthly payments of $1,074.65.

The percentage to be applied to the principal amount of the assumed loan is computed by dividing the actual required monthly payment by the payment required for a loan at the prevailing rate:

$$\frac{\$858.91}{\$1{,}074.65} = 0.80, \text{ or } 80\%$$

The remaining principal amount of the loan is then multiplied by that percentage to find its adjusted value:

$$\$150{,}000 \times 0.80 = \$120{,}000$$

The cash equivalency value of the sale can be reached by adding the down payment to the adjusted value of the assumed loan:

$$\$120{,}000 + \$50{,}000 = \$170{,}000$$

The cash equivalency value of this sale is $170,000.

If the cash equivalency technique is used to adjust the sales price of any comparable, all of the comparable properties should be so treated. *Note:* Use of a cash equivalency technique as the sole method of determining value is not permitted by Fannie Mae. Ideally, comparable properties will have comparable terms of sale, and no adjustment for financing will be necessary. If the appraiser has no choice but to use properties with varying financing terms, their selling prices should be adjusted to reflect realistically the effect of financing in the marketplace, rather than simply being the result of a mechanical formula.

A cash equivalency technique may be useful when a buyer has assumed an existing mortgage loan or when the seller provides financing by giving the buyer a credit for some or all of the purchase price. In either situation, the appraiser will be interested in the effect on the sales price of financing that may be more or less favorable than that currently available from conventional lenders.

Seller financing may be the only alternative for a buyer who has difficulty qualifying for a loan from any other source. Another advantage of seller financing is elimination of the up-front loan fees charged by financial institutions such as banks and savings associations—termed **conventional lenders**. If the buyer doesn't have a large enough down payment for a conventional loan, a short-term second mortgage carried by the seller may enable the buyer to secure the bulk of the financing from an institution. In return for carrying all or part of the financing on the purchase, the seller may expect to receive a rate of interest that is higher than the prevailing market rate. This is most often the case when the seller's extension of credit for part of the purchase price is secured by a second lien, also called a junior lien, on the property.

The opposite situation also may occur, however. If the property has been difficult to sell because of its location or features, or if the market has few buyers for the available properties, the seller may tempt a buyer by offering financing at a rate the same as or less than the market rate. A favorable rate, combined with an easier qualifying process and no loan origination fees, can make the seller-financed home a very desirable property, even in a "buyer's market."

Exercise 8-6

A house sells for $250,000 with a down payment of $50,000 and a seller-financed $200,000 mortgage at 5% interest. The mortgage is amortized over 20 years with a balloon payment due in 5 years. The appraiser checks the market for sales financed by similar mortgage provisions and finds that a $175,000, 5% note was sold for $150,000. What is the cash equivalency value of the $200,000 mortgage?

Check your answer against the one in the answer key at the back of the book.

Arm's-Length Transactions

Every comparable property must have been sold in an **arm's-length transaction**, in which neither buyer nor seller is acting under duress (greater duress, that is, than what is felt by the buyer and seller in the average transaction), the property is offered on the open market for a reasonable time, and both buyer and seller have a reasonable knowledge of the property, its assets, and its defects.

In most cases, the slightest indication of duress on the part of either of the principals automatically excludes a transaction from consideration. If the sale has been forced for any reason (a foreclosure, a tax sale, an estate liquidation, or the need to purchase adjoining property or sell before the owner is transferred), it is not an arm's-length transaction. If the principals are related individuals or corporations, this must be assumed to have affected the terms of the sale. Again, financing should be considered. If the down payment was extremely small, or none was required, such an exceptional situation might disqualify the sold property from consideration as a comparable, or at least require an adjustment.

Sources of Data

The preliminary search, as well as the collection of specific data, will be made from one or more of the sources listed here. All sales data, however, must be verified by one or more of the principals to the transaction. The sources are as follows:

- *The appraiser's own records*. These offer the best sources of data. If four comparable properties are available from the appraiser's own records, only the sales prices will remain to be independently verified. (Even though the appraiser has researched the market value as thoroughly as possible, the actual selling price may not have been the same figure.)
- *Official records of deeds*. The appraiser may keep a file of transactions held within the area, but all records will be available in the county or city clerk's office. Much of the specific information needed can also be culled from these records. In localities where transfer tax stamps must be recorded on deeds, such stamps may give an indication of selling price; they are not generally reliable sources of exact selling price, however. The tax rate may be based only on the actual cash amount paid at the closing of the sale, thereby excluding assumed mortgages, for instance. Tax stamps are also usually based on rounded amounts, such as $0.50 per each $500 of financial consideration, or a fraction thereof. Merely multiplying the number of stamps by $500 in such a case could result in a final estimate that is as much as $499 more than the actual cash amount. Too many or too few stamps may also be put on the deed deliberately to mislead anyone trying to discover the property's selling price.
- *The real estate assessor's office*. If property cards can be examined, these will ordinarily reveal sales price, deed book and page, zoning, age of dwelling, lot and dwelling dimensions, and dates of additions to the house. Many assessors now make property records available via the taxing jurisdiction's website.
- *Records of sales*. These are published by some local real estate boards or compiled by sales research services, often on the internet.

- *Internet valuation services*. Care should be taken to use only a reliable source, such as a local data compiler, rather than one that may not accurately reflect current market conditions and sales.

Usually, information will be sought only on sales that have already closed escrow; that is, sales that have already been completed. Information on pending sales would ordinarily not be used and would be exceedingly difficult to come by in any event, given that real estate brokers, attorneys, and other agents of the principals could be in breach of their fiduciary duties if they revealed such information. Nevertheless, the fact that some sales are pending could be a strong indicator that a previously depressed market is on the rebound. In the same way, asking prices of properties currently listed but not yet sold are generally not considered in a property appraisal, but could be very revealing of the current market status. If there have been relatively few sales in the area recently, for instance, and current asking prices are lower than previous sales prices, that fact should be noted by the appraiser. When combined with other factors, such as increasing length of time on the market, the appraiser may have reason to discount the value of previously recorded sales.

The appraiser should also note previous sales of the subject property that occurred within at least three years. Close analysis of prior sales of the subject property may also indicate general market conditions.

Exercise 8-7

1. The subject of an appraisal is a house that is six years old and has three bedrooms. Name four places you would look for sales data.

2. You are appraising a subject property fitting the following description:

   Built 30 years ago, has five rooms, 1½ baths, of average-quality construction, in a neighborhood where average annual family income is $36,000.

   There are five properties that have sold recently. These five properties are similar to the subject property except for these differences:

   - Sale 1 has only one bath.
   - Sale 2 is about 20 years old.
   - Sale 3 needs paint.
   - Sale 4 is in a close-by, but similar, neighborhood.
   - Sale 5 has eight rooms and one bath.

   Which sales should be dropped from consideration as comparables, and why?

Check your answer against the one in the answer key at the back of the book.

■ SUMMARY

The appraisal process begins with a description of the property being appraised and a statement of the type of value being sought. The ownership or other interest being appraised also must be specified. The market value of a lease depends on the length of the remaining lease term. The value of a life estate depends on the probable life expectancy of the person against whose life the estate is measured.

An appraisal can be made as of any date, but an opinion of value based on a future date requires that the appraiser make clear the assumptions on which the opinion is based.

The appraisal process involves the collection of many types of data. The appraiser must identify the kinds and sources of data necessary for an accurate property appraisal. General data on the region, city, and neighborhood, as well as specific data on the sites and buildings involved and sales, cost, and income data must be collected.

The appraiser must follow national and regional trends closely to gauge accurately their impact on market value. Individual communities with a stable economic base are most likely to thrive in any set of circumstances. In addition to providing employment and shopping opportunities, local businesses can help bolster a community's tax base.

A parcel of real estate may be worth considerably more when it is combined with other parcels by the process of assemblage to allow construction of a much larger structure or other improvement than would otherwise be possible. The increase in value of the parcels, called plottage, will be enjoyed by the developer who takes the time and effort to assemble the individual lots.

The sales comparison approach, also called the market data approach, makes use of the principle of substitution to compare the property being appraised with comparable properties. The homebuyer who intends to occupy the home generally is less concerned than is the investor with the property's investment value based on its potential cash flow. For most homebuyers, the most important consideration is the price that other similar properties have sold for recently.

Most appraisals are based on fee simple ownership of the real estate being appraised, but some properties do not include all of the rights of ownership. Lesser interests, such as mineral or air rights, might be excluded. The property might include an extra benefit of ownership, such as an easement to travel over land owned by someone else. Leased fee and leasehold interests can be appraised separately.

The effect of unusual financing terms on the sales price of a comparable property must be analyzed and an adjustment made for any impact on value. Seller financing might indicate an interest rate above or below the market rate.

Uniform Appraisal Dataset (UAD) requirements enable the appraiser to produce more accurate and consistent appraisal reports.

■ Review Questions

1. The sales comparison approach relies on the principle of
   a. anticipation.
   b. leverage.
   c. substitution.
   d. highest and best use.

2. Another name for the sales comparison approach is
   a. the cost approach.
   b. the income capitalization approach.
   c. the market data approach.
   d. the substitution approach.

3. The transaction price of a property is its
   a. sales price.
   b. market value.
   c. insurance value.
   d. asking price.

4. *MOST* residential appraisals are based on
   a. the leased fee.
   b. fee simple ownership.
   c. the leasehold interest.
   d. less than fee simple ownership.

5. The appraisal process requires that the appraiser collect, record, and verify
   a. only data on the subject property's neighborhood.
   b. data on all neighborhoods in the city with which the appraiser is unfamiliar.
   c. data on an annual basis.
   d. data on the region, city, and neighborhood.

6. Ideally, the appraiser of a residential property will collect data on comparable property sales that occurred no earlier than
   a. 6 months prior to the date of appraisal.
   b. one year prior to the date of appraisal.
   c. 18 months prior to the date of appraisal.
   d. two years prior to the date of appraisal.

7. When choosing comparable sales for the sales comparison approach, property characteristics that should be identical or very similar to those of the subject property include
   a. the size of lot and building.
   b. the age of building and type of construction.
   c. the number and type of rooms.
   d. all of these.

8. One method of compensating for sales that involved different terms of financing is use of
   a. the financing readjustment grid.
   b. the cash equivalency technique.
   c. the loan-to-value ratio.
   d. the operating statement ratio.

9. To be considered comparable to the subject property, a comparable must have been sold
   a. in an arm's-length transaction.
   b. with a conventional mortgage.
   c. without any form of secondary financing.
   d. for all cash.

10. All sales data must be verified by
    a. one of the principals to the transaction.
    b. an internet resource.
    c. the county assessor.
    d. another appraiser.

11. To be considered comparable sales, properties should be
    a. close to the subject property.
    b. recently sold.
    c. very similar to the subject property.
    d. all of these.

12. The value of adjustments to the sales prices of comparable properties is set by
    a. the appraiser.
    b. the assessor.
    c. the market.
    d. the Appraisal Foundation.

13. What is the range of UAD condition entries?
    a. C1 to C6
    b. Q1 to Q6
    c. A to E
    d. A to Z

14. An area with set geographic boundaries and similar property uses is called
    a. a market.
    b. a geographic base.
    c. an economic base.
    d. a neighborhood.

15. The combination of two or more adjacent parcels is known as
    a. assemblage.
    b. plottage.
    c. unification.
    d. combination.

16. The increase in value that can occur when parcels are combined is called
    a. assemblage.
    b. plottage.
    c. unification.
    d. combination.

17. The agency that creates federal flood hazard maps is
    a. HUD.
    b. FNMA.
    c. FEMA.
    d. FHFO.

18. A transaction in which neither the seller nor the buyer is acting under duress is called
    a. arm's-length.
    b. conventional.
    c. cash equivalent.
    d. seller financing.

19. The first step in the appraisal process is
    a. collecting data.
    b. stating the problem.
    c. verifying data.
    d. collecting the fee from the client.

20. The level of business activity in a community is known as its
    a. market.
    b. market base.
    c. economic base.
    d. comprehensive base.

Check your answers against those in the answer key at the back of the book.

UNIT NINE

SITE VALUATION

LEARNING OBJECTIVES

When you have completed this unit, you will be able to

- distinguish vacant land from a building site,
- list reasons why a separate site valuation may be necessary,
- explain the concept of highest and best use,
- explain the importance of zoning in land valuation,
- describe some of the environmental concerns that can affect land value, and
- identify and demonstrate methods of site valuation.

KEY TERMS

abstraction method
allocation method
building residual technique
capitalization rate
condemnation
cost approach
eminent domain
entrepreneurial profit
environmental property assessment (EPRA)
environmental site assessment (ESA)
extraction method
forecast absorption
ground lease
ground rent
highest and best use
homeowners' association
interim use
land development method
nonconforming use
private restrictions
projected gross sales method
sales comparison method
subdivision development method
theory of consistent use
zoning
zoning variance

■ OVERVIEW

This unit discusses the basic principles and techniques that enable an appraiser to form an opinion of the market value of land after identifying it and gathering, recording, verifying, and analyzing the necessary data. You will learn some of the reasons for separate valuation of a site. You will also learn some of the red flags that indicate possible environmental problems on or near the site. Finally, you will be introduced to five methods of site valuation, with examples and exercises for four of them.

■ SEPARATE SITE VALUATIONS

There are two basic facts that affect all real estate appraisals:

- Land value is the primary determinant of overall real estate value.
- Land value is determined by market demand.

The most luxurious building constructed with the finest materials and the greatest attention to detail, regardless of its construction cost, will be only as valuable as the demand for that kind of property in that location warrants. As explained in earlier units, market demand is a reflection of the number of possible buyers competing for the available products and services. The number of buyers and sellers in the marketplace for real estate is subject to many variables, including the same factors that affect the country's overall economy, such as income and employment levels. The real estate appraiser's job is to identify the market variables that affect land value as well as possible and to determine their impact on value.

IN PRACTICE

A three-bedroom, two-bathroom house with an attached two-car garage is constructed on a suburban building lot in a neighborhood called Sorrento. At the same time, an exact duplicate of the house is constructed by the same builder on a lot of the same size and topography in a neighboring town called The Oaks. The same kinds of materials are used, the same craftspeople are hired to perform the work, and both houses are fitted with the same brand of appliances. Yet the asking price for the house in Sorrento is $330,000 and the asking price for the house in The Oaks is $290,000. Why is there a price differential? The answer lies in the value of the two parcels of land on which the houses were built. The lot in Sorrento cost the builder $95,000, while the lot in The Oaks cost the builder only $55,000.

Although vacant land can be appraised, most land valuations consider the property's value as a building site. A site is land that has been prepared for its intended use by the addition of such improvements as grading, utilities and road access. These improvements do not include structures, even though the same term can be used to include both. A site, then, is land that is ready for building or that already has a building on it but is being valued separately from the building. The major reasons for separate valuations are reviewed next.

Cost Approach

One of the primary reasons for a separate site valuation is use of the **cost approach** to value. The cost approach is based on the following formula:

$$\text{Cost of improvements new} - \text{Depreciation on improvements} + \text{Site value} = \text{Property value}$$

Even though the elements of site preparation, such as access and utilities, are improvements to the land, in the cost approach formula the term *improvements* refers to structures. An appraiser using the cost approach will calculate the value of the land separately and then add that value to the depreciated construction cost of the structures. The cost approach is covered in detail in Units 10 and 11.

Assessments and Taxation

Local communities frequently assess individual property owners for the cost of installation or upkeep of utilities and roads that benefit their property. The amount of the individual assessment is typically based on the value of the site, exclusive of any structures.

Real property taxes are generally *ad valorem* taxes; that is, they are based on a percentage of property value. Most states require separate valuations of site and structure(s) when determining the base property value to which the property tax rate will be applied.

Structures owned for investment purposes can be depreciated. Their value can be deducted from income produced by the investment over the term allowed by the applicable provision of federal income tax law. Because land is not considered a wasting or depreciating asset, its value must be subtracted from the overall property value before the amount of the allowable deduction can be calculated.

Land held as an investment, whether or not improved with structures, may lose value due to market factors, but any loss cannot be realized until the property is sold by the investor. Even though a homeowner realizes several income tax advantages, such as the deductibility of mortgage interest, the homeowner is not allowed to deduct any loss on the sale of the home.

Condemnation Appraisals

In **condemnation** proceedings under the government's right of **eminent domain**, courts will frequently require separate site and building valuations as part of the determination of the property's fair market value.

Income Capitalization

Using the income capitalization approach, the appraiser must determine the present value of the right to receive the income stream estimated to be produced by the subject property. One method that relies on income data to determine value is the **building residual technique** (covered in detail in Unit 14), which requires the appraiser to find land value separately. The appraiser subtracts an appropriate return on land value from the net income produced by the property to indicate the income available to the building.

Highest and Best Use

A **highest and best use** study can be a very complex process. The appraiser who is asked to consider the entire range of uses to which a property could be put must consider the value of the land separately from the value of any particular structure that can be erected on it. The property will be valued both with and without structures. The appraiser will consider not only the most valuable present and prospective use of the site, but also whether a zoning change or other approval necessary for a particular use is likely.

Every appraisal will include at least a brief statement of the property's highest and best use. Although many appraisals will be limited to present permitted land uses, occasionally the appraiser will be asked to make a broader recommendation that will require a thorough analysis of the feasibility and profitability of the entire range of uses to which the property could be put—a highest and best use study.

IN PRACTICE

Most urban and suburban land is zoned for a particular purpose. The few highly developed areas that do not have zoning (such as Houston, Texas) usually rely heavily on private deed restrictions to limit density and kinds of development. Site approval and building permits also may be required.

The requirements of purchasers in the marketplace will define the type of property that will be most desirable. The factors that contribute to desirability are what the appraiser must consider in determining a property's probable market value. The optimum combination of factors—resulting in the optimum value—is termed the property's highest and best use.

Of course, a purchaser in the marketplace will have some constraints on the fulfillment of a "wish list" of real estate objectives. Those constraints—physical, legal, and financial—are discussed next.

Four tests

In a highest and best use analysis, the appraiser must determine the use that fulfills the following four tests. The site use must be

1. physically possible,
2. legally permitted,
3. financially (or economically) feasible, and
4. maximally productive.

1. The use must be physically possible. A site's use may be limited by its size, shape, and topography. Does the site have sufficient access for development? Are utilities present or available? If they must be brought in, what cost is involved? Would the site be more promising as part of a larger parcel? As pointed out in Unit 8, an individual building lot may be more valuable if it can be combined with other adjacent properties in the process called assemblage.

2. The use must be legally permitted. Some concerns that begin as geologic considerations may result in legal prohibitions, such as restrictions on building in the vicinity of an earthquake fault line. Other legal restrictions are more subjective.

Zoning is an exercise of police power by a municipality or county to regulate private activity by enacting laws that benefit the health, safety, and general welfare of the public. The concept of zoning was upheld by the U.S. Supreme Court in *Euclid v. Ambler*, 272 U.S. 365 (1926). Ambler Realty Company, which owned 68 acres of land in the Village of Euclid, Ohio, a suburb of Cleveland, sued the village for passing a zoning ordinance that set permissible building sizes and uses in different parts of the village. The lower court agreed with Ambler's position that the ordinance denied the company its 14th Amendment right to due process and equal protection, but the Supreme Court held that zoning was a legitimate use of the village's police power.

Zoning regulations typically include the following:

- Permitted uses
- Minimum lot-size requirements
- Types of structures permitted
- Limitations on building size and height
- Minimum setbacks from lot lines
- Permitted density (for example, the number of buildings per acre)

An appraisal report should always include the property's current zoning classification. Any proposed changes to the current zoning classification also should be mentioned and commented on. Property sometimes is purchased subject to the condition that the present zoning will be changed—never a foregone conclusion. A request for a change of zoning may be made by appeal to the local zoning authority, usually a zoning administrator, zoning board, or board of zoning adjustment. If a property owner is unfairly burdened by a zoning restriction, a **zoning variance** may be granted. The variance allows a change in the specifications ordinarily required under the zoning regulations.

IN PRACTICE

A frequently encountered example of a zoning variance involves building setback requirements for residential property. If the rear of the property is a steep downslope that is unusable for all practical purposes, a variance may be granted to permit the homeowner to build a deck that would ordinarily be too close to the rear property line but that allows at least some use of what would otherwise be an inaccessible area. The circumstances in each case must be considered by the local zoning board or other authority, and approval of the request should never be taken for granted.

An existing property improvement is termed a **nonconforming use** if it would not be allowed under the site's present zoning. A building that represents a nonconforming use may still be a legal use of the property, however, if the structure was in conformance with applicable zoning at the time it was erected. Zoning ordinances typically allow an existing structure to remain when property is rezoned for a different use, although expansion or rebuilding based on the existing use may be prohibited or limited. If that is the case, an appraisal should include an estimate of the number of years that the existing structure can be expected to remain economically viable.

A nonconforming use may represent an underimprovement, such as residential property in an area rezoned for commercial use, or it may represent an overimprovement, such as a child care business in an area rezoned for residential use only. Another frequent example of an overimprovement is the church in a residential area. Although the church use may be allowed under a conditional use permit (permission allowing a use inconsistent with zoning but necessary for the common good), use of the property for any other purpose would require separate consideration by the zoning authority.

Not all property restrictions are imposed by government. **Private restrictions** include the covenants, conditions, and restrictions (CC&Rs) found in the typical declaration of restrictions filed by a subdivision developer and incorporated by reference in the deed to each subdivision lot.

IN PRACTICE

Residential deed restrictions typically are enacted to ensure that property owners observe a degree of conformity in construction and upkeep of improvements and may cover such topics as architectural style, building materials and exterior colors, landscaping, and maintenance.

Although deed restrictions can be enforced by any property owner who is benefited by them, they are most effective when a **homeowners' association** is formed and given the authority to act on behalf of all property owners. In many cases, the relatively minimal fee charged property owners to pay for the expenses of the homeowners' association is far outweighed by the financial benefits that flow from the improved appearance and desirability of the neighborhood.

3. The use must be financially feasible. A site use may be both physically possible and legally permitted, yet still be undesirable if using the site in that manner will not produce a commensurate financial return. Because market conditions affect financial feasibility, it is also possible that a use that is not financially feasible at present may become so in the future or vice versa. Often a site in what is apparently a very desirable location will remain vacant for a long time simply because the cost to develop it cannot be justified on the basis of estimated market demand for any permitted type of improvement.

IN PRACTICE

A site near an airport may be designated by zoning as suitable for either a hotel or a light manufacturing complex. If the area already has a relatively large number of hotels in the vicinity, resulting in a very low percentage rate of hotel-room occupancy, another hotel may not be advisable from an investment perspective. The expected rate of return per room may not justify the cost to build and maintain the facility. The same analysis would have to be made of the other allowed use; that is, would the development of the site for light manufacturing produce an adequate investment return?

4. The use must be maximally productive. If there is more than one legally permitted, physically possible, and financially feasible property use, which use will produce the highest financial return and thus the highest price for the property? The appraiser analyzes and compares the estimated net operating income of each present or prospective property use, in light of the rate of return typically expected by investors in that type of property, to determine which use offers the highest estimated financial return and thus makes the property more valuable.

IN PRACTICE

A vacant site in an almost completely developed suburban area that is zoned for limited commercial uses could be used for either a department store or a theater, and the terrain of the site would allow development of either. Using the income capitalization approach, the appraiser deducts from the expected net operating income for each type of structure an amount that represents the expected rate of return for property of that type. The income remaining is then divided by the capitalization rate assigned to the land to estimate the market value of the property for each purpose. The higher figure indicates the most productive use of the site and thus its highest and best use.

Each of these four areas of analysis is affected by the others. The amount of income that a particular use could generate is meaningless if legal approval for the use cannot be obtained. Conversely, not every legally permitted use will warrant the expenditure of funds required to bring it about. The appropriate combination of all four factors results in the single use that can be identified as the property's highest and best use.

Vacant (or as if vacant)

The traditional approach to determining highest and best use is to analyze vacant land or, if the land is improved, to study it as though it were vacant. There are several reasons why land may be studied and valued separately. First, in the cost approach and sometimes in the income capitalization approach to appraising, land value is estimated apart from the value of structures. Second, the purpose of the appraisal may be to consider the economic consequences of removing or converting an existing structure. The present structure, if any, is disregarded in the analysis of highest and best use, although the feasibility and cost of demolition and removal of an existing structure should be noted. The appraiser will then be correctly applying what has been termed the **theory of consistent use**. Both site and improvements will be valued based on the same use.

If an improved parcel is studied for its highest and best use as if vacant, that fact should be noted in the appraiser's report.

As improved

The expense and legal approval process associated with demolition of an existing structure may make it a necessary component of the parcel. Nevertheless, there may still be some possibility of a changed use that might result in higher income potential for the property. An older building that has outlived its usefulness for one purpose may undergo a sometimes startling transformation. This is especially true during a period of intense competition that results from an overbuilt market or economic downturn. Then, a state institution that has fallen into disuse may be deemed entirely appropriate for redevelopment into condominiums, rental units, and a golf course. (For more details of the economic realities that can result in such a transaction, see "Yesterday's Grim Asylums, Tomorrow's Grand Apartments," by Michael Corkery, *Wall Street Journal*, July 27, 2005, page B1.)

IN PRACTICE

Unlike commercial property, which may allow a variety of uses, residential property usually is zoned for exactly that, and any new structure must conform to that use. Despite the cost of demolition and removal of an existing building, however, many homes are purchased for the value of the underlying land and the prospect of tearing down the existing dwelling and erecting a new one, usually on a grand and luxurious scale. Understandably, some residents of areas where these earthbound phoenixes have arisen have taken offense at the brash and often conspicuous newcomers, and permits for conversion of such "teardown" properties have become more difficult to obtain in some communities.

Interim use

Some properties are appraised at a time when they are not yet at their expected highest and best use. The present use in such a case is considered an **interim use.**

The classic example of an interim use is farmland in the path of development. While considering the present use to be an interim use and appraising it as such may appear to be a logical assumption based on the population growth trend, surrounding land uses, and present zoning, a note of caution is in order. More than one landowner has been dismayed to find that being in the path of development is no guarantee that the land will ever be allowed to develop more than grass and wildflowers. Even if present zoning allows for a range of uses, including the potential for subdivision development, a zoning ordinance can be amended by the city or county government that enacted it in the first place.

IN PRACTICE

If property is "downzoned" to prohibit future development, can the property owner make a claim for compensation based on the economic loss of an expected property use? Not at the present time, unless the owner is denied all economically viable uses of the property (the "total takings" test), as decided by the U.S. Supreme Court in *Lucas v. South Carolina Coastal Council*, 505 U.S. 1003 (1992).

Exercise 9-1

The major reasons for valuing sites separately from buildings have been discussed. List as many of these reasons as you can.

Check your answer against the one in the answer key at the back of the book.

■ SITE DATA

Identification

The appraiser performing a site appraisal must determine and then collect the necessary data. The first step in site analysis, as required by the appraiser's scope of work, is to identify the property. A complete and legally accurate description of the site's location must be obtained. The plot plan used to illustrate the property description should include the site's property line dimensions and show its location within a given block.

IN PRACTICE

A visual inspection of the property should be made to confirm its approximate shape and size, as well as the existence of any structures or other improvements. The appraiser is not a surveyor and should not be expected to verify property boundaries. If there is any question as to the accuracy of the property description, such as the presence of a structure that was not reported, a property survey should be recommended. It is not unusual for a home in a brand-new subdivision to be erected on the wrong building lot.

Analysis

Once the subject property has been properly identified and described, it must be analyzed in detail. A report on the site's highest and best use should be an integral part of the analysis and should include the study of trends and factors influencing value, the data collection program, and the physical measurement of the site. Important features of the site are its size, location in terms of position on the block, utilities, improvements, soil composition (especially as related to grading, septic system, or bearing capacity for foundations), and whether it is located in a flood zone or an earthquake fault zone.

Knowledge of the subject site's zoning, which will affect its future use, is necessary, as is knowledge of the current zoning or imminent rezoning of surrounding properties in the area.

Finally, easements, deed restrictions, or publicly held rights-of-way should be noted. Any part of the site that cannot be used for building purposes should be clearly designated, along with other limitations on the use of the site.

IN PRACTICE

Vacant land requires a soil engineer's report to determine its suitability for building. Conditions that may make construction physically impossible or financially impractical, such as an underground stream, will not be apparent on a visual inspection.

■ ENVIRONMENTAL CONCERNS

With a wide range of environmental legislation now in place at both federal and state levels, identification and remediation of contaminants has become a necessary and sometimes very expensive component of property ownership. Federal regulations covering water, air, toxic substances, endangered species, wetlands, and other environmental concerns can have a profound impact on property condition as well as permitted property uses. State regulations pick up where federal regulations leave off, in many cases providing even more stringent requirements.

The first concern of the appraiser will be to identify potential or actual environmental factors that are likely to affect property value. This does not mean that every appraisal will serve as an evaluation of all environmental problems present on or affecting the subject property but, rather, that the appraiser should at least note obvious conditions and recommend further inspection. For commercial real estate, an **environmental site assessment (ESA)** or **environmental property assessment (EPRA)** is probably well advised to protect the property owner, lender, and others involved in the transaction. Either type of inspection and analysis is beyond the scope of the average appraiser and should be undertaken only by one who is especially trained in the physical, economic, and legal ramifications of environmental conditions.

What the average appraiser can do is conduct a conscientious inspection of the subject property and note suspicious conditions. These may include (and are by no means limited to) the following:

- Ponds, lakes, creeks, and other bodies of water
- Standing water or wetlands, even if seasonal
- High-power transmission lines
- Evidence of past commercial or agricultural land use
- Underground or above-ground storage tanks or drums
- Deteriorating paint
- Insulation around water pipes or ducts
- Smoke, haze, or other airborne condition
- Excessive noise
- Old building foundations or other evidence of an earlier structure
- A dump site

WEB LINK
www.epa.gov

Even a pristine site can be problematic if it is found to be the habitat for an endangered species. In short, any factor that could affect property use should be noted in the appraisal report. More information on a wide variety of topics can be found at www.epa.gov.

WEB LINK
www.epa.gov/brownfields

Brownfields

The Environmental Protection Agency (EPA) has estimated that there are approximately 450,000 parcels of real estate in the United States that can be described as brownfields—abandoned or underutilized property that may or may not be contaminated. Pilot programs aimed at promoting a unified approach to environmental assessment, cleanup, and redevelopment have begun in 40 jurisdictions. More information about the Brownfields Action Agenda, including telephone numbers for 10 regional offices, can be obtained from the EPA's Washington office at 202-566-2777, or at www.epa.gov/brownfields.

■ METHODS OF SITE VALUATION

The following six valuation methods are commonly used in appraising building sites:

- *Sales comparison method.* Sales of similar vacant sites are analyzed and compared. After any necessary adjustments to sales prices are made, the appraiser arrives at an opinion of value for the subject site.
- *Allocation method.* The allocation method is used when the land value of an improved property must be found. The ratio of land value to building value typical of similar improved properties in the area is applied to the total value of the subject property to arrive at the land value of the subject.
- *Abstraction method,* also called *extraction method.* When the sales price of a property is known, the cost of all improvements can be subtracted from it to find land value.
- *Subdivision development method.* The costs of developing and subdividing a parcel of land are subtracted from the total expected sales prices of the separate sites, adjusting for the time required to sell all of the individual sites, to determine the value of the undivided raw land.
- *Ground rent capitalization method.* When a landowner leases land to a tenant who agrees to erect a building on it, the lease is usually called a ground lease. Ground rents can be capitalized at an appropriate rate to indicate the market value of the site. For example, assume that a site is on a long-term lease with a ground rent of $100,000 per year. If the appropriate rate for capitalization of ground rent is 10%, the estimated value by direct capitalization is

  $$\$100{,}000 \div 0.10 = \$1{,}000{,}000$$

- *Land residual method.*[1] The net income earned by the building is deducted from the total net income of the property; the balance is attributed to the land. The residual or leftover income is then capitalized to indicate the land value. The formula used for this method is

  Property net income – Building net income = Land net income

  Land net income ÷ Land capitalization rate = Land value

Sales Comparison Method

There are no basic differences between the data valuation of improved properties and unimproved sites in the **sales comparison method**. Sales comparison analysis and valuation are discussed and illustrated in detail in Units 8 and 12; the basic points are simply reviewed here.

Of all the methods of site valuation, the sales comparison method generally provides the most reliable indicator of market value. Just as the value of an existing

---

1. Because a comprehensive treatment of the residual techniques and the capitalization process is contained in Unit 14, "Direct and Yield Capitalization," this method of site valuation is not covered here.

(not newly constructed) house is estimated by the most recent sales prices of comparable houses in the neighborhood, the value of a site is judged largely by the same comparison method.

The appraiser's objective is to determine the probable market value of the property being appraised by interpreting the data from sales of similar properties. The appraiser's first task in applying this method is to find sales data on comparable properties. Because no two parcels of land are identical, an appraiser will always have to compensate for some differences when comparing sales properties to the subject property. Typical differences include date of sale, location, physical characteristics, zoning and land-use restrictions, terms of financing, and conditions of sale. Of course, the appraiser is also concerned that the comparable properties have been sold fairly recently. If any sale occurred more than six months before the date of the appraisal, an adjustment is probably indicated.

The adjustment process is an analysis designed to eliminate the effect on value of the significant property differences. Each comparable property is likened as much as possible to the subject property. In adjusting the sales price of a comparable property, lump-sum dollar amounts or percentages are customarily used. Adjustments are always applied to the sales price of the comparable property, not the value of the subject property. If the comparable property is inferior in some respect to the subject property, its sales price is increased by an appropriate dollar amount or percentage. If the comparable property is superior to the subject property in some category, its sales price is decreased commensurately. The appraiser then uses the adjusted sales prices of the comparable properties to determine the most likely value to assign to the subject property.

In comparing site data, whether vacant or improved, the appraiser should take care always to use the same units of measurement. For example, the sales price of a site may be expressed as a certain amount per front foot, based on the site's street frontage. Rural property usually is valued in acres; a residential subdivision lot may be valued in square feet or, if large enough, in acres. If lots are all very close in size or utility, value may be expressed per lot.

IN PRACTICE

An appraisal is being made of Lot 81, Hilltop Acres Subdivision. Lot 81 is very similar to Lot 78, which sold recently for $28,000, but Lot 81 has a view of a nearby lake. By analyzing sales of other lots in Hilltop Acres, the appraiser determines that a lake view contributes $10,000 to lot value. The adjusted sales price of Lot 78 thus is $38,000, which is the indicated value of Lot 81 using this comparable in the sales comparison approach.

Exercise 9-2

Assume that a residential lot, 75 feet by 150 feet, sold one year ago for $20,000. In analyzing the market, you arrive at the following conclusions:

1. The subject site is 12% or $2,400 more valuable as a result of price increases over the year since the comparable site was sold.
2. The subject site is 10% or $2,000 more valuable than the comparable site with respect to location.
3. The subject site is 15%, or $3,000, less valuable with respect to physical features.

Based on the information provided, complete the adjustment table:

	Sales Price	Date	Location	Physical Features	Net Adjustment + or –	Adjusted Price
Dollar basis						
Percentage basis						

Check your answers against those in the answer key at the back of the book.

Allocation Method

In the **allocation method**, land value is treated as a percentage or proportion of the total value of an improved property. Often, a consistent relationship exists between land and building values. For example, an area may tend to have a one-to-four land-to-building ratio. This means that the building value will be four times the land value. If the total property value is $200,000, $40,000 will be allocated to the land and $160,000 to the structure. As a rough rule of thumb, such a ratio will serve as a very broad indicator of what buyers in the marketplace are likely to expect.

As demand for buildable land increases, the ratio of land-to-building value tends to narrow as their relative values come closer together. The one-to-four ratio may become one-to-three or even one-to-two. This occurs because the total cost of the land and building will be limited by what buyers in the marketplace are prepared to pay, although the affordability ceiling will tend to rise as demand increases and supply dwindles.

Property tax assessors make such an allocation in apportioning the amount of property tax owed between land and improvements, by determining the ratio of land value to value of improvements. The allocation method is weak because it fails to take individual property differences into account.

IN PRACTICE

The allocation method should be used only in situations where there is a lack of current sales data for vacant sites that are similar to and competitive with the subject site. It may also be useful as a broad check of an appraisal by another method.

Exercise 9-3

In a high-income suburban residential area, the ratio of building value to land value approximates three-to-one. What is the land value of a typical property valued at $347,000, using the allocation method?

Check your answer against the one in the answer key at the back of the book.

Abstraction (Extraction) Method

Abstraction or **extraction** is similar to the allocation method. As shown in Figure 9.1, all improvement costs less depreciation ($129,000) are deducted from the sales price ($178,000), and the remaining value of $49,000 is considered land value..

FIGURE 9.1
Abstraction Method

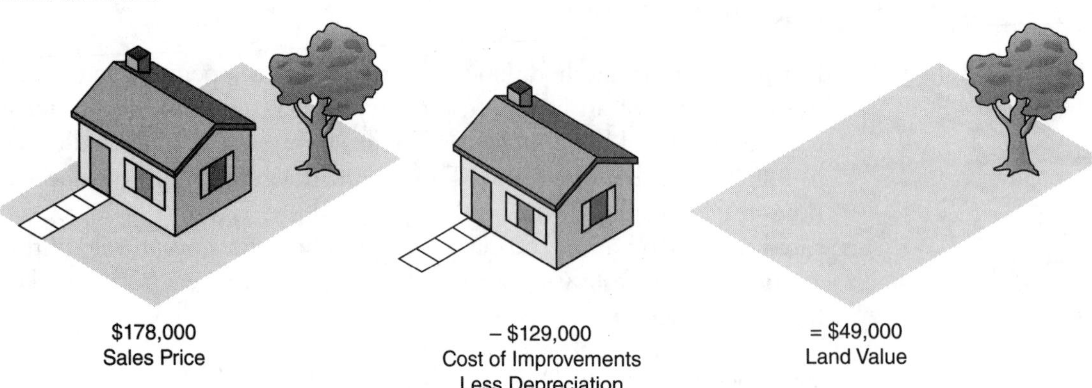

IN PRACTICE

The abstraction method, though imprecise, may be useful in appraising property when there are few sales for comparison. This is often the case with rural properties, particularly for larger parcels with improvements that represent a relatively small portion of the property's total value.

Subdivision Development Method

The **subdivision development method** is a land valuation method that concerns the value of raw (undeveloped) land that is suitable for single-family residential building lots. Residential development in and around urban areas is a fact of life, and most sites suitable for single-family houses are part of subdivisions that started out as large tracts of undeveloped land. Once the building sites are prepared and construction is ready to begin, the individual lots will be priced as the market allows. How can a fair value for raw land be determined?

One method that can be used factors out the expenses of development to determine a fair market value for the land prior to development. In the **subdivision development method,** also called the **land development method,** all probable costs of development, including the developer's profit and cost of financing, are subtracted from the total projected sales prices of the individual units. The figure that results is the raw land value. The method relies on accurate forecasting of market demand, including both **forecast absorption** (the rate at which properties will sell) and **projected gross sales** (total income that the project will produce).

IN PRACTICE

A 40-acre subdivision is expected to yield 160 single-family homesites after allowances for streets, common areas, et cetera. Each site should have an ultimate market value of $30,000, so that the projected sales figure for all the lots is $4,800,000 (160 × $30,000).

Based on an analysis of comparable land sales, it is concluded that lots can be sold at the rate of 60 in year 1, 70 in year 2, and 30 in year 3.

Engineers advise that the cost of installing streets, sewers, water, and other improvements will be $10,000 per lot. Other costs (sales expenses, administration, accounting, legal, taxes, overhead, etc.) are estimated at 20% and developer's profit at 10% of gross lot sales.

Problem: Assume that the highest and best use of the land is for subdivision development and that there is an active demand for home sites. What price should a developer pay for this acreage based on a sales program taking three years to complete?

Solution: Total projected sales:		
160 lots at $30,000 per lot		$4,800,000
Total projected development costs:		
Street grading and paving, sidewalks, curbs, gutters, sanitary and storm sewers for 160 lots at $10,000 per lot	$1,600,000	
Other costs, 20% of $4,800,000 (total projected sales)	960,000	
Developer's profit, 10% of $4,800,000 (total projected sales)	480,000	
Total development costs		3,040,000
Estimated value of raw land		$1,760,000
Raw land value per lot, $1,760,000 ÷ 160		$11,000

The amount that a developer should pay now in anticipation of the land's future value can be computed by using a financial calculator, as you will learn in Unit 12. It can also be computed by applying a reversion factor to the land's present estimated value undeveloped. The future value of the investment is reduced by the compound interest it could earn from the present time until the time when the investment is returned. This process of discounting indicates the value of the investment today.

Note that even if the developer is also the contractor on the project, the amount of profit attributable to the development function (also referred to as **entrepreneurial profit**) usually is considered a separate item.

IN PRACTICE

To continue our example, the developer's expected yield of 10% discounted to present worth for one year indicates a reversion factor of 0.909; two years, a reversion factor of 0.826; and three years, a reversion factor of 0.751.

The present worth of lot sales is as follows:

First year:	60 lots at $11,000 per lot = $660,000 $660,000 discounted to present worth at 10% for one year (0.909)	$ 599,940
Second year:	70 lots at $11,000 per lot = $770,000 $770,000 discounted to present worth for two years (0.826)	636,020
Third year:	30 lots at $11,000 per lot = $330,000 $330,000 discounted to present worth for three years (0.751)	247,830
	Present value of $1,760,000 discounted partially one, two, and three years	$1,483,790

In this very simplified example, a developer would be justified in paying $1,483,790 for the raw land for subdivision purposes.

Exercise 9-4

The following building costs have been predicted for a 72-unit residential subdivision planned to utilize a 30-acre tract:

Engineering and surveying	$ 23,000
Roads	117,000
Grading and leveling all sites	46,000
Utilities	129,000
Marketing	72,000
Financing	182,000
Taxes	47,000
Administration, accounting, and other professional services	118,000
Developer's profit	200,000

Projected sales figures for the lots are as follows:

- 48 lots at $27,000 each, discounted to present worth at 12% for one year (factor: 0.893);

- 16 lots at $32,000 each, discounted to present worth at 12% for two years (factor: 0.797); and
- 8 lots at $36,000 each, discounted to present worth at 12% for three years (factor: 0.712).

(The higher lot prices reflect expected price increases over time.)

Estimate the market value of the raw acreage using the subdivision development method.

Determine how much a subdivider would be justified in paying for the raw land for development.

Check your answers against those in the answer key at the back of the book.

Ground Rent Capitalization Method

The owner of land to be developed for commercial or other purposes may choose to retain the fee simple title to the land yet lease the right to use it for building. When a landowner leases land to a tenant who agrees to erect a building or other improvement on the land, the lease is usually called a **ground lease.** A ground lease must be for a long enough term to make the transaction desirable to the tenant investing in the building. Such leases often run for terms of 50 years or longer, and a lease for 99 years is not uncommon.

The terms of a ground lease, including the **ground rent** (payment made by the tenant under a ground lease) to be paid, will vary according to the desirability of the land and the relative negotiating strengths of the parties. Tenants can range from individual property owners in a subdivision of manufactured homes to a major corporation in a high-rise office building.

The value of a ground lease usually is determined by dividing the ground rent by an appropriate **capitalization rate**. Unit 14 of the text explains how the capitalization rate is derived. The provisions of the lease agreement must be known for a complete and accurate appraisal. The appraiser must consider the remaining length of the lease term as well as both the present rent paid and the possibility for a rent increase if the lease contains an escalation clause.

■ SUMMARY

Site value often is a separate appraisal consideration, even for property that has already been improved by the addition of structures. The site's optimum value will depend on its highest and best use, which is the use that is physically possible, legally permitted, financially feasible, and maximally productive.

A site's present legally permitted uses are determined by zoning and other public regulations, as well as private restrictions such as those found in the declaration of restrictions that often accompanies subdivision parcels. A preexisting use of land that does not conform to the present zoning ordinance is called a nonconforming use. A nonconforming use may ordinarily remain; however, certain restrictions are usually imposed, such as a limitation on expansion of the present use. A zoning variance may be requested from the local governing body; a conditional use permit will allow continuation of a use that does not comply with present zoning but is of benefit to the community.

The appraiser can choose among a variety of site valuation methods, making use of sales of comparable sites (sales comparison method), income streams (land residual method), costs of development compared with projected sales income (subdivision development method), analysis of income expectation for land alone (ground rent capitalization), site-to-building value ratios (allocation method), or cost of improvements (abstraction, or extraction, method).

Property may be appraised for the value of its current, interim use, with the expectation that the use will change in the future. By extracting all other costs from total property value, the appraiser will arrive at the amount that is attributable solely to land value. This method primarily is useful when there are few sales of such property available for comparison. The subdivision development, or land development, method takes into account all costs, including both contractor's profit and developer's entrepreneurial profit.

A ground lease can be appraised, and its value will depend on the ground rent being paid, the length of the remaining lease term, and other specific features of the underlying lease agreement.

■ Review Questions

1. Explain how the terms *land* and *site* differ.

2. Why would an appraiser need to know site valuation
   a. in the cost approach?
   b. for tax purposes?

3. Name six site valuation techniques. Which method is preferred, and why?

4. Another term for *developer's profit* is
   a. contractor's profit.
   b. entrepreneurial profit.
   c. project profit.
   d. management profit.

5. A church in a residential area is an example of
   a. police power.
   b. forecast absorption.
   c. a nonconforming use.
   d. a private restriction.

6. Zoning is an exercise of a government's
   a. police power.
   b. power of eminent domain.
   c. right of condemnation.
   d. right of priority.

7. All improvement costs, less depreciation, are subtracted from sales price to derive land value in the process called
   a. ground rent capitalization.
   b. extraction.
   c. entrepreneurial enterprise.
   d. assemblage.

8. Private deed restrictions often are enforced through
   a. a zoning variance.
   b. a zoning board.
   c. a homeowners' association.
   d. a housing cooperative.

9. A land-to-building (L:B) ratio is used in which site valuation technique?
   a. Allocation
   b. Extraction
   c. Sales comparison
   d. Abstraction

10. If the L:B ratio is 1:3, the percentage of land value to overall value is
    a. 20%.
    b. 25%.
    c. 33%.
    d. 50%.

11. A parcel of land has a L:B ratio of 1:4. If overall property values average $200,000 in the neighborhood, the land value of the parcel under consideration is
    a. $33,333.
    b. $40,000.
    c. $50,000.
    d. $100,000.

12. If a property's total value is $350,000, and the building value is $275,000, the land value is
    a. $55,000.
    b. $75,000.
    c. $150,000.
    d. $625,000.

13. A building's current construction cost is $200,000 and it has depreciated 10%. If the total property value is $220,000, the land value is
    a. $20,000.
    b. $30,000.
    c. $40,000.
    d. $50,000.

14. If the highest and best use of a parcel of land is its development potential, the method most often used to value it is
    a. the allocation method.
    b. the extraction method.
    c. the sales comparison method.
    d. the subdivision development method.

15. A condemnation appraisal might be required when the government exercises its right of
    a. escheat.
    b. eminent domain.
    c. taxation.
    d. police power.

16. Site value is determined separately in
    a. the cost approach.
    b. the sales comparison approach.
    c. the income approach.
    d. all of these.

17. Highest and best use is
    a. the most efficient land value.
    b. the maximally productive use of the land.
    c. the same as the current use of the land.
    d. analyzed after the three approaches are used.

18. Land and building must be valued at the same highest and best use according to the theory of
    a. contribution.
    b. substitution.
    c. anticipation.
    d. consistent use.

19. If land is rented, the rent might be analyzed to render an opinion of value in
    a. the ground rent capitalization method.
    b. the allocation method.
    c. the extraction method.
    d. the land residual method.

20. The amount of profit attributed to the land development function is
    a. excess profit.
    b. overage income.
    c. entrepreneurial profit.
    d. normalized income.

Check your answers against those in the answer key at the back of the book.

10

UNIT TEN

THE COST APPROACH—PART I: REPRODUCTION/REPLACEMENT COST

LEARNING OBJECTIVES

When you have completed this unit, you will be able to

- distinguish between reproduction cost and replacement cost;
- determine reproduction/replacement cost using the index, square-foot, unit-in-place, and quantity survey methods;
- explain what is meant by regional multipliers;
- use cost manuals; and
- compute the reproduction cost of a building based on building component costs.

KEY TERMS

comparative unit method
cost manuals
cost service index method
direct costs
entrepreneurial profit
gross living area
index method
indirect costs
principle of sibstitution
quantity survey method
regional multipliers
replacement cost
reproduction cost
square-foot method
summation method
unit-in-place method

■ OVERVIEW

One approach to appraising that is especially appropriate for certain types of property is the cost approach. In the cost approach, the value of all property improvements (reproduction or replacement cost less depreciation) is added to site value to determine market value. In this unit, the distinction between reproduction and replacement cost and the methods of computing building cost are explained. In Unit 11, the different types of depreciation are analyzed.

■ COST APPROACH FORMULA

To reach an opinion of value by the cost approach, the appraiser (1) calculates the cost to reproduce or replace the existing structures, (2) subtracts from the cost estimate any loss in value because of depreciation, and (3) adds the value of the site alone to the depreciated cost figure. The basic principle involved is the **principle of substitution**. The cost of a new building is substituted for that of the existing one, with some adjustment to compensate for depreciation of the existing building due to general deterioration and other factors.

The cost approach can be expressed as a formula:

$$\text{Reproduction or replacement cost of improvements} - \text{Accrued depreciation} + \text{Site value} = \text{Property value}$$

The value of the land must be figured separately and then added to the depreciated construction cost of the structure. Because the cost approach involves the addition of separately derived building and site values, it is also called the **summation method** of appraising.

The basic premise of the cost approach is this: Under normal market conditions, buyers of real estate typically do not want to pay more for a parcel with an existing structure than they would have to pay to build an identical structure on a vacant parcel. In the same manner, they would not want to pay as much for an older building as they would pay for a brand-new one. Over time, even if vacant, every building will suffer some of the effects of decay and ordinary wear and tear. In addition, an older structure will not be of the currently most desirable design or contain the most up-to-date fixtures. As a result, an older building should not be as expensive as a new building of the same size that offers the features that are currently in the greatest demand.

There are exceptions to every rule, of course. Some properties are more valuable *because* of their age and are priced accordingly. Many urban areas have a historic district in which the historical landmark designation can be either a blessing or an annoyance. It can be a blessing if it means that property will retain its character and charm for the enjoyment of all who live or work in the community. It can be an annoyance for the property owner if considerable effort and financial commitment is required to bring the property to livable standards within the limitations typically placed on historic structures. Fortunately, our tax laws may offer incentives to those who choose to invest in rehabilitating historic buildings. Partly because of that advantage, habitable buildings with historic status may be more valuable than similar buildings without such a designation.

The realities of the marketplace may sometimes appear to make a mockery of the cost approach. Most regions of the United States, at one time or another, have experienced the red-hot seller's market—the kind of market in which the typical property elicits multiple bids soon after being offered for sale. When an overabundance of buyers confronts a market with relatively few properties for sale, prices tend to rise at sometimes incomprehensible rates. Often, the cost of a used house rises to meet or even surpass that of a new house that may be less accessible or may not be immediately available for occupancy. Most areas of the country have experienced the effects of a real estate boom at one time or another. Property owners in recent times can attest to the ease with which property can be sold in the seller's market that accompanies a real estate boom.

Unfortunately for sellers, but fortunately for buyers, most markets tend to cool off eventually. Sometimes the cooling off is so precipitous that the boom turns into a bust and produces the opposite effect—the buyer's market. Many homeowners who anticipated their potential profits during the hot days of a seller's market know the cold feeling of desperation that comes from having to sell a house that no one is interested in buying. Even worse, some of those buyers who purchased when prices were at all-time highs are forced to sell their properties at a loss, the ultimate market dilemma that most of us don't like to think of in relation to one of our most valuable financial assets—our home.

Several other, more technical, drawbacks to the application of the cost approach exist, particularly when it is applied to residential property.

First, the existing property use may not be the land's highest and best use. If the structure being appraised is inappropriate and not easily adaptable to the site's highest and best use, a cost approach analysis may be an idle exercise. One example that occurs frequently in urban areas is the residential neighborhood that is rezoned to allow commercial development. As properties in the area are converted to commercial use, their land value typically increases. The value of other structures may increase as well, but the structures with the greatest increase in value will be those that are adaptable for business use.

Second, builder's costs always vary to some extent depending on the number of projects undertaken and the individual builder's profit margin, among other factors. The real estate appraiser's job is to be aware of the range of construction costs in the area in order to select the figure that is most appropriate for the property being appraised.

Nevertheless, the cost approach must be used when a value opinion via either the income capitalization approach or the sales comparison approach is not possible. For example, in the appraisal of special-purpose properties such as churches, schools, museums, and libraries, there are no income figures available and few, if any, comparable sales.

An opinion of value by the cost approach is also needed in establishing value for insurance purposes. Insurance claims are based on the cost of restoration, or reimbursement for loss, as determined by the appraised insurance value; therefore, an insurance appraiser is mainly concerned with reproduction cost. Condemnation proceedings and real estate tax assessments are other instances in which an opinion of value by the cost approach is necessary.

Site value is a critical part of the cost approach; however, it is not developed through a costing process. Site value, as the last part of the cost approach equation, usually is computed by the sales comparison approach, as explained in Unit 9. The location and amenities of the subject site (except for improvements) are compared with those of similar nearby sites. Adjustments are made for any significant differences, and the adjusted prices of the properties most like the subject site are used to form an opinion of the value of the subject site.

REPRODUCTION COST VS. REPLACEMENT COST

The appraiser always begins the cost approach valuation by estimating the construction cost of a new building that is physically or functionally identical to the subject building at current prices. The physical condition of the building and the outside factors that may affect its value are not considered at this stage. The construction cost computed by the appraiser will be either the reproduction cost or the replacement cost of the subject structure. Although the terms *reproduction cost* and *replacement cost* may appear synonymous, they have very different meanings in a real estate appraisal.

Reproduction cost is the dollar amount required to construct an exact duplicate of a building at prices current as of the date of appraisal. The appraiser must take into account the expense of finding materials of the same design, manufacture, and quality as the subject property, constructed with the same techniques.

For newer properties, this is usually a feasible task that results in a cost analysis in keeping with other structures of similar age. For older buildings, however, particularly those that have attained historic status, the task of estimating current reproduction cost is considerably more challenging. The appraiser is confronted with materials that may no longer be available or that may be impossible to duplicate except at an exorbitant cost. In addition, certain property features requiring sophisticated carpentry, masonry, or other skills may be beyond the expertise of today's craftspeople.

Because most existing structures are fairly recent in origin, finding the reproduction cost is usually not a problem and is how appraisers normally use the cost approach. For properties that do not have an economically viable reproduction cost, the appraiser will calculate the **replacement cost** of the structures instead.

Replacement cost is the current construction cost of a building with the same utility as the subject structure. The appraiser is actually estimating the reproduction cost, but it is the reproduction cost of a theoretical building that contains the same number, type, and size of rooms as the building being appraised and that can be used in the same way. The appraiser does not take into account the many details of material and workmanship that may make the subject property unique. The theoretical building against which the subject is measured should possess the same overall quality as the subject, but as defined by contemporary standards.

Of course, the appraiser will note as a condition of the appraisal that it is impossible to duplicate the subject property exactly in today's marketplace. The appraiser will also have to gauge the effect of this condition on the property's value. The existing property features may be more or less valuable, depending on the desirability of those features in the marketplace.

For example, an older home may have intricate exterior and interior carpentry well beyond the type of work available today. In such a case, the appraiser will estimate the cost to produce features of a similar quality, using currently available construction materials and methods. Many architectural details, such as elaborate moldings (ceiling trim) can be found in materials that look identical to the originals from which they are copied. Yet because the copies are formed from lightweight, synthetic materials, they are relatively inexpensive and easy to install. Replacement cost will be sought when finding reproduction cost is impossible or economically impractical.

IN PRACTICE

The exacting details of workmanship present in an older home may make it impossible to duplicate today at a reasonable price. Instead, the appraiser estimates the replacement cost of a home with the same number, type, size of rooms, and comparable construction quality as the subject property.

The construction cost, whether reproduction or replacement, will be for a new structure at current prices as of the effective appraisal date. The condition of the improvements at the time of the appraisal is not a factor at this point. Construction cost is a measure of the quality of a structure in terms of how expensive it would be to rebuild or replace and is not a measure of the structure's condition. An allowance for the condition of the subject property, as well as any other adverse influences, is made when accrued depreciation is subtracted in the second part of the cost approach equation.

If the cost approach section of the URAR form is completed, reproduction cost or replacement cost must be indicated.

Exercise 10-1

Replacement cost (rather than reproduction cost) would likely be used in valuing which of the houses shown here?

Why?

Check your answers against those in the answer key at the back of the book.

FINDING REPRODUCTION/REPLACEMENT COST

An appraiser using the cost approach will compute the cost to duplicate property improvements, whether of the subject property itself (reproduction cost) or a functionally identical replacement (replacement cost). Four basic methods can be used to find the reproduction cost of a structure. The most complex are used primarily for commercial and industrial properties.

- *Index method.* A factor representing the percentage increase of construction costs up to the date of value is applied to the original cost of the subject building.
- *Square-foot method.* The cost per square foot of a recently built comparable structure is multiplied by the number of square feet in the subject building.
- *Unit-in-place method.* The construction cost per unit of measure of each component part of the subject structure (including material, labor, overhead, and builder's profit) is multiplied by the number of units of that component part in the subject. Most components are measured in square feet, although certain items, such as plumbing fixtures, are estimated as complete units. The sum of the cost of the components is the cost of the new structure.
- *Quantity survey method.* The itemized costs of erecting or installing all of the component parts of a new structure are added. Indirect costs (building permit, land survey, overhead expenses such as insurance and payroll taxes, and builder's profit) are totaled, as well as direct costs (site preparation and all phases of building construction, including fixtures).

The **square-foot method** is the one typically used by appraisers in estimating construction costs. The quantity survey method is the one generally used by cost estimators, contractors, and builders because all of a structure's components are analyzed, which yields the most accurate cost estimate. This method, as well as the unit-in-place method, can be quite accurate when used by qualified cost estimators, although both are more time-consuming than the square-foot method. Because it does not take into account individual property variables, the index method generally is used only as a check of the estimate reached by one of the other methods, or when the lower level of reliability achieved is deemed acceptable.

Index Method

With the **index method**, the appraiser applies a factor representing the change in building costs over time to the original cost of the subject property. Although the index method of finding reproduction cost is rarely accurate enough to be used alone, it may serve as a useful way to verify cost figures arrived at by one of the other methods provided the original construction cost of the improvements is known.

Cost reporting or indexing services keep records of building cost changes over time, and sometimes from area to area. All dollar amounts are given a numerical factor relative to whatever base year is being used. By comparing the current cost index with the cost index at the time construction took place and then applying that factor to the original construction cost, an estimate of current cost can be derived. The formula used is as follows:

$$\frac{\text{Present index}}{\text{Index at time of construction}} \times \text{Original cost} = \text{Present cost}$$

IN PRACTICE

An office building constructed in 1988 for $149,000 had a cost index at that time of 177. The present cost index is 354. Using the formula:

$$\frac{354}{177} \times \$149{,}000 = \$298{,}000$$

In this example, $298,000 is the estimated reproduction cost of the subject building.

Using cost indices successfully requires that the building cost of the subject property be fairly typical; any additions or changes to the original structure must be taken into consideration. If a building or one of its components is fairly standard, the method can be useful.

The index method of finding reproduction cost is also called the **cost service index method.**

Exercise 10-2

A residence cost $39,000 to construct in 1975. A cost index published at that time was 158.2. The current cost index from the same cost reporting service is 537.8.

What is the current indicated reproduction cost of the residence by the index method?

Check your answer against the one in the answer key at the back of the book.

Square-Foot Method

WEB LINK

www.rsmeans.com

WEB LINK

www.construction.com/dodge

WEB LINK

www.marshallswift.com

With experience, the appraiser can become as familiar with local building costs as a contractor. One of the ways in which both building and appraisal professionals keep up to date on current costs is by using a cost manual. Information on building specifications and typical construction costs is provided in manuals published by such national companies as R. S. Means, F.W. Dodge Corporation, and Marshall & Swift. **Cost manuals** give building specifications and typical construction costs. They are customized for specific geographic regions and are usually updated quarterly, sometimes even monthly. Cost estimating services offer online cost databases for the most efficient and up-to-date cost estimates.

Figure 10.1 shows a page from a typical residential construction cost manual. The overall quality of construction and type of structure are specified (in this case, the structure is an economy-quality two-story house). Other features of the house, such as an asphalt shingled roof, are listed to the left of the illustration.

Figure 10.1
Sample Page from a Residential Construction Cost Manual

RESIDENTIAL	**Economy**	**2 Story**

- **Mass produced from stock plans**
- **Single family – 1 full bath, 1 kitchen**
- **No basement**
- **Asphalt shingles on roof**
- **Hot air heat**
- **Gypsum wallboard interior finishes**
- **Materials and workmanship are sufficient to meet codes**
- **Detail specifications on page 19**

Note: The illustration shown may contain some optional components (for example: garages and/or fireplaces) whose costs are shown in the modifications, adjustments, & alternatives below or at the end of the square foot section.

Base cost per square foot of living area

	Living Area										
Exterior Wall	**1000**	**1200**	**1400**	**1600**	**1800**	**2000**	**2200**	**2600**	**3000**	**3400**	**3800**
Wood Siding - Wood Frame	109.15	98.55	93.65	90.20	86.80	83.00	80.40	75.60	70.90	68.80	66.85
Brick Veneer - Wood Frame	114.00	103.05	97.80	94.25	90.55	86.60	83.85	78.70	73.75	71.50	69.45
Stucco on Wood Frame	101.10	91.15	86.70	83.60	80.55	76.95	74.65	70.40	66.05	64.25	62.50
Painted Concrete Block	109.00	98.40	93.50	90.10	86.70	82.85	80.25	75.55	70.80	68.65	66.75
Finished Basement, Add	15.85	15.20	14.65	14.30	13.95	13.65	13.40	12.85	12.50	12.25	12.05
Unfinished Basement, Add	7.15	6.55	6.15	5.90	5.55	5.35	5.15	4.75	4.45	4.25	4.10

Modifications

Add to the total cost

Upgrade Kitchen Cabinets	$ + 810
Solid Surface Countertops	+ 570
Full Bath - including plumbing, wall and floor finishes	+ 5458
Half Bath - including plumbing, wall and floor finishes	+ 3082
One Car Attached Garage	+ 11,736
One Car Detached Garage	+ 15,096
Fireplace & Chimney	+ 6068

Adjustments

For multi family - add to total cost

Additional Kitchen	$ + 4218
Additional Bath	+ 5458
Additional Entry & Exit	+ 1602
Separate Heating	+ 1468
Separate Electric	+ 1133

For Townhouse/Rowhouse - Multiply cost per square foot by

Inner Unit	+ .93
End Unit	+ .96

Alternatives

Add to or deduct from the cost per square foot of living area

Composition Roll Roofing	– .50
Cedar Shake Roof	+ 1.45
Upgrade Walls and Ceilings to Skim Coat Plaster	+ .74
Upgrade Ceilings to Textured Finish	+ .48
Air Conditioning, in Heating Ductwork	+ 2.52
In Separate Ductwork	+ 5.13
Heating Systems, Hot Water	+ 1.49
Heat Pump	+ 2.35
Electric Heat	– 1.09
Not Heated	– 3.26

Additional upgrades or components

Kitchen Cabinets & Countertops	Page 58
Bathroom Vanities	59
Fireplaces & Chimneys	59
Windows, Skylights & Dormers	59
Appliances	60
Breezeways & Porches	60
Finished Attic	60
Garages	61
Site Improvements	61
Wings & Ells	25

22 **Important: See the Reference Section for Location Factors (to adjust for your city) and Estimating Forms.**

Figure 10.2
Typical Page from a Commercial Construction Cost Manual

FACTORY AND OFFICE

One-story brick and concrete block building. Size—50' × 79'

FOUNDATION—Concrete walls, footings, and piers.
WALLS—150 L/F8" concrete block, 10' high, continuous steel sash windows, 8' high, including gutters and downspouts.
100 L/F 8" concrete block, 20' high, including 50 L/F 4" brick veneer front, 10' high, stone coping.
FLOOR—Concrete.
ROOF—Flat, tar and gravel roofing, insulated, steel decking, steel bar joists, beams, and columns.

MECHANICAL FEATURES

Electric—Pipe conduit wiring, metal reflectors.
Heating—Gas unit heaters.
Plumbing—3 water closets, 3 lavatories, 1 urinal, 1 water heater.
Sprinkler—None.
OTHER FEATURES—Miscellaneous steel crane girders on building columns. One-story brick office addition—22' × 50' × 10' high.

Office—Cost per square foot of ground area $70.65
Factory—Cost per square foot of ground area $40.95

Next, the base cost per square feet of living space is shown—ranging from 1,000 to 3,800 square feet. For example, the base cost per square feet of living area of a 2,000 square foot house of this quality and type, with exterior walls of brick veneer over a wood frame is $86.60. That figure would be adjusted to account for regional differences.

The house may also contain some optional components whose costs are shown in the Modifications, Adjustments and Alternatives sections and would be added to the base cost.

A sample page from a typical commercial construction cost manual is reproduced in Figure 10.2. The type of building is specified (in this case, it includes both factory and office space), and its dimensions are given. Construction features are itemized, with utilities (mechanical features) listed separately.

Because office and factory spaces have dissimilar features (such as windows and wall height), their costs have been listed separately. Because the appraiser is interested only in the cost per square foot of a particular type and construction of building, the total cost of the structure is not given. This example indicates a cost per square foot for office space of $70.65; factory space is $40.95 per square foot.

If the closest example in the cost manual still has significant differences from the subject building, a cost differential could be added to (or subtracted from) the cost per square foot given in the cost manual. Although cost estimates of high-ceilinged structures may utilize the cubic-foot method of estimating reproduction cost, a height adjustment made to the figure arrived at by the square-foot method is usually sufficient.

Both the square-foot method of estimating reproduction cost and the cubic-foot method may be referred to by the term **comparative unit method**. If that term is used, the appraiser should be sure to state the unit of measurement (square feet or cubic feet).

IN PRACTICE

The following floor plan is that of a factory building with contiguous office space that approximates the example building shown in Figure 10.2. There are no significant differences between the buildings.

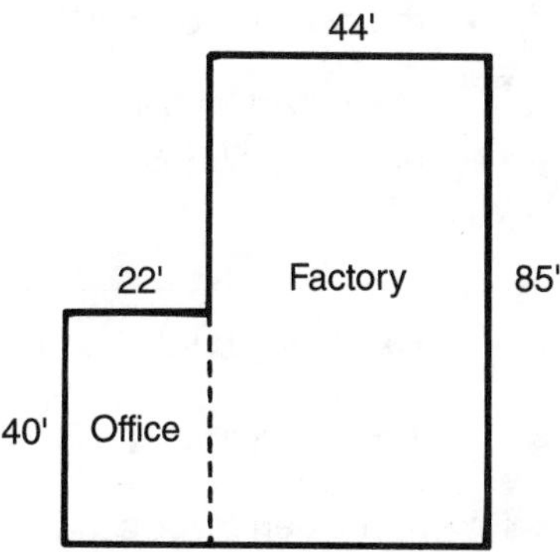

The area of the office space is 22' × 40', or 880 square feet; the area of the factory space is 44' × 85', or 3,740 square feet. Approximately 20% of floor area is thus office space, making this building comparable to the example, which has 22% office space. The reproduction cost of the office space is 880 square feet × $70.65, or $62,172. The reproduction cost of the factory space is 3,740 square feet × $40.95, or $153,153. The total estimate of the reproduction cost for the subject building is $62,172 + $153,153, or $215,325. If this building differed from the base building in the manual, then height, perimeter, or other extra adjustments to the estimate of reproduction cost would be necessary.

Regional multipliers

By using an online costing service, the appraiser should avoid the time lapse (sometimes substantial) between the appraisal date of a property and the publication date of a printed cost manual. The appraiser using a printed cost manual should keep informed of price increases in the area. Some cost manuals meant for national use have **regional multipliers**, so that a given example can be used for any area of the country, provided the cost estimate obtained is multiplied by the adjustment factor for that region.

Residential appraisals

The widespread use of the appraisal report forms prepared by Fannie Mae and Freddie Mac has made the square-foot method of calculating reproduction cost a commonly used technique for residential appraisals. An example of such an appraisal form, the Uniform Residential Appraisal Report (URAR), appears at the end of Unit 15.

With the URAR form, **gross living area** (derived by using the outside measurements of the house, less nonliving areas) is multiplied by cost per square foot. That figure is then added to the cost of nonliving areas and other improvements, such as garage and patio, to arrive at the total estimated cost new of all improvements. Note: Even though the URAR form provides space for a cost approach calculation of property value, it is not required unless the appraiser feels that it is necessary.

IN PRACTICE

A single-family residence is being appraised. The house has 1,800 square feet of living area, based on exterior building measurements. Current construction cost is $73 per square foot. Garage space of 550 square feet has a current construction cost of $25 per square foot. The house has a patio valued at $1,500. Other site improvements, including a driveway and landscaping, are valued at $8,500. What is the reproduction cost of the property?

The improvements have a present reproduction cost new of $131,400 (1,800 × $73) plus $13,750 (550 × $25) plus $1,500 plus $8,500, for a total of $155,150.

Exercise 10-3

The drawing that follows shows the perimeter of a residence you are appraising.

A residence of similar construction, 45 feet by 50 feet and in the same area, was recently completed at a cost of $184,500. What is your cost estimate of the subject?

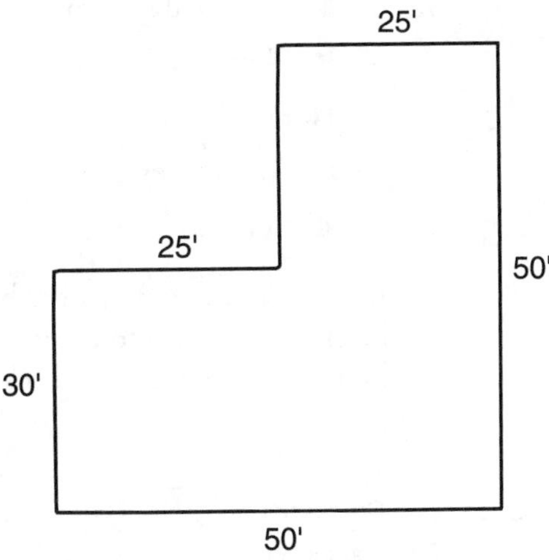

Check your answer against the one in the answer key at the back of the book.

Unit-in-Place Method

In the **unit-in-place method** of determining building reproduction cost, the costs of the various components of the subject structure are estimated separately, then added together to find the total cost. All the components are itemized, each is measured where necessary, and the current construction cost per unit of measure of each component is multiplied by the number of measured units of that component in the subject building.

The unit-in-place method provides a much more detailed breakdown of the type of structure being appraised than does the square-foot method. As such, it is much more time-consuming but is likely to be more accurate than the square-foot method. As with the square-foot method, the unit-in-place method relies on cost manuals, with some allowances made (if necessary) for regional differences or recent cost increases.

A detailed breakdown of residential building costs (such as that provided in the publications of the Marshall and Swift Company) typically includes the following building components:

- Foundation
- Floor structure
- Floor covering
- Exterior walls
- Gable roof
- Ceiling
- Roof dormers
- Roof structure and covering
- Interior construction
- Heating and cooling system

- Electrical system
- Plumbing
- Fireplace(s)
- Appliances
- Stairway

If the costs for an industrial building were to be found in a cost manual, they might be given as shown in Figure 10.3. Cost data given at the end of Unit 11 also show how cost figures may be broken down. Note: Prices shown are for illustration purposes only.

FIGURE 10.3
Cost Data

Component	Cost per Measured Unit
Foundation	
12" concrete wall and footings	$30.70 per linear foot
Floor Construction	
8" reinforced concrete	$3.60 per sq. ft. of floor area
Framing	
14' steel columns, beams, and purlins	$4.50 per sq. ft. of support area
Roof Construction	
sheathing, 2" polystyrene insulation, 4-ply asphalt and gravel covering	$3.70 per sq. ft.
Exterior Walls	
12" concrete block backup	$10.20 per sq. ft.
Windows	
industrial sash, steel, 50% vented	$14.20 per sq. ft.
Doors	
hollow metal, 3' × 7'	$355 per door
rolling steel, chain hoist operated, 12' × 12'	$1,425 per door
Interior	
painting	$3.10 per sq. ft. of building area
Electrical	
wiring and fixtures	$5.30 per sq. ft. of building area
Heating and A/C	$5.30 per sq. ft. of building area
Plumbing	
including fixtures	$2.25 per sq. ft. of building area
Parking Area	
3" asphalt on 3" stone base	$7.20 per sq. yd.

An example costing problem is presented next. The problem is based on a commercial property of standard specifications.

IN PRACTICE

Using the cost data in Figure 13.3, we will compute the reproduction cost of the industrial building shown here, with an adjacent 50' × 125' parking area. The cost of the following items will be determined separately, then totaled to find the reproduction cost of the subject building: concrete foundation, roof, exterior walls, building frame, interior construction, floor, electrical, heating and air-conditioning, plumbing, and parking area. Later in this unit, you will be asked to analyze and appraise a similar type of property, so study this example carefully.

Foundation: The measured unit used for computing the construction cost of the foundation is the linear foot, which is a measurement of length, in this case the perimeter of the building. So 100' + 125' + 100' + 125' = 450'

Because the cost is $30.70 per linear foot, 450' × $30.70 = $13,815

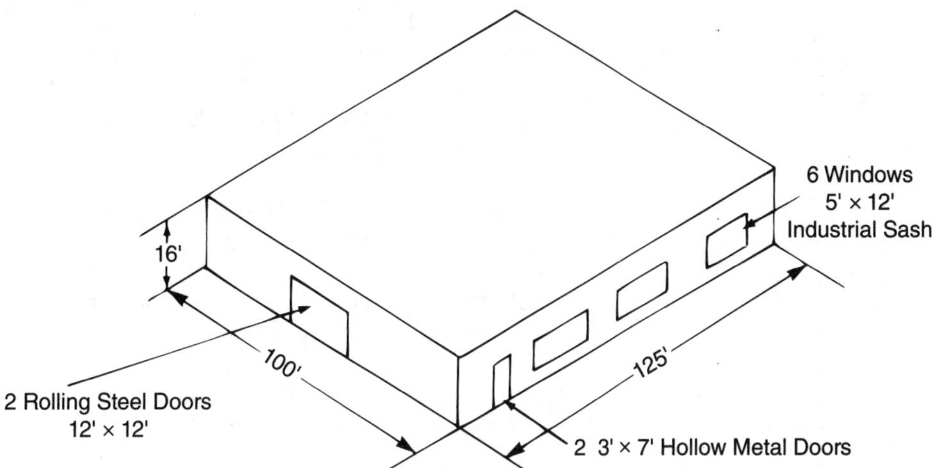

Frame: The space occupied by the steel frame is measured in square feet of support area. The subject building has bearing walls, along with steel columns that support part of the roof area, so the portion supported by bearing walls must be subtracted from the total roof area. The roof area supported by bearing walls is considered to be halfway to the nearest frame columns. The frame columns of the subject building, as shown in the following illustration, are 25 feet apart; thus 12½ feet will be subtracted from each side dimension to find the roof area supported by the frame columns. In the illustration, the area supported by bearing walls is shaded, and the area supported by the steel frame is not shaded.

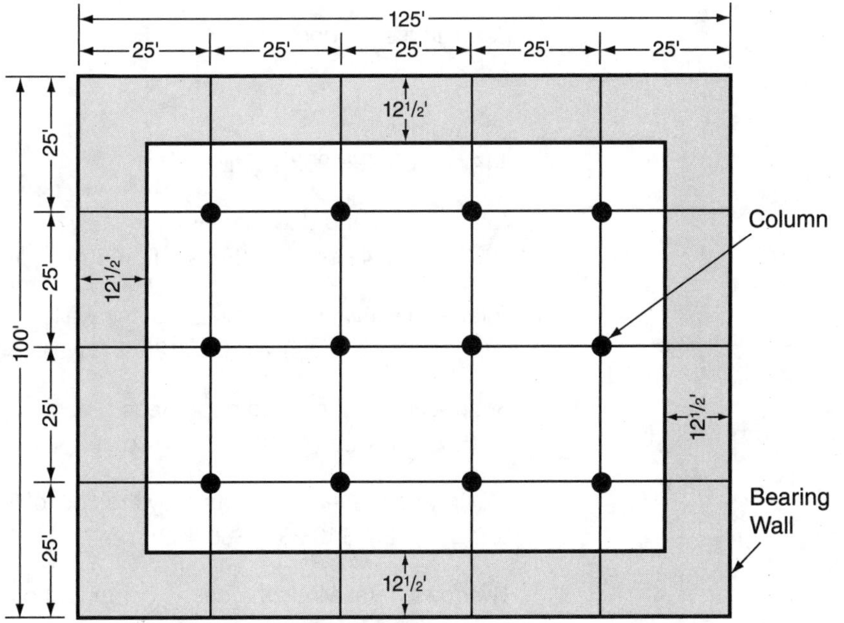

So
100' – (12½' + 12½') = 100' – 25' = 75'
125' – (12½' + 12½') = 125' – 25' = 100'
75' × 100' = 7,500 sq. ft.

The area supported by frame columns is multiplied by the cost of the steel frame, which is $4.50 per square foot.
7,500 × $4.50 = $33,750

Floor: The floor is measured in square feet, so
100' × 125' = 12,500 sq. ft.

Because the cost is $3.60 per square foot,
12,500 sq. ft. × $3.60 = $45,000

Roof: The roof is measured in square feet, so
100' × 125' = 12,500 sq. ft.

Because the cost is $3.70 per square foot,
12,500 sq. ft. × $3.70 = $46,250

Exterior walls: The walls are measured in square feet, but window and door areas must be subtracted. Per window,
5' × 12' = 60 sq. ft.

For six windows,
60 sq. ft. × 6 = 360 sq. ft.

Per hollow metal door,
3' × 7' = 21 sq. ft.

For two doors,
21 sq. ft. × 2 = 42 sq. ft.

Per rolling steel door,
12' × 12' = 144 sq. ft.

For two doors,
144 sq. ft. × 2 = 288 sq. ft.

Total window and door area is
360 sq. ft. + 42 sq. ft. + 288 sq. ft. = 690 sq. ft.

Total area within the perimeters of the walls is
(16' × 100' × 2 walls) + (16' × 125' × 2 walls) = 7,200 sq. ft.

Subtracting window and door areas,
7,200 sq. ft. – 690 sq. ft. = 6,510 sq. ft.

Multiplying the remaining area by the cost of $10.20 per square foot,
6,510 sq. ft. × $10.20 = $66,402

Windows: Total window area, as computed previously, is 360 square feet. At $14.20 per square foot,
360 sq. ft. × $14.20 = $5,112

Doors: There are two 3' × 7' hollow metal doors. At $355 per door,
2 × $355 = $710

There are two 12' × 12' rolling steel doors. At $1,425 per door,
2 × $1,425 = $2,850

Total cost, for all doors, is
$710 + $2,850 = $3,560

Interior: Interior wall space, subtracting door and window areas, is the same as exterior wall space, or 6,510 square feet. At a cost of $.35 per square foot for painting,
6,510 sq. ft. × $0.35 = $2,279

Electrical: Necessary electrical wiring and lighting fixtures for standard industrial illumination are measured per square foot of floor space. Because there are 12,500 square feet of floor space (as measured earlier), at $3.10 per square foot,
12,500 sq. ft. × $3.10 = $38,750

Heating and air-conditioning: Measured per square foot of area served, in this case, the entire floor area. At $5.30 per square foot,
12,500 sq. ft. × $5.30 = $66,250

Plumbing: The cost of plumbing, including standard fixtures, is measured in square feet of building area. At $2.25 per square foot,
12,500 sq. ft. × $2.25 = $28,125

Parking area: The parking area adjacent to the building is illustrated here.

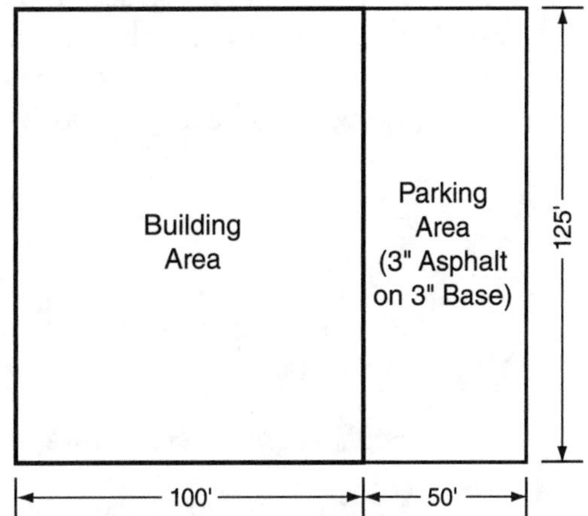

The cost of asphalt paving is measured in square yards, so
125' × 50' = 6,250 sq. ft.
6,250 sq. ft. ÷ 9 = 694.4 sq. yd.

At a cost of $7.20 per square yard for 3" asphalt paving on a 3" stone base,
694.4 sq. yd. × $7.20 = $5,000

In our sample cost analysis, no adjustments are necessary to allow for price increases since the cost data were compiled. Add all costs to arrive at the total reproduction cost of all improvements:

Foundation	$ 13,815
Frame	33,750
Floor	45,000
Roof	46,250
Exterior walls	66,402
Windows	5,112
Doors	3,560
Interior	2,279
Electrical	38,750
Heating and A/C	66,250
Plumbing	28,125
Parking area	5,000
	$354,293

The reproduction cost of the improvements on the subject property is $354,293. If this problem were to be carried through to find the market value estimate by the cost approach, the value of any depreciation on the improvements would have to be subtracted from the reproduction cost and the resultant figure added to the land value.

Exercise 10.4 requires that you apply what you have learned in the example problem to a similar structure. Although the measurements and construction cost information you will need are provided for you, remember that the unit-in-place method is based on accurate building specifications and measurements as well as knowledge of current construction costs.

Exercise 10-4

Based on the following unit-in-place costs, what is the reproduction cost estimate of a rectangular warehouse, 125' by 250'?

Foundation: concrete walls and footings at $37.30 per linear foot

Floor: reinforced concrete at $3.10 per sq. ft.

Roof: built-up tar and gravel at $2.40 per sq. ft.; roof sheathing at $.65 per sq. ft.; fiberboard insulation at $.55 per sq. ft.

Interior construction: painting and some partitions, at total cost of $4,500

Front exterior wall: common brick on concrete block, 125' long by 15' high, at $9.50 per sq. ft.; 2 windows, each 6' by 12', at $15.30 per sq. ft.; 10' by 12' drive-in door at a total cost of $1,300

Rear exterior wall: same as front wall with drive-in door, but no windows

Side exterior walls: concrete block, 250' long by 15' high, at $7.10 per sq. ft.; windows covering about 20% of wall area at $14.20 per sq. ft.

Steel framing: area supported by frame, 100' by 225'; with 14' eave height, at $4.50 per sq. ft.

Electrical: $3.25 per sq. ft. of floor area

Heating: $2.75 per sq. ft. of floor area

Plumbing: $1.60 per sq. ft. of floor area

Check your answer against the one in the answer key at the back of the book.

Quantity Survey Method

A builder or contractor estimating construction cost will need precise, up-to-date cost figures. Such an estimate usually is made by the **quantity survey method,** which necessitates a thorough itemization of all the costs expected in the construction of the building. As a result, this is the most comprehensive and accurate method of estimating reproduction cost.

Using the quantity survey method, **direct costs** (those related to materials and labor, and also known as *hard costs*) are computed more precisely than in the unit-in-place method. Every stage of construction is broken down into separate costs for materials and labor. The required expenditure for the electrical system, for instance, will take into account both the cost of materials at an estimated price per unit and the cost of labor for the required number of hours at the going rate per hour. Thus, the appraiser must be able to estimate material unit quantities and costs as well as work times and labor rates. **Indirect costs** (those involved in necessary but not construction-related expenses, such as surveys, payroll taxes, and profit, and also known as *soft costs*) are also added. A typical cost itemization for a 14-unit apartment building, using the quantity survey method, could include the following totals for the separate building components:

Direct Costs	
Clearing the land	$ 723
Rough and fine grading	16,753
Footings	8,760
Slabs	8,341
Entrance and stoops	4,200
Balconies	12,350
Interior stairs	575
Dampproofing	938
Rough and finished carpentry	127,390
Furring	3,480
Doors	3,560
Rough and finished hardware	11,722
Kitchen cabinets	14,250
Flooring	18,764
Refrigerators	11,920

Disposals	2,330	
Gas ranges	7,386	
Venetian blinds	4,800	
Bathroom tile	7,297	
Painting	13,750	
Insulation	1,070	
Glazing	2,483	
Structural steel and lintels	4,747	
Ornamental iron	8,190	
Masonry	79,423	
Drywall	35,961	
Heating and air-conditioning	39,467	
Plumbing	44,200	
Electrical wiring	21,870	
Water mains	4,102	
Water and sewer connections	790	
Roofing and sheet metal	6,200	
Incidentals	9,340	
Cleaning, general and contract	5,900	
Landscaping	7,450	
Fence	1,800	
Temporary utilities	4,728	
Temporary roads and structures	2,857	
Streets, parking area, sidewalks, curbs, and gutters	33,689	
Sanitary and storm sewers	15,042	
Supervision and timekeeping	21,785	$ 630,383
Indirect Costs		
Permit	$ 35	
Survey	1,980	
Layout	465	
Appraisal fee	5,000	
Architect's fee	15,000	
Payroll taxes and insurance	8,570	
Builder's overhead and profit	64,000	$ 95,050
Subtotal		725,433
Entrepreneurial profit ($725,433 × .10)		72,543
Total Reproduction Cost New		$ 797,976

The last item often included in the construction cost calculation is **entrepreneurial profit** (also known as developer's profit), discussed briefly in Unit 9. The management functions associated with major construction projects may be broken down into various areas of specialization. The development function may be separate from the building/contracting function; the developer may even hire a construction management firm to supervise the building contractor. As a result, the profit associated with the development function is itemized separately from the contractor's profit and other indirect costs. The developer basically is the risk taker. The amount of entrepreneurial profit ultimately received by the developer will depend on the success of the project. Of course, the element of risk also includes the possibility of loss if the project is unsuccessful.

The preceding simplified list of direct and indirect costs assumes that the builder is not the person developing the project, and the entry for "builder's overhead and profit" is included in indirect costs. It is more accurate (and realistic) to add the cost category for entrepreneurial profit to direct and indirect costs. In some cases, particularly when the builder/contractor works for the owner on a "build-to-suit" project, no separate entrepreneurial profit is identified. In other situations, as in this example, the contracting function is handled entirely apart from the development function and the developer has a separate profit expectation. This profit estimate should be based on market analysis. In the example, 10%, or $72,543, was added to reflect the market's expectation of profit.

Depending on market practice, entrepreneurial profit can be estimated as a percentage of

- direct costs,
- direct and indirect costs,
- direct and indirect costs plus land value, or
- the value of the completed project.

An appraiser using the quantity survey method obviously needs a more comprehensive knowledge of building construction than would be used in the square-foot or unit-in-place method. The appraiser must know every facet of building construction—almost as well as the builder does.

Exercise 10-5

Identify each of the following building costs as direct or indirect:

Payment to plumbing subcontractor

Site preparation

Contractor's performance bond

Barricade around construction site

Builder's profit

Building permit

Check your answer against the one in the answer key at the back of the book.

■ SUMMARY

The cost approach can be a helpful tool to the appraiser in the appraisal of certain special purpose properties that are not normally bought and sold in the open market, and for all properties where there is inadequate market data. It can also be a misleading tool if solely relied on when adequate market data is available to the appraiser.

In the cost approach, accrued depreciation is subtracted from the reproduction or replacement cost of the improvement(s), and the resulting figure is added to site value.

Replacement cost (current cost of a structure of comparable quality and utility) is computed when reproduction cost (current cost to construct an exact duplicate) is impractical. Reproduction or replacement cost is always based on a new structure, at current prices.

Reproduction/replacement cost can be found using the square-foot, unit-in-place, quantity survey, or index methods. Each has its utility, although the quantity survey method results in the most accurate cost estimate.

■ Review Questions

1. The cost of improvements identical in design and material to those of the subject property is called the subject's
   a. reproduction cost.
   b. sales price.
   c. replacement cost.
   d. market value.

2. The cost of improvements identical in utility to those of the subject is called
   a. reproduction cost.
   b. sales price.
   c. replacement cost.
   d. market value.

3. In using the cost approach to appraising, the estimated construction cost of improvements usually will be based on
   a. their original cost.
   b. the cost of new improvements at current prices.
   c. book value.
   d. the national cost average of all components.

4. The index method of estimating construction cost is based on
   a. the original cost of improvements.
   b. the cost of new improvements at current prices.
   c. book value.
   d. the national cost average of all components.

5. If a commercial structure is rectangular with sides of 65 feet and 135 feet and the current local cost to build a similar structure is $45 per square foot, what is the estimated construction cost of the structure using the square-foot method?
   a. $18,000
   b. $180,000
   c. $394,875
   d. $364,500

6. A nationally based construction cost manual is acceptable for appraisal purposes if it
   a. is updated frequently.
   b. is based on median construction cost estimates.
   c. is published by a nationally recognized firm.
   d. contains regional cost multipliers.

7. In a residential appraisal utilizing the URAR form, gross living area is derived by
   a. totaling individual room areas.
   b. finding the area of the whole house based on outside measurements.
   c. finding the area of the whole house based on outside measurements, then subtracting the area of nonliving spaces.
   d. estimating all spaces based on room width, room length, and ceiling height.

8. The cost of supervising workers on a construction site is considered
   a. a direct cost.
   b. an overhead expense.
   c. an indirect cost.
   d. an incidental expense.

9. The term *entrepreneurial profit* refers to
   a. the subcontractors' profit.
   b. the construction management firm's profit.
   c. the developer's profit.
   d. the real estate agent's profit.

10. The amount of entrepreneurial profit
    a. reflects the success of the project.
    b. is based on how project expenses are categorized.
    c. will always be the same, provided the project is completed within budget.
    d. cannot be estimated accurately.

11. An indirect cost also is known as
    a. a hard cost.
    b. a soft cost.
    c. a replacement cost.
    d. a reproduction cost.

12. A direct cost also is known as
    a. a hard cost.
    b. a soft cost.
    c. a replacement cost.
    d. a reproduction cost.

13. An example of an indirect cost is a property's
    a. foundation.
    b. HVAC.
    c. appraisal fee.
    d. carpentry.

14. An example of a direct cost is a property's
    a. foundation.
    b. appraisal fee.
    c. survey.
    d. permit process.

15. Which cost estimation method must take current costs into account?
    a. Square-foot method
    b. Unit-in-place method
    c. Quantity survey method
    d. All of these

16. Which cost estimation method must take geographic differences into account?
    a. Square-foot method
    b. Unit-in-place method
    c. Quantity survey method
    d. All of these

17. Gross living area includes heated, finished space measured using
    a. interior dimensions.
    b. exterior dimensions.
    c. retail space.
    d. office space.

18. The original cost of a house was $50,000. The original index is 1.50 and the current index is 3.00. The current estimated cost of the house, using the index method, is
    a. $50,000.
    b. $75,000.
    c. $100,000.
    d. $200,000.

19. The *MOST* accurate cost estimation method is
    a. the index method.
    b. the square-foot method.
    c. the rectangular survey method.
    d. the quantity survey method.

20. The *LEAST* accurate cost estimation method is
    a. the index method.
    b. the square-foot method.
    c. the rectangular survey method.
    d. the quantity survey method.

Check your answers against those in the answer key at the back of the book.

UNIT ELEVEN

THE COST APPROACH—PART II: DEPRECIATION

LEARNING OBJECTIVES

When you have completed this unit, you will be able to

describe the various forms of depreciation;

compare and contrast: economic life, physical life, remaining economic life, effective age, and chronological age;

compute depreciation using the age-life (straight-line), observed condition, capitalized value, and market extraction methods;

determine reproduction cost, cost per square foot of living area, accrued depreciation, and total property value using the cost approach; and

complete the Cost Approach section of the URAR form.

KEY TERMS

accrued depreciation
age-life method
capitalized value method
curable functional obsolescence
curable physical deterioration
depreciation
economic age-life method
economic life
effective age
external obsolescence
functional obsolescence
incurable external obsolescence
incurable functional obsolescence
incurable physical deterioration
long-lived items of depreciation
market extraction method
observed condition method
physical deterioration
physical life
remaining economic life
short-lived items of depreciation
straight-line method
superadequacy
United States Access Board

OVERVIEW

In the second part of the cost approach equation, depreciation is subtracted from the reproduction or replacement cost of improvements as of the date of valuation. Property value is then derived by adding site value to the depreciated value of improvements.

This unit explains the general types of depreciation and the methods most commonly used to estimate the amount by which a structure has depreciated. At the end of the unit, you will complete a sample appraisal of a commercial building using the cost approach.

ACCRUED DEPRECIATION

Depreciation is the kind of term that everyone can define, yet few people can apply.

Depreciation is a loss in value from any cause. The loss in value may come from decay, wear and tear, or the presence of features that are deficient, excessive, or simply currently undesirable. There also may be external factors that cause a loss in value. **Accrued depreciation** is the total loss in value from all causes as of the date of appraisal.

Generally, there are three categories of depreciation: physical deterioration, functional obsolescence, and external obsolescence.

Physical Deterioration

Physical deterioration is the gradual decay or wearing out of the structure, usually the most obvious form of depreciation. A building that needs painting or tuck-pointing or has broken windows, cracked plaster, or water-damaged walls from a leaky roof are all the ordinary effects of wear and tear. Some form of depreciation, at least physical deterioration, begins the moment a building is completed.

Physical deterioration can be either curable or incurable. If a defect can be repaired or replaced economically, it is considered **curable physical deterioration**; that is, the cost to cure the defect will result in an equal or greater increase in overall property value. The classic example is the cosmetic "fixer-upper" that is structurally sound but needs cleaning, minor repairs, and new paint to bring its appearance and appeal up to the standard of other properties in the neighborhood.

If a defect is not economically justified, it is considered **incurable physical deterioration**. Examples of incurable physical deterioration include structures that have been "stripped" of valuable building components, including plumbing and light fixtures, cabinetry, and electrical wiring. Such building components could be repaired or replaced only with great expense. Other damage may be caused by natural elements, such as a foundation that has suffered mudslide damage. Ordinarily, such building components are expected to last for the life of the building.

Loss caused by physical deterioration of all kinds can be valued as a percentage of total building value, or the appraiser can value each depreciated item separately.

Functional Obsolescence

Functional obsolescence takes place when a building's layout, design, or other features are considered undesirable in comparison with features designed for the same functions in newer properties. Functional obsolescence can be the result of a deficiency, the presence of a feature that should be replaced or modernized, or the presence of a feature that is superfluous (superadequate) for the structure's intended purpose.

A two-story, five-bedroom house with one bathroom and only one of the bedrooms on the first floor and no bathroom on the second floor would be functionally undesirable; the same house might still be functionally undesirable if it had a second bathroom on the first floor and none on the second floor. Functional obsolescence depends on the changing requirements of homebuyers. When family rooms came into great demand, many homes were built with little or no dining room space to allow for a family room at no major cost increase. In some areas, however, dining rooms and family rooms are both desirable, and a formal (separate) dining room may be a valuable feature.

The use of replacement cost, rather than reproduction cost, eliminates the need to estimate some forms of functional obsolescence. For example, consider an older house with exceptionally high ceilings and a poor overall layout. Inherent in a replacement cost estimate would be an adjustment for the high ceilings, but not for the poor layout.

Like physical deterioration, functional obsolescence can be either curable or incurable. If a defect is not easily remedied or economically justified, it is considered **incurable functional obsolescence**. For example, a house with a poor floor plan suffers from functional obsolescence that is not easily corrected or cured. If a defect can be added, replaced, redesigned, or removed at a cost no greater than the resulting increase in property value, it is considered **curable functional obsolescence**. An example might be the replacement of the original, outdated plumbing fixtures in an older house.

The Americans with Disabilities Act

The category of functional obsolescence has been greatly expanded for commercial properties by the provisions of Title III of the Americans with Disabilities Act of 1991 (ADA). Title III requires that new places of public accommodation (as defined by the law) be built so that there are no architectural or communication barriers to prevent their accessibility to persons having a disability. Any such barriers to full accessibility that are found in existing buildings must be removed if doing so is readily achievable.

For the purposes of the law, places of public accommodation include virtually all places to which members of the public are invited, including hotels, motels, restaurants, bars, theaters, movie houses, convention centers, retail and service establishments, public transportation terminals, museums and libraries, zoos, amusement parks, schools, social service centers, and places of exercise or recreation (such as gyms and golf courses).

Examples of accommodations that may be required by the law include constructing a ramp or widening a doorway to accommodate a wheelchair, lowering counters or display shelves, providing an accessible lavatory sink and toilet, and repositioning a water fountain. The decision as to whether a particular accommodation is readily achievable is made on a case-by-case basis but is based on the nature and cost of the action needed, the overall financial resources available, and the relationship of the site to the business or other enterprise using it, including the availability of other locations.

Unfortunately, many buildings that predate enactment of ADA require accommodations to make them fully accessible; in fact, the inspections and appraisal performed at the time of a sale or other transaction may represent the first analysis of the structure's compliance with the law. The effect on market value of necessary modifications or additions can be estimated using paired sale analysis, as described in Unit 12.

The penalty for noncompliance with ADA can be costly. Builders are now aware of the necessity to make model homes and other marketing sites accessible, even when the homes themselves would not fall within the law's requirements. But the issue of accessibility has also been addressed by HUD. In 1997, HUD took an unprecedented action by fining a Minnesota builder for false claims that the company's town homes and condominiums met federal requirements for accessibility by the handicapped. (Features noted by HUD that would have required little or no additional cost by the builder in order to make the units accessible included placement of wall outlets and thermostats; other features promised but not delivered included lowered thresholds and reinforcement of bathroom walls to allow future addition of grab bars.) The builder was fined $10,000, denied FHA insurance for one year, and required to make $160,000 in repairs and put funds in escrow for future repairs.

A copy of the Americans with Disabilities Act, as well as the text of the Americans with Disabilities Act Accessibility Guidelines for Buildings and Facilities (ADAAG) promulgated by the Architectural and Transportation Barriers Compliance Board, can be found at the website of the United States Access Board, www.access-board.gov. The site includes videos on accessibility issues, information on training programs and publication, and links to a variety of other government sites.

WEB LINK

www.access-board.gov

External Obsolescence

External obsolescence (also called environmental, economic, or locational obsolescence) is any loss in value from causes outside the property itself and is almost always considered incurable. Zoning changes, proximity to nuisances, changes in land use, and market conditions can all be causes of **incurable external obsolescence**. If a drive-in restaurant is constructed on a vacant lot, an adjacent residential property will probably lose value because of increased noise and traffic. The most conspicuous source of external obsolescence may be the environmental hazard. Proximity to a known hazard, even when the subject property can be scientifically demonstrated to be unaffected directly by the hazard, will tend to lower property value.

External obsolescence can be created by a variety of factors. It is locational when the property's neighborhood, community, state, or region becomes less desirable and value subsequently declines. It is economic when market conditions lower demand, as during a recession. It is political when a nearby land use is changed by the local governing body to permit a less desirable use, such as a landfill. An example of how the national political process can affect local land values was the closure and subsequent sale of military bases across the country in the 1980s and 1990s. For many communities, particularly those with few other sources of employment or business revenue, the closing of a military facility will have a major impact on the local economy, including real estate values. When the property undergoes redevelopment, however, the impact on the community can be reversed.

Evaluating Depreciation Sources

Care must be taken to determine whether the cause of external obsolescence has already been reflected in the appraiser's estimate of land value. While it is true that land does not depreciate, the value of land can (and does) go down. Because land is always valued as if vacant, external obsolescence frequently affects highest and best use, resulting in the existing improvements being an overimprovement. In that instance, the depreciation is functional, not external.

Depreciation is the most difficult part of the cost approach equation to estimate accurately. The older the structure, the more likely it is to have deteriorated to a marked degree, often in ways not easily observable (such as corroded plumbing lines or cracked plaster hidden by wallpaper or paneling). Physical deterioration begins the moment a building is constructed and continues until it is no longer usable. Even if a new building is unoccupied, care must be taken to maintain it adequately.

Depreciation (deterioration and obsolescence) may vary significantly, depending on market conditions as of the date of valuation. If demand exceeds supply, buyers may overlook many "typical" items of depreciation. For example, a single-family house located on a busy street normally suffers from external obsolescence due to the proximity of the traffic and all of the obnoxious and noxious conditions associated with traffic. In a tight market, however, buyers may overlook, or at least not penalize as heavily, frontage on a major arterial.

A buyer's measure of depreciation may vary considerably, depending on the price range of homes in the area; for example, the lack of car storage in an urban neighborhood convenient to public transportation may not be an item of depreciation at all. The lack of car storage in a suburban neighborhood, on the other hand, would probably be a major item of depreciation—particularly if there was no room to add car storage or if the cost to do so was high. Similarly, in neighborhoods of modest homes, buyers often are willing to do their own painting and decorating. So if a house in such a neighborhood needs painting, a buyer's informal measure of depreciation may be simply the cost of paint. In an upscale neighborhood, however, a house that needs painting and decorating may suffer significant deterioration because prospective buyers will take into account the cost of having professionals perform those tasks.

Every structure has an **economic life**, also called its useful life, the period during which it can be used for its originally intended purpose. When a structure no longer can be used without extensive repairs or renovation, it ceases to serve any profitable purpose. At that point, the value of the site is no higher with the improvement than it would be without it. In some cases, the existence of a structure may make a site less valuable because the cost of demolition and removal of the structure must be taken into account.

Economic life is not necessarily the length of time that the structure is expected to remain standing, which is its **physical life**. In fact, more buildings are torn down in still-usable condition than fall down from deterioration. Most buildings that are torn down are not totally derelict but have instead become unprofitable in terms of the highest and best use of the site they occupy.

A structure's **effective age** reflects the quality of its construction and the degree of maintenance and repair it has received. Any structure will suffer some physical defect eventually, whether from the elements or from the way in which it is used. Those defects will have a greater effect on improvements that were poorly constructed. If necessary maintenance and repairs are neglected, the process of deterioration is enhanced, and the physical life of the structure is shortened. On the other hand, well-constructed and well-maintained improvements benefit from a prolonged physical life.

Effective age will be greater or less than chronological age when a structure's condition differs significantly from that of similar structures in its market area that have had normal maintenance and upkeep but no remodeling or updating of any kind. The benchmark is a typical residence that has been maintained with no significant improvements but no significant neglect.

IN PRACTICE

The subject residence was constructed 20 years ago. The owners have maintained the home in excellent condition, including repainting the exterior several times and remodeling the kitchen. Similar properties in the neighborhood are adequately maintained but not as well as the subject residence. The subject residence thus has an effective age of only 15 years.

For appraisal purposes, the most important time measure is the building's **remaining economic life**. This is the period from the date of the appraisal during which the building can be expected to remain useful for its original purpose. In determining that period, the appraiser must consider not only the present condition of the structure but also other known factors that might affect its future use or desirability, such as the use or condition of nearby property. Houses adjacent to a shopping mall may suffer from increased traffic noise, fumes, and congestion. Over time, those houses may be sold more frequently and receive less investment in upkeep and repairs than others in the same neighborhood but not as close to the shopping area.

The appraiser should always keep in mind the reaction of the market (buyers) to similar properties. The phenomenon of gentrification of urban neighborhoods is an example of the desirability that even run-down properties may have if other factors, such as location and high demand, are strong enough.

By depreciating a structure's cost, the appraiser takes into account the probable past and future effects of its economic life, considering both its condition and outside factors.

Appraisers use several methods to measure depreciation. The age-life method and observed condition method measure depreciation directly. The capitalized value and sales comparison methods measure depreciation indirectly.

Age-Life Method

The **age-life method** of computing depreciation (also called the **straight-line method** or **economic age-life method**) is the simplest to understand and use. It is based on the assumption that depreciation occurs at an even rate throughout the projected life of a structure. In the age-life method, accrued depreciation is estimated by comparing the effective age of the structure at the time of valuation with its total economic life. Figure 11.1 shows how the relationship between building cost and projected age can be graphed along a straight line. The remaining building value at any building age can be found by finding the point on the graphed line where the age factor intersects the cost factor.

In the example plotted in Figure 11.1, the current building cost is $200,000, and the estimated economic life of the building is 60 years. When the building has an economic life of 30 years, its remaining value will be $100,000 because it will have depreciated by $100,000.

Because of differences in quality of construction and the degree of maintenance received, similar structures do not necessarily depreciate at the same rate. For this reason, appraisers normally base depreciation estimates on the effective age of the structure rather than the actual age.

The appraiser does not have to draw a graph to estimate depreciation by this method. A structure's loss in value can be assumed to be the ratio of its effective age to its total economic life. The formula for estimating depreciation thus is:

$$\text{Effective age} \div \text{Total economic life} = \text{Accrued depreciation}$$

A decimal figure, which may be converted to a percentage, results from this equation. This percentage is applied to the structure's reproduction or replacement cost to estimate lump-sum depreciation from all causes. The depreciation estimate is then subtracted from the cost figure to arrive at value.

IN PRACTICE

The reproduction cost of a commercial building is estimated to be $800,000. The building should have an economic life of 50 years, and it is now 5 years old, which is also its effective age. What is its rate of depreciation, and what is its value by the cost approach (exclusive of land value)?

FIGURE 11.1
Age-Life Depreciation

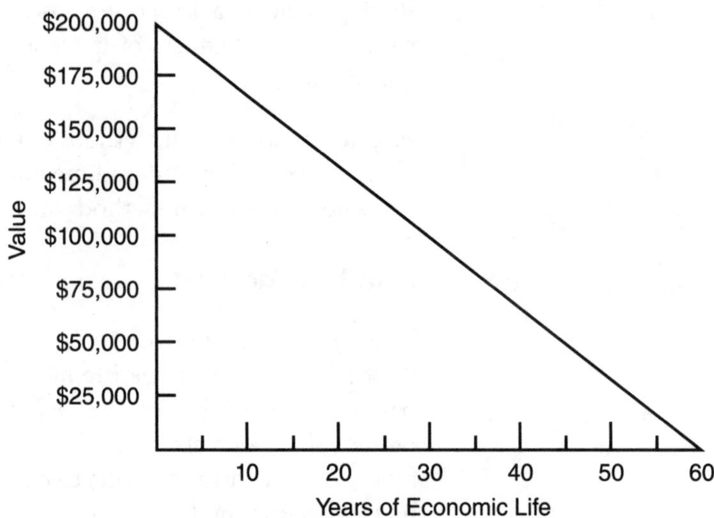

Using the age-life ratio, total depreciation is 10% (5 ÷ 50). In this example, the building is now worth $720,000:

Reproduction cost	$800,000
Less total accrued depreciation ($800,000 × 0.10)	– 80,000
Building value by the cost approach	$720,000

Although the age-life method is easy to apply and understand, it does have limitations:

- It assumes that every building depreciates on a straight-line basis over the span of its economic life. This is generally not true. Depreciation varies with market conditions and the economic cycles of a neighborhood.
- It lumps value loss from all causes into an overall estimate of depreciation.
- It does not distinguish between curable and incurable deterioration.
- Total economic life may be difficult to predict because it refers to a future time. Effective age is also subjective.

Variations of the age-life method

In one variation of the age-life method of estimating accrued depreciation, known as the modified effective age-life method, the cost to cure all curable items of depreciation, both physical and functional, is estimated first. This sum is then deducted from reproduction or replacement cost new of the improvements. Finally, the age-life ratio is applied to the remaining cost to arrive at depreciation from all other causes. For example:

Replacement cost new	$500,000
Less curable items	– 50,000
Remaining cost	$450,000
Less age-life ratio (15 ÷ 75 = .20 × $450,000)	– 90,000
Building value	$360,000

This variation of the age-life method is most useful when the subject property has curable depreciation not typically found in sales of properties in the subject market. When the curable items of depreciation are handled separately, the appraiser may determine that utilizing a shorter effective age and/or a longer economic life expectancy in calculating the age-life ratio is appropriate.

This same kind of analysis can be applied in situations where external obsolescence is present in the subject property but not in sales of other properties in the subject market. The dollar amount of external obsolescence is estimated first and deducted from reproduction or replacement cost new; then, the age-life ratio is applied to the remaining cost to derive depreciation from all causes except external obsolescence. The estimated depreciation from external obsolescence is added to the estimated depreciation from the age-life method to arrive at an estimate of total depreciation.

Exercise 11-1

A company bought a building for $450,000 and estimated its economic life at 25 years. Compute the amount of the building's total depreciation under the age-life method after 7 years.

Check your answer against the one in the answer key at the back of the book.

Observed Condition Method

Because many properties will require a more detailed depreciation analysis, another method may have to be used, at least for certain items.

In the **observed condition method** of computing depreciation (also known as the breakdown method), the appraiser estimates the loss in value for curable and incurable items of depreciation. A curable item is one that can be easily and economically restored or replaced, resulting in an immediate increase in appraised value. An item that would be impossible, too expensive, or not cost-effective to replace is labeled incurable. Following are examples in each of the three depreciation categories (physical deterioration, functional obsolescence, and external obsolescence).

Physical deterioration—curable

This category includes repairs that are economically feasible and would result in an increase in appraised value equal to or exceeding their cost. Items of routine maintenance fall into this category, as do simple improvements that may add far more than their cost to the value of the property. Fixtures and appliances should be in good working order, broken windows replaced, and landscaping tended. Exterior and interior painting often will return more than its cost by improving the overall appearance of a structure, particularly a residence.

The loss in value due to curable physical deterioration is the cost to cure the item(s) of depreciation.

Physical deterioration—incurable

This category includes the separate physical components of a structure, which do not deteriorate at the same rate. If roof, foundation, electrical system, et cetera did deteriorate at the same rate, the economic life of a structure would simply be the economic life of its components. Unfortunately (or fortunately), the foundation of a structure typically will last far longer than its roofing material, and other items will need replacing at other times.

Generally, the individual components of a structure can be divided into **short-lived items** and **long-lived items** of incurable physical deterioration. Short-lived items are those that may be replaced or repaired once or more over the economic life of the structure. These include roof, gutters, wall coverings, cabinets, and other finishing materials. Painting and decorating could be included here or under curable physical deterioration. Loss in value due to depreciation of these items can be estimated on an individual basis or by assigning an average percentage of depreciation to the total value of all items.

Long-lived items are those that should last as long as a structure's remaining economic life. Foundation, framework, walls, ceilings, and masonry would fall within this category.

Loss in value can be based on a percentage reflecting the number of years of remaining economic life of all such items as a group, or they can be depreciated individually.

Functional obsolescence—curable

This category includes physical or design features that are inadequate or undesirable by current standards or that are not necessary for the structure's intended use but could be added, replaced, redesigned, or removed economically (at a cost no greater than the resulting increase in value). Outmoded plumbing fixtures are usually easily replaced. Room function might be redefined at no cost if the basic room layout allowed for it, such as converting a bedroom adjacent to a kitchen to use as a family room. A closet converted to a darkroom might be easily converted back to a closet.

Loss in value from an item of curable functional obsolescence takes into account the fact that an item of remodeling or repair is more expensive when done separately than when work of the same design and specifications is performed as part of the construction of the entire structure. Thus, loss in value is the difference between the increase in total reproduction cost that would cure the item and what it would cost to cure only that item. If a kitchen suffers from lack of updated cabinets, countertops, and appliances, its depreciated value is the difference between the addition to reproduction cost represented by an updated kitchen and the cost to update the kitchen separately. If a kitchen with currently desirable materials would add $9,000 to reproduction cost and the cost to update the existing kitchen by remodeling is $10,500, then $1,500 is the loss in value due to an out-of-date kitchen. Remodeling an existing structure to cure a defect is more expensive with regard to that defect than a comparable improvement in an entirely new structure.

If replacement rather than reproduction cost is used, physical or design features that exceed current requirements (a **superadequacy**) represent a loss in value equal to the cost to remove them; their initial construction cost and degree of physical deterioration are not considered.

Functional obsolescence—incurable

This category includes currently undesirable physical or design features that could not be easily or economically remedied. The feature might be the result of a deficiency, a lack of modernization, or a superadequacy. Many older multistory industrial structures are considered less suitable than one-story structures. Older apartments with large rooms and high ceilings might not bring as high a rent per cubic foot of space as smaller, newer apartments. The cost to correct these deficiencies is not justified. The single-family house with three or more bedrooms but only one bathroom clearly suffers from functional obsolescence that is not readily cured.

Another form of incurable functional obsolescence is the misplaced improvement, a structure that is inappropriate for the site on which it is located. Why would anyone put an inappropriate structure on a site? Most misplaced improvements are not planned to be that way. The reasons that an improvement is considered misplaced usually come about some time after the improvement is made. For example, a structure that is perfectly suited to its site and neighborhood may become inappropriate if the area's zoning is changed and most other properties are adapted to the new permitted use. Or a structure built in a mostly undeveloped area may eventually be surrounded by a different type of development.

IN PRACTICE

The Houser family lives in a single-family residence near a downtown area. Zoning in the area, which was once solely residential, now allows limited retail and other commercial use. As a result, almost every lot on the Housers' block in this highly desirable area has been converted to a professional office or other use. The Houser residence, now located between an insurance agency and a real estate broker's office, may be considered a misplaced improvement.

The loss in value caused by incurable functional obsolescence could be estimated by comparing either the selling prices or rents of similar structures with and without the defect. Whether a misplaced improvement will result in a lowering of estimated market value will most likely depend on how adaptable the property is to any other use.

External obsolescence—incurable only

External obsolescence is considered incurable only. Because this form of depreciation is caused by factors outside the property, the owner most likely has no immediate, practical way of remedying it. The interstate highway that creates noise and pollution for nearby residents may be an annoying fact of life, but a fact of life, nonetheless. External obsolescence can be caused by economic factors also. The appraiser should be acutely aware of the effect on value of a depressed real estate market. The appraiser's market analysis should be thorough enough to reveal any economic or other factors likely to affect market value. In particular, the appraiser should note the apparent effect of economic conditions on recent sales or rentals of comparable properties.

When estimating accrued depreciation by the observed condition method, the appraiser must decide on the amount of value lost through applicable depreciation in each of the categories, as described earlier. The appraiser must be careful not to depreciate the same item more than once.

The loss in value due to external obsolescence also could be measured by comparing the selling prices or rents of similar properties, including some that are and some that are not affected by this type of depreciation. The response of buyers in the market to properties exhibiting the same type of depreciation is probably the best value indicator, but it may be difficult to isolate the loss in value due solely to that factor. For income-producing property, another way to measure loss in value due to external depreciation is by the capitalized value method, discussed next.

Exercise 11-2

Determine the depreciation category of each of the following items as specifically as you can.

Residential location on heavily traveled highway

Severe termite damage throughout a structure

Need for tuckpointing (repair of mortar between bricks) on exterior of house in overall good condition

Office space adjacent to extremely noisy factory

Newer two-story house in good condition but with potholes in asphalt driveway

Dry rot in attic beams

Major commercial airport built in 1940, with runways too short for modern jet planes

Three-bedroom house with one bathroom

Hot water-radiator heating system

20,000-seat sports arena with no drinking fountains

Check your answers against those in the answer key at the back of the book.

Capitalized Value Method

The **capitalized value method** of determining depreciation is also referred to as the rent loss method. In this method, the appraiser determines the loss in income resulting from depreciation by comparing the income produced by similar properties, then applying a capitalization rate to that amount of income to determine its effect on overall property value. It is necessary to have comparable properties that possess the same defect and some that do not, to isolate the difference in rental value due solely to that cause. The following example shows how a gross rent multiplier (GRM) can be used to determine the loss in value attributable to an item of incurable functional obsolescence. A GRM relates the sales price of a property to its rental income. The GRM is computed by dividing the sales price of a property by its gross monthly unfurnished rent. The development, analysis, and use of multipliers is covered in Unit 13, "The Income Capitalization Approach." More complex methods of developing a capitalization rate are discussed in Unit 14.

IN PRACTICE

A single-family residence has four bedrooms and one and one-half bathrooms. Comparable properties with the same number of bathrooms rent for $1,295 per month, while comparables with two full bathrooms rent for $1,350 per month.

The monthly difference in rent attributable to the lack of two full bathrooms is $55. That number is multiplied by a factor of 135, which is the monthly gross rent multiplier for the area. The resulting figure of $7,425 is the loss in value to the reproduction cost of the subject property that is attributable to one item of incurable functional obsolescence.

Exercise 11-3

A structure with an obsolete floor plan is being appraised. A comparable structure with the same floor plan rents for $980 per month. A comparable structure with a more desirable floor plan rents for $1,100 per month. If the monthly rent multiplier is 125, what is the loss in value caused by the obsolete floor plan?

Check your answer against the one in the answer key at the back of the book.

Market Extraction Method

With the **market extraction method** of computing depreciation, also referred to as the market comparison or sales comparison method, the appraiser uses the sales prices of comparable properties to derive the value of a depreciated feature. By analyzing enough comparable properties, the appraiser can isolate the value of the depreciated feature.

Total accrued depreciation applicable to the subject property can be estimated by following four steps:

1. The land value of a comparable property is subtracted from its selling price to find the depreciated value of the improvements.
2. The depreciated value is subtracted from the reproduction cost of the improvements to find the dollar amount of depreciation.
3. The dollar amount of depreciation is divided by the age of the improvements to find the depreciation rate, expressed as a percent of total depreciation per year.

4. If the depreciation rate is fairly consistent for at least several comparables, the appraiser applies that percent, multiplied by the age of the subject property's improvements, to the reproduction cost of those improvements. The resulting figure is the dollar amount of depreciation for the subject property.

IN PRACTICE

Property A, a lot and warehouse, sold for $350,000, has an appraised land value of $87,500, and is 16 years old. The reproduction cost of improvements is $437,500. Property B, also a lot and warehouse, sold for $400,000, has an appraised land value of $100,000, and is 12 years old. The reproduction cost of improvements is $428,600.

Property A has an improvement value of $262,500 ($350,000 – $87,500), indicating depreciation of $175,000 ($437,500 – $262,500), or 40% of reproduction cost ($175,000 ÷ $437,500), for a yearly depreciation rate of 2.5% (40% ÷ 16 years).

Property B has an improvement value of $300,000 ($400,000 – $100,000), indicating depreciation of $128,600 ($428,600 – $300,000), or 30% of reproduction cost ($128,600 ÷ $428,600), for a yearly depreciation rate of 2.5% (30% ÷ 12 years).

In the preceding example, a yearly rate of 2.5% could be multiplied by the age in years of the subject improvements to find the percentage of depreciation to be multiplied by the reproduction cost of the improvements.

While market extraction is a reliable method of measuring accrued depreciation, its accuracy depends on the existence of truly comparable sales of both improved properties and vacant sites. It also requires an accurate estimate of reproduction cost new of the subject improvements.

Exercise 11-4

A structure with an obsolete floor plan is being appraised. A comparable structure with the same floor plan recently sold for $142,000. A comparable structure with a more desirable floor plan recently sold for $156,000. What is the loss in value attributable to the floor plan?

Check your answer against the one in the answer key at the back of the book.

Itemizing Accrued Depreciation

To make the most accurate and thorough use of the cost approach, the appraiser must compute applicable depreciation in each category (physical deterioration, functional obsolescence, and external obsolescence), then subtract those figures from the reproduction or replacement cost of the improvements. The appraiser does so by listing each item within a category and determining the amount of depreciation attributable to each.

While one of the indirect methods of calculating depreciation (capitalized value or sales comparison) may be the only available method for some types of depreciation or property, in general the better approach is to estimate a percentage of depreciation for each feature. Those percentages can be computed and the resulting figures added to find the total loss in reproduction cost. Remember, a given item should not be depreciated more than once; that is, it should not appear in more than one category when values are calculated.

IN PRACTICE

The following chart gives the items of curable and short-lived incurable physical deterioration found in a one-story house, as well as the reproduction cost of each item. What amount will be subtracted from the house's reproduction cost of $192,750 as curable physical deterioration, the first step in the observed condition method of determining depreciation?

Item	Reproduction Cost	Percent Depreciation	Amount of Depreciation
Exterior painting	$2,400	60%	$1,440
Carpeting	3,600	20	720
Air conditioner compressor	2,400	70	1,680
Water heater	400	100	400

Total reproduction cost of items of curable and short-lived incurable physical deterioration is $8,800 ($2,400 + $3,600 + $2,400 + $400).

Total amount of curable and short-lived incurable physical deterioration is $4,240 ($1,440, + $720 + $1,680 + $400).

Because long-lived incurable physical deterioration is usually based on general wear and tear of items not separately measured by the appraiser, the age-life method of computing depreciation is applied to the reproduction cost remaining after the full value of other items of physical deterioration has been subtracted.

IN PRACTICE

In the previous example, the house is 10 years old (also its effective age) and has an estimated remaining economic life of 40 years. The appraiser has determined that the amount of long-lived incurable physical deterioration is 10/50, or 20% of the house's remaining reproduction cost. After the full value of all items of physical deterioration is subtracted, the remaining reproduction cost is $183,950 ($192,750 – $8,800). The amount attributable to long-lived incurable physical deterioration is $36,790 (1/5 of $183,950). Total depreciation due to physical deterioration is $41,030 ($4,240 + $36,790).

The next categories, functional and external obsolescence, may be derived by one of the methods outlined in this unit. When all categories of depreciation have been applied to the reproduction cost, the land value of the property being appraised is added to the depreciated value to determine market value by the cost approach.

IN PRACTICE

There is no functional obsolescence in the house described in the preceding examples. External obsolescence due to location too close to a highway is estimated by the sales comparison method at $10,000. Land value is estimated at $61,000. Therefore,

Reproduction cost	$192,750
Physical deterioration	– 41,030
Functional obsolescence	N/A
External obsolescence	– 10,000
Depreciated building cost	$141,720
Site value	61,000
Property value opinion by cost approach	$202,720

Exercise 11-5

You are estimating the market value of a lot with a one-story industrial building that is 12 years old and has a remaining economic life of 48 years. You believe that 20% is an adequate depreciation deduction for everything except the following:

	Reproduction Cost	Observed Depreciation
Heating system	$12,800	60%
Plumbing	15,200	30
Electric and power	23,000	40
Floors	18,200	25
Roof	16,500	55

Additional information: The building is 125' by 160'. You estimate that it would cost $55 per square foot to reproduce the building. You estimate site value at $180,000.

What is your opinion of the property's market value?

Check your answer against the one in the answer key at the back of the book.

Exercise 11-6

The property you are asked to appraise is a ten-year-old, one-story, single-family dwelling with 1,900 square feet of living area.

Given the following data, estimate reproduction cost, cost per square foot of living area, accrued depreciation, and total property value using the cost approach.

Cost data

Direct costs (including labor, materials, equipment, and subcontractors' fees):	$98,500
Indirect costs (including profit and overhead, architect's fees, survey, legal fees, permits, licenses, insurance, taxes, financing charges, and selling expenses):	$98,500

Depreciation data

Physical deterioration	
Curable physical deterioration (deferred maintenance):	$5,250
Incurable physical deterioration—short-lived items:	$12,250
Incurable physical deterioration—long-lived items:	
Observed effective age (after curing physical curable and physical incurable short-lived items and curable functional obsolescence):	5 years
Estimated economic life expectancy:	50 years
Functional obsolescence	
Curable functional obsolescence:	none
Incurable functional obsolescence:	none
External obsolescence (location too close to highway; estimated by the sales comparison method):	$9,000

Site value

Estimated value of site by sales comparison approach:	$40,000

Check your answers against those in the answer key at the back of the book.

Cost Approach Using the URAR Form

In the Cost Approach analysis section of the URAR form (Figure 11.2), the appraiser is required to complete the following tasks:

- Develop an opinion of the site value
- Compute the area of the dwelling
- Estimate the reproduction or replacement cost of the dwelling at current market prices (additional lines are provided for calculating the cost of any property features not included as part of the square-foot estimate of the main living space, such as a porch, deck, or patio)

- Compute the area of any garage, carport, or other structure and estimate reproduction cost at current market prices
- Estimate the amount by which the structures have depreciated
- Estimate the "as is" value of any other site improvements, such as landscaping, driveway, fences, et cetera, provided they are not included in the Opinion of Site Value line
- Add site value to the depreciated cost of improvements to find the indicated value
- Explain in the Comments section how the cost approach was applied and comment on items such as the source of cost data, types of depreciation found, and how the site value was derived

The appraisal usually will include an addendum showing a rough sketch of the perimeter of the subject structure(s), with dimensions given in feet.

FIGURE 11.2
Cost Approach

COST APPROACH TO VALUE (not required by Fannie Mae)					
Provide adequate information for the lender/client to replicate the below cost figures and calculations.					
Support for the opinion of site value (summary of comparable land sales or other methods for estimating site value)					
ESTIMATED ☒ REPRODUCTION OR ☐ REPLACEMENT COST NEW	OPINION OF SITE VALUE			= $	50,000
Source of cost data	Dwelling	2,000 Sq. Ft. @ $ 95		=$	190,000
Quality rating from cost service Effective date of cost data		Sq. Ft. @ $		=$	
Comments on Cost Approach (gross living area calculations, depreciation, etc.)			Extras (pool)		20,000
	Garage/Carport	625 Sq. Ft. @ $ 25		=$	15,625
See sketch for measurement analysis. Cost estimate based on	Total Estimate of Cost-New			= $	225,625
current costs of local contractors and verified by current cost manual.	Less	Physical	Functional	External	
The depreciation estimate reflects observed effective age. Site value	Depreciation	36,000			=$(36,000)
supported by market data on comparable sites.	Depreciated Cost of Improvements			=$	189,625
	"As-is" Value of Site Improvements			=$	8,000
Estimated Remaining Economic Life (HUD and VA only) Years	Indicated Value By Cost Approach			=$	247,625

Exercise 11-7

Complete the blank URAR Cost Approach section provided in Figure 11.3 using the following information:

The subject property is a rectangle, 75 feet wide and 35 feet deep. There is a center front entrance but no front porch. There is a rear sliding glass door to the left of the house, opening onto a deck that is 25 feet wide by 18 feet deep. The built-in garage is 26 feet by 26 feet. The energy-efficient items on the property are the same as those enjoyed by other homes in the neighborhood—well-insulated walls, ceilings, and floors. There are no special energy-efficient fixtures.

The appraiser gathered current costs from local contractors actively engaged in building similar houses in the area. These costs were then compared to known costs published by current cost manuals. Cost estimates are based on $112 per square foot for residential construction of this quality, $20 per square foot for decking, and $30 per square foot for the garage.

The subject property is 22 years old and in good overall condition. Depreciation due to physical deterioration is estimated at 20% and is based on the effective age of the house in relation to other houses in the area. There is no evidence of functional or external obsolescence.

Site value, including all amenities commonly found in comparable sites (such as underground utilities, storm and sanitary sewers, and concrete curbs and gutters) is estimated by analysis of comparable properties at $98,000. The value "as is" of site improvements not considered in any other category (such as the driveway and landscaping) is estimated to be $12,000.

FIGURE 11.3
URAR Cost Approach Section

COST APPROACH TO VALUE (not required by Fannie Mae)	
Provide adequate information for the lender/client to replicate the below cost figures and calculations.	
Support for the opinion of site value (summary of comparable land sales or other methods for estimating site value)	
ESTIMATED ☐ REPRODUCTION OR ☐ REPLACEMENT COST NEW	OPINION OF SITE VALUE = $
Source of cost data	Dwelling Sq. Ft. @ $ =$
Quality rating from cost service Effective date of cost data	Sq. Ft. @ $ =$
Comments on Cost Approach (gross living area calculations, depreciation, etc.)	
	Garage/Carport Sq. Ft. @ $ =$
	Total Estimate of Cost-New = $
	Less Physical Functional External
	Depreciation =$( )
	Depreciated Cost of Improvements =$
	"As-is" Value of Site Improvements =$
Estimated Remaining Economic Life (HUD and VA only) Years	Indicated Value By Cost Approach =$

Check your answer against the one in the answer key at the back of the book.

Usefulness of the Cost Approach

The reproduction cost of a building tends to set the upper limit of its value. There can be, however, a significant difference between the current cost to reproduce a structure and its market value. If the improvements are not new, the appraiser must estimate the amount of accrued depreciation that the property has suffered and deduct that amount from the reproduction cost. For very old buildings, estimating depreciation will be much more difficult. Added to that problem is the fact that today's marketplace may not produce any suitable equivalents to the construction materials and techniques used in an older structure. For those buildings, the sales comparison or income capitalization approach may be most appropriate.

The cost approach is especially useful when valuing buildings for which the sales comparison approach or income capitalization approach is impractical. Examples include schools, museums, libraries and other institutional structures. Generally, few, if any, comparable sales for such properties will exist, and no income figures will be available.

For certain appraisal purposes, the cost approach may be the only feasible approach. In an appraisal for insurance purposes, for instance, insured value will be based on the cost of restoration, which will dictate the amount of reimbursement for loss.

Exercise 11-8
Cost Approach Case Problem

You now have the opportunity to apply what you have learned in Units 10 and 11. You will be guided through a detailed simulation of an industrial appraisal problem, in which you have to perform cost and depreciation analyses to arrive at an opinion of property value by the cost approach. You will estimate reproduction cost, depreciation, land value, and total property value.

Each computation you must record is numbered so that you can check your answer in the answer key at the back of the book. To make the best use of this case problem, you should check each answer as it is derived, rather than waiting until you have reached your opinion of value.

You will be using the following data in this problem:

Identification of property:
The subject property is located at the corner of Parker Avenue and Plymouth Road (see Exhibit A) and is improved with a one-story office and factory building, approximately 20 years old. The lot is rectangular. The building is on the west section of the lot, with parking space to the east.

Neighborhood:
The neighborhood is located approximately four miles from the center of a small city. The immediate area is developed with various types of industrial and commercial properties, such as auto showrooms, gas stations, tool and die factories, and photographic and instrument manufacturers. The subject property is accessible to both employee automobile and truck traffic.

Public utilities and zoning:
All the public utilities are installed and in service. These include gas, electricity, sewers, telephone, and water. The zoning is light industrial.

Land value:
On the land comparison table in Exhibit F, there are four plots of land that are reliable indications of value for the subject property. Adjustments were made for size, location, date of sale, and desirability. In estimating land value for this type of property, the square foot rate is the most practical measurement used in this area.

Exterior construction:
Foundation—12" concrete wall and footings
Floor—6" reinforced concrete
Exterior walls—12" common brick with block backup; jumbo face brick veneer
Framing—steel frame with 14' eave height
Roof—sheathing, 17/8", fiberglass insulation, four-ply tar and gravel covering
Windows—industrial sash, aluminum, 50% vented
Doors—six 3' × 7' hollow metal; one rolling steel 12' × 12', chain hoist-operated

Interior construction:
Walls—painted drywall on 8' wood stud partitions in office; perimeter walls in office are painted at a cost of $0.25 per square foot of wall area; 12" concrete block dividing wall (14' high) separating factory area from office area
Floor covering—vinyl tile in office
Ceiling—suspended mineral fiber acoustic tile
Doors—six 3' × 7' hollow metal within office; one 3' × 7' hollow metal leading from office to factory
Interior of factory—unfinished
Electrical fixtures—fluorescent lights, normal lighting requirements
Plumbing—standard fixtures
Heating and air conditioning—both office and factory
Miscellaneous—3" asphalt paving on 3" stone base

Physical deterioration (curable): None

Physical deterioration (short-lived incurable):
Brickwork—40%
Roof (asphalt and gravel)—60%
Exterior doors—75%
Floor covering (vinyl tile)—55%
Acoustic tile ceiling—45%
Electric—35%
Plumbing—30%
Heating and air-conditioning—30%
Asphalt paving—40%

Depreciation deduction for balance of building—physical deterioration (long-lived incurable)—25%

Functional obsolescence (curable): None

Functional obsolescence (incurable): 5% of net value after physical deterioration

External obsolescence: None

Exhibit A: Plat Plan and Building Layout

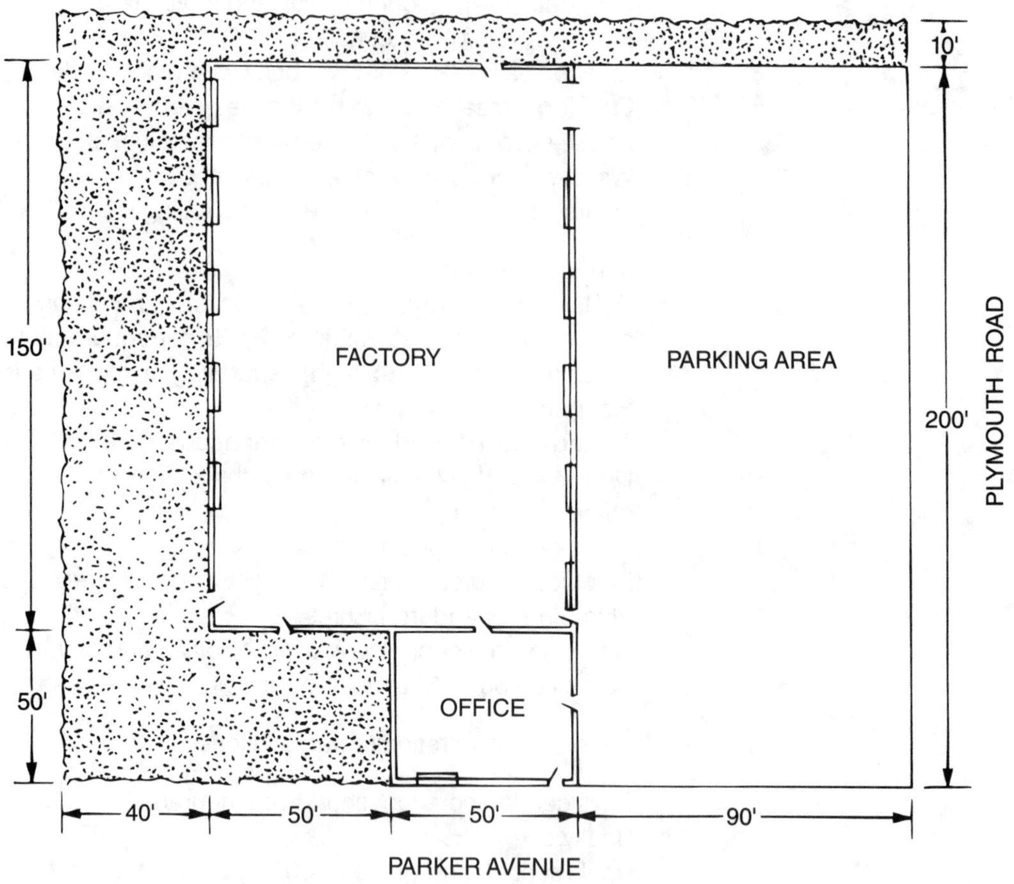

Compute the following:

Total factory area	________
Total office area	________
Total building area	________
Building perimeter (including foundation wall between factory and office areas)	________
Total parking area	________

Exhibit B: Exterior Wall Area

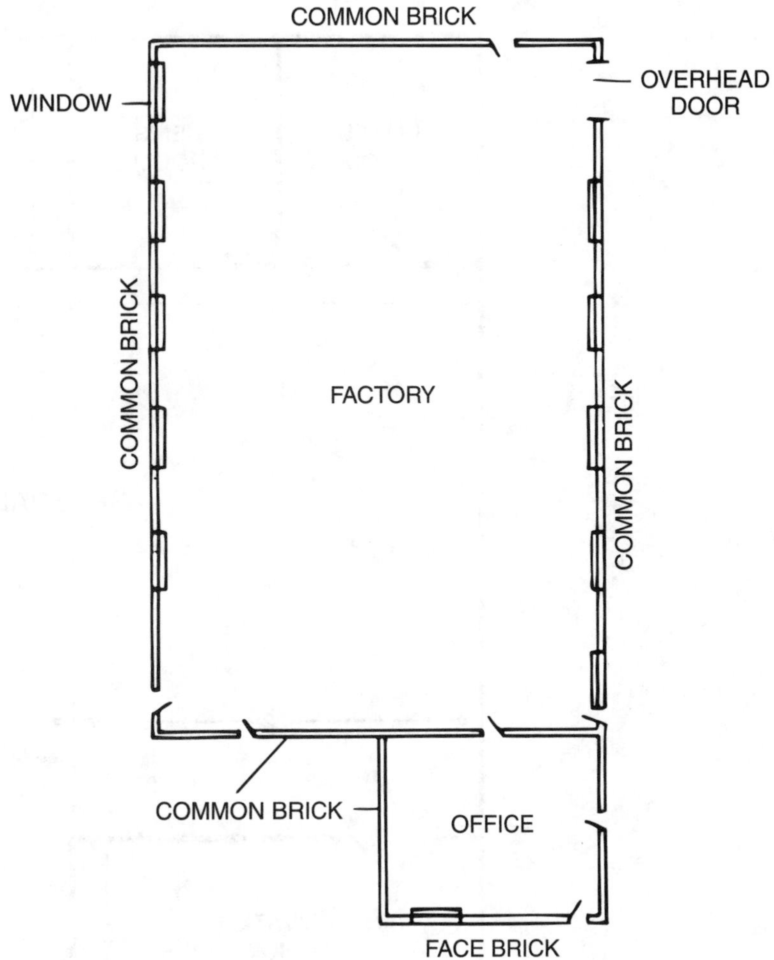

Data:

Factory height—14'
Office height—10'
Overhead door—12' × 12'
All other exterior doors—3' × 7'
All windows—6' × 12'

Compute the following:

Total area covered by common brick (including factory area above office roof and side walls) ________________

Total area covered by face brick ________________

CAUTION: Door and window areas must be deducted.

Exhibit C: Interior Wall Area (Excluding Perimeter of Office)

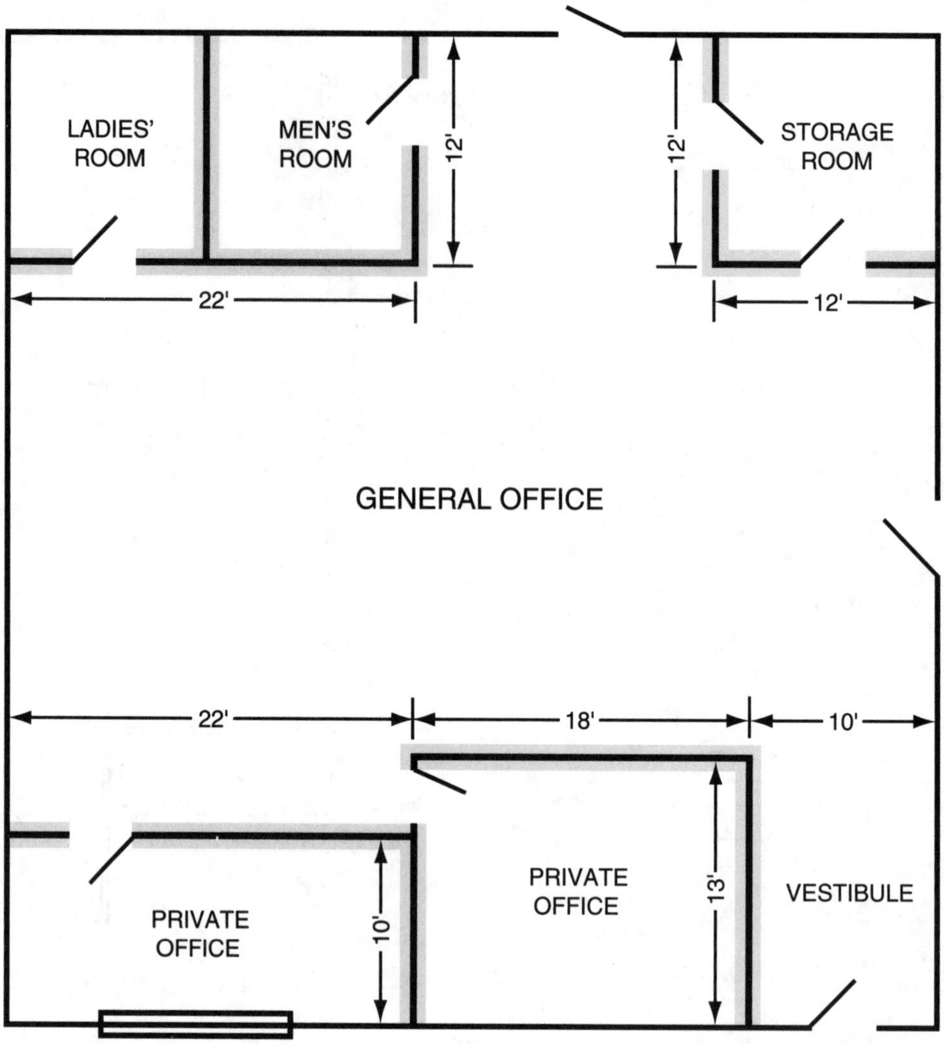

LADIES' ROOM
MEN'S ROOM
STORAGE ROOM
12'
12'
22'
12'
GENERAL OFFICE
22'
18'
10'
PRIVATE OFFICE
PRIVATE OFFICE
VESTIBULE
10'
13'

Data:

Ceiling height—8'
Doors—3' × 7'
Construction is drywall on wood studs.

Compute the interior wall area for the office portion of the building ________________

CAUTION: Both sides of a wall and door opening must be accounted for.

Exhibit D: Interior Wall Area (Perimeter of Office)

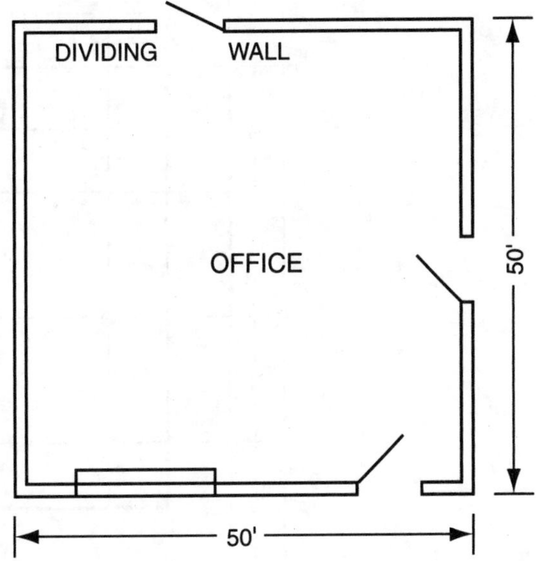

Data:

Dividing wall height—14'
Ceiling height—8'
Doors—3' × 7'
Window—6' × 12'

Compute the total wall area (perimeter of office only) ______________

Compute area of concrete block dividing wall ______________

Exhibit E: Frame Support

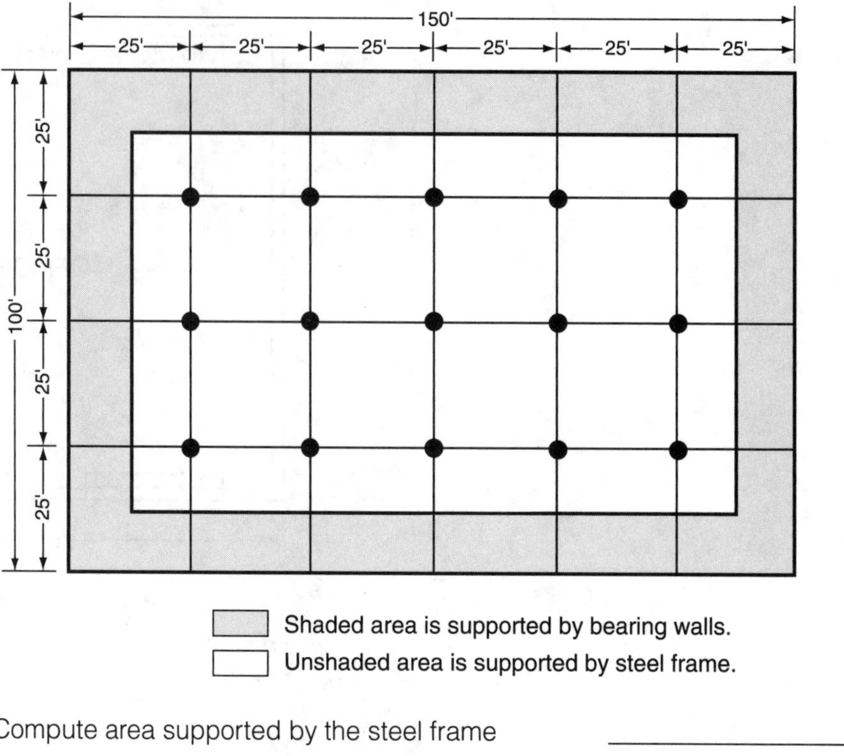

Compute area supported by the steel frame ______________

Exhibit F: Land Comparisons

Parcel	Sq. Ft. of Area	Sales Price	Sales Price per Sq. Ft.	Adjustments	Adjusted Sales Price per Sq. Ft.
A	45,000	$ 90,000	$2.00	+10%	$2.20
B	46,217	129,400	2.80	−20%	2.24
C	25,900	60,900	2.35	−15%	2.00
D	47,900	115,500	2.41	−10%	2.17

Compute the total land area of the subject property ______________

Compute the land value ______________

Using the cost data table in this exercise, compute your cost estimate for each building component listed on this and the next page. Where a cost range is given, use the highest estimate. Round off all of your answers to the nearest dollar.

Foundation ______________

Exterior walls ______________

Roof construction ______________

Framing ______________

Floor construction ______________

Windows ______________

Exterior doors ______________

Interior construction ______________

Electric __________
Plumbing __________
Heating and air-conditioning __________
Miscellaneous __________

Enter and total your reproduction cost figures in the following list.

Reproduction Costs

Exterior construction:
- Foundation __________
- Floor construction __________
- Exterior walls __________
- Framing __________
- Roof construction __________
- Windows __________
- Doors __________

Interior construction:
- Walls __________
- Floor covering __________
- Ceiling __________
- Doors __________
- Electric __________
- Plumbing __________
- Heating and air-conditioning __________
- Miscellaneous __________

Total reproduction cost __________

Observed depreciation:
- Brickwork __________
- Roof __________
- Exterior doors __________
- Floor covering __________
- Acoustic tile ceiling __________
- Electrical __________
- Plumbing __________
- Heating __________
- Air-conditioning __________
- Asphalt paving __________
- Depreciation deduction for balance of building: __________
- Deduction for incurable functional obsolescence: __________

Use the list below to determine a total property value

Cost Valuation

Reproduction cost ______

Depreciation:

Deterioration—curable ______

Short-lived incurable ______

Long-lived incurable ______

Functional obsolescence—curable ______

incurable ______

External obsolescence ______

Total accrued depreciation ______

Building value estimate ______

Land value estimate ______

Total property value indicated by cost approach ______

Check your answers against those in the answer key at the back of the book.

Cost Data

	Material	Specification	Cost per Unit of Measurement*
Foundation	Concrete wall and footing, 4' deep, incl. excavation	8" wide	$20.50 per linear foot of wall
		12"	30.70
		6"	37.30
Floor Construction	Reinforced concrete, poured in place, including forms and reinforcing	4"	$2.50 per sq. ft. of floor
		6"	3.10
		8"	3.60
Floor Covering	Nylon carpet		$12.00 per sq. yd.
	Vinyl tile		1.90 per sq. yd.
Framing	Steel frame, with steel columns, beams, and purlins	10' eave height	$3.70 per sq. ft. of support area
		14'	4.50
		20'	5.60
Roof Construction	Wood deck		
	Sheathing	½" thick	$0.65 per sq. ft.
	Fiberboard R-2.78	1"	0.55
	Fiberglass R-7.7	1⅞"	1.10
	Polystyrene R-8	2"	0.52
Roof Covering	Asphalt and gravel	3-ply	$2.10 per sq. ft.
		4-ply	2.40
	Polyurethane spray-on	1" thick	1.35
		3"	2.50

Cost Data			
	Material	Specification	Cost per Unit of Measurement*
Exterior Walls	Common brick facing with block backup	8" thick	$9.50 per sq. ft. of wall area
	Jumbo face brick veneer	12"	10.20
	Roman brick veneer		3.80
	Ribbed aluminum siding, 4" profile		7.50
	Steel siding, beveled, vinyl coated	0.40" thick	2.40 per sq. ft.
		8" wide	1.25 per sq. ft.
Doors	Hollow metal, 3' x 7', including frame, lockset, and hinges	Exterior	$355 each
		Interior	275
	Rolling steel, chain hoist operated	8' × 8'	$840 each
		10' × 10'	1,175
		12' × 12'	1,425
		20' × 16'	3,200
	Pine, 3' x 7', including frame, lockset, and hinges	Exterior	$290 each (incl. storm & screen)
		Interior	95
	Oak, including frame, lockset, and hinges	3' × 7' × 1¾'	$245 each
Windows	Industrial sash		$11.40 per sq. ft. of window area
	steel, fixed		14.20
	steel, 50% vented		17.50
	aluminum, fixed		20.10
	aluminum, 50% vented		
Interior Walls and Partitions	Concrete block	4"	$3.20 per sq. ft. of wall area
		6"	3.70
		8"	4.05
		12"	4.40
	Drywall on wood studs, including two coats of paint		$3.15 per sq. ft. of wall area
	Drywall on metal studs, including two coats of paint		$2.70
Ceiling	Mineral fiber acoustic tile, including suspension system		$1.65 per sq. ft. of ceiling area
Electrical Wiring	Fluorescent fixtures, normal lighting requirements		$3.10 per sq. ft. of building area
Heating and Cooling	Heating and central air-conditioning with ducts and controls		$5.75 per sq. ft. of building area
Plumbing	Plumbing, including fixtures		$2.75 per sq. ft. of building area
Misc.	Asphalt paving on 3" stone base	1½" thick	$4.25 per sq. yd.
		3"	7.20

*The figures given here are for purposes of illustration only.

■ SUMMARY

Accrued depreciation must be estimated, then subtracted from the reproduction or replacement cost of the improvement(s), and the resulting figure added to site value to determine value by the cost approach.

In the appraisal of older structures in particular, the problem of measuring depreciation accurately and convincingly may be impossible. In such a case, greater emphasis should be placed on the sales comparison and/or income capitalization approaches. On the other hand, the cost approach may be the best (or only) method of evaluating special-purpose properties, such as schools.

Accrued depreciation must be estimated for each category: physical deterioration, functional obsolescence, and external obsolescence.

Depreciation may be determined using the economic age-life method, observed condition method, capitalized value method, or market extraction method.

In the age-life method of computing depreciation, the building's construction cost is divided by the number of years of its economic life to find a yearly dollar amount of depreciation. In the observed condition method, the appraiser analyzes the property in terms of each of the separate categories of depreciation. In the capitalized value method, the appraiser computes depreciation by determining loss in rental value attributable to a depreciated item and then applying a gross rent multiplier to that figure. With the market extraction method, the appraiser uses the sales prices of comparable properties to derive the present value of a depreciated feature.

■ Review Questions

1. The total difference between a building's cost new and its market value is called
   a. accrued depreciation.
   b. replacement value.
   c. physical deterioration.
   d. functional obsolescence.

2. Any loss of value from causes outside the property itself is called
   a. physical deterioration.
   b. functional obsolescence.
   c. external obsolescence.
   d. modified depreciation.

3. A bedroom that can be entered solely through another bedroom is an example of
   a. functional obsolescence.
   b. locational obsolescence.
   c. incurable physical deterioration.
   d. economic obsolescence.

4. The number of years of useful life left to a building from the date of appraisal is the building's
   a. effective age.
   b. remaining economic life.
   c. useful life.
   d. physical life.

5. Physical or design features that exceed current requirements are called
   a. a capitalized value.
   b. a long-lived item.
   c. a superadequacy.
   d. a misplaced improvement.

6. A method of computing accrued depreciation in which the cost of a building is depreciated at a fixed annual percentage rate is called
   a. the capitalized value method.
   b. the observed condition method.
   c. the market extraction method.
   d. the age-life method.

7. Which method of estimating depreciation is the easiest to apply?
   a. Observed condition method
   b. Age-life method
   c. Market extraction method
   d. Capitalized value method

8. The chronological age of a house is 47 years. The appraiser renders an opinion of the structure's effective age of 25 years and remaining economic life of 75 years. What is the percentage of accrued depreciation?
   a. 20%
   b. 25%
   c. 30%
   d. 33%

9. The name of the method used to calculate depreciation in question 8 is
   a. age-life.
   b. extraction.
   c. index.
   d. observed condition.

10. In question 8, the replacement cost of the house is estimated at $500,000. What is the current estimated value of the structure?
    a. $375,000
    b. $400,000
    c. $425,000
    d. Not enough information to determine

11. In the cost approach, depreciation is a factor in
    a. the value of land.
    b. the value of the overall property.
    c. the value of the structure.
    d. the residual cost.

12. When does building cost equal value?
    a. When building cost is less than land value
    b. When building cost equals overall value
    c. Building cost never equals value
    d. When depreciation is zero; that is, the building is new

13. When depreciation is greater than the value added by curing it, the depreciation is
    a. observable.
    b. curable.
    c. incurable.
    d. feasible.

14. When depreciation is less than the value added by curing it, the depreciation is
    a. incurable.
    b. curable.
    c. observable.
    d. infeasible.

15. The market rent of a house with four bedrooms is $2,000 per month. The market rent of a house with three bedrooms is $1,750 per month. The gross rent multiplier in the subject neighborhood is 100, indicating the value of a fourth bedroom is
    a. $20,000.
    b. $25,000.
    c. $30,000.
    d. $40,000.

16. The technique used in question 15 is called
    a. the observed rent method.
    b. the gross income multiplier method.
    c. the rent loss method.
    d. the modified observed method.

17. The amount of functional obsolescence in question 15 is
    a. $20,000.
    b. $25,000.
    c. $30,000.
    d. $40,000.

18. The form of depreciation that is always incurable is
    a. physical obsolescence.
    b. functional obsolescence.
    c. external obsolescence.
    d. physical deterioration.

19. Which of the following components MOST likely suffers from incurable deterioration?
    a. Storms and screens
    b. Carpets
    c. Furniture
    d. Studs and joists

20. A weakness of the age-life method is that it is
    a. more subjective than other methods.
    b. less subjective than other methods.
    c. quantitative.
    d. rarely used.

Check your answers against those in the answer key at the back of the book.

UNIT TWELVE

12

THE SALES COMPARISON APPROACH

LEARNING OBJECTIVES

When you have completed this unit, you will be able to

- identify the property characteristics that are included in the sales comparison approach matrix,
- determine the suitability of properties as comparables,
- compute adjustment values,
- determine whether a dollar adjustment or percentage adjustment is appropriate,
- adjust the sales prices of comparable properties to reflect their differences from the subject property,
- complete a sales comparison analysis, and
- enter data on the Sales Comparison Approach section of the URAR form that complies with the requirements of the Uniform Appraisal Dataset (UAD).

KEY TERMS

dollar adjustment
highest and best use
matched pairs analysis (MPA)
paired data set analysis
paired sales analysis
percentage adjustment
Uniform Residential Appraisal Report (URAR) form
zoning

■ OVERVIEW

This unit continues the discussion of the sales comparison approach that began in Unit 8, following the steps in the appraisal process. Figure 6.1 shows the process the appraiser follows when carrying out an assignment. If the steps in the flowchart are followed carefully, all the necessary information will be collected to arrive at an accurate appraisal. The process begins with a definition of the problem and ends with the final opinion of value.

The exercises in this unit continue the sample appraisal of a single-family home and lot. At the end of this unit, you will complete an appraisal analysis of a single-family residence using the sales comparison approach.

Basics of the Sales Comparison Approach

In the sales comparison approach, the appraiser collects, classifies, analyzes, and interprets market data to determine the most probable selling price of a property.

The sales comparison approach requires the appraiser to do the following:

- Identify the sources of value or characteristics of the subject property that would produce market demand. This takes into account the viewpoint of the typical buyer.
- Find recently sold comparable properties that are reasonable alternatives for the typical buyer. The appraiser also considers asking prices of properties currently being marketed for a possible indication of a market downturn.
- Compare the comparable properties to the subject property and adjust for differences.
- Reach a final conclusion of value as of the indicated date.

The sales comparison approach is based on the principle of substitution; that is, the value of a property tends to equal the cost of acquiring a comparable property on the open market. This is just one of the principles that helps determine property value.

■ GATHER, RECORD, VERIFY, AND ANALYZE THE NECESSARY DATA

In Step 1 of the appraisal process, the appraiser defines the problem, and in Step 2, the appraiser determines the scope of work to be performed. These were discussed in earlier units. In Step 3, discussed next, the appraiser gathers, records, verifies, and analyzes the data required to complete the appraisal.

When using the sales comparison approach, data is collected on sales of comparable properties. If possible, only properties that have been sold within the last six months should be considered. A sale made a year or two before the appraisal will most likely not reflect current market value. Finally, the sales must have been arm's-length transactions, and the properties sold must be substantially similar to the subject property.

Comparison Grid

The Sales Comparison Approach section of the **Uniform Residential Appraisal Report (URAR) form**, shown in Figure 12.1, lists the common significant property variables that warrant price adjustments. The analysis grid provides space to describe the subject property and its comparables and space to adjust the sales price of each comparable to account for significant property differences.

The easiest way to complete the grid is to enter all the details of the subject property and then do the same for each comparable property in turn.

Although years of experience may give an appraiser some intuitive knowledge of the value of property, the figure presented in the appraisal report must be as factual as possible. It is important to remember that the adjustment value of a property feature is not simply the cost to construct or add that feature but instead what a buyer is willing to pay for it, typically a lesser amount. An opinion of market value must always consider the demands of the marketplace.

The appraiser's report to the client must present the facts on which the final opinion of value was reached rather than a preconception of value. The appraiser's intuition is useful, however, if the adjusted property value is far removed from what it should be. If the value seems too high or too low, there may be adjustment factors that the appraiser has failed to consider, indicating that more information must be gathered.

Usually, there will be some dissimilarity between the subject property and a comparable. The accuracy of the sales comparison approach relies on the categories selected for adjustments and the amount of any adjustments made. The appraiser should avoid making unnecessary adjustments; that is, the appraiser should make only those adjustments considered by buyers, sellers, and tenants involved with this type of property. The categories listed on the sales comparison approach grid are the most significant factors because they have the greatest effect on value in standard residential appraisals.

Finally, the appraiser should always be careful to use properties of similar construction quality when estimating the market value of property variables. Just as the properties themselves should be similar in overall quality of construction, so should individual components or details be similar, such as updated kitchen and bathroom design and fixtures.

FIGURE 12.1
URAR Sales Comparison Approach Section

There are comparable properties currently offered for sale in the subject neighborhood ranging in price from $ to $.
There are comparable sales in the subject neighborhood within the past twelve months ranging in sale price from $ to $.

FEATURE	SUBJECT	COMPARABLE SALE # 1		COMPARABLE SALE # 2		COMPARABLE SALE # 3	
Address	2130 W. Franklin	1901 Parkside Blvd.					
Proximity to Subject		.50 miles SE					
Sale Price	$		$ 226,000		$		$
Sale Price/Gross Liv. Area	$ sq. ft.	$ 125.56 sq. ft.		$ sq. ft.		$ sq. ft.	
Data Source(s)		Public records					
Verification Source(s)		Sales agent					
VALUE ADJUSTMENTS	DESCRIPTION	DESCRIPTION	+(-) $ Adjustment	DESCRIPTION	+(-) $ Adjustment	DESCRIPTION	+(-) $ Adjustment
Sale or Financing Concessions		ArmLth Conv					
Date of Sale/Time		6 weeks ago					
Location	N; Res	A; Bsy Rd					
Leasehold/Fee Simple	fee simple	fee simple					
Site	10,000 SF	10,000 SF					
View	N; Res	N; Res					
Design (Style)	Ranch	Ranch					
Quality of Construction	Q4	Q4					
Actual Age	6	8					
Condition	C3	C3					
Above Grade	Total / Bdrms / Baths	Total / Bdrms / Baths		Total / Bdrms / Baths		Total / Bdrms / Baths	
Room Count	7 / 3 / 2.1	7 / 3 / 2.0					
Gross Living Area	1,825 sq. ft.	1,800 sq. ft.		sq. ft.		sq. ft.	
Basement & Finished Rooms Below Grade	0	0					
Functional Utility	Average	Average					
Heating/Cooling	FWA/CAC	FWA/CAC					
Energy Efficient Items	none	none					
Garage/Carport	2-car att.	2-car att.					
Porch/Patio/Deck	none	none					
Net Adjustment (Total)		☐ + ☐ -	$	☐ + ☐ -	$	☐ + ☐ -	$
Adjusted Sale Price of Comparables		Net Adj. % Gross Adj. %	$	Net Adj. % Gross Adj. %	$	Net Adj. % Gross Adj. %	$

I ☐ did ☐ did not research the sale or transfer history of the subject property and comparable sales. If not, explain

My research ☐ did ☐ did not reveal any prior sales or transfers of the subject property for the three years prior to the effective date of this ap praisal.
Data source(s)
My research ☐ did ☐ did not reveal any prior sales or transfers of the comparable sales for the year prior to the date of sale of the comparable s ale.
Data source(s)
Report the results of the research and analysis of the prior sale or transfer history of the subject property and comparable sales (report additional prior sales on page 3).

ITEM	SUBJECT	COMPARABLE SALE # 1	COMPARABLE SALE # 2	COMPARABLE SALE # 3
Date of Prior Sale/Transfer				
Price of Prior Sale/Transfer				
Data Source(s)				
Effective Date of Data Source(s)				

Analysis of prior sale or transfer history of the subject property and comparable sales

Summary of Sales Comparison Approach

Indicated Value by Sales Comparison Approach $

Compliance with UAD

As mentioned in Unit 8, as of September 1, 2011, it became mandatory for appraisers to record data on the URAR form in compliance with the Uniform Appraisal Dataset (UAD) requirements for conventional mortgage loans sold to Freddie Mac and Fannie Mae.

On the following pages, the sales comparison section of the URAR form is analyzed line by line and the biggest changes resulting from implementation of the UAD are highlighted. The URAR form itself hasn't changed—only some of the guidelines for entering data on the form. The goal is to report appraisal data that is more specific, consistent, and accurate. You can view the complete UAD Field-Specific Standardization Requirements by going to www.efanniemae.com and entering "UAD Appendix D" in the search box at the top right of the page.

Refer to the Sales Comparison Approach section of the URAR form, shown in Figure 12.1, as each line item is discussed.

Address

Enter the physical address of the subject property and each comparable sale.

Sample entry: 313 Degas Dr., Nokomis, FL 34275

Proximity to subject

Enter the approximate distance of the comparable sales to the subject property in terms of miles or fraction of miles. Enter also the direction of each comparable property from the subject property.

You should comment on any comparable property located a substantial distance away from the subject property.

Sample entry: 1 mile S or 0.20 mile SE or ½ mile NW

Sale price

Enter the reported sale price of each comparable property. If there is no current pending sale price for the subject, leave that space blank.

Sample entry: 150,000

Sale price gross liv. area

Enter the price per square foot of gross living area for the subject and comparables. Divide the sale price of the property by the number of square feet of gross living area in the house. For example, if the sale price is $150,000 and the gross living area is 1,500 square feet, then the Sale Price/Gross Liv. Area is $150,000 ÷ 1,500, or $100 per square foot.

Sample entry: 100.00

Data source(s)

Enter the source of the market data used, such as the lender, public records, or multiple listing service or some similar response. Enter also the number of days on the market (Dom).

Sample entry: M.L.S#35698; Dom 155

Verification source(s)

Enter the source from which you verified the accuracy of the data collected. Basic sources may include public records, the appraiser's own files, multiple listing services, assessor, courthouse, REALTORS®, and lenders.

Sample entry: assessor

Value adjustments

Up to this point you have recorded only descriptive or factual data about the subject and comparables. The remaining items in the property variables list may require plus or minus adjustments. In most home appraisals, good comparables usually are available, thus requiring few adjustments. Remember, however, that all adjustments must be supported by documented market evidence. In most cases market-based price adjustments can be developed through matched pairs analysis, which will be discussed later in this unit.

WEB LINK

www.appraisalfoundation.org

The Appraisal Practices Board has issued valuation advisories that can be accessed through www.appraisalfoundation.org. Valuation Advisory 4 covers the selection of comparable properties in general, and Valuation Advisory 3 discusses issues that will be encountered when appraising residential property in a declining market. Some of those issues are touched on here, but the advisories should be consulted for detailed, updated information.

Sale or financing concessions

Indicate the sale type for each comparable property, such as arms length sale (see Figure 12.3). Then enter the financing type, such as FHA, VA, or conventional. Finally, enter the estimated value of the adjustment, if any.

Sample entry: ArmLth
Conv; $0

This is the first value adjustment to consider. Describe any special sale or financing arrangement that may have affected the sale price of a comparable property, such as a mortgage assumption, buydown, installment sales contract, or wrap-around loan. As you will see later, the final step is to enter the estimated value of the adjustment, if any, and provide an explanation in the Additional Comments section or in an addendum attached to the report form.

Since the advent of the recent subprime mortgage crisis, the real estate marketplace has been far from "normal" in many parts of the country. Lack of sales, or abundance of forced sales, has resulted in the creation by Fannie Mae and Freddie Mac of the Market Conditions Addendum to the Appraisal Report, shown in Figure 12.2. As of April 1, 2009, the addendum became a requirement for appraisals on loans to be purchased by Fannie Mae or Freddie Mac. The form helps define the marketplace by providing a fuller description of the rate of sales and range of sales prices, as well as the effect on the market of foreclosure sales.

IN PRACTICE

Ordinarily, a foreclosure sale would be excluded from consideration as a comparable property because, by definition, it does not qualify as an arm's-length transaction. In areas in which a high number of foreclosures have occurred, however, those may be the only available recent property sales to use for comparables. If that is the case, foreclosures have become the market. Each sale should be noted as a foreclosure and the appraiser should explain why it was used. An isolated foreclosure sale could also be used as a comparable (again, with an explanation), if there are few sales in the area and the appraiser believes it is a good indicator of current market value. With any foreclosure sale, property condition is an important issue. If possible, the appraiser should inspect both the exterior and interior of any foreclosed property used as a comparable; at a minimum, the appraiser should inspect the property exterior and obtain from a reliable source a report of the condition of the property interior at the time of the foreclosure sale.

Date of sale/time

An adjustment will probably be necessary if market conditions and price levels change between the date of sale of the comparable property and the date of appraisal. The question must be asked: Have housing prices increased, decreased, or stayed the same in the last six months? In an active market, comparable properties that sold within the past six months should be readily available. Most underwriters require the appraiser to explain the use of any comparable sale that occurred more than six months before the date of appraisal. In a slow market, however, it may be necessary to use comparable sales from as long as a year ago. In that event, market conditions may have changed, thus creating the need for a time adjustment.

For each comparable property, enter the status type from the list shown in Figure 12.4. Then enter the appropriate date(s).

Sample entry: s11/12/11; c10/01/11

FIGURE 12.2
Market Conditions Addendum to the Appraisal Report

Uniform Residential Appraisal Report

File #

SALES COMPARISON APPROACH

There are comparable properties currently offered for sale in the subject neighborhood ranging in price from $ to $.

There are comparable sales in the subject neighborhood within the past twelve months ranging in sale price from $ to $.

FEATURE	SUBJECT	COMPARABLE SALE # 1		COMPARABLE SALE # 2		COMPARABLE SALE # 3	
Address							
Proximity to Subject							
Sale Price	$		$		$		$
Sale Price/Gross Liv. Area	$ sq. ft.	$ sq. ft.		$ sq. ft.		$ sq. ft.	
Data Source(s)							
Verification Source(s)							
VALUE ADJUSTMENTS	DESCRIPTION	DESCRIPTION	+(-) $ Adjustment	DESCRIPTION	+(-) $ Adjustment	DESCRIPTION	+(-) $ Adjustment
Sale or Financing Concessions							
Date of Sale/Time							
Location							
Leasehold/Fee Simple							
Site							
View							
Design (Style)							
Quality of Construction							
Actual Age							
Condition							
Above Grade Room Count	Total Bdrms. Baths	Total Bdrms. Baths		Total Bdrms. Baths		Total Bdrms. Baths	
Gross Living Area	sq. ft.	sq. ft.		sq. ft.		sq. ft.	
Basement & Finished Rooms Below Grade							
Functional Utility							
Heating/Cooling							
Energy Efficient Items							
Garage/Carport							
Porch/Patio/Deck							
Net Adjustment (Total)		☐ + ☐ -	$	☐ + ☐ -	$	☐ + ☐ -	$
Adjusted Sale Price of Comparables		Net Adj. % Gross Adj. %	$	Net Adj. % Gross Adj. %	$	Net Adj. % Gross Adj. %	$

I ☐ did ☐ did not research the sale or transfer history of the subject property and comparable sales. If not, explain

My research ☐ did ☐ did not reveal any prior sales or transfers of the subject property for the three years prior to the effective date of this appraisal.

Data source(s)

My research ☐ did ☐ did not reveal any prior sales or transfers of the comparable sales for the year prior to the date of sale of the comparable sale.

Data source(s)

Report the results of the research and analysis of the prior sale or transfer history of the subject property and comparable sales (report additional prior sales on page 3).

ITEM	SUBJECT	COMPARABLE SALE # 1	COMPARABLE SALE # 2	COMPARABLE SALE # 3
Date of Prior Sale/Transfer				
Price of Prior Sale/Transfer				
Data Source(s)				
Effective Date of Data Source(s)				

Analysis of prior sale or transfer history of the subject property and comparable sales

Summary of Sales Comparison Approach

Indicated Value by Sales Comparison Approach $

RECONCILIATION

Indicated Value by: Sales Comparison Approach $ Cost Approach (if developed) $ Income Approach (if developed) $

This appraisal is made ☐ "as is", ☐ subject to completion per plans and specifications on the basis of a hypothetical condition that the improvements have been completed, ☐ subject to the following repairs or alterations on the basis of a hypothetical condition that the repairs or alterations have been completed, or ☐ subject to the following required inspection based on the extraordinary assumption that the condition or deficiency does not require alteration or repair:

Based on a complete visual inspection of the interior and exterior areas of the subject property, defined scope of work, statement of assumptions and limiting conditions, and appraiser's certification, my (our) opinion of the market value, as defined, of the real property that is the subject of this report is $, as of , which is the date of inspection and the effective date of this appraisal.

Freddie Mac Form 70 March 2005 Page 2 of 6 Fannie Mae Form 1004 March 2005

FIGURE 12.3
Sales or Financing Concessions Entries

Abbreviated Entry	Sale Type
REO	REO Sale
Short	Short sale
CrtOrd	Court ordered sale
Estate	Estate sale
Relo	Relocation sale
ArmLth	Arms length sale
Listing	Listing

Abbreviated Entry	Financing Type
FHA	FHA
VA	VA
Conv	Conventional
Seller	Seller
Cash	Cash
RH	USDA—Rural housing

FIGURE 12.4
Date of Sale/Time Entries

STATUS TYPE
Active
Contract
Expired
Withdrawn
Settled sale

Abbreviated Entry	Status Type Date
C	Contract Date
S	Settlement Date
W	Withdrawn Date
E	Expiration Date

- If the comp is an **active** listing, the appraiser must specify **active**.
- If the comp is under **contract**, a **settled** sale, an **expired** or **withdrawn** listing, the appraiser must first enter the appropriate abbreviation followed by the corresponding date in mm/yy format.
- If the comp is a settled sale and the contract date is known, the appraiser must first enter s followed by the settlement date and then c followed by the contract date.
- In settled sales for which the contract date is unavailable to the appraiser, the abbreviation **Unk**, for unknown, must be entered in place of the contract date.

Location

Because similar properties might differ in value from neighborhood to neighborhood, comparable properties should be located in the same neighborhood as the subject property, if possible. There may be no recourse but to find comparable properties outside the immediate area if few sales have been made in the neighborhood, if the subject property is in a rural area, or if the subject property is atypical—such as the only three-apartment building in an area of single-family houses. In such a case, the buildings chosen as comparables should at least come from comparable neighborhoods.

Two comparisons are required in this entry. Select one of these ratings to describe the overall effect on value and marketability of the location factor associated with the subject property and each comparable property: N (neutral), B (beneficial), or A (adverse). Then, enter a location factor, such as residential, commercial, busy road, waterfront, adjacent to park, and so on. See Figure 12.5.

Sample entry: N; res

FIGURE 12.5
Location Entries

Abbreviated Entry	Overall Location Rating
N	Neutral
B	Beneficial
A	Adverse

Abbreviated Entry	Location Factor
Res	Residential
Ind	Industrial
Comm	Commercial
BsyRd	Busy Road
WtrFr	Water Front
GlfCse	Golf Course
AdjPrk	Adjacent to Park
AdjPwr	Adjacent to Power Lines
Lndfl	Landfill
PubTrn	Public Transportation

IN PRACTICE

Even within the same neighborhood, locations can offer significant variances, such as proximity to different land uses or frontage on a heavily traveled street. A property across the street from a golf course would tend to be more valuable than one across the street from a commercial site.

Leasehold/fee simple

All comparable property sales chosen should reflect the same type of property interest as that of the subject property. In most cases the property interest appraised will be a fee simple interest—which would be entered on the URAR form. If the property interest appraised is a leasehold interest, special considerations come into play. Then, you must consider and analyze the effect on value, if any, of the terms and conditions of the lease(s). Appraising lease interests is covered in a later unit.

Sample entry: fee simple

Site

The size of the subject site and each comparable sale must be entered. If a site has an area of less than one acre, the size must be given in square feet. If a site has an area of one acre or more, the size must be given in acres to two decimal places.

Sample entry: 12,000 sq. ft., or 1.40 acres

View

You must provide at least one specific view for the subject property; then rate the view as N (neutral), B (beneficial) or A (adverse). Words such as typical, average and good are now unacceptable. See Figure 12.6.

Sample entry: Mtn;B

Adjustments for houses with water or mountain views or the like may be very substantial.

FIGURE 12.6
View Entries

Abbreviated Entry	Overall View Rating
N	Neutral
B	Beneficial
A	Adverse

Abbreviated Entry	View Factor
Wtr	Water View
Pstrl	Pastoral View
Woods	Woods View
Prk	Park View
Glfvw	Golf Course Views
CtySky	City View Skyline View
Mtn	Mountain View
Res	Residential View
CtyStr	City Street View
Ind	Industrial View
PwrLn	Power Lines
LtdSght	Limited Sight

Design (style)

The style of a house probably should follow the rule of conformity; that is, the design should be compatible with that of others in the neighborhood.

Appraisers can no longer simply list single-story or 2-story to describe the design of a house. Instead, they must be more specific and identify the architectural design or style of the subject property and comparable properties as contemporary, ranch, colonial, Victorian, cottage, cape cod and the like.

Sample entry: colonial

IN PRACTICE

In some subdivisions of custom homes, owners take pride in the uniqueness of their properties, and conformity is not a desirable neighborhood characteristic. Such properties may be located on well-landscaped lots that are large enough to obscure the view of adjoining structures and make the lack of conformity less jarring. As a rule, however, houses that are similar in design, construction, and amenities provide a more pleasing look to the neighborhood.

Quality of construction

If not the same as or equivalent to the subject property, quality of construction will be a major adjustment. Remember that this entry covers all aspects of construction, from foundation to finish work. The quality of workmanship and quality and durability of materials used in the construction of the structure must be considered. Available comparables within a particular builder's subdivision typically will be of the same construction quality. Instead of appraisers using words like low, average, good, or excellent to describe quality of construction, they must now use a rating system from Q1 to Q6. See Figure 12.7. The appraiser must select the rating that best describes the overall quality of the property.

Sample entry: Q3

FIGURE 12.7
Quality of Construction Entries

Q1—These dwellings are unique structures that are individually designed by an architect for a specific user, and typically feature an exceptionally high level of workmanship and exceptionally high-grade materials throughout both exterior and interior.

Q2—Dwellings that are often custom-designed for construction on the property owner's site, but which can also be found in high-quality tract developments featuring residences constructed from individual plans or highly modified or upgraded plans. The design features detailed, high-quality exterior ornamentation and interior refinements. Workmanship, materials, and finishes throughout are generally of high or very high quality.

Q3—Dwellings of higher quality built from individual or readily available designer plans in above-standard residential tract developments or on the property owner's site. The design includes significant exterior ornamentation and well-finished interiors. Workmanship exceeds acceptable standards and any materials and finishes throughout the dwelling have been upgraded from "stock" standards.

Q4—Dwellings that meet or exceed the requirements of applicable building codes, utilizing standard or modified standard building plans. Design includes adequate fenestration and some exterior ornamentation and interior refinements. Materials, workmanship, finish, and equipment are of stock or builder grade and may feature some upgrades.

Q5—Dwellings that feature economy of construction and basic functionality as main consideration, with a plain design that uses readily available or basic floor plans featuring minimal fenestration and basic finishes with minimal exterior ornamentation and limited interior detail. Dwellings meet minimum building codes and are constructed with inexpensive, stock materials with limited refinements and upgrades.

Q6—Dwellings of basic quality and lower cost, which may not be suitable for year-round occupancy. Such dwellings are often built with simple plans or even without plans, often built or expanded by persons who are professionally unskilled or possessing only minimal construction skills, and often utilizing the lowest-quality building materials. Electrical, plumbing, and other mechanical systems and equipment may be minimal or nonexistent. Older dwellings may feature one or more substandard or nonconforming additions to the original structure.

IN PRACTICE

Building materials can be a good indicator of the quality of construction and can also indicate market preferences. A subdivision in which every home has a brick exterior—or at least a brick facade on the front of the home—will tend to have more expensive finishing materials than a subdivision in which the exterior of every home is covered in vinyl siding. Regional preferences may dictate the range of materials. In New Mexico, an adobe structure usually is more desirable than one finished with wood siding; in Ohio, a brick exterior usually is more desirable than one finished with stucco.

Actual age

Because most subdivisions are completed within a relatively short period, there may be no significant differences among comparables with respect to age. A brand-new home would likely be valued by the builder according to actual costs, overhead, and profit. With older homes in good general condition, an age difference of five years in either direction usually is not significant. Overall upkeep is of greater importance, although the age of the house may alert the appraiser to look for outmoded design or fixtures or any needed repairs.

Enter the actual age of the subject property and each comparable property. For new construction that is less than one year old, enter 0 (zero). If the actual age is not known, enter the estimated age. Do not enter any additional information, such as years.

Sample entry: 23

Condition

Instead of using words like average, fair or good to describe the house's condition, appraisers must now use a specific rating system from C1 to C6, with C1 being best and C6 being worst. Figure 8.5. Select the rating that best describes the overall quality of the property.

Sample entry: C3

An adjustment is indicated if the comparable is in better or worse condition than the subject property.

Above-grade room count/gross living area

Enter the number of finished above-grade rooms (excluding baths and basement), the number of bedrooms and baths, and the total above-grade square-foot living area for the subject and comparable properties. A major adjustment is needed if the subject property has fewer than three bedrooms and the comparables all have at least three, or vice versa. The total number of full baths (sink, toilet, and tub/shower) and half-baths (sink and toilet) are tallied in this category.

In the new UAD system, instead of entering 2.5 baths on the URAR form as before—meaning 2-1/2 baths—it must now be shown as 2.1. The figure to the left of the decimal point indicates the number of full bathrooms and the figure to the right of the decimal indicates the number of half baths. For example, 2.2 indicates two full baths and two half baths above grade.

Modern plumbing is assumed, with an adjustment made for out-of-date fixtures.

The appraiser should confirm that the comparables were measured using a method similar to that used to measure the subject property. Total gross living area of a home generally includes only above-grade, finished living areas and not basement areas, whether completely or partially below grade, even if they are finished with the same materials and quality of construction used in the rest of the house. This is the rule applied to homes appraised for Fannie Mae. An exception to the general rule is allowed if the below-grade living space is typical of homes in the area and is considered to add to property value; then, comparables with the same type(s) of space should be found. This is often the case in California, where hillside homes with one or more levels at least partially below grade are common.

Large variances between the subject property and a comparable property should be carefully analyzed to determine whether the comp should be kept or thrown out.

Sample entries: 7 3 2.2
2,300

Basement and finished rooms below grade

The appraiser should note any below-grade improvements, such as a finished basement. In some areas, the walk-out, or English, basement is considered a desirable feature.

On Line 1 indicate the following:

- Total square footage of the property improvements below grade. If there is no basement, enter 0 (zero)
- Finished square footage of the property improvements below grade, if applicable.
- The type of access to the basement—walk-out (wo), Walk-up (wu), or interior only (in)

On Line 2, indicate whether there are any finished rooms below grade (including the basement). If there are, identify the room types; for example: recreation room (rr), bedroom (br), bathroom (ba), and other (o).

Sample entries: Line 1: 1,000 sq. ft.; 700 sq. ft. fin
Line 2: 1rr1.0ba

Functional utility

Functional utility refers to a dwelling's overall compatibility with its intended use and environment, as defined by market standards. This category includes design features (such as layout and room size) that are in line with current trends in the market area. Marketability is the ultimate test of functional utility. When judging the functional utility of homes, the appraiser must interpret the reaction of typical buyers in the subject market area.

Rate the subject and comparables as good, average, fair or poor.

Sample entry: average

Heating/cooling

Identify the types of heating and cooling system present in the subject house and comparable houses. Common types are forced warm air (FWA), central air-conditioning (CAC) and heat pump (HP).

Sample entry: WFA/CAC

Energy-efficient items

Energy-efficient windows, high R-factor insulation, solar heating units, and any other energy conservation features contained in the subject and comparable properties should be noted. As with all price adjustments, any made for energy-conservation features, should reflect how much more the market will pay for the property because of the existence of the feature.

Enter any energy efficient items for the subject property and each comparable property. If there are no energy efficient items, enter "none."

Sample entry: solar heat

Garage/carport

Indicate whether the subject and comparables have garages or carports and the number of cars they hold. If a property does not have a garage/carport, enter none. Adjustments should be based on the typical value buyers place on garages or carports, not on cost data.

Sample entry: 2-car garage

Porch, patio, deck

Porches, patios, decks, fireplaces, and any other special feature of the basic structure should be noted here. Indicate also the presence of a fence, Florida room, swimming pool, spa, greenhouse, or any other structure not considered part of the primary house. Blank lines provide additional space for entries. An adjustment factor is indicated if the subject property or one of the comparables has any other interior property improvements that adds to or subtracts from value.

Sample entry: deck/spa

IN PRACTICE

Such amenities as a fireplace, whirlpool bathtub, or luxurious finishing material (marble, granite, wood parquet, etc.) ordinarily add to a home's value. Adjustments for these features should reflect local market expectations and buyer requirements.

■ FORM OPINION OF VALUE BY EACH OF THE THREE APPROACHES

The appraiser may begin this part of the appraisal process by determining the highest and best use of the subject property. To review what was covered in Unit 9, the **highest and best use** of real estate, whether vacant or with improvements, is its most profitable legally permitted, physically possible, and financially feasible use. The highest and best use of real estate that has been improved by the erection of a structure or structures on it may take into account the existing improvements, or the land may be treated as if vacant.

Because of the wide use of **zoning** throughout the United States, consideration of highest and best use is generally limited to the property's present legally permitted uses. In the case of areas zoned for single-family residences, this use is usually accepted as the highest and best use. A change of zoning is occasionally possible, particularly when a subsequent nearby land use creates adverse conditions for enjoyment of residential property. As an example, property along a roadway that has become very heavily traveled by commercial vehicles as a result of nearby development may be rezoned for commercial use. Rezoning can never be assumed, however, and it usually entails a lengthy application and approval process. For the appraiser's purpose, only existing permitted land uses are considered unless otherwise specified by the client.

IN PRACTICE

The client requests a conditional value based on land-use changes that have a reasonable probability of occurring. The appraiser must disclose the special circumstances and assumptions of the report to ensure that the report will not be misleading.

For purposes of this unit, the present use of all properties used in the case study and exercises will be considered their highest and best use.

Because house and lot are valued together in the sales comparison approach, we will not make a separate estimate of land (site) value for the sample appraisal we are carrying out in this unit. (Site valuation techniques were discussed in Unit 9.)

FORM OPINION OF VALUE BY SALES COMPARISON APPROACH

Because no two parcels of real estate are exactly alike, each comparable property must be analyzed and adjusted for differences between it and the subject property.

The most difficult step in using the sales comparison approach is determining the amount of each adjustment. The accuracy of an appraisal using this approach depends on the appraiser's use of reliable adjustment values. Because adjustments must reflect the activities of buyers and sellers in the market, it is the appraiser's job to research, analyze, and draw supportable conclusions from market-derived data. Unfortunately, the value of the same feature may vary for different types, sizes, and overall values of property. Until an appraiser has the background of many appraisals in a given area, more comparable properties will have to be studied than just the three to six presented in the typical appraisal report. If the appraiser completes an adjustment chart for as many as 10 to 20 or more properties, a market pattern may be more evident, and with better documentation, the value of individual differences may be estimated fairly accurately. When there have been few recent sales, the appraiser's own files can be the best source of adjustment values.

IN PRACTICE

Ordinarily, an appraisal of real estate does not include any personal property on the premises. If the sales price of a comparable property includes such items, the value of the items should be noted as an adjustment factor.

Adjustment Process

At this point, all the data the appraiser will need to arrive at a fair market value opinion of the subject property has been gathered. The next step is to compare properties and make adjustments where needed. Although adjustments may be made for some differences between the subject property and the comparables, most of the following factors should be similar:

- Style of house
- Age
- Number of rooms
- Number of bedrooms
- Number of bathrooms
- Size of lot
- Size of dwelling
- Terms of sale
- Type of construction
- General condition

Naturally, wherever differences exist, adjustments must be made to bring the comparable properties into conformity with the subject property. The four major categories in which adjustments for differences must be made are the following:

- *Date of sale*. An adjustment must be made if market conditions change between the date of the sale of the comparable property and the date of the appraisal. Changes in market conditions may be caused by such things as fluctuations in supply and demand, inflation, and economic recession.
- *Location*. An adjustment may be necessary to compensate for locational differences between comparables and the subject property. For example, similar properties might differ in price from neighborhood to neighborhood or even in more desirable locations within the same neighborhood.
- *Physical features*. Physical features that may require adjustments include the age of the structure, the number of rooms, the layout of the room (functional utility), the square feet of living space, the exterior and interior condition, and the presence or absence of special features such as a garage, central air-conditioning, fireplace, swimming pool, energy-efficient items, and the like. Not every feature will add to the property's value. The swimming pool that is a desirable amenity in Florida may actually decrease the value of a home in Wisconsin.
- *Terms and conditions of sale*. This consideration becomes important if a sale is not financed by a standard mortgage.

Comparable sales must be adjusted to the subject property. That is, the subject property is the standard against which the comparable sales are evaluated and adjusted. Thus, if a feature in the comparable property is superior to that in the subject property, a minus (–) adjustment is required to make that feature equal to that in the subject property. Conversely, if a feature in the comparable property is inferior to that in the subject property, a plus (+) adjustment is required to make the feature equal to that in the subject property.

Types of Adjustments

The adjustments that will be made to the sales prices of the selected comparable properties may be expressed in several ways. Most often, a **dollar adjustment** is used, to indicate

- the value of a desirable feature present in the subject property but not in the comparable, resulting in a plus (+) adjustment to the sales price of the comparable; and
- the value of a desirable feature present in the comparable but not in the subject property, resulting in a minus (–) adjustment to the sales price of the comparable.

The amount of the dollar adjustment is determined by using one of the methods discussed in the next section of this unit.

Another way to adjust the sales price of a comparable is to use a **percentage adjustment**, indicating the overall effect on market value of the factor valued. This is the method often used to account for changes in market conditions as well as other changes that affect the property as a whole, such as the time from the date of sale or the property's location.

IN PRACTICE

Market evidence shows that comparable properties located in the subject property's immediate vicinity typically have a market value that is 10% higher than that of properties in the vicinity of one of the comparable properties. There are many factors that could contribute to such a difference, even among properties that are in the same general neighborhood. Homes within walking distance of a school may be considered more desirable; homes near a highway with the accompanying noise and pollution may be considered less desirable. In either case, an appropriate adjustment to the sales price of the comparable property is necessary.

Another common use of a percentage adjustment is to take into account the change in market value over time. If the sale of a comparable property took place one year before the date of appraisal, and average property appreciation in the area for the same type of property has been 6% over the same period, the selling price of the comparable can be adjusted by increasing it by 6%.

The dollar amount of the adjustment is the appraiser's estimate of the effect on value of the identified factor. The adjustment thus is the appraiser's measurement of typical buyer reaction to the noted property difference.

Compute Adjustment Values

The most difficult step when using the sales comparison approach is determining the dollar amount of each adjustment. The accuracy of an appraisal applying this approach depends on the appraiser's use of reliable adjustment values. The adjustment value of a property feature is not simply the cost to construct or add that feature but what a buyer is willing to pay for it, typically a lesser amount. An opinion of market value must always consider the demands of the marketplace.

Ideally, if properties could be found that were exactly alike except for one variable, the adjustment value of that variable would be the difference in selling prices of the two properties.

The sales price adjustment chart (or matrix) is a source of information for adjustment values that can be used in the sales comparison approach. The appraiser can develop such a chart and use it to substantiate dollar amounts for adjusted values.

IN PRACTICE

House A is very similar to house B, except that it has a two-car attached garage, and B does not. A sold for $194,000; B sold for $181,500. Because the garage is the only significant difference between the two properties, its value is the difference between the selling price of $194,000 and the selling price of $181,500. So the value of the garage is $194,000 – $181,500, or $12,500.

This type of analysis is called **matched pairs analysis (MPA)**, **paired sales analysis**, or **paired data set analysis**. In matched pairs analysis, the appraiser compares the features and sales prices of comparable properties. A sufficient number of sales must be found to allow the appraiser to isolate the effect on value of the pertinent factor. Often this is not possible, and the appraiser's judgment becomes especially critical in determining the relative values to assign to multiple property variables.

The number of sales needed for an accurate opinion of market value cannot be easily specified, but the fewer the sales, the more carefully they must be investigated. If the appraiser analyzes 10 to 20 or more properties, a market pattern may be more evident and, with better documentation, the value of individual differences may be estimated fairly accurately.

The appraiser may also study the changes in sales price of the same property that has sold more than once within a defined period. Those prices may indicate the change in overall market conditions in that period. Of course, the appraiser must check the other factors involved in the sales to ensure that they do not involve related parties or that the presence of some other factor has not made a sale less than an arm's-length transaction. For instance, a quick resale may be necessitated by an unexpected job transfer and could have the effect of lowering the sales price. A sudden illness of the buyer and subsequent transfer of the property could also indicate a sale that does not accurately reflect market conditions. The property also could have been a "fixer-upper" with a considerably higher resale price, indicative of the extent of its rehabilitation rather than the state of the market.

There may be property differences that require no adjustment because they have no effect on the typical buyer's decision to purchase.

IN PRACTICE

House A has intricately hand-painted wainscoting in the family room, and house B has wallpaper in the family room. Neither property difference will require an adjustment because the houses are perceived by buyers in the marketplace as identical to ones with plain painted walls.

FIGURE 12.8
Sales Price Adjustment Chart: Comparables

	A	B	C	D	E	F	G	H	I	J
Sales price	$242,000	$233,000	$243,000	$247,000	$241,000	$220,000	$286,000	$221,000	$252,000	$242,000
Financing	Conv	Conv	Conv	Conv	Conv	Conv	Conv	Conv	Conv	Conv
Date of sale	6 wks.	2 mos.	3 wks.	5 wks.	6 wks.	5 wks.	3 wks.	1 yr.	5 wks.	11 wks.
Location	N;res	N;res	N;res	N;res	N;res	highway	Commercial	N;res	N;res	N;res
Leasehold/ fee simple	Fee simple	Fee simple	Fee simple	Fee simple	Fee simple	Fee simple	Fee simple	Fee simple	Fee simple	Fee simple
View	B;water	B;water	B;water	B;water	B;water	B;water	B;water	B;water	B;water	B;water
Site	10,000sf	10,000sf	10,000sf	10,000sf	10,000sf	10,000sf	10,000sf	10,000sf	10,000sf	10,000sf
Design (style)	Colonial	Colonial	Colonial	Colonial	Colonial	Colonial	Colonial	Colonial	Colonial	Colonial
Quality of construction	Q4;brick	Q5; aluminum siding	Q4;brick	Q4;brick	Q4;brick	Q4;brick	Q4;brick	Q4;brick	Q4;brick	Q4;brick
Age	8	7	8	6	6	7	6	7	6	7
Condition	C4	C4	C4	C4	C4	C4	C4	C4	C4	C4
No. of rms./ bedrms./ baths	7/3/2	7/3/2	7/3/2	7/3/2½	7/3/2	7/3/2	7/3/2	7/3/2	8/4/2	7/3/2
Sq. ft. of living space	1,275	1,300	1,290	1,300	1,300	1,325	1,300	1,350	1,400	1,300
Other space (basement)	1,275sf	1,300sf	1,290sf	1,300sf	1,300sf	1,325sf	1,300sf	1,350sf	1,400sf	1,300sf
Functional utility	Average	Average	Average	Average	Average	Average	Average	Average	Average	Average
Heating/ cooling	FWA/ CAC	FWA/ CAC	FWA/ CAC	FWA/ CAC	FWA/ CAC	FWA/ CAC	FWA/ CAC	FWA/ CAC	FWA/ CAC	FWA/ CAC
Energy-efficient items	None	None	None	None	None	None	None	None	None	None
Garage/ carport	2-car att.	2-car att.	2-car att.	2-car att.	2-car att.	2-car att.	2-car att.	2-car att.	2-car att.	2-car att.
Other ext. improvements	Patio	Patio	Patio	Patio	Patio	Patio	Patio	Patio	Patio	Patio
Other int. improvements; fireplace	One	One	One	One	One	One	One	One	One	One
Typical house value	$242,000	$242,000	$242,000	$242,000	$242,000	$242,000	$242,000	$242,000	$242,000	$242,000
Variable feature		Aluminum siding		Extra half-bath		Poor location	Commercial area	Year-old sale	4th bedroom	
Adjustment value of variable										

Figure 12.8 is a sales price adjustment chart that has been completed for 10 properties, all comparable to each other. Each relevant adjustment variable has been highlighted by a screen. Although an appraiser ordinarily will need two or more instances of each variable as a check on the accuracy of an adjustment value, for the sake of brevity, only one comparable with each variable is presented here.

Because properties A, C, E, and J exhibit no variables, they will be used to define the standard against which the worth of each variable will be measured. A sold for \$242,000, C for \$243,000, E for \$241,000, and J for \$242,000. Because C shows only a slight price increase and E only a slight price decrease, \$242,000 will be used as the base house value for a typical property in the neighborhood, that is, one having the most typical property features. Each variable can now be noted and valued.

Time adjustment

The time factor refers to the economic changes from the date of the sale to the date of the appraisal. To isolate the time factor, those sales that differ from each other in the date of sale only are selected. If several properties are alike except for the length of time since the date of sale, then it is logical to assume that the time factor is reflected in the difference in selling prices.

Property H is identical in features to properties A, C, E, and J, except for the length of time since the date of sale. Market conditions over the past year indicate a period of general inflation. Property H was sold one year ago; properties A, C, E, and J were all sold within the past 3 to 11 weeks. The adjustment value to be made in the case of a year-old sale is, therefore,

$$\$242{,}000 - \$221{,}000 = \$21{,}000$$

The \$21,000 adjustment value can be expressed as a percentage of the total cost of the property:

$$\frac{\$21{,}000}{\$221{,}000} = 0.09502 = 9.502\%, \text{ or simply } 9.5\%$$

In this case, the adjustment value of the variable is \$21,000. If a one-year time adjustment were required for another property, the dollar value of the adjustment would be the amount derived by applying the percentage of value to that property's sales price.

Location

Property F, on a less desirable site facing a busy highway, sold for \$22,000 less than the standard; therefore, this poor location indicates an adjustment of \$22,000.

Commercial area

In this example, the \$286,000 selling price of property G is considerably higher than that of properties in the residential area. On closer analysis, the appraiser discovered that G was adjacent to the site of a new shopping mall and had been purchased by the mall developers for use as a parking area. Because G represents an extraordinary situation, it should not be considered representative of the adjustment value warranted by location.

In the next exercise, you will find the remaining adjustment values used in the sample appraisal being carried out in this unit.

Exercise 12-1

Complete the adjustment valuations for construction, number of bedrooms, and number of bathrooms, as indicated by the data in the sales price adjustment chart in Figure 12.8. Record all of the adjustments computed thus far, and those you will compute yourself, in the appropriate boxes in the chart.

Time: One year ago
9.5% per year

Location: Highway

\$242,000 – \$220,000 = \$22,000

Construction:

No. of bedrooms:

No. of baths:

Check your completed chart adjustments against the ones in the answer key at the back of the book.

Sequence of Adjustments

Some of the adjustments made to the sales prices of comparables will reflect overall property value, such as an adjustment due to sales or financing concessions. Other adjustments will be due to a specific property feature, such as the presence or absence of air-conditioning. The appraiser also may use a combination of adjustment methods, including both percentage and dollar valuations.

To reflect all adjustments accurately, the appraiser should make adjustments in sequence, with those affecting the overall property value being made first, followed by those affecting only individual property features. For example, if any adjustment is required to account for sales or financing concessions, the adjustment is made to the sales price before any other adjustment is made to determine a normal sales price. If an adjustment is required to account for a change in market value over time since the date of sale of the comparable, that adjustment is made next, the result being a time-adjusted normal sales price (TANSP). Only after those adjustments have been made does the appraiser make a final adjustment on the basis of differences in individual property features.

The sequence of adjustments would make no difference if all the adjustment factors were based on a dollar value rather than a percentage value. The recommended sequence of adjustments is crucial, because an adjustment in either of the first two adjustment categories—financing and time—usually is based on a percentage of total sales price. Any percentage adjustment for financing should be based on total sales price before any other adjustment is made. Any percentage adjustment for time should be based on the total sales price after any adjustment required for financing has been made. (The only other percentage adjustment that could be made before the adjustment for time would be an adjustment for seller motivation, as in the case of a forced sale due to employee transfer or serious illness. Seller motivation also may be referred to as condition of sale.)

Although no hard and fast rule can be applied to all cases, total gross adjustments, no matter how they are calculated, should probably not exceed 25% of a comparable's sales price.

Exercise 12-2

In the sample appraisal, five properties, all within one-half mile south of the subject, have been selected as comparables. A description of each property and its sale is given in the following list. In each case, property information from the public records was supplied by the sales agent. All sales were arm's-length transactions. Complete the URAR Sales Comparison Approach sections of the URAR form in Figures 12.9 and 12.10 down to the Net Adj (total) line. Needed information on the subject property and comparable 1 has already been recorded. In the same way, you are to insert the necessary information for comparables 2 through 5. A map of the neighborhood is shown on page 215. Current market rate financing available for the purchase of homes in this price range is 5¼–5½%, with a minimum down payment of 20%. All the homes are ranch style, with no functional obsolescence. The quality of construction for each home—except for sale #3—exceeds acceptable standards.

1. 1901 Parkside Boulevard—fee simple interest in an eight-year-old, seven-room brick ranch with living room, kitchen, family room, three bedrooms, and two full baths. The improvements are well maintained and feature limited physical deterioration due to normal wear and tear. There are no common areas and no homeowners' association. The house, which has forced warm air heating and central air-conditioning, has a total of 1,800 square feet of living space. Landscaping is very attractive, with several large trees, shrubs, and flower beds, but the street is heavily traveled. There is a two-car attached garage. The lot is 50 feet by 200 feet. The buyer obtained a 5½% mortgage loan, making a down payment of 25% on the $226,000 sales price. The arm's-length sale took place six weeks before the date of appraisal of the subject property.
2. 2135 Hastings Avenue—fee simple interest in a seven-year-old, seven-room ranch, with 1,875 square feet of space and forced warm air heating and cooling. The house is well maintained and has little depreciation due to wear and tear; it is brick, with an attached two-car garage. There are three bedrooms, two full baths, living room, dining room, kitchen, and family room. The lot is 50 feet by 200 feet, with good landscaping and a residential view with shade trees in front and back yards. There are no common areas and no homeowners' association. The buyer obtained a 5½% mortgage; the exact amount of the down payment is not known, but it was probably at least 25 or 30%. The purchase price was $239,000; the sale took place one year before the date of appraisal of the subject property.

3. 2129 Osceola Way—fee simple interest in a seven-room, 1,825-square-foot aluminum-sided ranch on a 50-foot-by-200-foot corner lot, with attached two-car garage. The house has forced warm air heating and central air-conditioning. Landscaping is good, and the house has an attractive view of the residential area. The house is eight years old with a living room, dining room, kitchen, family room, three bedrooms, and two full baths. There are no common areas and no homeowners' association. The sales price was $238,000, and the purchase, two months before the date of this appraisal, was financed by the buyer's obtaining a 5¼% loan with a 25% cash down payment. The house is well maintained with little physical depreciation. Quality of construction is a cut below the other homes.

4. 2243 Parkside Boulevard—fee simple interest in an eight-room, 1,925-square-foot brick ranch on a 50-foot-by-200-foot lot, with attached two-car garage. Landscaping is good and well kept, and the six-year-old house is also well maintained. The view is of a quiet residential scene. There is a living room, dining room, kitchen, family room, four bedrooms, and two full baths. The house has forced warm air heating and central air-conditioning. There are no common areas and no homeowners' association. The purchase price of $256,500 was financed by the buyer's paying 20% down and obtaining a 5¼% mortgage. The sale took place five weeks before the date of the subject appraisal.

5. 2003 Franklin Street—fee simple interest in a seven-room, 1,825-square-foot brick ranch, on a 50-foot-by-200-foot lot, with good landscaping, pretty views, and attached two-car garage. The house is seven years old, in good condition, and has a living room, dining room, kitchen, family room, three bedrooms, two full baths, and one half-bath. The house has forced warm air heating and central air-conditioning. There are no common areas and no homeowners' association. The house is well maintained with little physical deterioration and an appealing residential view. The sale, which took place five weeks ago, was financed by the buyer's down payment of 25% on a 5½% mortgage loan. The purchase price was $251,000.

Each of the comparables is functionally adequate. Record all the data in this exercise on the Sales Comparison Approach sections of the URAR form in Figures 12.9 and 12.10.

At this point in many appraisals, properties considered comparables are found to be unacceptable for one or more reasons. In this group of comparables for the sample appraisal, do any of the properties seem unacceptable? If so, why?

____

Check your answers and your completed Sales Comparison Approach sections with those in the answer key at the back of the book.

FIGURE 12.9
Comparables 1 through 3 for Exercise 12-2

There are comparable properties currently offered for sale in the subject neighborhood ranging in price from $ to $.

There are comparable sales in the subject neighborhood within the past twelve months ranging in sale price from $ to $.

FEATURE	SUBJECT	COMPARABLE SALE # 1		COMPARABLE SALE # 2		COMPARABLE SALE # 3	
Address	2130 W. Franklin	1901 Parkside Blvd.					
Proximity to Subject		.50 miles SE					
Sale Price	$		$ 226,000		$		$
Sale Price/Gross Liv. Area	$ sq. ft.	$ 125.56 sq. ft.		$ sq. ft.		$ sq. ft.	
Data Source(s)		Public records					
Verification Source(s)		Sales agent					
VALUE ADJUSTMENTS	DESCRIPTION	DESCRIPTION	+(-) $ Adjustment	DESCRIPTION	+(-) $ Adjustment	DESCRIPTION	+(-) $ Adjustment
Sale or Financing Concessions		ArmLth Conv					
Date of Sale/Time		6 weeks ago					
Location	N; Res	A; Bsy Rd					
Leasehold/Fee Simple	fee simple	fee simple					
Site	10,000 SF	10,000 SF					
View	N; Res	N; Res					
Design (Style)	Ranch	Ranch					
Quality of Construction	Q4	Q4					
Actual Age	6	8					
Condition	C3	C3					
Above Grade	Total / Bdrms / Baths	Total / Bdrms / Baths		Total / Bdrms / Baths		Total / Bdrms / Baths	
Room Count	7 / 3 / 2.1	7 / 3 / 2.0					
Gross Living Area	1,825 sq. ft.	1,800 sq. ft.		sq. ft.		sq. ft.	
Basement & Finished Rooms Below Grade	0	0					
Functional Utility	Average	Average					
Heating/Cooling	FWA/CAC	FWA/CAC					
Energy Efficient Items	none	none					
Garage/Carport	2-car att.	2-car att.					
Porch/Patio/Deck	none	none					
Net Adjustment (Total)		☐ + ☐ -	$	☐ + ☐ -	$	☐ + ☐ -	$
Adjusted Sale Price of Comparables		Net Adj. % Gross Adj. %	$	Net Adj. % Gross Adj. %	$	Net Adj. % Gross Adj. %	$

I ☐ did ☐ did not research the sale or transfer history of the subject property and comparable sales. If not, explain

My research ☐ did ☐ did not reveal any prior sales or transfers of the subject property for the three years prior to the effective date of this appraisal.

Data source(s)

My research ☐ did ☐ did not reveal any prior sales or transfers of the comparable sales for the year prior to the date of sale of the comparable sale.

Data source(s)

Report the results of the research and analysis of the prior sale or transfer history of the subject property and comparable sales (report additional prior sales on page 3).

ITEM	SUBJECT	COMPARABLE SALE # 1	COMPARABLE SALE # 2	COMPARABLE SALE # 3
Date of Prior Sale/Transfer				
Price of Prior Sale/Transfer				
Data Source(s)				
Effective Date of Data Source(s)				

Analysis of prior sale or transfer history of the subject property and comparable sales

Summary of Sales Comparison Approach

Indicated Value by Sales Comparison Approach $

FIGURE 12.10
Comparables 4 and 5 for Exercise 12-2

There are comparable properties currently offered for sale in the subject neighborhood ranging in price from $ to $.
There are comparable sales in the subject neighborhood within the past twelve months ranging in sale price from $ to $.

FEATURE	SUBJECT	COMPARABLE SALE # 4		COMPARABLE SALE # 5		COMPARABLE SALE # 6	
Address	2130 W. Franklin						
Proximity to Subject							
Sale Price	$		$		$		$
Sale Price/Gross Liv. Area	$ sq. ft.	$ sq. ft.		$ sq. ft.		$ sq. ft.	
Data Source(s)							
Verification Source(s)							
VALUE ADJUSTMENTS	DESCRIPTION	DESCRIPTION	+(-) $ Adjustment	DESCRIPTION	+(-) $ Adjustment	DESCRIPTION	+(-) $ Adjustment
Sale or Financing Concessions							
Date of Sale/Time							
Location	N; Res						
Leasehold/Fee Simple	fee simple						
Site	10,000 SF						
View	N; Res						
Design (Style)	Ranch						
Quality of Construction	Q4						
Actual Age	6						
Condition	C3						
Above Grade Room Count	Total Bdrms Baths 7 3 2.1	Total Bdrms Baths		Total Bdrms Baths		Total Bdrms Baths	
Gross Living Area	1,825 sq. ft.	sq. ft.		sq. ft.		sq. ft.	
Basement & Finished Rooms Below Grade	0						
Functional Utility	Average						
Heating/Cooling	FWA/CAC						
Energy Efficient Items	none						
Garage/Carport	2-car att.						
Porch/Patio/Deck	none						
Net Adjustment (Total)		☐ + ☐ -	$	☐ + ☐ -	$	☐ + ☐ -	$
Adjusted Sale Price of Comparables		Net Adj. % Gross Adj. %	$	Net Adj. % Gross Adj. %	$	Net Adj. % Gross Adj. %	$

I ☐ did ☐ did not research the sale or transfer history of the subject property and comparable sales. If not, explain

My research ☐ did ☐ did not reveal any prior sales or transfers of the subject property for the three years prior to the effective date of this appraisal.
Data source(s)
My research ☐ did ☐ did not reveal any prior sales or transfers of the comparable sales for the year prior to the date of sale of the comparable sale.
Data source(s)
Report the results of the research and analysis of the prior sale or transfer history of the subject property and comparable sales (report additional prior sales on page 3).

ITEM	SUBJECT	COMPARABLE SALE # 1	COMPARABLE SALE # 2	COMPARABLE SALE # 3
Date of Prior Sale/Transfer				
Price of Prior Sale/Transfer				
Data Source(s)				
Effective Date of Data Source(s)				

Analysis of prior sale or transfer history of the subject property and comparable sales

Summary of Sales Comparison Approach

Indicated Value by Sales Comparison Approach $

Record Information

Using the adjustment values you computed in Exercise 12.1, you are ready to complete the Sales Comparison Approach section of the URAR form in Figure 12.11 and Figure 12.12 for the sample appraisal being carried out in Unit 8 and this unit.

First, the details of the subject property are recorded, as well as the selling prices of the comparables.

Then the adjustment values for the features that differ significantly from the subject property must be recorded. For example, comparable 1 is located on a major thoroughfare, while the subject property is on a quiet residential street. So the adjustment value computed earlier for location can be assigned to comparable 1 and entered in the location box for that comparable. Keep in mind that selling prices of comparable properties are adjusted to reflect the probable market value of the subject property. Because the subject property's location is generally considered a more desirable one than that of comparable 1, the adjustment value of $22,000 computed earlier must be added to the sales price of the comparable to find what the subject property would be worth. So, "+$22,000" is recorded.

An adjustment will be a plus (+) if that feature is found in the subject but not the comparable or otherwise represents a higher value for the subject property. An adjustment will be a minus (–) if that feature is present in the comparable but not the subject or otherwise represents a lower value for the subject property.

Exercise 12-3

Record the remaining adjustments on the Sales Comparison Approach sections of the URAR form in Figures 12.11 and 12.12. You will be recording the following adjustments, using the adjustment values you computed in the last exercise:

Comparable 1—No. of baths

Comparable 2—No. of baths
Date of Sale

Comparable 3—Construction
No. of baths

Comparable 4—No. of bedrooms
No. of baths

Check your answers against those in the answer key at the back of the book.

FIGURE 12.11

Comparables 1 through 3 for Exercise 12-3

There are comparable properties currently offered for sale in the subject neighborhood ranging in price from $ to $.

There are comparable sales in the subject neighborhood within the past twelve months ranging in sale price from $ to $.

FEATURE	SUBJECT		COMPARABLE SALE # 1		COMPARABLE SALE # 2		COMPARABLE SALE # 3	
Address	2130 W. Franklin		1901 Parkside Blvd.		2135 Hastings Ave.		2129 Osceola Way	
Proximity to Subject			.50 miles SE		.50 miles SE		.50 miles SE	
Sale Price	$			$ 226,000		$ 239,000		$ 238,000
Sale Price/Gross Liv. Area	$ sq. ft.		$ 125.56 sq. ft.		$ 127.47 sq. ft.		$ 130.41 sq. ft.	
Data Source(s)			Public records		Public records		Public records	
Verification Source(s)			Sales agent		Sales agent		Sales agent	
VALUE ADJUSTMENTS	DESCRIPTION		DESCRIPTION	+(-) $ Adjustment	DESCRIPTION	+(-) $ Adjustment	DESCRIPTION	+(-) $ Adjustment
Sale or Financing Concessions			ArmLth Conv		ArmLth Conv		ArmLth Conv	
Date of Sale/Time			6 weeks ago		1 year ago		2 months ago	
Location	N; Res		A; Bsy Rd		N; Res		N; Res	
Leasehold/Fee Simple	fee simple		fee simple		fee simple		fee simple	
Site	10,000 SF		10,000 SF		10,000 SF		10,000 SF	
View	N; Res		N; Res		N; Res		N; Res	
Design (Style)	Ranch		Ranch		Ranch		Ranch	
Quality of Construction	Q4		Q4		Q4		Q5	
Actual Age	6		8		7		8	
Condition	C3		C3		C3		C3	
Above Grade	Total / Bdrms / Baths		Total / Bdrms / Baths		Total / Bdrms / Baths		Total / Bdrms / Baths	
Room Count	7 / 3 / 2.1		7 / 3 / 2.0		7 / 3 / 2.0		7 / 3 / 2.0	
Gross Living Area	1,825 sq. ft.		1,800 sq. ft.		1,875 sq. ft.		1,825 sq. ft.	
Basement & Finished Rooms Below Grade	0		0		0		0	
Functional Utility	Average		Average		Average		Average	
Heating/Cooling	FWA/CAC		FWA/CAC		FWA/CAC		FWA/CAC	
Energy Efficient Items	none		none		none		none	
Garage/Carport	2-car att.		2-car att.		2-car att.		2-car att.	
Porch/Patio/Deck	none		none		none		none	
Net Adjustment (Total)			☐ + ☐ -	$	☐ + ☐ -	$	☐ + ☐ -	$
Adjusted Sale Price of Comparables			Net Adj. % Gross Adj. %	$	Net Adj. % Gross Adj. %	$	Net Adj. % Gross Adj. %	$

I ☐ did ☐ did not research the sale or transfer history of the subject property and comparable sales. If not, explain

My research ☐ did ☐ did not reveal any prior sales or transfers of the subject property for the three years prior to the effective date of this appraisal.

Data source(s)

My research ☐ did ☐ did not reveal any prior sales or transfers of the comparable sales for the year prior to the date of sale of the comparable sale.

Data source(s)

Report the results of the research and analysis of the prior sale or transfer history of the subject property and comparable sales (report additional prior sales on page 3).

ITEM	SUBJECT	COMPARABLE SALE # 1	COMPARABLE SALE # 2	COMPARABLE SALE # 3
Date of Prior Sale/Transfer				
Price of Prior Sale/Transfer				
Data Source(s)				
Effective Date of Data Source(s)				

Analysis of prior sale or transfer history of the subject property and comparable sales

Summary of Sales Comparison Approach

Indicated Value by Sales Comparison Approach $

FIGURE 12.12

Comparables 4 and 5 for Exercise 12-3

There are comparable properties currently offered for sale in the subject neighborhood ranging in price from $ to $.

There are comparable sales in the subject neighborhood within the past twelve months ranging in sale price from $ to $.

FEATURE	SUBJECT	COMPARABLE SALE # 4		COMPARABLE SALE # 5		COMPARABLE SALE # 6	
Address	2130 W. Franklin	2243 Parkside Blvd.		2003 Franklin St.			
Proximity to Subject		.50 miles SE		.50 miles SE			
Sale Price	$		$ 256,500		$ 251,000		$
Sale Price/Gross Liv. Area	$ sq. ft.	$ 133.25 sq. ft.		$ 137.53 sq. ft.		$ sq. ft.	
Data Source(s)		Public records		Public records			
Verification Source(s)		Sales agent		Sales agent			
VALUE ADJUSTMENTS	DESCRIPTION	DESCRIPTION	+(-) $ Adjustment	DESCRIPTION	+(-) $ Adjustment	DESCRIPTION	+(-) $ Adjustment
Sale or Financing Concessions		ArmLth Conv		ArmLth Conv			
Date of Sale/Time		5 weeks ago		5 weeks ago			
Location	N; Res	N; Res		N; Res			
Leasehold/Fee Simple	fee simple	fee simple		fee simple			
Site	10,000 SF	10,000 SF		10,000 SF			
View	N; Res	N; Res		N; Res			
Design (Style)	Ranch	Ranch		Ranch			
Quality of Construction	Q4	Q4		Q4			
Actual Age	6	6		7			
Condition	C3	C3		C3			
Above Grade	Total / Bdrms / Baths	Total / Bdrms / Baths		Total / Bdrms / Baths		Total / Bdrms / Baths	
Room Count	7 / 3 / 2.1	8 / 4 / 2.0		7 / 3 / 2.1			
Gross Living Area	1,825 sq. ft.	1,925 sq. ft.		1,825 sq. ft.		sq. ft.	
Basement & Finished Rooms Below Grade	0	0		0			
Functional Utility	Average	Average		Average			
Heating/Cooling	FWA/CAC	FWA/CAC		FWA/CAC			
Energy Efficient Items	none	none		none			
Garage/Carport	2-car att.	2-car att.		2-car att.			
Porch/Patio/Deck	none	none		none			
Net Adjustment (Total)		☐ + ☐ -	$	☐ + ☐ -	$	☐ + ☐ -	$
Adjusted Sale Price of Comparables		Net Adj. % Gross Adj. %	$	Net Adj. % Gross Adj. %	$	Net Adj. % Gross Adj. %	$

I ☐ did ☐ did not research the sale or transfer history of the subject property and comparable sales. If not, explain

My research ☐ did ☐ did not reveal any prior sales or transfers of the subject property for the three years prior to the effective date of this appraisal.

Data source(s)

My research ☐ did ☐ did not reveal any prior sales or transfers of the comparable sales for the year prior to the date of sale of the comparable sale.

Data source(s)

Report the results of the research and analysis of the prior sale or transfer history of the subject property and comparable sales (report additional prior sales on page 3).

ITEM	SUBJECT	COMPARABLE SALE # 1	COMPARABLE SALE # 2	COMPARABLE SALE # 3
Date of Prior Sale/Transfer				
Price of Prior Sale/Transfer				
Data Source(s)				
Effective Date of Data Source(s)				

Analysis of prior sale or transfer history of the subject property and comparable sales

Summary of Sales Comparison Approach

Indicated Value by Sales Comparison Approach $

Net Adjustments

Total the dollar amounts of the positive (+) and negative (–) adjustments for each comparable to find the net adjustment and enter that amount, checking the + or – box as appropriate. The Sales Comparison Approach section in Figure 12.13 shows the net adjustment for comparable 1. The location adjustment factor of +$22,000 is added to the adjustment factor of +$5,000 for an extra half bath, for a total adjustment of +$27,000. Therefore, the + box is checked.

The proper selection of comparable properties minimizes both the need for and the size of adjustments. Very substantial adjustments suggest that the properties are not comparable.

Adjusted Sales Price of Comparables

The net adjustment is added to or subtracted from the sale price of the comparable property to obtain an adjusted sale price. This is the appraiser's opinion of what the comparable property would have sold for had it possessed all the significant characteristics of the subject property. To find the adjusted value of comparable 1, its sales price and net adjustments are totaled. In this case, $226,000 plus $27,000 results in an adjusted sale price of $253,000.

Fannie Mae has established guidelines for the net and gross percentage adjustments that review appraisers or loan underwriters may rely on as a general indicator of whether a property should be used as a comparable sale. Generally, the total dollar amount of the net adjustment should not exceed 15% of the comparable's sale price. Further, the dollar amount of the gross adjustment should not exceed 25% of the comparable's sales price. The amount of the gross adjustment is determined by adding all individual adjustments without regard to the plus or minus signs.

If adjustments do not fall within Fannie Mae's net and gross percentage adjustment guidelines but the appraiser believes the comparable sales used to be the best available, as well as the best indicators of value for the subject property, an appropriate explanation must be provided.

A large total adjustment could indicate that the property is not a reliable comparable for the subject property.

Net adjustment %

Divide total net dollar adjustment by comparable property's sale price.

Gross adjustment %

Divide total dollar adjustment by comparable property's sale price.

Exercise 12-4

Complete the net adjustment and adjusted sales price computations for comparables 2, 3, 4, and 5 and record them on the Sales Comparison Approach sections in Figures 12.13 and 12.14.

Check your answers against those in the answer key at the back of the book.

FIGURE 12.13
Comparables 1 through 3 for Exercise 12-4

There are comparable properties currently offered for sale in the subject neighborhood ranging in price from $ to $.

There are comparable sales in the subject neighborhood within the past twelve months ranging in sale price from $ to $.

FEATURE	SUBJECT	COMPARABLE SALE # 1		COMPARABLE SALE # 2		COMPARABLE SALE # 3	
Address	2130 W. Franklin	1901 Parkside Blvd.		2135 Hastings Ave.		2129 Osceola Way	
Proximity to Subject		.50 miles SE		.50 miles SE		.50 miles SE	
Sale Price	$		$ 226,000		$ 239,000		$ 238,000
Sale Price/Gross Liv. Area	$ sq. ft.	$ 125.56 sq. ft.		$ 127.47 sq. ft.		$ 130.41 sq. ft.	
Data Source(s)		Public records		Public records		Public records	
Verification Source(s)		Sales agent		Sales agent		Sales agent	
VALUE ADJUSTMENTS	DESCRIPTION	DESCRIPTION	+(-) $ Adjustment	DESCRIPTION	+(-) $ Adjustment	DESCRIPTION	+(-) $ Adjustment
Sale or Financing Concessions		ArmLth Conv		ArmLth Conv		ArmLth Conv	
Date of Sale/Time		6 weeks ago		1 year ago	+22,700	2 months ago	
Location	N; Res	A; Bsy Rd	+22,000	N; Res	(rounded)	N; Res	
Leasehold/Fee Simple	fee simple	fee simple		fee simple		fee simple	
Site	10,000 SF	10,000 SF		10,000 SF		10,000 SF	
View	N; Res	N; Res		N; Res		N; Res	
Design (Style)	Ranch	Ranch		Ranch		Ranch	
Quality of Construction	Q4	Q4		Q4		Q5	+9,000
Actual Age	6	8		7		8	
Condition	C3	C3		C3		C3	
Above Grade	Total Bdrms Baths	Total Bdrms Baths		Total Bdrms Baths		Total Bdrms Baths	
Room Count	7 3 2.1	7 3 2.0	+5,000	7 3 2.0	+5,000	7 3 2.0	+5,000
Gross Living Area	1,825 sq. ft.	1,800 sq. ft.		1,875 sq. ft.		1,825 sq. ft.	
Basement & Finished Rooms Below Grade	0	0		0		0	
Functional Utility	Average	Average		Average		Average	
Heating/Cooling	FWA/CAC	FWA/CAC		FWA/CAC		FWA/CAC	
Energy Efficient Items	none	none		none		none	
Garage/Carport	2-car att.	2-car att.		2-car att.		2-car att.	
Porch/Patio/Deck	none	none		none		none	
Net Adjustment (Total)		☒ + ☐ -	$ 27,000	☐ + ☐ -	$	☐ + ☐ -	$
Adjusted Sale Price of Comparables		Net Adj. % Gross Adj. %	$ 253,000	Net Adj. % Gross Adj. %	$	Net Adj. % Gross Adj. %	$

I ☐ did ☐ did not research the sale or transfer history of the subject property and comparable sales. If not, explain

My research ☐ did ☐ did not reveal any prior sales or transfers of the subject property for the three years prior to the effective date of this appraisal.

Data source(s)

My research ☐ did ☐ did not reveal any prior sales or transfers of the comparable sales for the year prior to the date of sale of the comparable sale.

Data source(s)

Report the results of the research and analysis of the prior sale or transfer history of the subject property and comparable sales (report additional prior sales on page 3).

ITEM	SUBJECT	COMPARABLE SALE # 1	COMPARABLE SALE # 2	COMPARABLE SALE # 3
Date of Prior Sale/Transfer				
Price of Prior Sale/Transfer				
Data Source(s)				
Effective Date of Data Source(s)				

Analysis of prior sale or transfer history of the subject property and comparable sales

Summary of Sales Comparison Approach

Indicated Value by Sales Comparison Approach $

FIGURE 12.14
Comparables 4 and 5 for Exercise 12-4

There are comparable properties currently offered for sale in the subject neighborhood ranging in price from $ to $.

There are comparable sales in the subject neighborhood within the past twelve months ranging in sale price from $ to $.

FEATURE	SUBJECT			COMPARABLE SALE # 4				COMPARABLE SALE # 5				COMPARABLE SALE # 6			
Address	2130 W. Franklin			2243 Parkside Blvd.				2003 Franklin St.							
Proximity to Subject				.50 miles SE				.50 miles SE							
Sale Price	$						$ 256,500				$ 251,000				$
Sale Price/Gross Liv. Area	$ sq. ft.			$ 133.25 sq. ft.				$ 137.53 sq. ft.				$ sq. ft.			
Data Source(s)				Public records				Public records							
Verification Source(s)				Sales agent				Sales agent							
VALUE ADJUSTMENTS	DESCRIPTION			DESCRIPTION			+(-) $ Adjustment	DESCRIPTION			+(-) $ Adjustment	DESCRIPTION			+(-) $ Adjustment
Sale or Financing Concessions				ArmLth Conv				ArmLth Conv							
Date of Sale/Time				5 weeks ago				5 weeks ago							
Location	N; Res			N; Res				N; Res							
Leasehold/Fee Simple	fee simple			fee simple				fee simple							
Site	10,000 SF			10,000 SF				10,000 SF							
View	N; Res			N; Res				N; Res							
Design (Style)	Ranch			Ranch				Ranch							
Quality of Construction	Q4			Q4				Q4							
Actual Age	6			6				7							
Condition	C3			C3				C3							
Above Grade	Total	Bdrms	Baths	Total	Bdrms	Baths		Total	Bdrms	Baths		Total	Bdrms	Baths	
Room Count	7	3	2.1	8	4	2.0	−10,000	7	3	2.1					
Gross Living Area	1,825 sq. ft.			1,925 sq. ft.			+5,000	1,825 sq. ft.				sq. ft.			
Basement & Finished Rooms Below Grade	0			0				0							
Functional Utility	Average			Average				Average							
Heating/Cooling	FWA/CAC			FWA/CAC				FWA/CAC							
Energy Efficient Items	none			none				none							
Garage/Carport	2-car att.			2-car att.				2-car att.							
Porch/Patio/Deck	none			none				none							
Net Adjustment (Total)				☐ + ☐ -			$	☐ + ☐ -			$	☐ + ☐ -			$
Adjusted Sale Price of Comparables				Net Adj. % Gross Adj. %			$	Net Adj. % Gross Adj. %			$	Net Adj. % Gross Adj. %			$

I ☐ did ☐ did not research the sale or transfer history of the subject property and comparable sales. If not, explain

My research ☐ did ☐ did not reveal any prior sales or transfers of the subject property for the three years prior to the effective date of this appraisal.

Data source(s)

My research ☐ did ☐ did not reveal any prior sales or transfers of the comparable sales for the year prior to the date of sale of the comparable sale.

Data source(s)

Report the results of the research and analysis of the prior sale or transfer history of the subject property and comparable sales (report additional prior sales on page 3).

ITEM	SUBJECT	COMPARABLE SALE # 1	COMPARABLE SALE # 2	COMPARABLE SALE # 3
Date of Prior Sale/Transfer				
Price of Prior Sale/Transfer				
Data Source(s)				
Effective Date of Data Source(s)				

Analysis of prior sale or transfer history of the subject property and comparable sales

Summary of Sales Comparison Approach

Indicated Value by Sales Comparison Approach $

Opinion of Value

Using the adjusted values thus compiled, the appraiser can determine the appropriate opinion of market value for the subject property using the sales comparison approach.

Even when the appraiser is dealing with comparable properties that are virtually identical, the adjusted values will rarely be identical. Usually, there will be at least some differences in real estate transactions, however minor, that will cause selling prices to vary. A seller in one transaction may be less inclined to make a counteroffer than a seller in another transaction. Or the buyers may think that they have to offer a certain amount less than the asking price. After all, we are dealing with an imperfect market.

Whatever the reasons, the adjusted values of the comparable properties probably will not be identical.

No formula exists for reconciling the indicated values. Rather, this involves the application of careful analysis and judgment for which no mathematical formula can be substituted. The appraiser's task is to choose the adjusted value that seems to best reflect the characteristics of the subject property. In other words, which comparable is most like the subject property? The adjusted value of that property will most likely represent the market value of the subject property.

In the next step in the appraisal process, the appraiser compares the values reached by the cost and income approaches with that reached by the sales comparison approach. You will learn more about that step in Unit 15, "Reconciliation and the Appraisal Report."

Exercise 12-5

You have already completed the Sales Comparison Approach section for this unit's sample appraisal. Based on what you have just read, which adjusted value indicates the appropriate opinion of market value of the subject property? Why?

Check your answers against those in the answer key at the back of the book.

■ APPLICATION OF SALES COMPARISON APPROACH

The most obvious advantage of the sales comparison approach is its simplicity and rationale; by definition, it reflects the actions of market participants. It is not complex either as a concept or as a mechanical technique. Furthermore, its simplicity and directness appeal to both clients and the courts. When there are sufficient, recent and reliable market transactions, the sales comparison approach is probably the most logical and objective approach to value.

The chief limitation of the sales comparison approach is that it depends on a substantial volume of reliable information for its validity. When the number of market transactions is insufficient, the reliability of the approach is seriously reduced. Another difficulty is the need for making accurate adjustments, because two properties are seldom identical. Even under the best of circumstances, differences in value due to variations among properties may be difficult to measure. Adjustments may be lengthy and complex in some cases, with relatively little available basis for evaluating differences. Finally, it is sometimes difficult to determine whether a transaction is a bona fide, arm's-length sale or whether the sale price was distorted by a hidden motive.

Above all, the appraiser must be keenly attuned to market conditions and trends. The sales comparison approach should not become a mechanical exercise. The appraiser must always question the reliability of sales data in light of economic, political, and social market pressures.

In addition to its wide use in the appraisal of homes, the sales comparison approach is the preferred method for the appraisal of vacant land, as discussed in Unit 9.

■ SUMMARY

The sales comparison approach relies on the collection of accurate data on both the general market and recent sales of specific properties comparable to the subject property.

The appraiser adjusts the sales price of a comparable property to reflect any differences between it and the property that is the subject of the appraisal. Either a dollar adjustment or a percentage adjustment can be made. The value of an adjustment can be computed using matched pairs analysis, also called paired sales analysis and paired data set analysis. Necessary adjustments to account for differences in financing terms or date of sale are made before other adjustments.

■ REVIEW QUESTIONS

At the conclusion of this three-part problem, you will be asked for your opinion of the market value of a single-family residence.

1. First, determine the adjustment value for each of the significant variables by completing the sales price adjustment chart in Figure 12.15.

2. The subject property is a seven-room house with three bedrooms and two baths. It is situated on land 65 feet by 145 feet. The property is located in the central part of the neighborhood. The house is seven years old and is in good condition. Additional details on the subject property are listed in Figure 12.16. Using the adjustment values you computed in the preceding step, complete the Sales Comparison Approach sections of the URAR form in Figures 12.16, 12.17, and 12.18.

3. In your opinion, what is the market value of the subject property?

Check your answers against those in the answer key at the back of the book.

FIGURE 12.15
Sales Price Adjustment Chart Comparables

	1	2	3	4	5	6	7
Sales price	$185,500	$190,000	$178,600	$186,000	$169,000	$173,500	$190,000
Financing	FHA	FHA	FHA	FHA	FHA	FHA	FHA
Date of sale	2 mos. ago	3 wks. ago	1 yr. ago	2 wks. ago	1 mo. ago	8 wks. ago	3 wks. ago
Location	N;res	N;res	N;res	N;res	N;res	N;res	N;res
Leasehold/ fee simple	Fee simple	Fee simple	Fee simple	Fee simple	Fee simple	Fee simple	Fee simple
View	B;Glfvw	B;Glfvw	B;Glfvw	B;Glfvw	B;Glfvw	B;Glfvw	B;Glfvw
Site	9425sf	9425sf	9425sf	9425sf	9425sf	9425sf	9425sf
Design (style)	Ranch	Ranch	Ranch	Ranch	Ranch	Ranch	Ranch
Quality of construction	Q4	Q4	Q4	Q4	Q4	Q4	Q4
Age	7	6½	6	7½	7	7	7
Condition	C3	C3	C3	C4	C3	C3	C3
No. of rms./ bedrms./baths	7/3/2	7/3/2	7/3/2	7/3/2	7/3/2	7/3/2	7/3/2
Sq. ft. of living space	1,600	1,600	1,600	1,575	1,575	1,575	1,590
Other space (basement)	1600sf; 800sf fin 1rr0.1ba	1600sf; 800sf fin 1rr0.1ba	1600sf; 800sf fin 1rr0.1ba	1575sf; 800sf fin 1rr0.1ba	1575sf; 800sf fin 1rr0.1ba	1575sf; 800sf fin 1rr0.1ba	1590sf; 800sf fin 1rr0.1ba
Functional utility	Average	Average	Average	Average	Average	Average	Average
Heating/cooling	FWA	FWA/CAC	FWA/CAC	FWA/CAC	FWA	FWA/CAC	FWA/CAC
Energy-efficient items	None	None	None	None	None	None	None
Garage/carport	2-car att.	2-car att.	2-car att.	2-car att.	carport	carport	2-car att.
Other ext. improvements	Porch	Porch	Porch	Porch	Porch	Porch	Porch
Other int. improvements;	Brick fireplace	Brick fireplace	Brick fireplace	Brick fireplace	Brick fireplace	Brick fireplace	Brick fireplace
Typical house value							
Variable feature							
Adjustment value of variable							

FIGURE 12.16

Comparables 1 through 3 for Review Questions

There are comparable properties currently offered for sale in the subject neighborhood ranging in price from $ to $.

There are comparable sales in the subject neighborhood within the past twelve months ranging in sale price from $ to $.

FEATURE	SUBJECT	COMPARABLE SALE # 1		COMPARABLE SALE # 2		COMPARABLE SALE # 3	
Address							
Proximity to Subject							
Sale Price	$		$		$		$
Sale Price/Gross Liv. Area	$ sq. ft.	$ sq. ft.		$ sq. ft.		$ sq. ft.	
Data Source(s)							
Verification Source(s)							
VALUE ADJUSTMENTS	DESCRIPTION	DESCRIPTION	+(-) $ Adjustment	DESCRIPTION	+(-) $ Adjustment	DESCRIPTION	+(-) $ Adjustment
Sale or Financing Concessions							
Date of Sale/Time							
Location	N; Res						
Leasehold/Fee Simple	fee simple						
Site	9,425 SF						
View	B; GlfVw						
Design (Style)	Ranch						
Quality of Construction	Q4						
Actual Age	7						
Condition	C3						
Above Grade	Total Bdrms Baths	Total Bdrms Baths		Total Bdrms Baths		Total Bdrms Baths	
Room Count	7 3 2						
Gross Living Area	1,600 sq. ft.	sq. ft.		sq. ft.		sq. ft.	
Basement & Finished Rooms Below Grade	800 SF Fin 1rr; 0.1ba						
Functional Utility	Average						
Heating/Cooling	FWA/CAC						
Energy Efficient Items	none						
Garage/Carport	2-car att.						
Porch/Patio/Deck	porch						
Fireplace	brick						
Net Adjustment (Total)		☐ + ☐ -	$	☐ + ☐ -	$	☐ + ☐ -	$
Adjusted Sale Price of Comparables		Net Adj. % Gross Adj. %	$	Net Adj. % Gross Adj. %	$	Net Adj. % Gross Adj. %	$

I ☐ did ☐ did not research the sale or transfer history of the subject property and comparable sales. If not, explain

My research ☐ did ☐ did not reveal any prior sales or transfers of the subject property for the three years prior to the effective date of this appraisal.

Data source(s)

My research ☐ did ☐ did not reveal any prior sales or transfers of the comparable sales for the year prior to the date of sale of the comparable sale.

Data source(s)

Report the results of the research and analysis of the prior sale or transfer history of the subject property and comparable sales (report additional prior sales on page 3).

ITEM	SUBJECT	COMPARABLE SALE # 1	COMPARABLE SALE # 2	COMPARABLE SALE # 3
Date of Prior Sale/Transfer				
Price of Prior Sale/Transfer				
Data Source(s)				
Effective Date of Data Source(s)				

Analysis of prior sale or transfer history of the subject property and comparable sales

Summary of Sales Comparison Approach

Indicated Value by Sales Comparison Approach $

FIGURE 12.17

Comparables 4 through 6 for Review Questions

There are comparable properties currently offered for sale in the subject neighborhood ranging in price from $ to $.

There are comparable sales in the subject neighborhood within the past twelve months ranging in sale price from $ to $.

FEATURE	SUBJECT	COMPARABLE SALE # 4		COMPARABLE SALE # 5		COMPARABLE SALE # 6	
Address							
Proximity to Subject							
Sale Price	$		$		$		$
Sale Price/Gross Liv. Area	$ sq. ft.	$ sq. ft.		$ sq. ft.		$ sq. ft.	
Data Source(s)							
Verification Source(s)							
VALUE ADJUSTMENTS	DESCRIPTION	DESCRIPTION	+(-) $ Adjustment	DESCRIPTION	+(-) $ Adjustment	DESCRIPTION	+(-) $ Adjustment
Sale or Financing Concessions							
Date of Sale/Time							
Location	N; Res						
Leasehold/Fee Simple	fee simple						
Site	9,425 SF						
View	B; GlfVw						
Design (Style)	Ranch						
Quality of Construction	Q4						
Actual Age	7						
Condition	C3						
Above Grade Room Count	Total / Bdrms / Baths: 7 / 3 / 2	Total / Bdrms / Baths		Total / Bdrms / Baths		Total / Bdrms / Baths	
Gross Living Area	1,600 sq. ft.	sq. ft.		sq. ft.		sq. ft.	
Basement & Finished Rooms Below Grade	800 SF Fin 1rr; 0.1ba						
Functional Utility	Average						
Heating/Cooling	FWA/CAC						
Energy Efficient Items	none						
Garage/Carport	2-car att.						
Porch/Patio/Deck	porch						
Fireplace	brick						
Net Adjustment (Total)		☐ + ☐ -	$	☐ + ☐ -	$	☐ + ☐ -	$
Adjusted Sale Price of Comparables		Net Adj. % Gross Adj. %	$	Net Adj. % Gross Adj. %	$	Net Adj. % Gross Adj. %	$

I ☐ did ☐ did not research the sale or transfer history of the subject property and comparable sales. If not, explain

My research ☐ did ☐ did not reveal any prior sales or transfers of the subject property for the three years prior to the effective date of this appraisal.

Data source(s)

My research ☐ did ☐ did not reveal any prior sales or transfers of the comparable sales for the year prior to the date of sale of the comparable sale.

Data source(s)

Report the results of the research and analysis of the prior sale or transfer history of the subject property and comparable sales (report additional prior sales on page 3).

ITEM	SUBJECT	COMPARABLE SALE # 1	COMPARABLE SALE # 2	COMPARABLE SALE # 3
Date of Prior Sale/Transfer				
Price of Prior Sale/Transfer				
Data Source(s)				
Effective Date of Data Source(s)				

Analysis of prior sale or transfer history of the subject property and comparable sales

Summary of Sales Comparison Approach

Indicated Value by Sales Comparison Approach $

FIGURE 12.18
Comparable 7 for Review Questions

There are comparable properties currently offered for sale in the subject neighborhood ranging in price from $ to $.
There are comparable sales in the subject neighborhood within the past twelve months ranging in sale price from $ to $.

FEATURE	SUBJECT	COMPARABLE SALE # 7		COMPARABLE SALE # 8		COMPARABLE SALE # 9	
Address							
Proximity to Subject							
Sale Price	$		$		$		$
Sale Price/Gross Liv. Area	$ sq. ft.	$ sq. ft.		$ sq. ft.		$ sq. ft.	
Data Source(s)							
Verification Source(s)							
VALUE ADJUSTMENTS	DESCRIPTION	DESCRIPTION	+(-) $ Adjustment	DESCRIPTION	+(-) $ Adjustment	DESCRIPTION	+(-) $ Adjustment
Sale or Financing Concessions							
Date of Sale/Time							
Location	N; Res						
Leasehold/Fee Simple	fee simple						
Site	9,425 SF						
View	B; GlfVw						
Design (Style)	Ranch						
Quality of Construction	Q4						
Actual Age	7						
Condition	C3						
Above Grade Room Count	Total 7 / Bdrms 3 / Baths 2.0	Total / Bdrms / Baths		Total / Bdrms / Baths		Total / Bdrms / Baths	
Gross Living Area	1,600 sq. ft.	sq. ft.		sq. ft.		sq. ft.	
Basement & Finished Rooms Below Grade	800 SF Fin 1rr; 0.1ba						
Functional Utility	Average						
Heating/Cooling	FWA/CAC						
Energy Efficient Items	none						
Garage/Carport	2-car att.						
Porch/Patio/Deck	porch						
Fireplace	brick						
Net Adjustment (Total)		☐ + ☐ -	$	☐ + ☐ -	$	☐ + ☐ -	$
Adjusted Sale Price of Comparables		Net Adj. % Gross Adj. %	$	Net Adj. % Gross Adj. %	$	Net Adj. % Gross Adj. %	$

I ☐ did ☐ did not research the sale or transfer history of the subject property and comparable sales. If not, explain

My research ☐ did ☐ did not reveal any prior sales or transfers of the subject property for the three years prior to the effective date of this appraisal.
Data source(s)
My research ☐ did ☐ did not reveal any prior sales or transfers of the comparable sales for the year prior to the date of sale of the comparable sale.
Data source(s)
Report the results of the research and analysis of the prior sale or transfer history of the subject property and comparable sales (report additional prior sales on page 3).

ITEM	SUBJECT	COMPARABLE SALE # 1	COMPARABLE SALE # 2	COMPARABLE SALE # 3
Date of Prior Sale/Transfer				
Price of Prior Sale/Transfer				
Data Source(s)				
Effective Date of Data Source(s)				

Analysis of prior sale or transfer history of the subject property and comparable sales

Summary of Sales Comparison Approach

Indicated Value by Sales Comparison Approach $

UNIT THIRTEEN

13

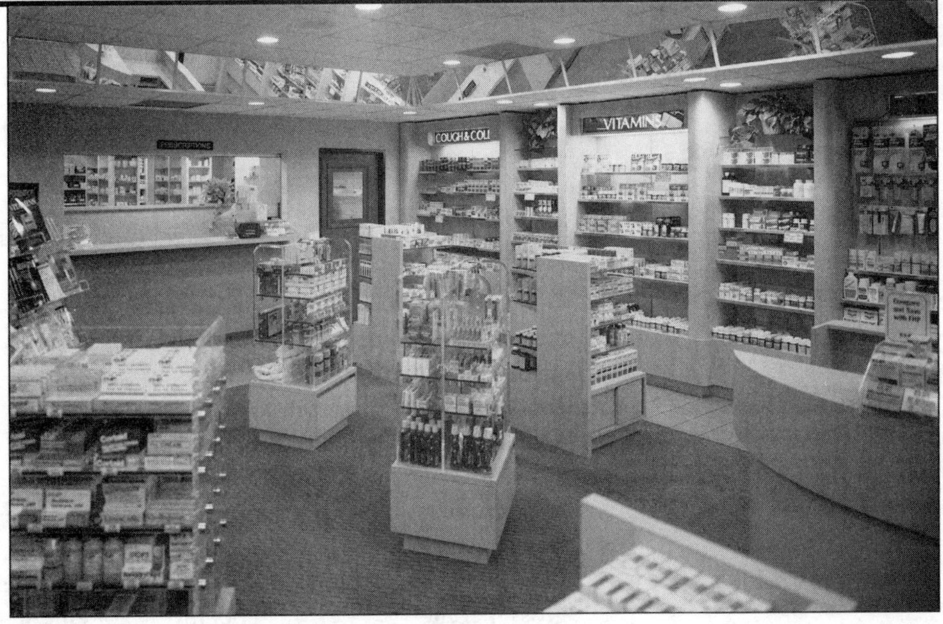

THE INCOME CAPITALIZATION APPROACH

■ LEARNING OBJECTIVES

When you have completed this unit, you will be able to

- identify the principle that is fundamental to the income capitalization approach;
- define gross income and potential gross income;
- compare and contrast market rent, scheduled rent, and historical rent;
- define effective gross income and net operating income;
- calculate vacancy and collection loss;
- classify operating expenses as variable expenses, fixed expenses, or reserves for replacement;
- distinguish expenses for accounting purposes from expenses for appraisal purposes;
- reconstruct an operating statement;
- develop a GRM (or GIM) and opinion of value for a subject property;
- complete the Income section of the URAR form; and
- derive an operating expense ratio, net income ratio, and breakeven ratio.

KEY TERMS

accrual basis accounting
breakeven ratio
capital improvements
cash basis accounting
contract rent
economic life
economic rent
effective gross income multiplier
effective gross income
fixed expenses
gross income
gross income multiplier
gross rent multiplier
historical rent
income capitalization
lessee
lessor
market rent
net income ratio
net operating income (NOI)
operating expense ratio
operating statement
potential gross income
potential gross income multiplier
principle of anticipation
property manager
real estate agent
reserves for replacement
scheduled rent
useful life
vacancy and collection losses
variable expenses

OVERVIEW

Although the income capitalization approach has a formidable title, it is based on a relatively simple premise: the value of a property is related to the income it can produce. The more income the property produces, the more the property tends to be worth. The process requires an accurate estimation of income and expenses and the selection of a capitalization rate and capitalization technique by which net income is processed into value.

The primary advantage of the income capitalization approach is that it approximates the thinking of the typical investor, who is interested in the dollar return on, as well as the return of, an investment in income-producing real estate.

The disadvantages of the income capitalization approach stem from the fact that in some cases, a complex set of relationships must be developed, and the complexities of income capitalization tend to confuse nonappraisers. Despite these difficulties, the income capitalization approach is an important valuation tool and must be understood by every real estate appraiser.

In this unit, you will learn what is meant by the terms *gross income*, *effective gross income*, and *net operating income*. You will also learn how to formulate and use gross rent and gross income multipliers. In Unit 14, the capitalization rate is defined, and you will learn a direct capitalization technique by which market value may be derived. Unit 14 also covers the techniques of yield, or annuity, capitalization.

THE INCOME-BASED APPROACHES TO APPRAISAL

Income Capitalization and the Principle of Anticipation

The **income capitalization** approach is based on the premise that there is a relationship between the income a property can earn and the property's value. Income capitalization thus is a process of converting income into value, and the concept of anticipation is fundamental to the approach. The **principle of anticipation** asserts that value is created by the expectation of benefits to be derived in the future. The price a buyer should be willing to pay for a property, therefore, would be equal to the present worth of these future benefits.

In the income capitalization approach, the appraiser discounts (reduces) a property's anticipated future income to its present worth. The discount recognizes the fact that an anticipated future dollar is worth less than a dollar in hand. For example, when you deposit $100 in a savings account to earn 2% annual interest, you are accepting the fact that the $102 you will receive at the end of the first year has a present value of only $100. Thus, $100 is the present value of $102 when discounted for one year at 2%. As you will see in Unit 14, yield capitalization uses discount rates to find the present value of projected future income.

Many commercial properties are purchased to be leased to other parties. The future net income the property is capable of earning and the eventual return (residual) of the investment capital are the main benefits to the owner. For this reason, the worth of the property to a prospective buyer is based largely on its earning capacity. The income capitalization approach to value translates the estimated potential income of a property into a determination of market value by the use of certain data and one of numerous income models that link different income variables to value.

The usefulness of the income capitalization approach depends on the type of property under appraisal and the data available. Obviously, it is most useful for income-producing investment properties. These typically include commercial properties, such as office buildings and retail stores. Less often, investors purchase industrial properties, such as manufacturing plants, for their income potential. The same can be said of residential property with more than four dwelling units. The buyer of an apartment building will be interested in the cash flow the property generates; that is, the amount of profit that can be expected over and above the expenses of ownership.

Smaller multiunit buildings with only two to four apartments can also be purchased primarily for their income-producing potential, but very often they are owner-occupied, and the benefits of living in the building have to be weighed against the loss of income from the owner-occupied unit.

Single-family houses, on the other hand, are not usually purchased for their income-producing potential. Even though many single-family houses are purchased by investors, the majority of single-family residences are owner-occupied, and the amount of income they could generate is not a factor in the decision to buy. Still, a variation of the income capitalization approach can be used in analyzing the income-producing capability of a single-family house. This simpler version of the income capitalization approach, called the **gross income multiplier** or **gross rent multiplier** method, is similar in application to the sales comparison approach because it compares rents of similar properties with their selling prices to arrive at a determination of value for the subject property. Gross rent multipliers frequently are used to determine the value of single-family residences because such properties usually produce only rental income. Although these may never be rented, they usually have rental income potential, which is particularly important when an oversupply of properties, inflated prices, high mortgage interest rates, or other factors result in a weak resale market. Because industrial and commercial properties generate income from many sources other than rent, the term gross income multiplier is used.

This unit and Unit 14 cover the types of information required to apply either version of the income approach, as well as the ways in which the information is derived.

■ POTENTIAL GROSS INCOME

Gross income is the income generated by a property before subtracting any of the expenses of ownership. Because the income capitalization approach is concerned with the amount of income a piece of real estate produces, the appraiser using this method must obtain complete information on the potential gross income the property can generate. **Potential gross income** is a property's total potential income from all sources during a specific period of time, usually a year. The appraiser takes into account both rental income and income from other sources, such as vending machines, laundry services, parking fees, and the like.

Rent

Rent is the major source of income from most investments in real estate. Even though a building may be fully occupied by reliable, long-term tenants, the appraiser must consider not only the present rents paid, but also past rents as well as rents paid for comparable properties in the area. An appraiser who is gathering data for a market value appraisal using the income capitalization approach needs to know the amount of the property's market rent. **Market rent**, also called **economic rent**, is an estimate of a property's rent potential—what an investor can expect to receive in rental income if the subject space is currently available for a new tenant. In a competitive market, market rent is the standard to which the subject's rent will eventually be drawn. To find market rent, the appraiser must consider not only the present rents paid by tenants but also past rents and rents currently paid for comparable properties in the area. By comparing present and past performances of the subject and similar properties, the appraiser should be able to recognize what the subject property's rent potential is and whether the property is living up to that potential.

Scheduled (contract) rent

Rent currently being paid by agreement between tenant and landlord is called **scheduled rent** or **contract rent**. Although local custom may vary, scheduled rent is usually computed per square foot per year on income properties such as stores, offices, and warehouses. The usual practice in stating apartment rents is to quote the scheduled rent per unit per year, which then is broken down to the rent per room per year. The appraiser's data on scheduled rent usually comes from the

- **lessee** (the tenant), the person or company renting or leasing the property;
- **lessor** (the landlord), the owner of the property;
- **property manager**, who maintains the rent roll; and
- **real estate agent**, if the property has been recently sold.

Historical rent

The appraiser will also be interested in **historical rent**, which is scheduled rent paid in past years. Historical rent data for both the subject property and similar properties will tell the appraiser whether the market rent appears to be following a trend and whether current rent information is likely to be reliable. For instance, rents in a given area may be increasing at the rate of 4% annually. If the current scheduled rent of either the subject or any of the comparable properties is not in line with the trend, the appraiser should find the reason for the discrepancy to justify the estimate of the rental value the property could command on the current market. Recent rental trends should, of course, be emphasized in estimating the current market rental income for the appraised property.

Again, the appraiser can acquire the needed data for estimating market rental rates from the tenant, landlord, property management firms, real estate brokers in the area, or perhaps from the appraiser's own files. The following example shows how to develop and use comparable property data in determining market rent for a property to be appraised by the income capitalization approach.

IN PRACTICE

The first chart that follows shows some of the information collected on the subject and other commercial properties in the vicinity. The second chart shows how data can be converted into like units of measurement to make the comparative data more meaningful.

Properties 2 and 4 are roughly the same size as the subject; both are one-floor structures, and the rents are close. Properties 1 and 3 probably do not apply because of the big difference in size.

Data for Finding Market Rent

Subject	Use	Hardware store
	Size	90' x 95' (one floor)
	Scheduled rent	$12,850
Property 1	Use	Clothing store
	Size	70' x 100' (two floors)
	Scheduled rent	$21,700
Property 2	Use	Drugstore
	Size	85' x 100' (one floor)
	Scheduled rent	$18,105
Property 3	Use	Cleaners
	Size	105' x 120' (one floor)
	Scheduled rent	$20,500
Property 4	Use	Grocery store
	Size	90' x 100' (one floor)
	Scheduled rent	$18,450

	Use	Square Feet	Scheduled Rent	Rent per Square Foot per Year
Subject	Hardware	8,550	$12,850	$1.50
Property 1	Clothing	14,000	21,700	1.55
Property 2	Drugstore	8,500	18,105	2.13
Property 3	Cleaners	12,600	20,500	1.63
Property 4	Grocery store	9,000	18,450	2.05

Property 2 rents for $2.13 per square foot, and property 4 rents for $2.05 per square foot. This suggests that the market (potential) rent of the subject property may be higher than the current scheduled rent of $1.50 per square foot.

In an actual appraisal, other factors of similarity and/or dissimilarity for selecting comparable properties must be considered. Such factors include location, construction of the building, its age and condition, parking facilities, front footage, air-conditioning, and responsibilities of the tenant. If comparable properties rent for more or less than the subject, the appraiser must search for clues as to why there are rental differences. Another important factor that should be considered is the age of the leases. Although the properties may be similar, an older lease could reflect a rental level lower than prevailing rentals.

Exercise 13-1

You are asked to appraise a six-unit apartment building. Each apartment has one bath and five rooms: living room, dining room, kitchen, and two bedrooms. Each apartment is presently leased at $900 per room per year. For this problem, historical rent will be ignored. There are three other six-unit apartment buildings in the area of similar room size and construction:

- Property 1 contains two-bedroom apartments with living room, dining room, kitchen, and bath, renting for $3,780 per room per year.
- Property 2 contains three-bedroom apartments with living room, dining room, kitchen, and bath, renting for $4,320 per room per year.
- Property 3 contains two-bedroom apartments with living room, dining room, kitchen, and bath, renting for $3,528 per room per year.

What is the scheduled rent for the subject property?

What is the expected (market) rent for the subject property?

Check your answers against those in the answer key at the back of the book.

Outside Economic Factors

Various national, regional, and local factors also might have to be analyzed in deriving market rent. For example, suppose the country has been in a period of recession for the year before the date of an appraisal. Historical rental data may indicate a 6% increase per year over the preceding five years, but this rate of increase will be too high for the year immediately before the appraisal. Thus, the appraiser must keep informed of economic trends at all levels.

Assume a distribution facility that will employ hundreds of people is being built close to a town. If no new construction has begun on housing facilities, rent for dwelling space in that area most likely will increase because of the relatively low supply of and high demand for housing. The appraiser should be aware of this factor and take it into consideration when estimating market rent.

Using both historical and scheduled rent information for the subject and similar properties, the appraiser can derive the subject property's market rent—the amount for which the competitive rental market indicates the property should rent. This figure may be the same as, higher than, or lower than the property's current rent. The appraiser will base the potential gross income estimate on market rent added to any other income derived from the property during a one-year period.

Other Income

Rents may not be the only source of income. Even a small apartment building may provide coin-operated laundry machines for the use of tenants. Or the owner of an office building may offer food and other vending machines for the convenience of tenants. In larger buildings, the lessor may operate a convenience store on the premises. A parking area may provide substantial additional income. Any income received must be taken into consideration, because it will be a factor in determining market value.

IN PRACTICE

An appraisal for ABC Office Management, Inc., estimates the potential gross income from one of its buildings as $230,000 in scheduled rent and $9,000 from parking fees. Show the building's income in an itemized statement.

Potential Gross Income	
Scheduled rent	$230,000
Parking fees	9,000
	$239,000

The total potential gross income for the building under appraisal is $239,000.

In making up a statement of potential gross income, the appraiser will list rent and nonrent income separately, then total them.

Potential gross income often includes (or fails to include) items that are reported improperly by owners or accountants not experienced in real estate. Among the more important errors are these:

- Leaving out any percentage income that may be paid if the lease is on a minimum-plus-percentage basis. This type of lease is most often found with retail stores. The lessee pays a stipulated minimum rent plus a percentage of the gross business income over a stated amount. This percentage may increase automatically as gross sales (or business) income rises. For instance, the rent may be $25,000 per year plus 8% of annual gross sales over $100,000 and 6% of gross sales over $150,000.
- Reporting only the actual income for a year and not the total potential gross income.
- Leaving out equivalent rents for owner-occupied areas and/or manager's quarters. These can materially affect the capitalized value of the property if the owner and/or the manager occupy substantial space.
- Leaving out any "other" income not derived from rents, such as income from parking garages or lots and from the resale of electricity, heat, or air-conditioning to the tenant.

The appraiser should not accept figures and statements without verifying them by questioning either the tenants or the real estate broker or rental agent involved.

Exercise 13-2

You are appraising a six-unit residential property, and the only information available is the following yearly income and expense data. List the income information in statement form, then compute the estimated potential gross income.

Apartment rental income is $96,000. Outlay for janitorial service is $14,700, with another $1,700 for supplies. Utilities are $10,600, and maintenance and repairs amount to about $3,000. Taxes are $5,700. Income from washers and dryers is $1,900. Building depreciation is estimated at $4,500 per year. Rental spaces in the adjacent parking lot bring in $5,400 per year.

Check your answers against those in the answer key at the back of the book.

EFFECTIVE GROSS INCOME

As discussed earlier, the appraiser's estimate of potential gross income is based on a combination of market rent plus all other income earned by the property. It is reasonable to assume, however, that some rental properties will not be fully occupied 100% of the time, and some tenants will fail to pay the scheduled rent. Normally, especially during times of economic recession or overbuilt markets, many properties have vacancies. Vacancies, as well as instances of nonpayment of rent, can significantly reduce a property's income. An allowance for vacancy and collection loss is usually estimated as a percentage of potential gross income.

To derive **effective gross income**, the appraiser totals potential income from all sources, then subtracts an allowance for **vacancy and collection losses**. In equation form:

Potential gross income – Vacancy & collection losses = Effective gross income

The appropriate rate to allow for anticipated vacancy and collection losses is based on market conditions. Vacancy and collection losses rise as competition for tenants increases; they fall when the demand for desirable properties exceeds supply. In short, there is no standard rate for vacancy and collection losses that can take into account all market conditions. If comparable properties are experiencing vacancy rates of 15%, then that is the rate that should be assigned to the property being appraised to best reflect market conditions.

For example, assume that the potential gross income of an apartment building that derives all of its income from rent is $650,000. Historically, the subject property has had a 10% vacancy rate. If the rate of vacancies in the current year, based on market data analysis, does not differ from that of past years, the real or effective gross income of the property would be $585,000. To calculate the effective gross income for a property, the appraiser first determines the potential market rent, then adds any nonrent income. Finally, the appraiser reduces the resulting estimated potential gross income by the percentage of market rent that probably will be lost due to vacancies, collection losses, or both.

In summary, factors to be taken into account for estimating an allowance for vacancy and collection losses are as follows:

- Current and past rental losses of the subject property
- Current and past rental levels for other properties in the area that are in competition with the subject property
- Area population and economic trends
- Length of existing leases

Under ordinary market conditions (neither boom nor bust), the allowance for vacancy and collection losses is typically 5–10%. If the area has experienced any amount of overbuilding or for whatever reason has many more properties available than current market demand warrants, the vacancy factor may be considerably higher. If the area's economy is experiencing a recession or depression, collection losses as well as vacancies will tend to be higher than normal. On the other hand, if there is a heavier-than-normal demand for space relative to the number of available properties, the appraiser may determine that a lower allowance for vacancy and collection losses is indicated. Each appraisal assignment, then, requires that this allowance be derived from pertinent market facts.

IN PRACTICE

An eight-unit apartment building historically has a 4% vacancy rate and a 4% collection loss rate. A current survey of the local market also supports these vacancy estimates. The projected income for the building over the next year is $146,400 market rent, $8,000 parking income, $4,300 from vending machine income, and $2,800 income from laundry facilities. What is the property's effective gross income?

The effective gross income can be found most easily by first making an itemized statement of potential gross income:

Market rent	$146,400
Parking	8,000
Vending machines	4,300
Laundry facilities	2,800
Potential gross income	$161,500

Then vacancy and collection losses based on rental income can be computed and subtracted from potential gross income to arrive at effective gross income:

Vacancy and collection losses @ 8% of potential gross income	12,920
Effective gross income	$148,580

The effective gross income of the subject property is $148,580.

Exercise 13-3

Using the income and expense information given in Exercise 13-2, draw up an effective gross income statement for the subject property. The effective gross income will be based on the following vacancy and rental losses:

- The apartment units are vacant for an average of one week of each year.
- There has also been a total rental loss of 3% for each of the past three years.

Check your answer against the one in the answer key at the back of the book.

■ NET OPERATING INCOME

Having found the effective gross income, the appraiser can deduct the property's operating expenses to derive the net operating income (NOI). The value of an income-producing property is measured by the NOI it can be expected to earn during its remaining economic life or forecast income period. Operating expenses are those costs incurred to maintain the property and to continue the income stream. Such expenses include the cost of all goods and services used or consumed in the process of obtaining and maintaining rental income. Net operating income is customarily expressed as an annual amount. In equation form, it is

Effective gross income – Operating expenses = NOI

The expenses incurred depend on the property and the services provided by the owner. Apartment buildings may require a doorman, and staffs for housekeeping and common areas, in addition to maintenance, insurance, property taxes, employee salaries and benefits, utility payments, legal and accounting fees and management fees. Some owners of retail store properties provide the real estate and pay for the exterior maintenance of the building, insurance, and property taxes. All utilities and inside maintenance and repairs may be the responsibility of the tenant.

Classification of Operating Expenses

Operating expenses are usually grouped according to the nature of the cost incurred. Expenses may be classified as follows:

- **Variable expenses** are the out-of-pocket costs incurred for management, wages and benefits of building employees, fuel, utility services, decorating, repairs, and other items required to operate the property. These expenses tend to vary according to the occupancy level of the property.
- **Fixed expenses** are those costs that are more or less permanent and do not vary according to occupancy, such as real estate taxes and insurance for fire, theft, and hazards.

- **Reserves for replacement** are allowances set up for replacement of building and equipment items that have a relatively short life expectancy. For example, reserves should be set up for heating systems, roof replacements, elevators, air conditioners, ranges, refrigerators, carpeting, and other items that routinely wear out and have to be replaced during the economic life of the building. The appraiser provides for the replacement of an item by estimating its replacement cost and its remaining **economic life** or **useful life**. Using a straight-line recapture method, the annual charge is found by dividing the cost of the item by the number of years of economic life. (Other methods of recapture are discussed in Unit 14.)

Expenses for Accounting Purposes vs. Expenses for Appraisal Purposes

Operating expenses for appraisal purposes do not include expenditures that are beyond the direct operation of an income-producing property. There are four types of expenses to the owner that are not operating expenses of real estate:

- *Financing costs*. Property is appraised without considering available or probable financing, except under the mortgage equity capitalization method. The focus of a market value opinion is the property's productivity—its NOI.
- *Income tax payments*. Income taxes are a powerful force and exert an influence on investment behavior, but they relate to the owner, not the property. Personal income taxes depend on the total income of a person, personal expenses, age, health, size of family, et cetera, and are not treated as expenses of the property for market value appraisal purposes.
- *Depreciation charges on buildings or other improvements*. An annual depreciation charge is an accounting method of recovering the cost of an investment over a period of time. The process of capitalization, which will be explained later, automatically provides for the recovery of the investment.
- *Capital improvements*. Although payments may have been made for **capital improvements**, such as new refrigerators, ranges, or storm windows, the payments themselves are not treated as operating expenses but are taken from the replacement reserve monies.

Reconstructing the Operating Statement

The appraiser's estimates and computations are summarized in an **operating statement** for the property being appraised. Because the appraiser's operating statement will include some important differences from the accountant's operating statement for the same property, this process is referred to as reconstructing the operating statement. It may also be described as the stabilization of income and expenses. Estimates of current income or expenses may be adjusted if the appraiser's study indicates that they are out of line for comparable properties or do not accurately reflect typical market conditions. Figure 13.1 is an example of a reconstructed operating statement that shows the accountant's figures, as well as the appraiser's calculations.

The operating statement can be prepared using either

- **cash basis accounting** in which revenue is recorded only when received and expenses recorded only when actually paid; or
- **accrual basis accounting** in which revenue recorded for the period includes all revenue earned, whether or not it has actually been received during the period; and expenses recorded for the period include all expenses incurred, whether or not they have actually been paid during the period.

Individuals usually choose to keep their personal accounts on a cash basis, while businesses generally prefer accrual basis accounting and may be required by the Internal Revenue Service to use this method. The basis of the accounting system used must be identified for the appraiser to reconstruct the operating statement accurately.

Figure 13.1 is an operating statement for an apartment building in which the appraiser considered its past, present, and expected future rental performance. The first column of figures was prepared by the owner's accountant. The second column of figures was reconstructed by the appraiser (rounding amounts to the nearest $100). The footnotes to Figure 13.1 explain the items in the operating statement with corresponding circled numbers. All amounts on the operating statement are expressed on an annual basis.

Exercise 13-4

You are gathering data for the appraisal of a 32-unit apartment building. Using the form Operating Statement included in this exercise, list the yearly income and expense data given in the following accountant's summary. Then compute the property's effective gross income, total expenses, and net operating income. Natural gas rates are expected to increase, perhaps by 25%. Because of a general increase in the tax rate, taxes should be increased by about 20%. Round all figures to the nearest $100.

Property address: 759 Fourteenth Street

Rental income	$210,000.00
Vacancy and collection losses	9,850.00
Salaries—Janitor	9,248.17
Employee benefits	612.00
Management	6,000.00
Natural gas	12,375.00
Water	3,845.67
Electricity	8,674.32
Property taxes	6,000.00
Janitorial supplies	673.00
Redecorating	2,000.00
Reserves for building replacements	2,500.00
Legal and accounting fees	2,400.00

Operating Statement

Potential Gross Income		______
Allowance for Vacancy and Collection Losses		______
Effective Gross Income		______
Operating Expenses	______	
Variable Expenses	______	
	______	
	______	
	______	
	______	
	______	
	______	
	______	
	______	
	______	
	______	
	______	
	______	
Fixed Expenses	______	
Reserves for Replacement	______	
Total Operating Expense		______
Net Operating Income		______

Check your answers against those in the answer key at the back of the book.

FIGURE 13.1
Sample Operating Statement

		Accountant's Figures	Appraiser's Adjusted Estimate
	① Gross Income (Rent)	$56,000.00	$58,700
	② Allowance for Vacancies and Bad Debts	____	2,900
	Effective Gross Income	____	55,800
	Operating Expenses		
VARIABLE EXPENSES	Salaries and wages	6,000.50	6,000
	Employees' benefits	519.00	500
	Electricity	900.12	900
	Gas	3,014.60	3,000
	Water	400.10	400
	Painting and decorating	1,000.00	1,000
	Supplies	525.56	500
	Repairs	2,024.30	2,000
	Management	3,000.00	3,000
	Legal and accounting fees	800.00	800
	Miscellaneous expenses	400.00	400
FIXED EXPENSES	Insurance (three-year policy)	1,500.00	500
	Real estate taxes	5,100.00	5,100
RESERVES FOR REPLACEMENT	Reserves—		
	③ Roof replacement	____	500
	④ Plumbing and electrical	____	1,000
	⑤ Payments on air conditioners	1,200.00	____
	⑥ Principal on mortgage	1,500.00	____
	⑦ Interest on mortgage	10,000.00	____
	⑧ Depreciation—building	8,000.00	____
	Total Expenses	$45,884.38	$25,600
	Net Operating Income	$10,115.62	$30,200

1 Income was adjusted upward to reflect the rental value of an apartment occupied by the owner.
2 Vacancy and collection losses, based on an area study, typically amount to 5 percent of gross rental income.
3 Roof replacement is expected every 20 years at a cost of $10,000, or $500 per year ($10,000 ÷ 20).
4 Plumbing and electrical replacements are based on a 20-year service life for fixtures costing $20,000, or $1,000 per year ($20,000 ÷ 20).
5 Payments for capital improvements such as air conditioners are not operating expenses.
6 & 7 Principal and mortgage interest payments are personal income deductions, not property expenses, when appraising on a "free and clear basis."
8 Depreciation is included in the accountant's figures as the owner's expense, to allow for the loss of income that will result when the property reaches the end of its useful life. (For more information on how accrued depreciation is estimated in judging the value of a property, see Chapter 9.)

■ OPERATING STATEMENT RATIOS

The effect on value of varying expense levels in relation to income can be seen by studying what are called the operating statement ratios. These ratios, which are derived from sales and rental data and/or the operating statements of properties similar to the subject, can be used to test the validity of the subject's estimated operating expenses.

The **operating expense ratio** is the ratio of total operating expenses to effective gross income. As a formula, the relationship can be expressed as follows:

$$\frac{\text{Operating expenses}}{\text{Effective gross income}} = \text{Operating expense ratio}$$

The **net income ratio** is the ratio of net operating income to effective gross income. The formula for this relationship is as follows:

$$\frac{\text{Net operating income}}{\text{Effective gross income}} = \text{Net income ratio}$$

The operating expense ratio and net income ratio complement each other; that is, the two ratios added together equal 1. For example, consider a building that has an effective gross income of $100,000 and total operating expenses of $25,000. The building's operating expense ratio is $25,000 divided by $100,000, or 0.25. The net operating income is $100,000 less $25,000, or $75,000, making the net income ratio $75,000 divided by $100,000, or 0.75. The two ratios added together (0.25 + 0.75) equal 1.

The **breakeven ratio** is the ratio of the operating expenses plus the property's annual debt service to potential gross income. In other words, it is the ratio of funds flowing out of the property (before income taxes) to funds coming in.

The formula for the breakeven ratio is:

$$\frac{\text{Operating expenses} + \text{Debt service}}{\text{Potential gross income}} = \text{Breakeven ratio}$$

The breakeven ratio also can be based on effective gross income. The ratio indicates the breakeven point at which all expenses of ownership, including financing costs, are covered by the income generated. For example, consider a building that has a potential gross income of $100,000, has operating expenses of $25,000, and requires a debt service of $55,000 at current interest rates. The property's breakeven ratio is $80,000 ($25,000 + $55,000) divided by $100,000, or 0.80. At 80% occupancy (20% vacancy), the property will break even. Any additional reduction in the vacancy factor brought about by an increase in the occupancy rate will be profit.

Ratios vary according to the type of property being studied. For instance, a hotel usually has a breakeven point that is somewhat lower than that of an office building. A 75% occupancy level may be considered adequate for a hotel, even though the same occupancy level (representing a vacancy factor of 25%) may be considered poor for an office building. By comparing the various ratios for properties comparable to the one being appraised, the appraiser can learn what kind of return is expected in the marketplace for properties producing that level of income. Ratios are particularly useful tools when they either confirm that a property's income and expenses are in line with those of other properties or indicate an abnormality that warrants further investigation.

Exercise 13-5

1. The ratio of total operating expenses to effective gross income is
   a. the operating expense ratio.
   b. the net income ratio.
   c. the effective gross income ratio.
   d. the breakeven ratio.
2. The ratio of net operating income to effective gross income is
   a. the operating expense ratio.
   b. the net income ratio.
   c. the effective gross income ratio.
   d. the breakeven ratio.
3. The ratio of the operating expenses plus annual debt service to potential gross income is
   a. the operating expense ratio.
   b. the net income ratio.
   c. the effective gross income ratio.
   d. the breakeven ratio.
4. A building that has an effective gross income of $50,000 and total operating expenses of $10,000 has what operating expense ratio?
   a. 0.10
   b. 0.15
   c. 0.20
   d. 0.25
5. The building described in problem 4 has what net income ratio?
   a. 0.80
   b. 0.90
   c. 1
   d. 5

Check your answers against those in the answer key at the back of the book.

Gross Income and Gross Rent Multipliers

As a substitute for the more elaborate and very detailed income capitalization approach, a much simpler form of income analysis can be used to develop an opinion of market value.

For single-family residences, the gross income used will be the amount of the monthly rent, with no other source of income from the property. For this reason, this approach is referred to as the gross rent multiplier (GRM) method. When appraising commercial and industrial properties, the amount of annual income from all sources is likely to include more than just rents, and the gross income multiplier (GIM) is the more appropriate term.

The theory behind the use of the GIM or GRM is that rental prices and sales prices generally react to the same market influences, and so they tend to move in the same direction and in the same proportion. If rental prices go up or down, sales prices will usually follow suit, and to the same degree. Of course, not all factors will affect both rental prices and sales prices equally or at the same time. If property taxes go up, rents may rise well ahead of the time that the taxed property is sold. If a sudden drop in demand for rental units occurs because of overbuilding, rental prices and sales prices will both drop as new leases are begun and sales occur.

The relationship between the sales price and rental price can be expressed as a factor or ratio, which is the gross income or gross rent multiplier. The ratio is expressed as follows:

$$\frac{\text{Sales price}}{\text{Gross income}} = \text{GIM}$$

or

$$\frac{\text{Sales price}}{\text{Gross rent}} = \text{GRM}$$

IN PRACTICE

A commercial property sold a month ago for $900,000. The annual gross income was $100,000. What is the GIM for the property?

Because the property is commercial, the annual gross income is used in the formula for finding the GIM:

$$\frac{\$900{,}000}{\$100{,}000} = 9\text{, the GIM for this property}$$

To establish a reasonably accurate GIM, the appraiser should have recent sales and income data from at least 10 properties similar to the subject property that have sold in the same market area and were rented at the time of sale. The resulting GIM can then be applied to the actual or projected rental of the subject property to develop an opinion of its market value. The formula would then be as follows:

$$\text{Gross income} \times \text{GIM} = \text{Market value}$$

IN PRACTICE

Determination of Market Value—Gross Income Multiplier Analysis

Sale No.	Market Value	Annual Gross Income	GIM
1	$400,000	$40,000	10.0
2	450,000	50,000	9.0
3	361,000	38,000	9.5
4	467,500	55,000	8.5
5	427,500	45,000	9.5
Subject	?	42,000	?

The range of GIMs applied to the subject's gross income gives the following:

$42,000 × 8.5 = $357,000
$42,000 × 10 = $420,000

These comparisons bracket the opinion of value within reasonable limits. By using sales 1, 3, and 5 as most comparable, the appraiser concludes that the subject property's GIM should be 9.5. Therefore, $42,000 × 9.5 = $399,000, the indicated value of the subject property.

The **gross income multiplier** method of determining property value also is called the **potential gross income multiplier** method. Potential gross income is income (usually annual) from all sources before any deduction for vacancy and collection losses or operating expenses. If vacancy and collection losses are deducted from gross income before the multiplier is derived, it is termed the **effective gross income multiplier**.

Because the potential gross income multiplier converts gross, rather than net, income into value, the result can be misleading. For example, consider two similar properties, each with an asking price of eight times gross income, but one property netting $150,000 per year and the other netting only $75,000 per year. (The lower net income could be caused by excessive operating expenses.) According to the GIM method, the investor ought to pay the same price for either property. This is not actually the case, however. The property with the larger net income is certainly more valuable than the other. The length of the lease term also may be a significant factor. A property nearing the end of a five-year lease term in a period of high inflation may well be generating less income than it might if the lease had been renegotiated during that period.

In other methods of direct capitalization, the multiplier concept is refined by considering not only gross income but also the lease term as well as the operating expenses incurred. It is important to use comparable properties that have similar operating expense ratios.

Exercise 13-6

The subject property has a gross income of $18,000 per year. Information on comparable properties is listed here, with adjustment factors indicated.

Sale No.	Adjustment	Sales Price	Gross Income	GIM
1	New, long-term lease	$835,000	$93,750	
2	High operating expenses	625,000	57,500	
3	Old lease	978,000	57,500	
4	Low operating expense	720,000	67,000	
5	Customized property	735,000	140,000	

Compute the GIM for each property. Then derive the GIM for the subject property, taking into account the adjustment factors that indicate that a GIM should be raised or lowered to reflect special circumstances. Finally, develop an opinion of value for the subject property.

Check your answers against those in the answer key at the back of the book.

Applying the GRM to Residential Properties

As you have seen, the gross rent multiplier is a number that expresses the relationship between the sales price of a residential property and its gross monthly unfurnished rental:

$$\frac{\text{Sales price}}{\text{Gross rent}} = \text{GRM}$$

To derive a reasonably accurate GRM, the appraiser should make an effort to obtain and evaluate data on at least 10 comparable rental sales—more if the subject property is located in an area in which there is a high percentage of rentals. The formula for this step is as follows:

$$\text{Gross rent} \times \text{GRM} = \text{Market value}$$

The four steps in applying the gross rent multiplier can be summarized:

1. Estimate the subject property's monthly market rent
2. Calculate gross rent multipliers from recently sold comparable properties that were rented at the time of sale
3. Based on rent multiplier analysis, derive the appropriate GRM for the subject property
4. Estimate market value by multiplying the amount of the monthly market rent by the subject property's GRM

Because even very similar properties rarely have the same rent or sales price, GRM analysis is likely to produce a range of multipliers. The appraiser must decide which multiplier is most appropriate for the subject property. No mathematical or mechanical formula can be substituted for careful analysis and judgment.

Following is an example of the range of data that might be collected by an appraiser trying to determine an appropriate GRM for a single-family home.

IN PRACTICE

Sale No.	Sales Price	Monthly Rental	GRM (rounded)
1	$100,000	$825	121
2	110,500	875	126
3	105,500	850	124
4	112,000	890	126
5	105,250	850	124
6	104,000	845	123
Subject	?	850	?

In this example, the appraiser has estimated that the market rent for the subject property is $850. The range of GRMs derived from recent sales of comparable properties is from 121 to 126. When applied to the subject's market rent estimate, the GRMs place value between $102,850 ($850 × 121) and $107,100 ($850 × 126). These comparisons bracket the estimate of value within reasonable limits.

Because property sales 3 and 5 are most comparable to the subject property, the appraiser concludes that the subject property's GRM should be 124. The indicated value of the subject property by the gross rent multiplier method then is $850 × 124, or $105,000 (rounded).

The gross rent multiplier method can be a valid indicator of market value if the subject property is located in a rental-oriented area where an abundance of viable information is available. In areas that are almost exclusively owner-occupied, rental data may be too scarce to permit the use of this method.

If the right kinds of data are available to develop valid market rent and GRM estimates, the gross rent multiplier method can be used as a check against the value reached by the sales comparison approach.

FIGURE 13.2
URAR Income Approach Section

INCOME	INCOME APPROACH TO VALUE (not required by Fannie Mae)			
	Estimated Monthly Market Rent $	X Gross Rent Multiplier	= $	Indicated Value by Income Approach
	Summary of Income Approach (including support for market rent and GRM)			

Income Approach Using the URAR Form

In the Income Approach section of the URAR form shown in Figure 13.2, the appraiser is required to

- enter the subject property's monthly market rent estimate derived from the marketplace,
- enter the GRM applicable to the subject property,
- multiply the monthly market rent estimate by the GRM, and
- enter the value opinion indicated by the income approach.

SUMMARY

In the income capitalization approach, the appraiser estimates the market value of property based on its anticipated income.

Gross income includes potential property income from all sources during a specified period. Rent is the major source of income from real estate. Historical rent is scheduled, or contract, rent paid in past years. Current scheduled rent may not be the same as a property's projected market rent.

A gross income or rent multiplier can be multiplied by the amount of gross income to derive an estimate of property value. A monthly multiplier is used for single-family residences; a yearly multiplier is used for multifamily and commercial buildings. The income multiplier method of determining value can be based on either potential gross income or effective gross income, in which case vacancy and collection losses are deducted.

By analyzing a property's operating statement, an appraiser can determine the operating expenses that are deducted from effective gross income to find net operating income. The appraiser must know whether account entries are made on a cash or an accrual basis.

The relationship of effective gross income, operating expenses, and net operating income can be expressed in several operating statement ratios that may indicate whether the property's income production is typical of the marketplace.

■ Review Questions

1. To arrive at net operating income, expenses are deducted from
   a. operating profit.
   b. gross income.
   c. effective gross income.
   d. none of these.

2. In the following list, check each item that is *NOT* an expense from an appraiser's point of view.
   a. Gas and electricity
   b. Depreciation on building
   c. Water
   d. Real estate taxes
   e. Building insurance
   f. Income tax
   g. Supplies
   h. Payments on air conditioners
   i. Janitor's salary
   j. Management fees
   k. Maintenance and repairs
   l. Legal and accounting fees
   m. Principal and interest on mortgage
   n. Advertising
   o. Painting and decorating
   p. Depreciation on equipment
   q. Value of janitor's apartment (rent free)
   r. Water and sewer tax
   s. Salaries and wages of employees
   t. Reserves for replacement
   u. Payments on stoves and refrigerators

3. If a property's net income ratio is 0.85, what is its operating expense ratio?
   a. 0.15
   b. 1.50
   c. 0.58
   d. 0.015

4. Another name for contract rent is
   a. market rent.
   b. scheduled rent.
   c. economic rent.
   d. surplus rent.

5. Another name for market rent is
   a. contract rent.
   b. scheduled rent.
   c. economic rent.
   d. surplus rent.

6. A commercial property producing an annual gross income of $39,000 was sold two months ago for $341,250. What is the property's gross income multiplier?
   a. 7
   b. 7.75
   c. 8.5
   d. 8.75

7. A single-family residence that sold for $285,000 was rented for $1,400 per month when it was sold. The property's gross rent multiplier is
   a. 17.
   b. 204.
   c. 207.
   d. 210.

8. Vacancy and collection losses are deducted from gross income using
   a. a potential gross income multiplier.
   b. an effective gross income multiplier.
   c. a gross income multiplier.
   d. a gross rent multiplier.

9. In the formula for the operating expense ratio,
   a. operating expenses are divided by effective gross income.
   b. effective gross income is divided by operating expenses.
   c. potential gross income is divided by effective gross income.
   d. effective gross income is divided by potential gross income.

10. In the formula for the net income ratio,
    a. effective gross income is divided by potential gross income.
    b. potential gross income is divided by effective gross income.
    c. effective gross income is divided by net operating income.
    d. net operating income is divided by effective gross income.

11. If a property's net operating income remains stable, but the cap rate rises, the property's value
    a. rises.
    b. declines.
    c. stays the same.
    d. cannot be determined.

12. If the risk of an investment rises, the cap rate will
    a. rise.
    b. fall.
    c. stay the same.
    d. cannot be determined.

13. An investor owns a four-unit apartment building. Two units are rented for $800 per month each. Two units are rented for $1,000 per month each. The building's vacancy rate is 5% and the property's net income ratio is .40. What is the property's potential gross income?
    a. $38,400
    b. $40,000
    c. $43,200
    d. $50,200

14. An investor owns a four-unit apartment building. Two units are rented for $800 per month each. Two units are rented for $1,000 per month each. The building's vacancy rate is 5% and the property's net income ratio is .40. What is the property's anticipated vacancy loss?
    a. $2,160
    b. $1,900
    c. $2,000
    d. $2,500

15. An investor owns a four-unit apartment building. Two units are rented for $800 per month each. Two units are rented for $1,000 per month each. The building's vacancy rate is 5% and the property's net income ratio is .40. What is the property's effective gross income?
    a. $40,000
    b. $41,040
    c. $41,200
    d. $48,200

16. An investor owns a four-unit apartment building. Two units are rented for $800 per month each. Two units are rented for $1,000 per month each. The building's vacancy rate is 5% and the property's net income ratio is .40. What is the property's net operating income?
    a. $14,600
    b. $16,416
    c. $18,236
    d. $20,236

17. An investor owns a four-unit apartment building. Two units are rented for $800 per month each. Two units are rented for $1,000 per month each. The building's vacancy rate is 5% and the property's net income ratio is .40. If the property's cap rate is 8.5%, its indicated value is
    a. $173,800.
    b. $183,294.
    c. $189,300.
    d. $193,129.

18. A house built in 1923 is rented for $2,500 per month. Property tax and other expenses total $17,000 annually. With a gross rent multiplier of 125, the indicated value of the house is
    a. $250,000.
    b. $300,000.
    c. $312,500.
    d. $625,000.

19. If a property's cap rate is 10%, estimated gross income is $100,000, and operating expense ratio is .60, its indicated value is
    a. $400,000.
    b. $450,000.
    c. $500,000.
    d. $550,000.

20. Which of the following properties is likely to be appraised using the income approach?
    a. A factory that has no comparable rentals in the area
    b. A house of worship that has no comparable rentals in the area.
    c. A single-family dwelling that has never been rented, in a neighborhood with many comparable rental sales
    d. A single-family dwelling that has never been rented, in a neighborhood with few comparable rental sales

Check your answers against those in the answer key at the back of the book.

UNIT FOURTEEN

DIRECT AND YIELD CAPITALIZATION

■ LEARNING OBJECTIVES

When you have completed this unit, you will be able to

identify the two ways of capitalizing income;

compare and contrast direct capitalization and yield capitalization;

develop a capitalization rate;

develop a cap rate using the band of investment method;

explain the relationship between cap rate and risk;

compute the value of a property using the building, land, and property residual techniques;

explain the effects of the annuity and straight-line methods of recapture on income; and

find the present worth of a property using the annuity method of capitalization.

KEY TERMS

annuity
annuity method
band of investment method
building residual technique
capitalization rate
capital recapture
direct capitalization
discount rate
effective gross income
equity capitalization rate
estimated remaining economic life
interest rate
land residual technique
mortgage constant
net operating income
potential gross income
pretax cash flow
recapture rate
remaining economic life
six functions of a dollar
straight-line method of recapture
yield capitalization

OVERVIEW

As discussed in Unit 13, the income capitalization approach is most useful for investment properties—those that are purchased strictly for their ability to produce income. These typically include commercial properties such as retail stores and office buildings. An income-based property appraisal can be made considering

- the return a property is capable of producing in a single stabilized year, using a method called *direct capitalization*, or
- the present value of the anticipated future income stream that can be expected from the property over a period of years, using a method called *yield capitalization*.

Using direct capitalization, the appraiser analyzes the market value of an income-producing property from the perspective of a new investor. The appraiser next studies the relationship between sales prices and income levels of comparable properties to derive a capitalization rate. That rate is then applied to the subject property's annual operating income, based on the income that can be expected during the first stabilized year of ownership. The resulting figure is a determination of the market value warranted by the stated level of income, assuming the same return received by comparable properties.

Using yield capitalization, the appraiser estimates the income that the property may be expected to produce in the future and then estimates the present worth of the right to receive that income. The appraiser develops a capitalization rate based on the typical investor's required return and applies that rate to the present value of the income stream to derive market value.

If there are adequate data on comparable sales with similar income expectations, direct capitalization can produce a very reliable value conclusion. If information on comparable sales is lacking, yield capitalization may provide a more reliable value opinion because an appropriate yield rate can be selected by determining what rate of return investors are requiring on investments of comparable risk.

DIRECT CAPITALIZATION

The capitalization rate can be developed by evaluating net income figures and sales prices of comparable properties. This process is called direct capitalization.

The **direct capitalization** formula is

$$\frac{\text{Net operating income}}{\text{Capitalization rate}} = \text{Value}$$

For example, if a property produces an income of $20,000 per year, with a cap rate of 10%, its value is $200,000.

The four categories of data needed for an appraisal by the income approach using direct capitalization are as follows:

- **Potential gross income** from the property, which includes the annual income from all sources
- Amount of expected annual **effective gross income** from the property, estimated by subtracting anticipated vacancy and collection losses from potential gross income
- **Net operating income**, found by deducting normal annual operating and other expenses from the effective gross income
- **Capitalization rate** for the property—that is, the rate that can be applied to the property's net annual income, the result being the appraiser's opinion of the property's value

CAPITALIZATION RATE

The average investor will expect an income-producing property to provide both a return on the investment (profit on the amount invested) and a return of the investment (the amount invested). The real estate investment shares the same basic rationale as any investment. The first investment most people make is to deposit cash into a bank account. The depositor expects to earn a certain rate of interest on the funds deposited, which can be withdrawn or left in the account to accumulate additional interest. The depositor also expects to be able to withdraw the principal, the original amount invested. These are the same types of considerations that guide investments in real estate.

The rate of return that the investor in real estate receives is called the **capitalization rate** or overall capitalization rate, which can be expressed as a relationship between the annual net operating income a property produces and its value. In equation form, it can be expressed as follows:

$$\frac{\text{Net operating income}}{\text{Value}} = \text{Capitalization rate} \quad \text{or} \quad \frac{I}{V} = R$$

IN PRACTICE

An investor paid $500,000 for a building that earns a net income of $50,000 per year. What is the capitalization rate of the investment?

Using the formula $\frac{I}{V} = R$, the capitalization rate is $\frac{\$50,000}{\$500,000}$ or 10%.

The formula for the capitalization rate is particularly useful for appraisal purposes because of its two corollaries:

Capitalization rate × Value = Net operating income, or R × V = I

$$\frac{\text{Net operating income}}{\text{Capitalization rate}} = \text{Value or } \frac{I}{R} = V$$

By dividing the estimated net operating income (NOI) of a property by the appropriate capitalization (cap) rate, the property's value may be determined.

There are several ways an appraiser can find a property's capitalization rate. The appraiser can study comparable properties that have recently sold and assume that the capitalization rate of a comparable property would be approximately the same as that of the subject property. For example, if a comparable property that sold recently for $200,000 produces an income of $10,000 per year, it has a capitalization rate of 0.05, or 5%, using the formula I/V = R, and dividing $10,000 by $200,000. To find the value of the subject property, the income that the appraiser estimates the subject property will produce is divided by the cap rate of 0.05%. In this case, using the formula I/R = V, the subject property's income of $12,000 is divided by 0.05% to derive a value opinion of $240,000.

Or the appraiser can analyze the component parts of a capitalization rate and construct a rate for the subject property. Both methods of direct capitalization are discussed in this unit.

In Unit 13, we saw that the appraiser must analyze income and operating expense data to accurately estimate a property's potential gross income and compute its NOI. Using these two types of data, the appraiser compiles information from even more sources to arrive at the property's capitalization rate.

IN PRACTICE

An appraiser has determined that the annual NOI of the subject property is $130,000. By screening the market data the appraiser has compiled, a comparable property is located with an NOI of $128,000 a year that sold recently for $1,820,000. Using information on this comparable property only, what is the capitalization rate of the subject property?

The overall capitalization rate of the comparable property is

$$\frac{I}{V} = \frac{\$128,000}{\$1,820,000} = 7\%$$

The NOI for the subject property is $130,000, so its value is

$$\frac{I}{R} = \frac{\$130{,}000}{0.07} = \$1{,}857{,}000$$

Of course, the appraisal would be more reliable if additional comparable properties were studied to find the most appropriate capitalization rate for the subject.

By definition, comparable properties should have comparable capitalization rates. If a property the appraiser thought was comparable turns out to have a capitalization rate significantly higher or lower than that of other comparable properties, the appraiser should consider discarding that sample. Closer examination of the property or sales transaction would probably reveal extenuating circumstances (such as a transaction between related companies) that should have kept the property from consideration as a comparable.

When the income capitalization approach is used, even a slight difference in the assigned capitalization rate will have a substantial effect on the opinion of property value. If a property were assigned a capitalization rate of 9% and its NOI were $180,000, its indicated value would be $180,000 ÷ 0.09, or $2,000,000. If the capitalization rate assigned were 8%, the value opinion would be $180,000 ÷ 0.08, or $2,250,000.

One percentage point difference in the capitalization rate would make a 12½% difference in value. By discarding extremes, the appraiser should have a narrow range of capitalization rates from which the subject property's capitalization rate can be estimated; the appraiser must use judgment in selecting a capitalization rate that is reflective of the most comparable properties.

Exercise 14-1

You are appraising an industrial building with an NOI of $170,000. You have previously appraised or studied the comparable properties listed here. Use all of the information you have on hand to find a suitable capitalization rate for the subject, then the subject's value. Round your answer to the nearest $100.

Property	Selling Price	Net Operating Income	Capitalization Rate
A	$1,360,000	$148,000	
B	940,000	110,000	
C	1,270,000	150,000	
D	1,105,000	126,000	
E	1,500,000	320,000	

Check your answers against those in the answer key at the back of the book.

Building a Capitalization Rate

Another way of determining a capitalization rate for the subject property is by analyzing the capitalization rate's component parts and estimating each of those components for the subject property. The two basic components of the capitalization rate are the recapture rate and the interest rate, which will be discussed next.

As stated previously, an investor who purchases an income-producing property expects two things:

- Return of the investment. This is the right to get back the purchase price at the end of the term of ownership and is ordinarily expressed as an annual rate. Appraisers call this **capital recapture**.
- Return on the investment. This return is the investor's profit on the money used to purchase the property and is expressed as the **interest rate**. The interest rate is also referred to as the **discount rate**, risk rate, or return on rate.

Because land usually does not depreciate, its sales price at the end of the investor's period of ownership is considered adequate compensation. Buildings depreciate, however, and the investor has an asset of continually decreasing value. This anticipated future depreciation is provided for in the recapture part of the capitalization rate.

These two investment objectives can be illustrated by the following example.

IN PRACTICE

The ABC Corporation owns a lot on which it builds an office building for $3 million. The building has an economic life of 20 years. The company expects to receive an annual NOI of 10% from the building during its economic life and also expects to have the building investment repaid over that period of time. To achieve these two objectives, the NOI of the property would have to be as follows:

$3,000,000 × 0.10 = $300,000 interest (return on investment)
$3,000,000 ÷ 20 = $150,000 annual recapture (return of investment)
$300,000 + $150,000 = $450,000 annual NOI

In the previous example, with an NOI of $450,000 and a value of $3 million, the building capitalization rate is I/V or $450,000 ÷ $3,000,000 or 15%. The return on the investment (interest) makes up 10% of the capitalization rate, and the return of the investment (recapture) makes up 5% of the total capitalization rate of 15%.

By analyzing the factors that constitute the interest and recapture rates, the appraiser can determine a property's capitalization rate and use that and the property's net income to find its value. The recapture and interest rates are discussed next.

Selecting the Rate for Capital Recapture

Every good investment provides for a return on the invested capital, called the interest or discount, and a return of the invested capital, called capital recapture. In processing income produced by land only, a recapture provision is usually unnecessary. The assumption (which does not necessarily reflect the reality of the marketplace) is that land will not depreciate, and recapture can therefore be accomplished entirely through resale. A building, however, does depreciate. That is, its value decreases with the passing of time. Therefore, the appraiser must add to the interest rate a percentage that will provide for the recapture of the investment in the building.

Straight-line method of recapture

The simplest, most widely used method of computing the recapture rate is the **straight-line method of recapture.** Under this method, total accrued depreciation is spread over the useful life of a building in equal annual amounts. Thus, when the building is 100% depreciated and presumably economically useless, all of the investment will have been returned to the investor. To find the recapture rate by the straight-line method, divide the total accrued depreciation (100%) by the estimated useful years of life of the building:

$$\frac{100\%}{\text{Years of useful life}} = \text{Annual recapture rate}$$

If, for example, a building has a remaining useful life of 20 years, 5% of the building's value should be returned annually out of NOI:

$$\frac{100\%}{20} = 5\% \text{ recapture rate}$$

The straight-line method of recapture requires a good deal of knowledge about the useful life of a given type of property. As a starting point, the appraiser may refer to tables, contained in various cost manuals, that deal with the useful lives of buildings by type. Then the appraiser must consider the factors unique to the subject property, such as its age, its condition, and the area in which it is located.

A building most frequently becomes useless through external or functional obsolescence, rather than through physical deterioration; that is, more buildings are torn down in still-usable condition than become unusable through deterioration. For this reason, the recapture period is often referred to as **estimated remaining economic life.** An appraiser estimates the remaining economic life of a property after considering the physical, functional, and external factors involved.

Selecting the Interest Rate by the Market Extraction Method

In the market extraction method, the appraiser finds the interest rate of a comparable property by subtracting the portion of the property's NOI attributable to building recapture from total NOI, then dividing the remainder by the selling price of the property.

IN PRACTICE

Property X sold for $200,000. The site is valued at $50,000, and the building has a remaining economic life of 40 years. Total NOI is $30,000.

The building value is $150,000 ($200,000 – $50,000), and the recapture rate is 0.025 (1/n, or 1 ÷ 40 years), so

$150,000 × 0.025 = $3,750

The annual recapture of $3,750 is applied to the entire property value of $200,000 to produce an interest rate of 1.875%.

$3,750 ÷ $200,000 = 0.01875

The net operating income available for building recapture of $3,750 leaves $26,250 ($30,000 – $3,750) as NOI available for the property. Dividing that amount by the property's sales price:

$26,250 ÷ $200,000 = 0.13125

The interest rate for property X is 13.125%, and the overall cap rate for the subject property is .13125 + 0.01875, or 0.15, which is 15%.

Exercise 14-2

Construct an interest rate for a recently sold commercial property with the following known facts: The selling price was $435,000. The site value is $125,000, and the building's estimated remaining economic life is 25 years. Total net operating income is $57,000.

What is the overall cap rate for the property?

Check your answer against the one in the answer key at the back of the book.

Band of Investment Method—Mortgage and Equity Elements

Another method commonly used to calculate an overall capitalization rate is the **band of investment method**, which considers the financial components, or "bands," of debt and equity capital required to support the investment. This method thus takes into account everyone who has a financial interest in the real estate being appraised. Not every investor will be satisfied with the same rate of return on an investment. For example, owners may regard their position as riskier than that of the first or second mortgage holders. Each mortgage creates a lien on the property. If the owner defaults, the property may be sold to pay such liens, and the owner will receive only those proceeds that may remain from the sale of the property after the lienholders have been paid. Because the owner's interest is generally considered inferior to those of lienholders, the owner may require a higher total return on the investment but accept a lower cash flow return, given the value of the owner's residual interest in the property in addition to the owner's subordinated claim on the cash flow.

The band of investment method must take into account both the rate required by the lender and the rate necessary for the equity investor's desired pretax cash flow. The rate required by the lender is called the mortgage constant and is annual debt service expressed as a percentage of the original principal amount. For example, a $100,000, 30-year mortgage loan at 8% has monthly payments of $733.78. Annual debt service is $8,805.36 ($733.78 × 12). The mortgage constant is $8,805.36 divided by $100,000, which is 0.088, or 8.8%.

The rate required by the equity investor, which is the ratio of the investor's expected **pretax cash flow** to the investment's value, is called the **equity capitalization rate**. The equity capitalization rate also may be called the cash on cash rate, cash flow rate, or equity dividend rate.

The overall rate developed by the band of investment method thus is based on (1) the capitalization rate for debt, called the **mortgage constant**, and (2) the rate of return required (yield) on equity, called the equity capitalization rate. For example, assume a case in which a mortgage with a 30-year amortization period covering 80% of the value of the property can be obtained at 8% interest, and the buyer requires a return of 10% on the equity portion (the 20% of the value of the property the buyer will invest). Using the band of investment method, the overall rate could be developed as follows:

	Percent of property's total value	Return required	
Loan	0.80	× 0.088 (mortgage constant)	= 0.07
Equity	0.20	× 0.10 (equity cap rate)	= 0.02
Overall rate			0.09 or 9%

In the previous example, the overall capitalization rate of 9% reflects the rate of return required to attract money into the type of ownership position that results when the interests of all participants are taken into account.

Relationship of Capitalization Rate and Risk

Several generalizations can be made about the relationship between the capitalization rate and the risk of an investment:

High risk = High capitalization rate

Low risk = Low capitalization rate

Because high risk implies a high possibility of investment loss, a property with a high risk will have a lower selling price or value than one with a relatively low risk factor. Each of the preceding generalizations thus can be carried one step farther:

High risk = High capitalization rate = Low value

Low risk = Low capitalization rate = High value

Exercise 14-3

Assuming the following data, what capitalization rate would you use in appraising the subject property?

- A 30-year mortgage covering 75% of property value can be obtained from a bank at 8½%. The mortgage constant is 0.092.
- Equity for this type of property requires a 12% return.

Check your answer against the one in the answer key at the back of the book.

CAPITALIZATION TECHNIQUES USING RESIDUAL INCOME

With the property's net operating income and the investor's desired capitalization rate determined, the appropriate capitalization technique must be selected and applied.

Two techniques by which net operating income (NOI) can be capitalized into value using residual income are (1) the building residual technique and (2) the land residual technique.

In appraising, a residual is the income remaining after all deductions have been made. It may refer to

- the NOI attributable to the building after return on land value has been deducted (building residual technique); or
- the NOI attributable to the land after return on and recapture of the building value have been deducted (land residual technique).

In estimating the value of real estate, each technique will produce approximately the same answer, provided the return (interest rate) and recapture assumptions remain the same for each technique.

Building Residual Technique

To use the **building residual technique**, the appraiser must know the value of the land, usually found by analyzing comparable sales.

First, the appraiser deducts the amount of NOI that must be earned by the land to justify its value. The balance of the NOI must be earned by the building. This building income is then capitalized at the interest rate plus the rate of recapture to arrive at the building's value.

IN PRACTICE

A commercial property is being appraised. The land value has been estimated at $80,000, and the typical rate of return is 12%, so the land itself must earn $9,600 ($80,000 × 0.12) if it is to justify its purchase price. The property should yield a total NOI of $37,000 yearly. The residual income to the building, therefore, is $27,400 ($37,000 – $9,600).

The capitalization rate for the building will be based on the interest rate of 12% (already applied to the land value) and a recapture rate of 5% based on an estimated remaining economic life of 20 years (100% ÷ 20 years = 5% per year). The building capitalization rate, therefore, is 17% (12% + 5%). The estimated building value is $27,400 ÷ 0.17, or $161,200 (rounded to the nearest hundred dollars).

Finally, the value of the building is added to the value of the land to arrive at the total property value, which is $241,200 ($161,200 + $80,000).

The information in this example problem could be itemized as follows:

Estimated land value			$80,000
NOI		$37,000	
Interest on land value ($80,000 × 0.12)		– 9,600	
Residual income to building		$27,400	
Capitalization rate for building			
Interest rate	12%		
Recapture rate	+ 5		
	17%		
Building value ($27,400 ÷ 0.17)			161,200
Total property value			$241,200

The building residual technique is most useful when land values are stable and can be determined easily by recent sales of similar sites. This technique is also used when the construction cost of the building and the amount of accrued depreciation are difficult to measure accurately because of the building's age or unusual design.

Exercise 14-4

The property under appraisal is a 25-year-old apartment building producing an NOI of $50,000 a year.

Compute the value of the property, assuming a remaining economic life of 40 years for the building, a 10½% interest rate, and land value estimated at $100,000.

Check your answer against the one in the answer key at the back of the book.

Land Residual Technique

The **land residual technique** follows the same procedure as the building residual technique—but with the building and land calculations reversed.

IN PRACTICE

Assume that the NOI for a commercial property is $45,000 annually, and the value of the building has been determined at $225,000. The appropriate interest rate for the building is 117/8%, and the estimated recapture rate is 4%. What is the value of the property to the nearest $100?

Assumed building value			$225,000
NOI		$45,000	
Capitalization rate for building			
Interest rate	11.875%		
Recapture rate	4.0		
Total	15.875%		
Interest and recapture on building value ($225,000 × .15875)		– 35,700	
Residual income to land		$ 9,300	
Land value ($9,300 ÷ .11875)			78,300
Total property value			$303,300

In this example, the value of land and building together is $303,300.

The land residual technique is used (1) when the land value cannot be estimated from comparable sales or (2) when the building is new or in its early life and represents the highest and best use of the land. When a building is new, value usually is assumed to be equal to reproduction cost.

Exercise 14-5

A new office building valued at $3 million produces an annual NOI of $530,000. A first mortgage of 60% can be obtained from a bank at 10¼%. This type of property requires a 12% return, and the building's remaining economic life is estimated at 50 years. Estimate the total property value by the land residual technique.

Check your answer against the one in the answer key at the back of the book.

Valuing the Land and Building as a Whole

The land and building are valued as a single unit, rather than as separate units, when the building is very old or when it is difficult to make reliable opinions of either the land or the building value.

The appraiser analyzes sales of comparable properties and develops an NOI for each property. Then, using the formula for the capitalization rate, I / V = R, the appraiser computes a range of overall rates from which a rate appropriate to the subject property can be selected.

IN PRACTICE

A comparable property produces an NOI of $12,000 and was sold for $100,000. By dividing $12,000 by $100,000, an overall rate of 12% is derived, which includes both interest and recapture. Several additional properties comparable to the subject also produce NOIs that, when divided by their selling prices, indicate a yield of approximately 12%, making it reasonable to capitalize the NOI of the subject property at the same overall rate—12%. If the NOI of the subject is $10,000, its value by direct capitalization is $10,000 ÷ 0.12, or approximately $83,000.

Exercise 14-6

You have been asked to appraise an income-producing property in a rural area where it is difficult to substantiate either building or land values. You have obtained the following income and sales price data on comparable properties:

	Net Operating Income	Sales Price
Property 1	$15,000	$115,400
Property 2	20,000	166,700
Property 3	12,500	100,000
Property 4	18,000	140,600
Subject	16,000	

Because all these properties are highly comparable, you feel that an average cap rate will probably be applicable to the subject. What is your estimate of value for the subject property?

Check your answer against the one in the answer key at the back of the book.

YIELD CAPITALIZATION

In the process called **yield capitalization**, real estate investment return is broken down into two components: (1) an income flow for a specified number of years and (2) a capital change (a gain or loss) realized at the end of the multiyear investment period from an actual or assumed sale of the property. Yield capitalization is computed on a cash accounting basis from the investor's perspective.

Yield capitalization is an appropriate technique to use for the investor who intends to buy an income-producing property and wants to know the value of the income stream that can be expected in the future from the property. An investor planning to obtain a mortgage loan to help pay for the property will also want to know how the mortgage payments will affect the property's expected cash flow.

All of these factors can be understood only after the appraiser has made a thorough analysis of the subject property and the degree of risk it carries as an investment. The relative permanence of the investment is considered; that is, the length of the lease term coupled with the reliability of the tenant. The capitalization method chosen by the appraiser depends on the potential stability of the income stream. The examples included here assume a relatively long-term lease and a very reliable tenant.

VALUE OF ONE DOLLAR

In Unit 2, we discussed the six functions of an investment of one dollar. When is a dollar worth more than a dollar? When it will be received at some time in the future. An investor who puts a dollar into an investment today wants to receive more than the dollar back when the investment matures. Sometimes a dollar is worth less than a dollar. An investor may be interested in an investment that pays back x number of dollars at a certain time in the future, based on an initial investment that is some amount less than x dollars. What is the present value of either investment? The answer to that question depends on the length of the investment term, the interest paid, and whether the interest will be compounded during the investment term.

A financial calculator, computer program, or smartphone app can enable an appraiser or real estate professional to perform quickly and accurately the calculations that once required time-consuming application of arduous formulas or skilled consultation of lengthy charts. The best way to use a calculator or specialized program, however, is with an understanding of the basis for the underlying computations.

The chart in Figure 14.1 is itself a shortcut method that shows the final figures derived from application of the formulas required to determine the value of $1 to an investor under different circumstances at an interest rate of 10% over an annual term from 1 to 50 years. The **six functions of a dollar**, as shown in columns one through six, are:

1. *Future value of $1*. This column indicates the value of $1 one year from now if the dollar accumulates 10% interest. An investment of $1 at 10% interest per year will yield $1.10 at the end of one year.
2. *Future value of an annuity of $1 per year*. This column shows the total amount contributed to an annuity if a total of $1 is contributed every year and every year the cumulative total contributed earns 10% interest. At the end of year one, the total contributed is $1. At the end of year two, the total contributed is $1 for the first year, plus interest of $0.10 on that dollar over the second year, plus $1 for the second year, for a total of $1 + $0.10 + $1, or $2.10.
3. *Sinking fund factor*. This column shows the amount that must be invested each year of the stated term at 10% interest to accumulate $1. If an investor wants to accumulate $1,000,000 at the end of five years, $163,797 must be invested every year at 10% interest.
4. *Present value of a $1 reversion*. This column shows the amount that must be invested at 10% interest now in order to return $1 at the end of the stated number of years (the reversionary interest). To receive a return of $1,000,000 at the end of five years, an investment of $620,921 must be made at the beginning of the five-year term, provided interest accumulates at the rate of 10% per year.

5. *Present value of an annuity of $1 per year.* This column shows the present value of the right to receive an annuity of $1 per year for the stated period. An investor who wants to be paid $10,000 every year for 10 years from an annuity must contribute $61,445.67 at the start of the annuity period, provided the amount invested accumulates 10% interest per year.
6. *Payment to amortize $1.* This column indicates the payment amount needed to pay off a loan of $1 for the stated number of years. If $100,000 is borrowed for 15 years, the yearly payment (including both principal and interest) needed to pay the loan off in full in 15 years is $13,147.40.

When is a dollar worth more than a dollar? When it is loaned, borrowed, or spent on income-producing property. Some of the values of a dollar discussed previously will be referred to in the remaining sections of this unit. We will make use of the factors shown in Figure 14.1 and also demonstrate how basic computations are carried out on a financial calculator.

FIGURE 14.1
Six Functions of a Dollar

10.00% Annual Interest Rate							
Years	1 Future Value of $1	2 Future Value Annuity of $1 per Year	3 Sinking Fund Factor	4 Present Value of $1 (Reversion)	5 Present Value Annuity of $1 per Year	6 Payment to Amortize $1	Years
1	1.100000	1.000000	1.000000	0.909091	0.909091	1.100000	1
2	1.210000	2.100000	0.476190	0.826446	1.735537	0.576190	2
3	1.331000	3.310000	0.302115	0.751315	2.486852	0.402115	3
4	1.464100	4.641000	0.215471	0.683013	3.169865	0.315471	4
5	1.610510	6.105100	0.163797	0.620921	3.790787	0.263797	5
6	1.771561	7.715610	0.129607	0.564474	4.355261	0.229607	6
7	1.948717	9.487171	0.105405	0.513158	4.868419	0.205405	7
8	2.143589	11.435888	0.087444	0.466507	5.334926	0.187444	8
9	2.357948	13.579477	0.073641	0.424098	5.759024	0.173641	9
10	2.593742	15.937425	0.062745	0.385543	6.144567	0.162745	10
11	2.853117	18.531167	0.053963	0.350494	6.495061	0.153963	11
12	3.138428	21.384284	0.046763	0.318631	6.813692	0.146763	12
13	3.452271	24.522712	0.040779	0.289664	7.103356	0.140779	13
14	3.797498	27.974983	0.035746	0.263331	7.366687	0.135746	14
15	4.177248	31.772482	0.031474	0.239392	7.606080	0.131474	15
16	4.594973	35.949730	0.027817	0.217629	7.823709	0.127817	16
17	5.054470	40.544703	0.024664	0.197845	8.021553	0.124664	17
18	5.559917	45.599173	0.021930	0.179859	8.201412	0.121930	18
19	6.115909	51.159090	0.019547	0.163508	8.364920	0.119547	19
20	6.727500	57.274999	0.017460	0.148644	8.513564	0.117460	20

Source: Jeffrey D. Fisher and Robert S. Martin, Income Property Appraisal, 2nd Edition (Chicago: Dearborn™ Real Estate Education, 2005).

FIGURE 14.1
Six Functions of a Dollar (continued)

10.00% Annual Interest Rate							
Years	1 Future Value of $1	2 Future Value Annuity of $1 per Year	3 Sinking Fund Factor	4 Present Value of $1 (Reversion)	5 Present Value Annuity of $1 per Year	6 Payment to Amortize $1	Years
21	7.400250	64.002499	0.015624	0.135131	8.648694	0.115624	21
22	8.140275	71.402749	0.014005	0.122846	8.771540	0.114005	22
23	8.954302	79.543024	0.012572	0.111678	8.883218	0.112572	23
24	9.849733	88.497327	0.011300	0.101526	8.984744	0.111300	24
25	10.834706	98.347059	0.010168	0.092296	9.077040	0.110168	25
26	11.918177	109.181765	0.009159	0.083905	9.160945	0.109159	26
27	13.109994	121.099942	0.008258	0.076278	9.237223	0.108258	27
28	14.420994	134.209936	0.007451	0.069343	9.306567	0.107451	28
29	15.863093	148.630930	0.006728	0.063039	9.369606	0.106728	29
30	17.449402	164.494023	0.006079	0.057309	9.426914	0.106079	30
31	19.194342	181.943425	0.005496	0.052099	9.479013	0.105496	31
32	21.113777	201.137767	0.004972	0.047362	9.526376	0.104972	32
33	23.225154	222.251544	0.004499	0.043057	9.569432	0.104499	33
34	25.547670	245.476699	0.004074	0.039143	9.608575	0.104074	34
35	28.102437	271.024368	0.003690	0.035584	9.644159	0.103690	35
36	30.912681	299.126805	0.003343	0.032349	9.676508	0.103343	36
37	34.003949	330.039486	0.003030	0.029408	9.705917	0.103030	37
38	37.404343	364.043434	0.002747	0.026735	9.732651	0.102747	38
39	41.144778	401.447778	0.002491	0.024304	9.756956	0.102491	39
40	45.259256	442.592556	0.002259	0.022095	9.779051	0.102259	40
41	49.785181	487.851811	0.002050	0.020086	9.799137	0.102050	41
42	54.763699	537.636992	0.001860	0.018260	9.817397	0.101860	42
43	60.240069	592.400692	0.001688	0.016600	9.833998	0.101688	43
44	66.264076	652.640761	0.001532	0.015091	9.849089	0.101532	44
45	72.890484	718.904837	0.001391	0.013719	9.862808	0.101391	45
46	80.179532	791.795321	0.001263	0.012472	9.875280	0.101263	46
47	88.197485	871.974853	0.001147	0.011338	9.886618	0.101147	47
48	97.017234	960.172338	0.001041	0.010307	9.896926	0.101041	48
49	106.718957	1057.189572	0.000946	0.009370	9.906296	0.100946	49
50	117.390853	1163.908529	0.000859	0.008519	9.914814	0.100859	50

Source: Jeffrey D. Fisher and Robert S. Martin, Income Property Appraisal, 2nd Edition (Chicago: Dearborn™ Real Estate Education, 2005).

■ ANNUITY METHOD OF CAPITALIZATION

An **annuity** is a fixed yearly return on an investment. It may be for any number of years, if the investment is high enough to provide the return desired. The return also may be paid weekly, monthly, or quarterly, rather than yearly.

An investor who wants a return of $1,100 on a one-year investment that pays 10% interest has to invest $1,000. The $1,000 will be returned to the investor at the end of the year, along with interest of $100 ($1,000 × 10%), making a total of $1,100. A total return of $1,000 at 10% interest for one year requires an investment of $909. The investor will receive interest income of $91. In effect, the investor is paying $909 for the right to receive income of $91 and have the amount of original investment returned.

As shown previously, the mathematics of computing investment amounts for one year is simple. The total return is 100% of the original investment plus the interest for the time period involved (in the preceding example, 10%); thus, the total return is 110% of the original investment. Most income properties, however, are expected to yield income for more than one year. Before the advent of financial calculators, tables of factors based on different interest rates over different periods of time could be consulted to find the factor applicable to the desired investment term and rate of return. This meant that the person performing the calculation had to have access to a book of factor tables.

IN PRACTICE

An investor wishes to receive an annual income of $6,000 for four years by making an investment earning 10%. What should be the amount of the original investment?

Using the annuity method. Column 5 in Figure 14.1 indicates that the annuity factor for an interest rate of 10% over an investment period of four years is 3.169865, which we will round to 3.17. Multiplied by the annual income sought ($6,000 × 3.17), an initial investment figure of $19,020 is derived. In other words, a $19,020 investment for four years at 10% interest will yield yearly income of $6,000. At the end of the four years, the entire amount invested, plus all interest earned, will have been returned to the investor.

Using a financial calculator. HP 12 C keystrokes and results displayed are:

f Cl x	clears the memory
6000 pmt	6,000.00
4 n	4.00
10 n	10.00
PV	–19,019.19

The answer is stated as a negative because it is the amount that must be invested, making it a cash outflow. Note also that the answer provided by the calculator differs from that generated by using an annuity factor; because the HP 12C carries the problem out to 30 decimal places, it provides a more accurate answer.

To learn how to use a financial calculator, consult the manual provided by the manufacturer. Courses are also available to provide an introduction or refresher in the use of a specific device.

As stated earlier, annuity table factors may not be appropriate for every investment in real estate. The investment should be a stable one. The sound financial status of the tenant and a long-term lease should indicate a reliable income stream. In addition, the number of years that the investment will be expected to yield income should be based on the remaining economic life of the property, which may or may not coincide with the length of the lease term or projected holding period.

With the proper data available, use of a financial calculator can eliminate the need to have access to financial tables and provide less opportunity for error. While a financial calculator requires training and practice to use it efficiently and accurately, the results achieved can make the time and effort worthwhile.

Building Residual Technique

Ideally, the income stream over the remaining economic life of the property will be ensured by a lease signed by a reliable client. In such a case, if land value can be estimated, the total property value can be found by using the building residual technique.

IN PRACTICE

An appraiser is analyzing the current market value of an investment property with a land value of $100,000 (estimated by analyzing comparable sales). The retail store on the land is being leased by a major supermarket chain, which has been financially successful for 20 years and should remain so. The lease, as of the date of appraisal, will run for another 23 years. The yield rate on land and building has been calculated at 13%. The property provides an annual net operating income (NOI) of $36,000. What is its current market value?

The interest on the land value of $100,000 is $13,000 ($100,000 × 13%). When $13,000 is subtracted from the total annual NOI of $36,000, a net income residual of $23,000 ($36,000 – $13,000) may be used to derive the building value.

Using the annuity method. An annuity table indicates a factor of 7.230 for a 13% interest rate over 23 years. The building value is the building income multiplied by the annuity factor, or

$23,000 × 7.230 = $166,290

The value of the building is $166,290. The total property value is $166,290 plus the land value of $100,000, or $266,290. The appraiser records the following information:

Indicated land value		$100,000
Annual NOI before recapture of building	$36,000	
Interest on indicated land value		
(@ 13% per year on $100,000)	13,000	
Annual residual income to building	$23,000	
Annuity factor (7.230, based on 13% interest over 23 years)		
Building value ($23,000 × 7.230)		166,290
Total property value		266,290
Rounded to		$266,000

Using a financial calculator. HP 12 C keystrokes and results displayed are:

f Cl x	clears the memory
100,000 enter	100,000.00
.13 enter x	13,000.00
36000 enter	36,000.00
13,000	13,000
–	23,000.00
23000 PMT	23,000.00
23 n	23.00
13 i	13.00
PV	–166,282.13
–166,282.13 CHS	166,282.13
100,000	266,282.13

The answer provided by the calculator is slightly different from the answer generated by using the annuity factor but is more accurate because the calculations were carried out to more decimal places.

Exercise 14-7

Use the building residual technique to estimate the value of a property that produces an NOI before recapture of $26,400 per year. The land is valued at $75,000, and the interest rate on land and building is calculated at 11% per year, indicating an annuity factor of 8.694. The current tenant has 30 years remaining on the lease.

Check your answer against the one in the answer key at the back of the book.

Land Residual Technique

If building value can be estimated, the total property value can be found by using the land residual technique. Using the facts in the preceding example, value is figured as follows:

Indicated building value		$166,000 (rounded)
Annual NOI	$36,000	
Interest on indicated building value		
(@ 13% per year on $166,000)	21,000 (rounded)	
Annual residual income to land	$14,400	
Annuity factor (7.230)		
Land value ($14,000 × 7.230)		104,112
Total property value		270,112
Rounded to		$270,100

Exercise 14-8

Use the land residual technique and the annuity table to estimate the value of a property that produces an NOI of $50,000 per year. The building is valued at $300,000, interest rate on land and building is 10% annually, the applicable annuity factor is 9.077, and the current tenant has 25 years remaining on the lease.

Check your answer against the one in the answer key at the back of the book.

Valuing the Property as a Whole

If the property used to explain the building residual technique in the preceding example were to be treated as a whole (both land and building), the present worth of the property, with an income stream of $36,000 and an annuity factor of 7.230, would be estimated at $260,280:

Total annual NOI	$ 36,000
Annuity factor (23 years @ 13%)	× 7.230
Present worth of NOI	$260,280

Using the HP 12 C:

f CI x	clears the memory
36000 PMT	36,000.00
13 i	13.00
23 n	23.00
PV	–260,267.68

At the end of the income stream of 23 years, however, the land will revert back to the owner. That is, although the building will have reached the end of its economic life, the land will still be valuable. The future, or reversionary, value of the land may be quite difficult to predict. The reversionary value of the land may be assumed by the appraiser to be the same as its present value, based on the appraiser's judgment of the future market value of the property.

The present worth of the whole property will be what the investor is willing to pay for the specified income stream, plus the right to the reversionary value of the land at the end of the income-producing period.

The amount that the investor should pay for the land's future value can be computed by applying a reversion factor to the land's present estimated value.

In the preceding example problem, for an investment valued at 13% interest for 23 years, we can apply a reversion factor of .060. Because the present (and assumed future) value of the land was estimated at $100,000, the value of the reversion at the end of 23 years is, thus, $6,000 ($100,000 × 0.060). When the present worth of the reversion ($6,000) is added to the present worth of the net income stream ($260,280), the resulting property value is $266,280. This value is almost exactly that reached by the building residual technique. The slight discrepancy results from rounding off the annuity and reversion factors. Even this small discrepancy would be reduced if the factors were carried out to more decimal places.

Using a financial calculator helps reduce the discrepancy even further. With the HP 12 C:

f Cl x	clears the memory
100000 FV	100,000.00
13 i	13.00
23 n	23.00
FV	-6,014.45
CHS	6,014.45
260,267.68	266,282.13

Exercise 14-9

Using the annuity and reversion factors provided, estimate the value of the following property.

The property is a two-acre site with an industrial warehouse leased to a major auto parts manufacturer at an annual rental of $30,000, which is also the NOI. The lease term will expire in 25 years, which is the estimated remaining economic life of the building. The value of the site in 25 years is expected to be $75,000 per acre. The investment should yield an income stream at 12% interest. The applicable annuity factor is 7.843 and the reversion factor based on these facts is 0.059.

Check your answer against the one in the answer key at the back of the book.

Recapture Rate

The **recapture rate** is a periodic allowance for the recovery of investment capital from the property's income stream. In other words, part of the income produced is attributed to the original investment. The land value is treated as remaining the same over the term of the investment, so it is not recaptured. Because structures on the property are considered wasting (depreciating) assets, their value is recaptured.

The calculations involved in computing a recapture rate using the annuity method do not assume a static (unchanging from year to year) recapture rate. Slow changes in building value are assumed in the early years of the investment term, with greater changes in the last years of the investment. In the straight-line method of recapture, however, the same recapture rate is assumed for each year of the investment. The annuity method thus allows for a slower decrease in building value over the early years of a building's life, providing a higher value in later years. The straight-line method applies an equal decrease in value to be recaptured for every year of the building's economic life.

■ SUMMARY

Capitalization is the relationship between income and market value. Generally speaking, income capitalization is the most important approach used in valuing income-producing property and is the one appraisers normally rely on most heavily in the final value conclusion. The reliability of this approach is directly related to the quality of the data used and the proper application of income capitalization techniques.

The two ways of capitalizing income are direct capitalization and yield capitalization. Direct capitalization is the simplest mathematical process to apply, and when the rate used is supported adequately by comparable sales in the market, it is a most convincing method for estimating value.

The process of developing a capitalization rate by comparing net income figures and sales prices of comparable properties is one of the techniques of direct capitalization. A capitalization rate can also be developed by breaking down the rate's component parts and estimating each separately. The rate developed will be composed of recapture rate (return of investment) and interest rate (return on investment). The recapture rate is often derived by using the straight-line method. The interest rate is developed by using the market extraction method.

The band of investment method takes into account both the rate required by the lender (called the mortgage constant) and the rate necessary for the equity investor's desired pretax cash flow (called the equity capitalization rate). An investment with a high degree of risk will have a corresponding high capitalization rate, resulting in a low property value. A low-risk investment will have a corresponding low capitalization rate and high value.

NOI can be capitalized into value by using the building residual or land residual techniques, or by valuing the property as a whole.

Using yield capitalization, investment property value is considered the present worth of the right to receive a fixed return of both the amount invested and the interest on that amount. Yield capitalization uses discount rates to find the present value of projected future income. The discount rate used in yield capitalization should be the rate of return that typical investors in the marketplace would expect to earn on comparable properties of similar risk.

Use of a financial calculator can alleviate the need for the appraiser to consult a table of lengthy factors and help produce the necessary calculations more efficiently and more accurately.

■ Review Questions

1. In income property investments,
   a. Low risk = Low cap rate = High value.
   b. Low risk = Low cap rate = Low value.
   c. Low risk = High cap rate = Low value.
   d. Low risk = High cap rate = High value.

2. All other factors being equal, as the location of an income property becomes less desirable, the cap rate used will be
   a. lower.
   b. higher.
   c. less reliable.
   d. unaffected.

3. Recapture generally applies to
   a. wasting assets, such as buildings.
   b. nonwasting assets, such as land.
   c. both of these.
   d. neither of these.

4. In the land residual technique, the appraiser starts with an assumption of
   a. replacement cost.
   b. building value.
   c. net capitalization.
   d. land value.

5. In the building residual technique, the appraiser starts with an assumption of
   a. replacement cost.
   b. building value.
   c. net capitalization.
   d. land value.

6. The cash on cash rate is the same as
   a. the yield capitalization rate.
   b. the equity dividend rate.
   c. the overall capitalization rate.
   d. the breakeven point.

7. Name the two component rates that are inherent in every capitalization rate.

8. Under which method are the recapture installments lowest in the earlier years?
   a. Annuity
   b. Straight-line

9. Under which method are the installments highest?
   a. Annuity
   b. Straight-line

10. An overall capitalization rate that considers the financial components of debt and equity capital required to support an investment is
    a. the market extraction method.
    b. the building residual technique.
    c. the band of investment method.
    d. the land residual technique.

11. A fixed yearly return on an investment is called
    a. a reversion.
    b. capital recapture.
    c. an annuity.
    d. the cap rate.

12. Using the following data, compute value by (a) the building residual technique and (b) the land residual technique. Round your figures to the nearest $1,000.
    a. The net operating income is $400,000.
    b. The land value is $500,000.
    c. Sixty-five percent of the value of the property can be borrowed at 11%, and equity capital for this type of investment requires a 12% return.
    d. The building's remaining economic life is 25 years.

13. In this case problem, you will determine the market value of a property by the income capitalization approach. Round all figures to the nearest $1.

    You have been asked to appraise a one-story commercial building located in a small neighborhood shopping center. The building is about 20 years old and is divided into four separate stores, all of equal size. Each store pays a yearly rental of $10,200, which is well in line with comparable properties analyzed.

    The owner of the subject property lists the following items of expense for the previous year:

    - Real estate taxes—$4,000
    - Insurance—three-year policy—$3,000
    - Repairs and maintenance—$2,800
    - Mortgage payments—$8,400
    - Legal and accounting fees—$550
    - Miscellaneous expenses—$500

    In addition to the expense listing, you obtain the following information:

    - Tenants pay for their own water, heating, electricity, and garbage removal.
    - Repairs and general maintenance should be based on 12% of effective gross income.
    - Miscellaneous expenses should be increased to 2% of potential gross income.

The records of property managers indicate that vacancy and collection losses in the area run about 4%.

A new roof, costing $2,000 and having an average life of 20 years, was installed last year.

The gas furnace in each store can be replaced for $950 and will carry a ten-year guarantee.

Recent land sales in the area indicate that the land value of the subject property should be estimated at $55,000.

You have determined from banks in the area that 75% of the value of the property can be borrowed at 11% interest, and equity money for this type of investment requires a 13% return.

The building is 20 years old and appears to have depreciated about one-third.

a. On the basis of the information provided, reconstruct the operating statement.
b. Determine the appropriate capitalization rate.
c. Estimate the total property value.

14. You are appraising a commercial building earning an annual NOI before recapture of $50,000. Based on supportable information, the interest rate has been established at 15%. Land value has been estimated at $100,000, and the building's remaining economic life at 25 years.

    Determine the estimated value of the property in each of the following cases.

    a. The property has year-to-year tenants of average credit risk.
    b. The property is leased for the entire 25 years to a national concern with an excellent credit rating.

15. As the risk of an investment rises, the cap rate
    a. rises.
    b. stays the same.
    c. lowers.
    d. cannot be determined.

16. As the risk of an investment is reduced, the cap rate
    a. rises.
    b. stays the same.
    c. lowers.
    d. cannot be determined.

17. As the risk of an investment rises, the value of the property
    a. rises.
    b. stays the same.
    c. lowers.
    d. cannot be determined.

18. As the risk of an investment is lowered, the value of the property
    a. rises.
    b. stays the same.
    c. lowers.
    d. cannot be determined.

19. Use of a financial calculator is preferable to use of financial tables because
    a. a financial calculator is less cumbersome to carry than a book of financial tables.
    b. the result produced by using a financial calculator will be more accurate than the result produced by consulting a financial table.
    c. a financial calculator can handle a broader range of factors than it is possible to find in a list of factors.
    d. all of these.

20. Yield capitalization makes use of discount rates to find
    a. the present value of the indicated income stream.
    b. the present value of proven past income.
    c. the future value of projected future income.
    d. the present value of projected future income.

Check your answers against those in the answer key at the back of the book.

15

UNIT FIFTEEN

RECONCILIATION AND THE APPRAISAL REPORT

LEARNING OBJECTIVES

When you have completed this unit, you will be able to

- define the process of reconciliation;
- review each appraisal approach considering the value sought and subject property;
- analyze data collected for each of the approaches used to reach a final opinion of value;
- describe the two types of appraisal reports permitted by *USPAP*;
- explain the uses of the form appraisal report and the narrative appraisal report;
- state the purpose of Fannie Mae Form 2075; and
- work through an appraisal using the URAR form.

KEY TERMS

appraisal report
correlation
form report
Form 2075
narrative report
reconciliation
restricted report

■ OVERVIEW

The last step in the appraisal process, before the final report is prepared, is the reconciliation of the values indicated by each of the three appraisal approaches. In the cost approach, the cost of reproducing or replacing the structure less depreciation plus site value was calculated. In the income capitalization approach, value was based on income the property should be capable of earning. In the sales comparison approach, the analysis of comparable sales produced adjusted sales prices that were used to derive an opinion of value for the subject property.

The value opinions reached by using the different approaches rarely will be exactly the same. Even if the appraiser had all the relevant data and had carried out the steps in each approach without error, each value indication, in almost every case, would be different. In the reconciliation process (also called correlation), the validity of the methods and the result of each approach are weighed objectively to arrive at the single best and most supportable conclusion of value. Almost all appraisal clients want a single opinion of value and won't accept a value range.

After the value opinions reached by the different approaches to value are reconciled or correlated, the resulting final opinion of value is presented by the appraiser to the client in as much detail as requested by the client. Although the appraiser must always fully document the research and reasoning leading to the conclusion of value, all of that background information may not be presented in the report to the client.

In this unit, you will learn what the process of reconciliation is and how it is accomplished. In addition, you will learn the types of appraisal reports that may be used.

■ DEFINITION OF RECONCILIATION

In theory, all the values derived using the three major approaches should be exactly the same; that is, if the appraiser had all of the relevant data and had carried out the steps in each approach without error, each value indication should be the same. In actual practice, this seldom happens. In fact, if an appraiser reaches the same value indication for all three approaches, the credibility of the appraisal report could be seriously questioned. In almost every case, the application of the three approaches naturally results in three different indications of value.

The Process of Reconciliation

Many appraisers believe that all three approaches to value should be used in every appraisal assignment—if the appropriate kinds of data are available. Other appraisers feel that only one or two of the approaches are really necessary in typical assignments. For instance, it may be argued that the income capitalization approach does not lend itself to valuing single-family residences, because such properties are not typically bought for their income-producing capacities. The sales comparison approach would not be appropriate in valuing a special-purpose property, such as a public library or museum, because no useful comparable sales information would be available. The cost approach cannot be used to value vacant land. In reaching a decision about which approach or approaches to use, the appraiser must first understand the nature of the property and the objective of the assignment.

In the process of **reconciliation**, or **correlation**, the appraiser reviews his or her work and considers at least the following four factors:

- Definition of value sought
- Amount and reliability of the data collected in each approach
- Inherent strengths and weaknesses of each approach
- Relevance of each approach to the subject property and market behavior

The process of reconciliation is not a simple averaging of the differing value opinions. After the factors listed are considered, the most relevant approach—cost, sales comparison, or income—receives the greatest weight when determining the value opinion that most accurately reflects the value sought. In addition, each approach serves as a check against the others.

Exercise 15-1

Why is it unlikely that application of the three approaches to the same property will result in identical opinions of value?

Check your answer against the one in the answer key at the back of the book.

Review of the Three Approaches

To begin the reconciliation process, the appraiser reviews the steps followed in each approach to substantiate the accuracy and consistency of all data and the logic leading to the value opinion.

In reviewing the sales comparison approach, the appraiser should check:

- that properties selected as comparables are sufficiently similar to the subject property,
- amount and reliability of sales data,
- factors used in comparison,
- logic of the adjustments made between comparable sale properties and the subject property,
- soundness of the value derived from the adjusted sales prices of comparable properties, and
- mathematical accuracy of the adjustment computations.

A check of all mathematical calculations is an important part of the review process because errors can lead to incorrect value indications and can destroy the credibility of the entire appraisal.

In reviewing the cost approach, the appraiser should check:

- that sites used as comparables are, in fact, similar to the subject site;
- amount and reliability of the comparable sales data collected;

- appropriateness of the factors used in comparison;
- logic of the adjustments made between comparable sales sites and the subject site;
- soundness of the value derived from the adjusted sales prices of comparable sites;
- mathematical accuracy of the adjustment computations;
- appropriateness of the method of estimating reproduction or replacement cost;
- appropriateness of the unit cost factor;
- accuracy of the reproduction or replacement cost computations;
- market values assigned to accrued depreciation charges; and
- for double-counting and/or omissions in making accrued depreciation charges.

In reviewing the income capitalization approach, the appraiser should check the logic and mathematical accuracy of the:

- market rents;
- potential gross income estimate;
- allowance for vacancy and collection losses;
- operating expense estimate, including reserves for replacement;
- net income estimate;
- estimate of remaining economic life; and
- capitalization rate and method of capitalizing.

In reviewing the gross rent multiplier method, the appraiser should check:

- that properties analyzed are comparable to the subject property and to one another in terms of locational, physical, and investment characteristics;
- that adequate rental data are available;
- that comparable sales were drawn from properties that were rented at the time of sale;
- that the gross rent multiplier for the subject property was derived from current sales and current rental incomes; and
- the mathematical accuracy of all computations.

Weighing the Choices

Once assured of the validity of the indicated values, the appraiser then must decide which is the most reliable, in terms of the value sought, for the subject property. Inherent factors may make a particular method automatically more significant for certain kinds of property (such as the income approach for investment properties or the cost approach for special purpose properties). But other factors, of which the appraiser should be aware, may negate part of that significance. An economically depressed neighborhood, for instance, may make any structure virtually worthless. If the appraiser is trying to arrive at an opinion of market value, and if the market for property in a certain neighborhood is likely to be extremely small, this fact should be reflected in the appraiser's final opinion of value.

IN PRACTICE

An appraiser forming an opinion of the market value of a home in a neighborhood composed predominantly of owner-occupied, single-family houses arrived at the following initial figures:

Sales comparison approach	$422,500
Cost approach	431,500
Income capitalization approach	426,800

Based on these indications of value, the range is from $422,500 to $431,500, a difference of $9,000 between the lowest indication of value and the highest. This relatively narrow range suggests that the information gathered and analyzed is both a reasonable and a reliable representation of the market.

After value indications are reached by each of the three approaches, the appraiser produces a single opinion of value based on the approach(es) supported by the most convincing factual evidence. This figure may be the same as one of the values produced by the three approaches, or it may differ from all of them but still fall somewhere within the value range. The appraiser should have no reservations about reaching a final determination of value at either end of the range, provided his or her opinion is supported by market facts and persuasive analysis.

When reviewing the data collected for the sales comparison approach and the results drawn, the appraiser realized that an opinion of value based on this information should be very reliable. Other houses in the same general condition, and with the same types of improvements, were selling from $416,000 to $430,000. Because all comparable sales used in the analysis required few adjustments, considerable weight was given to the sales comparison approach, as normally would be expected. After allowing for specific differences, an indicated value of $422,500 was determined for the subject property by applying the sales comparison approach.

Next, the appraiser analyzed the information collected and the result obtained using the cost approach. The cost approach tends to set an upper limit of value when the property is new, without functional or external obsolescence, and at its highest and best use. The older a structure becomes, however, the more difficult it is to accurately estimate the proper amount of accrued depreciation. The fact that the subject house is relatively new, only a few years old, strengthens the $431,500 opinion of value by the cost approach.

Finally, the appraiser considered the market value derived from the income approach. This approach seemed to be the least valid for this particular property, because few houses in the subject neighborhood are rentals and even fewer rental homes have been sold currently, making it difficult to establish a reasonably accurate GRM. The property's current income indicates a market value of $426,800.

As stated previously, the final opinion of value is not an average but an opinion the appraiser makes based on the type of property being appraised, the results of the research compiled, and the valuation techniques used. In this case, the appraiser placed the most weight on the sales comparison approach. The appraiser's final opinion of market value for the subject property was $422,500.

Exercise 15-2

You are appraising a residential duplex in a well-maintained community. One unit of the property will be owner occupied and the other unit rented, as in the past. There are many similar properties in the neighborhood, most owner occupied with one unit used as a rental. Rents have increased slowly but consistently over the years, and there are no indications of any change in demand. No buildable lots are available in the area.

Your estimate of value by the sales comparison approach is $173,000; by the cost approach, $168,000; and by the income capitalization approach, $170,000. What will be your final opinion of market value, and why?

Check your answer against the one in the answer key at the back of the book.

■ RECONCILIATION IS NOT . . .

The reconciliation process can be summarized best by a discussion of what it is not. Value reconciliation is not the correction of errors in thinking and technique. Any corrections to be made are actually part of the review process that precedes the final conclusion of value. The appraiser reconsiders the reasons for the various choices that were made throughout the appraisal framework as they affect the values reached by the three approaches.

No formula exists for reconciling the various indicated values. Rather, reconciliation involves applying careful analysis and judgment for which no mathematical or mechanical formula can be substituted.

Reconciliation also is not merely a matter of averaging the three values. Using a simple arithmetic average implies that the data and logic applied in each of the three approaches are equally reliable and should therefore be given equal weight. Certain approaches obviously are more valid and reliable with some kinds of properties than with others. But even if each value opinion were multiplied by a different factor, the appraiser would still be substituting mechanical formulas for judgment and analysis.

Finally, value reconciliation is not a narrowing of the range of values reached by the three appraisal approaches. Those values are never changed—unless an error is found. Reconciliation is the final statement of reasoning and weighing of the relative importance of the facts, results, and conclusions of each of the approaches that culminates in a fully justified final opinion of market value.

Weighted Average (Mean)

As you have learned, the arithmetic average or mean is calculated by summing the data and dividing it by the number of items. For example, let's say you have three different opinions of market value under the three approaches: Sales comparison—$160,000, Cost—$167,000, Income—$170,000.

The arithmetic average or mean is \$160,000 + \$167,000 + \$170,000 = \$497,000 ÷ 3, or \$165,667.

With a weighted average, each value is assigned a percentage factor based on its importance. The values are then multiplied by their respective factors. Finally, the values are added together, and divided by the sum of the factors. For example:

	Value	% Factor		
Sales comparison	\$160,000	0.50	=	\$ 80,000
Cost	167,00	0.30	=	50,100
Income	170,000	0.20	=	34,000
		1.00		Sum \$164,100

\$164,100 ÷ 1.00 = \$164,100. This is the appraised value of the house using a weighted average.

Although it's not the approach we emphasize in this text, many appraisers use the weighted average concept in forming an opinion of market value.

■ TYPES OF APPRAISAL REPORTS

WEB LINK

www.uspap.org

Before 2014, the *Uniform Standards of Professional Appraisal Practice (USPAP)* recognized three types of appraisal report options for real property appraisal assignments: self-contained, summary, and restricted use. *USPAP* now permits just two appraisal report options, which are discussed in the following. These descriptions are subject to change with future revisions of *USPAP*. The latest edition of *USPAP* can be found at www.uspap.org.

The two types of appraisal reports permitted by *USPAP* are the following:

- **Appraisal report.** The report must contain sufficient information to lead the client to the appraiser's conclusion. The URAR form is an example of this type of report.
- **Restricted report.** Made for a specific client and for a stated limited purpose, the restricted report contains virtually none of the information the appraiser used to arrive at the value conclusion.

As you can see, the key difference between the reports is the content and level of information presented. But, regardless of type, *USPAP* requires that each written or oral appraisal report must:

- clearly and accurately set forth the appraisal in a manner that will not be misleading;
- contain sufficient information to enable the intended users of the appraisal to understand the report properly; and
- clearly and accurately disclose all assumptions, extraordinary assumptions, hypothetical conditions, and limiting conditions that are used in the assignment.

It should be clear from this that there is no substitute for a thorough understanding of *USPAP* requirements.

■ STYLES OF WRITTEN APPRAISAL REPORTS

Form Report

The appraisal report can present the final opinion of value to the client in basically two ways: a form report or a narrative report.

A **form report** makes use of a standardized form or format to provide in a few pages a synopsis of the data supporting the conclusion of value. The form report usually is accompanied by one or more exhibits. These include location and plat maps, plot and floor plans, and photographs of the subject property and comparables. The type of property as well as the definition of value sought will determine the exact form to be used.

Form reports are used by agencies such as the Federal Housing Administration, Fannie Mae, banks, and insurance companies for routine property appraisals. A form is usually designed for a particular type of property being appraised for a particular purpose. The most common form report in use today for residential appraisals is the URAR. Figure 15.1 is a sample appraisal showing the first thee pages of the URAR form plus the Market Conditions Addendum, which is required for appraisals on mortgage loans sold to Fannie Mae and Freddie Mac. Fannie Mae has also developed a form, Form 2075, to be used in conjunction with its computerized underwriting program. This form is shown in Figure 15.2.

The ease of recording information makes the form report an efficient, time-saving method of presenting appraisal data. But the final opinion of value does not gain accuracy simply because it is supported by a report. The data on which the opinion is based and the experience and judgment of the appraiser are the important elements that give the appraisal validity.

Narrative Report

The most thorough presentation of the appraiser's assumptions, data, analyses, findings, and conclusions is provided in a **narrative report**. The purpose of the narrative report is to give the client not only the facts about the property but also the reasoning that the appraiser used to develop the final opinion of value. That is, in a narrative appraisal report, the appraiser summarizes the important background research and presents all the relevant data for each appraisal method that contributed to the final conclusion of value. A number of exhibits may be included, such as photographs of the subject property and its comparables and maps showing demographic, topographical, soil, and other analyses of the subject and its comparables. Narrative reports can contain just a few pages to several hundred pages. The remainder of this unit examines the requirements of the narrative style appraisal report.

Every appraisal report, regardless of its length, should contain the following items:

- Name of person for whom the report is made
- Date of appraisal
- Identification and description of the subject property
- Purpose of the appraisal

- Value conclusion
- Appraiser's certification and signature

A narrative style appraisal report ordinarily contains most or all of the sections described as follows.

Introduction

Title page

An identifying label, or title page, gives the name of the appraiser and the client, the date of appraisal, and the type of property and its address.

Letter of transmittal

Page 1 of a narrative appraisal report is the letter of transmittal, which formally presents the report to the person for whom the appraisal was made. The letter should be addressed to the client and contain the following information: street address and a complete and accurate legal description of the subject property, property rights to be appraised, type of value sought (most often, market value), appraiser's opinion of value, effective date of the appraisal, and the appraiser's signature. Any state appraiser license or certification held should be indicated, as should any professional designations.

Table of contents

A complete listing of the separate parts of the appraisal and all appendices will be of great help to both the client and the appraiser and will provide an overview of the entire appraisal process.

Summary of important facts and conclusions

The summary page highlights the important facts and conclusions of the report. This section should include the opinion of land value and highest and best use, the reproduction or replacement cost estimate per square foot or cubic foot, the age of the improvement(s) and its depreciated value(s), the gross rental value on a stated occupancy basis, the net income expectancy, the value opinions derived under the three approaches, and the final opinion of value.

Suppositions of the Appraisal

Type of appraisal and report format

The report should include the report format (appraisal report or restricted report).

Purpose of the appraisal

The purpose of an appraisal is a statement of the appraiser's objective, which is usually to form an opinion of market value as of a specified date. Although market value has been the main subject of this book, the content and result of the appraisal can vary greatly with its purpose. For example, in appraisals for inheritance tax, condemnation, or the sale of property, the sales comparison approach is important. For certain mortgage loan purposes, the income-producing capacity of the property would be stressed. For insurance purposes, reproduction or replacement cost data and construction features and materials would be most significant.

Definition of value

Because the word *value* can have many interpretations, the type of value sought should always be defined in the report so the client fully understands the basis for the reported value.

Date of opinion of value

The report must indicate the date as of which the value conclusion is applicable.

Property rights

In most cases, the property rights to be appraised will be a fee simple interest. The appraiser, however, may be asked to estimate the value of fractional interests, or to estimate the effect on value of a change in zoning or a deed restriction, et cetera. Whatever property rights are involved, they must be given in exact detail.

Statement of assumptions and limiting conditions

Some general assumptions and limiting conditions typically found in an appraisal report include the following:

- It is assumed that the legal description of the property as stated in the appraisal is correct.
- The named owner of the property is assumed to be its true owner.
- Unless otherwise stated, there is no legal impediment to the marketability of the property (no "cloud on the title").
- The land has been valued at its highest and best use and the improvements at their contributory value.
- Unless otherwise stated, it is assumed that there are no hidden or unapparent property defects or adverse environmental conditions that would affect the opinion of value. No responsibility is assumed for such conditions or for any engineering or testing that might be required to discover them.
- Although information, estimates, and opinions taken from a variety of sources are considered reliable, no responsibility is taken for the accuracy of such information. Such a statement does not relieve the appraiser of the responsibility to independently verify certain data, as discussed in this book, and to follow generally accepted appraisal methods and techniques.
- Unless otherwise agreed, the appraiser will not be required to testify in court concerning the appraisal.
- Disclosure of the contents of the appraisal report is governed by *USPAP*.

Presentation of Data

National, regional, and city data

In a typical appraisal, most of the general data about the nation, region, and city are gathered initially from office files or previous appraisal reports. Such information should be included in the appraisal report only if it is useful in measuring the future marketability of the property—its economic life, the stability of its location, area trends, et cetera. For this reason, national and regional data are generally not included in the appraisal report. Any relevant maps should be included in an appendix to help describe the region or city. When necessary, the body of the report should contain cross-references to such exhibits.

Neighborhood data

Neighborhood data provide important background information that may influence value. Cross-references to photographs and maps can be helpful here, too. Factors such as distance to schools, public transportation, and shopping and business areas may affect property values. Such information is especially useful if the report is to be submitted to someone unfamiliar with the area. If any form of external obsolescence exists, it should be described in some detail because it must be measured later in the appraisal report.

Financing

The report should include a brief statement about financing available in the area.

Site data

A factual presentation of site data is needed, with cross-references to the plat map, also included in an appendix. A description of the site, including its shape, area, contour, soil, and subsoil, must be given. Census tract identification should be included when available to the appraiser.

Utilities

The important site utilities, their capacities, and how adequately they serve the present or proposed highest and best use(s) should be inventoried.

Zoning

A statement about current zoning regulations is not enough. The report should indicate whether zoning regulations are strictly enforced or a change could be easily effected. Information about the uses permitted and to what extent they conform under the present zoning also should be included. This would have an important bearing on both highest and best use and value.

Amenities

This section should contain community features, such as schools, places of worship, shopping facilities, and public services.

Description of improvements

Among the items this section should contain are construction details and finishing, including quality, floor plan, dimensions, design and layout, age and condition, list of equipment or fixtures, and needed repairs or deferred maintenance. If physical deterioration or functional obsolescence exists, it should be described in some detail, because it will have to be valued later.

Taxes

Current assessed value, tax rate, taxes, and the likelihood of tax changes and their effects should be included.

Sales history

The price and terms of any sale of the subject property within the past three years should be included, as well as the sale of any of the comparable properties within one year before the sale date noted in the appraisal.

Data Analyses and Conclusions

Highest and best use analysis

Most appraisals are based on the highest and best use for which the subject property is suited. Overimprovements or underimprovements are a part of the highest and best use concept, as is use of the site, whether proper or improper. It is not enough simply to say that the existing improvements reflect the highest and best use of the site. Some explanation or justification must be given. Remember, this is a highest and best use analysis—not simply an unsupported statement.

Next, each approach to value is developed separately and in enough detail for the reader to understand the basis for the appraiser's final conclusion of value.

The cost approach

The basic unit cost used to arrive at reproduction or replacement cost must be explained. Two buildings are seldom if ever identical, so a square-foot cost or a cubic-foot cost taken from known cost data is almost always subject to some adjustment. The measurement of depreciation resulting from physical wear and tear, layout and design, and neighborhood defects must also be explained.

The sales comparison approach

In the sales comparison approach, the selling prices of properties considered comparable are used to arrive at the value of the appraised property. These comparable properties must be described in detail to illustrate the points of comparison and convince the reader that the appraiser's choices are valid comparables.

Usually, it is possible to list the comparable properties on one page, bringing out both similarities and differences. A second page might show the adjustments the appraiser has developed, with a third page explaining the adjustments. Sometimes, an adjustment grid showing the required adjustments is followed by a description of each comparable sale and an explanation of the adjustments made. Very large adjustments suggest that the properties are not sufficiently comparable.

The income capitalization approach

In the income capitalization approach, the value of the property is based on the income it produces. Rent and expense schedules of comparable properties should be included in this section to support the appraiser's net income estimate. When available, the income history of the subject property should be listed, along with some explanation of vacancy expectations and anticipated changes in expense items.

Reconciliation and final conclusion of value

Reconciliation of the value opinions derived under the sales comparison, cost, and income capitalization approaches to value is presented. The reasons for emphasizing one opinion over another should be explained clearly.

Certification of value

The appraiser's certification is a guarantee that the appraiser or the appraiser's agent has personally inspected the property, has no present or contemplated interest in the property, and that the statements contained in the report are correct to the best of the appraiser's knowledge.

Qualifications of appraiser

The reader of the report will be interested in knowing the qualifications of the appraiser because experience and sound judgment are essential in the appraisal process. For this reason, a description of the appraiser's education, professional background, and appraisal experience is needed. If the appraiser is state licensed or state certified, this should be noted as well. It serves no purpose to include civic and social offices held or other extraneous information.

Supporting Material

Addenda

The addenda usually include tables of supporting data, maps, photographs, plat and floor plans, and résumés of leases, deeds, contracts, or other items that influenced the appraiser in reaching the final conclusion of value.

Exhibits must be neat, uncluttered, and professionally executed. An area or neighborhood plan, if included, should clearly indicate the important aspects of the area or neighborhood. When plot plans and floor plans are included in the addenda, such plans should be drawn to scale and, as in the case of other exhibits, should have a professional appearance.

Exercise 15-3

A suburban strip shopping center, built four years ago, is being appraised. The property is fully rented to a major supermarket chain, a variety of retail businesses, a pizzeria, and a nationally franchised ice cream parlor. The area is growing, and such businesses have flourished. As a result, there is high demand for property such as the subject, and vacant land prices in the area have increased dramatically over the past four years. Which appraisal approach(es) will probably be most important in finding the market value of the subject property, and why?

Check your answer against the one in the answer key at the back of the book.

SAMPLE APPRAISAL REPORT

A sample URAR-based appraisal report is provided in Figure 15.1. The first three pages of the URAR form are shown, along with a Market Conditions Addendum that the appraiser prepared. The three pages of the URAR form that include the Statement of Assumptions and Limiting Conditions, and the addenda for this appraisal showing photos, floor plan, and plat for the subject property, and photos of the comparable properties, have been omitted. As indicated in Unit 12, use of the URAR form for a mortgage to be purchased by Fannie Mae or Freddie Mac would also require inclusion of the Market Conditions Addendum to the Appraisal Report.

Form 2075

Because of advanced technology and the demands of the marketplace, Fannie Mae is developing new reporting options for lenders. One such option is the Desktop Underwriter Property Inspection Report (Form 2075), to be used in conjunction with Fannie Mae's Desktop Underwriter computer program.

Form 2075 is not an appraisal report. (See Figure 15.2) It is used in conjunction with the automated valuation model (AVM) provided by the Desktop Underwriter software.

Form 2075 allows a drive-by inspection option based on a risk assessment of the loan. The appraiser's description of the physical characteristics of the subject property is based on the drive-by inspection and what he or she believes to be reliable data sources. Such sources may include prior inspections, appraisal files, MLS data, assessment and tax records, information provided by the property owner, or other sources of information available to the appraiser.

If the property inspection reveals adverse physical deficiencies or conditions, Fannie Mae requires the lender to provide a complete interior and exterior appraisal.

Form 2075 consists of five basic sections:

1. Subject
2. Neighborhood
3. Site
4. Improvements
5. Certification and limiting conditions

If Form 2075 is used, the only exhibits required are a photograph that shows the front scene of the subject property and a street map that shows the location of the subject property and comparables.

If both exterior and interior inspections of the property are required, the standard exhibits needed to support appraisal report forms such as the URAR must be included.

FIGURE 15.1
Sample Appraisal Report

The Appraisal Group, 156

Uniform Residential Appraisal Report

File # Sample 1

The purpose of this summary appraisal report is to provide the lender/client with an accurate, and adequately supported, opinion of the market value of the subject property.

SUBJECT

Property Address 123 State St | City Blablablaville | State IL | Zip Code 00000

Borrower Mary Cook | Owner of Public Record Burns/Allen | County Happy

Legal Description LOT 3 IN SMILEY SUBDIVISION, TOWNSHIP 44, RANGE 11, SECTION 29, EAST OF THE 5TH MERIDIAN IN HAPPY COUNTY

Assessor's Parcel # 12-34-567-890 | Tax Year 2016 | R.E. Taxes $ 6,200

Neighborhood Name Bigtown Park | Map Reference 53421 | Census Tract 007.00

Occupant [X] Owner [ ] Tenant [ ] Vacant | Special Assessments $ 0 | [ ] PUD | HOA $ 0 | [ ] per year [ ] per month

Property Rights Appraised [X] Fee Simple [ ] Leasehold [ ] Other (describe)

Assignment Type [X] Purchase Transaction [ ] Refinance Transaction [ ] Other (describe)

Lender/Client Sample Mortgage Company | Address 235 Main Street, Your Town, IL 00000

Is the subject property currently offered for sale or has it been offered for sale in the twelve months prior to the effective date of this appraisal? [X] Yes [ ] No

Report data source(s) used, offering price(s), and date(s). DOM 65;The had an original list date of 07/14/2017 for $345,000 (MLS #017235) for 30 days. There was a price reduction to $330,000 (MLS #017382). A contract date was posted for 09/11/2017. No other listings noted in past 12 months.

CONTRACT

I [X] did [ ] did not analyze the contract for sale for the subject purchase transaction. Explain the results of the analysis of the contract for sale or why the analysis was not performed. Arms length sale;Contract = 6 pages; disclosures = 5 pages. An offering for $300,000 was presented on 09/10/2017 and signed by Mary Cook. The seller accepted on 09/11/2017, and signed by Bill Burns and Janet Allen. All appliances and window treatments included. $5,000 down payment, closing scheduled for 10/31/2017.

Contract Price $ 300,000 | Date of Contract 09/11/2017 | Is the property seller the owner of public record? [X] Yes [ ] No | Data Source(s) Recorder of Deeds

Is there any financial assistance (loan charges, sale concessions, gift or downpayment assistance, etc.) to be paid by any party on behalf of the borrower? [ ] Yes [ ] No

If Yes, report the total dollar amount and describe the items to be paid. $0;;

NEIGHBORHOOD

Note: Race and the racial composition of the neighborhood are not appraisal factors.

Neighborhood Characteristics				One-Unit Housing Trends				One-Unit Housing			Present Land Use %	
Location	[ ] Urban	[X] Suburban	[ ] Rural	Property Values	[ ] Increasing	[X] Stable	[ ] Declining	PRICE $ (000)		AGE (yrs)	One-Unit	80 %
Built-Up	[X] Over 75%	[ ] 25-75%	[ ] Under 25%	Demand/Supply	[ ] Shortage	[X] In Balance	[ ] Over Supply				2-4 Unit	0 %
Growth	[ ] Rapid	[X] Stable	[ ] Slow	Marketing Time	[ ] Under 3 mths	[X] 3-6 mths	[ ] Over 6 mths	215	Low	10	Multi-Family	0 %
								450	High	35	Commercial	0 %
								325	Pred.	22	Other	20 %

Neighborhood Boundaries Bigtown Park: Random St (2000S) south; Main St (300E) east; Wisdom Ave (600S) north; and the Monopoly Rail Road Tracks/1st Ave (600W) west.

Neighborhood Description The subject is located 1 block east of Bigtown Park, which features baseball fields, play lots, and an indoor recreation center. Access to the downtown business district is via commuter train, which is 5 blocks northeast of the subject, and via primary highway, which is 3 miles northwest. The subject is in the Jones Elementary and Clark High School Districts. Business district is 10 miles northwest of subject.

Market Conditions (including support for the above conclusions) The subject's Market Segment is detached single family houses with 3 - 4 bedrooms, 2 - 3 baths, aged from 15 - 30 years in Bigtown Park See attached 1004MC form for supporting information for the above conclusions. In all of Blablablaville, there are stable property values, balanced inventory levels, and marketing times between 3 - 6 months.

SITE

Dimensions 50 x 125 | Area 6250 sf | Shape Rectangular | View N;Res;

Specific Zoning Classification R-1 | Zoning Description Single Family Residence

Zoning Compliance [X] Legal [ ] Legal Nonconforming (Grandfathered Use) [ ] No Zoning [ ] Illegal (describe)

Is the highest and best use of subject property as improved (or as proposed per plans and specifications) the present use? [X] Yes [ ] No If No, describe The Highest and Best Use is in "as is" condition as a residential, single family house.

Utilities	Public	Other (describe)		Public	Other (describe)	Off-site Improvements - Type		Public	Private
Electricity	[X]	[ ]	Water	[X]	[ ]	Street	Asphalt	[X]	[ ]
Gas	[X]	[ ]	Sanitary Sewer	[X]	[ ]	Alley	None	[ ]	[ ]

FEMA Special Flood Hazard Area [ ] Yes [X] No | FEMA Flood Zone X | FEMA Map # 36093D | FEMA Map Date 01/08/2014

Are the utilities and off-site improvements typical for the market area? [X] Yes [ ] No If No, describe

Are there any adverse site conditions or external factors (easements, encroachments, environmental conditions, land uses, etc.)? [ ] Yes [X] No If Yes, describe

The subject is located in a Zone X. The Federal Emergency Management Agency identifies Zone X as: "Areas determined to be outside the 500 year flood plain or Areas of 500 - year flood; areas of 100 - year flood with average depths of less than 1 foot or with drainage areas less than 1 square mile, and areas protected by levees from 100 - year flood." Fannie Mae and Freddie Mac identify Special Flood Hazard Areas that require flood insurance as Zones: V, VE, V1-30, A, AE, A1-30, AH, AO and A99.

IMPROVEMENTS

General Description		Foundation		Exterior Description	materials/condition	Interior	materials/condition
Units [X] One [ ] One with Accessory Unit		[ ] Concrete Slab [ ] Crawl Space		Foundation Walls	Concrete/Average	Floors	Wood/Carpet Avg
# of Stories	2	[X] Full Basement [ ] Partial Basement		Exterior Walls	Brick/Cedar/Average	Walls	Drywall/Average
Type [X] Det. [ ] Att. [ ] S-Det./End Unit		Basement Area	952 sq.ft.	Roof Surface	Asphalt Shingle/Avg	Trim/Finish	Stained Paint Wd
[X] Existing [ ] Proposed [ ] Under Const.		Basement Finish	100 %	Gutters & Downspouts	Aluminum/Average	Bath Floor	Ceramic/Wood Avg
Design (Style)	2 ST	[ ] Outside Entry/Exit [X] Sump Pump		Window Type	Double Hung/Avg	Bath Wainscot	Ceramic/Average
Year Built	1994	Evidence of [ ] Infestation		Storm Sash/Insulated	No/Yes	Car Storage [ ] None	
Effective Age (Yrs)	7	[ ] Dampness [ ] Settlement		Screens	Yes	[X] Driveway # of Cars	2
Attic	[ ] None	Heating [X] FWA [ ] HWBB [X] Radiant		Amenities	[ ] Woodstove(s) # 0	Driveway Surface	Asphalt
[ ] Drop Stair	[ ] Stairs	[ ] Other	Fuel Gas	[ ] Fireplace(s) # 0	[X] Fence Wood	[X] Garage # of Cars	2
[ ] Floor	[X] Scuttle	Cooling [X] Central Air Conditioning		[X] Patio/Deck Patio	[ ] Porch None	[ ] Carport # of Cars	0
[ ] Finished	[ ] Heated	[ ] Individual [ ] Other		[ ] Pool None	[ ] Other None	[ ] Att. [X] Det.	[ ] Built-in

Appliances [X] Refrigerator [X] Range/Oven [X] Dishwasher [X] Disposal [X] Microwave [X] Washer/Dryer [ ] Other (describe)

Finished area **above** grade contains: 6 Rooms 3 Bedrooms 2.1 Bath(s) 1,903 Square Feet of Gross Living Area Above Grade

Additional features (special energy efficient items, etc.). See page 3 of this report for room by room written explanation of interior features. See attached interior photograph pages included in this report. Basement is finished with a rec room, bedroom, full bath, laundry room, and utility room.

Describe the condition of the property (including needed repairs, deterioration, renovations, remodeling, etc.). C3;Kitchen-remodeled-eleven to fifteen years ago;Bathrooms-remodeled-one to five years ago;12 years ago the current owners remodeled the kitchen with wood cabinets, granite countertops, glass tile backsplash, under cabinet lighting, and black appliances. Also, 3 years ago the master bath was remodeled with ceramic tile floor and wainscot, new toilet, soaking tub, glass enclosed shower, double bowl granite vanity top, and wood cabinets; no remodeling to powder room and other full bath.

Are there any physical deficiencies or adverse conditions that affect the livability, soundness, or structural integrity of the property? [ ] Yes [X] No If Yes, describe

Does the property generally conform to the neighborhood (functional utility, style, condition, use, construction, etc.)? [X] Yes [ ] No If No, describe

Freddie Mac Form 70 March 2005 | UAD Version 9/2011 | Page 1 of 6 | Fannie Mae Form 1004 March 2005

Form 1004UAD - "TOTAL" appraisal software by a la mode, inc. - 1-800-ALAMODE

FIGURE 15.1
Sample Appraisal Report (continued)

Uniform Residential Appraisal Report

File # Sample 1

There are 8 comparable properties currently offered for sale in the subject neighborhood ranging in price from $ 285,000 to $ 475,000 .
There are 22 comparable sales in the subject neighborhood within the past twelve months ranging in sale price from $ 275,000 to $ 425,000 .

FEATURE	SUBJECT	COMPARABLE SALE # 1		COMPARABLE SALE # 2		COMPARABLE SALE # 3	
Address	123 State St Blablablaville, IL 00000	435 Maple Ave Blablablaville, IL 00000		448 Maple Ave Blablablaville, IL 00000		275 Union St Blablablaville, IL 00000	
Proximity to Subject		0.19 miles S		0.19 miles S		0.22 miles S	
Sale Price	$ 300,000		$ 325,000		$ 295,000		$ 310,000
Sale Price/Gross Liv. Area	$ 157.65 sq.ft.	$ 147.73 sq.ft.		$ 155.26 sq.ft.		$ 140.91 sq.ft.	
Data Source(s)		MLS #090697;DOM 72		NI MLS #081186;DOM 5		NI MLS #092982;DOM 69	
Verification Source(s)		Assessor #260111		Assessor #986067		Assessor #310024	
VALUE ADJUSTMENTS	DESCRIPTION	DESCRIPTION	+(-) $ Adjustment	DESCRIPTION	+(-) $ Adjustment	DESCRIPTION	+(-) $ Adjustment
Sales or Financing Concessions		ArmLth Conv;0		ArmLth Conv;0		ArmLth Cash;0	
Date of Sale/Time		s08/17;c07/17	0	s07/17;c05/17	0	s05/17;c03/17	0
Location	N;Res;	N;Res;		N;Res;		N;Res;	
Leasehold/Fee Simple	Fee Simple	Fee Simple		Fee Simple		Fee Simple	
Site	6250 sf	6250 sf		6250 sf		6250 sf	
View	N;Res;	N;Res;		N;Res;		N;Res;	
Design (Style)	DT2;2 ST	DT2;2 ST		DT2;2 ST		DT2;2 ST	
Quality of Construction	Q3	Q3		Q3		Q3	
Actual Age	23	24	0	23		22	0
Condition	C3	C3		C3		C3	
Above Grade Room Count (Total / Bdrms. / Baths)	6 / 3 / 2.1	6 / 3 / 3.0	-5,000	6 / 3 / 2.0	+5,000	6 / 3 / 3.0	-5,000
Gross Living Area	1,903 sq.ft.	2,200 sq.ft.	-12,000	1,900 sq.ft.	0	2,200 sq.ft.	-12,000
Basement & Finished Rooms Below Grade	952sf952sfin 1rr1br1.0ba1o	1000sf1000sfin 1rr1br1.0ba1o	0	950sf950sfin 1rr1br1.0ba1o	0	1000sf1000sfin 0rr0br0.0ba0o	0 +15,000
Functional Utility	3 Bedroom	3 Bedroom		3 Bedroom		3 Bedroom	
Heating/Cooling	FA/CAC	FA/CAC		FA/CAC		FA/CAC	
Energy Efficient Items	Radiant Floors	Radiant Floors		Radiant Floors		Radiant Floors	
Garage/Carport	2gd2dw	2gd2dw		2gd2dw		2gd2dw	
Porch/Patio/Deck	Patio	Deck	-5,000	Patio		Deck	-5,000
Kitchen and Bath Finishes	Good	Good		Good		Good	
Fireplace	None	One	-4,000	None		None	
Net Adjustment (Total)		☐ + ☒ -	$ -26,000	☒ + ☐ -	$ 5,000	☐ + ☒ -	$ -7,000
Adjusted Sale Price of Comparables		Net Adj. 8.0 % Gross Adj. 8.0 %	$ 299,000	Net Adj. 1.7 % Gross Adj. 1.7 %	$ 300,000	Net Adj. 2.3 % Gross Adj. 11.9 %	$ 303,000

I ☒ did ☐ did not research the sale or transfer history of the subject property and comparable sales. If not, explain

My research ☐ did ☒ did not reveal any prior sales or transfers of the subject property for the three years prior to the effective date of this appraisal.
Data Source(s) MLS and Recorder of Deeds
My research ☒ did ☐ did not reveal any prior sales or transfers of the comparable sales for the year prior to the date of sale of the comparable sale.
Data Source(s) MLS and Recorder of Deeds
Report the results of the research and analysis of the prior sale or transfer history of the subject property and comparable sales (report additional prior sales on page 3).

ITEM	SUBJECT	COMPARABLE SALE #1	COMPARABLE SALE #2	COMPARABLE SALE #3
Date of Prior Sale/Transfer	11/01/2006	07/07/2006	10/31/2007	04/15/2011
Price of Prior Sale/Transfer	$275,000	$280,000	$300,000	$260,000
Data Source(s)	Assessor #092064	Assessor #966540	Assessor #005116	Assessor #905610
Effective Date of Data Source(s)	09/22/2017	09/22/2017	09/22/2017	09/22/2017

Analysis of prior sale or transfer history of the subject property and comparable sales All sales are similar styled properties from the subject's Market Segment. No sale or transfer of the subject in the past 36 months. No sale of all sales in the past 12 months from their current sale. The most recent sale of all sales are profiled above. By comparing the prior sales to their current sales, I conclude the subject's market is increasing in value. By comparing sales 1 and 2, I conclude the subject's market has recovered from the 2008 Housing Crash. This supports the information profiled in the Market Conditions section of this report.

Summary of Sales Comparison Approach All sale have remodeled kitchens with granite countertops, as well as remodeled master baths with granite vanity tops. All sales are judged to be in similar condition to the subject. Sale 3 does not have a finished basement and has been adjusted accordingly.
The sales considered reflect a value range between $299,000 to $303,000; market conditions as of September 25, 2017 caused me to conclude within the adjusted value range which is well supported by the data. Sales 1 and 2 are the most recent sales are closest in proximity to the subject, therefore, given most emphasis in my determination of the subject's opinion of market value.

Indicated Value by Sales Comparison Approach $ 300,000

SALES COMPARISON APPROACH

Indicated Value by: Sales Comparison Approach $ 300,000 **Cost Approach (if developed) $** **Income Approach (if developed) $**

The sales comparison approach was given most weight as it displays the actions of the buyers and sellers. Because there is insufficient market evidence to credibly support the derivation of total appreciation, the cost approach was not developed, nor given any consideration in the appraiser's final analysis. The income approach not developed because the subject area is primarily owner occupied properties.

This appraisal is made ☒ "as is", ☐ subject to completion per plans and specifications on the basis of a hypothetical condition that the improvements have been completed, ☐ subject to the following repairs or alterations on the basis of a hypothetical condition that the repairs or alterations have been completed, or ☐ subject to the following required inspection based on the extraordinary assumption that the condition or deficiency does not require alteration or repair:

Based on a complete visual inspection of the interior and exterior areas of the subject property, defined scope of work, statement of assumptions and limiting conditions, and appraiser's certification, my (our) opinion of the market value, as defined, of the real property that is the subject of this report is $ 300,000 **, as of** 09/22/2017 **, which is the date of inspection and the effective date of this appraisal.**

RECONCILIATION

Freddie Mac Form 70 March 2005 UAD Version 9/2011 Page 2 of 6 Fannie Mae Form 1004 March 2005

Form 1004UAD - "TOTAL" appraisal software by a la mode, inc. - 1-800-ALAMODE

Figure 15.1
Sample Appraisal Report (continued)

Uniform Residential Appraisal Report

File # Sample 1

ADDITIONAL COMMENTS

INTERIOR FEATURES: The subject features the following: brick facade with cedar frame exterior at sides and back; ceramic tile foyer floor, hardwood floors throughout levels 1 and 2, 9 foot ceilings on levels 1 and 2, powder room with wood floors and pedestal sink, wood cabinet kitchen with granite countertops, glass tile backsplash, black appliances, under cabinet lighting, and kitchen island with granite countertop; pantry with added shelves, bedroom closets with built-in closet organization systems, bath 1 with laminate vanity top, wood cabinet, ceramic tile floor and wainscot; scuttle attic, master bath was remodeled 3 years ago with ceramic tile floor and wainscot, new toilet, soaking tub, glass enclosed shower, double bowl granite vanity top, and wood cabinets; rec room with ceramic tile floor and ceiling fan, basement with 9 foot ceilings, bedroom with carpeted floors, bath with cultured marble vanity, ceramic tile floor and wainscot; basement with radiant heated floors, 200 amp circuit breaker electrical service, tankless water heater, sump pump, brick patio, 2 car detached garage, home security system.

Appraisal Development and Reporting Process: This is an Appraisal Report, which is intended to comply with the reporting requirements set forth under Standards Rule 2 - 2 of the Uniform Standards of Professional Appraisal Practice for an Appraisal Report. The depth of the discussion contained in this report is specific to the needs of the lender/client and for the intended use stated in the report.Supporting documentation that is not provided with the report concerning the data, reasoning, and analyses is retained in the appraiser's file; this includes interior photographs of the subject. The appraiser is not responsible for unauthorized use of this report.

COST APPROACH

COST APPROACH TO VALUE (not required by Fannie Mae)

Provide adequate information for the lender/client to replicate the below cost figures and calculations.

Support for the opinion of site value (summary of comparable land sales or other methods for estimating site value)

ESTIMATED ☐ REPRODUCTION OR ☐ REPLACEMENT COST NEW	OPINION OF SITE VALUE =$
Source of cost data	DWELLING Sq.Ft. @ $ =$
Quality rating from cost service Effective date of cost data	Sq.Ft. @ $ =$
Comments on Cost Approach (gross living area calculations, depreciation, etc.)	=$
	Garage/Carport Sq.Ft. @ $ =$
	Total Estimate of Cost-New =$
	Less Physical Functional External
	Depreciation =$( )
	Depreciated Cost of Improvements =$
	"As-is" Value of Site Improvements =$
Estimated Remaining Economic Life (HUD and VA only) Years	INDICATED VALUE BY COST APPROACH =$

INCOME

INCOME APPROACH TO VALUE (not required by Fannie Mae)

Estimated Monthly Market Rent $ X Gross Rent Multiplier = $ Indicated Value by Income Approach

Summary of Income Approach (including support for market rent and GRM)

PUD INFORMATION

PROJECT INFORMATION FOR PUDs (if applicable)

Is the developer/builder in control of the Homeowners' Association (HOA)? ☐ Yes ☐ No Unit type(s) ☐ Detached ☐ Attached

Provide the following information for PUDs ONLY if the developer/builder is in control of the HOA and the subject property is an attached dwelling unit.

Legal Name of Project

Total number of phases Total number of units Total number of units sold

Total number of units rented Total number of units for sale Data source(s)

Was the project created by the conversion of existing building(s) into a PUD? ☐ Yes ☐ No If Yes, date of conversion.

Does the project contain any multi-dwelling units? ☐ Yes ☐ No Data Source

Are the units, common elements, and recreation facilities complete? ☐ Yes ☐ No If No, describe the status of completion.

Are the common elements leased to or by the Homeowners' Association? ☐ Yes ☐ No If Yes, describe the rental terms and options.

Describe common elements and recreational facilities.

Freddie Mac Form 70 March 2005 UAD Version 9/2011 Page 3 of 6 Fannie Mae Form 1004 March 2005

Form 1004UAD - "TOTAL" appraisal software by a la mode, inc. - 1-800-ALAMODE

FIGURE 15.1
Sample Appraisal Report (continued)

Market Conditions Addendum to the Appraisal Report

File No. Sample 1

The purpose of this addendum is to provide the lender/client with a clear and accurate understanding of the market trends and conditions prevalent in the subject neighborhood. This is a required addendum for all appraisal reports with an effective date on or after April 1, 2009.

Property Address 123 State St City Blablablaville State IL ZIP Code 00000

Borrower Mary Cook

Instructions: The appraiser must use the information required on this form as the basis for his/her conclusions, and must provide support for those conclusions, regarding housing trends and overall market conditions as reported in the Neighborhood section of the appraisal report form. The appraiser must fill in all the information to the extent it is available and reliable and must provide analysis as indicated below. If any required data is unavailable or is considered unreliable, the appraiser must provide an explanation. It is recognized that not all data sources will be able to provide data for the shaded areas below; if it is available, however, the appraiser must include the data in the analysis. If data sources provide the required information as an average instead of the median, the appraiser should report the available figure and identify it as an average. Sales and listings must be properties that compete with the subject property, determined by applying the criteria that would be used by a prospective buyer of the subject property. The appraiser must explain any anomalies in the data, such as seasonal markets, new construction, foreclosures, etc.

MARKET RESEARCH & ANALYSIS

Inventory Analysis	Prior 7–12 Months	Prior 4–6 Months	Current – 3 Months	Overall Trend		
Total # of Comparable Sales (Settled)	11	6	5	☐ Increasing	☒ Stable	☐ Declining
Absorption Rate (Total Sales/Months)	1.83	2.00	1.67	☐ Increasing	☒ Stable	☐ Declining
Total # of Comparable Active Listings	9	12	8	☐ Declining	☐ Stable	☐ Increasing
Months of Housing Supply (Total Listings/Ab.Rate)	4.9	6.0	4.8	☐ Declining	☐ Stable	☐ Increasing
Median Sale & List Price, DOM, Sale/List %	Prior 7–12 Months	Prior 4–6 Months	Current – 3 Months	Overall Trend		
Median Comparable Sale Price	327,500	322,000	325,000	☐ Increasing	☒ Stable	☐ Declining
Median Comparable Sales Days on Market	93	98	95	☐ Declining	☒ Stable	☐ Increasing
Median Comparable List Price	335,675	328,500	335,000	☐ Increasing	☐ Stable	☐ Declining
Median Comparable Listings Days on Market	69	62	64	☐ Declining	☐ Stable	☐ Increasing
Median Sale Price as % of List Price	97.5%	98%	97%	☐ Increasing	☐ Stable	☐ Declining
Seller-(developer, builder, etc.)paid financial assistance prevalent?	☐ Yes ☒ No			☐ Declining	☐ Stable	☐ Increasing

Explain in detail the seller concessions trends for the past 12 months (e.g., seller contributions increased from 3% to 5%, increasing use of buydowns, closing costs, condo fees, options, etc.). Seller's Concessions are not commonly utilized as incentives to expedite sales in the subject's market. Market data reviewed by the appraiser indicates that seller's concessions have remained stable.

Are foreclosure sales (REO sales) a factor in the market? ☐ Yes ☒ No If yes, explain (including the trends in listings and sales of foreclosed properties).

Out of the 22 closed sales in the subject's market segment, there are 0 foreclosure or short sales. Foreclosures and short sales are not a factor in the subject's Market Segment.

Cite data sources for above information. Sources for the above information include the local MLS, recorder of deeds files, local news sources, and/or internet housing sites.

Summarize the above information as support for your conclusions in the Neighborhood section of the appraisal report form. If you used any additional information, such as an analysis of pending sales and/or expired and withdrawn listings, to formulate your conclusions, provide both an explanation and support for your conclusions.

The subject's Market Segment is detached single family houses with 3 - 4 bedrooms, 2 - 3 baths, aged from 15 - 30 years in Bigtown Park. When this market is examined, there are 22 closed sales and 8 active listings. There are also 3 pending sales, which have a median list price of $337,500. By examining the above data, I conclude inventory levels are in balance and property values are stable. It is noted that the average days on market for active sales are 112 days, and for closed sales in the past 12 months is 97 days. Marketing times are between 3 - 6 months.

Exposure time for the subject is estimated to be between three (3) to six (6) months.

CONDO/CO-OP PROJECTS

If the subject is a unit in a condominium or cooperative project, complete the following: **Project Name:**

Subject Project Data	Prior 7–12 Months	Prior 4–6 Months	Current – 3 Months	Overall Trend		
Total # of Comparable Sales (Settled)				☐ Increasing	☐ Stable	☐ Declining
Absorption Rate (Total Sales/Months)				☐ Increasing	☐ Stable	☐ Declining
Total # of Active Comparable Listings				☐ Declining	☐ Stable	☐ Increasing
Months of Unit Supply (Total Listings/Ab.Rate)				☐ Declining	☐ Stable	☐ Increasing

Are foreclosure sales (REO sales) a factor in the project? ☐ Yes ☐ No If yes, indicate the number of REO listings and explain the trends in listings and sales of foreclosed properties.

Summarize the above trends and address the impact on the subject unit and project.

APPRAISER

Signature	Signature
Appraiser Name Randolph Sertrez	Supervisory Appraiser Name
Company Name ABC Appraisal Company	Company Name
Company Address 100 Perfection Ave, Overbydare, IL 12345	Company Address
State License/Certification # CR123456 State IL	State License/Certification # State
Email Address RUSertrez@sampleappraisal.com	Email Address

Freddie Mac Form 71 March 2009 Page 1 of 1 Fannie Mae Form 1004MC March 2009

Form 1004MC2 - "TOTAL" appraisal software by a la mode, inc. - 1-800-ALAMODE

Exercise 15-4

Read the following information carefully and refer to it as often as necessary to complete the residential appraisal form in Figure 15.4. Fill in as many items on the form as you can, then compare your own form against the one shown in the answer key at the back of the book. Correct any errors you made and add any information you omitted.

Legal description:
Lot 31 in Block 4 in Hickory Gardens Unit I, being a subdivision of part of the Southeast ¼ of Section 5, Township 30 North, Range 15, East of the Third Principal Meridian, according to the plat thereof registered in the Office of the Registrar of Titles of Dakota County, Illinois, and commonly known as: 4807 Catalpa Road, Woodview, IL 60000.

Purpose of the appraisal:
To give an opinion of the fair market value of the subject property, held in fee simple, for possible sale purposes.

Real estate taxes:
The subject property is assessed for ad valorem tax purposes at $29,092. The tax rate is $7.828 per $100 of assessed value, which compares favorably with comparable sub-urban areas.

Neighborhood data:
The subject property is located in a desirable neighborhood in the Central Eastern sec-tion of the Village of Woodview. The 25-year-old neighborhood is 100% developed with single-family residences currently ranging in value from $150,000 to $210,000. Most are valued at about $180,000, and virtually all are owner occupied. There is no homeowners' association.

The subject's neighborhood is bounded on the East by the Village of Willow; on the South by 40th Avenue; to the West by Grand Street; and to the North by Park District land. The surrounding neighborhoods are residential communities of approximately the same age as the subject's neighborhood, with homes ranging in value from $160,000 to $250,000.

The occupants of the subject's area are mostly blue-collar workers, with median incomes ranging from $26,000 to $43,000. Employment opportunities in this area have historically been better than the national average. The neighborhood is within walking distance of public grade schools of good reputation, shopping, and transportation, and also offers several nearby parks and playgrounds. Police and fire protection have been above average. The subject's neighborhood has been well-maintained and there has been a steady demand for housing with a gradual uptrend in values during the past several years. Most houses are sold within two months of being put on the market.

Amenities:
Downtown Metroville is eight miles away, accessible by car, bus, and train; local shop-ping, six blocks; grade school, two blocks; high school, one mile, but accessible by bus; commuter railroad station, four blocks; expressway, two miles.

There are no detrimental influences.

FIGURE 15.2
Form 2075

FannieMae

Desktop Underwriter Property Inspection Report File No.

THIS PROPERTY INSPECTION REPORT IS INTENDED FOR USE BY THE LENDER/CLIENT FOR A MORTGAGE FINANCE TRANSACTION ONLY.

SUBJECT

Property Address City State Zip Code
Legal Description County
Assessor's Parcel No. Tax Year R.E. Taxes $ Special Assessments $
Borrower Current Owner Occupant ☐ Owner ☐ Tenant ☐ Vacant
Neighborhood or Project Name Project Type ☐ PUD ☐ Condominium HOA$ /Mo.
Property rights ☐ Fee Simple ☐ Leasehold Map Reference Census Tract

NEIGHBORHOOD

Location	☐ Urban	☐ Suburban	☐ Rural	Property values	☐ Increasing	☐ Stable	☐ Declining	Single family housing PRICE $ (000) AGE (yrs)	Condominium housing PRICE (if applic.) $ (000) AGE (yrs)
Built up	☐ Over 75%	☐ 25-75%	☐ Under 25%	Demand/supply	☐ Shortage	☐ In balance	☐ Over supply		
Growth rate	☐ Rapid	☐ Stable	☐ Slow	Marketing time	☐ Under 3 mos.	☐ 3-6 mos.	☐ Over 6 mos.	Low	Low
								High	High
								Predominant	Predominant

Neighborhood boundaries

SITE

Does the site generally conform to the neighborhood in terms of size and shape? ☐ Yes ☐ No If No, describe:

Does the property conform to zoning regulations? ☐ Yes ☐ No If No, describe:

Does the present use represent the highest and best use of the property as improved? ☐ Yes ☐ No If No, describe:

Utilities	Public	Other		Public	Other	Off-site Improvements	Type	Public	Private
Electricity	☐		Water	☐		Street		☐	☐
Gas	☐		Sanitary sewer	☐		Alley		☐	☐

Do the utilities and off-site improvements conform to the neighborhood? ☐ Yes ☐ No If No, describe:

Are there any apparent adverse site conditions (easements, encroachments, special assessments, slide areas, etc.)? ☐ Yes ☐ No If Yes, describe:

IMPROVEMENTS

Source(s) used for physical characteristics of property: ☐ Exterior inspection from street ☐ Previous appraisal files ☐ Assessment and tax records ☐ MLS ☐ Prior inspection ☐ Property owner ☐ Other (Describe):

No. of Stories Type (Det./Att.) Exterior Walls Actual Age (Yrs.) Manufactured Housing ☐ Yes ☐ No

Does the property generally conform to the neighborhood in terms of style, condition, and construction materials? ☐ Yes ☐ No If No, describe:

Are there any apparent physical deficiencies or conditions that would affect the soundness or structural integrity of the improvements or the livability of the property? ☐ Yes ☐ No If Yes, describe:

Are there any apparent adverse environmental conditions (hazardous wastes, toxic substances, etc.) present in the improvements, on the site, or in the immediate vicinity of the subject property? ☐ Yes ☐ No If Yes, describe:

CERTIFICATION AND LIMITING CONDITIONS

APPRAISER'S CERTIFICATION: The appraiser certifies and agrees that:
1. I personally inspected from the street the subject property and neighborhood.
2. I stated in this report only my own personal unbiased, and professional analysis, opinions, and conclusions, which are subject only to the contingent and limiting conditions specified in this form.
3. I have not knowingly withheld any significant information and I believe, to the best of my knowledge, that all statements are true and correct.
4. I have no present or prospective interest in the property that is the subject of this report, and I have no present or prospective personal interest or bias with respect to the participants in the transaction.
5. I have no present or contemplated future interest in the subject property, and neither my current or future employment nor my compensation for performing this inspection is contingent on the outcome of the inspection.

SUPERVISORY APPRAISER'S CERTIFICATION: If a supervisory appraiser signed this report, he or she certifies and agrees that; I directly supervise the appraiser who prepared this report, agree with the statements and conclusions of the appraiser, agree to be bound by the appraiser's certifications numbered 4 and 5 above, and am taking full responsibility for this report.

CONTINGENT AND LIMITING CONDITIONS: The above certification is subject to the following conditions: The appraiser has noted in this report any adverse conditions (such as, but not limited to, needed repairs, the presence of hazardous substances, etc.) observed during the exterior inspection of the subject property and neighborhood. Unless otherwise stated in this report, the appraiser has no knowledge of any hidden or unapparent conditions of the property or adverse environmental conditions that would make the property more or less valuable, and has assumed that there are no such conditions and makes no guarantees or warranties, expressed or implied, regarding the condition of the property. The appraiser will not be responsible for any such conditions that do exist or for any engineering or testing that might be required to discover whether such conditions exist. Because the appraiser is not an expert in the field of environmental hazards, this report must not be considered as an environmental assessment of the property.

APPRAISER:	**SUPERVISORY APPRAISER (ONLY IF REQUIRED):**
Signature:	Signature:
Name:	Name:
Company Name:	Company Name:
Company Address:	Company Address:
Date of Report/Signature:	Date of Report/Signature:
State Certification #:	State Certification #:
or State License #:	or State License #:
State:	State:
Expiration Date of Certification or License:	Expiration Date of Certification or License:
	☐ Did ☐ Did not inspect subject property from street

10 CH. PAGE 1 OF 1 Fannie Mae Form 2075 7-97

Site data:
The site is at 4807 Catalpa Road in Woodview, Dakota County, IL 60000. The site is on the north side of Catalpa between Salem and Third. The lot is a rectangle, 65' × 130' or 8,450 square feet, providing a large rear yard. There is an asphalt driveway but no alley, and there are no common areas. The street paving is also asphalt.

Sanitary and storm sewers are maintained by the city. Drainage is very good, and there is no danger of flooding. A review of the applicable flood-zone map indicates that the subject property is not located in a flood hazard area. Water is city supplied; public utility companies provide electricity and gas. There have been no major fuel supply problems in this area, and none are foreseen. Streetlights are city maintained. Electric and tele-phone lines are underground.

Landscaping is typical of the neighborhood, with a sodded lawn, shrubs, and trees. The rear yard has a six-foot redwood fence.

Zoning:
The subject property is zoned "R-2, Single-Family Residence District." The subject conforms to the zoning ordinance.

Highest and best use:
The subject property conforms to existing zoning regulations and constitutes the highest and best use of the site.

Easements and encroachments:
There are no easements or encroachments affecting this property, either of record or as noted by visual inspection.

Description of improvements:
General description—a single-family residence, ranch style, containing seven rooms, three bedrooms, and two baths; contemporary open floor plan and typical room layout and dimensions

Age—25 years (effective age 15 years); remaining economic life, 45 years

Condition—both the exterior and the interior of the structure have been well maintained with normal physical depreciation from wear and tear

Rooms—living room, dining room, family room, kitchen, three bedrooms, two full baths and one half bath, six closets, and two-car garage

Exterior—concrete foundation, 100% brick veneer walls, wood-framed, double-hung windows with thermopane glass, galvanized and painted gutters, hip and gable roof with asphalt shingles, and aluminum combination storms and screens; the structure meets or exceeds the requirements of applicable building codes

Interior (principal rooms)—vinyl tile in kitchen and bathrooms, finished oak flooring covered with wall-to-wall carpeting in other rooms; wall covering of drywall, taped and painted or papered; ceilings of drywall, taped and painted; average trim of painted pine; materials, workmanship, finish and equipment are of stock grade

Kitchen—modern, with maple cabinets, Formica counters, vinyl flooring with carpet in dinette, double-bowl porcelain sink, hood-type exhaust fan, built-in gas oven and range, garbage disposal (new), dishwasher, and refrigerator; no pantry

Bathrooms—two full baths, each with ceramic tile floor and wainscoting, built-in tub with shower, single-bowl vanity sink with mirrored medicine cabinet, and a two-piece built-in toilet and one half bath with a toilet and sink

Construction—plywood subflooring covered with oak or tile, 2" × 10" joists, steel beams and columns; galvanized pipes in good condition

Basement—none

Heating—very good, gas-fired, forced warm air furnace with adequate 190,000 BTU output

Cooling—very good three-ton central air conditioner with adequate 190,000 BTU output

Water heater—one-year-old, 40-gallon, gas-fired water heater

Electrical wiring—100-amp, 220-volt system with 12 circuit breakers

Insulation—six inches above ceilings and behind drywall

Garage—two-car detached, 20' × 25' with frame walls, asphalt roof, concrete floor, and wood overhead door

Miscellaneous and extras:
The foyer of the home has a ceramic tile floor. There is wall-to-wall plush carpeting of good quality in the living room, dining room, hall, stairs, and bedrooms. The dinette and family room have wall-to-wall indoor/outdoor carpeting. The family room has a masonry fireplace. A low attic accessible by drop-stair could be used for storage, but is not floored or heated.

General condition:
Overall, the house and garage are in good condition, with limited wear and tear. Materials and finish are better than average but comparable to other homes in this area.

Current market conditions:
The current housing market is strong, reflecting a healthy local economy. Typical fi-nancing in the area is through conventional mortgages, with up to 90% financed at in-terest rates ranging from 6% to 8%, depending on the down payment. Mortgage funds are readily available.

Cost data:

House		$90 per square foot
Extra insulation	$1,200	
Garage		$30 per square foot
Landscaping, driveway, fencing	$8,400	
Land value by allocation	$45,000	
Depreciation factors (to date)		

Garage	physical	25%
	functional	0
	external	0
House	physical	25%
	functional	0
	external	0

Market data:
Adjustment value of fireplace is $5,000.

Adjustment value of finished basement is $10,000.

The subject has an assumable mortgage.

Information on comparable properties is provided in the sales price adjustment chart in Figure 15.3.

There are two comparable properties currently offered for sale in this neighborhood, priced at $178,900 and $184,500. The county tax assessor's records indicate no prior sale of any of the comparable properties within the year before each of those sales.

Income data:
House like subject, but without fireplace, rents for $1,500.
House like subject, but without garage, rents for $1,250.
House like subject, but without garage and fireplace, rents for $1,100.

Typical sales and rental statistics:
House (A) sold for $160,000 and rented for $1,200.
House (B) sold for $166,550 and rented for $1,275.
House (C) sold for $173,500 and rented for $1,300.

The square footage of the house may be computed by using the figures indicated in the following diagram.

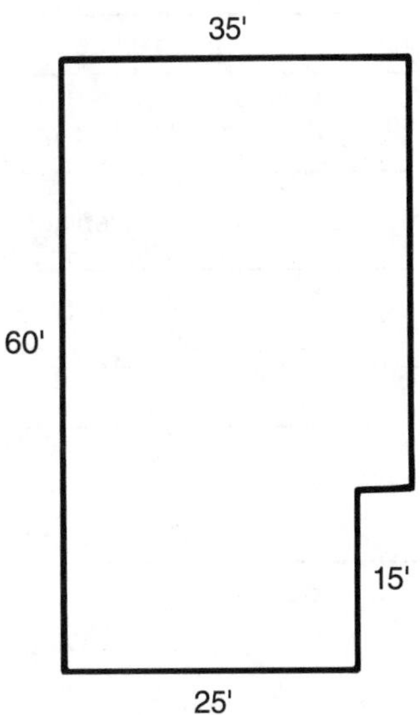

Check your answers against those in the answer key at the back of the book.

FIGURE 15.3
Sales Price Adjustment Chart for Exercise 15-4

Sales Price Adjustment Chart Comparables					
	1160 Central Park	**25 Jackson**	**310 W. Gladys**	**3840 W. Monroe**	**316 Iowa**
Sales price	$152,000	$165,000	$177,750	$180,000	$186,240
Financing	Cash	Conv.	Conv.	Conv.	Conv.
Date of sale	4 wks. ago	1 yr. ago	6 wks. ago	3 wks. ago	6 wks. ago
Location	Quiet res.	Quiet res.	Quiet res .	Quiet res.	Quiet res.
Leasehold/fee simple	Fee	Fee	Fee	Fee	Fee
View	res	res	res	res	res
Site	8,400 sq. ft.	8,400 sq. ft.	8,400 sq. ft.	8,400 sq. ft.	8,400 sq. ft.
Design (style)	Ranch	Ranch	Ranch	Ranch	Ranch
Construction	Q4	Q4	Q4	Q4	Q4
Age	25	25	25	25	25
Condition	C5	C3	C3	C3	C3
No. of rms./bedrms./baths	7/3/2	7/3/2	7/3/2	7/3/2	7/3/2
Sq. ft. of living space	1,950	2,300	1,975	1,950	1,940
Other space (basement)	None	None	None	None	1940sf;970sffin 1rro.1ba.
Functional utility	Average	Average	Average	Average	Average
Heating/cooling	Central heat/air	Central heat/air	Central heat/air	Central heat/air	Central heat/air
Energy efficient items	Extra insulation	Extra insulation	Extra insulation	Extra insulation	Extra insulation
Garage/carport	Carport	2-car garage.	2-car garage	2-car garage.	2-car garage
Other ext. Improvements	Fence	Fence	Fence	Fence	Fence
Other int. Improvements	Masonry fireplace	Masonry fireplace	None	Masonry fireplace	Masonry fireplace
Typical house value					
Variable feature					
Adjustment value of variable					

FIGURE 15.4

URAR for Exercise 15-4

Uniform Residential Appraisal Report

File #

The purpose of this summary appraisal report is to provide the lender/client with an accurate, and adequately supported, opinion of the market value of the subject property.

SUBJECT

Property Address City State Zip Code

Borrower Owner of Public Record County

Legal Description

Assessor's Parcel # Tax Year R.E. Taxes $

Neighborhood Name Map Reference Census Tract

Occupant ☐ Owner ☐ Tenant ☐ Vacant Special Assessments $ ☐ PUD HOA $ ☐ per year ☐ per month

Property Rights Appraised ☐ Fee Simple ☐ Leasehold ☐ Other (describe)

Assignment Type ☐ Purchase Transaction ☐ Refinance Transaction ☐ Other (describe)

Lender/Client Address

Is the subject property currently offered for sale or has it been offered for sale in the twelve months prior to the effective date of this appraisal? ☐ Yes ☐ No

Report data source(s) used, offering price(s), and date(s).

CONTRACT

I ☐ did ☐ did not analyze the contract for sale for the subject purchase transaction. Explain the results of the analysis of the contract for sale or why the analysis was not performed.

Contract Price $ Date of Contract Is the property seller the owner of public record? ☐ Yes ☐ No Data Source(s)

Is there any financial assistance (loan charges, sale concessions, gift or downpayment assistance, etc.) to be paid by any party on behalf of the borrower? ☐ Yes ☐ No

If Yes, report the total dollar amount and describe the items to be paid.

NEIGHBORHOOD

Note: Race and the racial composition of the neighborhood are not appraisal factors.

Neighborhood Characteristics	One-Unit Housing Trends	One-Unit Housing		Present Land Use %	
Location ☐ Urban ☐ Suburban ☐ Rural	Property Values ☐ Increasing ☐ Stable ☐ Declining	PRICE	AGE	One-Unit	%
Built-Up ☐ Over 75% ☐ 25–75% ☐ Under 25%	Demand/Supply ☐ Shortage ☐ In Balance ☐ Over Supply	$ (000)	(yrs)	2-4 Unit	%
Growth ☐ Rapid ☐ Stable ☐ Slow	Marketing Time ☐ Under 3 mths ☐ 3–6 mths ☐ Over 6 mths	Low		Multi-Family	%
Neighborhood Boundaries		High		Commercial	%
		Pred.		Other	%

Neighborhood Description

Market Conditions (including support for the above conclusions)

SITE

Dimensions Area Shape View

Specific Zoning Classification Zoning Description

Zoning Compliance ☐ Legal ☐ Legal Nonconforming (Grandfathered Use) ☐ No Zoning ☐ Illegal (describe)

Is the highest and best use of the subject property as improved (or as proposed per plans and specifications) the present use? ☐ Yes ☐ No If No, describe

Utilities	Public	Other (describe)		Public	Other (describe)	Off-site Improvements—Type	Public	Private
Electricity	☐	☐	Water	☐	☐	Street	☐	☐
Gas	☐	☐	Sanitary Sewer	☐	☐	Alley	☐	☐

FEMA Special Flood Hazard Area ☐ Yes ☐ No FEMA Flood Zone FEMA Map # FEMA Map Date

Are the utilities and off-site improvements typical for the market area? ☐ Yes ☐ No If No, describe

Are there any adverse site conditions or external factors (easements, encroachments, environmental conditions, land uses, etc.)? ☐ Yes ☐ No If Yes, describe

IMPROVEMENTS

General Description		Foundation		Exterior Description	materials/condition	Interior	materials/condition
Units ☐ One ☐ One with Accessory Unit		☐ Concrete Slab ☐ Crawl Space		Foundation Walls		Floors	
# of Stories		☐ Full Basement ☐ Partial Basement		Exterior Walls		Walls	
Type ☐ Det. ☐ Att. ☐ S-Det./End Unit		Basement Area	sq. ft.	Roof Surface		Trim/Finish	
☐ Existing ☐ Proposed ☐ Under Const.		Basement Finish	%	Gutters & Downspouts		Bath Floor	
Design (Style)		☐ Outside Entry/Exit ☐ Sump Pump		Window Type		Bath Wainscot	
Year Built		Evidence of ☐ Infestation		Storm Sash/Insulated		Car Storage ☐ None	
Effective Age (Yrs)		☐ Dampness ☐ Settlement		Screens		☐ Driveway # of Cars	
Attic	☐ None	Heating ☐ FWA ☐ HWBB ☐ Radiant		Amenities	☐ Woodstove(s) #	Driveway Surface	
☐ Drop Stair	☐ Stairs	☐ Other	Fuel	☐ Fireplace(s) #	☐ Fence	☐ Garage # of Cars	
☐ Floor	☐ Scuttle	Cooling ☐ Central Air Conditioning		☐ Patio/Deck	☐ Porch	☐ Carport # of Cars	
☐ Finished	☐ Heated	☐ Individual	☐ Other	☐ Pool	☐ Other	☐ Att. ☐ Det. ☐ Built-in	

Appliances ☐ Refrigerator ☐ Range/Oven ☐ Dishwasher ☐ Disposal ☐ Microwave ☐ Washer/Dryer ☐ Other (describe)

Finished area **above** grade contains: Rooms Bedrooms Bath(s) Square Feet of Gross Living Area Above Grade

Additional features (special energy efficient items, etc.)

Describe the condition of the property (including needed repairs, deterioration, renovations, remodeling, etc.).

Are there any physical deficiencies or adverse conditions that affect the livability, soundness, or structural integrity of the property? ☐ Yes ☐ No If Yes, describe

Does the property generally conform to the neighborhood (functional utility, style, condition, use, construction, etc.)? ☐ Yes ☐ No If No, describe

Freddie Mac Form 70 March 2005 Page 1 of 6 Fannie Mae Form 1004 March 2005

FIGURE 15.4
URAR for Exercise 15-4 (continued)

Uniform Residential Appraisal Report

File #

There are comparable properties currently offered for sale in the subject neighborhood ranging in price from $ to $.

There are comparable sales in the subject neighborhood within the past twelve months ranging in sale price from $ to $.

SALES COMPARISON APPROACH

FEATURE	SUBJECT	COMPARABLE SALE # 1		COMPARABLE SALE # 2		COMPARABLE SALE # 3	
Address							
Proximity to Subject							
Sale Price	$		$		$		$
Sale Price/Gross Liv. Area	$ sq. ft.	$ sq. ft.		$ sq. ft.		$ sq. ft.	
Data Source(s)							
Verification Source(s)							
VALUE ADJUSTMENTS	DESCRIPTION	DESCRIPTION	+(-) $ Adjustment	DESCRIPTION	+(-) $ Adjustment	DESCRIPTION	+(-) $ Adjustment
Sale or Financing Concessions							
Date of Sale/Time							
Location							
Leasehold/Fee Simple							
Site							
View							
Design (Style)							
Quality of Construction							
Actual Age							
Condition							
Above Grade Room Count	Total / Bdrms. / Baths	Total / Bdrms. / Baths		Total / Bdrms. / Baths		Total / Bdrms. / Baths	
Gross Living Area	sq. ft.	sq. ft.		sq. ft.		sq. ft.	
Basement & Finished Rooms Below Grade							
Functional Utility							
Heating/Cooling							
Energy Efficient Items							
Garage/Carport							
Porch/Patio/Deck							
Net Adjustment (Total)		☐ + ☐ -	$	☐ + ☐ -	$	☐ + ☐ -	$
Adjusted Sale Price of Comparables		Net Adj. % Gross Adj. %	$	Net Adj. % Gross Adj. %	$	Net Adj. % Gross Adj. %	$

I ☐ did ☐ did not research the sale or transfer history of the subject property and comparable sales. If not, explain

My research ☐ did ☐ did not reveal any prior sales or transfers of the subject property for the three years prior to the effective date of this appraisal.

Data source(s)

My research ☐ did ☐ did not reveal any prior sales or transfers of the comparable sales for the year prior to the date of sale of the comparable sale.

Data source(s)

Report the results of the research and analysis of the prior sale or transfer history of the subject property and comparable sales (report additional prior sales on page 3).

ITEM	SUBJECT	COMPARABLE SALE # 1	COMPARABLE SALE # 2	COMPARABLE SALE # 3
Date of Prior Sale/Transfer				
Price of Prior Sale/Transfer				
Data Source(s)				
Effective Date of Data Source(s)				

Analysis of prior sale or transfer history of the subject property and comparable sales

Summary of Sales Comparison Approach

Indicated Value by Sales Comparison Approach $

RECONCILIATION

Indicated Value by: Sales Comparison Approach $ Cost Approach (if developed) $ Income Approach (if developed) $

This appraisal is made ☐ "as is", ☐ subject to completion per plans and specifications on the basis of a hypothetical condition that the improvements have been completed, ☐ subject to the following repairs or alterations on the basis of a hypothetical condition that the repairs or alterations have been completed, or ☐ subject to the following required inspection based on the extraordinary assumption that the condition or deficiency does not require alteration or repair:

Based on a complete visual inspection of the interior and exterior areas of the subject property, defined scope of work, statement of assumptions and limiting conditions, and appraiser's certification, my (our) opinion of the market value, as defined, of the real property that is the subject of this report is $, as of , which is the date of inspection and the effective date of this appraisal.

Freddie Mac Form 70 March 2005 Page 2 of 6 Fannie Mae Form 1004 March 2005

FIGURE 15.4
URAR for Exercise 15-4 (continued)

Uniform Residential Appraisal Report

File #

ADDITIONAL COMMENTS

COST APPROACH TO VALUE (not required by Fannie Mae)

Provide adequate information for the lender/client to replicate the below cost figures and calculations.

Support for the opinion of site value (summary of comparable land sales or other methods for estimating site value)

ESTIMATED ☐ REPRODUCTION OR ☐ REPLACEMENT COST NEW	OPINION OF SITE VALUE = $
Source of cost data	Dwelling Sq. Ft. @ $ =$
Quality rating from cost service Effective date of cost data	Sq. Ft. @ $ =$
Comments on Cost Approach (gross living area calculations, depreciation, etc.)	
	Garage/Carport Sq. Ft. @ $ =$
	Total Estimate of Cost-New = $
	Less Physical / Functional / External
	Depreciation =$( )
	Depreciated Cost of Improvements =$
	"As-is" Value of Site Improvements =$
Estimated Remaining Economic Life (HUD and VA only) Years	Indicated Value By Cost Approach =$

INCOME APPROACH TO VALUE (not required by Fannie Mae)

Estimated Monthly Market Rent $ X Gross Rent Multiplier = $ Indicated Value by Income Approach

Summary of Income Approach (including support for market rent and GRM)

PROJECT INFORMATION FOR PUDs (if applicable)

Is the developer/builder in control of the Homeowners' Association (HOA)? ☐ Yes ☐ No Unit type(s) ☐ Detached ☐ Attached

Provide the following information for PUDs ONLY if the developer/builder is in control of the HOA and the subject property is an attached dwelling unit.

Legal name of project

Total number of phases Total number of units Total number of units sold

Total number of units rented Total number of units for sale Data source(s)

Was the project created by the conversion of an existing building(s) into a PUD? ☐ Yes ☐ No If Yes, date of conversion

Does the project contain any multi-dwelling units? ☐ Yes ☐ No Data source(s)

Are the units, common elements, and recreation facilities complete? ☐ Yes ☐ No If No, describe the status of completion.

Are the common elements leased to or by the Homeowners' Association? ☐ Yes ☐ No If Yes, describe the rental terms and options.

Describe common elements and recreational facilities

Freddie Mac Form 70 March 2005 Page 3 of 6 Fannie Mae Form 1004 March 2005

■ SUMMARY

In reconciling the values reached by the three appraisal approaches, the appraiser considers the value sought, the data collected and their reliability, the strengths and weaknesses of each approach, and the relevancy of each approach to the subject property.

Reconciliation is not an averaging; it is a process of reasoning and judgment by which the appraiser identifies the specific factors that result in the final opinion of value.

The appraiser's final task is to present the conclusion of value determined by reconciling the results of the appraisal approaches to the client.

Two appraisal reporting options are permitted by *USPAP*:

- *Appraisal report*—presents the highlights of all significant data.
- *Restricted report*—provides required information only. The client is the only intended user.

USPAP does not dictate the style of the appraisal report. In the form report important facts and conclusions are recorded by checking boxes and/or filling in blanks. The narrative report includes even more details of both the appraiser's research and the reasoning leading to the final conclusion of value.

In conclusion, it should be obvious to the reader that an appraiser is not a magician and does not consult a crystal ball to forecast property value. Also, an appraisal is not an exercise in stargazing or fortune-telling, but a process that should lead to a well-reasoned judgment based on available facts.

■ REVIEW QUESTIONS

1. Which statement is *TRUE*?
   a. All value approaches are equally valid and reliable and should be given equal weight.
   b. Certain value approaches are more valid and reliable with some kinds of properties than with others.
   c. The cost approach is most effective when the structure is older.
   d. The income approach can't be used to value single-family homes.

2. The term *reconciliation* refers to
   a. a process by which an appraiser determines the highest and best use for a parcel of land.
   b. a process by which the validity and reliability of the results of the value approaches are weighed objectively to form a final opinion of value.
   c. a process by which an appraiser averages the three opinions of value.
   d. a method of separating the land value from the total value of the property.

3. Overall, the approach likely to receive the *MOST* weight in appraising a single-family residence is
   a. the cost approach.
   b. the income approach.
   c. the sales comparison approach.
   d. all approaches because all should be given equal weight.

4. Which statement is *TRUE*?
   a. Reconciliation is the correction of errors in thinking and technique.
   b. Reconciliation results in averaging the three value opinions.
   c. Reconciliation is a narrowing of the range of value opinions.
   d. None of these is true.

5. The essential difference between the two reporting options is
   a. the number of comparables needed for the appraisal.
   b. the number of value approaches required.
   c. the accuracy of the value conclusion.
   d. the level of detail required.

6. Which is one of the reporting options sanctioned by *USPAP*?
   a. Unlimited appraisal report
   b. Self-contained appraisal report
   c. Appraisal report
   d. None of these

7. As a rule, the *MOST* reliable approach for valuing single-family residences is
   a. the cost approach.
   b. the sales comparison approach.
   c. the income capitalization approach.
   d. all of these.

8. Normally, the *MOST* reliable approach for valuing special-purpose properties is
   a. the cost approach.
   b. the sales comparison approach.
   c. the income capitalization approach.
   d. all of these.

9. Normally, the *MOST* reliable approach for valuing income-producing properties is
   a. the cost approach.
   b. the sales comparison approach.
   c. the income capitalization approach.
   d. all of these.

10. One kind of written appraisal report allowed by *USPAP* is
    a. the restricted report.
    b. the summary report.
    c. the short form report.
    d. the long form report.

11. The written appraisal report limited to a specific client for a stated limited purpose is
    a. the restricted report.
    b. the appraisal report.
    c. the short form report.
    d. the long form report.

12. The method of forming an opinion of market value that relies on assigning a percentage factor to each of the values derived in the appraisal process makes use of
    a. the average.
    b. the mean.
    c. the weighted average.
    d. the median.

13. Fannie Mae allows which of the following form reports?
    a. FHA
    b. VA
    c. 1050
    d. URAR

14. A newer four-unit apartment building is being appraised. The building has never been rented, and there are no other similar properties in the subject neighborhood. Which approach to value will probably be given the most weight by the appraiser?
    a. Income approach
    b. Sales comparison approach
    c. Cost approach
    d. All approaches will be given equal weight

15. An older single-family dwelling is being appraised. The building is rented for $1,500 per month and there are many rentals and comparable sales in the subject neighborhood. Which approach to value will probably be given the most weight by the appraiser?
    a. Income approach
    b. Sales comparison approach
    c. Cost approach
    d. All approaches will be given equal weight.

16. What is the last step in forming an opinion of value?
    a. Reconciliation
    b. Identifying the problem
    c. Reporting assignment results
    d. Determining highest and best use

17. What is the last step in the appraisal process?
    a. Reconciliation
    b. Identifying the problem
    c. Reporting assignment results
    d. Determining highest and best use

18. A shopping center is being appraised for ABC Bank. ABC wants to save money and asks the appraiser to complete a restricted appraisal report. Which statement is *TRUE*?
    a. The restricted report requires less appraisal work than an appraisal report.
    b. The restricted report requires the same appraisal work as an appraisal report.
    c. The appraisal report is longer, so the valuation process is also longer.
    d. The restricted report is longer, so the valuation process is also longer.

19. The choice of report option is determined by
    a. the appraiser.
    b. the client.
    c. the property owner.
    d. communication between client and appraiser.

20. The appraiser's guarantee that the appraiser did (or did not) inspect the subject property is
    a. the certification.
    b. the warranty.
    c. the limiting condition.
    d. the reconciliation.

Check your answers against those in the answer key at the back of the book.

16

UNIT SIXTEEN

APPRAISING PARTIAL INTERESTS

LEARNING OBJECTIVES

When you have completed this unit, you will be able to

- define common partial interests, such as the condominium and tenancy in common;
- explain the difference between a time-share estate and a time-share use;
- identify when Fannie Mae Form 1073 is appropriate;
- state the differences between a tenancy in common and joint tenancy;
- define the terms applicable to leased fee and leasehold interests; and
- use a basic method for valuing leased fee and leasehold interests.

KEY TERMS

condominium
deficit rent
escalator clause
excess rent
expense-stop clause
Form 1073
gross lease
ground lease
joint tenant
leased fee
leasehold estate
lessee
lessor
manufactured home
net lease
partial interest
percentage lease
planned unit development (PUD)
purchase option
renewal option
sandwich lease
subleasehold
tax-stop clause
tenant improvements
tenant in common (TIC)
time-share
triple-net lease

OVERVIEW

Although we have already considered a variety of types of real estate, including single-family homes, multiunit apartment buildings, retail, and other commercial and industrial properties, there are still more forms of property interests that can be appraised. In this unit, you will learn about some of these property interests, including condominiums and time-shares. You also will learn how the interest of a lessee (tenant) can be valued.

TYPES OF PARTIAL INTERESTS

Thus far we have referred to real estate (land and improvements) owned outright—what is termed *fee simple* ownership. You also should be familiar with other forms of property ownership, some of which have come into use in the United States fairly recently. **Partial interests** include any interest that is less than full fee simple ownership of the entire property conveyed.

Condominiums

The **condominium** form of ownership, long popular in Europe, has been used widely in this country only since the early 1960s. It is particularly attractive to those who want the security of owning property without the maintenance and care that a house requires. The owner of each unit holds a fee simple title to the unit. Ownership includes exclusive right to the airspace that encompasses that unit, as well as an interest in the common areas. Common areas typically include such items as the land, courtyard, walkways, parking spaces, foundation, outside walls, roof, lobby, hallways, elevators, and stairways, as well as recreational facilities such as swimming pools, golf courses, and tennis courts (see Figure 16.1). Unit owners must pay a proportional share of the maintenance and upkeep expenses of the common areas. Many residential apartments, townhouses, offices, and retail stores now are held in the condominium form of legal ownership.

The apartment condominium has some of the same benefits and drawbacks as rental apartment living—lack of privacy being a primary consideration. The townhouse condominium offers greater privacy and generally more living and storage space. For those who cannot afford or choose not to invest in other types of property, however, the condominium is a way to own property (with all the tax and estate planning advantages that entails) yet avoid onerous yard and building maintenance.

Special appraisal considerations for condominiums include specification of both private and public areas, mention of the exact location of the subject property within the building or site, and consideration of the upkeep of both public areas and other units. The appraiser should note the condominium and/or management association that cares for common areas, the amount of monthly fees or other assessments charged, and any special facilities provided (such as a tennis court or swimming pool).

Appraisers generally use the sales comparison approach to value individual condominium units. In areas of high population density, well-designed and well-maintained residential condominiums have appreciated in value, though typically not as much as detached homes, if those are available. If a surfeit of building has resulted in more condominiums than the available demand has warranted, prices will decrease to reflect the reduced demand. When a substantial number of condominium units are owned for rental investment purposes, maintenance may be more difficult, particularly if absentee landlords are slow in paying homeowner assessments. Investors contributed to the run-up of property prices in many areas, particularly in Florida.

Comparable condominium properties should be similar in building size, unit size, number of owner-occupied units, extent of common areas, and type of amenities.

Planned Unit Developments

A **planned unit development (PUD)** is a subdivision consisting of individually owned parcels or lots, as well as areas owned in common.

A PUD may feature detached residences, condominiums, or townhouses (houses on separately owned lots that have adjacent or party walls) and may include both residential and commercial property. Security and convenience are major advantages of planned unit developments. Some PUDs comprise hundreds of separately owned lots with detached residences, one or more swimming pools, tennis courts, a clubhouse, and other amenities. Property owners pay fees and assessments to the property owners' association for upkeep of common areas. Of course, the more extensive the common areas, the higher will be the fees and other assessments required for proper maintenance, although spreading costs over many units can help keep expenses manageable.

The best valuation method for a PUD home or condominium unit is the sales comparison approach, ideally using similar properties in the same development.

FIGURE 16.1
Condominium Ownership

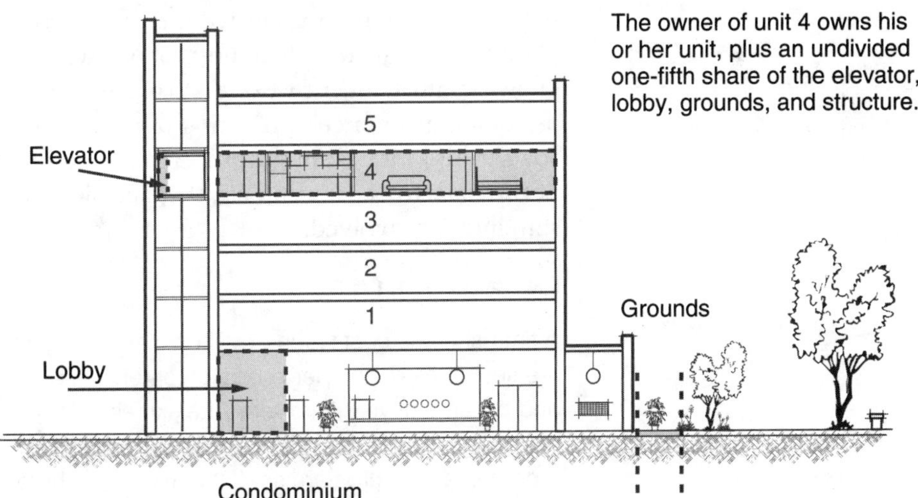

Fannie Mae Form 1073: Individual Condominium Unit Appraisal Report

Fannie Mae **Form 1073**, shown in Figure 16.2, is used to appraise a unit in a condominium project or a condominium unit in a PUD. Entries to this form must comply with UAD requirements and the Market Conditions Addendum must be included.

Form 1073 contains sections that

- describe the scope of work to be performed (see page 4 of the form);
- identify the intended use of the appraiser's opinions and conclusions;
- identify the client and other intended users;
- define market value;
- list the appraiser's assumptions and limiting condition; and
- list the appraiser's certifications.

The appraiser is not permitted to make changes to this form, with the following exceptions: Fannie Mae will allow additional certifications to be added on a separate page if such certifications are required by state law, or if they cover such things as the appraiser's continuing education or membership in an appraisal organization. The appraiser may expand the scope of work to include any additional research or analysis necessary, based on the complexity of the appraisal assignment.

Time-Share Projects

The **time-share** is a relatively new and heavily promoted form of vacation property ownership, ranging from campgrounds to city apartments. A time-share purchaser receives the right to exclusive use of a portion of the property for a particular period each year (usually in units of one week) or a fractional or percentage share of ownership, frequently expressed as a number of points that can be traded for the use of a unit for a certain period of time. A time-share estate includes an estate (ownership) interest in the property; a time-share use, on the other hand, consists of the right to occupy and use the facilities for a specified period with no ownership interest involved.

IN PRACTICE

A time-share is best valued by the sales comparison approach. Initial sales prices are set by the developer based on amenities of the unit (size, special features, view) and the time of year involved. At a ski resort, for instance, a week in January is more valuable than a week in May. Holiday periods typically have the highest premium. If percentage shares are sold, the minimum share available typically will purchase the right to use the smallest unit for the minimum time, usually at least one week. The owner is assessed for maintenance and common area expenses based on the percentage of ownership in the property.

For some time-share projects, high initial marketing costs and limited resale potential have resulted in heavily discounted resale prices. The appraiser should examine the local market carefully, especially noting the exact ownership interest involved and the sales price and length of time on the market for resales.

FIGURE 16.2
Form 1073

Individual Condominium Unit Appraisal Report

File #

The purpose of this summary appraisal report is to provide the lender/client with an accurate, and adequately supported, opinion of the market value of the subject property.

SUBJECT

Property Address Unit # City State Zip Code
Borrower Owner of Public Record County
Legal Description
Assessor's Parcel # Tax Year R.E. Taxes $
Project Name Phase # Map Reference Census Tract
Occupant ☐ Owner ☐ Tenant ☐ Vacant Special Assessments $ HOA $ ☐ per year ☐ per month
Property Rights Appraised ☐ Fee Simple ☐ Leasehold ☐ Other (describe)
Assignment Type ☐ Purchase Transaction ☐ Refinance Transaction ☐ Other (describe)
Lender/Client Address
Is the subject property currently offered for sale or has it been offered for sale in the twelve months prior to the effective date of this appraisal? ☐ Yes ☐ No
Report data source(s) used, offering price(s), and date(s).

CONTRACT

I ☐ did ☐ did not analyze the contract for sale for the subject purchase transaction. Explain the results of the analysis of the contract for sale or why the analysis was not performed.

Contract Price $ Date of Contract Is the property seller the owner of public record? ☐ Yes ☐ No Data Source(s)
Is there any financial assistance (loan charges, sale concessions, gift or downpayment assistance, etc.) to be paid by any party on behalf of the borrower? ☐ Yes ☐ No
If Yes, report the total dollar amount and describe the items to be paid.

NEIGHBORHOOD

Note: Race and the racial composition of the neighborhood are not appraisal factors.

Neighborhood Characteristics	Condominium Unit Housing Trends	Condominium Housing		Present Land Use %	
Location ☐ Urban ☐ Suburban ☐ Rural	Property Values ☐ Increasing ☐ Stable ☐ Declining	PRICE	AGE	One-Unit	%
Built-Up ☐ Over 75% ☐ 25–75% ☐ Under 25%	Demand/Supply ☐ Shortage ☐ In Balance ☐ Over Supply	$ (000)	(yrs)	2-4 Unit	%
Growth ☐ Rapid ☐ Stable ☐ Slow	Marketing Time ☐ Under 3 mths ☐ 3–6 mths ☐ Over 6 mths	Low		Multi-Family	%
Neighborhood Boundaries		High		Commercial	%
		Pred.		Other	%

Neighborhood Description

Market Conditions (including support for the above conclusions)

PROJECT SITE

Topography Size Density View
Specific Zoning Classification Zoning Description
Zoning Compliance ☐ Legal ☐ Legal Nonconforming – Do the zoning regulations permit rebuilding to current density? ☐ Yes ☐ No
☐ No Zoning ☐ Illegal (describe)
Is the highest and best use of the subject property as improved (or as proposed per plans and specifications) the present use? ☐ Yes ☐ No If No, describe

Utilities	Public	Other (describe)		Public	Other (describe)	Off-site Improvements—Type	Public	Private
Electricity	☐	☐	Water	☐	☐	Street	☐	☐
Gas	☐	☐	Sanitary Sewer	☐	☐	Alley	☐	☐

FEMA Special Flood Hazard Area ☐ Yes ☐ No FEMA Flood Zone FEMA Map # FEMA Map Date
Are the utilities and off-site improvements typical for the market area? ☐ Yes ☐ No If No, describe
Are there any adverse site conditions or external factors (easements, encroachments, environmental conditions, land uses, etc.)? ☐ Yes ☐ No If Yes, describe

PROJECT INFORMATION

Data source(s) for project information
Project Description ☐ Detached ☐ Row or Townhouse ☐ Garden ☐ Mid-Rise ☐ High-Rise ☐ Other (describe)

General Description	General Description	Subject Phase		If Project Completed		If Project Incomplete	
# of Stories	Exterior Walls	# of Units		# of Phases		# of Planned Phases	
# of Elevators	Roof Surface	# of Units Completed		# of Units		# o f Planned Units	
☐ Existing ☐ Proposed	Total # Parking	# of Units For Sale		# of Units for Sale		# of Units for Sale	
☐ Under Construction	Ratio (spaces/units)	# of Units Sold		# of Units Sold		# of Units Sold	
Year Built	Type	# of Units Rented		# of Units Rented		# of Units Rented	
Effective Age	Guest Parking	# of Owner Occupied Units		# of Owner Occupied Units		# of Owner Occupied Units	

Project Primary Occupancy ☐ Principle Residence ☐ Second Home or Recreational ☐ Tenant
Is the developer/builder in control of the Homeowners' Association (HOA)? ☐ Yes ☐ No
Management Group – ☐ Homeowners' Association ☐ Developer ☐ Management Agent – Provide name of management company.

Does any single entity (the same individual, investor group, corporation, etc.) own more than 10% of the total units in the project? ☐ Yes ☐ No If Yes, describe

Was the project created by the conversion of an existing building(s) into a condominium? ☐ Yes ☐ No If Yes, describe the original use and the date of conversion.

Are the units, common elements, and recreation facilities complete (including any planned rehabilitation for a condominium conversion)? ☐ Yes ☐ No If No, describe

Is there any commercial space in the project? ☐ Yes ☐ No If Yes, describe and indicate the overall percentage of the commercial space.

Freddie Mac Form 465 March 2005 Page 1 of 6 Fannie Mae Form 1073 March 2005

FIGURE 16.2
Form 1073 (continued)

Individual Condominium Unit Appraisal Report

File #

PROJECT INFORMATION

Describe the condition of the project and quality of construction.

Describe the common elements and recreational facilities.

Are any common elements leased to or by the Homeowners' Association? ☐ Yes ☐ No If Yes, describe the rental terms and options.

Is the project subject to ground rent? ☐ Yes ☐ No If Yes, $ per year (describe terms and conditions)

Are the parking facilities adequate for the project size and type? ☐ Yes ☐ No If No, describe and comment on the effect on value and marketability.

PROJECT ANALYSIS

I ☐ did ☐ did not analyze the condominium project budget for the current year. Explain the results of the analysis of the budget (adequacy of fees, reserves, etc.), or why the analysis was not performed.

Are there any other fees (other than regular HOA charges) for the use of the project facilities? ☐ Yes ☐ No If Yes, report the charges and describe.

Compared to other competitive projects of similar quality and design, the subject unit charge appears ☐ High ☐ Average ☐ Low If High or Low, describe

Are there any special or unusual characteristics of the project (based on the condominium documents, HOA meetings, or other information) known to the appraiser?
☐ Yes ☐ No If Yes, describe and explain the effect on value and marketability.

UNIT DESCRIPTION

Unit Charge $ per month X 12 = $ per year Annual assessment charge per year per square feet of gross living area = $
Utilities included in the unit monthly assessment ☐ None ☐ Heat ☐ Air Conditioning ☐ Electricity ☐ Gas ☐ Water ☐ Sewer ☐ Cable ☐ Other (describe)

General Description	Interior materials/condition	Amenities	Appliances	Car Storage
Floor #	Floors	☐ Fireplace(s) #	☐ Refrigerator	☐ None
# of Levels	Walls	☐ Woodstove(s) #	☐ Range/Oven	☐ Garage ☐ Covered ☐ Open
Heating Type Fuel	Trim/Finish	☐ Deck/Patio	☐ Disp ☐ Microwave	# of Cars
☐ Central AC ☐ Individual AC	Bath Wainscot	☐ Porch/Balcony	☐ Dishwasher	☐ Assigned ☐ Owned
☐ Other (describe)	Doors	☐ Other	☐ Washer/Dryer	Parking Space #

Finished area **above** grade contains: Rooms Bedrooms Bath(s) Square Feet of Gross Living Area Above Grade
Are the heating and cooling for the individual units separately metered? ☐ Yes ☐ No If No, describe and comment on compatibility to other projects in the market area.

Additional features (special energy efficient items, etc.)

Describe the condition of the property (including needed repairs, deterioration, renovations, remodeling, etc.).

Are there any physical deficiencies or adverse conditions that affect the livability, soundness, or structural integrity of the property? ☐ Yes ☐ No If Yes, describe

Does the property generally conform to the neighborhood (functional utility, style, condition, use, construction, etc.)? ☐ Yes ☐ No If No, describe

PRIOR SALE HISTORY

I ☐ did ☐ did not research the sale or transfer history of the subject property and comparable sales. If not, explain

My research ☐ did ☐ did not reveal any prior sales or transfers of the subject property for the three years prior to the effective date of this appraisal.
Data source(s)
My research ☐ did ☐ did not reveal any prior sales or transfers of the comparable sales for the year prior to the date of sale of the comparable sale.
Data source(s)
Report the results of the research and analysis of the prior sale or transfer history of the subject property and comparable sales (report additional prior sales on page 3).

ITEM	SUBJECT	COMPARABLE SALE # 1	COMPARABLE SALE # 2	COMPARABLE SALE # 3
Date of Prior Sale/Transfer				
Price of Prior Sale/Transfer				
Data Source(s)				
Effective Date of Data Source(s)				

Analysis of prior sale or transfer history of the subject property and comparable sales.

Freddie Mac Form 465 March 2005 Page 2 of 6 Fannie Mae Form 1073 March 2005

FIGURE 16.2
Form 1073 (continued)

Individual Condominium Unit Appraisal Report

File #

SALES COMPARISON APPROACH

There are comparable properties currently offered for sale in the subject neighborhood ranging in price from $ to $.

There are comparable sales in the subject neighborhood within the past twelve months ranging in sale price from $ to $.

FEATURE	SUBJECT	COMPARABLE SALE # 1		COMPARABLE SALE # 2		COMPARABLE SALE # 3	
Address and Unit #							
Project Name and Phase							
Proximity to Subject							
Sale Price	$		$		$		$
Sale Price/Gross Liv. Area	$ sq. ft.	$ sq. ft.		$ sq. ft.		$ sq. ft.	
Data Source(s)							
Verification Source(s)							
VALUE ADJUSTMENTS	DESCRIPTION	DESCRIPTION	+(-) $ Adjustment	DESCRIPTION	+(-) $ Adjustment	DESCRIPTION	+(-) $ Adjustment
Sale or Financing Concessions							
Date of Sale/Time							
Location							
Leasehold/Fee Simple							
HOA Mo. Assessment							
Common Elements and Rec. Facilities							
Floor Location							
View							
Design (Style)							
Quality of Construction							
Actual Age							
Condition							
Above Grade Room Count	Total | Bdrms. | Baths	Total | Bdrms. | Baths		Total | Bdrms. | Baths		Total | Bdrms. | Baths	
Gross Living Area	sq. ft.	sq. ft.		sq. ft.		sq. ft.	
Basement & Finished Rooms Below Grade							
Functional Utility							
Heating/Cooling							
Energy Efficient Items							
Garage/Carport							
Porch/Patio/Deck							
Net Adjustment (Total)		☐ + ☐ -	$	☐ + ☐ -	$	☐ + ☐ -	$
Adjusted Sale Price of Comparables		Net Adj. % Gross Adj. %	$	Net Adj. % Gross Adj. %	$	Net Adj. % Gross Adj. %	$

Summary of Sales Comparison Approach

Indicated Value by Sales Comparison Approach $

INCOME

INCOME APPROACH TO VALUE (not required by Fannie Mae)

Estimated Monthly Market Rent $ X Gross Rent Multiplier = $ Indicated Value by Income Approach

Summary of Income Approach (including support for market rent and GRM)

RECONCILIATION

Indicated Value by: Sales Comparison Approach $ Income Approach (if developed) $

This appraisal is made ☐ "as is", ☐ subject to completion per plans and specifications on the basis of a hypothetical condition that the improvements have been completed, ☐ subject to the following repairs or alterations on the basis of a hypothetical condition that the repairs or alterations have been completed, or ☐ subject to the following required inspection based on the extraordinary assumption that the condition or deficiency does not require alteration or repair:

Based on a complete visual inspection of the interior and exterior areas of the subject property, defined scope of work, statement of assumptions and limiting conditions, and appraiser's certification, my (our) opinion of the market value, as defined, of the real property that is the subject of this report is $, as of , which is the date of inspection and the effective date of this appraisal.

Freddie Mac Form 465 March 2005 Page 3 of 6 Fannie Mae Form 1073 March 2005

FIGURE 16.2
Form 1073 (continued)

Individual Condominium Unit Appraisal Report

File #

This report form is designed to report an appraisal of a unit in a condominium project or a condominium unit in a planned unit development (PUD). This report form is not designed to report an appraisal of a manufactured home or a unit in a cooperative project.

This appraisal report is subject to the following scope of work, intended use, intended user, definition of market value, statement of assumptions and limiting conditions, and certifications. Modifications, additions, or deletions to the intended use, intended user, definition of market value, or assumptions and limiting conditions are not permitted. The appraiser may expand the scope of work to include any additional research or analysis necessary based on the complexity of this appraisal assignment. Modifications or deletions to the certifications are also not permitted. However, additional certifications that do not constitute material alterations to this appraisal report, such as those required by law or those related to the appraiser's continuing education or membership in an appraisal organization, are permitted.

SCOPE OF WORK: The scope of work for this appraisal is defined by the complexity of this appraisal assignment and the reporting requirements of this appraisal report form, including the following definition of market value, statement of assumptions and limiting conditions, and certifications. The appraiser must, at a minimum: (1) perform a complete visual inspection of the interior and exterior areas of the subject unit, (2) inspect and analyze the condominium project, (3) inspect the neighborhood, (4) inspect each of the comparable sales from at least the street, (5) research, verify, and analyze data from reliable public and/or private sources, and (6) report his or her analysis, opinions, and conclusions in this appraisal report.

INTENDED USE: The intended use of this appraisal report is for the lender/client to evaluate the property that is the subject of this appraisal for a mortgage finance transaction.

INTENDED USER: The intended user of this appraisal report is the lender/client.

MARKET VALUE: The most probable price which a property should bring in a competitive and open market under all conditions requisite to a fair sale, the buyer and seller, each acting prudently, knowledgeably and assuming the price is not affected by undue stimulus. Implicit in this definition is the consummation of a sale as of a specified date and the passing of title from seller to buyer under conditions whereby: (1) buyer and seller are typically motivated; (2) both parties are well informed or well advised, and each acting in what he or she considers his or her own best interest; (3) a reasonable time is allowed for exposure in the open market; (4) payment is made in terms of cash in U. S. dollars or in terms of financial arrangements comparable thereto; and (5) the price represents the normal consideration for the property sold unaffected by special or creative financing or sales concessions* granted by anyone associated with the sale.

*Adjustments to the comparables must be made for special or creative financing or sales concessions. No adjustments are necessary for those costs which are normally paid by sellers as a result of tradition or law in a market area; these costs are readily identifiable since the seller pays these costs in virtually all sales transactions. Special or creative financing adjustments can be made to the comparable property by comparisons to financing terms offered by a third party institutional lender that is not already involved in the property or transaction. Any adjustment should not be calculated on a mechanical dollar for dollar cost of the financing or concession but the dollar amount of any adjustment should approximate the market's reaction to the financing or concessions based on the appraiser's judgment.

STATEMENT OF ASSUMPTIONS AND LIMITING CONDITIONS: The appraiser's certification in this report is subject to the following assumptions and limiting conditions:

1. The appraiser will not be responsible for matters of a legal nature that affect either the property being appraised or the title to it, except for information that he or she became aware of during the research involved in performing this appraisal. The appraiser assumes that the title is good and marketable and will not render any opinions about the title.

2. The appraiser has provided a sketch in this appraisal report to show the approximate dimensions of the improvements. The sketch is included only to assist the reader in visualizing the property and understanding the appraiser's determination of its size.

3. The appraiser has examined the available flood maps that are provided by the Federal Emergency Management Agency (or other data sources) and has noted in this appraisal report whether any portion of the subject site is located in an identified Special Flood Hazard Area. Because the appraiser is not a surveyor, he or she makes no guarantees, express or implied, regarding this determination.

4. The appraiser will not give testimony or appear in court because he or she made an appraisal of the property in question, unless specific arrangements to do so have been made beforehand, or as otherwise required by law.

5. The appraiser has noted in this appraisal report any adverse conditions (such as needed repairs, deterioration, the presence of hazardous wastes, toxic substances, etc.) observed during the inspection of the subject property or that he or she became aware of during the research involved in performing this appraisal. Unless otherwise stated in this appraisal report, the appraiser has no knowledge of any hidden or unapparent physical deficiencies or adverse conditions of the property (such as, but not limited to, needed repairs, deterioration, the presence of hazardous wastes, toxic substances, adverse environmental conditions, etc.) that would make the property less valuable, and has assumed that there are no such conditions and makes no guarantees or warranties, express or implied. The appraiser will not be responsible for any such conditions that do exist or for any engineering or testing that might be required to discover whether such conditions exist. Because the appraiser is not an expert in the field of environmental hazards, this appraisal report must not be considered as an environmental assessment of the property.

6. The appraiser has based his or her appraisal report and valuation conclusion for an appraisal that is subject to satisfactory completion, repairs, or alterations on the assumption that the completion, repairs, or alterations of the subject property will be performed in a professional manner.

FIGURE 16.2
Form 1073 (continued)

Individual Condominium Unit Appraisal Report

File #

APPRAISER'S CERTIFICATION: The Appraiser certifies and agrees that:

1. I have, at a minimum, developed and reported this appraisal in accordance with the scope of work requirements stated in this appraisal report.

2. I performed a complete visual inspection of the interior and exterior areas of the subject property. I reported the condition of the improvements in factual, specific terms. I identified and reported the physical deficiencies that could affect the livability, soundness, or structural integrity of the property.

3. I performed this appraisal in accordance with the requirements of the Uniform Standards of Professional Appraisal Practice that were adopted and promulgated by the Appraisal Standards Board of The Appraisal Foundation and that were in place at the time this appraisal report was prepared.

4. I developed my opinion of the market value of the real property that is the subject of this report based on the sales comparison approach to value. I have adequate comparable market data to develop a reliable sales comparison approach for this appraisal assignment. I further certify that I considered the cost and income approaches to value but did not develop them, unless otherwise indicated in this report.

5. I researched, verified, analyzed, and reported on any current agreement for sale for the subject property, any offering for sale of the subject property in the twelve months prior to the effective date of this appraisal, and the prior sales of the subject property for a minimum of three years prior to the effective date of this appraisal, unless otherwise indicated in this report.

6. I researched, verified, analyzed, and reported on the prior sales of the comparable sales for a minimum of one year prior to the date of sale of the comparable sale, unless otherwise indicated in this report.

7. I selected and used comparable sales that are locationally, physically, and functionally the most similar to the subject property.

8. I have not used comparable sales that were the result of combining a land sale with the contract purchase price of a home that has been built or will be built on the land.

9. I have reported adjustments to the comparable sales that reflect the market's reaction to the differences between the subject property and the comparable sales.

10. I verified, from a disinterested source, all information in this report that was provided by parties who have a financial interest in the sale or financing of the subject property.

11. I have knowledge and experience in appraising this type of property in this market area.

12. I am aware of, and have access to, the necessary and appropriate public and private data sources, such as multiple listing services, tax assessment records, public land records and other such data sources for the area in which the property is located.

13. I obtained the information, estimates, and opinions furnished by other parties and expressed in this appraisal report from reliable sources that I believe to be true and correct.

14. I have taken into consideration the factors that have an impact on value with respect to the subject neighborhood, subject property, and the proximity of the subject property to adverse influences in the development of my opinion of market value. I have noted in this appraisal report any adverse conditions (such as, but not limited to, needed repairs, deterioration, the presence of hazardous wastes, toxic substances, adverse environmental conditions, etc.) observed during the inspection of the subject property or that I became aware of during the research involved in performing this appraisal. I have considered these adverse conditions in my analysis of the property value, and have reported on the effect of the conditions on the value and marketability of the subject property.

15. I have not knowingly withheld any significant information from this appraisal report and, to the best of my knowledge, all statements and information in this appraisal report are true and correct.

16. I stated in this appraisal report my own personal, unbiased, and professional analysis, opinions, and conclusions, which are subject only to the assumptions and limiting conditions in this appraisal report.

17. I have no present or prospective interest in the property that is the subject of this report, and I have no present or prospective personal interest or bias with respect to the participants in the transaction. I did not base, either partially or completely, my analysis and/or opinion of market value in this appraisal report on the race, color, religion, sex, age, marital status, handicap, familial status, or national origin of either the prospective owners or occupants of the subject property or of the present owners or occupants of the properties in the vicinity of the subject property or on any other basis prohibited by law.

18. My employment and/or compensation for performing this appraisal or any future or anticipated appraisals was not conditioned on any agreement or understanding, written or otherwise, that I would report (or present analysis supporting) a predetermined specific value, a predetermined minimum value, a range or direction in value, a value that favors the cause of any party, or the attainment of a specific result or occurrence of a specific subsequent event (such as approval of a pending mortgage loan application).

19. I personally prepared all conclusions and opinions about the real estate that were set forth in this appraisal report. If I relied on significant real property appraisal assistance from any individual or individuals in the performance of this appraisal or the preparation of this appraisal report, I have named such individual(s) and disclosed the specific tasks performed in this appraisal report. I certify that any individual so named is qualified to perform the tasks. I have not authorized anyone to make a change to any item in this appraisal report; therefore, any change made to this appraisal is unauthorized and I will take no responsibility for it.

20. I identified the lender/client in this appraisal report who is the individual, organization, or agent for the organization that ordered and will receive this appraisal report.

Freddie Mac Form 465 March 2005 | Page 5 of 6 | Fannie Mae Form 1073 March 2005

FIGURE 16.2
Form 1073 (continued)

Individual Condominium Unit Appraisal Report

File #

21. The lender/client may disclose or distribute this appraisal report to: the borrower; another lender at the request of the borrower; the mortgagee or its successors and assigns; mortgage insurers; government sponsored enterprises; other secondary market participants; data collection or reporting services; professional appraisal organizations; any department, agency, or instrumentality of the United States; and any state, the District of Columbia, or other jurisdictions; without having to obtain the appraiser's or supervisory appraiser's (if applicable) consent. Such consent must be obtained before this appraisal report may be disclosed or distributed to any other party (including, but not limited to, the public through advertising, public relations, news, sales, or other media).

22. I am aware that any disclosure or distribution of this appraisal report by me or the lender/client may be subject to certain laws and regulations. Further, I am also subject to the provisions of the Uniform Standards of Professional Appraisal Practice that pertain to disclosure or distribution by me.

23. The borrower, another lender at the request of the borrower, the mortgagee or its successors and assigns, mortgage insurers, government sponsored enterprises, and other secondary market participants may rely on this appraisal report as part of any mortgage finance transaction that involves any one or more of these parties.

24. If this appraisal report was transmitted as an "electronic record" containing my "electronic signature," as those terms are defined in applicable federal and/or state laws (excluding audio and video recordings), or a facsimile transmission of this appraisal report containing a copy or representation of my signature, the appraisal report shall be as effective, enforceable and valid as if a paper version of this appraisal report were delivered containing my original hand written signature.

25. Any intentional or negligent misrepresentation(s) contained in this appraisal report may result in civil liability and/or criminal penalties including, but not limited to, fine or imprisonment or both under the provisions of Title 18, United States Code, Section 1001, et seq., or similar state laws.

SUPERVISORY APPRAISER'S CERTIFICATION: The Supervisory Appraiser certifies and agrees that:

1. I directly supervised the appraiser for this appraisal assignment, have read the appraisal report, and agree with the appraiser's analysis, opinions, statements, conclusions, and the appraiser's certification.

2. I accept full responsibility for the contents of this appraisal report including, but not limited to, the appraiser's analysis, opinions, statements, conclusions, and the appraiser's certification.

3. The appraiser identified in this appraisal report is either a sub-contractor or an employee of the supervisory appraiser (or the appraisal firm), is qualified to perform this appraisal, and is acceptable to perform this appraisal under the applicable state law.

4. This appraisal report complies with the Uniform Standards of Professional Appraisal Practice that were adopted and promulgated by the Appraisal Standards Board of The Appraisal Foundation and that were in place at the time this appraisal report was prepared.

5. If this appraisal report was transmitted as an "electronic record" containing my "electronic signature," as those terms are defined in applicable federal and/or state laws (excluding audio and video recordings), or a facsimile transmission of this appraisal report containing a copy or representation of my signature, the appraisal report shall be as effective, enforceable and valid as if a paper version of this appraisal report were delivered containing my original hand written signature.

APPRAISER

Signature ______________________
Name ______________________
Company Name ______________________
Company Address ______________________
____
Telephone Number ______________________
Email Address ______________________
Date of Signature and Report ______________________
Effective Date of Appraisal ______________________
State Certification # ______________________
or State License # ______________________
or Other ____________ State # ____________
State ______________________
Expiration Date of Certification or License ______________________

ADDRESS OF PROPERTY APPRAISED
____
____

APPRAISED VALUE OF SUBJECT PROPERTY $ ______________________

LENDER/CLIENT
Name ______________________
Company Name ______________________
Company Address ______________________
Email Address ______________________

SUPERVISORY APPRAISER (ONLY IF REQUIRED)

Signature ______________________
Name ______________________
Company Name ______________________
Company Address ______________________
____
Telephone Number ______________________
Email Address ______________________
Date of Signature ______________________
State Certification # ______________________
or State License # ______________________
State ______________________
Expiration Date of Certification or License ______________________

SUBJECT PROPERTY
☐ Did not inspect subject property
☐ Did inspect exterior of subject property from street
Date of Inspection ______________________
☐ Did inspect interior and exterior of subject property
Date of Inspection ______________________

COMPARABLE SALES
☐ Did not inspect exterior of comparable sales from street
☐ Did inspect exterior of comparable sales from street
Date of Inspection ______________________

Manufactured Homes

Factory-built homes now account for one-third of all new single-family home purchases in the United States. The federal government refers to a home constructed in a factory, including both completely enclosed homes and those that consist of components to be assembled on site, as a **manufactured home**. Such homes must meet the National Manufactured Home Construction and Safety Standards covering design, construction, durability, fire resistance, and energy efficiency.

Well-maintained manufactured home subdivisions, offering generous lot space with lawn areas, well-paved streets, swimming pools, and other facilities, can be inviting places to live and may increase in value. Manufactured homes offer housing that usually is much more affordable than alternatives. Unfortunately, strict zoning has limited their availability in most urban areas.

Special considerations for manufactured homes appraised by the sales comparison approach include the age and size of the home, its location, and, if applicable, space rental cost, lease term, subdivision amenities, and upkeep of the subdivision grounds and other units.

Some forms of manufactured housing, such as those using panelized construction, may be required to conform to local building codes and thus are considered equivalent to homes constructed entirely on site.

Other Forms of Ownership

Other partial interests include the life estate, easement, cooperative, and various forms of co-ownership. **Tenants in common (TICs)** share an undivided interest in the property that is the subject of the cotenancy. This means that each tenant has the right to use the entire property, regardless of the fractional interest owned. The value of a tenant in common's interest is based on that fraction.

Joint tenants, who share the unities of title, time, interest, and possession, cannot have unequal interests. A joint tenancy also includes the right of survivorship, which means that a joint tenant cannot convey the property interest without destroying the joint tenancy. The joint tenancy has value while the tenant lives because the tenant is entitled to full use of the property, but the ultimate value of a joint tenant's interest depends on the actuarial likelihood that the joint tenant will be the last survivor.

If all cotenants are willing to join in a conveyance of co-ownership property, the property's value should be the same as it would be under individual ownership of the fee simple title. An individual tenant's interest, valued separately, will depend on the type of property and the terms of the cotenancy. The appraiser must consider the likely desirability of the property to a potential buyer. If use of the property is easily divisible, such as a three-unit building owned by three tenants in common under an agreement giving each the right to occupy a separate unit, the valuation process will be less complicated.

Exercise 16-1

What special considerations would be taken into account when appraising the following property interests?

1. Condominium
2. PUD
3. Time-share
4. Manufactured home

Check your answers against those in the answer key at the back of the book.

■ APPRAISING LEASE INTERESTS

In previous units, we referred to the owner of a leased property as the **lessor**, or landlord, and to the person who leases the property as the **lessee**, or tenant. When the scheduled rent the lessee pays is the same as the market rent, or economic potential of the property, both parties receive full value for their lease and investment dollar. If the scheduled rent (contract rent) is lower or higher than market rent, however, one party gains and the other loses the amount of the difference. How the lessor's and lessee's interests are defined and evaluated is discussed next.

Lease Terminology

Leaseholds and leased fee interests, first mentioned in Unit 4, are reviewed here and additional terms are discussed.

Leased fee

An owner who leases property for a given period owns a **leased fee**, which represents the lessor's interest and rights in the real estate. In return for the lease that permits the tenant to occupy and use the property, the lessor receives a stipulated fee or rental and retains the right to repossess the property at the termination of the lease. The value of the rental payments plus the remaining property value at the end of the lease period, known as the reversion, make up the lessor's interest in the property. This leased fee interest may be sold or mortgaged, subject to the rights of the tenant.

Leasehold estate

A second interest created by a lease belongs to the tenant. It is referred to as the **leasehold estate**, or the lessee's interest and rights in the real estate. Because the lessee is obligated under the terms of the lease to pay rent, the lessee's interest in the property can have value only if the agreed-on scheduled rent is less than the prevailing market rental, or economic rent. If the agreed-on scheduled rent is higher than the prevailing market rent, the difference is termed excess rent and the tenant has a negative leasehold interest.

A lessee may make substantial improvements to a parcel under the terms of a ground lease. A **ground lease** is defined as a lease of land only, on which the tenant usually owns a building or is required to build as specified in the lease. The ground lease has been used most often with commercial property, but is also used for residential complexes in areas of high property values.

An important benefit of the lessee's leasehold estate is the right to mortgage leasehold improvements by using them as security for the repayment of a debt. The lessee's interest in the improvements usually is subordinated (made secondary) to the interest of the mortgagee (the holder of the mortgage).

Sandwich lease

When a tenant has a leasehold estate of value, the tenant may sublet that interest. By doing so, the tenant creates what is known as a **sandwich lease**, and the value of the property is then divided among three interests: the lessor's, the original or prime lessee's, and the sublessee's. The interest of the sublessee under a sandwich lease is called a **subleasehold**.

Creation of Lease Interests

The statute of frauds in most states requires that a lease that will terminate more than one year from the date of agreement must be in writing to be enforceable in a court of law. Oral agreements for leases of one year or less are usually enforceable; however, it is good business practice to put all lease agreements in writing.

A lease agreement may cover one or more of the following topics.

Gross lease

In a **gross lease**, the tenant usually pays a fixed rental over the period of the lease, and the landlord pays all expenses of ownership, such as taxes, assessments, and insurance.

Net lease

Under a **net lease**, in addition to the rent, the tenant pays part or all of the property charges, such as taxes, assessments, insurance, and maintenance.

Triple-net lease

In a **triple-net lease**, also known as a net, net, net lease, absolute net lease, or 3N lease, the tenant pays all operating and other expenses plus a fixed rent. These expenses include taxes, assessments, insurance, utilities, and maintenance.

Percentage lease

In a **percentage lease**, the tenant usually pays a minimum guaranteed base rent plus a percentage of gross income earned by the business. The amount paid over the base is called overage rent. The percentage paid may change (usually, it decreases) as gross income increases. For example, the rent may be $1,000 per month plus 3% of gross income over $6,000 per month and 1% of gross income over $10,000 per month.

Either a gross lease or a net lease may be a percentage lease.

Excess rent and deficit rent

Excess rent is the amount by which scheduled rent exceeds market rent at the time of the appraisal. Excess rent is created by a lease that is favorable to the lessor and is likely the result of a strong rental market. **Deficit rent**, on the other hand, is the amount by which market rent exceeds scheduled rent at the time of the appraisal. Deficit rent is created by a lease favorable to the tenant and is usually the result of a weak rental market. Because excess rent and deficit rent result from a lease contract rather than the income potential of the property, their effect is often considered a nonrealty element of value.

Escalator clause

An **escalator clause** provides for periodic increases in rents based on any increase in one of a number of indices, such as the consumer price index (CPI) or the wholesale price index (WPI).

Renewal options

The lease may provide that the lessee has the right at the end of the lease term to renew the lease for the same term or some other stated period. A **renewal option** usually includes a rent increase at a stated percentage or based on an index or other formula. The existence of a renewal option at a rate favorable to the lessee will make the lessee's interest that much more valuable and the lessor's interest that much less valuable. Because the right to exercise a renewal option is entirely at the discretion of the lessee, it usually is considered a benefit to the lessee rather than the lessor.

Tenant improvements

Most leased office and other commercial buildings are built, finished, or remodeled according to the requirements of a particular tenant. Frequently, original construction does not include interior partitioning, which is completed only after a lease is entered into so that the space can be finished to suit the tenant's needs. Either the lessor or the lessee may be obligated to pay for such **tenant improvements**, as the lease provides. If the lessor pays, the rent will be higher than it would be otherwise; if improvements are made by the tenant, the rent may be lower than otherwise.

Other lease provisions

A lease may contain a **tax-stop clause** that allows the landlord to charge the tenant for any increase in taxes over a specified level. An **expense-stop clause** works in the same way to pass increases in building maintenance expenses on to tenants on a pro rata basis. A **purchase option**, or right of first refusal, may accompany a lease of real property. The purchase price may be provided in the lease agreement or it may be based on a stated formula.

Exercise 16-2

1. Scheduled rent that is higher than market rent creates
   a. overage rent.
   b. gross rent.
   c. excess rent.
   d. escalator rent.
2. The amount paid over minimum base rent in a percentage lease is
   a. overage rent.
   b. gross rent.
   c. excess rent.
   d. escalator rent.
3. The lease under which the tenant pays a fixed rental and the landlord pays all expenses of ownership is
   a. the gross lease.
   b. the triple-net lease.
   c. the net lease.
   d. the percentage lease.
4. An index will be referred to in
   a. a gross lease.
   b. a triple-net lease.
   c. an escalator clause.
   d. an expense-stop clause.
5. The interest of a sublessee is
   a. a leasehold.
   b. a leased fee.
   c. a subleasehold.
   d. a sandwich lease.
6. Increases in maintenance costs are passed on to tenants under
   a. a tax-stop clause.
   b. an expense-stop clause.
   c. a gross lease.
   d. an escalator clause.

Check your answers against those in the answer key at the back of the book.

■ LEASED FEE AND LEASEHOLD VALUATIONS

Because changing conditions affect the value of real estate, leases made prior to the current period may be for amounts above or below the current market figures. If market rent exceeds scheduled rent, the property owner is, in effect, transferring part of the property interest to the tenant, thus creating a positive leasehold interest. On the other hand, if scheduled rent exceeds market rent, a negative leasehold interest (called a lease premium) exists, and the unfavorable lease, in a sense, is a liability of the lessee. If the difference between scheduled rent and market rent becomes too heavily weighted in the owner's favor, the tenant may try to renegotiate the terms of the lease (perhaps exchanging a longer lease term for a lower lease payment). If scheduled rent and market rent are the same, the tenant's interest in the property is of zero value.

The principle involved in the valuation of lease interests is similar to that of capitalized income valuation under the annuity or Inwood method. The value of the lessor's and the lessee's interests is found by capitalizing the present value of the income each receives and adding the reversionary value of the land, or land and building, at the expiration of the lease term. Ordinarily, the lessor receives the reversionary value of the property. But some leases provide for payments to the lessee by the lessor for any improvements made by the lessee that will ultimately revert to the lessor.

In valuing lease interests, the appraiser must first carefully study the detailed provisions of the lease to determine the rights and obligations of the owner and tenant. Then, the valuation of leased fee and leasehold interests is basically a matter of dividing the value of the property into separate values attributable to each of the various interests. As a rule, the total of the various interests in the property will approximate the value of the property under free and clear ownership, but may be somewhat more or less.

The examples in this unit give leased property situations and suggested methods of appraisal. The In Practice examples shown next are typical of situations involving relatively long-term leases and assume no remaining building value at the end of the lease term. Other leases require different assumptions. Note, too, that capitalization rates must always have adequate market support. The first example illustrates the valuation of an investment property free and clear of any lease interests.

IN PRACTICE

A property earning a net operating income of $48,000 per year is rented on an annual basis to one tenant. The remaining economic life of the building is 25 years, and the current market value of the land is estimated at $100,000. The rate of interest for similar investments is 14%. Based on these facts, and using the building residual technique, the value of the property is obtained:

Estimated land value			$100,000
Net operating income		$48,000	
Interest on land value ($100,000 × 14%)		– 14,000	
Residual income to building		$34,000	
Capitalization rate for building	14%		
Interest rate	4%		
Recapture rate	18%		
Building value ($34,000 ÷ 18%)			188,889
Total property value			$288,900 (rounded)

The following series of In Practice examples, all based on the same hypothetical property but with varying conditions as to term of lease and amount of rent under the lease, illustrate the valuation of leased fee and leasehold interests.

IN PRACTICE

Assume that the property described in the previous example is now leased to a nationally known company on a 25-year lease at the same net annual rent of $48,000, equal to market rent. The building is considered of no value at the end of the lease term. Because of the increased security, and therefore the decreased risk, in having the property leased for a long period of time by a national company, the interest rate (sometimes called risk rate) has been lowered from 14% to 12%. The interest rate applicable to reversion is assumed to be 14%.

Based on these facts, and using the Inwood method of capitalization, the value of the leased fee is derived as follows:

Net operating income	$ 48,000
Annual factor (25 yrs @ 12%)	× 7.843
Present worth of net income	$376,500 (rounded)
Present worth of reversion	
(25 yrs @ 14%)	
($100,000 × 0.038 reversion factor)	3,800
Total property value	$380,300

In the preceding example, the lower risk rate of 12% results in an increase in the value of the investment (from $288,900 to $380,300).

IN PRACTICE

The property is leased to a nationally known company on a 25-year lease, but the net operating income is only $40,000, $8,000 below the market rent. The appraiser in this instance must estimate the value of the two affected interests—leased fee and leasehold. Because of the greatly reduced risk brought on by the long lease to a national company at a scheduled rent well below the market rent, the interest rate has been lowered to 11%. The interest rate applicable to reversion is unchanged at the 14% rate assumed earlier.

The leased fee interest can be computed as follows:

Net operating income	$ 40,000
Annuity factor (25 yrs @ 11%)	× 8.422
Present worth of net income	$336,900 (rounded)
Present worth of reversion	
(25 yrs @ 14%)	
($100,000 × 0.038 reversion factor)	3,800
Value of the leased fee interest	$340,700

The leasehold interest can be computed as follows:

Market rent	$ 48,000
Scheduled rent	40,000
Excess rent	$ 8,000
Present worth of excess rent discounted @ 15%	6.464
Value of leasehold interest	$ 51,700 (rounded)
Total value of leased fee and leasehold interests ($340,700 + $51,700)	$392,400

In the preceding example, it is obvious that the lessee has an interest in the property that can be measured annually in terms of the difference between the rental value of the property today and the actual rent paid to the landlord. This would also be the value of the lessee's interest if a sandwich lease were to be created, with (under these facts) the sublessee's scheduled rent equal to the market rent. To measure the lessee's leasehold interest, the excess rent must be capitalized over the term of the lease. Because the excess rent arises out of a leasehold interest, it is subject to the covenants and conditions of the lease and is less secure; therefore, the interest rate used (15%) is higher than the 14% rate used to value the property under free and clear ownership.

IN PRACTICE

The scheduled rent is $52,000 per year, or $4,000 higher than the current market rent. A higher interest rate (15%) will be applied to the excess rent portion of the total income because it may not continue for the length of the lease.

The leased fee interest can be computed as follows:

Present value of market rent (provided previously)	$376,500
Value of reversion	3,800
	$380,300
Excess rent discounted @ 15%	
($4,000 × 6.464 annuity factor)	25,900 (rounded)
Value of leased fee interest	$406,200

When scheduled rent is higher than market rent, as in the last example, the value of the lessor's interest increases. This happens even though the excess rent is capitalized at a higher rate because the tenant may default if paying more rent than what is ordinarily expected.

Exercise 16-3

1. Explain how a leasehold estate is created.

2. Using the figures given in the previous example, what is the value of the leased fee interest if scheduled rent is $54,000? If scheduled rent is $50,000?

Check your answers against those in the answer key at the back of the book.

■ SUMMARY

A property interest to be appraised is not always an undivided fee simple interest. A condominium is the undivided ownership of the airspace that a unit actually occupies, plus an undivided interest in the ownership of the common elements, which are owned jointly with the other condominium unit owners. A planned unit development (PUD) includes individual ownership of a detached home and lot, town home and lot, or condominium, along with shared ownership of common areas. A time-share divides ownership into increments of time or a percentage interest. Manufactured homes require special consideration of their location.

Property under co-ownership may be difficult to sell, and its value will be affected commensurately if all owners do not take part in the transaction.

Excess rent is any amount by which scheduled rent is greater than market rent. Deficit rent is the amount by which market rent exceeds scheduled rent. A lessee may mortgage property improvements. A subleasehold is the interest of a sublessee.

A lease may be described by the manner in which rent is determined, as in a gross lease, net lease, triple-net lease (net, net, net lease), or percentage lease. Overage rent is any amount paid over the base minimum under a percentage lease. With an escalator clause, lease payments can increase on the basis of an index (for example, the consumer price index).

The lessee may have the right to renew the lease under the same or revised terms. The lease also may provide the lessee a purchase option or right of first refusal. Tenant improvements are made to suit the tenant and may be paid for by either landlord or tenant. The tax-stop clause and expense-stop clause work to pass on to the lessee any increase in tax or expense payments that would otherwise be the obligation of the landlord.

Because the annuity method of capitalization is based on the premise that income will remain scheduled and predictable throughout the term of a long lease, it is almost always used in valuing leased fee and leasehold interests.

A leasehold interest can have value only if the scheduled rent under the lease is less than the market rent value of the property free of lease. A leasehold interest has many of the characteristics of first mortgage equity. If there is a sublessee who also has an interest (which may occur when scheduled rent is less than market rent), the sublessee's interest—the subleasehold—will have risk characteristics similar to a second mortgage. Thus, the capitalization of either the prime lessee's interest or the sublessee's interest normally will warrant a higher capitalization rate than that of the lessor's interest.

The sum of the values of the various lease interests tends to equal the value of the property under free and clear ownership. However, if the scheduled rent paid by a reliable lessee exceeds the market rent, the sum of the values of the various interests could exceed the value of the real estate free and clear.

REVIEW QUESTIONS

The following case study should be used to answer questions 1 through 3.

An industrial property with a 30-year lease to a highly rated tenant calls for an annual rental of $36,000. Data on comparative properties indicate that the market rent of the subject property is $45,000 per year.

The lessor is virtually assured of receiving the rent, as long as it remains below market rent. In the opinion of the appraiser, an appropriate rate of interest for a low-risk investment of this type is 11%. The lessee, on the other hand, has an interest that is subject to variation in value. If market conditions change and the per-year rental value is no longer a favorable one, the value of the leasehold estate will be reduced considerably or even eliminated. To reflect the lessee's risk, the appraiser estimates the leasehold rate at 14%. The annuity factor for 30 years at 14% is 7.003.

1. If land value at the expiration of the lease is determined to be $150,000, and the building is assumed to be worthless at the time, what is the value of the leased fee interest?
2. What is the value of the leasehold interest?
3. What is the total value of the leased fee and leasehold interests?

The following case study should be used to answer questions 4 through 20.

The subject property is a warehouse that is 50 feet by 200 feet by 16 feet high. The warehouse is cement block faced with brick on a concrete slab and was built in 1980 for $75 per square foot. The appraiser has estimated the property's current land value as $500,000. The current replacement cost of the structure is $150 per square foot and its effective age is 20 years, with a remaining economic life of 30 years.

Comparable warehouses in the subject neighborhood sell for $160 per square foot if the property has a rail spur. Without a rail spur, the sales price for a comparable warehouse is $140 per square foot. The subject warehouse lacks a rail spur.

Warehouses like the subject property rent for $25,000 per month, with a 5% vacancy rate and a net income ratio of 40%. Sales of comparable rentals indicate a capitalization rate of 8.15% for the subject.

The assignment is to appraise the fee simple absolute estate of the subject property to establish asset value for a purchase. The effective date of the appraisal is the date of the appraiser's inspection of the property.

4. The gross building area is
   a. 10,000 square feet.
   b. 15,000 square feet.
   c. 20,000 square feet.
   d. 25,000 square feet.

5. The volume of the structure is
   a. 100,000 cubic feet.
   b. 160,000 cubic feet.
   c. 250,000 cubic feet.
   d. 500,000 cubic feet.

6. The percentage of physical depreciation suffered by the structure is
   a. 20%.
   b. 30%.
   c. 40%.
   d. 50%.

7. The amount of physical depreciation suffered by the structure is
   a. $400,000.
   b. $500,000.
   c. $600,000.
   d. $800,000.

8. The value of the structure is
   a. $400,000.
   b. $500,000.
   c. $750,000.
   d. $900,000.

9. The property's value via the cost approach (rounded to the nearest $5,000) is
   a. $1,200,000.
   b. $1,300,000.
   c. $1,400,000.
   d. $1,500,000.

10. The property's value via the sales comparison approach (rounded to the nearest $5,000) is
    a. $1,200,000.
    b. $1,300,000.
    c. $1,400,000.
    d. $1,500,000.

11. The property's potential gross income is
    a. $250,000.
    b. $300,000.
    c. $400,000.
    d. $500,000.

12. The property's effective gross income is
    a. $158,000.
    b. $210,000.
    c. $285,000.
    d. $300,000.

13. The property's net operating income is
    a. $100,000.
    b. $114,000.
    c. $150,000.
    d. $175,000.

14. The property's value via the income approach (rounded to the nearest $5,000) is
    a. $1,200,000.
    b. $1,300,000.
    c. $1,400,000.
    d. $1,500,000.

15. The appraiser's likely opinion of the market value of the subject property (rounded to the nearest $5,000) is
    a. $1,200,000.
    b. $1,300,000.
    c. $1,400,000.
    d. $1,500,000.

16. The process used to arrive at the appraiser's final value conclusion is called
    a. reconciliation.
    b. conciliation.
    c. averaging.
    d. lowest common mean.

17. If the subject property could be rented for only $20,000 per month instead of $25,000, this would create
    a. a nonfreehold estate.
    b. an estate in severalty.
    c. a freehold estate.
    d. an estate in the entirety.

18. If the subject property was rented for $20,000 per month, that amount would be its
    a. market rent.
    b. contract rent.
    c. historical rent.
    d. graduated rent.

19. If a property's contract rent is less than current market rent, what could be the result?
    a. The surplus rent could result in a trade lease.
    b. The deficit rent could result in a sandwich lease.
    c. The surplus rent could result in a graduated lease.
    d. The deficit rent could result in a graduated lease.

20. Which of the following estates can be valued as of the effective date of appraisal?
    a. Fee simple absolute
    b. Leased fee
    c. Leasehold
    d. All of these

Check your answers against those in the answer key at the back of the book.

APPENDIX

WEBSITES

American Institute of Architects

www.aia.org

American Real Estate Society

www.aresnet.org

American Society of Appraisers

www.appraisers.org

American Society of Farm Managers and Rural Appraisers, Inc.

www.asfmra.org

American Society of Home Inspectors

www.ashi.org

Americans with Disabilities Act

www.ada.gov

Appraisal Foundation

www.appraisalfoundation.org

Appraisal Institute

www.appraisalinstitute.org

Appraisal Institute of Canada

www.aicanada.org

Appraisal Practices Board

www.appraisalfoundation.org/

Appraisal Qualifications Board

www.appraisalfoundation.org

Appraisal Standards Board

www.appraisalfoundation.org

Association of Appraiser Regulatory Officials

www.aaro.net

Building Owners and Managers Association International

www.boma.org

Bureau of Labor Statistics

stats.bls.gov

Bureau of Land Management

www.blm.gov

Bureau of Transportation Statistics

www.rita.dot.gov/bts/

Census Bureau

www.census.gov

A Citizen's Guide to Radon, Revised 2012 (EPA)

www.epa.gov/radon/pubs/citguide.html

Commercial Investment Real Estate Institute

www.ccim.com

Department of Energy

www.energy.gov

Department of Housing and Urban Development

www.hud.gov

Department of Veterans Affairs

www.va.gov

Energy Star Program

www.energystar.gov

Environmental Protection Agency

www.epa.gov

Fannie Mae

www.fanniemae.com

www.fanniemae.com/singlefamily

Federal Agricultural Mortgage Corporation (Farmer Mac)

www.farmermac.com

Federal Bureau of Investigation

www.fbi.gov/about-us/investigate/white_collar/mortgage-fraud

Federal Deposit Insurance Corporation

www.fdic.gov

Federal Emergency Management Agency

www.fema.gov

Federal Financial Institutions Examination Council, Appraisal Subcommittee

www.asc.gov/Home.aspx

Federal Housing Administration

www.hud.gov/offices/hsg/fhahistory.cfm

Federal Housing Finance Agency

www.fhfa.gov

Federal Reserve Board

www.federalreserve.gov

Freddie Mac

www.freddiemac.com

Fedworld Information Network

http://fedworld.ntis.gov/

F.W. Dodge Corporation

www.construction.com/dodge/

Ginnie Mae

www.ginniemae.gov

Inman News Service

www.inman.com

The Inside Story: A Guide to Indoor Air Quality (EPA)

www.epa.gov/iaq/pubs/insidest.html

Internal Revenue Service Publications

www.irs.gov/Forms-&-Pubs

International Association of Assessing Officers

www.iaao.org

International Code Council

www.iccsafe.org

International Right of Way Association

www.irwaonline.org

Manufactured Housing Institute

www.manufacturedhousing.org

Marshall & Swift Publication Company

www.marshallswift.com

Municipal Code Corporation

www.municode.com

National Appraisal Coalition

www.nationalappraisalcoalition.org/findacoalition.html

National Association of Home Builders

www.nahb.org

National Association of Independent Fee Appraisers

www.naifa.com

National Association of Real Estate Brokers

www.nareb.com

National Association of REALTORS®

www.realtor.com

www.realtor.org

National Innovation Research Labs

www.homeinnovation.com

National Lead Information Center

www2.epa.gov/lead

National Radon Information Center

www.epa.gov/radon

National Residential Appraisers Institute

www.nraiappraisers.com

National Safety Council

www.nsc.org

National Society of Real Estate Appraisers, Inc.

www.nsrea.org

Real Estate Educators Association

www.reea.org

Realty Times

www.realtytimes.com

R. S. Means Company

www.rsmeans.com

Uniform Standards of Professional Appraisal Practice

www.uspap.org

United States Access Board

www.access-board.gov

United States Green Building Council

www.usgbc.org

ANSWER KEY

UNIT 1

Exercise 1-1

An appraiser's compensation should not depend on the estimate of value obtained, to avoid even the appearance of impropriety. The appraiser's compensation may, however, reflect the complexity of the work required in dealing with the subject property.

Exercise 1-2

All the courses listed would benefit a professional appraiser because they touch on topics that must be understood in order to prepare a well-reasoned appraisal report.

Exercise 1-3

1. b
2. b
3. c
4. b

Exercise 1-4

The appraiser should maintain a backup system for all information gathered as part of the appraisal process and stay up to date on developments in technology that will be required by the appraiser's clients, but also of use to the appraiser.

Review Questions

1. Numerous courses, such as economics, geography, city planning, accounting, statistics
2. a
3. c
4. a
5. b
6. b
7. d
8. b
9. c
10. a

11. c
12. b
13. a
14. c
15. b
16. c
17. c
18. a
19. d
20. a

UNIT 2

Exercise 2-1

1. 0.4
2. 0.37
3. 0.166

Exercise 2-2

1. $190,000 × 108% = $205,200
2. $340,000 – $250,000 = $90,000 profit
   $90,000 ÷ $250,000 = 0.36, or 36% profit

Exercise 2-3

$30,000 × 102% = $30,600 end of year 1
$30,600 × 102% = $31,212 end of year 2
$31,212 × 102% = $31,836.24 end of year 3

Exercise 2-4

1. 3 square feet or 432 square inches
2. 1.875 square feet or 270 square inches
3. 42 square feet or 6,048 square inches
4. 144 square inches
5. 10.5 square feet
6. 75 feet × 125 feet = 9,375 square feet

Exercise 2-5

A = ½(BH) = ½(50' × 85') = ½(4,250 sq. ft.) = 2,125 sq. ft.

Exercise 2-6

1. Area of A = 25' × 19' = 475 sq. ft.
   Area of B = 13' × 8' = 104 sq. ft.
   Area of C = 9' × 7' = 63 sq. ft.
   Total area = 642 sq. ft.
2. Area of rectangle:
   A = L × W = 18' × 7' = 126 sq. ft.
   Area of triangle:
   A = ½(BH) = ½(22' – 18') × 7' = ½(4' × 7') = ½(28 sq. ft.) = 14 sq. ft.
   Total area = 126 sq. ft. + 14 sq. ft. = 140 sq. ft.
3. Area of A = ½(20' – 12') × 8' = 32 sq. ft.
   Area of B = 18' × 20' = 360 sq. ft.
   Area of C = ½(8' × 18') = 72 sq. ft.
   Area of D = ½(12' × 22') = 132 sq. ft.
   Area of E = ½ × (20' – 8') × 20' = 120 sq. ft.
   Area of F = 8' × 20' = 160 sq. ft.
   Total area = (32 + 360 + 72 + 132 + 120 + 160) sq. ft. = 876 sq. ft.

Exercise 2-7

AREA		
A = 5' × 16'	=	80 sq. ft.
B = 3' × (20' + 16') = 3' × 36'	=	108
C = 12' × 20'	=	240
D = 10' × (40' – 22') = 10' × 18'	=	180
E = (50' – 25') × 22' = 25' × 22'	=	550
F = (50' – 10') × (74' – 22') = 40' × 52'	=	2,080
TOTAL	=	3,238 sq. ft.

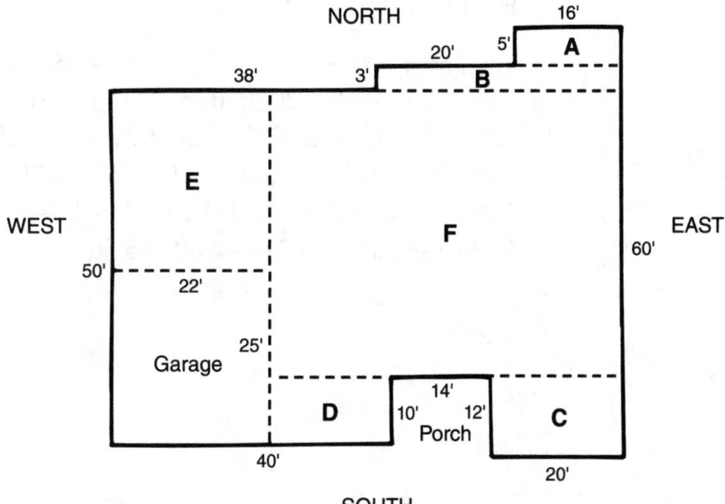

Exercise 2-8

1. 8' × 7' = 56 sq. ft. = 8,064 sq. in. = 6 sq. yd. (rounded)
2. 9' × 3' × 2' = 54 cu. ft. = 93,312 cu. in. = 2 cu. yd.
3. A. B = (33' + 55') – 83' = 5' ½ (5' × 16')
   = 40 sq ft

   B. 83' × 16' = 1,328 sq. ft.

   C. B = 132' – 110' = 22'; H = (16' + 82' + 28' + 28') – 110' = 44'

   ½ (22' × 44') = 484 sq. ft.

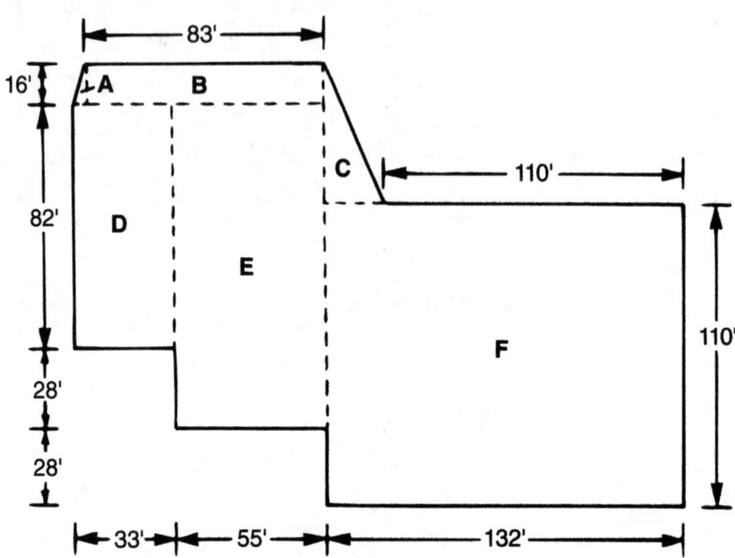

   D. 82' × 33' = 2,706 sq. ft.

   E. 55' × (82' + 28') = 55' × 110' = 6,050 sq. ft.

   F. 132' × 110' = 14,520 sq. ft.

   Total area = 40 sq. ft. + 1,328 sq. ft. + 484 sq. ft. + 2,706 sq. ft. + 6,050 sq. ft. + 14,520 sq. ft. = 25,128 sq. ft.
4. 80' × 35' × 10' = 28,000 cu. ft. ÷ 27 = 1,037.037 cu. yd.
   ½(80' × 35' × 6') = 8,400 cu. ft. ÷ 27 = 311.111 cu. yd.
   1,037.037 cu. yd. + 311.111 cu. yd. = 1,348.148 cu. yd.
   1,348.148 cu. yd. × $45 = $60,666.66

Exercise 2-9

x	$(x-\bar{x})$	$(x-\bar{x})^2$
12	−7.6	57.76
15	−4.6	21.16
18	−1.6	2.56
25	5.4	29.16
28	8.4	70.56
98		181.20

Mean = 98 ÷ 5 = 19.6

s = 181.20 ÷ 4 = 45.3

s = $\sqrt{45.3}$

s = 6.73

Review Questions

1. $45,000 ÷ 0.36 = $125,000
2. $24,000 ÷ $200,000 = 0.12 = 12%
3. A = 25' × 15' = 375 sq. ft.
   B = 65' × (30' + 25') = 65' × 55' = 3,575 sq. ft.
   C = ½(*BH*) B = 100' – (15' + 65') = 20'
   H = 30' + 25' = 55'
   ½ × (20' × 55') = 550 sq. ft.
   Total area = 375 sq. ft. + 3,575 sq. ft. + 550 sq. ft. = 4,500 sq. ft.

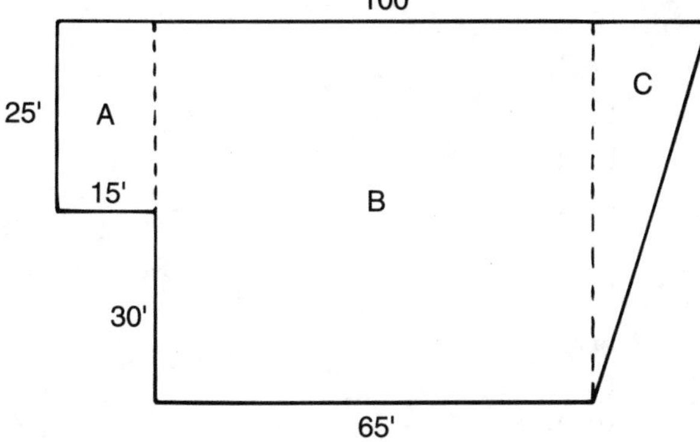

4. 35' × 20' × 14' = 9,800 cu. ft.
   ½(35' × 20' × 6') = 2,100 cu. ft.
   9,800 cu. ft. + 2,100 cu. ft. = 11,900 cu. ft.
   11,900 × $2.75 = $32,725
5. 40.83' × 60.67' = 2,477 sq. ft. (rounded)
   80.5' × 25.25' = 2,033 sq. ft. (rounded)
   Total area = 4,510 sq. ft. (rounded)

6. AREA

A = 26' × (24' – 2') = 26' × 22'	572 sq. ft.
B = 36' – (24' – 2') = 36' – 22' = 14' × 5	70
C = 21' × 5'	105
D = 59' × (45' – 5') = 59' × 40'	2,360
TOTAL	3,107 sq. ft.

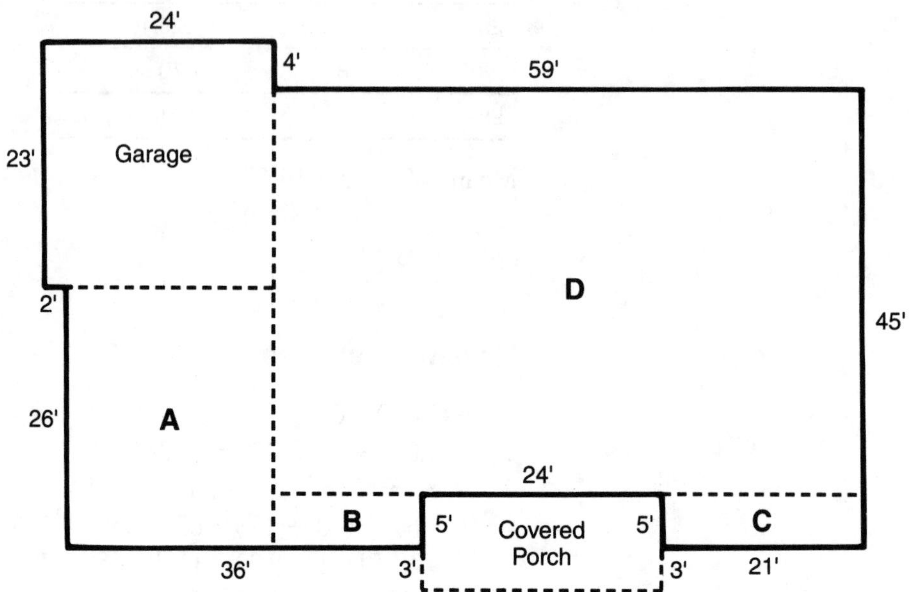

7. a
8. c
9. d
10. a
11. b
12. d
13. b
14. d
15. b
16. a
17. c
18. a
19. b
20. d

UNIT 3

Exercise 3-1

Real estate or real property: 1, 2, 3, 4, 5, 6, 9, 10

Personal property: 7, 8

If an item were personal property, it could not be considered in estimating the value of real property. On the other hand, if the item were real estate, then its contribution to the value of the real property would have to be estimated.

Exercise 3-2

1. 40 acres
2. 640 acres
3. No, the parcels are not contiguous. They total 320 acres.
4. 160 acres × $7,500 per acre = $1,200,000
5. The adjacent half-section is the N½ of Section 2, Tier 1 South and Range 3 East of the grant meridian and base line.
6. The section to the north of the described section is Section 32, Tier 2 South and Range 5 West.

Exercise 3-3

1. Leased fee; leasehold
2. Leased fee
3. Reversion

Exercise 3-4

1. Joint tenancy; tenancy by the entireties
2. Ownership in severalty
3. Joint tenancy or tenancy by the entireties

Exercise 3-5

1. Fee simple absolute, or fee simple
2. Tenant owns a leasehold estate; landlord owns a leased fee estate.
3. The property on which the house is located is the dominant tenement. The adjoining land over which the easement runs is the servient tenement.
4. Joint tenancy
5. Condominium

Review Questions

1. b
2. c
3. d
4. d

5. d
6. a
7. d
8. b
9. a
10. b
11. c
12. a
13. c
14. Whether something attached to real property is a fixture may be determined by considering the intention of the person who placed the item on the land, the method of attachment, the adaptability of the thing for the land's ordinary use, the agreement of the parties, and the relationship of the parties.
15. b
16. c
17. c
18. b
19. a
20. b

UNIT 4

Exercise 4-1

1. Because of the homeowner's possible mental impairment, she may not have legal capacity to transfer title to her house. Even if she is determined to have the legal capacity to do so, she may have acted under undue influence by her nephew.
2. The father offered to pay $10 for every A grade that his son earned, but has paid him only $50 even though the son had eight A grades. The father has failed to live up to the terms of their agreement by not paying adequate consideration to his son.
3. An oral agreement for the sale of real estate is not valid.
4. The appraiser should not provide any opinion of property value, no matter what it is called, without a clear understanding between her and the client of the nature of the assignment and the fact that it would be performed in an objective manner in compliance with *USPAP*.

Exercise 4-2

A contract to perform an appraisal of real estate should include, at a minimum, the name of the appraiser and client and contact information for each; address of the property and property interests to be appraised, purpose of the appraisal (such as a determination of market value), type of appraisal report required, effective date of the appraisal report, date by which the appraisal report is to be delivered to the client, appraiser's compensation, any statutory requirements, and other provisions intended to define the scope of work required by the appraisal assignment and make the liability of the appraiser subject to the stated conditions.

Exercise 4-3

1. The grantor of a quitclaim deed makes no warranty of actually owning any interest to convey in the described property; any interest that is owned, however, will be conveyed by the deed.
2. Recording a deed serves notice to the world of the title transfer if the deed is recorded in the county in which the property is located.

Exercise 4-4

The friends will probably want some type of percentage lease that will allow them to make a minimal base payment while their business is getting established, but will require higher lease payments as their income grows.

Review Questions

1. a
2. c
3. c
4. d
5. b
6. b
7. c
8. d
9. b
10. a
11. d
12. c
13. d
14. a
15. c
16. b
17. a
18. b
19. d
20. b

UNIT 5

Exercise 5-1

Likely to prevent an arm's-length transaction: 1, 3, 5, 6

Exercise 5-2

1. Highest and best use, change, conformity
2. Contribution, laws of increasing and decreasing returns
3. Contribution, laws of increasing and decreasing returns, competition
4. Competition, contribution
5. Laws of increasing and decreasing returns, contribution
6. Externalities

Review Questions

1. c
2. d
3. b
4. a
5. b
6. a
7. b
8. a
9. b
10. a
11. c
12. d
13. Market value is an estimate of the worth of a property. Sales price is the actual selling price of a property.
14. Progression
15. Substitution
16. Anticipation
17. Highest and best use
18. Highest and best use
19. Supply and demand
20. Contribution

UNIT 6

Exercise 6-1

Sales comparison approach: $778,000 – $27,000 = $751,000 (value of house X)

Cost approach: $230,000 – (30% × $230,000) + $52,000 = Property value
$230,000 – $69,000 + $52,000 = $213,000

Income capitalization approach: $64,500 ÷ 9% = $716,667

Exercise 6-2

1. Cost
2. Income capitalization
3. Cost
4. Sales comparison
5. Income capitalization
6. Sales comparison
7. Income capitalization
8. Sales comparison
9. Cost
10. Income capitalization

Review Questions

1. a
2. c
3. b
4. c
5. Value of property B: \$480,000 – \$36,000 = \$444,000
6. \$725,000 – (40% × \$725,000) + \$175,000 = Property value
   \$725,000 – 290,000 + \$175,000 = \$610,000
7. \$124,000 ÷ 9% = \$1,377,800 (rounded to nearest hundred dollars)
8. c
9. a
10. b
11. c
12. d
13. a
14. b
15. d
16. b
17. b
18. a
19. a
20. c

UNIT 7

Exercise 7-1

1. a. One-and-a-half-story house: there is economy in cost per cubic foot of habitable space and built-in expandability.
   b. Two-story house: plumbing can be lined up; winter heating is used to the best advantage (heat rises); more house can be built on a smaller piece of property.
   c. Split-entry house: the square footage of the house is doubled at a modest cost increase by finishing the rooms on the lower level.
2. If a house is oriented with the main living areas facing south, it can result in savings in heating and air-conditioning costs. Orientation also contributes to the enjoyment of a house if it takes advantage of a natural view and the maximum amount of land is allocated for private use.
3. The scale most often used is ¼-inch to 1-foot.
4. Curb appeal is a property's overall attractiveness as viewed from the street.
5. To provide a larger private zone.

Exercise 7-2

1. Solid cores are generally preferred for exterior doors because they provide better heat and sound insulation and are more resistant to warping. Hollow-core doors are about a third as heavy as the solid-core type and are commonly used for interior locations where heat and sound insulation are not as critical.

2. The water supply system brings water to the house from a well or city main and distributes hot and cold water through two sets of pipes. The vent piping system carries out of the house all sewer gases from drainage lines.
3. The main drawback to the heat pump is its initial cost. Once installed, however, the heat pump operates very economically and requires little maintenance.
4. 1. *Safety*—The system must meet all NEC requirements.
   2. *Capacity*—The system must meet the home's existing needs and have the capacity to accommodate room additions and new appliances.
   3. *Convenience*—There should be enough switches, lights, and outlets, and they should be located so that occupants will not have to walk in the dark or use extension cords.
5. Balloon construction differs from the platform method in that the studs are continuous, extending to the ceiling of the second floor, rather than shorter lengths, extending the length of one floor at a time. The platform method is usually preferred.
6. *Firestopping:* Boards or blocks nailed between studs or joists to stop drafts and retard the spread of fire.
7. *Circuit breaker box:* The distribution panel for the many electrical circuits in the house. If a circuit is overloaded, the heat generated by the additional flow of electrical power will cause the circuit breaker to open at the breaker box. By removing the overload and allowing the breaker to cool, the switch in the circuit breaker box may be turned to "on" and electrical service restored.
8. *Insulation:* Batts or loose fill placed in outside walls or ceilings to prevent loss of heat from structure in winter and transfer of heat into structure in summer.
9. *Monolithic slab:* Concrete slab forming foundation area of structure. Monolithic concrete is poured in a continuous process so there are no separations due to different setting times.
10. *Sills:* The horizontal members of the foundation that are secured to the piers by the anchor bolts to prevent the house from sliding from its foundation.

Review Questions

1. b
2. b
3. a
4. c
5. b
6. c
7. c
8. a
9. b
10. a
11. a
12. b
13. d

14. c
15. b
16. Monolithic concrete slab
17. Wood sheathing covered with building paper and siding
18. Plaster over wallboard
19. Could be either single or double hung
20. Finished wood on first floor; unfinished concrete in basement

UNIT 8

Exercise 8-1

The property being appraised is the single-family residence located at 2130 West Franklin Street, Lakeside, Illinois. Fee simple property rights are to be appraised. The purpose of the appraisal is to estimate market value, which is the most probable price the property should bring in a sale occurring under normal market conditions. The date of valuation is the date of the report.

As a rule, the sales comparison approach is most useful in valuing properties of this type.

Exercise 8-2

1. (1) Personal inspection
   (6) Register of deeds
   (42) Plats
2. (19) Building architects, contractors, and engineers
   (12) City hall or county courthouse
   (20) County or city engineering commission
   (24) Newspaper and magazine articles
3. (12) City hall or county courthouse
   (20) County or city engineering commission
   (22) Area planning commissions
4. (22) Area planning commissions
   (29) U.S. Bureau of the Census
   (32) Local chamber of commerce
   (33) Government councils
5. (1) Personal inspection
   (22) Area planning commissions
   (44) Area maps
6. (1) Personal inspection
   (12) City hall or county courthouse
   (22) Area planning commissions
   (32) Local chamber of commerce
   (44) Area maps
   (28) Public utility companies
7. (12) City hall or county courthouse
   (20) County or city engineering commission
   (22) Area planning commissions

8. (6) Register of deeds
   (7) Title reports
9. (7) Title reports
   (12) City hall or county courthouse
   (13) Assessor's office

Exercise 8.3

NEIGHBORHOOD

Note: Race and the racial composition of the neighborhood are not appraisal factors.

Neighborhood Characteristics				**One-Unit Housing Trends**				**One-Unit Housing**			**Present Land Use %**	
Location	[X] Urban	[ ] Suburban	[ ] Rural	Property Values	[X] Increasing	[ ] Stable	[ ] Declining	PRICE		AGE	One-Unit	%
Built-Up	[X] Over 75%	[ ] 25–75%	[ ] Under 25%	Demand/Supply	[ ] Shortage	[X] In Balance	[ ] Over Supply	$ (000)		(yrs)	2-4 Unit	95 %
Growth	[ ] Rapid	[ ] Stable	[X] Slow	Marketing Time	[ ] Under 3 mths	[X] 3–6 mths	[ ] Over 6 mths	160	Low	15	Multi-Family	1 %
Neighborhood Boundaries	Cedar, Parkside, Ellis, and Lombard define this predominantly residential							280	High	22	Commercial	1 %
neighborhood known as the Gunderson area.								240	Pred.	7	Other Vac	1 %

Neighborhood Description Fifteen-minute commute time to downtown Midstate and convenient schools, shopping and health care facilities continue to make the Gunderson area very desirable and demand for homes has been consistent.

Market Conditions (including support for the above conclusions) Although sales prices have kept pace with inflation, a seasonal slowdown has resulted in an average marketing time of three months. This remains a healthy market, however, with no indication of a downturn.

Exercise 8-4

SITE

Dimensions 50'× 200' Area 10,000 sf Shape Rectangular View N; Res

Specific Zoning Classification R-2 Zoning Description Residential, Single-Family

Zoning Compliance [X] Legal [ ] Legal Nonconforming (Grandfathered Use) [ ] No Zoning [ ] Illegal (describe)

Is the highest and best use of the subject property as improved (or as proposed per plans and specifications) the present use? [X] Yes [ ] No If No, describe

Utilities	**Public**	**Other (describe)**		**Public**	**Other (describe)**	**Off-site Improvements—Type**		**Public**	**Private**
Electricity	[X]	[ ]	Water	[X]	[ ]	Street	Asphalt	[X]	[ ]
Gas	[X]	[ ]	Sanitary Sewer	[X]	[ ]	Alley	None	[ ]	[ ]

FEMA Special Flood Hazard Area [ ] Yes [X] No FEMA Flood Zone FEMA Map # FEMA Map Date

Are the utilities and off-site improvements typical for the market area? [X] Yes [ ] No If No, describe

Are there any adverse site conditions or external factors (easements, encroachments, environmental conditions, land uses, etc.)? [X] Yes [ ] No If Yes, describe

Apparent utility easement across rear ten feet of site.

Exercise 8-5

IMPROVEMENTS

General Description	Foundation	Exterior Description materials/condition	Interior materials/condition
Units [X] One [ ] One with Accessory Unit	[ ] Concrete Slab [ ] Crawl Space	Foundation Walls Concrete	Floors Wd/tile/carpet
# of Stories 1	[X] Full Basement [ ] Partial Basement	Exterior Walls Brick	Walls Drywall
Type [X] Det. [ ] Att. [ ] S-Det./End Unit	Basement Area 1,825 sq. ft.	Roof Surface Mineral-fiber shingles	Trim/Finish Wd/paint
[X] Existing [ ] Proposed [ ] Under Const.	Basement Finish 50 %	Gutters & Downspouts Aluminum	Bath Floor Ceramic tile
Design (Style) Ranch/brick	[ ] Outside Entry/Exit [X] Sump Pump	Window Type Wood double-hung	Bath Wainscot Ceramic
Year Built 1990	Evidence of [ ] Infestation	Storm Sash/Insulated Aluminum	Car Storage [ ] None
Effective Age (Yrs) 20	[ ] Dampness [ ] Settlement	Screens Aluminum	[X] Driveway # of Cars
Attic [X] None	Heating [X] FWA [ ] HWBB [ ] Radiant	Amenities [ ] Woodstove(s) #	Driveway Surface Asphalt
[ ] Drop Stair [ ] Stairs	[ ] Other Fuel Gas	[ ] Fireplace(s) # [ ] Fence	[X] Garage # of Cars 2
[ ] Floor [ ] Scuttle	Cooling [X] Central Air Conditioning	[ ] Patio/Deck [ ] Porch	[ ] Carport # of Cars
[ ] Finished [ ] Heated	[ ] Individual [ ] Other	[ ] Pool [ ] Other	[X] Att. [ ] Det. [ ] Built-in

Appliances [X] Refrigerator [X] Range/Oven [X] Dishwasher [X] Disposal [ ] Microwave [ ] Washer/Dryer [X] Other (describe) Range Fan/Hood

Finished area **above** grade contains: 6 Rooms 3 Bedrooms 2.1 Bath(s) 1,600 Square Feet of Gross Living Area Above Grade

Additional features (special energy efficient items, etc.)

Describe the condition of the property (including needed repairs, deterioration, renovations, remodeling, etc.). C4; No updates in the prior 15 years; overall good exterior and interior condition of improvements noted with no indication of functional inadequacies.

Are there any physical deficiencies or adverse conditions that affect the livability, soundness, or structural integrity of the property? [ ] Yes [ ] No If Yes, describe

Does the property generally conform to the neighborhood (functional utility, style, condition, use, construction, etc.)? [X] Yes [ ] No If No, describe

Exercise 8-6

$$\frac{150{,}000}{175{,}000} = 0.8571428$$

$\$200{,}000 \times 0.8571 = 171{,}400$

Exercise 8-7

1. Records on previous appraisals; multiple listing data; assessor's office; brokers or salespeople
2. Sale 2 should be dropped from consideration because of its age. Sale 5 should be dropped because it has three more rooms than the subject; if the only difference was its having only one bathroom, it could still be considered as a comparable.

Review Questions

1. c
2. c
3. a
4. b
5. d
6. a

7. d
8. b
9. a
10. a
11. d
12. c
13. a
14. d
15. a
16. b
17. c
18. a
19. b
20. c

UNIT 9

Exercise 9-1

1. To value vacant sites
2. To apply the cost approach to value
3. To levy special assessments for public improvements
4. For taxation purposes
5. To estimate building depreciation
6. To apply the building residual technique
7. May be required in condemnation appraising
8. To determine if the site is realizing its highest and best use

Exercise 9-2

	Sales Price	Date	Location	Physical Features	Net Adjustment + or –	Adjusted Price
Dollar basis	$20,000	+ $2,400	+ $2,000	– $3,000	+ $1,400	$21,400
Percentage basis	$20,000	+12%	+ 10%	– 15%	+ 7%	$21,400

Exercise 9-3

Land value is $347,000 ÷ 4, or $86,750.

Exercise 9-4

Total projected sales:	
48 lots at $27,000 per lot	$1,296,000
16 lots at $32,000 per lot	512,000
8 lots at $36,000 per lot	288,000
72	$2,096,000
Total projected development costs	934,000
Estimated value of raw land	$1,162,000
Raw land value per lot: $1,162,000 ÷ 72	$16,139

Present worth of lot sales:

First year:	48 lots at $16,139 per lot = $774,672	
	$774,672 discounted to present worth at 12% for one year (0.893)	$691,782
Second year:	16 lots at $16,139 per lot = $258,224	
	$258,224 discounted to present worth at 12% for two years (0.797)	205,805
Third year:	8 lots at $16,139 per lot = $129,112	
	$129,112 discounted to present worth at 12% for three years (0.712)	91,928
Amount subdivider should pay for raw land		$989,515

Review Questions

1. The earth's surface, and everything under it or on it, is considered land. When the land is improved by the addition of utilities (water, gas, electricity) or other services (such as sewers), it becomes a site and may be considered suitable for building purposes.

2. a. In applying the cost approach, site value must be distinguished from the cost of improvements, as indicated by the following formula:

   Cost of improvements new − Depreciation on improvement(s) + Site value = Estimated property value

   b. In computing depreciation for tax purposes, site value must be subtracted from total property value, because land is not depreciable.

3. Sales comparison method; allocation method; abstraction method; subdivision development method; ground rent capitalization; land residual method.

   The sales comparison approach is preferred whenever sales of similar vacant sites are available. The underlying presumption is that recent sales of comparable sites competitive with the subject site are the most reliable guide to the probable current market behavior and reactions of informed buyers.

4. b
5. c
6. a

7. b
8. c
9. a
10. b
11. b
12. b
13. c
14. d
15. b
16. a
17. b
18. d
19. a
20. c

UNIT 10

Exercise 10-1

The house shown in the bottom photograph: It is an old house that cannot be economically produced today.

Exercise 10-2

537.8 ÷ 158.2 × \$39,000 = \$132,580

Exercise 10-3

Area of comparable building: 45' × 50' = 2,250 sq. ft.

\$184,500 ÷ 2,250 = \$82 (cost per square foot)

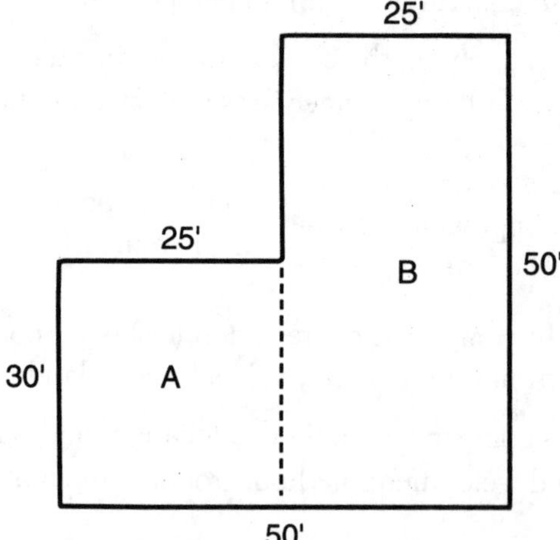

A = 30' × 25'	750 sq. ft.
B = 25' × 50'	1,250 sq. ft.
Total area	2,000 sq. ft.

Cost estimate: 2,000 sq. ft. × \$82 = \$164,000

Exercise 10-4

Unit-in-place costs:

Foundation		
Perimeter, 750 ft. @ $37.30		$27,975
Floor		
31,250 sq. ft. @ $3.10		96,875
Roof		
31,250 sq. ft. @ $3.60 ($2.40 + $0.65 + $.55)		112,500
Interior construction		
Painting and partitions		4,500
Front exterior wall		
125' × 15' = 1,875 sq. ft.		
– 144 sq. ft. for windows		
– 120 sq. ft. for door =		
1,611 sq. ft. @ $9.50	$15,305	
Windows 144 sq. ft. @ $15.30	2,203	
Door	1,300	18,808
Rear exterior wall		
1,875 sq. ft. – 120 sq. ft. = 1,755 sq. ft. @ $9.50	$16,673	
Door	1,300	17,973
Side exterior walls		
500' × 15' = 7,500 sq. ft. – 20% for windows = 6,000 sq. ft. @ $7.10	$42,600	
Windows 1,500 sq. ft. @ $14.20	21,300	63,900
Steel framing		
Area supported by frame		
100' × 225' = 22,500 sq. ft. @ $4.50		101,250
Electric		
31,250 sq. ft. @ $3.25		101,563
Heating		
31,250 sq. ft. @ $2.75		85,938
Plumbing		
31,250 sq. ft. @ $1.60		50,000
Total Reproduction Cost		$ 681,282

$681,282 ÷ 31,250 sq. ft. = ~ $21.80 per sq. ft.

Exercise 10-5

1. Direct
2. Direct
3. Indirect
4. Direct
5. Indirect
6. Indirect

Review Questions

1. a
2. c
3. b
4. a
5. c
6. d
7. c
8. a
9. c
10. a
11. b
12. a
13. c
14. a
15. d
16. d
17. b
18. c
19. d
20. a

UNIT 11

Exercise 11-1

Age-life method:

Total depreciation = 28% (7 ÷ 25)

Dollar amount of accrued depreciation = $126,000 ($450,000 × 0.28)

Exercise 11-2

1. External obsolescence—incurable
2. Physical deterioration—long-lived incurable
3. Physical deterioration—short-lived incurable
4. External obsolescence—incurable
5. Physical deterioration—curable

6. Physical deterioration—short-lived incurable
7. Functional obsolescence—incurable
8. Functional obsolescence—incurable
9. Functional obsolescence—incurable
10. Functional obsolescence—curable

Exercise 11-3

$1,100 – $980 = $120 loss in rent

$120 × 125 monthly rent multiplier = $15,000 loss in property value

Exercise 11-4

$156,000 – $142,000 = $14,000 loss in property value

Exercise 11-5

	Reproduction Cost	Observed Depreciation	Amount of Depreciation
Heating system	$12,800	60%	$ 7,680
Plumbing	15,200	30	4,560
Electric and power	23,000	40	9,200
Floors	18,200	45	8,190
Roof	16,500	55	9,075
Total	$85,700		$38,705

Reproduction cost: 125' × 160' = 20,000 sq. ft.		
20,000 × $55 = $1,100,000		
Depreciation itemized above	–85,700	
Balance of building depreciation	$1,014,300 × 0.20	202,860
Total depreciation		$241,565

Applying the formula for the cost approach:

$1,100,000 – $241,565 + $180,000 = $1,038,435 property value

Exercise 11-6

Estimated reproduction cost new of improvements		
Direct costs	$98,500	
Indirect costs	26,500	
Total reproduction cost		$125,000
Cost per square foot of living area		
($125,000 ÷ 1,900 sq. ft.), $65.79		
Estimated accrued depreciation		
Physical deterioration		
Curable	$ 5,250	
Incurable—short-lived	12,250	– 17,500
Reproduction cost of long-lived items		$107,500
Incurable—long-lived:		
5 (effective age) ÷ 50 (economic life)		× 0.10
Incurable—long-lived		$ 10,750
Total physical deterioration		
($5,250 + $12,250 + $10,750) = $28,250		

Summation and value indication by the cost approach to value

Estimated reproduction cost new of improvements		$125,000
Estimated accrued depreciation		
Physical deterioration	$28,250	
Functional obsolescence	0	
External obsolescence	9,000	
Total estimated accrued depreciation		– 37,250
Estimated reproduction cost less accrued depreciation		$ 87,750
Estimated site value		+ 40,000
Indicated value by the cost approach		$127,750

Exercise 11-7

COST APPROACH TO VALUE (not required by Fannie Mae)				
Provide adequate information for the lender/client to replicate the below cost figures and calculations.				
Support for the opinion of site value (summary of comparable land sales or other methods for estimating site value)				
ESTIMATED ☒ REPRODUCTION OR ☐ REPLACEMENT COST NEW	OPINION OF SITE VALUE			= $ 98,000
Source of cost data	Dwelling 2,625 Sq. Ft. @ $ 112			=$ 294,000
Quality rating from cost service Effective date of cost data	Deck 450 Sq. Ft. @ $ 20			=$ 9,000
Comments on Cost Approach (gross living area calculations, depreciation, etc.)				
	Garage/Carport 676 Sq. Ft. @ $ 30			=$ 20,280
Cost estimate supported by current costs of local contractors	Total Estimate of Cost-New			= $ 323,280
verified by current cost manual.	Less Physical	Functional	External	
Depreciation based on observed physical deterioration and age of	Depreciation 65,000			=$(65,000)
property. Site value suggested by market data on comparable sites.	Depreciated Cost of Improvements			=$ 258,280
	"As-is" Value of Site Improvements			=$ 12,000
Estimated Remaining Economic Life (HUD and VA only) Years	Indicated Value By Cost Approach			=$ 368,280

Exercise 11-8

1. Total factory area: 100' × 150' = 15,000 sq. ft.
2. Total office area: 50' × 50' = 2,500 sq. ft.
3. Total building area: 15,000 sq. ft. + 2,500 sq. ft. = 17,500 sq. ft.
4. Building perimeter:

   100' + 150' + 50' + 50' + 50' + 50' + 200' = 650 linear ft.
5. Total parking area: 90' × 200' = 18,000 sq. ft. = 2,000 sq. yd.
6. Area covered by common brick:

100' + 150' + 50' + 150' = 450' × 14'		6,300 sq. ft.
Plus area above office roof 50' × 4'	200	
Plus area along office walls		
50' + 50' = 100' × 10'	1,000	7,500 sq. ft.
Less—		
Door area 12' × 12'	144 sq. ft.	
5(3' × 7')	105	
Window area 10 (6' × 12')	720	– 969
Total area covered by common brick		6,531 sq. ft.

7. Area covered by face brick:

50' × 10'		500 sq. ft.
Less—		
Door area 3' × 7'	21 sq. ft.	
Window area 6' × 12'	72	– 93
Total area covered by face brick		407 sq. ft.

8. Interior wall area for office:

Private office 32' × 2 sides = 64' × 8'	512 sq. ft.	
Private office 34' × 2 sides = 68' × 8'	544	
Storage room 24' × 2 sides = 48' × 8'	384	
Washrooms 46' × 2 sides = 92' × 8'	736	2,176 sq. ft.
Less door area 6 (3' × 7') × 2 sides		– 252
Total interior wall area for office		1,924 sq. ft.

9. Perimeter of office:

50' + 50' + 50' + 50' = 200' × 8'		1,600 sq. ft.
Less—		
Door area 3(3' × 7')	63 sq. ft.	
Window area 6' × 12'	72	– 135
Total perimeter of office		1,465 sq. ft.

10. 50' × 14' — 700 sq. ft.

Less one door 3' × 7'	– 21
Total	679 sq. ft.

11. Steel frame: 75' × 125' = 9,375 sq. ft.
12. Total land area: 210' × 230' = 48,300 sq. ft.
13. Land value:

Of the four sales listed, the price of only the smallest parcel, C, appears to be out of line. The remaining sales are priced from $2.20 to $2.24 per square foot, a narrow range.

Because no additional information is given, and parcel D is closest to the subject lot in size, $2.17 per square foot seems appropriate in estimating the land value.

Land value = 48,300 sq. ft. × $2.17 = $104,811

14. Foundation: 650 linear feet, 12, concrete @ $30.70 = $19,955
15. Exterior walls:

Common brick, 12" block, 6,531 sq. ft. @ $10.2	$66,616
Jumbo face brick veneer 407 sq. ft. @ $3.80	1,547
Total for exterior walls	$68,163

16. Roof construction:

sheathing	$ .65
1½" fiberglass insulation	1.10
4-ply tar and gravel covering	2.40
Total	$4.15

17,500 sq. ft. of building area @ $4.15 = $72,625

17. Framing: 9,375 sq. ft. @ $4.50 = $42,188
18. Floor construction:

17,500 sq. ft. 6" reinforced concrete @ $3.10 = $54,250

19. Windows: 11(6' × 12') = 792 sq. ft. @ $20.10 = $15,919

20. Exterior doors:

6(3' × 7') metal @ $355	$2,130
12' × 12' rolling steel @ $1,425	1,425
Total for exterior doors	$3,555

21. Interior construction:

Wall area for office (drywall on wood studs),	
1,924 sq. ft. @ $3.15	$6,061
Concrete block dividing wall 679 sq. ft. @ $4.40	2,988
Perimeter of office	
1,465 sq. ft. @ $.25 (painting)	366
Total for walls	$9,415

Doors: 7(3' × 7') @ $275 = $1,925

Floor covering: 2,500 sq. ft. vinyl tile in office @ $1.90 = $4,750

Ceiling (office): 2,500 sq. ft. mineral fiber acoustic tile @ $1.65 = $4,125

22. Electric: 17,500 sq. ft. @ $3.10 = $54,250

23. Plumbing: 17,500 sq. ft. @ $2.75 = $48,125

24. Heating and air-conditioning: 17,500 sq. ft. @ $5.75 = $100,625

25. Miscellaneous:

Parking area: 2,000 sq. yd. @ $7.20 = $14,400

26. Reproduction Costs:

Exterior construction	
Foundation	$ 19,955
Floor construction	54,250
Exterior walls	68,163
Framing	42,188
Roof construction	72,625
Windows	15,919
Exterior doors	3,555
Interior construction	
Walls	9,415
Floor covering	4,750
Ceiling	4,125
Interior doors	1,925
Electrical	54,250
Plumbing	48,125
Heating and air-conditioning	100,625

Miscellaneous		
Parking	14,400	
Total reproduction cost	$514,270	

27. Depreciation

Observed depreciation, deterioration—short-lived incurable

brickwork $68,163 × 40%	$27,265	
roof (asphalt and gravel) $42,000 × 60%	25,200	
exterior doors $3,555 × 75%	2,666	
floor (vinyl tile) $4,750 × 55%	2,613	
acoustic tile ceiling $4,125 × 45%	1,856	
electrical $54,250 × 35%	18,988	
plumbing $48,125 × 30%	14,438	
heating and air-conditioning $100,625 × 30%	30,188	
asphalt paving $14,400 × 40%	5,760	
Deterioration—short-lived incurable	$128,974	
Total reproduction cost	$514,270	
Full cost of short-lived incurable items	–339,993	
Balance of building	$174,277	
Deterioration—long-lived incurable	× .25	43,569
Total physical deterioration		$172,543

Incurable functional obsolescence

Net value after physical deterioration: $514,270 – 172,543 = $341,727

Incurable functional obsolescence: $341,727 × 5% = $17,086

28. Cost valuation

Reproduction cost		$514,270
Depreciation:		
Deterioration—curable	0	
–short-lived incurable	$128,974	
–long-lived incurable	43,569	
Functional obsolescence		
–curable	0	
–incurable	17,086	
External obsolescence	0	
Total accrued depreciation		– 189,629
Building value estimate		324,641
Land value estimate		108,675
Total property value indicated by cost approach		$433,316

Review Questions

1. a
2. c
3. a
4. b
5. c
6. d
7. b
8. b
9. a
10. a
11. c
12. d
13. c
14. b
15. b
16. c
17. b
18. c
19. d
20. a

UNIT 12

Exercise 12-1 (See form on next page.)

Construction: Aluminum siding, rather than brick

\$242,000 – \$233,000 = \$9,000

No. of bedrooms: 4 (1 extra)

\$252,000 – \$242,000 = \$10,000

No. of baths: extra ½ bath

\$247,000 – \$242,000 = \$5,000

Exercise 12-1

Sales Price Adjustment Chart

Sales Price Adjustment Chart Comparables										
	A	B	C	D	E	F	G	H	I	J
Sales price	$242,000	$233,000	$243,000	$247,000	$241,000	$220,000	$286,000	$221,000	$252,000	$242,000
Financing	Conv	Conv	Conv	Conv	Conv	Conv	Conv	Conv	Conv	Conv
Date of sale	6 wks.	2 mos.	3 wks.	5 wks.	6 wks.	5 wks.	3 wks.	1 yr.	5 wks.	11 wks.
Location	N;res	N;res	N;res	N;res	N;res	highway	Commer-cial	N;res	N;res	N;res
Leasehold/fee simple	Fee simple	Fee simple	Fee simple	Fee simple	Fee simple	Fee simple	Fee simple	Fee simple	Fee simple	Fee simple
View	B;water	B;water	B;water	B;water	B;water	B;water	B;water	B;water	B;water	B;water
Site	10,000sf	10,000sf	10,000sf	10,000sf	10,000sf	10,000sf	10,000sf	10,000sf	10,000sf	10,000sf
Design (style)	Colonial	Colonial	Colonial	Colonial	Colonial	Colonial	Colonial	Colonial	Colonial	Colonial
Quality of construction	Q4;brick	Q5; aluminum siding	Q4;brick	Q4;brick	Q4;brick	Q4;brick	Q4;brick	Q4;brick	Q4;brick	Q4;brick
Age	8	7	8	6	6	7	6	7	6	7
Condition	C4	C4	C4	C4	C4	C4	C4	C4	C4	C4
No. of rms./bedrms./baths	7/3/2	7/3/2	7/3/2	7/3/2½	7/3/2	7/3/2	7/3/2	7/3/2	8/4/2	7/3/2
Sq. ft. of living space	1,275	1,300	1,290	1,300	1,300	1,325	1,300	1,350	1,400	1,300
Other space (basement)	1,275sf	1,300sf	1,290sf	1,300sf	1,300sf	1,325sf	1,300sf	1,350sf	1,400sf	1,300sf
Functional utility	Average	Average	Average	Average	Average	Average	Average	Average	Average	Average
Heating/cooling	FWA/CAC	FWA/CAC	FWA/CAC	FWA/CAC	FWA/CAC	FWA/CAC	FWA/CAC	FWA/CAC	FWA/CAC	FWA/CAC
Energy-efficient items	None	None	None	None	None	None	None	None	None	None
Garage/carport	2-car att.	2-car att.	2-car att.	2-car att.	2-car att.	2-car att.	2-car att.	2-car att.	2-car att.	2-car att.
Other ext. improvements	Patio	Patio	Patio	Patio	Patio	Patio	Patio	Patio	Patio	Patio
Other int. improvements	One	One	One	One	One	One	One	One	One	One
Typical house value	$242,000	$242,000	$242,000	$242,000	$242,000	$242,000	$242,000	$242,000	$242,000	$242,000
Variable feature		Aluminum siding		Extra half-bath		Poor location	Commer-cial area	Year-old sale	4th bedroom	
Adjustment value of variable		$9,000		$5,000		$22,000	$26,000	$21,000	$10,000	

Exercise 12-2

Sales Comparison Approach

Uniform Residential Appraisal Report

File #

There are comparable properties currently offered for sale in the subject neighborhood ranging in price from $ to $.

There are comparable sales in the subject neighborhood within the past twelve months ranging in sale price from $ to $.

FEATURE	SUBJECT	COMPARABLE SALE # 1		COMPARABLE SALE # 2		COMPARABLE SALE # 3	
Address	2130 W. Franklin	1901 Parkside Blvd.		2135 Hastings Ave.		2129 Osceola Way	
Proximity to Subject		.50 miles SE		.50 miles SE		.50 miles SE	
Sale Price	$		$ 226,000		$ 239,000		$ 238,000
Sale Price/Gross Liv. Area	$ sq. ft.	$ 125.56 sq. ft.		$ 127.47 sq. ft.		$ 130.41 sq. ft.	
Data Source(s)		Public records		Public records		Public records	
Verification Source(s)		Sales agent		Sales agent		Sales agent	
VALUE ADJUSTMENTS	DESCRIPTION	DESCRIPTION	+(-) $ Adjustment	DESCRIPTION	+(-) $ Adjustment	DESCRIPTION	+(-) $ Adjustment
Sale or Financing Concessions		ArmLth Conv		ArmLth Conv		ArmLth Conv	
Date of Sale/Time		6 weeks ago		1 year ago		2 months ago	
Location	N; Res	A; Bsy Rd		N; Res		N; Res	
Leasehold/Fee Simple	fee simple	fee simple		fee simple		fee simple	
Site	10,000 SF	10,000 SF		10,000 SF		10,000 SF	
View	N; Res	N; Res		N; Res		N; Res	
Design (Style)	Ranch	Ranch		Ranch		Ranch	
Quality of Construction	Q4	Q4		Q4		Q5	
Actual Age	6	8		7		8	
Condition	C3	C3		C3		C3	
Above Grade Room Count	Total 7, Bdrms 3, Baths 2.1	Total 7, Bdrms 3, Baths 2.0		Total 7, Bdrms 3, Baths 2.0		Total 7, Bdrms 3, Baths 2.0	
Gross Living Area	1,825 sq. ft.	1,800 sq. ft.		1,875 sq. ft.		1,825 sq. ft.	
Basement & Finished Rooms Below Grade	1600 sf; 800 sf fin; 1rr 0.1ba	1600 sf; 800 sf fin; 1rr 0.1ba		1600 sf; 800 sf fin; 1rr 0.1ba		1600 sf; 800 sf fin; 1rr 0.1ba	
Functional Utility	Average	Average		Average		Average	
Heating/Cooling	FWA/CAC	FWA/CAC		FWA/CAC		FWA/CAC	
Energy Efficient Items	none	none		none		none	
Garage/Carport	2-car att.	2-car att.		2-car att.		2-car att.	
Porch/Patio/Deck	none	none		none		none	
Net Adjustment (Total)		☐ + ☐ -	$	☐ + ☐ -	$	☐ + ☐ -	$
Adjusted Sale Price of Comparables		Net Adj. % Gross Adj. %	$	Net Adj. % Gross Adj. %	$	Net Adj. % Gross Adj. %	$

I ☐ did ☐ did not research the sale or transfer history of the subject property and comparable sales. If not, explain

My research ☐ did ☐ did not reveal any prior sales or transfers of the subject property for the three years prior to the effective date of this appraisal.

Data source(s)

My research ☐ did ☐ did not reveal any prior sales or transfers of the comparable sales for the year prior to the date of sale of the comparable sale.

Data source(s)

Report the results of the research and analysis of the prior sale or transfer history of the subject property and comparable sales (report additional prior sales on page 3).

ITEM	SUBJECT	COMPARABLE SALE # 1	COMPARABLE SALE # 2	COMPARABLE SALE # 3
Date of Prior Sale/Transfer				
Price of Prior Sale/Transfer				
Data Source(s)				
Effective Date of Data Source(s)				

Analysis of prior sale or transfer history of the subject property and comparable sales

Summary of Sales Comparison Approach

Indicated Value by Sales Comparison Approach $

Exercise 12-2

Sales Comparison Approach (continued)

Uniform Residential Appraisal Report

File #

There are comparable properties currently offered for sale in the subject neighborhood ranging in price from $ to $.

There are comparable sales in the subject neighborhood within the past twelve months ranging in sale price from $ to $.

FEATURE	SUBJECT	COMPARABLE SALE # 4		COMPARABLE SALE # 5		COMPARABLE SALE # 6	
Address	2130 W. Franklin	2243 Parkside Blvd.		2003 Franklin St.			
Proximity to Subject		.50 miles SE		.50 miles SE			
Sale Price	$		$ 256,500		$ 251,000		$
Sale Price/Gross Liv. Area	$ sq. ft.	$ 133.25 sq. ft.		$ 137.53 sq. ft.		$ sq. ft.	
Data Source(s)		Public records		Public records			
Verification Source(s)		Sales agent		Sales agent			
VALUE ADJUSTMENTS	DESCRIPTION	DESCRIPTION	+(-) $ Adjustment	DESCRIPTION	+(-) $ Adjustment	DESCRIPTION	+(-) $ Adjustment
Sale or Financing Concessions		ArmLth Conv		ArmLth Conv			
Date of Sale/Time		5 weeks ago		5 weeks ago			
Location	N; Res	N; Res		N; Res			
Leasehold/Fee Simple	fee simple	fee simple		fee simple			
Site	10,000 SF	10,000 SF		10,000 SF			
View	N; Res	N; Res		N; Res			
Design (Style)	Ranch	Ranch		Ranch			
Quality of Construction	Q4	Q4		Q4			
Actual Age	6	6		7			
Condition	C3	C3		C3			
Above Grade	Total Bdrms Baths	Total Bdrms Baths		Total Bdrms Baths		Total Bdrms Baths	
Room Count	7 3 2.1	8 4 2.0		7 3 2.1			
Gross Living Area	1,825 sq. ft.	1,925 sq. ft.		1,825 sq. ft.		sq. ft.	
Basement & Finished Rooms Below Grade	0	0		0			
Functional Utility	Average	Average		Average			
Heating/Cooling	FWA/CAC	FWA/CAC		FWA/CAC			
Energy Efficient Items	none	none		none			
Garage/Carport	2-car att.	2-car att.		2-car att.			
Porch/Patio/Deck	none	none		none			
Net Adjustment (Total)		☐ + ☐ -	$	☐ + ☐ -	$	☐ + ☐ -	$
Adjusted Sale Price of Comparables		Net Adj. % Gross Adj. %	$	Net Adj. % Gross Adj. %	$	Net Adj. % Gross Adj. %	$

I ☐ did ☐ did not research the sale or transfer history of the subject property and comparable sales. If not, explain

My research ☐ did ☐ did not reveal any prior sales or transfers of the subject property for the three years prior to the effective date of this appraisal.

Data source(s)

My research ☐ did ☐ did not reveal any prior sales or transfers of the comparable sales for the year prior to the date of sale of the comparable sale.

Data source(s)

Report the results of the research and analysis of the prior sale or transfer history of the subject property and comparable sales (report additional prior sales on page 3).

ITEM	SUBJECT	COMPARABLE SALE # 1	COMPARABLE SALE # 2	COMPARABLE SALE # 3
Date of Prior Sale/Transfer				
Price of Prior Sale/Transfer				
Data Source(s)				
Effective Date of Data Source(s)				

Analysis of prior sale or transfer history of the subject property and comparable sales

Summary of Sales Comparison Approach

Indicated Value by Sales Comparison Approach $

Exercise 12-3

Sales Comparison Approach

Uniform Residential Appraisal Report

File #

There are comparable properties currently offered for sale in the subject neighborhood ranging in price from $ to $.

There are comparable sales in the subject neighborhood within the past twelve months ranging in sale price from $ to $.

FEATURE	SUBJECT	COMPARABLE SALE # 1		COMPARABLE SALE # 2		COMPARABLE SALE # 3	
Address	2130 W. Franklin	1901 Parkside Blvd.		2135 Hastings Ave.		2129 Osceola Way	
Proximity to Subject		.50 miles SE		.50 miles SE		.50 miles SE	
Sale Price	$		$ 226,000		$ 239,000		$ 238,000
Sale Price/Gross Liv. Area	$ sq. ft.	$ 125.56 sq. ft.		$ 127.47 sq. ft.		$ 130.41 sq. ft.	
Data Source(s)		Public records		Public records		Public records	
Verification Source(s)		Sales agent		Sales agent		Sales agent	
VALUE ADJUSTMENTS	DESCRIPTION	DESCRIPTION	+(-) $ Adjustment	DESCRIPTION	+(-) $ Adjustment	DESCRIPTION	+(-) $ Adjustment
Sale or Financing Concessions		ArmLth Conv		ArmLth Conv		ArmLth Conv	
Date of Sale/Time		6 weeks ago		1 year ago	+22,700 (rounded)	2 months ago	
Location	N; Res	A; Bsy Rd	+22,000	N; Res		N; Res	
Leasehold/Fee Simple	fee simple	fee simple		fee simple		fee simple	
Site	10,000 SF	10,000 SF		10,000 SF		10,000 SF	
View	N; Res	N; Res		N; Res		N; Res	
Design (Style)	Ranch	Ranch		Ranch		Ranch	
Quality of Construction	Q4	Q4		Q4		Q5	+9,000
Actual Age	6	8		7		8	
Condition	C3	C3		C3		C3	
Above Grade Room Count (Total / Bdrms / Baths)	7 / 3 / 2.1	7 / 3 / 2.0	+5,000	7 / 3 / 2.0	+5,000	7 / 3 / 2.0	+5,000
Gross Living Area	1,825 sq. ft.	1,800 sq. ft.		1,875 sq. ft.		1,825 sq. ft.	
Basement & Finished Rooms Below Grade	0	0		0		0	
Functional Utility	Average	Average		Average		Average	
Heating/Cooling	FWA/CAC	FWA/CAC		FWA/CAC		FWA/CAC	
Energy Efficient Items	none	none		none		none	
Garage/Carport	2-car att.	2-car att.		2-car att.		2-car att.	
Porch/Patio/Deck	none	none		none		none	
Net Adjustment (Total)		☒ + ☐ -	$	☐ + ☐ -	$	☐ + ☐ -	$
Adjusted Sale Price of Comparables		Net Adj. % Gross Adj. %	$	Net Adj. % Gross Adj. %	$	Net Adj. % Gross Adj. %	$

I ☐ did ☐ did not research the sale or transfer history of the subject property and comparable sales. If not, explain

My research ☐ did ☐ did not reveal any prior sales or transfers of the subject property for the three years prior to the effective date of this appraisal.

Data source(s)

My research ☐ did ☐ did not reveal any prior sales or transfers of the comparable sales for the year prior to the date of sale of the comparable sale.

Data source(s)

Report the results of the research and analysis of the prior sale or transfer history of the subject property and comparable sales (report additional prior sales on page 3).

ITEM	SUBJECT	COMPARABLE SALE # 1	COMPARABLE SALE # 2	COMPARABLE SALE # 3
Date of Prior Sale/Transfer				
Price of Prior Sale/Transfer				
Data Source(s)				
Effective Date of Data Source(s)				

Analysis of prior sale or transfer history of the subject property and comparable sales

Summary of Sales Comparison Approach

Indicated Value by Sales Comparison Approach $

Exercise 12-3

Sales Comparison Approach (continued)

Uniform Residential Appraisal Report

File #

There are comparable properties currently offered for sale in the subject neighborhood ranging in price from $ to $.

There are comparable sales in the subject neighborhood within the past twelve months ranging in sale price from $ to $.

FEATURE	SUBJECT	COMPARABLE SALE # 4		COMPARABLE SALE # 5		COMPARABLE SALE # 6	
Address	2130 W. Franklin	2243 Parkside Blvd.		2003 Franklin St.			
Proximity to Subject		.50 miles SE		.50 miles SE			
Sale Price	$		$ 256,500		$ 251,000		$
Sale Price/Gross Liv. Area	$ sq. ft.	$ 133.25 sq. ft.		$ 137.53 sq. ft.		$ sq. ft.	
Data Source(s)		Public records		Public records			
Verification Source(s)		Sales agent		Sales agent			
VALUE ADJUSTMENTS	DESCRIPTION	DESCRIPTION	+(-) $ Adjustment	DESCRIPTION	+(-) $ Adjustment	DESCRIPTION	+(-) $ Adjustment
Sale or Financing Concessions		ArmLth Conv		ArmLth Conv			
Date of Sale/Time		5 weeks ago		5 weeks ago			
Location	N; Res	N; Res		N; Res			
Leasehold/Fee Simple	fee simple	fee simple		fee simple			
Site	10,000 SF	10,000 SF		10,000 SF			
View	N; Res	N; Res		N; Res			
Design (Style)	Ranch	Ranch		Ranch			
Quality of Construction	Q4	Q4		Q4			
Actual Age	6	6		7			
Condition	C3	C3		C3			
Above Grade	Total Bdrms Baths	Total Bdrms Baths		Total Bdrms Baths		Total Bdrms Baths	
Room Count	7 3 2.1	8 4 2.0	−10,000	7 3 2.1			
Gross Living Area	1,825 sq. ft.	1,925 sq. ft.	+5,000	1,825 sq. ft.		sq. ft.	
Basement & Finished Rooms Below Grade	0	0		0			
Functional Utility	Average	Average		Average			
Heating/Cooling	FWA/CAC	FWA/CAC		FWA/CAC			
Energy Efficient Items	none	none		none			
Garage/Carport	2-car att.	2-car att.		2-car att.			
Porch/Patio/Deck	none	none		none			
Net Adjustment (Total)		☐ + ☐ -	$	☐ + ☐ -	$	☐ + ☐ -	$
Adjusted Sale Price of Comparables		Net Adj. % Gross Adj. %	$	Net Adj. % Gross Adj. %	$	Net Adj. % Gross Adj. %	$

I ☐ did ☐ did not research the sale or transfer history of the subject property and comparable sales. If not, explain

My research ☐ did ☐ did not reveal any prior sales or transfers of the subject property for the three years prior to the effective date of this appraisal.

Data source(s)

My research ☐ did ☐ did not reveal any prior sales or transfers of the comparable sales for the year prior to the date of sale of the comparable sale.

Data source(s)

Report the results of the research and analysis of the prior sale or transfer history of the subject property and comparable sales (report additional prior sales on page 3).

ITEM	SUBJECT	COMPARABLE SALE # 1	COMPARABLE SALE # 2	COMPARABLE SALE # 3
Date of Prior Sale/Transfer				
Price of Prior Sale/Transfer				
Data Source(s)				
Effective Date of Data Source(s)				

Analysis of prior sale or transfer history of the subject property and comparable sales

Summary of Sales Comparison Approach

Indicated Value by Sales Comparison Approach $

Exercise 12-4

Sales Comparison Approach

Uniform Residential Appraisal Report

File #

There are comparable properties currently offered for sale in the subject neighborhood ranging in price from $ to $

There are comparable sales in the subject neighborhood within the past twelve months ranging in sale price from $ to $

FEATURE	SUBJECT	COMPARABLE SALE # 1		COMPARABLE SALE # 2		COMPARABLE SALE # 3	
Address	2130 W. Franklin	1901 Parkside Blvd.		2135 Hastings Ave.		2129 Osceola Way	
Proximity to Subject		.50 miles SE		.50 miles SE		.50 miles SE	
Sale Price	$		$ 226,000		$ 239,000		$ 238,000
Sale Price/Gross Liv. Area	$ sq. ft.	$ 125.56 sq. ft.		$ 127.47 sq. ft.		$ 130.41 sq. ft.	
Data Source(s)		Public records		Public records		Public records	
Verification Source(s)		Sales agent		Sales agent		Sales agent	
VALUE ADJUSTMENTS	DESCRIPTION	DESCRIPTION	+(-) $ Adjustment	DESCRIPTION	+(-) $ Adjustment	DESCRIPTION	+(-) $ Adjustment
Sale or Financing Concessions		ArmLth Conv		ArmLth Conv		ArmLth Conv	
Date of Sale/Time		6 weeks ago		1 year ago	+22,700	2 months ago	
Location	N; Res	A; Bsy Rd	+22,000	N; Res	(rounded)	N; Res	
Leasehold/Fee Simple	fee simple	fee simple		fee simple		fee simple	
Site	10,000 SF	10,000 SF		10,000 SF		10,000 SF	
View	N; Res	N; Res		N; Res		N; Res	
Design (Style)	Ranch	Ranch		Ranch		Ranch	
Quality of Construction	Q4	Q4		Q4		Q5	+9,000
Actual Age	6	8		7		8	
Condition	C3	C3		C3		C3	
Above Grade	Total / Bdrms / Baths	Total / Bdrms / (Baths)		Total / Bdrms / (Baths)		Total / Bdrms / (Baths)	
Room Count	7 / 3 / 2.1	7 / 3 / 2.0	+5,000	7 / 3 / 2.0	+5,000	7 / 3 / 2.0	+5,000
Gross Living Area	1,825 sq. ft.	1,800 sq. ft.		1,875 sq. ft.		1,825 sq. ft.	
Basement & Finished Rooms Below Grade	0	0		0		0	
Functional Utility	Average	Average		Average		Average	
Heating/Cooling	FWA/CAC	FWA/CAC		FWA/CAC		FWA/CAC	
Energy Efficient Items	none	none		none		none	
Garage/Carport	2-car att.	2-car att.		2-car att.		2-car att.	
Porch/Patio/Deck	none	none		none		none	
Net Adjustment (Total)		☒ + ☐ -	$ 27,000	☒ + ☐ -	$ 27,700	☒ + ☐ -	$ 14,000
Adjusted Sale Price of Comparables		Net Adj. % Gross Adj. %	$ 253,000	Net Adj. % Gross Adj. %	$ 266,700	Net Adj. % Gross Adj. %	$ 252,000

I ☐ did ☐ did not research the sale or transfer history of the subject property and comparable sales. If not, explain

My research ☐ did ☐ did not reveal any prior sales or transfers of the subject property for the three years prior to the effective date of this appraisal.

Data source(s)

My research ☐ did ☐ did not reveal any prior sales or transfers of the comparable sales for the year prior to the date of sale of the comparable sale.

Data source(s)

Report the results of the research and analysis of the prior sale or transfer history of the subject property and comparable sales (report additional prior sales on page 3).

ITEM	SUBJECT	COMPARABLE SALE # 1	COMPARABLE SALE # 2	COMPARABLE SALE # 3
Date of Prior Sale/Transfer				
Price of Prior Sale/Transfer				
Data Source(s)				
Effective Date of Data Source(s)				

Analysis of prior sale or transfer history of the subject property and comparable sales

Summary of Sales Comparison Approach

Indicated Value by Sales Comparison Approach $

Exercise 12-4

Sales Comparison Approach (continued)

Uniform Residential Appraisal Report

File #

There are comparable properties currently offered for sale in the subject neighborhood ranging in price from $ to $.

There are comparable sales in the subject neighborhood within the past twelve months ranging in sale price from $ to $.

FEATURE	SUBJECT	COMPARABLE SALE # 4		COMPARABLE SALE # 5		COMPARABLE SALE # 6	
Address	2130 W. Franklin	2243 Parkside Blvd.		2003 Franklin St.			
Proximity to Subject		.50 miles SE		.50 miles SE			
Sale Price	$		$ 256,500		$ 251,000		$
Sale Price/Gross Liv. Area	$ sq. ft.	$ 133.25 sq. ft.		$ 137.53 sq. ft.		$ sq. ft.	
Data Source(s)		Public records		Public records			
Verification Source(s)		Sales agent		Sales agent			
VALUE ADJUSTMENTS	DESCRIPTION	DESCRIPTION	+(-) $ Adjustment	DESCRIPTION	+(-) $ Adjustment	DESCRIPTION	+(-) $ Adjustment
Sale or Financing Concessions		ArmLth Conv		ArmLth Conv			
Date of Sale/Time		5 weeks ago		5 weeks ago			
Location	N; Res	N; Res		N; Res			
Leasehold/Fee Simple	fee simple	fee simple		fee simple			
Site	10,000 SF	10,000 SF		10,000 SF			
View	N; Res	N; Res		N; Res			
Design (Style)	Ranch	Ranch		Ranch			
Quality of Construction	Q4	Q4		Q4			
Actual Age	6	6		7			
Condition	C3	C3		C3			
Above Grade	Total / Bdrms / Baths	Total / Bdrms / Baths		Total / Bdrms / Baths		Total / Bdrms / Baths	
Room Count	7 / 3 / 2.1	8 / 4 / 2.0	-10,000	7 / 3 / 2.1			
Gross Living Area	1,825 sq. ft.	1,925 sq. ft.	+5,000	1,825 sq. ft.		sq. ft.	
Basement & Finished Rooms Below Grade	0	0		0			
Functional Utility	Average	Average		Average			
Heating/Cooling	FWA/CAC	FWA/CAC		FWA/CAC			
Energy Efficient Items	none	none		none			
Garage/Carport	2-car att.	2-car att.		2-car att.			
Porch/Patio/Deck	none	none		none			
Net Adjustment (Total)		☐ + ☒ -	$ 5,000	☐ + ☐ -	$ -0-	☐ + ☐ -	$
Adjusted Sale Price of Comparables		Net Adj. % Gross Adj. %	$ 251,000	Net Adj. % Gross Adj. %	$ 251,000	Net Adj. % Gross Adj. %	$

I ☐ did ☐ did not research the sale or transfer history of the subject property and comparable sales. If not, explain

My research ☐ did ☐ did not reveal any prior sales or transfers of the subject property for the three years prior to the effective date of this appraisal.

Data source(s)

My research ☐ did ☐ did not reveal any prior sales or transfers of the comparable sales for the year prior to the date of sale of the comparable sale.

Data source(s)

Report the results of the research and analysis of the prior sale or transfer history of the subject property and comparable sales (report additional prior sales on page 3).

ITEM	SUBJECT	COMPARABLE SALE # 1	COMPARABLE SALE # 2	COMPARABLE SALE # 3
Date of Prior Sale/Transfer				
Price of Prior Sale/Transfer				
Data Source(s)				
Effective Date of Data Source(s)				

Analysis of prior sale or transfer history of the subject property and comparable sales

Summary of Sales Comparison Approach

Indicated Value by Sales Comparison Approach $

Exercise 12-5

Because the value range (excluding comparable 2) is close and comparable 5 required no adjustment, it is reasonable to estimate that the subject property has a market value of $251,000.

Review Questions

See the following figures for the answers to questions 1 and 2.

3. $173,500 is the indicated market value of the subject property by the sales comparison approach.

Sales Price Adjustment Chart
Comparables

	1	2	3	4	5	6	7
Sales price	$185,500	$190,000	$178,600	$186,000	$169,000	$173,500	$190,000
Financing	FHA	FHA	FHA	FHA	FHA	FHA	FHA
Date of sale	2 mos. ago	3 wks. ago	1 yr. ago	2 wks. ago	1 mo. ago	8 wks. ago	3 wks. ago
Location	N;res	N;res	N;res	N;res	N;res	N;res	N;res
Leasehold/fee simple	Fee simple	Fee simple	Fee simple	Fee simple	Fee simple	Fee simple	Fee simple
View	B;Glfvw	B;Glfvw	B;Glfvw	B;Glfvw	B;Glfvw	B;Glfvw	B;Glfvw
Site	9425sf	9425sf	9425sf	9425sf	9425sf	9425sf	9425sf
Design (style)	Ranch	Ranch	Ranch	Ranch	Ranch	Ranch	Ranch
Quality of construction	Q4	Q4	Q4	Q4	Q4	Q4	Q4
Age	7	6½	6	7½	7	7	7
Condition	C3	C3	C3	C4	C3	C3	C3
No. of rms./bedrms./baths	7/3/2	7/3/2	7/3/2	7/3/2	7/3/2	7/3/2	7/3/2
Sq. ft. of living space	1,600	1,600	1,600	1,575	1,575	1,575	1,590
Other space (basement)	1600sf; 800sf fin 1rr0.1ba	1600sf; 800sf fin 1rr0.1ba	1600sf; 800sf fin 1rr0.1ba	1575sf; 800sf fin 1rr0.1ba	1575sf; 800sf fin 1rr0.1ba	1575sf; 800sf fin 1rr0.1ba	1590sf; 800sf fin 1rr0.1ba
Functional utility	Average	Average	Average	Average	Average	Average	Average
Heating/cooling	FWA	FWA/CAC	FWA/CAC	FWA/CAC	FWA	FWA/CAC	FWA/CAC
Energy-efficient items	None	None	None	None	None	None	None
Garage/carport	2-car att.	2-car att.	2-car att.	2-car att.	carport	carport	2-car att.
Other ext. improvements	Porch	Porch	Porch	Porch	Porch	Porch	Porch
Other int. improvements	Brick fireplace	Brick fireplace	Brick fireplace	Brick fireplace	Brick fireplace	Brick fireplace	Brick fireplace
Typical house value	$190,000	$190,000	$190,000	$190,000	$190,000	$190,000	$190,000
Variable feature	No central air	—	Yr-old sale	Condition	No central air; no garage	No garage	—
Adjustment value of variable	$4,500	—	$11,400	$4,000	$21,000	$16,500	—

Review Questions

Sales Comparison Approach

Uniform Residential Appraisal Report

File #

There are comparable properties currently offered for sale in the subject neighborhood ranging in price from $ to $

There are comparable sales in the subject neighborhood within the past twelve months ranging in sale price from $ to $

FEATURE	SUBJECT	COMPARABLE SALE # 1		COMPARABLE SALE # 2		COMPARABLE SALE # 3	
Address							
Proximity to Subject							
Sale Price	$		$ 185,500		$ 190,000		$ 178,600
Sale Price/Gross Liv. Area	$ sq. ft.	$ 115.94 sq. ft.		$ 118.75 sq. ft.		$ 111.63 sq. ft.	
Data Source(s)							
Verification Source(s)							
VALUE ADJUSTMENTS	DESCRIPTION	DESCRIPTION	+(-) $ Adjustment	DESCRIPTION	+(-) $ Adjustment	DESCRIPTION	+(-) $ Adjustment
Sale or Financing Concessions		ArmLth FHA		ArmLth FHA		ArmLth FHA	
Date of Sale/Time		2 months ago		3 weeks ago		1 year ago	+11,400
Location	N; Res	N; Res		N; Res		N; Res	
Leasehold/Fee Simple	fee simple	fee simple		fee simple		fee simple	
Site	9,425 SF	9,425 SF		9,425 SF		9,425 SF	
View	B; GlfVw	B; GlfVw		B; GlfVw		B; GlfVw	
Design (Style)	Ranch	Ranch		Ranch		Ranch	
Quality of Construction	Q4	Q4		Q4		Q4	
Actual Age	7	7		6 1/2		6	
Condition	C3	C3		C3		C3	
Above Grade Room Count	Total 7, Bdrms 3, Baths 2.0	Total 7, Bdrms 3, Baths 2.0		Total 7, Bdrms 3, Baths 2.0		Total 7, Bdrms 3, Baths 2.0	
Gross Living Area	1,600 sq. ft.	1,600 sq. ft.		1,600 sq. ft.		1,600 sq. ft.	
Basement & Finished Rooms Below Grade	1600 sf; 800 sf fin; 1rr 0.1ba	1600 sf; 800 sf fin; 1rr 0.1ba		1600 sf; 800 sf fin; 1rr 0.1ba		1600 sf; 800 sf fin; 1rr 0.1ba	
Functional Utility	Average	Average		Average		Average	
Heating/Cooling	FWA/CAC	FWA	+4,500	FWA/CAC		FWA/CAC	
Energy Efficient Items	none	none		none		none	
Garage/Carport	carport	2-car att.	−16,500	2-car att.	−16,500	2-car att.	−16,500
Porch/Patio/Deck	porch	porch		porch		porch	
Fireplace	brick fireplace	brick fireplace		brick fireplace		brick fireplace	
Net Adjustment (Total)		☐ + ☒ -	$ 12,000	☐ + ☒ -	$ 16,500	☐ + ☒ -	$ 5,100
Adjusted Sale Price of Comparables		Net Adj. % Gross Adj. %	$ 173,500	Net Adj. % Gross Adj. %	$ 173,500	Net Adj. % Gross Adj. %	$ 173,500

I ☐ did ☐ did not research the sale or transfer history of the subject property and comparable sales. If not, explain

My research ☐ did ☐ did not reveal any prior sales or transfers of the subject property for the three years prior to the effective date of this appraisal.

Data source(s)

My research ☐ did ☐ did not reveal any prior sales or transfers of the comparable sales for the year prior to the date of sale of the comparable sale.

Data source(s)

Report the results of the research and analysis of the prior sale or transfer history of the subject property and comparable sales (report additional prior sales on page 3).

ITEM	SUBJECT	COMPARABLE SALE # 1	COMPARABLE SALE # 2	COMPARABLE SALE # 3
Date of Prior Sale/Transfer				
Price of Prior Sale/Transfer				
Data Source(s)				
Effective Date of Data Source(s)				

Analysis of prior sale or transfer history of the subject property and comparable sales

Summary of Sales Comparison Approach

Indicated Value by Sales Comparison Approach $

Review Questions

Sales Comparison Approach (continued)

Uniform Residential Appraisal Report

File #

There are comparable properties currently offered for sale in the subject neighborhood ranging in price from $ to $.

There are comparable sales in the subject neighborhood within the past twelve months ranging in sale price from $ to $.

FEATURE	SUBJECT	COMPARABLE SALE # 4		COMPARABLE SALE # 5		COMPARABLE SALE # 6	
Address							
Proximity to Subject		.50 miles SE		.50 miles SE			
Sale Price	$		$ 186,000		$ 169,000		$ 173,500
Sale Price/Gross Liv. Area	$ sq. ft.	$ 118.10 sq. ft.		$ 107.30 sq. ft.		$ 110.16 sq. ft.	
Data Source(s)							
Verification Source(s)							
VALUE ADJUSTMENTS	DESCRIPTION	DESCRIPTION	+(-) $ Adjustment	DESCRIPTION	+(-) $ Adjustment	DESCRIPTION	+(-) $ Adjustment
Sale or Financing Concessions		ArmLth FHA		ArmLth FHA		ArmLth FHA	
Date of Sale/Time		2 weeks ago		1 mo ago		5 weeks ago	
Location	N; Res	N; Res		N; Res		N; Res	
Leasehold/Fee Simple	fee simple	fee simple		fee simple		fee simple	
Site	9425 SF	9425 SF		9425 SF		9425 SF	
View	B; GlfVw	B; GlfVw		B; GlfVw		B; GlfVw	
Design (Style)	Ranch	Ranch		Ranch		Ranch	
Quality of Construction	Q4	Q4		Q4		Q4	
Actual Age	7	7.5		7		7	
Condition	C3	C4	+4,000	C3		C3	
Above Grade	Total / Bdrms / Baths	Total / Bdrms / Baths		Total / Bdrms / Baths		Total / Bdrms / Baths	
Room Count	7 / 3 / 2.0	7 / 3 / 2.0		7 / 3 / 2.0		7 / 3 / 2.0	
Gross Living Area	1600 (sq. ft.)	1575 (sq. ft)		1575 (sq. ft)		1575 (sq. ft)	
Basement & Finished Rooms Below Grade	800 sq ft fin; 1rr 0.1ba	800 sq ft fin; 1rr 0.1ba		800 sq ft fin; 1rr 0.1ba		800 sq ft fin; 1rr 0.1ba	
Functional Utility	Average	Average		Average		Average	
Heating/Cooling	FWA/CAC	FWA/CAC		FWA	+4,500	FWA/CAC	
Energy Efficient Items	none	none		none		none	
Garage/Carport	carport	2-car att.	−16,500	carport		carport	
Porch/Patio/Deck	porch	porch		porch		porch	
Fireplace	brick fireplace	brick fireplace		brick fireplace		brick fireplace	
Net Adjustment (Total)		☐ + ☒ -	$ 12,500	☒ + ☐ -	$ 4,500	☐ + ☐ -	$ -0-
Adjusted Sale Price of Comparables		Net Adj. % Gross Adj. %	$ 173,500	Net Adj. % Gross Adj. %	$ 173,500	Net Adj. % Gross Adj. %	$ 173,500

I ☐ did ☐ did not research the sale or transfer history of the subject property and comparable sales. If not, explain

My research ☐ did ☐ did not reveal any prior sales or transfers of the subject property for the three years prior to the effective date of this appraisal.

Data source(s)

My research ☐ did ☐ did not reveal any prior sales or transfers of the comparable sales for the year prior to the date of sale of the comparable sale.

Data source(s)

Report the results of the research and analysis of the prior sale or transfer history of the subject property and comparable sales (report additional prior sales on page 3).

ITEM	SUBJECT	COMPARABLE SALE # 1	COMPARABLE SALE # 2	COMPARABLE SALE # 3
Date of Prior Sale/Transfer				
Price of Prior Sale/Transfer				
Data Source(s)				
Effective Date of Data Source(s)				

Analysis of prior sale or transfer history of the subject property and comparable sales

Summary of Sales Comparison Approach

Indicated Value by Sales Comparison Approach $

Review Questions

Sales Comparison Approach (continued)

Uniform Residential Appraisal Report

File #

There are comparable properties currently offered for sale in the subject neighborhood ranging in price from $ to $.

There are comparable sales in the subject neighborhood within the past twelve months ranging in sale price from $ to $.

FEATURE	SUBJECT	COMPARABLE SALE # 7		COMPARABLE SALE # 8		COMPARABLE SALE # 9	
Address							
Proximity to Subject							
Sale Price	$		$ 190,000		$		$
Sale Price/Gross Liv. Area	$ sq. ft.	$ 119.50 sq. ft.		$ sq. ft.		$ sq. ft.	
Data Source(s)							
Verification Source(s)							
VALUE ADJUSTMENTS	DESCRIPTION	DESCRIPTION	+(-) $ Adjustment	DESCRIPTION	+(-) $ Adjustment	DESCRIPTION	+(-) $ Adjustment
Sale or Financing Concessions		ArmLth FHA					
Date of Sale/Time		3 weeks ago					
Location	N; Res	N; Res					
Leasehold/Fee Simple	fee simple	fee simple					
Site	9,425 SF	9,425 SF					
View	B; GlfVw	N; Res					
Design (Style)	Ranch	Ranch					
Quality of Construction	Q4	Q4					
Actual Age	7	7					
Condition	C3	C3					
Above Grade	Total / Bdrms / Baths	Total / Bdrms / Baths		Total / Bdrms / Baths		Total / Bdrms / Baths	
Room Count	7 / 3 / 2.0	7 / 3 / 2.0					
Gross Living Area	1,600 sq. ft.	1,590 sq. ft.		sq. ft.		sq. ft.	
Basement & Finished Rooms Below Grade	800 sq ft fin; 1rr 0.1ba	800 sq ft fin; 1rr 0.1ba					
Functional Utility	Average	Average					
Heating/Cooling	FWA/CAC	FWA/CAC					
Energy Efficient Items	none	none					
Garage/Carport	carport	2-car att.	–16,500				
Porch/Patio/Deck	porch	porch					
Fireplace	brick fireplace	brick fireplace					
Net Adjustment (Total)		☐ + ☒ -	$ 16,500	☐ + ☐ -	$	☐ + ☐ -	$
Adjusted Sale Price of Comparables		Net Adj. % Gross Adj. %	$ 173,500	Net Adj. % Gross Adj. %	$	Net Adj. % Gross Adj. %	$

I ☐ did ☐ did not research the sale or transfer history of the subject property and comparable sales. If not, explain

My research ☐ did ☐ did not reveal any prior sales or transfers of the subject property for the three years prior to the effective date of this appraisal.

Data source(s)

My research ☐ did ☐ did not reveal any prior sales or transfers of the comparable sales for the year prior to the date of sale of the comparable sale.

Data source(s)

Report the results of the research and analysis of the prior sale or transfer history of the subject property and comparable sales (report additional prior sales on page 3).

ITEM	SUBJECT	COMPARABLE SALE # 1	COMPARABLE SALE # 2	COMPARABLE SALE # 3
Date of Prior Sale/Transfer				
Price of Prior Sale/Transfer				
Data Source(s)				
Effective Date of Data Source(s)				

Analysis of prior sale or transfer history of the subject property and comparable sales

Summary of Sales Comparison Approach

Indicated Value by Sales Comparison Approach $

UNIT 13

Exercise 13-1

Scheduled rent:

$2,700 per room per year or $2,700 × 5 rooms = $13,500 per year per unit
$13,500 per year per unit × 6 units = $81,000 per year

Market rent:

Because property 2 is an apartment building that contains apartments with three bedrooms, it has been dropped as a comparable sale.
Property 1: $3,780 × 5 rooms = $18,900 per year per unit
$18,900 per year per unit × 6 units = $113,400 per year
Property 3: $3,528 × 5 rooms = $17,640 per year per unit
$17,640 per year per unit × 6 units = $105,840 per year

If the comparable properties reflect typical rents in the area, then rental income ranges from $105,840 per year to $113,400 per year, or from $3,528 per room per year to $3,780 per room per year. The subject property should be expected to rent for about $3,660 per room per year, or $109,800 annually.

Exercise 13-2

Apartment rental income	$96,000
Income from washers and dryers	1,900
Rent on parking space	5,400
Potential gross income	$103,300

Exercise 13-3

Apartment rental income	$96,000
Income from washers and dryers	1,900
Rent on parking space	5,400
Potential gross income	$ 103,300
Six units provide 312 possible weeks of rent (6 × 52 = 312).	
Six weeks of vacancy means a 2% vacancy loss (6 ÷ 312 = 0.019).	
Vacancy and collection losses (2% + 3% = 5%) × $103,300	5,165
Effective gross income	$98,135

Exercise 13-4

Potential gross income		$210,000
Allowance for vacancy and collection losses		– 9,900
Effective gross income		$200,100
Variable expenses:		
Salaries—janitor	$ 9,200	
Employee benefits	600	
Management	6,000	
Natural gas (+25%)	15,500	
Water	3,800	
Electricity	8,700	
Janitorial supplies	700	
Redecorating	2,000	
Legal and accounting fees	2,400	
Fixed expenses:		
Taxes (+20%)	7,200	
Reserves for replacement	2,500	
Total operating expenses		58,600
Net operating income		$141,500

Exercise 13-5

1. a
2. b
3. d
4. c
5. a

Exercise 13-6

Sale No.	Adjustment	GIM
1	+	8.9
2	–	10.9
3	–	17.0
4	+	10.7
5	–	5.3

Sales 3 and 5 appear out of line. The range for the subject, then, is between 8.9 and 10.9, and weighted toward the high side by the indicated adjustments.

Our estimate:

GIM = 10.8

Value of subject property = $18,000 × 10.8 = $194,400

Review Questions

1. c
2. b, f, h, m, p, u
3. a
4. b
5. c
6. d
7. b
8. b
9. a
10. d
11. b
12. a
13. c
14. a
15. b
16. b
17. d
18. c
19. a
20. c

UNIT 14

Exercise 14-1

Property	Capitalization Rate (rounded)
A	10.9
B	11.7
C	11.8
D	11.4
E	21.3

The capitalization rate of property E appears out of line with the rest of the comparables and should be discarded.

Based on the four remaining comparables, the value of the subject property is in a range from about $144,100 ($17,000 ÷ 0.118) to about $156,000 ($17,000 ÷ 0.109).

Exercise 14-2

Sales price	$435,000
Site value	–125,000
Building value	$310,000
Recapture rate = 100% ÷ 25 years =	× 0.04
NOI available for building recapture	$ 12,400

Interest rate (building) = $12,400 ÷ $435,000 property value = 0.0285 = 2.85%

Total NOI	$ 57,000
NOI for building recapture	– 12,400
NOI available for site	$ 44,600

Interest rate = $44,600 ÷ $435,000 = .1025 = 10¼%

Overall cap rate = 10.25% + 2.85% = 13.10%

Exercise 14-3

Loan (0.75 × 0.092)	0.069
Equity (0.25 × 0.12)	0.030
Overall rate	0.099 or 9.9%

Exercise 14-4

Estimated land value		$100,000
Net operating income	$50,000	
Interest on land value		
($100,000 × 10½%)	– 10,500	
Residual income to building	$39,500	
Cap rate for building		
Interest rate	10.5%	
Recapture rate (100% ÷ 40)	2.5	
Building value (rounded)		
$39,500 ÷ .13	13.0%	303,800
Total property value		$403,800

Exercise 14-5

Estimated building value			$3,000,000
Net operating income		$530,000	
Cap rate for building			
Interest rate:	12%		
Recapture rate (100% ÷ 50)	2		
Total	14%		
Discount and recapture on building			
value ($3,000,000 × 0.14)		– 420,000	
Residual income to land		$110,000	
Land value $110,000 ÷ 0.12			917,000
Total property value			$3,917,000

Exercise 14-6

Average cap rate = 0.1257

Subject: $\frac{I}{R} = V$

$16,000 ÷ 0.1257 = $127,300 (rounded)

Exercise 14-7

Estimated land value		$75,000
Total net operating income	$26,400	
Interest on land value ($75,000 × 11%)	– 8,250	
Residual income to building	$18,150	
Building value (using annuity factor of 8.694 × $18,150)		157,796
Total property value		$232,796

Exercise 14-8

Indicated building value		$300,000
Annual NOI	$50,000	
Interest on building value		
(10% on $300,000)	30,000	
Annual residual income to land	$20,000	
Annuity factor 9.077		
Land value ($20,000 × 9.077)		$181,540
Total property value		481,540
Rounded to		$481,500

Exercise 14-9

Total operating net income	$ 30,000
Annuity factor (25 years at 12%)	× 7.843
Present worth of net operating income	$235,290
Reversion factor (25 years at 12% = 0.059)	
Present worth of reversion ($150,000 × 0.059)	8,850
Total value of property	$244,140

Review Questions

1. a
2. b
3. a
4. b
5. d
6. b

7. Interest rate
   Recapture rate
8. a
9. b
10. c
11. c
12. Interest rate: 65% × 11% = 7.15%
    35% × 12% = 4.20%
    Total = 11.35%

Recapture rate: 100% ÷ 25 yrs = 4%

a. Building residual technique:

Estimated land value			$500,000
Net operating income		$400,000	
Interest on land value			
($500,000 × 0.1135)		– 56,750	
Residual income to building			$343,250
Cap rate for building			
Interest rate	11.35%		
Recapture rate	4.00		
	15.35%		
Building value (rounded)			
($343,250 ÷ 0.1535)			2,236,000
Total property value			$2,736,000

b. Land residual technique:

Estimated building value			$2,236,000
Net operating income		$400,000	
Cap rate for building			
Interest rate	11.35%		
Recapture rate	4.00		
	15.35%		
Interest and recapture on building value ($2,236,000 × 0.1535)		– 343,226	
Residual income to land		$56,774	
Land value (rounded) $56,774 ÷ 0.1135			500,000
Total property value			$2,736,000

13. a. Reconstruction of operating statement:

Potential gross income (4 stores × $10,200 per yr)		$40,800
Allowance for vacancy and collection losses (4%)		– 1,632
Effective gross income		$39,168
Variable expenses:		
Repairs and maintenance (12% of effective gross income)	$4,700	
Legal and accounting fees	550	
Miscellaneous expense	816	

Fixed expenses:			
Insurance ($3,000 ÷ 3 yrs)		1,000	
Real estate taxes		4,000	
Reserves for replacement:			
Roof ($2,000 ÷ 20 yrs)		100	
Furnaces ($950 × 4 ÷ 10 yrs)		380	
Total operating expenses			– 11,546
Net operating income			$ 27,622

b. Capitalization rate estimate:

Interest rate			
First mortgage (75% × 11%)	8.25%		
Equity (25% × 13%)	3.25		
Total interest rate	11.5%		
Recapture rate (100% ÷ 40 yrs remaining economic life)			2.5
Total capitalization rate			14.0%

c. Estimate of total property value:

Building residual technique			
Estimated land value			$ 55,000
Net operating income		$27,622	
Interest on land value ($55,000 × 11.5%)		– 6,325	
Residual income to building		$21,297	
Cap rate for building			
Interest rate	11.5%		
Recapture rate	2.5		
	14.0%		
Building value rounded ($21,297 ÷ 0.14)			152,121
Total property value			$207,121

14. The value indications are different in cases "a" and "b" because of different assumptions in types of income streams and methods of recapturing capital.

a. Building residual—straight-line method

Estimated land value			$100,000
Net operating income		$50,000	
Return on land value ($100,000 × 0.15)		– 15,000	
Residual income to building		$35,000	
Cap rate for building			
Interest rate	15%		
Recapture rate	+ 4		
	19%		
Building value ($35,000 ÷ 0.19) (rounded)			184,211
Total value of property			$284,211

b. Property residual—annuity method

Total net operating income	$ 50,000
Annuity factor (25 years at 15%)	× 6.464
Present worth of net operating income	$323,200
Present worth of reversion—$100,000 × 0.030 (25 years at 15%)	3,000
Total value of property	$326,200

or

Building residual—annuity method		
Estimated land value		$100,000
Residual income to building	$35,000	
Annuity factor (25 years @ 15%)	× 6.464	
Value of building		226,240
Total value of property		$326,240

15. a
16. c
17. c
18. a
19. d
20. d

UNIT 15

Exercise 15-1

All three approaches involve many variables that will affect the estimate of value. In the cost approach, the many factors contributing to construction cost and property depreciation must be recognized and evaluated. The sales comparison approach is successful only when recent sales of comparable properties are available. Even single-family residences may have many individual differences, entailing price adjustments that in turn rely on accurate estimations of the value of property features. The income capitalization approach relies on accurate income analysis and may involve complex computations.

Exercise 15-2

The cost approach valuation is somewhat lower than the others, but because no new construction is possible in the area, reliance on this estimate would be unrealistic. The other estimates are roughly comparable. The income approach valuation reflects the fact that rents in the area have been fairly stable, and there are no economic indicators of a significant change in either direction. Because most such properties are owner occupied, a positive factor as indicated by the upkeep of the area, the market value estimate is probably more accurate than that reached solely by the income capitalization approach. The final opinion of market value, as the most probable price the property can command, thus should be $173,000.

Exercise 15-3

The income capitalization and cost approaches will be most important in valuing the subject property. The cost approach will set the upper limit of value, as there is land available for similar construction. The income capitalization approach is important because of the property's income-producing abilities and potential. The value reached by the income capitalization approach will be influenced by the existence of major tenants, who may be financially sound but who also may benefit from long-term contracts that may not reflect the recent dramatic increases in property values in the area.

Exercise 15-4

Uniform Residential Appraisal Report

Uniform Residential Appraisal Report

File #

The purpose of this summary appraisal report is to provide the lender/client with an accurate, and adequately supported, opinion of the market value of the subject property.

SUBJECT

Property Address 4807 Catalpa Road City Woodview State IL Zip Code 60000
Borrower Owner of Public Record County Dakota
Legal Description attached to this report
Assessor's Parcel # Tax Year R.E. Taxes $ 2,278
Neighborhood Name Map Reference Census Tract
Occupant [X] Owner [ ] Tenant [ ] Vacant Special Assessments $ [ ] PUD HOA $ [ ] per year [ ] per month
Property Rights Appraised [X] Fee Simple [ ] Leasehold [ ] Other (describe)
Assignment Type [ ] Purchase Transaction [ ] Refinance Transaction [ ] Other (describe)
Lender/Client Address
Is the subject property currently offered for sale or has it been offered for sale in the twelve months prior to the effective date of this appraisal? [X] Yes [ ] No
Report data source(s) used, offering price(s), and date(s).

CONTRACT

I [ ] did [ ] did not analyze the contract for sale for the subject purchase transaction. Explain the results of the analysis of the contract for sale or why the analysis was not performed.

Contract Price $ Date of Contract Is the property seller the owner of public record? [ ] Yes [ ] No Data Source(s)
Is there any financial assistance (loan charges, sale concessions, gift or downpayment assistance, etc.) to be paid by any party on behalf of the borrower? [ ] Yes [ ] No
If Yes, report the total dollar amount and describe the items to be paid.

NEIGHBORHOOD

Note: Race and the racial composition of the neighborhood are not appraisal factors.

Neighborhood Characteristics	One-Unit Housing Trends	One-Unit Housing		Present Land Use %	
Location [ ] Urban [X] Suburban [ ] Rural	Property Values [X] Increasing [ ] Stable [ ] Declining	PRICE	AGE	One-Unit	100 %
Built-Up [X] Over 75% [ ] 25–75% [ ] Under 25%	Demand/Supply [ ] Shortage [X] In Balance [ ] Over Supply	$ (000)	(yrs)	2-4 Unit	%
Growth [ ] Rapid [X] Stable [ ] Slow	Marketing Time [X] Under 3 mths [ ] 3–6 mths [ ] Over 6 mths	Low		Multi-Family	%
Neighborhood Boundaries Boundaries are shown on attached map		High		Commercial	%
		Pred.		Other	%

Neighborhood Description Subject property is located in a desirable subdivision in the Central Eastern section of the Village of Woodview. Schools, shopping, and other necessary facilities and services are within a reasonable distance.

Market Conditions (including support for the above conclusions) Steady demand for housing with a gradual uptrend in values reflects a relatively healthy local economy. Conventional financing readily available with interest rates at 6% to 8%. The desirability of this neighborhood is reflected by the fact that most homes are sold within 2 months of being put on the market.

SITE

Dimensions 65' × 130' Area 8,450 squre feet Shape rectangular View tree-lined st/typical
Specific Zoning Classification R-2 Zoning Description Single-family residence
Zoning Compliance [X] Legal [ ] Legal Nonconforming (Grandfathered Use) [ ] No Zoning [ ] Illegal (describe)
Is the highest and best use of the subject property as improved (or as proposed per plans and specifications) the present use? [X] Yes [ ] No If No, describe

Utilities	Public	Other (describe)		Public	Other (describe)	Off-site Improvements—Type	Public	Private
Electricity	[X]	[ ]	Water	[X]	[ ]	Street	[X]	[ ]
Gas	[X]	[ ]	Sanitary Sewer	[X]	[ ]	Alley	[ ]	[ ]

FEMA Special Flood Hazard Area [ ] Yes [X] No FEMA Flood Zone FEMA Map # FEMA Map Date
Are the utilities and off-site improvements typical for the market area? [X] Yes [ ] No If No, describe
Are there any adverse site conditions or external factors (easements, encroachments, environmental conditions, land uses, etc.)? [ ] Yes [X] No If Yes, describe
Underground electric and telephone lines; no easements or encroachments

IMPROVEMENTS

General Description	Foundation	Exterior Description materials/condition	Interior materials/condition
Units [X] One [ ] One with Accessory Unit	[ ] Concrete Slab [X] Crawl Space	Foundation Walls Concrete/gd	Floors Vinyl/cpt/oak/gd
# of Stories 1	[ ] Full Basement [ ] Partial Basement	Exterior Walls Brick veneer/gd	Walls Drywall/paint/gd
Type [X] Det. [ ] Att. [ ] S-Det./End Unit	Basement Area sq. ft.	Roof Surface Asphlt.shingle/gd	Trim/Finish Wood/Avg
[X] Existing [ ] Proposed [ ] Under Const.	Basement Finish %	Gutters & Downspouts Galv./paint/gd	Bath Floor Ceram/gd
Design (Style) Ranch	[ ] Outside Entry/Exit [ ] Sump Pump	Window Type Wood double-hung/gd	Bath Wainscot Ceram/gd
Year Built 25 years ago	Evidence of [ ] Infestation	Storm Sash/Insulated Comb.alum/gd	Car Storage [ ] None
Effective Age (Yrs) 15	[ ] Dampness [ ] Settlement	Screens Comb.alum/gd	[X] Driveway # of Cars 2
Attic [ ] None	Heating [X] FWA [ ] HWBB [ ] Radiant	Amenities [ ] Woodstove(s) #	Driveway Surface Asphalt
[X] Drop Stair [ ] Stairs	[ ] Other Fuel	[ ] Fireplace(s) # [ ] Fence	[X] Garage # of Cars
[ ] Floor [ ] Scuttle	Cooling [X] Central Air Conditioning	[ ] Patio/Deck [ ] Porch	[ ] Carport # of Cars
[ ] Finished [ ] Heated	[ ] Individual [ ] Other	[ ] Pool [ ] Other	[ ] Att. [X] Det. [ ] Built-in

Appliances [X] Refrigerator [X] Range/Oven [X] Dishwasher [X] Disposal [ ] Microwave [ ] Washer/Dryer [X] Other (describe) Oven fan/hood
Finished area **above** grade contains: 7 Rooms 3 Bedrooms 2.00 Bath(s) 1,950 Square Feet of Gross Living Area Above Grade
Additional features (special energy efficient items, etc.) 6" insulation above ceiling and behind drywall; 6' redwood fence around rear yard.

Describe the condition of the property (including needed repairs, deterioration, renovations, remodeling, etc.). Overall, house and garage are in good shape with normal wear and tear indicating 25% depreciation. There is no evidence of functional or external obsolescence.

Are there any physical deficiencies or adverse conditions that affect the livability, soundness, or structural integrity of the property? [ ] Yes [X] No If Yes, describe
No detrimental influences.

Does the property generally conform to the neighborhood (functional utility, style, condition, use, construction, etc.)? [X] Yes [ ] No If No, describe

Exercise 15-4

Uniform Residential Appraisal Report (continued)

Uniform Residential Appraisal Report

File #

There are 2 comparable properties currently offered for sale in the subject neighborhood ranging in price from $ 178,90.00 to $ 184,500.00 .

There are 5 comparable sales in the subject neighborhood within the past twelve months ranging in sale price from $ 152,000.00 to $ 186.240.00 .

SALES COMPARISON APPROACH

FEATURE	SUBJECT	COMPARABLE SALE # 1		COMPARABLE SALE # 2		COMPARABLE SALE # 3	
Address	4807 Catalpa Road	4310 W. Gladys		3840 W. Monroe		316 Iowa	
Proximity to Subject		.50 miles SE		.50 miles SE		.50 miles SE	
Sale Price	$		$ 177,750		$ 180,000		$ 186,240
Sale Price/Gross Liv. Area	$ sq. ft.	$ 90.00 sq. ft.		$ 92.31 sq. ft.		$ 96.00 sq. ft.	
Data Source(s)		Public records		Public records		Public records	
Verification Source(s)		Sales agent		Sales agent		Sales agent	
VALUE ADJUSTMENTS	DESCRIPTION	DESCRIPTION	+(-) $ Adjustment	DESCRIPTION	+(-) $ Adjustment	DESCRIPTION	+(-) $ Adjustment
Sale or Financing Concessions		Conv		Conv		Conv	
Date of Sale/Time		6 weeks ago		3 weeks ago		6 weeks ago	
Location	N; Res	N; Res		N; Res		N; Res	
Leasehold/Fee Simple	fee simple	fee simple		fee simple		fee simple	
Site	8,400 SF	8,400 SF		8,400 SF		8,400 SF	
View	N; Res	N; Res		N; Res		N; Res	
Design (Style)	Ranch	Ranch		Ranch		Ranch	
Quality of Construction	Q4	Q4		Q4		Q4	
Actual Age	25	25		25		25	
Condition	C3	C3		C3		C3	
Above Grade Room Count	Total 7 Bdrms. 3 Baths 2.0	Total 7 Bdrms. 3 Baths 2.0		Total 7 Bdrms. 3 Baths 2.0		Total 7 Bdrms. 3 Baths 2.0	
Gross Living Area	1,950 sq. ft.	1,975 sq. ft.		1,950 sq. ft.		1,940 sq. ft.	
Basement & Finished Rooms Below Grade	none	none		none		1900 sf; 970 sf fin	-10,000
Functional Utility	Average	Average		Average		Average	
Heating/Cooling	FWA/CAC	FWA/CAC		FWA/CAC		FWA/CAC	
Energy Efficient Items	extra insul	extra insul		extra insul		extra insul	
Garage/Carport	2-car garage	2-car garage		2-car garage		2-car garage	
Porch/Patio/Deck							
Fireplace	masonry	none	+5,000	masonry		masonry	
Fence	fence	fence		fence		fence	
Net Adjustment (Total)		[X] + [ ] -	$ 5,000	[ ] + [ ] -	$	[ ] + [X] -	$ 10,000
Adjusted Sale Price of Comparables		Net Adj. 2.80 % Gross Adj. 2.80 %	$ 182,750	Net Adj. % Gross Adj. %	$ 180,000	Net Adj. -5.40 % Gross Adj. -5.40 %	$ 176,240

I [X] did [ ] did not research the sale or transfer history of the subject property and comparable sales. If not, explain

My research [ ] did [X] did not reveal any prior sales or transfers of the subject property for the three years prior to the effective date of this appraisal.

Data source(s) County tax assessor

My research [ ] did [X] did not reveal any prior sales or transfers of the comparable sales for the year prior to the date of sale of the comparable sale.

Data source(s) County tax assessor

Report the results of the research and analysis of the prior sale or transfer history of the subject property and comparable sales (report additional prior sales on page 3).

ITEM	SUBJECT	COMPARABLE SALE # 1	COMPARABLE SALE # 2	COMPARABLE SALE # 3
Date of Prior Sale/Transfer				
Price of Prior Sale/Transfer				
Data Source(s)				
Effective Date of Data Source(s)				

Analysis of prior sale or transfer history of the subject property and comparable sales

Summary of Sales Comparison Approach

Indicated Value by Sales Comparison Approach $ 180,000

RECONCILIATION

Indicated Value by: Sales Comparison Approach $ 180,000 **Cost Approach (if developed) $** **Income Approach (if developed) $** 169,000

This appraisal is made [ ] "as is", [ ] subject to completion per plans and specifications on the basis of a hypothetical condition that the improvements have been completed, [ ] subject to the following repairs or alterations on the basis of a hypothetical condition that the repairs or alterations have been completed, or [ ] subject to the following required inspection based on the extraordinary assumption that the condition or deficiency does not require alteration or repair:

Based on a complete visual inspection of the interior and exterior areas of the subject property, defined scope of work, statement of assumptions and limiting conditions, and appraiser's certification, my (our) opinion of the market value, as defined, of the real property that is the subject of this report is $, as of , which is the date of inspection and the effective date of this appraisal.

Exercise 15-4

Uniform Residential Appraisal Report (continued)

Uniform Residential Appraisal Report

File #

ADDITIONAL COMMENTS

COST APPROACH TO VALUE (not required by Fannie Mae)

Provide adequate information for the lender/client to replicate the below cost figures and calculations.

Support for the opinion of site value (summary of comparable land sales or other methods for estimating site value)

ESTIMATED [X] REPRODUCTION OR [ ] REPLACEMENT COST NEW	OPINION OF SITE VALUE = $ 45,000
Source of cost data	Dwelling 1,950 Sq. Ft. @ $ 90 =$ 175,500
Quality rating from cost service Effective date of cost data	Sq. Ft. @ $ =$
Comments on Cost Approach (gross living area calculations, depreciation, etc.)	Extra insulation 1,200
Depreciation based on normal wear and tear for well-maintained	Garage/Carport 500 Sq. Ft. @ $ 30 =$ 15,000
property with effective age of 15 years.	Total Estimate of Cost-New = $ 191,700
	Less Physical Functional External
	Depreciation 47,925 =$(47,925)
	Depreciated Cost of Improvements =$ 143,775
	"As-is" Value of Site Improvements =$ 8,400
Estimated Remaining Economic Life (HUD and VA only) Years	Indicated Value By Cost Approach =$ 197,175

INCOME APPROACH TO VALUE (not required by Fannie Mae)

Estimated Monthly Market Rent $ 1,300 X Gross Rent Multiplier 130 = $ 169,000 Indicated Value by Income Approach

Summary of Income Approach (including support for market rent and GRM) Comparable home sales prices/monthly rental income: $160,000/$1,200; $166,500/$1,275; $173,500/$1,300.

PROJECT INFORMATION FOR PUDs (if applicable)

Is the developer/builder in control of the Homeowners' Association (HOA)? [ ] Yes [ ] No Unit type(s) [ ] Detached [ ] Attached

Provide the following information for PUDs ONLY if the developer/builder is in control of the HOA and the subject property is an attached dwelling unit.

Legal name of project

Total number of phases Total number of units Total number of units sold

Total number of units rented Total number of units for sale Data source(s)

Was the project created by the conversion of an existing building(s) into a PUD? [ ] Yes [ ] No If Yes, date of conversion

Does the project contain any multi-dwelling units? [ ] Yes [ ] No Data source(s)

Are the units, common elements, and recreation facilities complete? [ ] Yes [ ] No If No, describe the status of completion.

Are the common elements leased to or by the Homeowners' Association? [ ] Yes [ ] No If Yes, describe the rental terms and options.

Describe common elements and recreational facilities

Review Questions

1. b
2. b
3. c
4. d
5. d
6. c
7. b
8. a
9. c
10. a
11. a
12. c
13. d
14. c
15. d
16. a
17. c
18. b
19. d
20. a

UNIT 16

Exercise 16-1

1. Condominium building size, unit size, number of owner-occupied units, common areas, amenities, monthly fees, or other assessments
2. PUD size of development, common areas, amenities, fees, or assessments, use of comparable properties in the same development
3. Time-share ownership interest, amenities, time of year, resale market, maintenance fees
4. Manufactured home age and size of home, lot size, lawn areas, streets, park amenities, upkeep, space rental cost, and lease term

Exercise 16-2

1. c
2. a
3. a
4. c
5. c
6. b

Exercise 16-3

1. A leasehold estate is created (may be valued) when scheduled rent under the lease is less than the fair market rental, or economic rent.
2. $419,100
   $393,200

Review Questions

1. Leased fee interest:

Net operating income	$ 36,000
Annuity factor (30 years @ 11%)	× 8.694
Present worth of net income	$312,984
Present worth of reversion	
($150,000 × 0.044 reversion factor)	6,600
Value of the leased fee interest	$319,584

2. Leasehold interest:

Market rent	$ 45,000
Scheduled rent	– 36,000
Excess rent	$ 9,000
Present worth of excess rent discounted at 14%	× 7.003
Value of leasehold interest	$ 63,027

3. Total value of leased fee and leasehold interests = $319,584 + $63,027 = $382,611 rounded to $382,600.
4. a
5. b
6. c
7. c
8. d
9. c
10. c
11. b
12. c
13. b
14. c
15. c
16. a
17. a
18. b
19. b
20. d

GLOSSARY

abatement Stopping or reducing of amount or value, as when assessments for ad valorem taxation are abated after the initial assessment has been made.

absentee landlord An owner of an interest in income-producing property who does not reside on the premises and who may rely on a property manager to oversee the investment.

absolute fee simple title A title that is unqualified. Fee simple is the best title that can be obtained. (See also *fee simple*.)

absorption analysis A study of the number of units of residential or nonresidential property that can be sold or leased over a given period of time in a defined location. (See also *feasibility study*.)

abstraction Method of finding land value in which all improvement costs (less depreciation) are deducted from sales price. Also called *extraction method*.

access A way to enter and leave a tract of land, sometimes by easement over land owned by another. (See also *egress* and *ingress*.)

accessibility The relative ease of entrance to a property by various means, a factor that contributes to the probable most profitable use of a site.

accessory buildings Structures on a property, such as sheds and garages, that are secondary to the main building.

accretion Land buildup resulting from the deposit by natural action of sand or soil washed up from a river, lake, or sea.

accrual basis In accounting, a system of allocating revenue and expense items on the basis of when the revenue is earned or the expense incurred, not on the basis of when the cash is received or paid out.

accrued depreciation (1) For accounting purposes, total depreciation taken on an asset from the time of its acquisition. (2) For appraisal purposes, the difference between reproduction or replacement cost and the appraised value as of the date of appraisal.

accrued expenses Expenses incurred that are not yet payable. In a closing statement, the accrued expenses of the seller typically are credited to the purchaser (taxes, wages, interest, etc.).

acknowledgment A declaration of an act to give it legal validity; the signature of a person executing a legal document is acknowledged by the signor to the notary or official who verifies the signature.

acquisition appraisal A market value appraisal of property condemned or otherwise acquired for public use, to establish the compensation to be paid to the owner.

acre A measure of land, 208.71 by 208.71 feet in area, being 43,560 square feet, 160 square rods, or 4,840 square yards.

actual age The number of years elapsed since the original structure was built. Sometimes referred to as *historical* or *chronological age*.

adjustable-rate mortgage (ARM) A financing technique in which the lender can raise or lower the interest rate according to a set index, such as the rate on six-month Treasury bills or the average cost of funds of FDIC-insured institutions. (See also *amortized mortgage.*)

adjustment Decrease or increase in the sales price of a comparable property to account for a feature that the property has or does not have in comparison with the subject property. Either a dollar adjustment or a percentage adjustment can be made.

ad valorem According to value (Latin); generally used to refer to real estate taxes that are based on assessed property value.

adverse land use A land use that has a detrimental effect on the market value of nearby properties.

aesthetic value Relating to beauty, rather than to functional considerations.

age-life method of depreciation A method of computing accrued depreciation in which the cost of a building is depreciated at a fixed annual percentage rate; also called the *straight-line method.*

aggregate In statistics, the sum of all individuals, called *variates.*

air rights The right to use the open space above the physical surface of the land, generally allowing the surface to be used for some other purpose.

allocation method The allocation of the appraised total value of the property between land and building. The allocation may be accomplished either on a ratio basis or by subtracting a figure representing building value from the total appraised value of the property.

allowance for vacancy and collection losses The percentage of potential gross income that will be lost due to vacant units, collection losses, or both.

amenities The qualities and state of being pleasant and agreeable; in appraising, those qualities that are attached to a property and from which the owner derives benefits other than monetary; satisfaction of possession and use arising from architectural excellence, scenic beauty, and social environment.

amortized mortgage A mortgage loan in which the principal and interest are payable in periodic installments during the term of the loan so that at the completion of all payments, there is a zero balance.

annuity A fixed, regular return on an investment.

annuity factors table Provides a factor to be multiplied by the desired level of yearly income (based on the interest rate and length of time of the investment) to find the present worth of the investment.

annuity method A method of capitalization that treats income from real property as a fixed, regular return on an investment. For the annuity method to be applied, the lessee must be reliable and the lease must be long term.

anticipation, principle of The principle that the purchase price of property is affected by the expectation of its future appeal and value.

appraisal An estimate of quantity, quality, or value; the process through which conclusions of property value are obtained; also refers to the report setting forth the process of estimating value. (See also *appraisal process.*)

Appraisal Foundation, The Nonprofit corporation established in 1987 and headquartered in Washington, D.C., sponsored by major appraisal and appraisal-related professional and trade groups.

appraisal management companies (AMCs) Any corporation, partnership, sole proprietorship, subsidiary, unit, or other business entity that administers networks of independent contract appraisers to perform real estate appraisal services for clients.

appraisal methods The approaches used in the appraisal of real property. (See *cost approach*; *income capitalization approach*; *sales comparison approach*.)

Appraisal Practices Board Created by the Appraisal Foundation to issue voluntary guidance to appraisers on emerging valuation issues in the marketplace.

appraisal process A systematic analysis of the factors that bear on the value of real estate; an orderly program by which the problem is defined; the work necessary to solve the problem is planned; the data involved are acquired, classified, analyzed, and interpreted into an opinion of value; and the final opinion of value is presented in the form requested by the client.

appraisal report An appraiser's written opinion to a client of the value sought for the subject property as of the date of appraisal, giving all details of the appraisal process. Two appraisal reporting options are permitted by the *Uniform Standards of Professional Appraisal Practice (USPAP)*:

appraisal report This reporting option contains sufficient information to lead the client and other intended users of the report to the appraiser's opinions and conclusions.

restricted report Made for a specific client and for a limited purpose, this type of report contains virtually none of the information the appraiser used to arrive at the value conclusion.

Appraisal Standards Board (ASB) Created by the Appraisal Foundation and responsible for establishing minimum standards of appraisal competence.

appraised value An opinion of an appraiser of the amount of a particular value, such as assessed value, insurable value, or market value, based on the particular assignment.

appraiser One who forms an opinion of a specified value.

Appraiser Independence Requirements Fannie Mae directives that took effect October 15, 2010, to help insure that appraisals are objective and not subject to any form of coercion.

Appraiser Qualifications Board (AQB) Created by the Appraisal Foundation and responsible for establishing minimum requirements for licensed and certified appraisers and licensing and certifying examinations.

appreciation Permanent or temporary increase in monetary value over time due to economic or related causes.

approaches to value Any of the following three methods used to value real estate: cost approach, income capitalization approach, and sales comparison approach.

appurtenance Anything used with land for its benefit, either affixed to land or used with it, that will pass with the conveyance of the land.

area The space inside a two-dimensional shape (i.e., one with length and width but not volume).

arm's-length transaction A transaction in which both buyer and seller act willingly and under no pressure, with knowledge of the present conditions and future potential of the property, and in which the property has been offered on the open market for a reasonable length of time and there are no unusual circumstances.

array An arrangement of statistical data according to numerical size.

assemblage The combining of two or more adjoining lots into one larger tract to increase their total value.

assessed value The value placed on land and buildings by a government unit (assessor) for use in levying annual real estate taxes.

assessment The imposition of a tax, charge, or levy, usually according to established rates. (See also *special assessment.*)

assessor One who determines property values for the purpose of ad valorem taxation.

asset Property that is owned and has value, such as cash or real or personal property.

assignment The transfer of the right, title, and interest in property belonging to one person (the *assignor*) to another person (the *assignee*).

average deviation In statistics, the measure of how far the average individual, or variate, differs from the mean of all variates.

balance, principle of The appraisal principle that states that the greatest value of a property will occur when the type and size of the improvements are proportional to each other as well as to the land.

band of investment method A method of developing a discount rate based on (1) the rate of mortgage interest available, (2) the rate of return required on equity, and (3) the debt and equity share in the property. A variation of this method is used to compute an overall capitalization rate.

bargain and sale deed A deed that contains no warranties against liens or other encumbrances but implies that the grantor has the right to convey title.

base line A reference survey line of the government or rectangular survey, being an imaginary line extending east and west and crossing a principal meridian at a definite point.

base rent The minimum rent payable under a percentage lease.

bell curve The shape of a graph line indicating the normal distribution of values; if the data are perfectly symmetrical, the mean, median, and mode are all equal and are shown at the highest point of the curve.

bench mark A permanent reference mark (PRM) used by surveyors in measuring differences in elevation.

benchmark The standard or base from which specific estimates are made.

beneficiary The person who is to receive the benefits from a trust fund.

book value The value of a property as an asset on the books of account; usually, reproduction or replacement cost, plus additions to capital and less reserves for depreciation.

breach Failure to fulfill one or more of the terms of a contract; default.

breakdown method (See *observed condition depreciation.*)

breakeven point That point at which total income equals total expenses.

breakeven ratio The ratio of operating expenses plus the property's annual debt service to potential gross income.

building capitalization rate The sum of the discount and capital recapture rates for a building.

building codes Rules of local, municipal, or state governments specifying minimum building and construction standards for the protection of public safety and health.

building residual technique A method of capitalization using net income remaining to building after interest on land value has been deducted.

bundle of rights A term often applied to the rights of ownership of real estate, including the rights of using, renting, selling, or giving away the real estate or *not* taking any of these actions.

Cape Cod One-and-a-half story house with sufficient head room in the second floor to provide livable space.

capital Money and/or property comprising the wealth owned or used by a person or business enterprise to acquire other money or goods.

capital improvement A structure or other addition to property or an addition or alteration to an existing improvement that adds value to the property, substantially increases its useful life, or makes the property suitable for a new use.

capitalization The process employed in valuing a property by the use of an appropriate capitalization rate and the annual net operating income expected to be produced by the property. The formula is expressed as follows:

$$\frac{\text{Income}}{\text{Rate}} = \text{Value}$$

capitalization rate The percentage rate applied to the income a property is expected to produce to derive an estimate of the property's value; includes both an acceptable rate of return on the amount invested (yield) and return of the actual amount invested (recapture).

capital market The market for securities, including stocks and bonds, that allows companies and governments to raise funds.

capital recapture The return of an investment; the right of the investor to get back the amount invested at the end of the term of ownership or over the productive life of the improvements.

capitalized value method of depreciation A method of computing depreciation by determining loss in rental value attributable to a depreciated item and applying a gross rent multiplier to that figure.

cash basis accounting A system of recognizing revenue and expense items only at the time cash is received or paid out.

cash equivalency technique Method of adjusting a sales price downward to reflect the increase in value due to assumption or procurement by buyer of a loan at an interest rate lower than the prevailing market rate.

cash flow The net spendable income from an investment, determined by deducting all operating and fixed expenses from gross income. If expenses exceed income, a negative cash flow is the result.

cash flow rate (See *equity capitalization rate*.)

cash on cash rate (See *equity capitalization rate*.)

chain A surveyor's unit of measurement equal to four rods or 66 feet, consisting of 100 links of 7.92 inches each; ten square chains of land are equal to one acre.

chain of title The record of land ownership that establishes the present owner of the property as the grantee of a deed from the previous owner, that owner as the grantee in an earlier deed, et cetera in an unbroken line going back to the first legally recognized document of title.

change, principle of The principle that no physical or economic condition ever remains constant.

chattels Tangible personal property items.

client One who hires another person as a representative or agent for a fee.

closing statement The computation of financial adjustments required to close a real estate transaction, computed as of the day of closing the sale; used to determine the net amount of money the buyer must pay to the seller to complete the transaction, as well as amounts to be paid to other parties, such as the broker or escrow holder. (See also *settlement*.)

code of ethics Rules of ethical conduct, such as those that govern the actions of members of a professional group.

community property A form of property ownership in which spouses have an equal interest in property acquired by either spouse during the time of their marriage. Community property does not include property that each spouse owned prior to marriage or property received by gift or inheritance or as the proceeds of separate property.

comparables Properties that are substantially equivalent to the subject property.

comparative unit method A method used to estimate the cost of a structure based on the value of comparable structures that were recently constructed and adjusted for time and physical differences.

comparison method (See *sales comparison approach.*)

competition, principle of The principle that a successful business attracts other such businesses, which may dilute profits.

compound interest Interest paid on both the original investment and accrued interest.

computer-assisted mass appraisal (CAMA) Use of computerized databases and techniques in valuing commercial and residential properties for tax assessment purposes.

condemnation Taking private property for public use through court action, under the right of eminent domain, with compensation to the owner.

conditional use permit Approval of a property use inconsistent with present zoning because it is in the public interest. For example, a church or hospital may be allowed in a residential district.

condominium The absolute ownership of an apartment or a commercial unit, generally in a multiunit building, by a legal description of the airspace that the unit actually occupies, plus an undivided interest in the ownership of the common elements, which are owned jointly with the other condominium unit owners.

common elements All portions of the land, property, and space that make up a condominium property that include land, all improvements and structures, and all easements, rights, and appurtenances and exclude all space composing individual units. Each unit owner owns a definite percentage of undivided interest in the common elements.

parcel The entire tract of real estate included in a condominium development; also referred to as a *development parcel.*

unit One ownership space in a condominium building or a part of a property intended for independent use and having lawful access to a public way. Ownership of one unit also includes a definite undivided interest in the common elements.

conformity, principle of The principle that buildings should be similar in design, construction, and age to other buildings in the neighborhood to enhance appeal and value.

contiguous Adjacent; in actual contact; touching.

contract An agreement entered into by two or more legally competent parties who, for a consideration, undertake to do or to refrain from doing some legal act or acts.

contract rent (See *scheduled rent.*)

contribution, principle of The principle that any improvement to a property, whether to vacant land or a building, is worth only what it adds to the property's market value, regardless of the improvement's actual cost.

conventional lender One who makes loans that are neither insured by the FHA nor guaranteed by the VA.

conventional loan A mortgage loan that is neither insured by the FHA nor guaranteed by the VA.

conveyance A written instrument, such as a deed or lease, by which title or an interest in real estate is transferred.

cooperative A multiunit residential building with title in a trust or corporation that is owned by and operated for the benefit of persons living within it, who are the beneficial owners of the trust or the stockholders of the corporation, each possessing a proprietary lease granting occupancy of a specific unit in the building.

corporation An association of shareholders, created under law, having a legal identity separate from the individuals who own it.

correction lines A system of compensating for inaccuracies in the rectangular survey system due to the curvature of the earth. Every fourth township line (24-mile intervals) is used as a correction line on which the intervals between the north and south range lines are remeasured and corrected to a full six miles.

correlation (See *reconciliation*.)

cost The amount paid for a good or service.

cost approach The process of valuing a property by adding the appraiser's estimate of the reproduction or replacement cost of property improvements, less depreciation, to land value.

cost index Figure representing construction cost at a particular time in relation to construction cost at an earlier time, prepared by a cost reporting or indexing service.

cost manuals Publications, now often electronic, that provide updated information on building and component construction costs in various areas.

cost of credit The interest rate paid on a loan used to make a purchase.

cost service index method (See *index method*.)

counteroffer A reply to an offer to enter into a contract that introduces new terms and conditions and thus has the effect of rejecting the original offer.

covenant An agreement written into deeds and other instruments promising performance or nonperformance of certain acts or stipulating certain uses or non-uses of property.

covenants, conditions, and restrictions (CC&Rs) Private limitations on property use placed in the deed received by a property owner, typically by reference to a declaration of restrictions.

cubic-foot method A method of estimating reproduction cost by multiplying the number of cubic feet of space a building encloses by the construction cost per cubic foot.

curable depreciation A depreciated item that can be restored or replaced economically. (See also *functional obsolescence—curable and physical deterioration—curable*.)

curb appeal A property's overall attractiveness as viewed from the street.

data Information pertinent to a specific appraisal assignment. Data may be general (relating to the economic background, the region, the city, and the neighborhood) or specific (relating to the subject property and comparable properties in the market).

data source list Government offices, companies, and other locations at which information regarding real estate can be found.

datum A horizontal plane from which heights and depths are measured.

debt investors Investors who take a relatively conservative approach, typically taking a passive role in investment management while demanding a security interest in property financed.

decimal Numerical system based on representations of numbers in units of 10, with the decimal point indicating positive multiples of ten to the left of the decimal point, and negative multiples of ten to the right of the decimal point.

declaration of restrictions Document filed by a subdivision developer and referenced in individual deeds to subdivision lots that lists all restrictions that apply to subdivision properties. (See also *deed restrictions*.)

decline Period when property requires an increasing amount of upkeep to retain its original utility and becomes less desirable.

decreasing returns, laws of The situation in which property improvements no longer bring a corresponding increase in property income or value.

deed A written instrument that conveys title to or an interest in real estate when properly executed and delivered.

deed of trust (See *trust deed*.)

deed restrictions Provisions in a deed limiting the future uses of the property. Deed restrictions may take many forms: they may limit the density of buildings, dictate the types of structures that can be erected, and prevent buildings from being used for specific purposes or used at all. Deed restrictions may impose a myriad of limitations and conditions affecting the property rights appraised.

default Failure to perform a duty or meet a contractual obligation.

deficit rent The amount by which market rent exceeds scheduled rent at the time of the appraisal.

demised premises Property conveyed for a certain number of years, most often by a lease.

demography The statistical study of human populations, especially in reference to size, density, and distribution. Demographic information is of particular importance to people involved in market analyses and highest and best use analyses in determining potential land uses of sites.

Department of Housing and Urban Development (HUD) Created in 1965, HUD is the federal, cabinet-level agency that is charged with enhancing home ownership and rental options by providing affordable housing opportunities and establishing and enforcing fair housing guidelines under the Fair Housing Act.

Department of Veterans Affairs (VA) Federal agency that provides education, health, housing, and other benefits to qualified veterans of one of the military services.

depreciated cost For appraisal purposes, the reproduction or replacement cost of a building, less accrued depreciation to the time of appraisal.

depreciation For appraisal purposes, loss in value due to any cause, including physical deterioration, functional obsolescence, and external obsolescence. (See also *obsolescence.*)
depth factor An adjustment factor applied to the value per front foot of lots that vary from the standard depth.
development (See *neighborhood life cycle.*)
direct capitalization Selection of a capitalization rate from a range of overall rates computed by analyzing sales of comparable properties and applying the following formula to each:

$$\frac{\text{Income}}{\text{Value}} = \text{Rate} \qquad \frac{I}{V} = R$$

direct costs The costs of notifying customers of a data breach, such as printing, postage, and legal fees.
direct market comparison approach (See *sales comparison approach.*)
discount rate (See *interest rate.*)
disintegration (See *neighborhood life cycle.*)
Dodd-Frank Wall Street Reform and Consumer Protection Act (Dodd-Frank) Became law July 21, 2010, and greatly increases federal regulation of financial services through the Federal Reserve Board, including changes to the Truth in Lending Act (TILA) that prohibit use of coercion or other attempts to influence appraisals.
dollar adjustment Difference in value between property being appraised and a comparable property, measured by the net effect on market value of property features present in one and not the other, positively or negatively.
DUST (demand, utility, scarcity, transferability) The four elements of value. When all four elements of value are present, property has a value that can be estimated by an appraiser.
easement A right to use the land of another for a specific purpose, such as a right-of-way or for utilities; a nonpossessory interest in land. An easement appurtenant passes with the land when conveyed.
economic age-life method of depreciation (See *age-life method of depreciation.*)
economic base The level of business activity in a community—particularly activity that brings income into the community from surrounding areas.
economic life The period during which a structure may reasonably be expected to perform the function for which it was designed or intended.
economic obsolescence (See *external obsolescence.*)
economic rent (See *market rent.*)
Economic Stimulus Act of 2008 Legislation passed in early 2008 intended to assist taxpayers and homeowners at a time of economic downturn and increased home foreclosures.
EDI (electronic data interchange) Transmission of information, including completed appraisal forms or other documents, via modem from one computer to another.
effective age The age of a building based on the actual wear and tear and maintenance, or lack of it, that the building has received.
effective demand The desire to buy coupled with the ability to pay.
effective gross income Estimated potential gross income of a rental property from all sources, less anticipated vacancy and collection losses.

effective gross income multiplier Factor that can be applied to gross income less vacation and collection losses to determine market value.

egress A way to leave a tract of land; the opposite of ingress. (See also *access*.)

electrical system Building components that provide adequate electrical service for the needs of occupants, meeting all safety requirements of the National Electrical Code (NEC).

eminent domain The right of a federal, state, or local government or public corporation, utility, or service corporation to acquire private property for public use through a court action called condemnation, in which the court determines whether the use is a necessary one and what the compensation to the owner should be.

encroachment A building, wall, or fence that extends beyond the land of the owner and illegally intrudes on land of an adjoining owner or a street or an alley.

encumbrance Any lien (such as a mortgage, tax lien, or judgment lien), easement, restriction on the use of land, outstanding dower right, or other interest that may diminish the value of property to its owner.

Energy Star A U.S. government program to promote energy efficient consumer products. It was created in 1992 by the Environmental Protection Agency (EPA).

entrepreneurial profit The amount of profit attributable to the development function.

environmental obsolescence (See *external obsolescence*.)

environmental property assessment (EPRA) Term used to describe a study of the present and previous ownership, uses, and environmental conditions of a property for purposes of a transaction and to comply with requirements of the Environmental Protection Agency (EPA).

environmental site assessment (ESA) Term used to describe a study of the present and previous ownership, uses, and environmental conditions of a property for purposes of a transaction and to comply with requirements of the Environmental Protection Agency (EPA).

equalization The raising or lowering of assessed values for tax purposes in a particular county or taxing district to make them equal to assessments in other counties or districts.

equilibrium Period during which property undergoes little change; also called stability.

equity The interest or value that an owner has in real estate over and above any mortgage or other lien or charge against it.

equity capitalization rate A rate that reflects the relationship between a single year's before-tax cash flow and the equity investment in the property. The before-tax cash flow is the net operating income less the annual debt service payment, and the equity is the property value less any outstanding loan balance. The equity capitalization rate, when divided into the before-tax cash flow, gives an indication of the value of the equity. Also called *cash on cash rate*, *cash flow rate*, or *equity dividend rate*.

equity dividend rate (See *equity capitalization rate*.)

equity investors Investors making use of what is termed venture capital to take an unsecured and thus relatively risky part in an investment.

escalator clause A clause in a contract, lease, or mortgage providing for increases in wages, rent, or interest, based on fluctuations in certain economic indices, costs, or taxes.

escheat The reversion of property of a decedent who died intestate (without a will) and without heirs to the state or county as provided by state law.

escrow The closing of a transaction through a disinterested third person called an escrow agent or escrow holder, who holds funds and/or documents for delivery on the performance of certain conditions.

estate The degree, quantity, nature, and extent of ownership interest that a person has in real property.

estate in land The degree, quantity, nature, and extent of interest a person has in real estate.

estate in remainder The remnant of an estate that has been conveyed to take effect and be enjoyed after the termination of a prior estate; for instance, when an owner conveys a life estate to one party and the remainder to another. (For a case in which the owner retains the residual estate, see *estate in reversion.*)

estate in reversion An estate that comes back to the original holder, as when an owner conveys a life estate to someone else, with the estate to return to the original owner on termination of the life estate.

estimated remaining economic life The estimated time period over which a structure is expected to add value above the value of the land as if vacant and valued at its highest and best use.

eviction A legal process to evict a person from possession of real estate.

excess income (See *excess rent.*)

excess rent The amount by which scheduled rent exceeds market rent.

expense The cost of goods and services required to produce income.

expense-stop clause Lease provision to pass increases in building maintenance expenses on to tenants on a pro rata basis.

external obsolescence Loss of value from forces outside the building or property, such as changes in optimum land use, legislative enactments that restrict or impair property rights, and changes in supply-demand relationships, and always considered incurable.

externalities The principle that states that outside influences may have a positive or negative effect on property value.

extraction method Method of finding land value in which all improvement costs (less depreciation) are deducted from the sales price; also called *abstraction method.*

fair housing laws Federal, state, and local statutes and ordinances that prohibit discrimination in housing transactions against individuals who fall within one of the specified protected classifications; federal law prohibits discrimination on the basis of race, color, national origin, religion, sex, familial status, and disability.

Fannie Mae Formerly the Federal National Mortgage Association, created by Congress in 1968 to establish a secondary market for home mortgages and now privately owned although supervised by the federal government through the Office of Federal Housing Enterprise Oversight (OFHEO).

feasibility study An analysis of a proposed subject or property with emphasis on the attainable income, probable expenses, and most advantageous use and design. The purpose of such a study is to ascertain the probable success or failure of the project under consideration.

Federal Deposit Insurance Corporation (FDIC) An independent federal agency whose purpose is to insure the deposits in commercial banks.

Federal Housing Finance Agency (FHFA) Created in 2008 to serve as regulator and conservator of Fannie Mae and Freddie Mac and regulator of the 12 Federal Home Loan Banks.

Federal Reserve Bank System Central bank of the United States established to regulate the flow of money and the cost of borrowing.

fee simple The greatest possible right of ownership of real property, continuing without time limitation. Sometimes called *fee* or *fee simple absolute*.

fee simple defeasible Any limitation on property use that could result in loss of the right of ownership.

fee simple qualified Ownership of property that is limited in some way.

fenestration The design and placement of windows, doors, and other exterior openings of a building.

FHA The Federal Housing Administration; insures loans made by approved lenders in accordance with its regulations.

final opinion of value The appraiser's opinion of the defined value of the subject property, arrived at by reconciling (correlating) the estimates of values derived from the sales comparison, cost, and income approaches.

Financial Institutions Reform, Recovery, and Enforcement Act of 1989 (FIRREA) Federal legislation that mandates state licensing or certification for appraisers performing appraisals in certain federally related transactions.

first mortgage A mortgage that has priority as a lien over all other mortgages.

fixed expenses Those costs that are more or less permanent and do not vary in relation to the property's occupancy or income, such as real estate taxes and insurance for fire, theft, and hazards.

fixed-rate mortgage (See *amortized mortgage*.)

fixture Anything affixed to land, including personal property attached permanently to a building or to land so that it becomes part of the real estate.

floor plan A drawing to scale showing a two-dimensional view of a floor level in a house.

forecast absorption The rate at which properties in a subdivision are expected to sell.

foreclosure A court action initiated by a mortgagee or lienor for the purpose of having the court order that the debtor's real estate be sold to pay the mortgage or other lien (mechanic's lien or judgment).

form appraisal report Any of the relatively brief standard forms prepared by federal or federally supervised agencies such as Fannie Mae and Freddie Mac and others for routine property appraisals.

Form 1073 Individual Condominium Unit Appraisal Report of Fannie Mae and Freddie Mac.

Form 2075 Desktop Underwriter Property Inspection Report.

four factors of production The elements that contribute to value, which include capital, labor, land, and management.

foundation The substructure of a building on which the superstructure rests, providing support for the building and its interior furnishings and occupants.

fraction A portion of a whole number, with the numerator (above-the-line number) of the fraction divided by the denominator (below-the-line number) of the fraction.

framing The skeleton members of a structure, erected on a foundation, to which the exterior and interior walls are attached.

Freddie Mac Formerly the Federal Home Loan Mortgage Corporation, created by Congress in 1970 to provide a secondary market for mortgage-backed securities and now privately owned but under the supervision of the Office of Federal Housing Enterprise Oversight (OFHEO).

freehold An estate in land in which ownership is for an indeterminate length of time.

frequency distribution The arrangement of data into groups according to the frequency with which they appear in the data set.

front foot A standard of measurement, being a strip of land one foot wide fronting on the street or waterfront and extending the depth of the lot. Value may be quoted per front foot.

functional obsolescence Defects in a building or structure that detract from its value or marketability, usually the result of layout, design, or other features that are less desirable than features designed for the same functions in newer property.

functional obsolescence—curable Physical or design features that are no longer considered desirable by property buyers but could be replaced or redesigned at relatively low cost.

functional obsolescence—incurable Currently undesirable physical or design features that are not easily remedied or economically justified.

GEDR (See *growth*, *equilibrium*, *decline*, and *revitalization*.)

GIS (geographic information systems) Various types of software that make use of a computerized database to produce maps based on satellite imaging–derived reference points on the earth's surface.

going-concern value The value existing in an established business property compared with the value of selling the real estate and other assets of a concern whose business is not yet established. The term takes into account the goodwill and earning capacity of a business.

government sponsored enterprise (GSE) One of the organizations comprising the secondary mortgage market, such as Fannie Mae, that is supervised by the federal government through the Office of Federal Housing Enterprise Oversight (OFHEO).

grant deed A type of deed in which grantors warrant that they have not previously conveyed the estate being granted to another, have not encumbered the property except as noted in the deed, and will convey to the grantee any title to the property the grantors may later acquire.

grantee A person who receives a conveyance of real property from a grantor.

grantor The person transferring title to or an interest in real property to a grantee.

green building A building that takes maximum advantage of environmentally friendly building design and components.

gross building area All enclosed floor areas, as measured along a building's outside perimeter.

gross income (See *potential gross income*.)

gross income multiplier A figure used as a multiplier of the gross income of a property to produce an estimate of the property's value.

gross leasable area Total space designed for occupancy and exclusive use of tenants, measured from outside wall surfaces to the center of shared interior walls.

gross lease A lease of property under the terms of which the lessee pays a fixed rent and the lessor pays all property charges regularly incurred through ownership (repairs, taxes, insurance, and operating expenses).

gross living area (GLA) Total finished, habitable, above-grade space, measured along the building's outside perimeter.

gross market income (See *potential gross income*.)

gross rent multiplier (See *gross income multiplier*.)

ground lease A lease of land only on which the lessee usually owns the building or is required to build as specified by the lease. Such leases are usually long-term net leases; the lessee's rights and obligations continue until the lease expires or is terminated for default.

ground rent Rent paid for the right to use and occupy land according to the terms of a ground lease.

growing equity mortgage (GEM) A type of loan that rapidly increases the equity in a property by increasing the monthly payments a certain percentage each year and applying those increases to the principal.

highest and best use The legally and physically possible use of land that is likely to produce the highest land (or property) value. It considers the balance between site and improvements as well as the intensity and length of uses.

growth Period in the life cycle of a property when improvements are made to the property as demand for such property increases.

heating and air-conditioning Building systems, powered by one or more of a variety of sources, that warm the interior of a structure in cold weather and/or cool it in warm weather.

historical cost Actual cost of a property at the time it was constructed.

historical rent Scheduled (or contract) rent paid in past years.

holdover tenancy A tenancy in which the lessee retains possession of the leased premises after the lease has expired and the landlord, by continuing to accept rent from the tenant, thereby agrees to the tenant's continued occupancy.

homeowners' association Organization of property owners in a residential condominium or subdivision development, usually authorized by a declaration of restrictions to establish property design and maintenance criteria, collect assessments, and manage common areas.

Hoskold sinking fund table A table that supplies a factor by which a property's annual net income may be multiplied to find the present worth of the property over a given period at a given rate of interest.

House Price Index (HPI) Indicator of house price trends in various regions of the United States, developed by the Federal Housing Finance Agency (FHFA).

Housing and Economic Recovery Act of 2008 (HERA) Intended to help the housing market, HERA provided new guarantees for owners of subprime mortgages, provided funding for Fannie Mae and Freddie Mac and placed both organizations in conservatorship, and created the Federal Housing Finance Agency.

Housing Finance Board Federal agency created to replace the Federal Home Loan Bank Board and provide regulatory oversight of the Federal Home Loan Banks.

HUD Department of Housing and Urban Development.

improved land Real property made suitable for building by the addition of utilities and publicly owned structures, such as a curb, sidewalk, street-lighting system, and/or sewer.

improvements Structures of whatever nature, usually privately rather than publicly owned, erected on a site to enable its utilization; for example, buildings, fences, driveways, and retaining walls.

income capitalization approach The process of estimating the value of an income-producing property by capitalization of the annual net operating income expected to be produced by the property during its remaining economic life.

increasing returns, law of The situation in which property improvements increase property income or value.

incurable depreciation A depreciated item that would be impossible or too expensive to restore or replace. (See also *external obsolescence, functional obsolescence—incurable, and physical deterioration—incurable.*)

independent contractor A person who contracts to do work for another by using his or her own methods and without being under the control of the other person regarding how the work should be done. Unlike an employee, an independent contractor pays all of his or her expenses, personally pays income and Social Security taxes, and receives no employee benefits. Many real estate appraisers are independent contractors.

index method An appraisal technique used to determine reproduction or replacement cost. The appraiser multiplies the original cost of construction by a price index for the geographic area to allow for price changes.

indirect costs Costs of erecting a new building not involved with either site preparation or building construction; for example, building permit, land survey, overhead expenses such as insurance and payroll taxes, and builder's profit.

industrial district or park A controlled development zoned for industrial use and designed to accommodate specific types of industry, providing public utilities, streets, railroad sidings, and water and sewage facilities.

ingress The way to enter a tract of land; often used interchangeably with access. (See also *access.*)

installment contract A contract for the sale of real estate by which the purchase price is paid in installments over an extended period of time by the purchaser, who is in possession, with the title retained by the seller until a certain number of payments are made. The purchaser's payments may be forfeited on default.

insulation Materials used in building construction in walls, floors, and ceilings to help retain heat in cold weather and cool air in warm weather. The effectiveness of insulation is indicated by its R-value, which is a measure of its resistance to heat flow. The higher the R-value, the more effective the insulation.

insurable value The highest reasonable value that can be placed on property for insurance purposes.

interest A percentage of the principal amount of a loan charged by a lender for its use, usually expressed as an annual rate.

interest rate Return on an investment; an interest rate is composed of four component rates—*safe rate*, *risk rate*, *nonliquidity rate*, and *management rate*.

management rate Compensation to the owner for the work involved in managing an investment and reinvesting the funds received from the property.

nonliquidity rate A penalty charged for the time needed to convert real estate into cash.

risk rate An addition to the safe rate to compensate for the hazards that accompany investments in real estate.

safe rate The interest rate paid by investments of maximum security, highest liquidity, and minimum risk.

interim use A temporary property use awaiting transition to its highest and best use.

International Code Council (ICC) Organization of national and international building code officials that established and updates the International Building Code.

intestate Dying without a will or without having made a valid will. Title to property owned by someone who dies intestate will pass to his or her heirs as provided in the law of descent of the state in which the property is located.

investment value The worth of investment property to a specific investor.

Inwood annuity table A table that supplies a factor to be multiplied by the desired yearly income (based on the interest rate and length of time of the investment) to find the present worth of the investment.

joint tenancy Ownership of real estate between two or more parties who have been named in one conveyance as joint tenants. On the death of a joint tenant, the decedent's interest passes to the surviving joint tenant(s) by the right of survivorship.

joint venture The joining of two or more people to conduct a specific business enterprise. A joint venture is similar to a partnership in that it must be created by agreement between the parties to share in the losses and profits of the venture. It is unlike a partnership in that the venture is for one specific project only, rather than for a continuing business relationship.

land The earth's surface in its natural condition, extending down to the center of the globe, its surface and all things affixed to it, and the air space above the surface.

land capitalization rate The rate of return, including interest, on land only.

land development method (See *subdivision development method*.)

landlocked parcel A parcel of land without any access to a public road or way.

landlord One who owns property and leases it to a tenant.

land residual technique A method of capitalization using the net income remaining to the land after return on and recapture of the building value have been deducted.

land trust A trust originated by the owner of real property in which real estate is the only asset. Because the interest of a beneficiary is considered personal property and not real estate, a judgment against the beneficiary will not create a lien against the real estate. Thus land trusts are popular when there are multiple owners who seek protection against the effects of divorce, judgments, or bankruptcies of each other.

latent defect Physical deficiencies or construction defects not readily ascertainable from a reasonable inspection of the property, such as a defective septic tank or underground sewage system, or improper plumbing or electrical wiring.

law of decreasing returns Principle that there is a point after which improvements to land and structures no longer will result in a corresponding increase in the property's income or value.

law of increasing returns Principle that there is a period in which improvements to land and structures will produce a proportionate or greater increase in the property's income or value.

lease A written or oral contract for the possession and use of real property for a stipulated period of time, in consideration for the payment of rent. Leases for more than one year generally must be in writing.

leased fee The lessor's interest and rights in the real estate being leased.

leasehold estate The lessee's right to possess and use real estate during the term of a lease. This is generally considered a personal property interest.

leasehold interest (See *leasehold estate*.)

LEED (Leadership in Energy and Environmental Design) A rating system designed by the U. S. Green Building Council to promote construction practices that increase profitability while reducing the negative environmental impacts of buildings and improving occupant health.

legal description A statement identifying land by a system prescribed by law. (See also *lot and block system*, *metes and bounds description*, and *rectangular survey system*.)

lessee The person to whom property is leased by another; also called a *tenant*.

lessee's interest An interest having value only if the agreed-on rent is less than the market rent.

lessor The person who leases property to another; also called a *landlord*.

lessor's interest The value of lease rental payments plus the remaining property value at the end of the lease period.

letter of engagement Communication to an appraiser that includes a request to perform the specified appraisal assignment.

letter of transmittal First page of a narrative appraisal report in which the report is formally presented to the person for whom the appraisal was made.

levy To impose or assess a tax on a person or property; the amount of taxes to be imposed in a given district.

license (1) The revocable permission for a temporary use of land—a personal right that cannot be sold. (2) Formal permission from a constituted authority (such as a state agency) to engage in a certain activity or business (such as real estate appraisal).

lien A right given by law to certain creditors to have their debts paid out of the property of a defaulting debtor, usually by means of a court sale.

life cycle of property Four stages through which a property will pass: growth, equilibrium, decline, revitalization (GEDR).

life estate An interest in real or personal property that is limited in duration to the lifetime of its owner or some other designated person or persons.

living trust An arrangement in which a property owner (trustor) transfers assets to a trustee, who assumes specified duties in managing the asset. After the payment of operating expenses and trustee's fees, the income generated by the trust property is paid to or used for the benefit of the designated beneficiary. The living trust is gaining popularity as a way to hold title and avoid probate of trust assets.

long-lived items of depreciation Individual components of a structure that are not expected to be replaced over the structure's useful life. Foundation, framework, walls, ceilings, and masonry would fall within this category.

lot and block system Method of legal description of an individual parcel of land by reference to tract, block, and lot numbers and other information by which the parcel is identified in a recorded subdivision map. Also called *lot, block, and tract system* and *subdivision system.*

low-E glass Low-emissivity window glass that takes advantage of glazing techniques, such as double or triple panes, to increase its thermal efficiency.

maintenance expenses Costs incurred for day-to-day upkeep, such as management, wages and benefits of building employees, fuel, utility services, decorating, and repairs.

manufactured house A factory-built house, available in one or more pieces, that is attached to a foundation after being transported to a building site; must meet HUD requirements.

marital property (See *community property* and *tenancy by the entirety.*)

markers (See *monuments.*)

market A place or condition suitable for selling and buying.

market comparison approach (See *sales comparison approach.*)

market comparison method of depreciation (See *sales comparison method of depreciation.*)

market data approach (See *sales comparison approach.*)

market extraction method of depreciation (See *sales comparison method of depreciation.*)

market price (See *sales price.*)

market rent The amount for which the competitive rental market indicates property should rent; an estimate of a property's rent potential.

market value The most probable price real estate should bring in an arm's-length transaction occurring under normal market conditions.

matched pairs analysis (MPA) (See *paired sales analysis.*)

mean The average of all items included within a group, calculated by dividing the sum of the individual items, or variates, by the number of variates.

mechanic's lien A lien created by statute that exists in favor of contractors, laborers, or materialmen who have performed work or furnished materials in the erection or repair of a building.

median The single variate at the center of a group of variates, if the group is an odd number; the mean of the two variates at the center of a group, if the group is an even number.

meridian (See *principal meridian.*)

mesothelioma A cancer caused by extensive exposure to asbestos fibers that enter and settle in the lungs. Symptoms can take as long as 30 or more years to appear.

metes and bounds description A method of legal description specifying the perimeter of a parcel of land by use of measured distances from a point of beginning along specified boundaries, or bounds, using monuments, or markers, as points of reference.

mile A measurement of distance, being 1,760 yards or 5,280 feet.

mineral rights The right to share in the sale of minerals—such as oil and gas deposits—that may be extracted from land.

mode The most frequently occurring variate in a group.

money market The financial market that brings together investors who trade short-term money instruments, such as Treasury bills and commercial paper.

monuments Natural or artificial objects used to define the perimeter of a parcel of land using the metes and bounds method of legal description.

mortgage A conditional transfer or pledge of real property as security for the payment of a debt; also, the document used to create a mortgage lien.

mortgage constant The first-year debt payment divided by the beginning loan balance.

mortgagee The lender in a loan transaction secured by a mortgage.

mortgagor An owner of real estate who borrows money and uses the property as security for the loan.

narrative appraisal report A detailed written presentation of the facts and reasoning behind an appraiser's opinion of value.

neighborhood boundaries A residential or commercial area with similar types of properties, buildings of similar value or age, predominant land-use activities, and natural or fabricated geographic boundaries, such as highways or rivers.

net income ratio The ratio of net operating income to effective gross income.

net lease A lease requiring the tenant to pay rent and part or all of the costs of maintenance, including taxes, insurance, repairs, and other expenses of ownership. Sometimes known as an *absolute net lease*, *triple-net lease*, or *net, net, net lease*.

net operating income (NOI) Income remaining after operating expenses are deducted from effective gross income.

nonconforming use A once lawful property use that is permitted to continue after a zoning ordinance prohibiting it has been established for the area; a use that differs sharply from the prevailing uses in a neighborhood.

normal distribution How the variates in a group will be shown on a line graph, absent any deviation. (See also *bell curve*.)

novation A mutual agreement substituting a new debt or obligation in place of the original contract. For example, when a buyer assumes the seller's existing mortgage and the lender agrees to the assumption, a novation is executed, relieving the original borrower of any obligation to repay the loan; the buyer then becomes legally liable for payment of the mortgage debt.

observed condition depreciation A method of computing depreciation in which the appraiser estimates the loss in value for all items of depreciation. (See also *incurable depreciation* and *curable depreciation*.)

obsolescence Lessening of value from out-of-date features as a result of current changes in property design, construction, or use; an element of depreciation. (See also *external obsolescence* and *functional obsolescence*.)

occupancy Possession and use of property as owner or tenant.

occupancy rate The percentage of total rental units occupied and producing income.

offer to purchase An agreement between a prospective buyer of real estate to enter into a contract with the seller. If the document is accepted and signed by the seller, it becomes a contract of sale.

operating expense ratio The ratio of total operating expenses to effective gross income.

operating expenses The cost of all goods and services used or consumed in the process of obtaining and maintaining income. (See also *fixed expenses*, *maintenance expenses*, and *reserves for replacement*.)

operating statement The written record of a business's gross income, expenses, and resultant net income.

operating statement ratio Relationship of a property's expenses to income, found by dividing total operating expenses by effective gross income.

opinion of property value The conclusion of a property's defined value reached by an appraiser after consideration of the relevant data concerning the subject property, comparable properties, and the marketplace as of a specified date.

opportunity cost The value differential between alternative investments with differing rates of return.

option A right given for a valuable consideration to purchase or lease property at a future date, for a specified price and terms. The right may or may not be exercised at the option holder's (optionee's) discretion.

orientation Positioning a structure on its lot with regard to exposure to the sun, prevailing winds, privacy, and protection from noise.

OTS (Office of Thrift Supervision) A government agency created by the Financial Institutions Reform, Recovery, and Enforcement Act (FIRREA) that governs the practices of fiduciary lenders—such as commercial banks and savings associations.

outlier In statistics, an extreme variate of a population that is taken out of a calculation of the mean of the variates to avoid distorting the computation.

overage rent Rent paid over a base amount in a percentage lease.

overall capitalization rate A rate of investment return derived by comparing the net income and sales prices of comparable properties.

overall rate The direct ratio between a property's annual net income and its sales price.

overimprovement An improvement to property that is more than warranted by the property's highest and best use and thus not likely to contribute its cost to the total market value of the property.

ownership in severalty Individual ownership of real estate, not to be confused with the use of the word several to mean "more than one"; also called *tenancy in severalty*, *sole tenancy*, or *separate ownership*.

paired sales analysis A method of estimating the amount of adjustment for the presence or absence of any feature by pairing the sales prices of otherwise identical properties with and without the feature in question. A sufficient number of sales must be found to allow the appraiser to isolate the effect on value of the pertinent factor (also called *paired data set analysis* and *matched pairs analysis*).

parameter A single number or attribute of the individual things, persons, or other entities in a population.

parcel The entire tract of real estate included in a condominium development; also referred to as a development parcel.

partial interest Any property interest that is less than full fee simple ownership of the entire property.

partnership An association of two or more individuals who carry on a continuing business for profit as co-owners. Under the law a partnership is regarded as a group of individuals rather than as a single entity.

percent Parts of the whole, when the whole is divided into one hundred parts.

percentage lease A lease commonly used for commercial property that provides for a rental based on the tenant's gross sales at the premises. It generally stipulates a base monthly rental, plus a percentage of any gross sales exceeding a certain amount.

performance The fulfillment of a legal obligation—such as a contract—according to its terms and conditions.

personal property Items that are tangible and movable and do not fit the definition of realty; chattels.

physical deterioration—curable Loss of value due to neglected repairs or maintenance that are economically feasible and, if performed, would result in an increase in appraised value equal to or exceeding their cost.

physical deterioration—incurable Loss of value due to neglected repairs or maintenance of short-lived or long-lived building components that would not contribute comparable value to a building if performed.

physical life The length of time a structure can be considered habitable, without regard to its economic use.

planned unit development (PUD) A subdivision consisting of individually owned residential and/or commercial parcels or lots as well as areas owned in common.

plat A map representing a parcel of land subdivided into lots, showing streets and other details or a single site.

plottage value The subsequent increase in the unit value of a group of adjacent properties when they are combined into one property in a process called *assemblage*.

plumbing system Includes the building components that provide water, a method of warming the water, and disposal of waste water, including the water supply system, water heater, vent piping system, and drainage system.

point of beginning Place at which a legal description of land using the metes and bounds method starts.

police power The right of the government to impose laws, statutes, and ordinances to protect the public health, safety, and welfare; includes zoning ordinances and building codes.

population All of the individual variates (items or units) of a group.

possession The right of the owner to occupy property. When property is occupied by a tenant, the owner has constructive possession by right of title.

potential gross income A property's total potential income from all sources during a specified period.

potential gross income multiplier A ratio calculated by dividing the sales price of a comparable property by its potential gross income to form an opinion of the subject property's value.

prepaid items of expense Expense items, such as insurance premiums and tax reserves, that have been paid in advance of the time that the expense is incurred. Prepaid expenses typically are prorated and credited to the seller in the preparation of a closing statement.

pretax cash flow Income that remains from net operating income (NOI) after debt service is paid but before ordinary income tax on operations is deducted.

price The amount of money set or paid as the consideration in the sale of an item at a particular time.

principal (1) A sum lent or employed as a fund or investment—as distinguished from its income or profits; (2) the original amount (as of a loan) of the total due and payable at a certain date; or (3) a party to a transaction—as distinguished from an agent.

principal meridian One of 35 north and south survey lines established and defined as part of the U.S. government or rectangular survey system.

private restrictions The covenants, conditions and restrictions (CC&Rs) found in the typical declaration of restrictions filed by a subdivision developer and incorporated by reference in the deed to each subdivision lot.

profit-and-loss statement (See *operating statement.*)

progression An appraisal principle that states that the value of an inferior property is favorably affected by its association with better properties of the same type.

projected gross sales Total income that a project is expected to produce.

property manager Someone who manages real estate for another person in exchange for compensation.

prorations The adjustment of taxes, interest, insurance, and/or other costs on a pro rata basis as of the closing of a sale. (See also *closing statement.*)

purchase money mortgage A note secured by a mortgage or trust deed given by the buyer, as mortgagor, to the seller, as mortgagee, as part of the purchase price of real estate.

purchase option A right given to a prospective purchaser or lessee to buy or lease the owner's property at a fixed price within a specified period of time.

quantity survey method A method for finding the reproduction cost of a building in which the costs of erecting or installing all of the component parts of a new building, including both direct and indirect costs, are added.

quitclaim deed A conveyance by which a grantor's interest in the land is transferred, without warranties or obligations.

R-value (See *insulation.*)

radon gas A colorless, odorless, tasteless radioactive gas that results from the natural breakdown of uranium in the soil and is harmful to people at high levels; in many cases, a mitigation system can reduce the radon level in a structure to a safe level.

ranch house A one-story house that may be built over a concrete slab foundation, crawlspace, or basement.

random sample A subset of a population of variates in which every variate is chosen by chance, with an equal probability of being picked.

range A measure of the difference between the highest and lowest items in a data set.

real estate Land; a portion of the earth's surface extending downward to the center of the earth and upward into space including fixtures permanently attached thereto by nature or by man, anything incidental or appurtenant to land, and anything immovable by law; freehold estate in land.

real estate agent A person licensed to represent a buyer or a seller in a real estate transaction in exchange for a fee.

real estate broker Any person, partnership, association, or corporation that, for compensation or valuable consideration, sells or offers for sale, buys or offers to buy, or negotiates the purchase, sale, or exchange of real estate; or that leases or offers to lease, or rents or offers for rent any real estate or the improvement thereon for others. Such a broker must secure a state license. For a license to be issued to a firm, it is usually required that all active partners or officers be licensed real estate brokers.

real estate investment trust (REIT) Trust ownership of real estate by a group of individuals who purchase certificates of ownership in the trust, which in turn invests the money in real property and distributes the profits to the investors free of corporate income tax.

real estate salesperson Any person who, for compensation or valuable consideration, is employed either directly or indirectly by a real estate broker to sell or offer to sell; or to buy or offer to buy; or to negotiate the purchase, sale, or exchange of real estate; or to lease, rent, or offer for rent any real estate; or to negotiate leases thereof or improvements thereon. Such a salesperson must secure a state license.

real property The rights of ownership of real estate, often called the bundle of rights; for all practical purposes, synonymous with real estate.

recapture rate The percentage of a property's original cost that is returned to the owner as income during the remaining economic life of the investment.

reconciliation The step in the appraisal process in which the appraiser reconciles the estimates of value received from the sales comparison, cost, and income capitalization approaches to arrive at a final opinion of market value for the subject property.

reconstruction of the operating statement The process of eliminating the inapplicable expense items for appraisal purposes and adjusting the remaining valid expenses, if necessary.

reconveyance deed A deed used by a trustee under a deed of trust to return title to the trustor.

recording The act of entering documents affecting or conveying interest in real estate in the recorder's office of the county in which the real estate is located.

rectangular survey system A system established in 1785 by the federal government, which provides for the surveying and describing of land by reference to principal meridians and base lines; also called *U.S. government survey system* and *section and township system*.

reformation A legal action taken to correct or modify a contract or deed that has not accurately reflected the intentions of the parties because of some mechanical error.

regional multipliers Adjustment factors by which standard cost figures can be multiplied to allow for regional price differences.

regression An appraisal principle that states that the value of a superior property is adversely affected by its association with an inferior property of the same type.

release Document in which one party to a contract states that the contract obligation(s) of the other party to the contract need not be performed.

remainder The remnant of an estate that has been conveyed to take effect and be enjoyed after the termination of a prior estate; for instance, when an owner conveys a life estate to one party and the remainder to another. (For the case in which the owner retains the residual estate, see *reversion*.)

remainderman The party designated to receive a remainder estate. There are two types: vested remainderman (one who is known and named) and contingent remainderman (one whose identity is not certain or who is to be selected).

remaining economic life The number of years of useful life left to a building from the date of appraisal.

renewal option Lease provision that allows the lessee to renew the lease for the same term or some other stated period, usually with a rent increase at a stated percentage or based on an index or other formula.

rent Payment under a lease or other arrangement for use of a property.

rent loss method of depreciation (See *capitalized value method of depreciation.*)

replacement cost The current construction cost of a building having exactly the same utility as the subject property.

reproduction cost The current construction cost of an exact duplicate of the subject building.

rescission Legal action taken to terminate or cancel a contract either by mutual consent of the parties to the contract or by one party when the other party is in breach of the contract.

reserves for replacement Allowances set up for replacement of building and equipment items that have a relatively short life expectancy.

residual In appraising, the value remaining after all deductions have been made.

retrospective appraisal (also called historical appraisal) An appraisal of property to determine market value when the effective date of the appraisal is a date in the past.

reverse annuity mortgage (RAM) An instrument designed to aid elderly homeowners by providing them a monthly income over a period of years in exchange for equity they have acquired in their homes. RAM borrowers typically may obtain up to 80% of the appraised value of free-and-clear property.

reversion The remnant of an estate that the grantor (as opposed to a third party) holds after he or she has granted a limited estate such as a leasehold or life estate to another person and that will return or revert back to the grantor. (See also *remainder.*)

reversion table The amount that an investor should pay for the future value of land is computed by applying a reversion factor to the land's present estimated value. A reversion table lists the computed factors at specified interest rates for a specified investment term.

revitalization A period in a neighborhood's life cycle when demand increases, providing the stimulus needed for renovation; also called rehabilitation.

revocation The act of terminating, canceling, or annulling an offer to contract by the person making the original offer.

right-of-way The right that one has to travel over the land of another; an easement.

riparian rights Rights of an owner of land that borders on or includes a stream, river, lake, or sea. These rights include definition of (and limitations on) access to and use of the water, ownership of streambed, navigable water, and uninterrupted flow and drainage. (See also *accretion.*)

risk rate (See *interest rate.*)

rod A measure of length, 16½ feet.

safe rate (See *interest rate.*)

sales comparison approach The process of forming an opinion of the market value of property through examination and comparison of actual sales of comparable properties; also called the *direct market comparison* or *market data approach.*

sales comparison method of depreciation Way of determining loss in value through depreciation by using sales prices of comparable properties to derive the value of a depreciated item; also called the *market data method* and the *market extraction method.*

salesperson (See *real estate salesperson.*)

sales price The actual price that a buyer pays for a property.

sample Some of the units, or variates, of a population that accurately represents the population.

sandwich lease The ownership interest of a sublessee.

scheduled rent Rent paid by agreement between lessor and lessee; also called *contract rent.*

scope of work The amount and type of information researched and the analysis applied in an appraisal assignment.

secondary mortgage market A market in which existing first mortgages are bought and sold; also called the *secondary money market.*

second mortgage A mortgage loan secured by real estate that has previously been made security for an existing mortgage loan; also called a *junior mortgage* or *junior lien.*

segmentation Consideration of a market area by division into specific categories of consumer preferences, such as the income, work, or leisure activities of the population.

seller financing A loan made by the owner/seller of real estate to the purchaser to cover all or part of the sales price.

selling price The actual price that a buyer pays for a property.

settlement The process of closing a real estate transaction by adjusting and prorating the required credits and charges.

shared appreciation mortgage (SAM) A loan designed for borrowers whose current income is too low to qualify for another type of mortgage. The SAM loan makes the lender and the borrower partners by permitting the lender to share in property appreciation. In return, the borrower receives a lower interest rate.

sheriff's deed Deed given by a court to effect the sale of property to satisfy a judgment.

short-lived items of depreciation Depreciating building components that could be expected to be replaced at least several times over the structure's useful life, such as roofing.

simple interest Interest earned on only the original principal, and not on the accrued interest.

sinking fund method Use of a factor by which a property's annual net income may be multiplied to find the present worth of the property over a given period at a given rate of interest.

site Land suitable for building purposes, usually improved by the addition of utilities or other services.

six functions of dollar The six compound interest factors used in the mathematics of finance to adjust present or future payments for the time value of money.

skewness A measure of the lack of symmetry in a distribution of the variates of a population.

solar heating An active or passive system that makes use of the warmth provided by sunlight to heat water or all or part of the interior of a structure.

special assessment A charge against real estate made by a unit of government to cover the proportional cost of an improvement, such as a street or sewer.

special-purpose property Property that has unique usage requirements, such as a church or a museum, making it difficult to convert to other uses.

specific performance Legal action in which a party to a contract asks the court to enforce the contract obligations as agreed to by the parties.

split-entry A one-story house constructed on an elevated foundation, with the entry between the upper and lower floors, that allows additional living space in the lower level.

split-level A house that has three separate levels of space, with the entry to a single level that provides access to a second story that is over a garage space.

square foot A rectangle with four sides, each one foot long.

square-foot method A method for finding the reproduction cost of a building in which the cost per square foot of a recently built comparable structure is multiplied by the number of square feet in the subject property.

stages of life cycle (See *life cycle of property*.)

standard deviation A measure of the difference between individual entities, called *variates*, and an entire population, in which the square root of the sum of the squared differences between each variate and the mean of all the variates in the population is divided by the number of variates in the population.

statistics The science of collecting, classifying, and interpreting information based on the number of things.

statute of frauds Carryover from English law that specifies agreements must be in writing to be enforceable, such as a contract for the sale of real estate.

statute of limitations Carryover from English law that specifies the time period in which certain legal actions must be brought.

straight-line method of depreciation (See *age-life method of depreciation*.)

straight-line recapture A method of capital recapture in which total accrued depreciation is spread over the useful life of a building in equal amounts.

subdivision A tract of land divided by the owner into blocks, building lots, and streets by a recorded subdivision plat. Compliance with local regulations is required.

subdivision development method A method of valuing land to be used for subdivision development. It relies on accurate forecasting of market demand, including both forecast absorption (the rate at which properties will sell) and projected gross sales (total income that the project will produce); also called the *land development method*.

subleasehold The interest of a sublessee under a sandwich lease.

subletting The leasing of premises by a lessee to a third party for a part of the lessee's remaining term.

subprime lending Loans made to borrowers with credit scores that do not qualify for the lowest interest rates.

substitution, principle of The basic appraisal premise that the market value of real estate is influenced by the cost of acquiring a substitute or comparable property.

summation method Another name for the cost approach to appraising.

superadequacy A structural feature that is not fully valued by the marketplace; an item in which its cost exceeds its value.

supply and demand, principle of A principle that the value of a commodity will rise as demand increases and/or supply decreases.

surplus productivity Amount remaining after expenses of property ownership (capital, labor, and management) are deducted from net income, representing the investor's return on the use of the land.

survey The process of measuring land to determine its size, location, and physical description; also, the map or plat showing the results of a survey.

taxation Government-imposed charge to cover the cost of public amenities and services; real property is taxed on an *ad valorem* (according to value) basis.

tax base The value of taxable properties in a region.

tax deed The instrument used to convey legal title to property sold by a governmental unit for nonpayment of taxes.

tax-stop clause A clause in a lease providing that the lessee will pay any increase in taxes over a base or an initial year's taxes.

tenancy by the entirety The joint ownership, recognized in some states, of property acquired by spouses during marriage. On the death of one spouse the survivor becomes the owner of the property.

tenancy in common (TIC) A form of co-ownership by which each owner holds an undivided interest in real property as if he or she were sole owner. Each individual owner has the right to partition. Unlike joint tenants, tenants in common have the right of inheritance.

tenancy in partnership Co-ownership of property by all partners.

tenancy in severalty (See *ownership in severalty*.)

tenant One who has possession of real estate; an occupant, not necessarily a renter; the lessee under a lease. The estate or interest held is called a *tenancy*.

tenant improvements Interior finishing of leased property according to the tenant's specifications.

tenant in common (TIC) One of the co-owners in a tenancy in common who share the four unities of time, title, interest, and possession.

theory of consistent use Refers to the concept that land cannot be valued on the basis of one use while the improvements are valued on the basis of another.

time-share Estate or use interest in real property for a designated time period each year.

title The evidence of a person's right to the ownership and possession of land.

topography Surface features of land; elevation, ridges, slope, contour.

trade fixtures Articles of personal property installed by a commercial tenant under the terms of a lease. Trade fixtures are removable by the tenant before the lease expires and are not true fixtures.

triple-net lease (See *net lease*.)

trust A fiduciary arrangement whereby property is conveyed to a person or an institution, called a trustee, to be held and administered on behalf of another person or entity, called a beneficiary. The one who conveys the trust is called the trustor.

trust deed An instrument used to create a mortgage lien by which the borrower conveys title to a trustee, who holds it as security for the benefit of the note holder (the lender); also called a *deed of trust*.

trustee The holder of bare legal title in a deed of trust loan transaction.

trustor The borrower in a deed of trust loan transaction.

Truth in Lending Act (TILA) Enacted in 1968 and implemented by the Federal Reserve, TILA offers protections to consumers in credit transactions, including mortgages, primarily by requiring disclosure of loan terms and obligations.

underimprovement An improvement that is less than a property's highest and best use.

Uniform Appraisal Dataset (UAD) Fannie Mae and Freddie Mac requirements intended to standardize all data elements necessary to complete their residential and condominium appraisal report forms.

Uniform Residential Appraisal Report (URAR) The standardized appraisal report form created by Fannie Mae and Freddie Mac.

Uniform Standards of Professional Appraisal Practice (USPAP) Minimal criteria for appraisal competency promulgated by the Appraisal Foundation at the direction of Congress, to be applied to appraisals that require the services of a state-licensed or certified appraiser.

unit One ownership space in a condominium building or a part of a property intended for independent use and having lawful access to a public way. Ownership of one unit also includes a definite undivided interest in the common elements.

unit-in-place method A method for finding the reproduction cost of a building in which the construction cost per square foot of each component part of the subject building (including material, labor, overhead, and builder's profit) is multiplied by the number of square feet of the component part in the subject building.

United States Access Board An independent federal agency dedicated to accessibility for people with disabilities.

URAR form (See *Uniform Residential Appraisal Report.*)

useful life (See *economic life.*)

use value The value of the acquired right to use a property for a specific purpose or in a specific manner.

usury Charging interest in excess of the maximum legal rate.

vacancy and collection losses (See *allowance for vacancy and collection losses.*)

valuation principles Factors that affect market value, such as the principles of substitution, highest and best use, supply and demand, conformity, contribution, increasing and decreasing returns, competition, change, stage of life cycle, anticipation, externalities, balance, surplus productivity, opportunity cost, and agents of production.

value The power of a good or service to command other goods or services in exchange; the present worth of future rights to income and benefits arising from ownership.

value in exchange The value of goods and services in exchange for other goods and services, or money, in the marketplace; an economic concept of market value.

value in use Property value based on a particular use, often considered as part of a broader operation or process. An example is a driving range adjacent to a golf course.

VA mortgage A mortgage loan on approved property made to a qualified veteran by an authorized lender and guaranteed by the Department of Veterans Affairs to limit possible loss by the lender.

variable expenses Property expenses for management, wages, and benefits of building employees, fuel, utility services, decorating, and other ongoing costs of individual building ownership, as opposed to permanent expenses, such as property taxes.

variance (See *zoning variance*.)

variate In statistics, an individual thing, person, or other entity.

vendee Buyer.

vendor Seller.

warranty deed A deed in which the grantor fully warrants good clear title to the property.

yield Income produced by an investment; usually used to refer to equity investments.

yield capitalization Method used to estimate value from annual net operating income by applying a capitalization rate derived by analyzing each of the rate's component parts to provide both return on and return of the investment.

zoning Municipal or county regulation of land use within designated districts or *zones*. Zoning is an application of a state's *police power* to regulate private activity by enacting laws that benefit the public health, safety, and general welfare. Zoning may affect use of the land, lot sizes, type of structure permitted, building heights, setbacks, and density.

zoning ordinance Regulation of the character and use of property by a municipality or other government entity through the exercise of its police power.

zoning variance An exemption from a zoning ordinance or regulation permitting a structure or use that would not otherwise be allowed.

INDEX

Notes

Notes

Notes

Notes

Notes

Notes

Notes